THE
CHANGING
FAMILY

David A. Schulz

Division of Urban Affairs and the Department of Sociology
University of Delaware

THE CHANGING FAMILY

Its Function and Future

Prentice-Hall, Inc.
Englewood Cliffs, New Jersey

Library of Congress Catalog Card Number: 77-166140

0-13-128082-1

10   9   8   7   6   5   4   3   2   1

PRENTICE-HALL INTERNATIONAL, INC., London
PRENTICE-HALL OF AUSTRALIA, PTY., LTD., Sydney
PRENTICE-HALL OF CANADA, LTD., Toronto
PRENTICE-HALL OF INDIA PRIVATE LTD., New Delhi
PRENTICE-HALL OF JAPAN, INC., Tokyo

To Helené, Lisa, and Alison

Contents

Preface

With experimentation in a wide variety of family forms in communes, religious communities, and on the college campus, and with dramatic departures from traditional norms among sedate swingers of suburbia, many people come to know one or more alternatives to the typical middle-class family's style of life personally. They may even prefer these to the traditional style of life. The change in sexual norms and behavior commonly referred to as the "sexual revolution" has not only separated coitus from reproduction, it has encouraged a free expression of all forms of sexual behavior, much of which only recently was considered "perverted." Public policy issues such as the population explosion, environmental pollution, women's liberation, and welfare rights draw attention to family life styles and suggest, among other things, that the average American family should have fewer children; consume less; reallocate power, privilege and prestige in a redefinition of sex roles; and come to accept the single-parent family as a viable family form. The quest for intimacy and community, particularly among upper-middle-class youth, is a positive side of their political and cultural alienation, but the "generation gap" points to another dimension of conflict within the family. In such times, it becomes increasingly difficult to specify who holds what norm, much less who puts it into practice.

The author of a text on the family cannot ordinarily expect to completely cover all of the scholarly research. Today it is difficult to cover all of the issues connected with family life. The study of the family has become controversial and the author cannot assume much about what his "typical reader" thinks about the family. When talking about changing the family, especially, what is humdrum to one reader is revolutionary to another. Nevertheless, I believe that the sociologist of the family should address himself to these matters of how the family should be changed, even though the bulk of his effort may be directed to an examination of how the family has changed.

This text draws upon diverse disciplines and perspectives in order to create a synthesis—a new perspective on the family—that will encourage rather than retard further discussion and debate. It would be quite misleading to imply that it offers a plan for changing the normal American family or that it provides a coherent theory of family change. Both are beyond the scope of its intent. Data and conceptual frameworks from a variety of disciplines are assembled and their contribution to an understanding of family change is discussed. Particular stress is placed upon descriptive material that helps the reader understand families that are different from the common American family. The social context of family life is sketched wherever possible. Since the family changes in response to changes in its social situation, these factors cannot be left out even though it is often difficult to specify precisely how they affect the family.

This is an introductory text. The advanced student may be annoyed at its descriptive emphasis, but he may also find that material which might otherwise have been taken for granted is given new significance because it is placed in a different context. Throughout, I have tried to remain sensitive to the practical realities of family life as they are brought forward in research, in the mass media, and in my personal experience. Whatever theory of family change is developed, whatever rigor of analysis is achieved in the social sciences, neither can be legitimately accomplished without such an attempt. The unreality of much research on family life derives in large measure from the fact that the researcher has lost contact with the issues of everyday life. No amount of rigor will improve the *utility* of our conceptual frameworks if we continue to ignore these commonplace realities. In my opinion, whatever clarity sociologists achieve in the theoretical understanding of the family should not be at the expense of its usefulness to society. It is my hope that this text will be useful.

As a sociologist who is also a clergyman, I speak implicitly to a particular community. If this text has any "revolutionary" component to it at all, it will probably be for those who still "profess and call themselves Christian" but who have not yet felt the full freedom and the greater responsibility of the "new" morality. Simply put, I do not believe that the Christian must accept one form of marriage (monogamy) and one family structure (the conjugal family composed of a man, his wife, and their children) as the only ethical options. The fact that the law of the land allows only monogamy does not detract from this point. It does, however, call attention to some of the practical difficulties involved in choosing an alternative. The fact that my wife and I still live together with our children in the seclusion of suburbia testifies, in part, to our personal assessment of the magnitude of these difficulties. Nevertheless, for those who consider themselves bound by a set of principles, a discussion of how those principles should be changed is a first step toward changing those principles, and perhaps, eventually, behavior as well.

ACKNOWLEDGMENTS

I owe a great deal to many people for their assistance in the generation of this book. The manuscript at various stages of its development was read by Albert T. Mollegen, Lee Rainwater, and Neil Smelzer. I received very helpful criticisms from five anonymous readers selected by Alan B. Lesure. Several students in my sociology class on the family read the manuscript and gave it a detailed evaluation. I am especially indebted to Sharon Ely, Mary C. McKelvey, Geraldine O'Donnel, Ray Honaker, and Curtis Bauman. I am indebted to many colleagues at Washington University (St. Louis), Penn State, and the University of Delaware for their insights and ideas that have arisen in conversation. The magnitude of this indebtedness cannot adequately be reflected in the footnotes.

The staff at Prentice-Hall has been most helpful in seeing this book through to its completion. I particularly thank Ed Stanford for his encouragement when the revisions seemed endless and Ann Levine for her imaginative efforts as production editor in bringing this book to publication.

A number of persons have worked hard over long periods of time typing the manuscripts in its several revisions: Norma MacPherson, Louella P. Johnson, Patricia C. Keller, Joan E. Pierce, Linda D. Ritchie, and Diane V. Zankowsky. I must also thank Donald Kent, Chairman of the Department of Sociology at Penn State, and C. Harold Brown, Director of the Division of Urban Affairs, the University of Delaware, for allowing time for me to work on the manuscript.

1. Introduction

The abstractions of social scientists often seem incompatible with the rich complexities of family life as we know it tacitly through direct experience. Their models of family interaction appear to oversimplify the intricacies of real life, and we often have difficulty assessing what value, if any, these models have in helping us to understand our own families. And yet, at the same time, we must realize that a society cannot enact useful public policy pertaining to its families solely on the basis of tacit knowledge. Nor is it reasonable to assume that even a few families can come together to create consciously a new style of community if each has only a tacit understanding of its own internal dynamics.[1] Families must see their own experience as a special case and examine what they have in common with the other families in their group; and this is an elemental mode of analysis.

A moment's reflection should convince us further that it is almost impossible for a purely idiosyncratic understanding of a single family to emerge in our society. Such isolation is difficult to conceive of, if only because each family normally has two others—the families of both parents—as a part of its experience. These three families are never exactly alike. They differ in size and style of life; they may not even have the same structure. But on the basis of these varied experiences in three different families we know something about the nature of family change, and we probably have our own explanations of why they differ.

We know, furthermore, that some of us have deliberately changed the character of our families—with or without adequate information. We have seen that our families have changed as a result of changes in our society, although we cannot always specify how this has occurred. When it comes to changing our own families we cannot dismiss our past history or our ethnocentric preferences. Confronted with a range of possible alternative family styles and the likely consequences of each, we must make a decision to move in one direction or another. A community may opt for pluralism—the legitimization of a wide range of equally acceptable family styles—but the individual can only choose one style at a time. The choice of an individual may be thwarted by circumstances or in part determined by them, but it must be made, it is always personal, and it often has long-term effects.

When we talk about family change, therefore, we have in mind at one extreme the individual effort of a single person or family to change its style of life, and at the other the unintended changes brought about in the family life of perhaps millions of persons as a result of changes in their societies. The more we understand scientifically various alternative family styles and the processes by which they come about, the more we can act rationally and the more our compassion can be effectively expressed. In this introductory chapter I will examine two ways in which families can be understood—through personal experience and through social research—and briefly consider two

1. I use the term "intentional community" to refer to these attempts to create consciously a new style of community—which ordinarily involves the restructuring of the the family. Intentional communities may be either "utopian" in that the stress is on the objectives or ideals that the community attempts to realize in its life, or they may be "experimental" in that the stress is on the need to understand the processes of community and family life in order to improve their quality or capacity to adapt and survive. Experimental communities may or may not have explicit ideals beyond survival.

frameworks within which they can be analyzed—structure-functionalism and role theory. I will go on to discuss changes in family life and to investigate some of the social and personal elements that prompt these changes.

Understanding the Family

PERSONAL EXPERIENCE

We do know a great deal about the family as a result of having lived in one, but we understand it tacitly—as a concrete group of people—rather than analytically. We have interacted with our parents and siblings, shared the unique experiences that make our family what it is, come to grips with our environment both as individuals and as members of families. This accumulation of experiences gives us a detailed understanding of how at least one family operates. And regardless of whether the family into which we have been born is one of which we are proud or ashamed, our perception is influenced by this first experience. Our assessment of other families is based on the success or failure of our own. The degree of happiness or fear with which we anticipate starting a new family depends on the nature of our experiences in this first family. Thus our first family is aptly called our *family of orientation*. Most of us will establish at least one other family through marriage. This is called our *family of procreation* because in it we are expected to carry on the task of bringing new life into the world.[2]

Those of us who have lived in families in which serious disruptions are not a part of everyday life tend to accept without question the patterns of family interaction. However, when we are hurt or disappointed within the structure of the family—when our parents humiliate us, our brothers and sisters hurt our feelings, our children disappoint us, or our spouses misunderstand us—we no longer take this family interaction for granted. We begin to examine our relationships with a concern for finding out what went wrong.

Although we cease taking them as much for granted under such stressful circumstances, we do not, even then, come to study our families as a sociologist might. For example, we are not inclined to look much beyond the persons who live with us in our own families to explain why they have let us down. Children of poor families characteristically do not blame society or the economic system for the fact that their father cannot provide for them adequately. Instead, they tend to see their father as being personally at fault. Most of us fail to look beyond the individual as a cause of our personal hurt; we fail to see that a family member's behavior may be little more than an expression of much more impersonal processes over which he has little, if any, control. When we do this, however, we do not look at the family as a

---

2. If we call the family consisting of a married couple and their children (own or adopted) the nuclear family, we can define the family of orientation as "a nuclear family viewed from the standpoint of one of the children." The family of procreation is, then, "a nuclear family viewed from the standpoint of one of the parents." These definitions are after the usage of W. Lloyd Warner.

social institution[3] that exists to meet the needs of society as well as those of its individual members. We are not considering how the family functions, and we are not inclined to estimate the full consequences of its operations.

RESEARCH AND ANALYSIS

The sociologist studying the family, on the other hand, is not concerned primarily with individual families, although he may employ the case-study approach in his quest for generalizations. He is primarily interested in patterns of interactions that form a basis for generalizations about relationships within the family and between the family and its society. He is particularly concerned about the range of situations over which his generalizations are thought to hold true. The extent to which his own tacit understanding biases his generalizations is an important consideration.

In order to ensure "objectivity" most researchers impose various types of instruments (questionnaires, psychological or sociological scales, statistical tests, etc.) between themselves and the families they are studying and between themselves and the data they collect on these families. Researchers can thus be found working at varying "distances" from the object of their investigation. At one extreme is the family sociologist who studies the family primarily through statistics others have collected. The United States Census and the records of private corporations and public agencies provide a rich source of information about family patterns in America. A major weakness of such an approach, however, is that the interpretation is based on little or no personal experience of the family life reflected in the data. A case in point is the well-known interpretation of statistical data provided by Daniel Patrick Moynihan in his controversial, *"The Negro Family: The Case for National Action."*[4] At the other extreme is the participant observer who spends a great deal of time interacting with the families he is studying. Even though he, himself, is the primary "instrument" that he takes into the field, he attempts to distinguish between his own perception of a family's situation and their perception of that situation. In assessing this style of research, we must ask whether the generalizations made on the basis of intensive study of a few families are truly representative.

In addition to personal and methodological biases, researchers often order their investigations in terms of an explicit conceptual framework.[5] The two that have influenced this book are structure-functionalism and role theory.

---

3. While the term "institution" is commonly defined as an established practice or organized group of persons, the term is used by sociologists to mean a set of interrelated *norms* (rules of conduct such as folkways, mores, laws). Thus, after Winch, I understand an institution to be a "set of interrelated norms pertaining to the carrying out of a function." After Leslie, I understand that the family as a social institution "is a system of norms regulating adult sex relationship and procreation" (its basic functions). An excellent synopsis of basic definitions is found in Robert F. Winch, *The Modern Family*, rev. ed. (New York: Holt, Rinehart & Winston, 1966), pp. 8–14.

4. United States Department of Labor, Office of Policy Planning and Research, *The Negro Family: The Case for National Action* (Washington, D. C.: U.S.G.P.O., 1965).

5. A useful comparison of the various models or conceptual frameworks used in family study can be found in Ivan Nye and Felix Bernardo, *Emerging Conceptual Frameworks in Family Analysis* (New York: Macmillan, 1966).

Structure-Functionalism: This is perhaps the most widely employed conceptual framework in the social sciences. Its basic postulates are (1) that every society should be viewed as a whole or system; (2) that every part of a given system is influenced by every other part, so that a change in one part is likely to bring about a change in every other part; and (3) that a system is in dynamic equilibrium so that change occurs within limits. The analogy can be made to the thermostatic feedback system that regulates the temperature of our homes. The temperature is never exactly the same from moment to moment, but it only goes beyond the limits established by the thermostat when the system breaks down in some way. In society such a breakdown might be a revolution, although most structure-functionalists would prefer to view the revolution as a less dramatic change. When the equilibrium system breaks down, the society ceases to be. Short of such catastrophe, change is incremental and bounded by the system's equilibrating mechanism—the norms that govern behavior. The dominant concern of most structure-functionalists is this normative system and its components, not the factors that change it.

Since every society must be viewed as a whole, the analysis of details must always be couched in the context of the whole and the boundary between the whole and the part specified so that the nature of the interaction can be more readily observed. As bounded phenomena with recognizable identities, all societies are presumed to have certain "functional prerequisites" that must be met by their institutions or they will cease to exist. These institutions are thus analogous to the organs of the body. But because of the reciprocal relationship between man and his environment, institutions meet these basic needs in quite different ways. Different institutions (or the same institution) function in diverse societies in different ways in order to cope with the same basic problems presented by the primary need to survive.

In every society the family is the institution that is normatively entrusted with the responsibility of the reproduction and basic socialization of the children who are necessary to the perpetuation of that society. Some structure-functionalists argue that the family as a particular structure (a system of *positions*—such as father, mother, children—and *roles*—behavior deemed appropriate for persons in these positions) universally performs the same functions. A particularly clear case is made for this position by George Peter Murdock in his *Social Structure*.[6] This will be considered further in the next chapter.

Those using this approach are commonly divided into *macro functionalists*, who deal with large social systems, and *micro functionalists*, who concern themselves with small systems such as the family. In the macro functional approach, the family may be seen as one element or institution within the larger system. In the micro functional approach, the internal dynamics of family life are foremost. In both the interrelationship between the family and its environment is considered important. In both the family as an institution is often considered to be passive. Concentration upon how the family actively produces members through the process of socialization is more commonly the consideration of a second conceptual framework, role theory.

Role Theory: Two divergent traditions, *social behaviorism* and *symbolic*

---

6. George Peter Murdock, *Social Structure* (New York: Free Press, 1965).

interactionism, have developed from role theory. The behaviorists see socialization as an interaction process. Roles develop out of persons in interaction as they mutually define the situation in which their interaction occurs. Roles persist independently of the individual actors in the sense that they are retained as commonly held expectations of behavior appropriate to a social position.

Symbolic interactionism, on the other hand, concentrates on roles as they develop from individuals' attempts to communicate. As man's primary symbol system, language is seen as a determining factor in his development. In the view of symbolic interactionists, there is always the possibility of completely new or emergent elements being introduced. Individual autonomy is given great consideration. Thus, the *stability* of the role is amazing, not the fact that it changes.

Theorists such as George H. Mead and Charles H. Cooley assume that we have a social as well as a personal component. The social component—or the objectively perceivable "Me"—is essentially a repertoire of behaviors developed in response to the expectations of others. Especially of importance are those others who are significant to us, our parents, close friends, persons whom we consider mentors, etc. For Mead the "I," or perceiving subject, is almost an illusion. The self is so much determined by the particular social situation in which the individual finds himself, that the "I" is all but eliminated. We are little more than the sum total of our situational selves. To the *extent* that this is so (and that is a continuing debate) it does not make sense to speak of people as having a "personality," that is as being aggressive or docile. We should speak instead of aggressive or docile *behaviors* and seek to control them situationally.

Cooley's conception of the "looking-glass self" emphasizes the extent to which we are interdependent beings. In this view the "self" is composed of three elements: (*1*) an estimation of alter's conception of ego, (*2*) an assessment of alter's evaluation of that conception, and (*3*) ego's self-assessment such as a feeling of competence or guilt. We cannot become human unless others "call us forth" by giving us cues as to who we are. Such a view seems supported by studies of isolated and extremely deprived children. In Cooley's thought, the family is a *primary group* characterized by its small size, face-to-face interaction, persistence, intimacy, and the care and concern that its members have for one another. All of these characteristics contribute to its effectiveness as a socializing agent.

To this author it seems that when we are concerned with understanding how the family is related to other institutions in society, structure-functionalism is more appropriate. When we want to understand more about the internal processes of the family—particularly that of socialization—role theory seems better.[7]

---

7. George Herbert Mead's contribution to sociology is found in three volumes posthumously published by The University of Chicago Press: *Mind, Self and Society* (1934), *Movements of Thought in the Nineteenth Century* (1936), and *The Philosophy of the Act* (1938). A useful summary is found in Anselm Strauss (ed.), *The Social Psychology of George Herbert Mead* (Chicago: University of Chicago Press, 1962). Charles Horton Cooley's concept of the "Looking-Glass Self" is best developed in his *Human Nature and*

The Utility of Analytic Models: How useful are the models that are derived from analysis? This is always dependent upon the modification, "How useful to whom?" A model describing the buying habits of our family might well be invaluable to a consumer analyst who is interested in selling certain products, to a population expert interested in disseminating effective means of contraception, to an urban planner interested in middle-class behavior pertaining to residence choice, and to hundreds of other persons who might profit from such a very limited construct of the family and its processes. Indeed, many of these interested persons might require only a few significant facts about us (such as our income, stage of development, etc.) as one family in a known larger population in order to meet their needs. There is really no need for the model of our family to fit or reflect precisely the reality of our family in order for it to be useful to social scientists, politicians, social workers, and even to our own family itself.

A problem arises, however, when we cease to regard such constructs as simply models and think of them as accurate portrayals of reality. We then commit what Whitehead has called the "fallacy of misplaced concreteness." At the level of our tacit formulation of models from direct experience we call this "stereotyping." *Stereotyping* is the persistent retention of a characterization of a person as a member of a group in spite of the evidence he gives us about himself to the contrary. Thus all blacks are lazy, all Chinese sly. The problem with stereotyping is not the use of generalization about a group of people, but rather its inappropriate retention in the face of contrary evidence.

Because a particular model has been useful in one situation, we wish it to be so in another. We bend data to fit the needs of the model or simply cease to test it by further investigation of concrete situations. Most commonly in the social sciences we identify with a school of thought and attempt to see the whole world through its conceptual framework. Thus micro functionalists think of the family as a small group despite its obvious differences; macro functionalists contend that the nuclear family is the universal building block of social structure in spite of much evidence to the contrary; and role theorists commonly assume that socialization is a completely adequate schema with which to account for the development of children into adults.

The fact that most of us know about families tacitly leads us to recognize the shallowness of the social science models and makes us rightfully suspicious of much of that which is paraded about as knowledge. Our tacitly understood models further enable us to apply social science generalizations to our own situations with less distortion than if we behaved as though we thought the scientific model was real. But because we are so close to such knowledge, it is not readily available for long-range planning in the case of our own family's future—much less as a basis for a national family policy. Indeed, as I have indicated, such information can easily lead us to assume that

---

the *Social Order* (New York: Schocken, 1964). A discussion of his works is found in Lewis A. Coser, *Masters of Sociological Thought* (New York: Harcourt Brace Jovanovich, 1971). A more detailed discussion of the process of socialization is found in Chapter 11 of this book.

all families are like our own in all important details, or at least that they "ought" to be. We do not accept differences easily, therefore, in large part because we cannot intuitively understand them. While we may profess a desire to accept those who live differently from us, we tend to make our everyday decisions so as to spend most of our time among those who live similarly.

Thus, our cities—which, as Lewis Mumford points out, offer the largest stage for the fullest human drama—tend to be experienced by the average urbanite not in terms of their rich variety of peoples, places, and experiences, but rather in terms of homogeneous neighborhoods of like-minded, similarly attired, reasonable people like themselves. If we are white, Anglo-Saxon, protestants (wasps), we often know little about how Blacks or Jews or hobos or Italian- or Mexican- or Puerto Rican-Americans live. If we think about it at all, we might assume that they live much like we do. If we find otherwise, we might think such different behavior undesirable or at least a little eccentric, if not down right immoral. We want *them* to change their ways so that they will be more like us. We tend to feel that our way is the right way and that it should remain unchanged.

The two perspectives—the tacit understanding of family life derived from our personal experience and the more impersonal explicit "scientific" analysis —sometimes reinforce one another, sometimes raise questions or contradict each other. Each has its utility and its limitations. While the former concerns itself mainly with concrete families and the latter with abstract generalizations about "all families" or all families of a particular type, both use models that are distinguishable from the world as it is. The models derived from our direct experience tend to be limited expressions of ethnocentric preferences. The models derived from scientific analysis tend toward broad generalizations devoid of meaning or interest to anyone but an intellectual elite. We have a tendency today to prefer one or the other approach to the understanding of the family, but if we really are concerned about how we can improve the quality of its life, we cannot afford to accept or dismiss either approach without examination.[8] Both can enrich our capacity for rational, compassionate action.

Our Changing Families

OUTSIDE SOCIAL FACTORS

Despite ideological conservatism, our families have changed quite dramatically in response to developments in other areas of our social and economic life. And they will continue to do so as the result of even more dra-

8. My view of the need to include both approaches in any study of the family is reflected in methodological preferences. I have had most experience as a participant observer. Participant observation is a method in which the major instrument brought into the field is the researcher himself. It assumes that social reality cannot be understood without the researcher's taking a role in the situation he wishes to study. As such, it attempts to combine tacit understanding with more "objective" approaches. In many regards it is similar to the approach of an ethnologist studying a foreign culture. A more detailed examination of this method is found in Severyn Bruyn, *The Human Perspective in Sociology* (Englewood Cliffs, N. J.: Prentice-Hall, 1966).

matic changes introduced by science and technology in the future. The Industrial Revolution, in addition to its broad-scale effects, had an impact on family patterns: the automobile emancipated the teenager from the bosom of his family, and courtship was carried on away from the front porch or parlor where it had been supervised by adults. The pill has furthered the emancipation and freed us from the necessity to tie sexual activity to procreation. Coitus has become a form of recreation, a mode of communication, and even a form of religious expression for large numbers of people who enjoy sex without guilt regardless of their marital status.

We cannot anticipate, at present, the results of developments in the biological sciences upon the family of the future, but books such as *The Second Genesis* suggest that they will be quite dramatic.[9] The capacity to produce children of any specified sex, with predetermined special characteristics, without the necessity of sexual intercourse or perhaps without even the need to implant an egg in a mother's womb (the embryo developing inside a mechanical womb "in vitro" where it can be carefully watched and subjected to corrective surgery if necessary) might render obsolete our present forms of marriage and family. Indeed, much less dynamic factors have radically changed family life in the farm communities of the Kibbutz. In these pioneer communities of the Negeb desert, the children are raised by community-appointed *meteplets*, or nurses, quite apart from their parents' living quarters. The result is a different modal personality in the children of the second and third generations (see Chapter 16).

When we become alarmed over the increasing divorce rate, the growing numbers of illegitimate children, the increasing freedom in extramarital and premarital sexual activities, we tend to see these as evidence of the family's disorganization; but they could be viewed equally well as newly emergent ways of organizing family life in response to a rapidly changing world.

Families change in response to a number of factors—cultural norms that seem to exist independently of the individual members of society; technological developments (the invention of the automobile); new situations (a new home in a new place). They change in response to public policy whether or not such change was intended, as in the case of the ADC fathers who leave their homes so that their families can get help. Imperfections in the socialization process and the idiosyncracies of each new generation make children different from their parents. (The "generation gap" but highlights some of these problems.) Families change because they *decide* to change for a variety of reasons, and because they *develop* from the married couple, through child rearing, and the empty nest, to the death of one of the originally married pair. They cease to be when both are dead.

If we conceive of the family as constantly changing, we must be clear about what we mean by this. Accepting for the moment the view of the family as a system of roles (wife-mother, husband-father, sibling-sibling) that make up its structure, we see that this structure changes as the family grows or diminishes in size, providing different patterns of interacting individuals

9. Albert Rosenfeld, *The Second Genesis* (Englewood Cliffs, N. J.: Prentice-Hall, 1969).

with new roles that reflect the aging of the actors and the new demands of different interaction networks. This may occur as a result of its development or in response to crises (as when members die or must move away). It may result from decisions such as to participate in wife swapping or to adopt a child. Further, the behavior that is expected in these various roles may change —as when women were emancipated in the 1920s and encouraged to work in the factories during World War II, or when parents respond to fads in child-rearing advice and in one decade expect their children to be aggressively expressive and in another, submissive.

This structure of interacting roles can be considered to fulfill certain needs of society as well as the needs of its members (these constitute its "functions" in sociological terms). These functions can change. Clearly the family meets fewer needs of its members now than it did before the Industrial Revolution. It has suffered a loss in some of its functions, and altered its mode of involvement in the case of others. It is no longer the major source of protection for its members; it does not provide the formal education its children need to become effective members of an industrial society; and it is less likely to be an economically productive unit. On the other hand, its behavior as a consumer unit has increased in importance (to the society), and some argue that it has increased in its capacity to provide for the emotional gratification of its members as well. With regard to education, while it is no longer the formal educator, it spends a great deal of time and money (at least in the upper-middle class) making sure that its children are well educated.

We must note that some of these changes in family living are expected and some are not. Thus the family is expected to *develop* in a certain manner. Individual families may change quite dramatically over the course of their development, but the norms governing that development may remain relatively unchanged over several generations. On the other hand, the changing role of women and the implications of a mother's career for the raising of her children were largely unexpected.

It is probable that the rate of change in family life will increase as other changes in our society come ever more rapidly. The issue is not, therefore, whether the family will change, but rather whether we should become much more aware of this change and attempt to gain more control of it.

PERSONAL CHOICE

It is often difficult to evaluate the element of conscious choice in a given decision. We are as likely today to consider men able and willing to act in all situations and, therefore, responsible for their actions as we are at other times to think of them as determined. When individuals "decide" to live in a way that is different from the way we live, we often consider them immoral or unethical. On the other hand, some of us consider such free choice to be an illusion (even though at times we still infer that men are responsible). More frequently, however, the element of personal choice seems insignificant or irrelevant.

Public policy sometimes reflects a conscious attempt to change the family. The policy-maker is most frequently concerned with some other person's family. Families that become the object of public policy frequently belong to some relatively powerless portion of our population such as the poor. Daniel P. Moynihan's *The Negro Family: The Case for National Action* might seem quite plausible to a middle-class White who feels the burden of welfare expenditures and fears the consequences of crime in the ghetto, but it was seen as highly insulting and quite threatening to the black community—particularly the intellectual element within it.

Sometimes we simply support policy that affects our families without being directly aware of it. We give implicit endorsement to a "free-enterprise" system that forces the average professional man to make a choice between his *career* and his *family* in regard to the distribution of his time, interests, commitments (and indeed his very passions) so that we talk with some realism about "corporation widows." Or we support the school system and send our children off to public or private schools at increasingly early ages with the conviction that if they are not trained early they will have a greater chance of failure—thereby building into the motivational patterns of our children the *fear of failure*. We do not feel it inappropriate—even in such a context—that we are prevented by law from assuming the responsibility for personally educating our children (regardless of our qualifications) unless we are certified to teach.

Sometimes we become aware of the need to change as a result of an increasing awareness of our society's problems. We might search for better ways of rearing less aggressive children when we see the price that aggression is extracting from our nation's resources, or we might limit the number of our children because of a concern about the population explosion. We might come to understand behavior which we previously considered unacceptable because of a broader understanding of the problems and potentials of human sexuality. We might be motivated to alter our patterns of consumption as a result of a greater understanding of the market and our nation's economy or because of our conviction that environmental pollution directly relates to our need for conspicuous and wasteful consumption.

Confrontation with problems that demand action forces us to reconsider our family's style of living and its mode of coping with its world. We may be forced to consider various alternatives as one component of the solution to a social problem we are concerned about. But once we have made a commitment to change our style of family life we may find that we are unable to do so.

In part this may be the case because "the family" is not, after all, a single variable. It is a large number of variables interacting in a complex but reasonably patterned way—a subsystem within the larger social system. To the extent that alteration in one variable produces some alteration in many others, every part may resist the change in every other part. This is particularly true of the family because we are ideologically committed to its stability. The family is "the building block" of our society. We believe that all else depends upon its health, and we equate its health with a single normative definition (the nuclear family). This normative family receives strong support from the Judeo-Christian tradition and is embedded in our legal structure.

While we may not explicitly view the family as an element of a system, systemic constraint is felt concretely in the form of the handicaps placed upon us by our class situation. Persons of the lower class tend more often to live in family forms not of their choosing and, because of their relative lack of power, to experience the effect of others' efforts to change their style of life. They do not have the money or the leisure to pursue actively the alternatives that are available to, say, the jet set. Nor do they have the feeling of creativeness or the self-assurance that could provide the sense of freedom to experiment that is characteristic of the artistic subculture of the voluntary poor. Life in the lower-lower class is more likely to be experienced passively because of a realistic assessment of limited opportunity. In the consideration of intentional change, therefore, it is very important that we recognize that we are not all equally free to change our life styles.

A Brief Overview

In the first section of the book, I will look at the family comparatively in a wide range of contexts. I will take up first the matter of definition, which is essentially a means of helping us decide how concrete families in diverse cultures are alike or different. From the perspective of intentional change, the debate over the universality of the nuclear family is an attempt to discover what is essential and, therefore, what should not be changed. Research indicates that even though this family form is not essential, it is very widespread. The discussion of its limitations as a universal family form provides a rudimentary sense of both the limits and the possible variations in viable family structures.

The structure-functional framework will be utilized most heavily in this section to examine the relationship between diverse family forms and their cultures. I will document as fully as I can the simple truth that human beings adequately meet similar needs with a wide variety of functional family forms and life styles. It need not be assumed, therefore, that any change from our present arrangement is evidence of "disorganization" or decay. On the other hand, not all of these functional alternatives will work as well for us as for other peoples. The character of our society must be taken into consideration along with its particular needs and preferences. But, to the extent that we can perceive similarities between ourselves and others, we can hazard some guesses about the likelihood of similar changes resulting in similar consequences in our own case.

In the second section, I will discuss the family as it is found in the United States. A characterization of class-based patterns of family life will suggest that the normal American family is a grand abstraction indeed. While Americans may be able to agree on certain basic norms that *ought* to govern family life, they in fact live in a variety of styles that contradict this normative model and increasing numbers are rejecting the norms outright. A sketch of the upper-middle class family in its native habitat—the suburb—is contrasted with an examination of the lower-lower class black family of the ghetto in order to further question the assumption of a normal or typical American family and to provide further insight into the variety of life styles that in fact obtain.

In the third section, I will focus upon the internal dynamics of American families. In a discussion of the development of families through their life cycle, the emphasis will be placed upon the middle-class family. Their pattern most closely approximates the statistical average. Middle-class persons must change the pattern of their family life in order to cope with problems presented by particular stages of their *development* (raising children, coping with retirement, etc.). They must also make adjustments in their life styles in order to cope with *changes* in the life cycle pattern. Couples now spend more time together without children, the husband retires earlier, and both can expect to live longer than was true at the turn of the century. This trend seems likely to continue. I will discuss the dominant factors governing mate choice and note that, although our system has few formal rules governing the selection of a mate, those persons who choose the socially proper person can expect on the average to have less trouble with their neighbors and are more likely to remain married than those who violate the informal regulations. Thus the family promotes social stability on the one hand, but, by denying many an access to upward mobility, prompts revolt on the other. Finally, I will look at the changing patterns of child rearing advice and behavior. In the 1930s there was great optimism that children could be so effectively socialized that they could be "made to order." I will indicate why this optimism is not now widely shared.

Section four takes up four social issues that cry out for changes in American family life. The sexual revolution, the generation gap, women's liberation, and the population explosion all raise questions about the common conception of what a family ought to be and suggest that alternative styles might help our society to cope more effectively with some of its problems. Rather than assuming that to change is bad, they argue that not to change is to court disaster.

In the fifth section, therefore, I discuss the matter of planned or intentional change. Case studies will provide us with several examples of how the family has been altered intentionally. In the case of Oneida, the "experiment" lasted only thirty years; in the case of Russia, the family policy seems to have in some ways "backfired"; but in the case of the Kibbutz, a new social order is entering its third generation and seems to provide a richly rewarding life for over 90,000 persons. How were these changes possible? Then, approaching the problem from another perspective, I draw upon several studies that attempt to predict how the family in the United States will change. Again, most of these assume the middle-class model, and their utility for others—particularly the lower-lower class—is quite limited. I describe a number of trends and, finally, examine a number of prescriptions. These latter do not pretend to be predictive. They ask, rather, what is desirable and suggest how we might achieve it. They do not assume that we will do so inevitably. Indeed, some raise questions about our capacity to intentionally change the style of our family life.

In the Afterword, I discuss what I think desirable change might be and acknowledge that my ideal certainly will not meet the needs of everyone.

In this section I will describe some of the functional alternatives to our own family that are to be found in other cultures. Although all men face certain basic problems, the cultural solutions to these problems vary greatly. The family reproduces and socializes its young according to the cultural prescriptions of a particular society. These prescriptions change as a society's technology, its relations with its neighbors, its sex ratio, its natural resources, and the dreams of its visionaries change, but we seem to be more able to alter intentionally the character of our family life than most societies.

While it is true that much of the variation in behavior and family life styles given in these cross-cultural chapters can be seen in our own society, there is a much stronger tendency to view behavior variation negatively when it occurs "close to home." Thus, while we might accept the use of artificial penises as normal in other cultures, we would look on their use in our own society as perverted. While we deplore sexual experimentation among our children, we may be quite willing to examine the positive effects of such activities in another culture. It is for this reason that I have chosen a cross-cultural approach for this section.

Descriptions of how the family functions in various societies will not tell us how a similar form will function in our own because the family as a social institution is dependent upon its society. Our nuclear family, for example, is in many ways more suited to an industrial society than is an extended family. At the same time, our kinship system requires us to draw upon many secondary institutions to provide structure, whereas in pre-industrial societies the lineage (either one's mother's or one's father's kin) is often strong enough to be the only structure.

Neither can these descriptions tell us how we *ought* to live in families. We have a different set of priorities based on a unique history and face somewhat different problems. However, an awareness of how other people live in families should raise a question in our minds as to whether our own way is the only right way.

CROSS-CULTURAL VARIATIONS

2. Do All of Us Live in Families?

. . . the problem of the family should not be approached in a dogmatic way. As a matter of fact, this is one of the more elusive questions in the whole field of social organization. . . . When we consider the wide diversity of human societies which have been observed since, let us say, Heroditus's time until present days, the only thing which can be said is as follows: monogamic, conjugal family is fairly frequent. . . . It is [however] at least conceivable that a perfectly stable and durable society could exist without it. Hence the difficult problem: If there is no natural law making the family universal, how can we explain why it is found practically everywhere?

CLAUDE LÉVI-STRAUSS

It is difficult to not be dogmatic about what constitutes a family. To most of us it seems so obvious that it needs no further examination. This is particularly true when we come to see that a family not unlike our own is a very common one. Our ethnocentric preferences are apparently upheld by ethnographic data, and again we are motivated to look no further for a basic social structure. Lévi-Strauss contends, however, that it is, in fact, one of the most complex problems in the field of social organization.

If we begin our discussion of the "family" with the question, "Do all of us live in families?" we can clearly answer, "No!" Some persons never marry and, although they may have once lived in a family, they live alone—perhaps without any living kin. Some persons grow up without having known both of their biological parents. They may live in orphanages, or with kin, or with only one parent in "broken families." Others must live out their lives in prisons, asylums, reformatories, and the like. The fact that we consider all of these persons "deviant cases" (the unfortunate, the ill, the irresponsible, the criminal, and the anti-social) must not blind us to the fact that individuals can survive—indeed they often thrive—in spite of their not living in a family.

When we consider further that many persons live in "families" that we do not consider "proper" families (homosexuals, hippies, bigamists, swingers, and other experimenters in conjugal communism) and that some of these may make notable contributions to our society, we realize that "family" is, in large measure, an *ideal*. It reflects a common conception of a desirable way of living that *does not have to exist* "of necessity."[1] Indeed, when we hear someone speak about the "disorganization" that has fallen upon the American family (which can *usually* be taken to mean that a certain *normative* conception of the properly organized family has been violated), we might wonder if, in his view, any of us live in families.[2]

1. Data collected in 1968 on families in the United States by the Population Reference Bureau are interpreted in *Population Profile* (U.S.G.P.O., July 28, 1969) to mean that the American family is a "thriving institution." This is based largely on the fact that more people got married in the United States in 1968 than in any other year since 1946 and that 92 percent of all Americans lived in families in 1967 (99 percent of all persons under the age of 18 lived in families). On closer examination, however, we note that 87 percent of these families are formed around a husband and a wife—the rest are living in single-parent families. Furthermore, about fifteen million Americans did not live in families in 1967. If we add these to those living in "broken" families, we come up with a figure of about forty-one million Americans who are not living in what most Americans would consider the ideal family *structure*. These figures do not reflect the fact that many who now live in families have remarried one or more times and thus have family obligations that extend beyond their current spouse and the children of that spouse. We do know, in this regard, that the rate of remarriage for divorced men rose from 168 to 211 per thousand during the period 1960–1966 and that the rate for women increased from 122 to 130. How many of these are third marriages (or, for that matter, even fourth or fifth) and what proportion of the population thus lives in such family types we do not know given the present method of data collection. What is apparent from the above is that the number of persons living in households where husband and wife are married once is considerably smaller than the figures on married couples reflect. We have not collected data of persons confined to institutions for life, or for significant portions thereof, nor are we able to detect more subtle deviation from our family ideal with any accuracy. Kinsey suggests that 50 percent of the married men in the U.S. commit adultery, which might not affect family form directly but does violate the norm of life-long monogamy. It should not be inferred from the above data that the family is undergoing extreme disorganization. We should, however, be aware of the fact that when we speak of family as a man and woman living together in life-long monogamy with only the children of their union, we are not referring to quite as common a type in practice as we might naïvely imagine.

2. For example, Ruth Nanda Anshen writes, "the moral ambivalence of our society

In the examination of other societies (see Fig. 2–1 for a map of the societies discussed in this section) it becomes clear that many forms of "family" are able to function adequately in meeting the needs of the individuals and societies that depend upon them. But it is also true that even though this variation in family form and function might be potentially infinite, we can limit the variation to a small number of patterns.[3] There seems to be, as the anthropologists would say, some "logic" to these patterns of human interaction.

The family is, nevertheless, a complex variable, not a universal structure derived from biological necessity nor a universal normative ideal based upon religious or cultural dogma. From the perspective of family change, the concern to define a universal family form as a functional requisite can be seen as a quest for limits. Is there, in fact, a basic human institution that is to be found without exception in all societies because its functions are essential to a society's survival? If there is, then surely this family form must not be altered. If there is not such an elementary building block, then the range of experimentation seems wider. I am inclined to argue that there is no such building block. The discussion of the problems of definition that follows should help to clarify this position. In this discussion I will not try to produce a single definition, but will discuss the strengths and weaknesses of two conceptual approaches: structure-functionalism and role theory.

Problems of Definition

The fact that patterns are discernible does not mean that they are easy to discover. In the field it sometimes becomes difficult for even the trained

---

has penetrated to the very heart of the problem of our time—the family and the home in which our children must receive their precepts and guidance. The failure of society is reflected in the failure of parenthood, for it is within the family that the seeds of anxiety, fear, and delinquency are sown. . . . The family in its present state of dissolution reflects the spiritual poverty of modern man, man as the experiencing, responsible, and deciding self, endowed by nature with freedom and will, yet beset with confusion and isolation from the dynamic stream of living reality. . . . This volume is born out of the consciousness of the family's spiritual emptiness and conceptual failure. . . . [Anshen's conception of the family is not defined, but taken for granted to be that of the traditional American ideal whose value to society is self evident.] . . . We attempt to present a philosophy of the family which points out the fallacy inherent in the principles of negation and evolution in that theory and to indicate the error which contends that 'progress' consists in the abandonment of the basic family structure and the perceptual creation of novel types of families." *The Family: Its Function and Destiny,* rev. ed. (New York: Harper & Row, 1959), pp. xvi–4.

3. It should be obvious that the discernment of a pattern does not mean that it exists "out there" in the society. It may well be more a function of the organizing mind of the perceiver than a principle of organization within the society itself. The whole tradition in anthropology is an attempt to minimize this effect through detailed ethnographic data collected, insofar as possible, from the point of view of the individuals in the society studied. Nevertheless, these data are analyzed and broad generations are imposed upon them. Their utility depends upon how accurately they can predict behavior on the one hand, and what new and unsuspected insights are churned up on the other. Their major defect lies in our tendency to equate them with concrete reality, as I have suggested in Chapter 1.

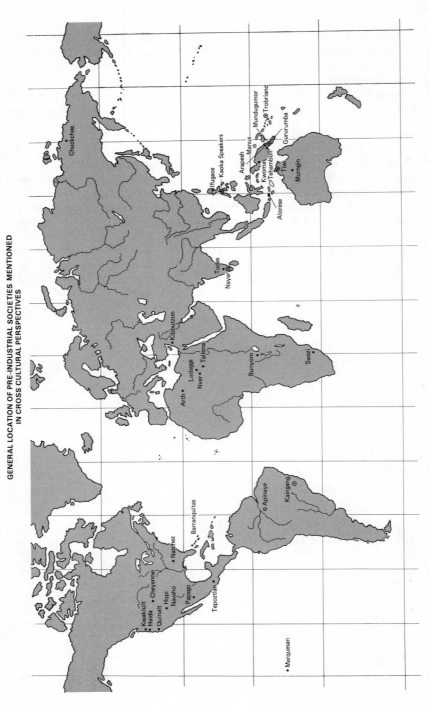

GENERAL LOCATION OF PRE-INDUSTRIAL SOCIETIES MENTIONED
IN CROSS CULTURAL PERSPECTIVES

FIGURE 2-1

eye to see anything resembling the family as we know it. The nuclear family (parents and their children) can be *recognized as a functional unity* in all but a few societies known to anthropologists. But it is by no means the *most preferred* family form.[4] The problem of conflicting preferences often makes it difficult for us to see what another people's preferences actually are. This, in turn, contributes to our problem in isolating the "family" as another society would see it. We can begin to appreciate the practical problems of definition by taking a brief look at the Kaingang.

THE KAINGANG

The Kaingang are a people of the high jungles of southeastern Brazil. With a population of 106 in 1932, the Kaingang lived on a small reservation in the state of Santa Catarina.[5] Some changes had taken place in their essentially nomadic way of life, but their culture was far from dead when studied by Jules Henry.

The following examples are taken from Henry's description of the Kaingang in his book, *Jungle People*:

> *The elaborate laws of sexual avoidance that chart the behavior of men and women in many primitive societies, dividing the entire community into the touchables and the untouchables, are undreamt of among the Kaingang. Little boys and girls play together in rough and tumble. Brothers and sisters, brothers and sisters-in-law and cousins, sleep next to one another, crosslegs, or embrace one another. The corollaries to this are the marriages and love affairs among almost all classes of relatives.* Only marriages between parents and children and between full brothers and sisters are avoided. *Marriages between half brothers and sisters are rare. . . .*
>
> *When a husband goes away, his wife becomes fair game for anyone who is interested, and she is generally willing prey for the enterprising hunter. . . .*
>
> *In our society the traditional, the ideal stabilizer of marriage is love —an exclusive sex interest in one person. The Kaingang have no tradition, no background for the development of such an interest.* Marriage in other primitive societies is sometimes stabilized by a large payment for the bride, but in Kaingang society there is no such payment. *If a woman leaves her husband she can always find a relative who will take care of her. Her brother or her cousin or her sister will always take her in, and although she lacks the full security that marriage gave her, she need not starve, for there are any number of men who will accept her as an added responsibility without complaint, even boasting a little that they took care of her and that she called them yugn [term applied to father, grandfather, and all males much older than oneself—men who have had relations with one's mother].*
>
> *A man separated from his wife may live with someone else and*

4. See George Murdock, *Social Structure* (New York: Free Press, 1965), p. 24.
5. This may seem to be a small number of people but many societies studied by anthropologists number only a few hundred.

share his fire. At the worst he can cook his own meals and spread his own bed, for no shame attaches to a man who does a woman's work. But after a woman has borne three children a marriage does not break up.

But separations before many children are born are legion. Young people frequently pass through one or two marriages before they finally settle down. The relationship between the sexes is informal, and there is no marriage ceremony. *In its early stages the only thing that distinguishes a marriage from a protracted affair is the announcement by the principals that they are married. There is no term for marriage. . . . "He sat with her 'means' he married her."* Sometimes people do not know whether a couple who have separated have ever been married. . . .

Once a couple are married they do not drop the liaisons formed before marriage. Their long training in philandering and the absence of an ideal of faithfulness have not suited them to the stability that marriage implies. Furthermore the absence of binding legal forms or big property stakes, as well as the knowledge that a meal can always be found at one's father's or brother's fire, that one's mother or sister-in-law is ready to cook the food and spread the bed, makes marriage brittle and its rupture not sharply felt. *Yet, in an utterly contradictory manner, the Kaingang believe that a man and woman, once they are "sitting together," belong to each other, and they use the same word to designate this possession as they use for the exclusive possession of material objects. . . . The young man who for years before his marriage has dallied with the wife of anyone from his father to his second cousin, who has day in and day out enjoyed adultery with an equally delighted adultress, decides suddenly, once he is married, that his possession should be exclusive. "I left my wife,"* Yuven said to me, *"because she took Kanyahe and Kundagn as lovers. She sleeps with everyone. All the women are that way. When their husbands go away they sleep with others; that is why I want to marry a Brazilian woman."*

The culture has so little immediate stake in marriage that it exercises itself very little about it. . . . Kaingang marriage, except when it becomes the temporary concern of some go-between, is the immediate affair only of the principals. . . .

Polygamy comes about in Kaingang society in the same informal, almost accidental manner as monogamic unions. In Kaingang ideology one of the primary causes of polygamy is that "There are no other men. . . ."

The children belong to their parents, if one can speak of "belonging" in a society in which children are not valued as property. What we so strongly idealize the Kaingang actually feel, for to them children are like highly charged emotional batteries. They are valued for their potentialities as emotionally satisfying living things, like most other pets. There is no idea expressed that when they grow up they will feed and protect their parents, for in nomadic days the latter knew only too well the whims that urged and the necessities that compelled their children to wander away from them. . . . But when children are left fatherless it often devolves upon the father's family to take care of them, for they feel that responsibility, and it is in this way that it comes about that a widow often marries someone of her husband's kin. She goes where her children are, and it is there, in the midst of her husband's close kin, that she begins her sex life anew and often finds her new husband. . . .[6]

The Kaingang, unlike many primitive societies, do not depend upon kinship to bring about a cohesive society through the regulation of marriage, parenthood, and descent. They weave what cohesiveness they have out of their sexual interests. The fact that they are a small society probably accounts for their emphasis upon these smaller units that form around the current sexual interests of the adults. With only thirty-six adult males and thirty adult females in their society, and with few restrictions on their sexual behavior, such interests could easily involve all of the people in the society. Nevertheless, the Kaingang remain something of an ethnographic enigma. Henry found that few commonly accepted generalizations about family and kinship systems adequately described Kaingang society. Going back over this brief description of the Kaingang should help us to appreciate the complexity involved in the understanding of the social organization of even a small primitive society.

Fortunately for the student of social structure, not all societies are as informal as the Kaingang. In most, marriage is very much a concern of the society, and the family is functionally interdependent with larger units of the kinship system. In order to understand such situations better, however, it is necessary to define more precisely what we mean by "family," to describe its more common forms and the manner in which they are interrelated with other kin units in a society.

The problem of defining the family lies not only in the complexity of the social structure being described but also in one's point of view. The definition used reflects not only social facts but also what we think are important about these facts. Definitions from our two major conceptual frameworks will be examined below, and others will be introduced later.

THE STRUCTURE-FUNCTIONAL APPROACH TO DEFINITION

Murdock's Nuclear Family: One of the most straightforward answers to the question of what we mean by "family" is given by George Peter Murdock:

> The family is a social group characterized by common residence, economic cooperation and reproduction. It includes adults of both sexes, at least two of whom maintain a socially approved sexual relationship, and one or more children, own or adopted, of the sexually cohabiting adults.[7]

He further classifies the family into three types: (1) the *nuclear family* consisting of a married man and woman with their offspring; (2) the *polyga-*

6. Jules Henry, *Jungle People* (New York: Vintage Books, 1964), pp. 17–36. [emphasis added]

7. Murdock *op cit.*, p. 1.

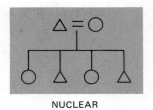

NUCLEAR

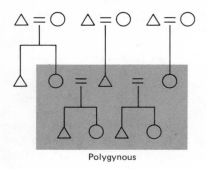

Polygynous

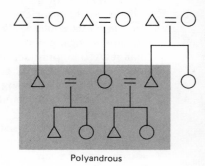

Polyandrous

POLYGAMOUS

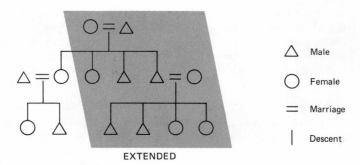

EXTENDED

△ Male

○ Female

= Marriage

| Descent

FIGURE 2–2
Three family types, after Murdock

mous family consisting of two or more nuclear families joined by multiple marriage (that is, a man or woman who has married two or more mates and had children by them, considered as one family); and (3) the *extended family* consisting of two or more nuclear families formed by adding the families of married children. Thus a woman, her husband, their children, and their married daughters with their husbands are one kind of extended family formed through extension of the female line. The male line may be extended analogously, and in some instances both lines may be extended.[8] Because polygamous and extended families are formed by adding nuclear families together, Murdock called both *composite* families (see Fig. 2–2).

The nuclear family, Murdock argues, should be our unit of comparison for it is found in every known society:

> *The nuclear family is a universal human social grouping. Either as the sole prevailing form of the family or as the basic unit from which more complex familiar forms are compounded, it exists as a distinct and strongly functional group in every known society. No exception, at least, has come to light in the 250 representative cultures surveyed for the present study.*[9]

He is not arguing that it is numerically the most common form in every culture or that all societies have the majority of their members living in such a family. This is not the case in fact. In primitive societies, the nuclear family is more frequently to be found enmeshed in either an extended family or a polygamous family. Murdock is arguing that it is, nevertheless, *discernible* and *functional* in all societies—even if only as an element in a larger composite family or kin unit.

Murdock's argument, however, is made more complex when he goes on to assert that not only is the nuclear family found in all known societies, but that it also is associated everywhere with four basic functions: sexual regulation, economic cooperation, reproduction, and education. These functions (which are essential to the survival of a society) are most expeditiously performed by persons living in nuclear families. The nuclear family structure is, therefore, necessary for a society's existence. This accounts for its universality.

Critique of Murdock's Position: Unfortunately, while Murdock's views have wide acceptance, the case for the universality of the nuclear family is far from made. Two well-known critiques of Murdock's position are those by Kathleen Gough in her study of the Nayar,[10] and Milford Spiro in his study of the Israeli Kibbutzim.[11] Each can help us understand this problem of definition

8. *Ibid.*
9. *Ibid.*, p. 2. [emphasis added] In light of what we have discussed in the introduction to this section, the debate over the universality of the family must be seen in a more limited perspective than the adjective "universal" might suggest. We do not have sufficient data to conclusively answer the question, "Is the family to be found in all human societies?" simply because we do not have access to data on all human societies—and never will have. Is it then found in *all for which we have sufficient data?* This depends upon how we define it.
10. E. Kathleen Gough, "The Nayars and the Definition of Marriage," *Journal of the Royal Anthropological Institute*, Vol. 85 (1955), 45–80. See also Joan P. Mencher, "The Nayars of South Malabar" in M. F. Nimkoff (ed.), *Comparative Family Systems* (Boston: Houghton Mifflin, 1965) pp. 163–91.
11. M. E. Spiro, "Is the Family Universal?" *American Anthropologist*, Vol. 56 (1954), 839–46. See also M. E. Spiro, *Children of the Kibbutz* (Cambridge, Mass.: Harvard University Press, 1958).

while providing additional ethnographic data about how different families live.

The Nayar: The Nayar as they are found today do not contradict Murdock's assertion that the nuclear family is functional in all societies. An estimated 30 percent of all Nayar households are *now* such nuclear family units. About 50 percent are extended family households, and the remaining 20 percent of the households are complicated by the fact that they contain a miscellaneous assortment of relatives.

The period during which they were supposed not to have utilized the nuclear family occurred prior to 1792 and British Rule. As a military caste within Indian society, the Nayar men were required to spend the major portion of their lives in arms. They were thus often away from home. The major institution that carried on the process of socialization was not the nuclear family, but the *matrilinear taravad*. Traditionally, the moderately well-to-do taravad consisted of several hundred persons broken down into many separate residential groups called *tavaris* which were headed by a living ancestress.

The Nayar acknowledged two forms of marriage. One was a ritual marriage or *talikettu kalyanam* which properly occurred before puberty. According to Gough, this tali rite was a ceremony in which a Nayar girl was married to a group of men in her caste, represented by a ritual husband. This rite established the girl as a sexually mature woman who was ready to bear children. Any child born to her by a man of appropriate caste was legitimate because the man who paid for the tali right was considered to be the child's father, even though the relationship between this man and the newly initiated girl typically lasted three to five days. After the tali rite was performed, a woman was free to receive men in a second form of marriage called a visiting husband or *sambandham* relationship. It was important that these men be of the same or higher caste than herself since children born to her by men of a lower caste were considered illegitimate.[12] (See Fig. 2–3.)

The major disruption of the nuclear family in the Nayar case derived from the required absence of the men and bore heavily upon the manner in which the children were socialized. Child care was the responsibility of the mother and her female relatives, maids, and older girls. A typical household was to be found in a large compound with its own food garden. It characteristically had a serpent grove, a large bathing tank, a well, a cowshed, and other small out-buildings. In such a dwelling each post-nuptial female had a room of her own generally on the first floor. Her children, if she had any, slept with her until they reached the age of six when they were placed in common rooms until later segregated by sex at puberty. Unmarried women occupied the second floor.

A child's life was, therefore, almost totally immersed in its mother's house and lineage. Its father was but a sporadic visitor. Men were ordinarily not in residence with the women who bore their children; women were permitted to change lovers quite frequently; and husbands and lovers did not

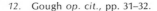

12. Gough *op. cit.*, pp. 31–32.

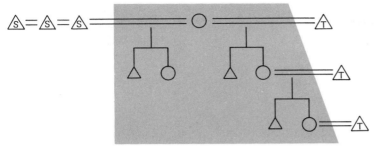

Matrilinear Taravad

⟨S⟩ Sambandam, or Visiting Husband

⟨T⟩ Husband by Virtue of the Tali Rite

FIGURE 2–3
The Nayar household

assist their women in the process of child rearing.

Finally, economic cooperation was not typically between husband and wife but among persons within the same *taravad*. If Gough's view of the Nayar *sambandham* is accepted, a form of group marriage more properly describes the relationship between adults than does a concept of linked nuclear families which assumes that certain male-female relationships are more important and are given greater social recognition than others.

Meyer Nimkoff interprets the overall rationale of the Nayar way from the male point of view:

> The family system meant they had no divided loyalties. The women formed the nucleus of the land-holding group. They were permanent, non-cultivating tenants, holding land on tenure from the Raja or other landlord, to whom they paid rent. They, in turn, subleased the land. The family system buttressed the matrilineage, since the men made no claim on the goods of their wives and the latter were not alienated from their lineage.[13]

In the case of the Nayar, the evidence is clear that they formed an exception to the nuclear family defined as a functioning unit of mother, father, and offspring who reside together and maintain a continuing functional relationship. Murdock's assertion that the nuclear family is universal and its form a prerequisite for the survival of a society thus seems to be called into question. However, the matter is complicated somewhat by the fact that the

13. M. F. Nimkoff (ed.), *op. cit.*, p. 15.

Nayar are a caste within a society and not a society in themselves. Clearly the fact that the majority of adult males were mercenary troops in the service of others in the caste system makes them functionally dependent upon these higher castes. Therefore, should they not be more properly viewed as but a section of the larger Indian society? In this larger society the nuclear family is clearly evident. If this qualification is accepted, then Murdock's position is technically upheld, but such a view really begs the point that a sizable number of persons could live satisfactorily without the nuclear family for an extended period of time. The matter is further complicated by Murdock's lack of specification. He really does not tell us just *how functional* the nuclear family structure must be. Malinowski contends that the family can be minimally defined by its capacity to legitimize children's status in a society. Could this, then, be a definition of a minimally functioning nuclear family?

The Kibbutzim: The second example frequently cited as contradicting Murdock's assertion that the nuclear family is universal is that of the Israeli Kibbutzim. These are small farming communities containing a total population of over 90,000 people. They will be discussed in greater detail in Chapter 16. Here I will describe briefly the early Kibbutzim in order to show how they were *not* composed of nuclear family units.

In these villages the responsibility of child rearing is turned over to community appointed nurses; the husband and wife do not live with their children and do not cooperate economically as a couple to any significant extent. In such communities greater emphasis is placed on peer relationships than on relationships resulting from blood or marriage. The whole community provides the major locus of a person's loyalty and his principal source of support. Since these communities frequently number only about 250 persons, they are small enough for everyone to know everyone else and tend to take on the characteristics of a family.

The strong emphasis on the community rather than on the nuclear family was more characteristic of the Kibbutz before the founding of the state of Israel in 1948 than it is now. Nevertheless, the type of family life characteristic of most Kibbutzim today is radically different from the traditional Jewish family, and although a nuclear family is discernable, it functions minimally.

Murdock would contend that here also there is no true society. The Kibbutzim are distinct from, but intimately interconnected with, the state of Israel. They are at best a sub-culture and not a relatively autonomous society. At this point it becomes rather difficult to decide just how much weight should be placed upon the definition of a society. No people in the world today are completely isolated, and most depend upon others in some degree. The examples of the Nayar and the Kitbbutzim both demonstrate that large numbers of people can live together over an extended period of time in meaningful and functional relationships—without depending on the nuclear family.

Marquesan Complexities: Perhaps the most damaging case against Murdock is one that receives comparatively little attention in the United States.

This concerns an examination of just what is meant by *nuclear family as a functioning unit*. Lévi Strauss, H. R. Rivers, and others find it difficult to distinguish between the nuclear family and larger kinship units such as a lineage. Keith Otterbein, in his examination of Marquesan family life,[14] points out that it is often not reasonable to see the household as built up of nuclear family units.

The problem can be seen in Fig. 2–4, which indicates that at least four types of households are common among the Marquesan: (I) Monogamous, (II) Polyandrous, (III) Polyandrous-Polygamous, and (IV) an unnamed type in which one or more unmarried men attach themselves to any of the three above household types, enjoy certain sexual rights with the women of the household, but do not marry them.[15]

Under Marquesan polyandry, a woman marries two men at the same time, or a man marries a woman who is already married and expects her and her husband to come and live with him. In the polyandrous-polygamous household, a married man marries a woman who is already married and invites her and her husband to move in with him and his wife. If they do, her husband has sexual privileges with the householder's wife but does not marry her. Under these circumstances, Otterbein asks how it is possible to speak of this family type as made up of nuclear families. It is not a true *composite family* as Murdock would view it. Should Case III, for example, be considered three nuclear families in composite form as Murdock would suggest, or should it be considered polygamous-polyandrous as Otterbein labels it? The latter would focus on the type of marriage contract negotiated by the two already married spouses—one of whom took another wife and the other of

---

14. Keith Otterbein, "Marquesan Polyandry," in *Marriage, Family, and Residence,* Paul Bohannan and John Middleton (eds.), (Garden City, N.Y.: The Natural History Press, 1968), pp. 287–96.
    15. *Ibid.,* pp. 293–94.

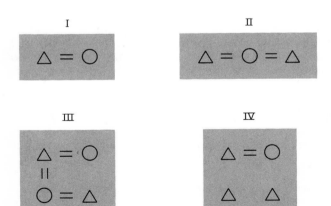

FIGURE 2–4
Marquesan household types.
From Keith Otterbein in
Bohannan and Middleton (eds.),
Marriage, Family, and Residence
(The Natural History Press,
1968), p. 293.

whom took another husband. In view of the extreme difficulty of determining family form in such cases, Otterbein suggests that the more fruitful unit of analysis is the *household*. A similar decision is often made by those studying Caribbean societies where a number of male-female relationships are recognized, and *family* forms become difficult to distinguish.

A household can simply be defined as consisting of the relatively permanent members of a dwelling unit.[16] Within the household two basic types of sexual union may exist between adult opposite-sexed members: legal unions (or marriages) and nonlegal unions. The case of the Marquesan households calls our attention to the fact that many complex households are significant units in a society and in no sense are "built up" from the nuclear family unit.

Whether or not the nuclear family is a functional requisite or only nearly so might seem to be simply a matter of semantics and a rather trivial academic debate. But, again, it must be remembered that in regard to changing the family, it is quite important. A single exception in the ethnographic record of people living without the use of a functioning nuclear family is convincing evidence that the form most common in our culture is *not essential*. Given other pressing social objectives (such as the necessity to maintain a large caste of mercenary troops) another family form has been found useful by the Nayar. With the coming of the British and the reduction in demand for Nayar mercenaries, the nuclear family has appeared as a workable family structure for a minority of Nayar households. The trend seems to be toward increasing the number of such families.

In the case of the Kibbutz, the dream of a better world through Zionist socialism and the return of the Jewish farmer brought about a radical departure from more traditional family forms. In the Kibbutz, the nuclear family is now discernible but only minimally functional.

Finally the various ways in which the "nuclear complex" can be "activated"[17] within composite families should make us quite unwilling to grant Murdock's contention that it functions everywhere in the areas of reproduction, socialization, economic cooperation, and the regulation of sexual activity. Murdock has contributed a great deal by demonstrating the extensiveness of a family type that is given some sort of recognition in almost every society. Yes, despite his assertions, it cannot be said to function similarly in all. The functions attributed to the nuclear family *may* be necessary for a society to survive, but the structure of the nuclear family is not everywhere linked with these functions.

Lévi-Strauss's Conjugal Family: Lévi-Strauss contends that the most important fact about the family is that it institutionalizes reciprocity between kin groups. The family is everywhere founded in marriage, and through marriage kin

---

16. *Ibid.*, p. 292.
17. Relationships which are called upon to perform various tasks or meet certain needs are said to be activated.

groups become obligated to one another. Among the Trobriand Islanders, for example, the bride's kin must provide the basic food for her family even though she lives with her husband and his kin. Because of the importance of marriage, Lévi-Strauss prefers to refer to the basic family unit as the conjugal family. This family has a certain autonomy, but it is most commonly enmeshed in an extended kinship system. Furthermore, kinsmen often exercise great control over the conjugal pair and frequently dictate the choice of mate. The characteristics of the conjugal family are: (1) It finds its origin in marriage. (2) It consists of husband, wife, and children born of their wedlock, though it can be conceived that other relatives may find their place close to that nuclear group. (3) The family members are united together by: (a) legal bonds, (b) economic, religious, and other kinds of rights and obligations, and (c) a precise network of sexual rights and prohibitions and varying and diversified feelings such as love, affection, respect, awe, etc.[18]

At first glance this description might not sound too different from that of Murdock's nuclear family. However, Lévi-Strauss does not argue that such a family is universal. He does not specify the precise structure that such a family must assume. He indicates, however, that the structure of the conjugal family is a common one. What primarily interests him are the rights and obligations that membership in a family confers on a person as a result of marriage. Indeed such a family is identifiable in the field because it originates in marriage:

> If there are many different types of marriage to be observed in human societies—whether monogamous or polygamous . . . the striking fact is that everywhere a distinction exists between marriage, i.e., a legal group-sanctioned bond between a man and a woman, and the types of permanent or temporary union resulting either from violence or consent alone. . . . It is almost a universal feature of marriage that it is originated, not by individuals but by groups concerned (families, lineages, clans, etc.) and that it binds the groups before and above the individuals. . . . Although marriage gives birth to the family, it is the family, or rather families, which produce marriage as the main legal device at their disposal to establish an alliance between themselves. As New Guinea natives put it, the real purpose of getting married is not so much to obtain a wife but to secure brothers-in-law.[19]

Such a view, of course, is quite different from our own romantic notion of marriage wherein love and the free choice of partners are paramount. This difference in marriage type has far-reaching implications for our way of life as I will suggest in Chapter 3.

Lévi-Strauss acknowledges that in some cases (such as that of the Kain-

---

18. Claude Lévi-Strauss, "The Family," in Harry L. Shapiro (ed.) *Man, Culture and Society* (New York: Oxford, 1966), pp. 266–67.
19. *Ibid.*, p. 268.

gang) it might be difficult to tell who is married. Nevertheless, the *normative* distinction between marital and nonmarital unions exists among even the Kaingang and is generally much more easily detected when studying other societies.

Lévi-Strauss differs from Murdock, furthermore, in the manner in which he holds this concept of the conjugal family. It is a *variable* of high universality but not one of basic necessity. I return to Lévi-Strauss's earlier question: "If there is no natural law making the family universal, how can we explain why it is found practically everywhere?"[20]

The explanation he advances is complex. Its simplest element concerns the importance of the mother and her children as a basic unit. Human infants are psychologically and physiologically dependent upon their mother for a long period of time. The father is added to this mother-child dyad because he can provide protection and greater economic security. A division of labor between the sexes enables an adult pair to survive more efficiently than they would be able to if they lived apart. Lévi-Strauss points out that the type of family that was most prevalent in western European experience was not the nuclear or the conjugal family but the *domestic* family. In the domestic family the oldest living ascendants or a community of brothers owned the land and homestead.[21] These groups, which sometimes became quite large, should not be designated as "extended" families because they were not in fact made up of smaller units of the conjugal family. This, again, questions the position taken by Murdock.

In Lévi-Strauss's view, the relationship between the conjugal family and its kinship network is very complex. The conjugal family reciprocally interacts and is interdependent with the lineage so that it is often impossible to distinguish them. In his view this predominance of larger units of social organization in most societies throughout the world would merit the designation of the conjugal family as "*the restricted family.*" This restricted unit of social organization may be more or less important in a society depending upon many circumstances:

> . . . *When the family is given a small functional value, it tends to disappear even below the level of the conjugal type. On the contrary, when the family has a great functional value, it becomes actualized much above that level. Our would-be universal conjugal family, then, corresponds* more to an unstable equilibrium between extremes than to a permanent and everlasting need coming from the deepest requirements of human nature.[22]

The values of a society have an independent effect upon the character of the conjugal family because its structure often derives from quite different

20. *Ibid.*, p. 266.
21. *Ibid.*, p. 272.
22. *Ibid.*, p. 273. [emphasis added]

evaluations of what is important in family life. For example, many societies believe that the social role of the spouse one should marry (example: one's mother's brother's daughter) is more important than the kind of match they will make together. Others accept unions that we would consider totally undesirable because they do not reflect our way of establishing a family. For example, the Chukchee Eskimo of Siberia consider it perfectly acceptable for a mature girl of twenty to marry a baby-husband of two or three. Then the woman, herself a mother by an authorized lover, can nurse both her own baby and her baby-husband. So also in parts of Africa women of high rank were permitted to marry other women who bore children for them through the services of socially acceptable male lovers. The noble woman assumed the role of the *father* to these children, and transmitted to them her own name, status, and wealth, according to the established father's right.[23] Finally, Lévi-Strauss points to cases where the conjugal family is thought to be necessary to *procreate* children but not to *raise* them. Under such arrangements a family ordinarily endeavors to rear someone else's children.

Thus, for Lévi-Strauss the family is much more of a variable, is more dynamically interrelated with its kin network, and is defined largely in terms of its contractual nature from its initiation in marriage to its fulfilling of the various rights and obligations placed upon it afterward. The reciprocity thus established is the basis of the social structure. Marriage and the founding of a family are, therefore, important in all cultures. They are frequently expressed as the monogamic marriage and the conjugal family because this unit is the minimal one necessary to establish a reciprocity between kin groups. But the family need not be limited to such an expression, and it frequently is not. The kind of flexibility that is built into this type of conceptual model is highly desirable for comparative purposes.

The matter of definition can be carried out indefinitely depending upon the interest of the definer. In the discussion to this point, I have shown that *no universally applicable definition can be stipulated simply by focusing upon what the family is as a structure or upon how it functions.* The same organizational structure functions differently in different societies, and the same functions are carried out by different structures.

A ROLE THEORY APPROACH TO DEFINITION

In the role theory frame of reference, the family is defined as a complex of interdependent roles. These roles can be conceptualized so that every society can be said to institutionalize them, but the agents that activate them may vary greatly. Thus the father role may be activated in the Trobriand society by both the biological father and mother's brother, who assumes the major responsibility for disciplining the children. Role theory has not been of major interest to anthropologists thus far.

23. *Ibid.*, p. 273.

Burgess, Locke, and Thomes: A classic role theory definition of the family comes from Burgess, Locke, and Thomes:

> *The family may . . . be defined as a group of persons united by ties or marriage, blood, or adoption; constituting a single household; interacting and communicating with each other in their respective roles of husband and wife, mother and father, son and daughter, brother and sister; and creating and maintaining a common culture.*[24]

Role theorists have not tried to discover any universal form of family as a unit of social organization. They have sought rather to investigate how the family operates in terms of its socially defined roles. Particular emphasis has been placed upon how it socializes its children. As a result the concepts advanced by role theorists reflect much more subtle nuances in the quality of family interaction than we have hitherto encountered. For example, a central type of family for Burgess, Locke, and Thomes is the emergent *companionship form*. Whereas in the past family behavior was governed by custom, social pressure, and law, a new form is emerging wherein "mutual affection" and "consensus of its members" unite the family.[25]

I will return to this point in Chapter 11. If their thesis is correct, however, another rationale for a role theory approach to family life becomes apparent. Clearly, in the modern family formal regulation by kin is not as significant a factor as it was in colonial days or particularly as it is in contemporary folk cultures. The investigation of its internal dynamics, therefore, becomes much more important in accounting for its behavior as an institution.

Goode's Synthesis: William J. Goode provides a particularly useful integration of structure-functionalism and role theory:

> *In all known societies, almost everyone lives his life enmeshed in a network of family rights and obligations called* role relations. *A person is made aware of his role relations through a long period of socialization during his childhood, a process in which he learns how others in his family expect him to behave, and in which he himself comes to feel this is both the right and the desirable way to act. . . . The strategic significance of the family is to be found in its mediating function in the larger society. It links the individual to the larger social structure. A society will not survive unless its many needs are met, such as the production and distribution of food, protection of the young and old, the sick and the pregnant, conformity to the law, the socialization of the young, and so on. . . .*
>
> *The family, then, is made up of individuals, but it is also part of the*

---

24. Ernest W. Burgess, Harvey J. Locke, and Mary Margaret Thomes, *The Family: From Institution to Companionship*, 3rd ed. (New York: American Book, 1963), p. 2. [emphasis added]

25. *Ibid.*, p. 3.

larger social network. Thus we are all under the constant supervision of
our kin, who feel free to criticize, suggest, order, cajole, praise, or
threaten, so that we will carry out our role obligations.[26]

Goode here avoids a precise definition that makes explicit claim to universality. He does not specify the structure that the family must assume, although he seems inclined to view the family that is quite stable over time as something not too different from the nuclear family. The family, he argues, fulfills the following functions in regard to its society: reproduction of the young, physical maintenance of family members, social placement of the child, socialization, and social control. These functions could all be separated theoretically. However, those experiments in communal child rearing—notably the Russian and the Israeli—have retreated to more conventional family forms in some measure. So it would seem that such functions are not readily separable. Goode concludes that the data suggest that the family is a very stable institution.[27]

The major contribution that role theory makes to the problem of definition is that it enables us to make further refinements in our qualifications of who does what. By assuming that roles, not persons, are the significant variables, it is possible to argue that persons in various institutions perform certain aspects of these roles. These persons may change over time. Thus the mother plays the central role of nurturance for the baby, but the teacher may play a dominant nurturant role when the child goes to school. The mother may be replaced in some instances or, more commonly, the number of socializers in a child's life will simply increase. Or, in primitive societies such as the Trobriand, mother's brother plays the role of disciplinarian, and father has a much more expressive role in the socialization of a child.

I have not exhausted all of the significant ways of looking at the family, each of which can produce a somewhat different definition.[28] No one has found a universal family structure that everywhere performs the same functions for society, but the quest has given us some idea of the extensiveness of such types as the nuclear family and the conjugal family. They both exhibit the same structure. Murdock sees the nuclear family as a "building block," but Lévi-Strauss's conception of the conjugal family as being a state of unstable equilibrium seems more apt. The introduction of role theory and the consequent examination of the quality of family dynamics succeeds in blurring the quest for the universal definition even more. Thus, what we intuitively perceive as a rather simple organization has proven to be difficult to define precisely. No common pattern is without exception.

26. William J. Goode, *The Family* (Englewood Cliffs, N.J.: Prentice-Hall, 1946), pp. 1–2.

27. *Ibid.*, p. 28.

28. See, for example, the various frameworks in F. Ivan Nye and Felix Bernardo, *Emerging Conceptual Frameworks in Family Analysis* (New York: Macmillan, 1966). These authors distinguish such frameworks although upon examination, some seem little more than slight modification of others.

Two Working Definitions of "Family"

At this point I have two alternatives. Following Levy and Fallers I could suggest that the concept of "family," to be useful for general comparative purposes, should be used to refer not to a single structure in each society, but rather to *any small, kinship-structured unit which carries aspects of the relevant functions.* Using the term in this way, one would find in most societies a series of "family units."[29] A common family function would be *socialization.*

In this tradition, Ira Reiss has narrowed the socialization function to mean *nurturance*—the emotional, not the physical, care of children. The family then becomes the small kinship-structured group whose primary functions is nurturance. Reiss goes further and argues that if—as in the case of the Kibbutz—nonkin socialize the children, then we might expect elements of kin structure to emerge (e.g., the children would consider all of the adults who raised them mother or father).[30] Reiss's emphasis on emotional care seems consonant with Raymond T. Smith's emphasis:

> However the family may be defined or structured, it always constitutes an area of diffuse and permanent solidarity between a limited number of individuals, and this is probably its most distinguishing characteristic.[31]

In such an approach, structure has been expanded to mean simply any kin structure (or structure that is evolving toward a kin structure). Function has been reduced to socialization or nurturance and not limited to any particular structure. In practice such a family would often be indistinguishable from a lineage (the kin group related through the father's or mother's side of the family). There are other problems. For example, which group should be called the family in the case of those societies where it is preferable that one couple give birth to a child and another raise it? The child's family of birth, the one that raised him, or both? Reiss's extension of kin structure to any group such as the Kibbutz community which performs the function of nurturance evades the issue of what a kinship structure really is.

Taking this route it seems as though the definitions examined in this chapter have become so vague as to be useless. Their prime function, however, is to sensitize us to the number of structures that can adequately provide nurturance or socialize the child. In such a perspective we can move

29. M. J. Levy and L. A. Fallers, "The Family: Some Comparative Considerations," *The American Anthropologist,* Vol. 61 (1959), 647–51.

30. Ira Reiss, "The Universality of the Family: A Conceptual Analysis," *Journal of Marriage and the Family,* Vol. 27 (Nov. 1965), 443–53.

31. Raymond T. Smith, "Family: Comparative Structure" in *International Encyclopedia of the Social Sciences,* Vol. V (1969), 312.

readily from structure-functionalism to role theory because of the mutual interest in socialization.

There is another alternative, however. After Morris Zelditch we can attempt to rescue a more precise definition by asking if there is some *norm* that is always associated with a group that we would recognize as a family. Zelditch argues that it is Malinowski's *Principle of Legitimacy*: ". . . according to this definition, a *family exists if, and only if, there is a pater role*, and a pater role is one that (1) determines the jural status, rights, and obligations of a child recognized as the pater's child and (2) is charged by members of the society with responsibility for the child's conduct."[32] This position combines significant elements in Lévi-Strauss's and George Peter Murdock's arguments.

Zelditch points out that any person or group can fill this role and that the person or group that fills this role need not instruct the child—it is simply held accountable by society for the child's conduct. Furthermore, it is a normative definition. It really says that a family *should* have a pater role. Concrete cases often violate it. Thus Goode upholds Malinowski's principle in the case of Caribbean peoples because he demonstrates that even though illegitimacy rates are commonly over 50 percent, legitimate birth is *preferred*. Almost everyone eventually does marry. The concrete cases should be viewed, therefore, as evidence of family disorganization.

Such a perspective takes us a long way from our own normative conceptions of family, because it suggests that the role of the father as *genitor* (biological father) is less important than his social role as *pater*. Fatherhood, as Malinowski observes, is a social invention—not a biological fact. It, furthermore, involves an assessment of normative structure that frequently is contradicted by concrete cases causing us to raise questions as to the extent of norm commitment on the one hand and of the utility of the definition on the other. A great deal of intensive study is necessary before it is possible to determine the degree of role commitment in cases such as the Caribbean. It is easy for "disorganization" to be merely a reflection of the views of the researcher.

Neither alternative offers us a foolproof approach to definition. Both have their utility and their limitations. If we consider a concrete group of persons in a specific society, we can ask to what extent this group exhibits the structure of a kin group and to what extent it socializes the young. If it seems to do both to a satisfactory extent (how much, precisely, being left unspecified), we can call it a family. A number of structurally different groups may fit this definition.

The definition of family as that group which legitimizes the birth of a child may also apply to a wide variety of concrete types so long as they institutionalize a pater role *in some way*. The *tali rite* of the Nayar, for exam-

---

32. Morris Zelditch, "Family, Marriage and Kinship," in *Handbook of Modern Sociology*, R. E. L. Faris (ed.) (Chicago: Rand McNally, 1964), p. 681. [emphasis added]

ple, qualifies as a means of institutionalizing the *pater* role. In this perspective, however, researchers are more inclined to uphold a normative definition and consider concrete cases as evidence of disorganization. In this approach, also, the evaluative element is left unspecified. To what extent must a society or a couple be committed to the norm of legitimacy before we can say that it is upheld in spite of contradictory behavior?

Both definitions, furthermore, focus upon the importance of the family as a social institution entrusted with bringing children into the world. Are married couples without children to be considered a "family"? Properly speaking, no. But what if they intend to have children? Marriage may institutionalize the pater role, but if it is not activated, should it still be considered a role? The answers to these questions may vary considerably.

Nevertheless, despite their limitation these definitions do have some utility. Their application to concrete cases will require a great deal of thought in some cases, but in others, where it is obvious that a group qualifies, it will not be so difficult.

What seems to be essential to both definitions is that *some* group must be responsible for socializing children (it may not carry out its responsibility), and some means must be provided for children's placement in the social structure so that their rights and obligations may be clearly specified (these means may not be used). We are forced by both approaches to make distinctions between what is normative and what is concrete and decide when the concrete case fits the definition.

Summary

The family, far from being the relatively simple social structure that Americans recognize as desirable and tend to take for granted as basic to the human venture, has proven to be a quite complex system. No general definition adequately fits all the data. The generalizations that many functionally oriented social scientists assert as universal are at best only nearly so.

If I define the family as any small kin-structured group whose primary function is that of the socialization of children, I have not done away with my problems. I must now recognize that many groups are entrusted with aspects of this function in primitive societies. Some of these—such as the matrilineage—I would not ordinarily conceive of as a family. I am encouraged, however, to examine the most commonly accepted function of the family—socialization—and its variations with a more open mind as to the strengths and weaknesses of each structural expression of family.

By defining the family as that group wherein the pater role is institutionalized as the primary means of legitimizing children, I focus upon a norm and run the risk of misunderstanding the degree of norm commitment.

The aim of this chapter has been to discuss the concept of family by appreciating some of its variety of expression without reducing the importance of certain central patterns. The family is a complex variable, not a universal structure derived from biological necessity nor a universal normative ideal based upon religious or cultural dogma.

To the extent that it arises from social necessity, the family is a variable of great richness. It both orients us to the world of our culture and yields to our changing conception of what a desirable family is. It can be seen as an unplanned "response" to other environmental changes. The family changes its structure from one culture to another and undergoes alterations within a given culture over time. Thus, if we take the anthropological evidence, there seems to be great latitude for successfully changing the family in order to improve its functioning.

3. The Web of Kinship

In the white way of doing things the family is not so important. The police and soldiers take care of protecting you, courts give you justice, the post office carries messages for you, the school teaches you. Everything is taken care of, even your children, if you die; but with us the family must do all of that.

POMO INDIAN

When he spoke of "family," this Pomo Indian did not mean the conjugal or nuclear unit familiar to us. He meant the larger kin unit we simply designate as "relatives." For most of us our conjugal family is more important than these relatives, but this is not true among many pre-industrial peoples. For some anthropologists the larger kinship system is a more useful unit of analysis than the nuclear family, because many of the functions that Murdock insists are characteristics of the nuclear family are delegated to larger kin units.

In many societies, moreover, larger kin units exercise more control over an individual's behavior than does the conjugal family. This is particularly true of societies in which descent is traced through either the mother's or the father's side—unilinear descent. Kin control is most powerfully manifested in the dictation of mate choice and residence. These strongly affect how "at ease" a person feels in public and, therefore, indirectly affect his personal behavior. I will examine in Chapter 4 the regulations they impose upon mate selection and marriage, and in a later section of this chapter I will look at residence rules. Here I will consider two major aspects of kin control over individuals: (1) the determination of rights of inheritance and succession and the designation of the line of descent—*status placement*; and (2) the formal constraints upon behavior such as patterns of avoidance, deference, and joking. These latter may govern how members of family units interact, or they may control the interaction between family members and kin or nonkin in public places. It is this control over expressive personal behavior that immediately distinguishes unilinear societies from our own.

We suffer from a serious handicap in viewing kinship systems in other societies. In our society the nuclear or conjugal family stands out in sharp relief, and kin ties are *relatively* less important. In most of the societies in the world, kin are much more significant. In some they completely overshadow the importance of the "family."

Kin Terminology as a Key to Social Structure

Anthropologists became aware of the importance of the kinship system when they began to realize that among pre-industrial peoples, kin terminology is important because there are few other ways of placing a person in his appropriate role. Our last name serves to identify us to strangers and, if we happen to belong to the "right" families, can even dictate certain rudimentary aspects of appropriate behavior in the face-to-face encounter. The kin designation precisely places a person in pre-industrial societies and often provides the cue to proper behavior in a wide range of situations:

> In aboriginal Australia, where preoccupation with kinship was carried to unusual lengths, it is said that a native could, at least theoretically, traverse the entire continent, stopping at each tribal boundary to compare notes on relatives, and at the end of his journey know precisely whom in the local group he should address as grandmother, father-in-law, sister, etc., whom he might associate freely with, whom he must avoid, whom he might or might not have sex relations with, and so on.[1]

1. Murdock, *Social Structure* (New York: Free Press, 1965), p. 96.

Sometimes the discernment of kin affiliation takes a great deal of time. Sometimes the exact nature of the relationship is not discernible and must be assumed. Sometimes the terms of kinship are extended to others who are not true kin for the purpose of establishing a more regulated, warm, and dependable relationship. The *compadre* system of Latin countries is an example. Kin terminology may be invoked with an enemy in a ceremony of blood brotherhood in order to placate his wrath. In no pre-industrial society are kin terms taken lightly. Everywhere they tend to mark off two groups (kin and nonkin) that stand in a significant relationship to one another. Frequently, the nonkin relationship is one of fear and mistrust, as in this instance reported by A. R. Radcliffe-Brown:

> I took with me on my journey a native of the Talainji tribe [of Australia], and at each native camp we came to, the same process had to be gone through. In one case, after a long discussion, they were still unable to discover any traceable relationship between my servant and the men of the camp. That night my "boy" refused to sleep in the native camp, as was his usual custom, and on talking to him I found he was frightened. These men were not his relatives, and they were therefore his enemies. This represents the real feeling of the natives on the matter. If I am a black-fellow and meet another black-fellow that other must be either my relative or my enemy. If he is my enemy, I shall take the first opportunity of killing him for fear he will kill me.[2]

While kin terminology is a key variable in understanding social structure, anthropologists are really focusing upon the *normative* structure of a society when they study kin terms. The actual functioning of a system is not always recorded with any precision in its terminology. What results, therefore, are *ideal types* of social structures. They describe the *social order* of a society. In some cases, the kin system cannot function as its *social order* prescribes or it would soon cease to exist. This discrepancy between the normative social order and the functioning social system may be due to many factors. A person may be unable to find the prescribed mate, and a substitute must be found. It may simply reflect inaccurate or incomplete understanding of the data by one or more ethnographers and/or their informants. Or it may simply result from a strong desire to preserve tradition despite its obvious lack of function. Thus a patrilineal society may retain terminology more appropriate to a matrilineal system.

Finally, there is great variation in the *extent* to which the kin system functions in any given society. Among the major variables are: (1) the extent to which blood and relationships based on marriage (affinal relationships) are recognized for social purposes; (2) the ways in which relatives so recognized are classified or grouped in social categories; (3) the particular customs by which the behavior of these relatives are regulated in daily life; (4) the

---

2. Reported in William F. Stephens, *The Family in Cross-Cultural Perspective* (New York: Holt, Rinehart & Winston, 1969), p. 101.

various rights and obligations which are mediated through kinship; and (5) the linguistic forms which are used to denote the various categories of kin.[3]

Unilinear Kin Groups

Aside from such notable exceptions as the American Indian tribes of the High Plains who were organized into bilateral bands (a system of descent wherein an individual has equal affiliation with each of his four grandparents), kinship in primitive societies is characterized by unilineal descent. In such cases descent is reckoned through one's father (patrilineal) or mother (matrilineal). Patrilineal societies are the dominant group. Both types are diagrammed in Figure 3–1.

While the mother's side of the family is never ignored in a patrilineal system, the father's side is recognized because it is primarily responsible for the transmission of property (inheritance), the transmission of offices such as kingship or chieftainship (succession), and the transmission of kin-group membership (descent). In actual operation these three items are not transmitted from one generation to the next in the same way in all patrilineal societies.

William F. Stephens suggests that the identifying characteristics of a unilinear kin group are: (1) a name such as Foxes, Bends-the-Knee, etc.; (2) a norm enjoining marriage outside of the group, called exogamy; (3) common religious obligations—particularly well exemplified in the cases where such groups are totemic and worship an ancestral animal; (4) corporate property ownership which gives rise to the frequent designation of these groups as "corporate groups" because they own property and normally persist beyond the lifetime of individual members; (5) corporate enterprise generally of an economic or religious type; (6) government—sometimes the only form of government a people has, but more commonly it is a strong supplementary form in addition to more centralized power as is the case among the Ashanti and Bunyoro; and (7) feuding—much like the feuding of the Hatfields and the McCoys in our own country.[4]

TWO EXAMPLES OF UNILINEAR KINSHIP SYSTEMS

Before going any further into the discussion of kinship systems and how they operate, I will examine a few cases from the ethnographic record. The first society, the Gururumba, is patrilineal.

The Gururumba: The Gururumba are a people numbering slightly over 1,100 who live in six large villages in the northern half of eastern New Guinea. Their territory consists of about thirty square miles. They have patrilineages,

3. Fred Eggan, "Kinship," in *International Encyclopedia of the Social Sciences,* Vol. 8, pp. 390–91.
4. Stephens *op cit.,* p. 269.

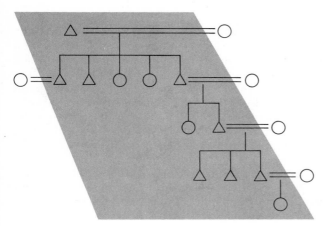

Patrilinear

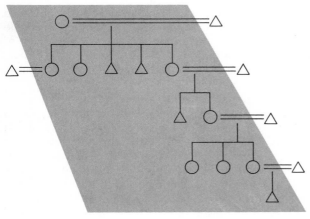

Matrilinear

FIGURE 3–1
Unilinear descent

but above the lineage group they only dimly reflect *agnatic* descent.[5] The term "Gururumba" applies to all persons willing to defend this territory against "those standing opposed to us." Philip Newman writes:

> The Gururumba consider themselves to be the descendants of a common set of ancestors [but] these ancestors are not specifically known nor do they form a descent group among themselves. The ancestors were simply

5. Patrilineal descent is also called agnatic descent.

the group to occupy this territory and defend it against outsiders. Similarly the Gururumba are the present day descendants of this heterogeneous group who remain committed to common defense of the territory.[6]

Thus it would seem that *territoriality* plays a much more important role in organizing kin than is commonly the case among pre-industrial peoples. This point is further exemplified by the fact that the Gururumba are divided into two groups called *phratries* which are normally based on the recognition of a common ancestry, but in this case extend membership to any group willing to commit itself to defend the territory of the phratry. Phratries feud among themselves but not to the death. War with outsiders—non-Gururumba—is not terminable short of the death of the vanquished. These two units, the tribe and the phratry, are the major units shaping the larger structure of the Gururumba society.

The smaller units, however, bear more directly upon the personal lives of the Gururumba. Each phratry has at least two *sibs* which do consider themselves to be descent groups and commonly sit together on such occasions as food distribution, ceremonials, and other public occasions. A man also calls upon his sib-mate to help him avenge a close kinsman's death. A sib is composed of many extended families that are linked together in several patrilineages. The sibs are the widest exogamous unit within Gururumba society—a man may choose a mate from any other sib except his own. Since sib-mates are regarded as consanguineal (blood) kin, kin terms appropriate to blood relatives are appropriate in their interchange. Any old man or woman in a person's sib may be addressed by the terms "father" or "mother," any slightly older man or woman as "elder brother" or "elder sister." This is a form of *classificatory* kinship terminology.

The geographical distribution of Gururumba lineages places them in villages which may have as many as sixteen lineages who do not recognize a common ancestor. While the village, as such, is thus not simply a group of kinsmen, it does exercise very important functions in Gururumba society. For example, it has a village name, its inhabitants frequently act as a unit in court cases, move together, gather nuts together, and perform the ritual to ensure the growth of nuts; it may also act as host and a food distribution center. If a sib does not give a funeral, a village may. The village is also the most important unit in the negotiation of the bride price. It can, therefore, be called a *clan* after Murdock.

Two groups which do not fit the classification based on culture traits, political alliance, territoriality, descent, and residence given above are (1) the age group and (2) the sex group. Age mates support each other in arguments, help in subsistence activities, and stand together in dance groups. While men do not stand against women as other social groups do, there is residential segregation by sex after puberty. Various activities of the men's cult are kept secret from the women. Also various activities connected with menstruation are women's rituals.

---

6. Philip L. Newman, *Knowing the Gururumba* (New York: Holt, Rinehart & Winston, 1965), p. 35. This brief sketch is based entirely on this book.

Among the Gururumba, men exercise control over the land and its products, while women have rights of usufruct over land, dwellings, or patches of forest containing usable plants that are contingent upon a woman's marriage or family affiliation. Various other aspects of work routine, ceremonial, and public office are assigned to either of the sexes, but not to both.

The Haida: The manner in which the kin system infiltrates the daily activities of primitive peoples can be seen from this second example of the *matrilineal* Haida as recorded by George Peter Murdock:

> The functions of the several Haida kin groups are quite distinctive. The moiety *regulates marriage*, which is[7] strictly exogamous. It also channelizes rivalries and regulates ceremonial property exchanges. Potlatches, for example, are inevitably given to members of the opposite moiety. The extended family is the unit of ordinary domestic life, or primary economic cooperation, of trade and of property accumulation. The nuclear family, in addition to its usual functions, is the group which gives a potlatch; the wife is technically the donor in major potlatches, but she is assisted by her husband, and their children are the beneficiaries of the resulting enhancement in status. The clan is the community, i.e., the face-to-face group of daily social intercourse. It is also the basic political unit, each clan being independent of all others. All property rights in land are held by the clan, under the trusteeship of its chief. Moveable goods are owned by the extended family or by individuals. Intangible property rights, on the other hand, are vested in the sib. This group owns a fund of personal names, of ceremonial titles for houses and canoes, of totemic crests, and of exclusive rights to songs and ceremonies. Mythology, too, is largely associated with the sib, and it is the group which regulates inheritance and succession. The sib, moreover, is the ceremonial unit; its members are invited collectively to feasts and potlatches, and they assist one another in preparing for and conducting these ceremonies when anyone of them is the host. Finally, the duty of blood vengeance for the murder or injury of one of its members falls upon the sib. Warfare, however, is the function of the clan, whether motivated by vengeance, self-defense, or the desire for booty and slaves.[8]

In these two instances the ethnographer was particularly sensitive to which kin unit exercised a particular right or demanded a particular obligatory behavior. In a large number of cases the ethnographies are not as specific, and so a more precise understanding of the dynamics of kin systems must await more detailed study in the field.

A comparatively rare variation of unilineal descent is called "double descent." In such situations a society recognizes *both* matrilineages and patri-

---

7. "Moiety" is a primary social division in which the tribe is made up of two groups. Each moiety often includes one or more interrelated clans, sibs, or phratries and moiety exogamy is common. The two groups may be of different size or function. The members of a moiety need not be related. A moiety may be formed for games or ceremonies. [Charles Winick, *Dictionary of Anthropology* (New York: Philosophical Library, 1956), p. 364.]

8. Murdock *op. cit.*, pp. 72–73.

lineages, "and a person is affiliated at the same time with the patrilineal group of his father and the matrilineal group of his mother, the relatives of his father's matrilineal and his mother's patrilineal group being discarded."[9] Under special conditions double descent produces certain rather unique types of consanguineal kin groups and might, therefore, be classified as a fourth form of descent rather than as simply a combination of patrilineal and matrilineal rules.

These two case studies illustrate the complexities of social organization. Kin structure is normally but one element in the total organization of a people, although it is usually the most important one in pre-industrial societies. Sometimes kin relationships are not demonstrable as in the case of the clan organization of the Gururumba village. Although the patrilineage is a significant organizational unit among these people, it serves chiefly the function of reckoning descent. The fact that a group of people occupy and are willing to defend a particular territory is a strong organizational principle among these people as recognized in their phratries. Age and sex distinctions are also important organizational elements.

Among the Haida, however, the matrilineage is quite prominent in the social organization. The clan is also an important organizational unit normally found occupying a village. Murdock clearly illustrates that various elements of the lineage are activated for different purposes. The household is more than a residence group.

THE FUNCTIONS OF THE KIN SYSTEM IN PRE-INDUSTRIAL SOCIETIES

The kin system in primitive society is frequently the primary means of placing a person in the social structure. This is accomplished by fixing his status and role precisely so that even strangers can, with some effort, determine the appropriate behavior in his presence. I will now consider how the kinship system controls interpersonal behavior.

The Regulation of Interpersonal Behavior: Societies control the behavior of their members in either a formal or an informal fashion. In the former case, the society is characterized by rigid rules governing such aspects of behavior as deference patterns, avoidance, and joking relationships. A society that is rigidly controlled by formal rules of behavior is one in which there is likely to be a great deal of tension. It is one that demands more of parents who must socialize their children into the intricate network of rules or suffer the consequences of continual social reproach.

Our society, on the other hand, is one in which there is relatively little regulation of interpersonal behavior by means of formal rules. While we rely heavily upon formal "standard operating procedures" in our bureaucratic organizations, these rules are primarily aimed at instrumental or task-oriented behavior. The controls of formal societies cover the whole repertoire of per-

9. Murdock *op. cit.*, p. 45.

sonal behavior. The examples that follow pertain primarily to expressive behavior.

Joking: The Mundugumor serve to illustrate the style of life in a society in which joking behavior is formally controlled:

> *A joking relative is not a person with whom one may joke if one wishes, but rather a relative towards whom joking is the correct behavior, a kind of behavior that is as culturally fixed as shaking hands. . . .*
>
> *A Mundugumor child is taught that everyone who is related to it as mother's brother, father's sister, sister's child of a male, brother's child of a female, and their spouses, is a joking relative with whom one engages in rough-house, accusations of unusual and inappropriate conduct, threats, mock bullying, and the like.*[10]

Avoidance: Along with joking relationships, there are also persons whom one must avoid in such formally regulated societies. A classic person to avoid is the mother-in-law. In some societies if a man should accidentally see his mother-in-law, he would be executed.

An example of avoidance behavior is provided by the Manus, a Melanesian people of the Admiralty Islands:

> *Women are aided in their avoidance outside the home by a calico cloak which has superseded the characteristic peaked rain mat of aboriginal days. . . . In a canoe gathering at which her kaleals [persons to be avoided] are present she sits huddled up on the canoe platform, her head bowed between her knees, her knees hunched, and her whole form wrapped in the cloak. . . .*
>
> *The women who labor under the greatest disadvantage are young women in their husbands' villages, and older women whose daughters have married into their own villages. A young wife in her husband's village may have to avoid half a dozen older men. An older woman may have several sons-in-law from whom she must hide or run away. Hiding her face is only acceptable in lieu of running away when running away is impossible, as in a canoe, or when a woman is surprised in a group. If a man appears on the edge of a group, the women who are his kaleals hastily cover their faces and drift away into the back of the house or out of the house altogether, or off the arakeu onto a canoe platform.*
>
> *Technically, for purposes of observing kaleals, a house is divided into two parts by one or more mats hung from the ceiling. Such a house can accommodate two households in which live a man and a woman whom he calls daughter-in-law and who must therefore avoid him, and never raise her voice so that he can hear it at the other end of a house. Nor can she ever go into his section of the house except when he is absent. This division of the house is designed to accommodate kaleals of the father-in-law–daughter-in-law type which are felt to be less drastic than those of the mother-in-law–son-in-law type. This occupation of a house by two brothers in which case the younger wife must avoid the older brother, as titular "father-in-law," is a common situation.*

10. Margaret Mead, *Sex and Temperament*, (New York: Mentor, 1950), pp. 142–43.

> *For a woman . . . as the weight of the "father-in-law" taboo drops from her shoulders, the weight of taboos based on her position as "mother-in-law" must be assumed. There is no respite for her with increasing age. She has had to avoid her "father-in-law" and now she must avoid her "sons-in-law." Her response to anyone naming a kaleal, or bringing a kaleal into the conversation is one of angry embarrassment.*[11]

The inconvenience and embarrassment caused by numerous avoidance rules makes us wonder why a society would choose to regulate its affairs in such a manner. Murdock argues that the avoidance behavior associated with mother, sister, and daughter supports the incest taboos in societies where such taboos are not strongly internalized—that is, taken for granted as rules that must be obeyed.[12] By extending the incest taboos to persons resembling spouses or potential spouses and observing that behavior tends to be generalized, Murdock enlarges this argument to cover others outside the nuclear family. This may account for the custom of avoidance in some societies, but not in all.

Deference: A final formality that is in some respects similar to avoidance (in that it requires one to respond in a negative manner upon encountering another) is deference. Unlike avoidance, however, deference behavior acknowledges a superior-inferior status relationship. One gives deference to another of higher status and does not reciprocally receive it. In the case of avoidance, both parties avoid each other, implying more of an equalitarian position. Typically forms of deference behavior are: kneeling, bowing, hand-kissing; speech etiquette, such as speaking in a low voice, not joking, not arguing, and not contradicting; mealtime etiquette, such as giving the deferred-to person the seat of honor, giving him the best food, letting him eat first; and body-elevation rules, such as not being higher than the deferred-to person, or standing upon greeting the deferred-to person, or sitting on the ground while the deferred-to person sits on a chair.[13]

Most frequently deference is offered to older by younger persons, to men by women. Examples of deference from our own society are found in the cases where women only eat after the men are fed or only sit at the foot of the table. Of the three types of patterned behavior, deference is the most widespread and does not seem as rigidly bound to more formal societies as is the case with avoidance and joking behavior.

The formal requirement to defer frequently obtains between members of the conjugal family, the wife being most frequently expected to defer to her husband, children to their parents.

Males over Females: In most pre-industrial societies women are excluded from politics and religious rites, are frequently barred from public gatherings, and are more likely to be killed at birth than men. The difference in the privilege extended to men and women is also manifested in the "dou-

---

11. Margaret Mead, "Kinship in the Admirality Islands," *Anthropological Papers of the American Museum of Natural History*, Vol. 34, Pt. 2 (1934), 266–69.
12. Murdock *op. cit.*, p. 276.
13. Stephens *op. cit.*, pp. 85–86.

ble standard" about which I will have more to say later. Sex restrictions are more heavily applied to women than to men. The permission to practice adultery, on the other hand, is not. The relatively inferior status accorded women is a characteristic of our own tradition going back at least as far as the Old Testament account of the fall where woman was created from Adam's rib and was responsible for his eating of the forbidden apple from the tree of the knowledge of good and evil.

Deference, involving the general posture of respect, submissiveness, and obedience, is more expected of women than of men. Deference rules imply unequal status involving privilege and power. Here also wife-to-husband practices are common, while husband-to-wife deference is rare. Waldemar Bogoras describes the custom among the Chuckchee:

> After the reindeer is slaughtered, the woman has to skin it and butcher it; then she must carry everything to its proper place. She prepares the food, and presents it to her husband. She cuts off the best and takes what is left, gnaws the bones, gathers all crumbs and scraps. Such delicacies as brains, marrow, and so forth, are eaten exclusively by men. Women are satisfied with licking their fingers when cutting the dainties into small pieces for the use of the men. 'Being women, eat crumbs,' is a saying of the Chuckchee.[14]

While deference practices are relatively easy to observe, difference in *power* is more difficult. Power differs from deference in that it pertains to who actually dominates and who submits. Because the exercise of power can be private, it is not readily observable. Thus while a wife may choose to be submissive in public, in the privacy of her home she may run the family. Further, how does one compare the various modes of regulating or controlling another's behavior? The Tepoztecan wife is publicly submissive, is ordinarily obedient to her husband, but utilizes her skill to control his behavior by more covert means. Likewise, William Madsen, reporting on lower-class Mexican American families in South Texas, notes that the traditional husband dominance is often undermined by a skillful wife. "The conservative Latin wife is, in fact, a skilled manipulator of her lord and master. The weapons she uses in disguised form are his own self-esteem, his machismo, and his role as provider and protector.[15]

So also, deference rules may be easy enough to discover, but individuals may well violate these rules in practice. When we are concerned with the matters of power, the extent of this infraction is important and very poorly documented in the ethnographies. The terms matriarchy and patriarchy also refer to the normative social structure. They may imply deference rules but do not give us sure evidence of the actual power relationships obtaining between husbands and wives in any given society.

14. Waldemar Bogoras, "The Chuckchee," *Part 3, Memoirs of the American Museum of Natural History*, Vol. 11 (1909), 288.
15. William Madsen, *The Mexican Americans of South Texas* (New York: Holt, Rinehart & Winston, 1964), p. 51.

Parents over Children: Patterns of power and deference extend to members of the conjugal family and include the children as well. Here, too, while formalized deference patterns are relatively easy to observe, the true balance of power is more difficult to determine. Nevertheless, here the formalized patterns more clearly reflect the actual power relationships. Cases of child dominance are extremely rare. Stephens notes two: Marquesans and Truck.[16] Among the Marquesans, a child of either sex may dominate:

> *The eldest child of either sex, or the child who was adopted to take the position of the eldest, became the official head of the household from the moment of birth or arrival. . . . Of course in practice, the father administered the household group until the child reached maturity, but socially the child outranked his father from the moment of birth. . . .*
> *Very little authority was exercised over children, and practically none over the eldest who, as has been explained, outranked the parents. These infant family heads could do practically anything they pleased. In the valley of Puamau, I once visited the local chief who had a boy eight or nine. When I arrived, the chief and his family were camping in the front yard and the boy was sitting in the house looking glum and triumphant. He had had a quarrel with his father a day or so before and had tabooed the house by naming it after his head. The family were thus uncomfortably camping in the open until the child could be persuaded to lift the taboo and allow them to enter the house again.[17]*

In the other instances, such as among the Tarong, the son is dominant over the father when the father is retired.

The opposite tendency is enforced even beyond the age of competence in Ireland. The father is normally owner and director of the enterprise. The farm and its income are vested in him. The farm bears his name in the community and the sons are spoken of as his "boys":

> *. . . even at forty-five and fifty, if the old couple have not yet made over the farm, the countryman remains a boy, both in farm work and in the rural vocabulary. . . . A countryman complained to me . . . "You can be a boy forever, as long as the old fellow is alive."[18]*

Because of the subordinate role of sons in rural Ireland, men and women do not marry until their late thirties. Even then they marry not because of love but because the "land needs a woman." Many women never marry because only one son inherits.

In Tepotzlan the father avoids intimacy with members of his family and expects them to demonstrate their respect for him by maintaining a proper social distance: "Not long ago, all children in Tepotzlan kissed the hands of

16. Stephens *op. cit.*, p. 312.
17. Ralf Linton, "Marquesan Culture," in *The Individual and His Society*, Abram Kardiner (ed.) (New York: Columbia University Press, 1939), pp. 154–59.
18. C. M. Arensberg, *The Irish Countryman* (Glouster, Mass.: Peter Smith, 1950), p. 123.

their parents, grandparents, and godparents in greeting; now only a few families continue this custom."[19]

Aside from the cases of Marquesans and Truck, the best that children can hope for in terms of power is a democratic relationship with their father. In marked contrast Stephens finds that the mother is only infrequently given deference by her children. This was true among the Papago, Tepotzlan, and seventeenth-century England in his sample.[20]

In summary, deference is almost always received by older men, is rarely given to women, and almost never given to younger children. "The father-child relationship appears to be the 'hub' of this pattern. If you defer to your father, you will also defer to some other elder kinsmen; if you don't defer to your father, you will not defer to other elder kin."[21] The general rules are:

1. Husband over wife.
2. Father over child.
3. Father is stricter than mother.
4. Elder men get deference; women and juniors do not.
5. If ego defers to father, he also defers to uncle and/or grandfather and/or brother. If he does not defer to father, he does not defer to uncle or grandfather or elder brother.
6. If father is dominant over some family members, he is dominant over all family members.

The first four are considered by Stephens to be strong trends, the last two, very weak ones.[22]

Status Placement: A person is established as "somebody" in a primitive society largely by virtue of his kin-group affiliation.

In any particular society, the inheritance of property, succession to office, and recruitment to kin groups usually follow the same mode of transmission. Indeed, the importance of descent groups lies in the fact that membership usually entails claiming basic productive and reproductive resources, as well as channeling succession to roles and offices. But this is not always the case.[23]

This is particularly true of the unilineal descent group:

> As with the wider ties of kinship, the disappearance of UDGs [unilinear descent groups] is linked with the growth of economic and social individualism in industrial societies, where a person tends to have direct ties with the political and economic agencies, mediated by specialized asso-

19. Oscar Lewis, *Life in a Mexican Village: Tepotzlan Revisited*, (Urbana, Ill.: University of Illinois Press, 1951), pp. 322–38.
20. Stephens *op. cit.*, p. 319.
21. *Ibid.*, p. 324.
22. *Ibid.*, p. 326.
23. Jack Goody, "Kinship: Descent Groups," in *International Encyclopedia of the Social Sciences*, Vol. 8, p. 402.

*ciations such as trade unions, and political parties rather than by multi-
functional units such as kin groups. In general, the role of UDGs diminishes with the importance of governmental institutions.*[24]

The property owning aspect of such groups is indicated by the term
corporate descent group. In the case of the Trobriand Islanders, for example,
the matrilineage—not the domestic group—owns the property and it is
passed on to the next generation through mother's brother.

Many people make office holding a matter of succession, particularly
that of high office such as the chieftainship or kingship. The Ashanti and
Bunyoro of Africa and the Hawaiians recognize hereditary heads. Among the
Hopi the matrilineage owns the property and much of the ceremonial para-
phernalia. The magical chants and incantations pass down through the matrilineage as a part of a person's "symbolic inheritance" although these latter
may also be sold.

Blood relationship, however, is not the only mode of reckoning descent.
There are several secondary modes of recruitment to a descent group such as
adoption or institutionalized illegitimacy. In the latter case a sterile woman
may marry another woman (such as in Dahomey) who bears children for the
former, or a slave may substitute for an infertile wife (such as Bilhah did for
Rachael in the Old Testament).

Major Mechanisms of Kin Control: The major mechanisms by which the kin
structure controls the family as an institution and not simply the behavior of
its individual members are the prescription of marriage partners and the
designation of rules of residence. Only extensive analysis will reveal the effect
of kin control in this area. (I will discuss the regulation of mate choice in
Chapter 10.)

Residence Rules: Our society specifies that the newly wedded couple
shall set up their own relatively independent residence. This form of residence is accordingly called *neolocal*. It is the only form of residence that is
quite incompatible with the extended family, since each generation is expected
to go forth on their own rather than to remain under one roof. The other
types of extended families are labeled after Kirchkoff according to which rule
of residence is recognized.[25] In *patrilocal* residence the young couple go to live
with or near the husband's family of orientation. In the case of *matrilocal* residence they go to live with or near the wife's family of orientation. With *bilocal*
rules they may live with either. A final case is that of *avunculocal* where they are
expected to live with the husband's maternal uncle. Again, since we are dealing
with the norms of the social order, we might expect that any concrete society
may have families living in violation of these expectations. We should expect
these to be in the minority, however, and should expect some stresses or
strains to result from such violations or discover some unusual extenuating
circumstance that can account for the exception. Of the 250 societies found

24. *Ibid.*, p. 402.
25. See Murdock *op. cit.*, p. 34.

in Murdock's World Ethnographic Sample, fifty-two were classified as patri-local extended, twenty-three as matrilocal extended, and ten as bilocal.[26]

The consequences of the various rules of residence are generally ac-knowledged by anthropologists as quite widespread. Murdock, for example, argues that change in the character of the entire kin structure is initiated by a change in the residence rule. The spouse who is living "at home" is in familiar surroundings, among kin in his own territory. The spouse who must move is always to some degree an alien who has, therefore, greater difficulty in establishing control over the family.

It would seem reasonable to expect that societies would synchronize the various rules governing their social structure so that, for example, patrilineal societies would in all cases have patrilocal or at least neolocal residence. This is not the case. The Trobriand Islanders are a matrilineal society with avuncu-local residence. Although descent is traced through the mother's lineage and her children inherit through her brother, she and her children must, never-theless, live in a village that is the property of her husband's lineage. Thus the integrative aspects of the kin structure are partially counterbalanced by friction between malintegrated components. This friction, however, can be conceived of as pressure toward change. Indeed Murdock considers the al-teration of residence rules and the consequent problems of adjustment to be a major source of social change in pre-industrial societies.

The Nuclear Family in Unilinear Societies

When we stop and recall that the discussion to this point has been about the control that lineages have over individual behavior, we can understand how comparatively insignificant the conjugal nuclear unit is in these societies. In our own case most of these control mechanisms are vested in the conjugal family. It is, therefore, really a distortion of emphasis to call these lineages "extended families" as does Murdock, even though there is a logical neat-ness in thinking of them as extensions of the nuclear unit through descent. Otterbein and others have demonstrated that composite families such as the extended family are not in fact formed by adding nuclear units. I have now indicated that even though this nuclear structure exists in pre-industrial so-cieties, it often has less control over individuals than the lineage. The loyalty of individuals is often greater toward their lineage than toward the members of their conjugal or nuclear family.

In societies where the lineage or larger kinship unit is more functional, change is less rapid. As I have shown, in such societies a great deal of em-phasis is placed upon inheritance, succession, and descent. All of these tend to ensure that the present generation will be much like its ancestors. Ancestor worship is a common feature of societies where there is great stress placed upon larger kin units, as in the case of the Chinese. What is transmitted through the lineage is a wide variety of things such as magical rites, canoes,

26. *Ibid.*, pp. 34–35.

and material possessions; and social positions such as kinships or rights to be a shaman. All of this tends to ensure continuity between the generations. When we realize that instead of two parents' being concerned over the personal behavior of their children it is not uncommon for a whole lineage to be directly involved, we see that it is more likely that children will exhibit conforming behavior in these societies. Such societies tend to be much more stable than ours, but the cost of stability is individual freedom.

I have saved our own type of kinship system until last. By so doing its uniqueness can be best appreciated. We have a *bilateral* system, that is we commonly reckon descent through both our mother and our father.

A Brief Examination of Our Own Kinship System

In comparison to pre-industrial societies, our society does not place as much importance on bonds of kinship beyond the primary kin of our own families.[27] Kinship as a factor in arranging marriages and in determining inheritance, succession, and descent is probably less important in the United States than in most industrialized countries. Although the extent to which we call upon kin for support is a subject of continuing debate, the fact that we do not live in communities surrounded by kin is well known. Our society depends upon many secondary organizations (corporations, schools, churches, government) to carry out its tasks and preserve its internal order and cohesion. Our kinship system is, furthermore, one of the most open in the world. In assigning an individual status or social position, we emphasize his achievement rather than simply accept his family's social position as sufficient (*ascription*). Of course, this is less true in upper-class families where ascription plays a more important role.

Figure 3–2 is a diagram of the ideal American kinship system. It can be modified in a number of ways. Most commonly such modification would come about through the addition of another family by the remarriage of persons in the line of descent. I am depicting the ideal and assuming that couples are bound in a single monogamous marriage until death. The diagram further suggests that most of us cease reckoning cousins beyond first cousins, although some may count kin much further removed from them. Notice, finally, that such a diagram does not include all persons who could be included. For example, the parents of ego's children-in-law and their families are not included in this diagram because they are not distinguished in our kinship terminology in relationship to ego.

Our kinship system is an uncommon form of kinship system in the World Ethnographic Sample. Seventy-five out of the 250 (30 percent) are bilateral.[28] As a type of bilateral system it has a number of distinctive features:

27. Much of the discussion in the following section is derived from Talcott Parsons, "The Kinship System of the Contemporary United States," *American Anthropologist*, Vol. 45 (Jan.–Mar., 1943), 22–38.
28. Murdock *op. cit.*, p. 57.

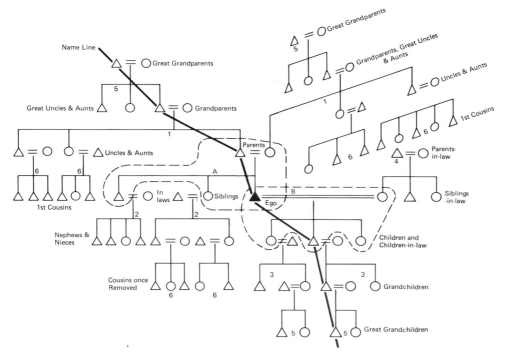

FIGURE 3–2. *The ideal American kinship system, after Parons. The* Inner Circle: *A–Ego's Family of Orientation (parents and siblings); and B–Ego's Family of Procreation (spouse and offspring); 1–First degree ascendant families (uncles and aunts); 2–First degree collateral families (nieces and nephews); 3–First degree descendant families (grandchildren); 4–In-law Family; 5—Second degree ascendants and descendants (great grandparents, great grandchildren); 6–Second degree collateral families (cousins). Adapted from "The Kinship System in the Contemporary United States," American Anthropologist, Vol. 45 (January–March 1943), 23.*

> *The most distinctive structural fact about the [bilateral] kindred is that,
> save through accident, it can never be the same for any two individuals
> with the exception of own siblings. For any given person, its member-
> ship ramifies out through diverse kinship connections until it is termi-
> nated at some degree of relationship—frequently with second cousins,
> although the limits are often drawn somewhat closer or farther away
> than this and may be rather indefinite. The kindreds of persons overlap
> or intersect rather than coincide. Those, for example, of first cousins, the
> sons of two brothers, have part of their membership in common—the
> near relatives through their respective fathers—and the rest distinct; the
> kinsmen of either cousin through his mother do not belong to the kin-
> dred of the other (except, of course, in those rare instances in which the
> brothers married a pair of sisters).*
>
> Since kindreds interlace and overlap, they do not and cannot form
> discrete or separate segments of the entire society (larger than the con-
> jugal family). *Neither a tribe, nor a community can be subdivided into
> constituent kindreds. . . . This intersecting or non-exclusive characteristic
> is found only with bilateral descent. Every other rule of descent produces
> only clearly differentiated, isolatable discrete kin groups, which never
> overlap with others of their kind.*[29]

Talcott Parsons characterizes our system as an "open, multilineal, conjugal
system." Our conjugal family is not broken up by another kin unit such as a
lineage. Thus, we have really only two kin units that we recognize termi-
nologically, the "family" and "relatives," which *do not refer to any specific
structural units*. None of the members of our conjugal family are identified by
the same kin term as other kinsmen (siblings are distinguished from cousins,
parents from aunts and uncles). Our system, therefore, is made up exclusively
of interlocking conjugal units.

With the exception of a designation of name line, we make no distinction between the maternal and paternal families of orientation. When we
move beyond the first ascending generation, any one of a number of lines
of descent may be treated as significant. The uniqueness of this reckoning of
descent can be seen best in our laws of inheritance which do not favor any
particular line of descent and grant to all children equal shares.

This relative absence of any structural bias in favor of solidarity with the
ascendant and descendant families in any one line of descent has enormously
increased the structural isolation of the individual conjugal family. This isolation, the almost symmetrical "onion" structure (best portrayed by Parsons'
original diagram), is the most distinctive feature of the American kinship system and underlies most of its peculiar functional and dynamic problems.[30]

Parsons acknowledges that his description best fits the urban middle
class. In rural America a form of the *stem family* (a nuclear family plus one
or more related individuals who do not comprise a second nuclear family)
still survives, especially where agriculture has not been commercialized.

29. Murdock *op. cit.*, p. 60. [emphasis added]
30. Parsons *op. cit.*, p. 28.

Among the upper class a tendency toward recognition of family solidarity along the lines of descent—particularly the patrilineal—is recognizable. It is coupled with a further tendency toward *primogeniture* (first-born son favored in inheritance). Finally, in the lower class there is a strong tendency toward mother-centered families in both black and white populations. The conjugal system encourages individual achievement rather than reliance upon ascription. The isolation of the conjugal family encourages the "romantic love complex" so characteristic of our society. Children are freed from socially prescribed roles to a much greater extent than in pre-industrial societies with unilineal descent. Marriage in our system involves not only a transition from a family of orientation to a family of procreation as it does in all societies, but also in a kind of emancipation. Members of the conjugal family of orientation —particularly the mother—play a much more important role in socializing the child in bilateral societies. However, they lose much of their control over a child when that child marries.[31] Hence, it is not surprising on structural analysis alone that the transition known as adolescence is particularly difficult in our society, giving rise to the "generation gap" and its related "youth culture."

In comparison with pre-industrial societies our society provides a high degree of emancipation for women. This is related to the fact that no priority is given to either sex in the maintenance of kin solidarity and in the *general* norm of achievement. This *relative* emancipation of women is associated, however, with a utilitarian division of labor within the conjugal family. In our society the status of the family depends largely upon the father's occupational achievement. If the wife works she normally has a job and not a career. She is expected to complement her husband's efforts on behalf of the family by her work in the home. She holds the family together; he provides for it. The tremendous importance placed upon the husband's career in our society, coupled with an ideal of equality between the sexes, creates a demand for a functional equivalent open to women. Hence women in America have traditionally tended to specialize in humanistic rather than technical achievements. They are the preservers of "good taste" in personal appearance, house furnishings, and literature and music—hence the finishing school. Traditional alternatives are becoming increasingly less satisfying for many women, however. Tensions are evident as the role of career girl becomes a viable alternative for more and more women.

Finally, in a society such as ours, the aged are quite alone. It is not normal for three generations to inhabit the same household. The emancipation of children is correlated with the expectation that aged parents will not come and live with them unless there is no other alternative. Thus, the aged are subjected to tremendous strains upon retirement when they are expected to make it on their own. Their economic support is ideally to be derived from retirement funds or social security rather than from their children's income.

31. *Ibid.,* p. 32.

Such are some of the implications of our kinship system as seen by one sociologist, Talcott Parsons. Each one of them will be discussed in more detail in the second section. They are discussed at this point not only to suggest something of the value of kinship analysis, but also in order to place Parsons' argument about the isolated conjugal family in the proper perspective. Much of the criticism that later will be directed at this position does not take into consideration that Parsons began his concern with a comparative kinship approach. In this light most of his comparisons are quite valid.

Summary

The lineage in primitive societies has as much control over the lives of individuals as the family does in our societies; in some cases it has more. The importance of the kinship system in pre-industrial societies can be seen in the native's concern with counting kin and determining relationships. Such an assessment of kin divides the world into two groups—kin and nonkin. With the former one can feel at home though away from home; with the latter one may fear for one's life.

Unilineal kinship systems in which the line of descent is reckoned through either the mother or the father (or both, in the unique situation of double descent) are characteristic of pre-industrial societies. Bilateral descent is characteristic of industrial societies. The change from unilineal to bilateral kinship systems is thus associated with industrialization, but the exact process by which the transformation occurs is poorly understood. From a society with strong tendencies to preserve the past way of life, to one that is open to the future is a great leap. In the former, change is comparatively slow. In the latter, it tends to become increasingly more rapid. The kinship system is one very significant element affecting the rate of change.

The kinship system functions in pre-industrial societies to regulate interpersonal behavior in a most formal manner. It prescribes those persons whom one must joke with, avoid, or defer to. It is also the most significant means of placing persons in the larger society through the mechanism of inheritance of property, succession of office, and the reckoning of descent. The kinship system further functions to control the family through determining residence rules and arranging marriages.

Analysis of our own kinship system indicates the extent to which we are free of such kin obligations and controls. Our system, which is commonly called a bilateral one, is composed of relatively isolated conjugal families and cannot be (by virtue of the fact that no two persons save siblings can have the same kindred) the basis of the social structure of our society. We must depend upon many nonkin organizations and institutions to perform this role.

As Stephens sees the comparative study of kinship structure, the societies of the world tend toward one of two poles: (1) those societies in which the kinship system is the basic social structure which are characterized by the formal control of behavior and ascription, and (2) those in which the kinship system plays a relatively insignificant role in structuring the society. These societies, such as our own, are characterized by informal behavior and a great emphasis upon achievement. As industrialization progresses, a common pattern is toward an informal society with its bilateral kin system and conjugal family. This is not an inevitable change, but the exceptions are few. I will return to this matter of development in Chapter 7.

4. Marriage and Family Structure

Romantic love as it occurs in our civilization, inextricably bound up with ideas of monogamy, exclusiveness, jealousy and undeviating fidelity . . . is a compound, the final result of many converging lines of development in Western Civilization, of the institution of monogamy, of the ideas of the age of chivalry, of the ethics of Christianity. Even a passionate attachment to one person which lasts for a long period and persists in the face of discouragement but does not bar out other relationships is rare among the Samoans. Marriage, on the other hand, is regarded as a social and economic arrangement in which relative wealth, rank, and skill of husband and wife, all must be taken into consideration. There are many marriages in which both individuals, especially if they are over thirty, are completely faithful. But this must be attributed to the ascendency of other interests over sex interests, rather than to a passionate fixation upon the partner in the marriage.

MARGARET MEAD

The passage from Margaret Mead's *Coming of Age in Samoa* on the preceding page was written in 1928. Romance was much more a component of love and lovemaking in America then than now. A sexual revolution has taken place in our country that has separated sex from marriage for a growing portion of our population, particularly those who are under thirty-five. (I will discuss the changes brought about in this revolution in Chapter 12.) It remains true, nevertheless, that in America marriage is less of a social contract and more of a personal commitment than in most primitive societies today, where bride wealth is often a more important reason for marriage than are sex and love.

An examination of the norms governing marriage and the family based on the world samples summarized in Table 4–1, and a description of some of the characteristics of family life in these societies will provide further documentation of the variation that is possible in marriage forms and will elaborate upon the relationship between the conjugal unit and the larger kinship system. I will begin this examination with a discussion of the interrelationships between the norms governing coitus and the institution of marriage.

Sex and Marriage

Marriage can be defined as:

> . . . *the established institution for starting a family. Both monogamous and polygamous marriage are found. There is often an exchange of economic goods in a marriage, and involved is a legal, physical and moral union between a man and a woman continuing through the raising of their children. Marriage regulates relations between the sexes and helps establish the child's relation to the community. It is usually associated with a ceremony, magical, religious, social or civil, which formalizes the group's approval. In marriage, the children produced by the women are usually accepted as the legitimate offspring of the married couple.*[1]

Marriage is the social institution wherein coitus is permitted if not encouraged in all but one society in the 250 societies of the World Ethnographic Sample.[2] It is not, however, *the* institution for the regulation of sexual behavior as it still tends to be in our society. Far too many societies prescribe coitus outside marriage to make this view tenable. On the other hand, no society prescribes *conception* outside of marriage. Some, such as those of the Caribbean, accept such an event as a second best alternative when marriage is difficult to negotiate or maintain. Marriage most characteristically functions in the sexual realm, therefore, to license parenthood and legitimize children.

Only three societies in the World Ethnographic Sample have a general

---

1. Charles Winick, *Dictionary of Anthropology* (New York: Philosophical Library, 1956), p. 344.
2. The World Ethnographic Sample was compiled by George Peter Murdock in the 1940s. It includes 70 societies from native North America, 65 from Africa, 60 from Oceana, 34 from Eurasia, and 21 from South America. It represents an attempt to obtain representative societies from these cultural areas, even though strict sampling procedures were departed from in some instances because of the lack of suitable material.

TABLE 4–1
The Regulation of Sexual Behavior in Relation to the Institution of Marriage

Premarital coitus	Murdock		Stephens		
Permitted	65	41%	20	59%	Permitted
Conditionally approved	43	28%			
			8	24%	Ineffective rule against
Mildly disapproved	6	2%			
Forbidden	44	29%	6	17%	Effective rule against
Totals	158		34		

Extramarital coitus	Murdock		Ford and Beach		Stephens		
No rule against	28	19%	54	39%	12	31%	No rule against
No rule against for men			69	39%	18	47%	No rule against for men
Rule against	128	81%	85	61%	14	37%	Ineffective rule against
Rule against for men and women			71	51%	6	16%	Effective rule against
Totals		148	139		38		

Common marriage type	Murdock
Strict monogamy	20%
Monogamy/pologamy	77%
Polyandry	3%
Group	—

Sources: Clellan S. Ford and Frank A. Beach, *Patterns of Sexual Behavior* (New York: Harper, 1951), p. 115; George Peter Murdock, *Social Structure* (New York: Free Press, 1965), pp. 24, 265; William F. Stephens, *The Family in Cross Cultural Perspective* (New York: Holt, Rinehart & Winston, 1963), pp. 246, 251–52.

taboo against sex. In all the rest the regulation of sexual behavior, particularly coitus, is interrelated with the maintenance of other social structures. The principal structures that are protected by the rules governing coitus are marriage, the family, social class, special social statuses, and special events. Thus there are widespread taboos against adultery, fornication, incest, breach of caste (also including class or racial boundaries), the violation of a special office (such as the priesthood), and incontinence.[3]

3. Murdock, *Social Structure* (New York: Free Press, 1965), p. 262.

In our *normative* frame of reference, every act of coitus outside marriage threatens to undermine the family either by reducing the desire to marry, by creating within the family jealousies over extra-marital affairs, or by generating uncontrollable tensions and rivalries as the result of incestuous relationships. This is not so in all countries.

THE REGULATION OF COITUS OUTSIDE MARRIAGE

Pre-Marital Coitus: In *Social Structure*, Murdock estimates that the sexual intercourse of a nonincestuous unmarried couple is fully permitted in sixty-five of the 250 societies in his sample, conditionally approved in forty-three, mildly disapproved in six, and forbidden in forty-four instances. Thus pre-marital sex is normatively endorsed in 70 percent of the societies in the World Ethnographic Sample. In the remaining 30 percent, restriction is directed primarily towards women and seems to be aimed at preventing birth out of wedlock.[4] In his smaller sample, Stephens calculates that premarital sex is permitted in twenty societies, ineffectively proscribed in eight, and effectively proscribed in six. In four of his societies (Barranquitas, Kwakiutl, Papago, and Tepotzlan) girls are severely restricted, but boys are not. Thus nearly half the societies in his sample forbid premarital sexual intercourse, but only one fourth "effectively restrict" it.[5]

The extent to which societies are consistent in their control over coitus outside marriage is not readily documented. Some inconsistency seems apparent. Norms against premarital or extra-marital coitus obtain in both informal and formal societies. However, even though such norms are established and sanctioned, *intimacy* between unmarried persons of the opposite sex may or may not be permitted. There is a tendency to reinforce strong negatively sanctioned taboos on coitus by formal restraints on intimacy demanding avoidance or deference behavior in regard to the tabooed group, but the tendency is weak. For example, premarital sex may be permissible in societies that also value virgin brides. This is our own situation under the "double standard." In the case of the Navaho, Kluckholm found that 90 percent of the men and about 50 percent of the women had experienced premarital sex. In our own society, despite our proscriptions, Kinsey concluded that most American men and women have experienced premarital sex. It must be remembered, however, that some societies which appear to be very permissive in their attitude regarding coitus outside marriage nevertheless restrict the permissible partners so that it becomes very difficult indeed to be guilty of excess. In some, half the population is excluded from being potential sex partners.

Something of the range in effective control over premarital sex can be seen in the cases of the Cheyenne, the Kaoka Speakers, and the Alorese.[6]

---

4. *Ibid.*, p. 265.
5. William F. Stephens, *The Family in Cross Cultural Perspective* (New York: Holt, Rinehart & Winston, 1969), p. 246.
6. See ethnographic accounts of these peoples in E. Adamson Hoebel, *The Cheyenne: Indians of the Great Plains* (New York: Holt, Rinehart & Winston, 1965); Ian Hogbin, *A Guadalcanal Society: The Kaoka Speakers* (New York: Holt, Rinehart & Winston, 1966); and Cora DuBois, *The People of Alor, Vol. I* (New York: Harper, 1944).

All three societies value virgin brides. In the case of the Cheyenne, the rules prohibiting fornication and adultery are explicit, severely sanctioned, and reinforced by myth and ceremonial. Consequently Cheyenne woman are noted for their chastity. The Kaoka Speakers of Guadalcanal also have norms against premarital coitus, but they pertain only to girls who wish to be considered respectable. Males are encouraged to have relations with prostitutes. If it were not for these women who were taken captive or born illegitimately, great stresses and strains would be introduced into the society. (See Fig. 4–1.) Finally, the Alorese are not con concerned about the enforcement of their taboos on premarital intercourse. There is no problem so long as one is not caught. There are checks after marriage, however. A difficult childbirth or a husband with a pain under his sternum tend to be diagnosed by Shamen as evidence of the wife's premarital unchastity. The penalties are severe once the act has been discovered, but, in practice, most couples feel free to engage in premarital coitus with discretion.

Studies such as Murdock's and Stephens' indicate further that in many societies premarital sex is positively sanctioned. The following example comes from the Ifugao of the Philippines (see Fig. 4–2.):

> *My father never gave me any advice about sexual relations with my wife because when I married, I already knew as much as he about that phase of life. But if a boy is big enough to begin his sex life and doesn't, his father will shame him. He will say, "Do not be bashful. If she runs away from you and goes where your 'sisters' are sleeping, they will know that*

FIGURE 4–1
The home of an important leader among the Kaoka Speakers. From Ian Hogbin, A Guadalcanal Society: The Kaoka Speakers (Holt, Rinehart & Winston, 1966), p. ix.

FIGURE 4–2
*An Ifugao bride preparing for
her wedding ceremonial. From
R. F. Barton,* Autobiography of
Three Pagans in the Philippines
(University Books, 1963).

*you are following her and will leave . . . so that you may come up." And
if a boy should be discouraged by a girl's rebuffs or running away, his
father advises him: "Chase her down. Don't be fooled, otherwise she'll
give it to somebody else. Follow her—it's well worth your while. Just
look at so-and-so (another boy of the same age). His wife is pregnant
already. Do as he did. It is well to learn even while you are a boy. Have
children when you are young. Let them slope evenly downward from you
through the first, second, third and so on down to the baby. My knees
are hungry for grandchildren (including great grandchildren). Whom can
you be taking after, that you are like this—afraid of the tadil of a girl?"*[7]

Some societies, however, while normatively permitting premarital coitus,
apparently exert subtle negative sanctions because such activity is carried
on with discretion and secrecy.

Finally, there are those societies that restrict premarital coitus to a very
narrow range of partners. Usually such permissiveness is associated with pref-
erential marriages such as cross-cousin marriages, and the preferred mate
is the permitted partner. As Murdock remarks, "Future marriages may be
said to cast their shadows before them." The behavior of cross-cousins in
such a permissive situation among the Murngin of Australia indicates that
even such permissiveness does not always go without some negative sanctions being applied:

*The young men and women older than the two usually tease the young
couple with somewhat obscene jokes about their relationship and its*

7. R. F. Barton, *Philippine Pagans: Autobiographies of Three Ifugaos* (London:
Routledge & Kegan Paul, 1938), p. 55.

meaning in their physical behavior. The youngsters are usually shy and ashamed when confronted with such humor; however, as small children, when away from the elders, they play house together. They are fully aware of the sexual act and of sex differences.

About the time facial hair appears upon a boy and the breasts of a girl swell, that is, when sexual intercourse is in their power and of interest to both, they start making love trysts in the bush. They may not copulate at first, but they simulate the act in close contact.

When a girl's first menses are over, her father . . . says to her mother . . . "You go make a house for them and fix a camp for them. She is big enough now."

After this, a young couple start living together and are recognized as husband and wife. They have been copulating before, frequently with the knowledge of the father and mother, but the latter pretend ignorance.[8]

Extra-Marital Coitus: The normative control of adultery—the intercourse of a married person with someone other than the spouse—is much less permissive. Yet adultery is widespread. As Lecky observes, "in all nations, ages, and religions a vast mass of irregular indulgence has appeared, which has probably contributed more than any other single cause to the misery and degradation of man."[9]

In a less judgmental view, Murdock observes simply that the norm is "sometimes more honored in the breach than in the observance." He records that 120 of the 148 societies in his sample have a rule against adultery.[10] In Ford and Beach's sample eighty-five, or 61 percent, have such a rule—although in fourteen cases it applied only to women.[11] Stephens' sample of thirty-nine yields six societies with harsh negative sanctions that apparently are effective; fourteen have an ineffective rule against it; six permit men but not women to copulate outside marriage; and twelve permit it for both men and women. In three other cases there is insufficient data.[12] Frequently extra-marital intercourse is confined to special occasions such as wife lending among the Copper Eskimo or periods of orgiastic celebrations such as occur among the Murngin, Kwoma, or Marquesan. In general more freedom is permitted the husband than the wife in such matters.

In Mexican and Mexican-American society the tradition of *machismo* prevails—a tradition that prescribes adultery for husbands and proscribes it for wives. But even in this case the husband is not permitted to do as he pleases:

Marital conflict often results from the male's desire to prove his machismo outside the home.

8. W. Lloyd Warner, *A Black Civilization* (New York: Harper and Row, 1939). p. 75.
9. William E. H. Lecky, *History of European Morals From Augustus to Charlemagne,* Vol. II (London: Longmans, Green, 1869), pp. 298–99.
10. Murdock *op. cit.,* p. 265.
11. Clellan S. Ford and Frank A. Beach, *Patterns of Sexual Behavior* (New York: Harper & Bro., 1951), p. 115.
12. Stephens *op. cit.,* pp. 251–52.

The young husband must show his male acquaintances that he has more sexual energy than his wife can accommodate. To prove his prowess, he often continues the sexual hunt of his premarital days. He may demonstrate his physical and financial resources by visiting Boys Town with his drinking companions after an evening in a tavern. The most convincing way of proving his machismo and financial ability is to keep a mistress in a second household known as a casa chica. Few men in the lower class can aspire to such luxury, which constitutes the height of manly success among middle- and upper-class husbands.

Mexican-American society maintains a system of checks to prevent the male from threatening his home life with extra-marital adventures. Foremost is the community's expectations that a husband will not allow any activity to interfere with his obligations to his wife and children. If the welfare of his family diminishes as a result of his sexual activities outside the home, the husband must face social disapproval and the intercession of his in-laws. His behavior damages his reputation in the community and brings dishonor on his parents. Exaggerated dedication to sex at the expense of friendship also demonstrates a lack of intellectual ability in social interaction. A third check on extra-marital excesses is fear of the venereal diseases. . . .

Sexual promiscuity on the part of the wife is a heinous crime. So fragile is a woman's purity—according to Mexican-American belief—that one sexual indiscretion inevitably leads to a life of complete sexual abandon. No man would remain with a promiscuous wife unless he is already so debased that nothing matters.[13]

The very strong emphasis on family solidarity coupled with the wife's ability to skillfully manipulate her husband serves as further control over the excesses of his extra-marital activities. The actual social constraints placed upon such activity, then, go far beyond the formal rules.

Whatever the norm, however, jealousies over such affairs seem common. The Mexican-American wife may be jealous, even though she expects her husband to express his *machismo*. Perhaps jealousy arises even in situations where the norm prescribes infidelity for both partners, but it seems equally likely that much of the apparent conflict between personal and social expectations that is implied by such observations results from a failure to specify more precisely the specific group which holds the norm of marital fidelity. In the case of Mexican society (and to a lesser extent perhaps even in our own) it can be argued that the expectations within the male sub-culture are such that infidelity is normal and within the female sub-culture such that it is deviant. On these and other matters there may not be an over-arching social norm. In any event a few societies do not proscribe extra-marital intercourse and apparently experience little marital strain as a result.

Thus nonmarital coitus is a quite common occurrence even in instances where the social norm gives it negative sanction. Premarital coitus is prescribed in the majority of the world's societies, and extra-marital coitus—

13. William Madsen, *The Mexican American of South Texas* (New York: Holt, Rinehart & Winston, 1963), pp. 49–50.

though proscribed in the majority of the world's societies—is, nevertheless, a very common occurrence. Because of other controls over the excesses of such behavior (the most common perhaps being public disapproval of excess, the common understandings worked out between husband and wife, and the heavy investment that most societies place in marriage as a significant socioeconomic contract undergirding their social structure), less permissiveness occurs in fact than the norms might suggest.

Incest Taboos: Incest taboos function to preserve the cohesiveness and authority structures of kin groups. In bilateral societies the kin group is the nuclear family. In unilinear societies, it is the lineage. The study of incest and its control has been a major concern of anthropologists because of their perception that these taboos reflect basic principles of organization within any social structure. As defined by the *Oxford Universal Dictionary* "incest" refers to "sexual intercourse or cohabitation between persons related within the degrees within which marriage is prohibited."[14] Under this definition, rules which prohibit intercourse between certain kin (incest taboos) are coextensive with rules which prohibit marriage (rules of exogamy). Stephens states it simply, "Incest taboos are prohibitions against sexual intercourse and marriage between kin. . . . Extended incest taboos applied to a more distant kin are sometimes termed 'exogamous rules' or simply 'exogamy'."[15] It is the further assumption of a number of anthropologists that incest taboos and their extensions cannot be explained unless it is understood that *the* kin group that is being protected is the nuclear family. In their view, the basic understanding of incest taboos must at least start with an explanation of why parents and children, brothers and sisters are almost everywhere prohibited from engaging in intercourse. The extension of the taboo to persons beyond the nuclear family may require some further assumptions such as the analogous social positions of classificatory kin systems.

Jack Goody takes Murdock and others to task for attempting to classify under the single term "incest" those diverse heterosexual offenses that are encountered universally. This classification reflects strongly the Western heritage of a bilateral reckoning of descent, the major weaknesses of which is a failure to distinguish between heterosexual offenses with group members and those with spouses of group members. Both are usually called "incest" by ethnographers, but the group-spouse offense is an offense for quite a different reason. A group-spouse is—before marriage—an eligible mate choice. The offense, therefore, occurs not because kin groups have been violated but rather because sexual rights in the spouse that have been more or less vested in a single group member have been violated. Such an offense is more properly seen as a form of adultery, not incest. Thus Goody would expand the categories of heterosexual offenses as follows[16]:

14. *The Oxford Universal Dictionary* (Oxford: Clarendon Press, 1964).
15. Stephens *op cit.*, p. 259.
16. Jack Goody, "A Comparative Approach to Incest and Adultery," in *Marriage, Family and Residence*, Paul Bohannan and John Middleton (eds.), (New York: The Natural History Press, 1968), p. 33.

	Offenses with	
Offenses that are:	Unmarried person	Married person
Intra-group	Incest	Incestuous adultery
Extra-group	Fornication	1. Spouse of group: Group-spouse adultery
		2. Other married person: Non-group adultery

A bilateral system does not generally distinguish between offenses with sibling or sibling-in-law, calling both "incest." Unilinear societies, on the other hand, do make such a distinction and sanction the offenses differently. As a general pattern, incestuous adultery is sanctioned more severely than incest and group-spouse adultery more severely than nongroup adultery, while nonincestuous fornication frequently goes without negative sanction.

A further complication is introduced into the above scheme with the recognition that societies differ in the extent to which they vest the group with rights over the women who marry into them. In patrilineal societies, rights to the sexual services of women are acquired in general by individuals, but the woman's procreative capacities are vested to some extent in the descent group. There is thus a contradiction involved in reckoning the descent of children, for the offspring of an individual is also the offspring of the entire clan. In order to reduce the contradiction in such situations and to prevent further complication in the reckoning of descent, the Brahmins make the rights over a woman so individualized that she may marry again after her husband's death. Among the Tallensi a widow *must* remarry but only into the same patriclan[17] as her husband, through the rule of widow inheritance. The LoDagga, also regard intercourse with the wife of a patri-clansman as the worst heterosexual offense, yet the younger of a pair of male twins, if unmarried, is supposed to be able to have his elder brother's wife as a sexual partner. The Nuer, on the other hand, tend to vest the *descent group* not only with rights to a woman's procreative capacities but also with rights to her sexual services. They must, therefore, permit kinsmen of the same descent group to court the same woman, whereas in most other African societies this is prohibited. The LoDagga and Tallensi most severely sanction full siblings negatively in this regard. So also, in the case of the Nuer, intercourse with wives of patriclansmen is not regarded with the same "horror" as it is among the Tallensi or LoDagga.

The severity of sanctions placed on intercourse between brother and sister as well as that between a man and the wife of a group member varies further depending upon whether the society is matrilineal or patrilineal. Among the matrilineal Trobrianders, brother-sister intercourse is regarded with the greatest horror. Among the patrilineal Tallensi, however, intercourse between brother and sister is merely regarded as disreputable. On the other

17. A group of relatives who live together and trace their descent from an original male ancestor.

hand, the Tallensi regard group-wife offenses with horror, while the matri-lineal Ashanti simply consider it disreputable. The reason for this difference in severity of negative sanction is that:

> . . . *in patrilineal societies the rights over a woman which are transferred at marriage include rights to her reproductive capacities as well as rights to her sexual services, whereas in matrilineal societies, it is only the latter which is transferred. Indeed, among the Ashanti, a male only acquires exclusive sexual rights by the payment of a special sum, known as the tiri-nsa, which is not intrinsic to the "marriage" itself.*[18]

For Goody, then, it is the descent group—not the family—that is the primary kin group being preserved by incest taboos in unilineal societies. His clarification of the concept of incest places doubt upon the applicability of Murdock's generalizations for they are based upon ethnographies that—by and large—do not make these distinctions. However, one generalization emerges with some clarity.

Incest taboos—defined by Goody as taboos on intercourse with *group members*—show a strong tendency to parallel rules of exogamy:

> *If therefore the rule of exogamy is to be related to the external value of the marriage alliance, . . . then the intra-group prohibition on intercourse cannot be dissociated from it. The rejection of temporary sexuality within the group is in part a reflection of the rejection of permanent sexuality, and the latter is related to the importance of establishing intergroup relationships by the exchange of rights in women.*[19]

Even here, however, there are exceptions. The Tallensi, for example, allow sexual intercourse with distant clansmen, where they do not permit marriage. The Lugbara of Uganda apparently do not classify intercourse between distant clansmen who are prohibited to marry as incest unless a child is born of the union. The latter would seem quite consistent with Goody's argument that sexual intercourse, when carried on secretly, does not require a realignment of kin groups whereas marriage does. So likewise the birth of an illegitimate child to distant clansmen creates the need for some reorganization. Interestingly the emphasis on the clandestine nature of the love affair is further stressed among the Lugbara in that a man would never have intercourse with a distant clan sister inside her hut. Rather, it must take place outside her compound in the grassland.

Incest taboos and rules of exogamy in unilineal societies thus serve to divide the population of a given society into two groups: a smaller one within which intercourse and marriage are prohibited, and a larger one within which they are permitted. The structure of the descent group is further preserved in unilineal societies by their recourse to an additional negative sanction on intercourse with group-spouses:

18. Goody, *op. cit.*, p. 36.
19. *Ibid.*, p. 44.

For where rights of sexual access are individualized, conflict over females may be a cause of internecine dispute, and this prohibition renders such disputes less likely. It is indeed closely related to the taboo, found among the Tallensi and among many other African peoples, against clansmen having sexual relationships with one woman during the same period.[20]

This offense he would call group-spouse adultery—not incest as it is most frequently referred to at present.

The function, then, of the incest taboo and its relationship to rules of exogamy (after redefinition) seem to be relatively clear and straightforward. They appear to be central mechanisms ensuring that social structures in unilineal societies can be built upon descent groups that are relatively precisely defined. In bilateral societies the kin group that is most directly protected by both, however, is the family—in our own case most frequently the nuclear family.

These, then, are the limited generalizations: (1) The incest taboo functions within the family to preserve parental authority in the control and socialization of children. (2) It functions externally to preserve the continuity of descent groups. This function is reinforced by taboos on group-spouse adultery. (3) In bilateral societies the social group that is most clearly protected by the incest taboo is the nuclear family. In unilinear societies it is the lineage. (4) In all societies the incest taboo is violated to some degree, and in some—such as the Trobriand—it is done with great relish. Natives are not "slaves of custom."

THE REGULATION OF MATE SELECTION

The regulation of mate selection is a quite different process from that of the regulation of sexual activities. Much more is at stake in the former instance. Marriage involves the realignment of segments of the social structure, while intercourse, when it produces no children, does not. Thus persons may be available as sexual partners but not as potential mates, and potential mates may not be available as sexual partners. A common pattern, however, is that persons who are not permitted to be potential mate choices are also not considered as possible sexual partners *in the normative social order.*

Exogamy and Endogamy: Two major principles govern mate selection. Exogamy *prohibits* marriage within a particular group. Endogamy *prescribes* marriage within a particular group. Exogamous and endogamous rules thus generally limit the choice of mates to a group of eligibles who are not so close to one's own blood lines as to be incestuous nor so distant from one's people as to be considered alien. Rules of exogamy, in particular, encourage one to marry out of one's own group, thus enabling the social structure to be firmly constructed not only upon blood lines clearly defined, but also upon affinal bonds that are carefully tied. Both types of rules may be either very

20. *Ibid.,* p. 45.

precise or very broad in their limitation of mate choice. Endogamous rules are frequently quite specific in their definition of eligible mates.

Ordinarily marriage is not permitted between members of one's own nuclear family. Rules of exogamy and incest taboos commonly coincide in this case. Frequently exogamous rules apply to extensions of the nuclear family in classificatory kinship terminology. A man, for example, may not be permitted to marry anyone called a "sister" even though that person may not be in fact related by blood. Traditionally the Chinese disapproved of marriage between two people with the same surname, even though they were unrelated by blood. Some peoples, such as the peasant villagers of Vasilika in Greece and the Kibutzniks in Israel, practice a kind of village exogamy, although no formal rules have been established against intravillage marriage. Typically, in unilineal societies such as the Trobriand and Bunyoro, *lineages* are exogamous. There are some instances of class or caste exogamy. For example, among the Natchez (lower Mississippi) a woman of the three noble classes is *required* to marry a commoner—a "Stinkard."

The rules of endogamy may be quite precise. A preferred mate among the Trobriander males is the father's sister's daughter. The Haida, on the other hand, prefer the other cross-cousin: mother's brother's daughter. Commonly, however, endogamous rules pertain to much larger groups of people. Kroeber reports that the Mohave disapprove not only of sexual relations but of any intercourse with other races, and regard such contact as a specific cause of sickness.[21] Under such circumstances interracial marriages are highly unlikely. The Arth, near the Algerian frontier, marry only among themselves and also refrain from all sexual intercourse with strangers. On the other hand, the Toda strongly oppose *marriage* to someone outside their community, but are not disturbed by a woman's relations with a stranger if she remains in the community.[22] The Quinault (coastal Washington) are most unusual in that they actually *prefer* marriages into other tribes.

When endogamous rules are quite precise in their stated preference of mate choice, it is customary for the society to make allowances for alternatives in instances where the preferred choice is not to be found. Thus a man who might be expected to marry his mother's mother's brother's daughter's daughter (a double cross-cousin) might have some difficulty in finding a mate if this rule were strictly enforced. Customarily he may select a spouse that fits this preferred choice as closely as possible.

Marriage Finance: Since most societies view marriage as a legal contract, they expect it to persist despite the personal desires of the married couple. The character of the marriage contract, therefore, frequently involves these larger kin groups directly so that they have something at stake in the preservation of the union. The elaborate marriage finance is but one mechanism that tends to ensure the involvement of the larger kin group and the continuance of the

21. Cited in Edward Westermarck, *The History of Human Marriage* (London: Macmillan 1921), p. 47.
22. *Ibid.*, p. 54.

marriage by exacting a price from one or the other or both kin groups should the marriage terminate.

Seventy percent of the societies in the World Ethnographic Sample have some form of marriage finance, the most frequently mentioned being a *bride price* which is a payment of some sort to the bride's family which, in effect, pays them for the loss of her services.[23] In the event of a broken marriage, such a price is usually refundable, and, therefore, at least one side of the family has a vested interest in keeping the relationship intact. In the Old Testament, Jacob served nine years under his father-in-law in lieu of a bride price for Rachael. Such compensation is called *bride service* and is a frequently acceptable alternative when the suitor cannot produce the bride price. Sometimes the payments go in the opposite direction, that is, they are paid to the groom's family or kinsmen, as in the case of the dowry. There may simply be an exchange of gifts or women cementing both sides in financial obligations. The higher frequency of payments going to the bride's kin does not indicate a higher status of women. Indeed, it suggests the opposite, since a *man* cannot be purchased, and most commonly a woman must be paid for because she goes to live with her husband, thus depriving her own kinsmen of her services. A much smaller number of societies requires the husband to go and live with his wife's family.

However, the bride price should not be seen as reducing women to the status of chattel or property if for no other reason than that in the vast majority of cases she cannot be sold again. As an economic transaction, the bride price can be seen as a gain on the more ancient custom of daughter exchange, accomplishing the same task of binding two kin groups together.

The first marriage in recorded history comes from Sumeria. Under this contract a groom was required to provide a gift to the bride's father on the announcement of their engagement. If he broke the engagement this was forfeited. If his fiancee broke the engagement, her father was obligated to return the gift plus an equal amount. In the happy event that the marriage was consummated the bride's father matched the engagement gift, and the sum became a gift to the groom.

Marriage and Child Bearing

Marriage is everywhere intimately associated with the bearing of children. No society encourages its members to bear children outside marriage. Sex is restricted to marriage in many societies because its function is presumed to be primarily that of reproduction. For some people a marriage is not consummated until a child is born.

CONCEPTION AND CONSUMMATION

Some societies see the relationships among marriage, sex, and procreation quite differently than we do. Under their reasoning a marriage is not finalized

23. Stephens *op. cit.*, p. 211.

until the woman has given birth to a child. Still practiced in such areas as rural Sweden, such reasoning ties marriage more strongly to the procreative function than to ideals of romantic love. If a woman is barren (and it is taken for granted that it is the woman who is barren), there is no reason to marry.

Some societies make allowances for barren wives by permitting other women to bear children for them. This custom is recorded in the Old Testament in such cases as Sarah and Abraham. The Swazi make both the requirement of the fruitfulness of the wife and the lifelong commitment of marriage a possibility through a similar arrangement:

> *Swazi marriage is essentially a linking of two families rather than of two persons, and the bearing of children is the essential consummation of wife-hood. Swazi marriage is of so enduring a nature that should the man himself die, the woman is inherited through the custom of the levirate by one of the male relatives to the deceased to raise children in his name. Similarly, since the production of children is the essential fulfillment of the woman's part of the contract, should she prove barren, her family must either return the cattle, or, following the custom of the sororate, provide her with a relative, preferably a younger full sister, as a junior co-wife to bear children to "put into her womb."*[24]

THE PRINCIPLE OF LEGITIMACY

Marriage, in the last analysis, is the principal means of licensing fatherhood and legitimizing the birth of a child. The principle of legitimacy formulated by Malinowski asserts that every child shall have a father and one father only.[25] Malinowski distinguishes here between the *pater* (the man who is the socially recognized father) and the *genitor* (the biological father). The principle asserts that every child *should* have a pater. As obvious as this might at first seem, a little reflection suggests that while the mother-child dyad could conceivably be self-sufficient economically and emotionally, it is never considered so sociologically. Even in those societies that are aware of the father's role of procreation, his role biologically might as well be that of a drone. Indeed, our more complete understanding of the techniques of reproduction limits the biological father's role even further to that of a donor in the case of artificial insemination, and theoretically it would be biologically useless should we be able to stimulate an egg to divide without impregnation by a sperm as occurs naturally in some lower life forms (parthenogenesis).

Nevertheless, despite his dispensability biologically, the father plays an important role sociologically. Some social scientists argue that the *couvade*— a custom common to South American and African tribes wherein the father "lies in" complaining of labor pains while his wife delivers the child—is an extreme instance of overcompensation, the sociological role being dramatized because the biological role is unknown or considered minimal.

24. Hilde Kuper, *The Swazi: A South African Kingdom* (New York: Holt, Rinehart & Winston, 1967), pp. 22–23.

25. See Part One, Section I of Coser, *op. cit.*, for several articles pertaining to this point.

In all societies the unmarried mother is proscribed and her child considered a bastard, although the consequences of illegitimacy vary considerably around the world. Therefore, the principle of legitimacy is a sociological concept—not the assertion of a biological tautology.

It is furthermore a normative concept and not a descriptive one. Every child *should* have one father and one father only, even though every child does not in fact have a sociologically recognized father. The form this principle takes in concrete cases further varies: (1) according to the laxity or stringency which obtains regarding premarital intercourse, (2) according to the value set upon virginity, (3) in relation to various ideas about procreation, and above all (4) according to whether the child is considered a burden or an asset to its parents.

In societies where premarital intercourse is regarded as immoral, marriage is the necessary prerequisite for legitimate children. In those societies where premarital intercourse is permitted and thus conception outside of marriage is a likely occurrence, marriage is still regarded as essential for the child's attainment of full status in the community. In those societies where children are considered assets, the unwed mother need not worry about her social status—she can quickly procure a husband as she is made more desirable by the fact that she has already provided evidence of her fertility.

Marriage should not, therefore, be seen as the licensing of sexual intercourse (which frequently is permitted outside of marriage) but rather as a mechanism for licensing parenthood and establishing the legitimacy of children.

Family Structure

While the conjugal or nuclear family is frequently enlarged by merging imperceptibly into the larger kinship network, as I have shown in Chapter 3, it can also be enlarged by extension of the marriage bond creating polygamous households.

The possible combination of spouses allows for three basic types of polygamous families: a husband with two or more wives—polygyny; a wife with two or more husbands—polyandry; and two or more husbands with two or more wives—group marriage. The naming of family types also coincides with that of marriage types in this instance. It must be remembered that there are quite different implications when one is talking about family forms rather than marriage types.

Polygyny is decidedly the *preferred* marriage form and family type, although the statistical majority of marriages and family forms reflected in the World Ethnographic Sample is monogamous and nuclear respectively. Polyandry is exceedingly rare as a preferred type, and group marriage has never been observed as the preferred type in any society.[26] Group marriage is found more

26. Murdock *op. cit.*, pp. 23–28 *passim*.

frequently in utopian communities within our own society such as Oneida or in subcultures such as the Hippies'. It would seem reasonable to infer from this that group marriage presents more problems than it solves for a society. Only rather adventuresome people within a social system seem able to sustain marriage in this form for even a couple of generations. There is no evidence of a promiscuous society—one wherein there is no preferred form of marriage and no restriction on sexual activity. The Kaingang come about as close to this extreme as any society.

POLYGYNY

In African societies polygyny has been quite successful, although not without problems. In most of these societies polygyny is not possible for the average man and is permitted most often only when sisters or relatives are co-wives, under living arrangements whereby each wife and her children have separate living quarters—often within the same compound of buildings. In such societies the senior wife is generally afforded higher status and may assume greater obligation for the care of the household. All wives, however, are granted equal sexual privileges. Thus a husband may have a preference for the youngest and most beautiful of his wives, but those who do not please his fancy at the moment are spared public mortification by the requirement that he spend the night with them when their turn comes up even though he might not engage in coitus. In the case of the Mormons in our own society, no such rule obtained, and a man could lavish his attention on his favorite as long as he could stay the anger of the dispossessed.

Nevertheless, jealousy among co-wives in polygamous societies is not uncommon. Furthermore, polygyny is highly correlated with sorcery and strict sexual taboos.[27] Who could be a more perfect practitioner of sorcery against a man than a jealous co-wife who has access to his person yet privacy enough to practice her craft? The strict sexual taboos (particularly those pertaining to prenatal, post-partum, and menstrual abstinence) are more observable in such a society, on the one hand because a man has other wives who are available to him and, on the other hand, because they serve to increase the likelihood that only properly related persons will be bound together in polygynous households.

Thus, it would seem that a plurality of wives is favored by a large part of the world's societies. Polygyny is not directly correlated with any particular set of economic conditions, as is seemingly the case with polyandry. It does not necessarily involve the low status of women, although the fact that polyandry is associated with female infanticide and polygyny is not associated with male infanticide leads one to conclude that the status of women is commonly lower than that of men. While female infanticide tends to reduce the problem of a surplus of women in polyandrous societies, the surplus of men in polygynous societies is usually counteracted by the early marriage of

27. Stephens, *op. cit.*, p. 68.

women. The result is that a typical polygynous society will have a number of young women married to one old man. A great many men will have only one wife or none.

Tiwi Polygyny: The Tiwi are a people who live on Melville and Bathhurst Islands off the northern coast of Australia.[28] This hunting and gathering people were studied during 1928–29 and again in 1953–54. The characteristics of their family life here described are thought to be more typical of them prior to the coming of the missionaries in 1911 (although the collaborating anthropologists, Hart and Pilling, were amazed to find how little they had changed between their respective contacts).

In their traditional organization they form nine bands of between 100 and 300 persons each, each of which occupies its own territory. Many bands cannot gather together for long periods of time for the purposes of conducting elaborate festivities because Tiwi technology is meager and the land upon which they live is unable to support large numbers of persons. Their environment is not as arid as that of the tribes of the Australian outback, however.

The basic unit of their social organization is not the band but the household built around polygymous marriage:

> The Tiwi household usually consisted of a man, his wife or wives, and their children, though in many would also be included a few leftovers or extras common to all cultures, such as bachelor uncles, visiting cousins, ancient widowers, and ambitious "big men" who came to dinner and were still there. Tiwi households did not include maiden aunts, female orphans, or ancient widows, since these could not exist in Tiwi culture. [A Tiwi woman was always married.][29]

For the Tiwi, women are treated as a medium of exchange. The negotiation of their marriage is of considerable concern to the men because having many wives is a commonly recognized indicator of a "big man." Such wives serve the function within a man's household, furthermore, of providing him with a better than average supply of food and leisure time for creative activities such as carving or writing songs.

Among the Tiwi, old age (especially in men) is honored. In fact the Tiwi represent a gerontological oligarchy—a society ruled by old men.

Under the Tiwi system, every woman is married. There are no single women, and therefore there is no possibility of illegitimate children. The Tiwi have defined marriage so precisely that it is impossible for a child not to have a father. This rather startling accomplishment is the result of two distinct mechanisms for acquiring a wife. Female babies are betrothed to their future husbands at birth—though they ordinarily do not go to live with their husband until they reach puberty. Such an exchange is called *infant bestowal*.

---

28. This section is based primarily on the ethnographic sketch of the Tiwi by C. W. M. Hart and Arnold R. Pilling, *The Tiwi of North Australia* (New York: Holt, Rinehart & Winston, 1960). The term "Tiwi" can be translated "we the only people."

29. *Ibid.*, p. 13. [emphasis added]

The second way a man can acquire a wife is through *widow remarriage,* wherein a woman is remarried at the graveside of her deceased husband. Since the exchange of infants and widows is of great importance to the older males, no female escapes marriage.

A man ordinarily acquires his first wife through the process of widow remarriage when he is about forty. After the acquisition of a first wife (and with sufficient aplomb to have convinced the older men that he is a young man who is going places) the Tiwi man of forty might then expect to acquire a number of wives in rapid succession through infant bestowal. Thus it is common for a Tiwi husband to be either much older or much younger than his wives. The typical Tiwi household is headed by a husband who is an average of fourteen years older than his younger wives.

In this household the senior wife ordinarily supervises the younger wives in the gathering of food and the carrying out of household tasks. She also serves as a guardian of the "harem," keeping a close eye on the young wives lest they engage in extra-marital affairs with some young Don Juan who is frequently to be found camping nearby. Indeed, so difficult is the matter of procuring a living, that frequently single young men seek scraps from the "big man's" table as well as the affection of his younger wives.

It is not difficult to imagine the problems inherent in such a system. Seduction is common, but elopement is virtually impossible, for there is no place to go. The tension between the young men and the gerontocrats might be totally unmanageable were it not for another fact of Tiwi life—the requirement that all young men between the ages of fourteen and twenty-four be isolated from the tribe for a considerable time in preparation for their rite of passage into adulthood.

The elders themselves frequently are "at war" with one another because of suspected or real betrayal in the negotiation for wives. Fortunately, Tiwi wars are not too deadly since the exchange of wives has bound the clans so closely to one another and intertwined each man's obligations so much that the combatants can rarely create enough dissension to split a gathering crowd into two warring groups. Instead, the offended parties usually stand at a relatively safe distance from one another and throw spears. Tiwi feuds generally end when blood is drawn from a wound that is rarely fatal. If a man desired to be "big" in Tiwi society, he had, first, to convince his elders that he was "promising" before he was twenty-five, and then be able to survive long enough to live with his wives. In practice there are few such big men.

POLYANDRY

While Murdock defines two societies in his World Ethnographic Sample as polyandrous, Stephens in his much smaller sample classified four societies—the Todas, Marquesan, Nayar, and Tibetan—as "predominantly polyandrous." The Nayar marriage, some argue, gives evidence of mixed polyandry and polygyny which might be labeled "group marriage." However one interprets the Nayar case, pure polyandry is quite rare as a dominant marriage type and family form.

Stephens makes the following generalizations about polyandry:

1. Group marriage is not uncommonly associated with polyandry.
2. The cohabiting husbands are often brothers.
3. An economic inducement to form such an arrangement is often mentioned by ethnographers.
4. It is strongly associated with female infanticide. As I have noted, polygynous societies do not practice male infanticide.
5. There is little evidence of jealousy between cohabiting husbands. It may be the case here that the *potential* for jealousy between cohabiting husbands is so great that it prohibits men who would tend to be jealous from joining polyandrous households in the first place.[30]

While polygyny is not as clearly associated with a particular kind of economy, economic factors seem to play an extremely important role in the development of polyandry. Jules Henry, for example, notes that among the Kaingang (where polyandry once flourished, but was never dominant), the motive for a man to join with a co-husband was always the security of his wife and family.[31]

Tolerance of a variety of family forms seems more characteristic of societies in which polyandry is to be found. If we reason that polyandry is usually a last resort, then it follows that where polyandry is found a greater variety of marriage forms will be likely. The preference for polygyny or at least a monogamous situation in societies where resources are scarce would motivate males to try to acquire such families and, in the process, accept various alternatives as second best—permissible but not preferred. Tibetan fraternal polyandry can be seen as the answer to the problem of land shortage and as such, is characteristic of the lower class. "Middle-class" Tibetans are characteristically monogamous, and Tibetan nobility polygynous. Among the Marquesans, nonfraternal polyandry ordinarily associates two to three men with a single wife. Upper-class families add one or two wives after the initial marriage of the household head, resulting in "group marriage" with the household head considered the father of the children for genealogical purposes.

Toda Polyandry: The Todas are a small pastoral tribe found in villages scattered throughout the plateaus of South India. They numbered between 500 and 600 at the time they were studied by W. H. R. Rivers.[32]

The Toda family is patrilocal and extends over three or more generations. Fraternal polyandry is a common form of marriage which is sometimes com-

30. Stephens *op. cit.*, pp. 44–45.
31. Henry, *Jungle People* (New York: Vintage Books, 1964), pp. 37–42 *passim*.
32. W. H. R. Rivers, *The Todas* (New York: Macmillan, 1906). Summaries are to be found in Stuart A. Queen and Robert Habenstein (eds.), *The Family in Various Cultures*, 3rd ed. (Philadelphia: Lippincott, 1967), pp. 18–44; and George Peter Murdock, *Our Primitive Contemporaries* (New York: Macmillan, 1934), pp. 107–34.

bined with polygyny to create a form of group marriage (see Fig. 4–3). Often each man has his own wife, plus access to his brother's wife. Under the marriage arrangements, a woman marries a man and at the same time becomes a wife to all his brothers. Among such co-husbands, jealousy is considered "bad form" and rarely occurs.

When a wife becomes pregnant, the father is determined through an unusual ceremony called "giving the bow." Usually the oldest brother gives the bow. By "giving the bow" he becomes recognized as the legal father of the unborn child and any other children that the woman might have. However, another brother frequently gives the bow to a woman after she has given birth to two or three children, and he then becomes recognized as the legal father of children born thereafter.

Toda males acquire wives through several means. Many are married when they are infants, and when this occurs it frequently results in a shortage of females for marriage at a later period (since the Todas practice female infanticide which more than compensates for the imbalance likely to be produced by polyandrous unions). Therefore, they have instituted a secondary marriage form which can be called *wife transfer*. Simply put, a man is permitted to seek a wife among those women who are already married. When he finds a suitable spouse, he will bargain for her with the permission of her father, two elders of the tribe, and her husband.

The Todas institutionalize a third form of sexual union between men and

FIGURE 4–3
A Toda household typically consists of a group of brothers and their
common wife (fraternal polyandry). Toda descent is patrilinear.
From the American Museum of Natural History.

women, that of the *consort-mistress*. This case occurs when the couple come from two groups (called moieties) within Toda society that are not permitted to marry (they are called, therefore, endogamous groups). The children born to such a union cannot be considered legitimate, and they become the children of the woman's legal husband. In this arrangement, the woman may live with her consort, or he—as is the more usual custom—may come to visit her at her husband's house. Their relationship is institutionalized through a ceremony after consent has been obtained and an exchange of gifts or money has been effected. The new consort "may claim marital privileges in scheduled visits or assume what actually amounts to a husband's role and live with the co-husband." His role as consort, then, approaches that of a husband. One outstanding difference, however, is that he cannot "give the bow" to his mistress.[33]

GROUP MARRIAGES

What constitutes group marriage is often a matter for debate among observers. For Otterbein there is no true group marriage among the Marquesans because one of the sexually cohabiting couples in his third case did not marry and, therefore, was not able to produce legitimate children. For Murdock the sexual privileges often extended to a group of males and females must be accompanied by economic responsibilities and, therefore, such examples as the wife exchange of the Chuckchee Eskimo are not cases of group marriage although they might appear to be so to the untrained observer. Further, Murdock notes that only "a handful" of such marriages appeared in his cross-cultural studies, and these appeared to be "exceptional individual" cases. Even among the Kaingang only 8 percent of recorded marriages were group marriages. Murdock concludes that "Group marriage, though figuring prominently in the early literature of anthropology, appears not to exist as a cultural norm."[34]

A principal reason for the variety in sexual unions to be found among the Kaingang, as we have seen, is that they have no system of clans, moieties, or lineages that would impose social obligations. Henry writes:

> A general lack of formal rules for marriage permitted the easy building up of large menages by gradual additions of men and women. A household might begin with either a monogamous or polygynous marriage; as time passed another man might be added to the household and become the cohusband; perhaps another wife was added and then another man. Through the years the family would expand and contract or simply change as the wives or husbands died or were killed off in feuds. . . .[35]

Henry does not employ the term "group marriage" but prefers "joint marriage" to describe the Kaingang case. Joint marriage, in his usage, is a

33. Queen and Habenstein *op. cit.*, pp. 21–25.
34. Murdock *op. cit.*, p. 24. See also Henry *op. cit.*, p. 45.
35. Henry *op. cit.*, p. 37.

situation in which several men live together with several women in mutual cohabitation under the headship of one male. Apparently such a relationship ought not to be called group marriage since a marriage ceremony is not performed for every union (although the status of children is not in doubt).

PATTERNS OF SEPARATENESS AND TOGETHERNESS

The American ideal marriage involves a great deal of sharing between spouses, a common residence, common property, mutual friends, and an exchange of ideas, opinions, and sentiments with a minimum of secrets. Ordinarily we believe in shared recreation—parties, vacations, and hobbies—as furthering the intimacy between spouses, and we encourage the development of as many common interests as possible. In short, we place a great deal of emphasis on togetherness—much more than is characteristic of the societies in the World Ethnographic Sample.

With about a fourth of the world's societies characterized by mother-child households, we can see at once a large population wherein intimacy between spouses is rendered very difficult indeed. They constitute, perhaps, the opposite of the "ideal" discussed above. In Moslem societies, where a man is permitted to have more than one wife, we find another departure from our ideal of togetherness. Although Moslem law prescribes that a man must treat all of his wives equally, he usually has a favorite to whom he is closer and with whom he shares more feeling. In any polygynous union, in which a man has a separate residence or alternates between residences of his several spouses or simply calls for a wife from his harem to sleep with him, a man will not be as close to all (or even to one) of his wives as will be a man in a monogamous marriage.

Perhaps the greatest degree of separation between husband and wife that we have found occurs among the Nayar and similar peoples of military bent where the husband is away at war a great deal of the time.

It should not be supposed, however, that monogamy in and of itself guarantees togetherness; nor does the fact of cohabitation guarantee intimacy. As Bott has pointed out, marriage among the working class of England, while monogamous, is characterized by a great deal of separateness.[36] In such monogamous families husbands and wives do not do a great deal together and do not expect to do so.

In some societies husbands and wives do not sleep together a great part of their married life because of the interference of numerous taboos; in other societies they do not eat together and do not share recreation. Opler tells us that among the Chiricahau Apache, husband and wife go to the same movie but will not sit together, preferring the company of their same-sexed friends. In rural Japan a husband and wife are rarely seen together in public; they walk down separate streets although going to the same destination, and they sit opposite each other in sexually segregated groups when visiting friends.

36. Elizabeth Bott, *Family and Social Network: Roles, Norms and External Relationships in Ordinary Urban Families* (London: Tavistock Publications, 1957).

Joint ownership of property seems to be a rarity. More commonly wives own certain property, and husbands own other. Among the Trobrianders, the husband's matrilineage owns the house and the village in which his family lives, but his children inherit from his wife's lineage. The Navaho wife owns her house and can terminate her marriage simply by placing her husband's saddle outside the door. Among the Hottentots, husband and wife each own their own cows.

The ban on public expression of intimacy is widespread. Malinowski writes of the Trobrianders:

> *There is an interesting and, indeed, startling contrast between the free and easy manner which normally obtains between husband and wife, and their rigid propriety in matters of sex, their restraint of any gesture which might suggest the tender relation between them. When they walk they never take hands or put their arms about each other in the way, called kaypapa, which is permitted to lovers and to friends of the same sex. Walking with a married couple one day, I suggested to the man that he might support his wife, who had a sore foot and was limping badly. Both smiled and looked on the ground in great embarrassment, evidently abashed by my improper suggestion. Ordinarily a married couple walk one behind the other in single file. On public and festival occasions they usually separate . . . you will never surprise an exchange of tender looks, loving smiles, or amorous banter between a husband and wife in the Trobriands.*[37]

Thus a great many societies demand a certain amount of public avoidance between husband and wife.[38] Indeed, while we permit terms of endearment to be exchanged between spouses, many societies do not permit husband and wife to call each other by name.

In communities such as Tepotzlan, a Mexican peasant village of the central highlands, the husband-wife relationship has a great deal of hostility built into both its public and its private expressions. Much of the conflict derives from the tradition of *machismo* wherein a man is *expected* to violate the norms of monogamous marriage and a woman is not. So also in the effort to retain the tradition of patriarchal dominance the husband "avoids intimacy with the members of his family with the purpose of gaining respect from them. . . . In many homes the husband's sense of security is a function of the extent to which he can control his wife and children or make them fear him . . . Tepotzlan women readily express hostility toward men and often characterize all men as 'bad.' "[39] Yet, despite this need to control, the husband characteristically turns all of his money over to his wife and expects her to provide him with the standard of living he desires whether or not his income is adequate.

37. Malinowski, *The Sexual Life of Savages* (New York: Harcourt, Brace and World, 1929), p. 111–12.
38. Stephens *op. cit.*, p. 51.
39. Oscar Lewis, *Tepotzlan: Village in Mexico* (New York: Holt, Rinehart & Winston, 1960), p. 56.

Summary

Generally throughout the world the regulation of sexual behavior does not reflect a general taboo against sex *per se*, but is rather an attempt to protect various social institutions such as marriage and the family. Traditionally our society has been among the very few that have such a general taboo against sex. The overcoming of this taboo is a major part of what we mean when we talk about the sexual revolution.

However, if we simply look at the formal regulations, we will not have an accurate understanding of how the overall way of life of a people controls the expression of sexuality. Not only do all people *not* live precisely as their social norms prescribe that they should live, but the actual control of sexual behavior may be more determined by customs and rituals than by any norm directed toward sexual behavior *per se*. Therefore, statistics on the number of societies permitting premarital or extra-marital coitus are at best only rough guides to the actual sexual behavior of a people. Because the selection of a mate and the consequent marriage have far-reaching consequences for most pre-industrial societies, the regulation of mate selection is formally prescribed and heavily sanctioned. Many societies enforce rules of exogamy or endogamy—the prohibition or prescription of marriage within a particular group—thereby making the range for the selection of mates much more narrow than that for the selection of legitimate sexual partners.

Marriage in pre-industrial societies is frequently accompanied by elaborate marriage finance. The exchange of gifts is one mechanism by which kin are bound together, increasing the stability of the social structure. To some extent the involvement of kin is correlated with the greater degree of expected social distance between the spouses. While we expect a great deal of sharing to take place in our middle-class conception of "togetherness," many societies tolerate a great deal of separateness in a marriage relationship. In a sizable minority of the world's societies, husband and wife do not live together. Frequently they are not seen in public together and are not expected to own mutual property.

The extension of the conjugal bond in multiple marriage becomes, finally, a means by which the structure of the family is enlarged and the network of kin reinforced. Polygynous households are common and are often the most preferred form of marriage. Monogamy remains the most common form of marriage and is found associated with all sorts of economies. Polyandry, which is rare, is associated with economic deprivation, and occurs in societies with the greatest variety of acceptable marriage forms.

The extent to which mate and residence choice are the prerogatives of individuals rather than kin groups is a good indicator of the extent to which a society is likely to be a rapidly changing one. Slow change is associated with kin regulation.

"That man wants to claim my pedigree. He says he's one of my descendants."

"Now, Mr. Darwin, how could you insult him so?"

5. Time and Circumstance: Theories of Family Change

. . . I do not believe for a moment that the system now emerging can be shown to yield greater "happiness" or "adjustment." . . . I do not believe we shall ever know how to balance the ecstasy and agony of the family systems now coming into being against that of older systems. . . . I see the world revolution in family patterns as part of a still more important revolution that is sweeping the world in our time, the aspiration on the part of billions of people to have the right for the first time to choose for themselves —an aspiration that has toppled governments both old and new, and created new societies and social movements.

For me, then, the major and sufficing justification for the newly emerging family patterns is that they offer people at least the potentialities of greater fulfilment, even if most do not seek it or achieve it.

WILLIAM J. GOODE

An examination of family forms and life styles in different cultures suggests something of the range of viable alternatives in family change, but it does not tell us much about *how* families have changed within a culture. I have assumed, in effect, a static view of the family by taking cross-cultural "snap shots" of different families without regard for the element of time. I turn now to a discussion of the time dimension in family change.

Family patterns are changing in the context of a world revolution characterized by urbanization and industrialization. Goode documents the trend away from an extended family system toward the conjugal system characteristic of the West, and highlights the importance of an ideology of the conjugal family in bringing about this change. But the rate of change, the processes by which it is occurring, and its likely consequences are only poorly understood. In large measure this is so because the data on family change are quite limited, cover a comparatively insignificant span of time, and are drawn largely from a period of rapid social change.

However inadequate, the information that social science can bring to bear upon family change during the Industrial Revolution is great indeed compared to the information it can muster on family change in earlier periods. Our ignorance can be dramatized by contrasting the amount of knowledge we have with the time span of human history.

The Historical Record

If we hold to the conservative figure of one million years as the length of time since the appearance of *Homo sapiens*, then an equally conservative estimate for the beginning of language is about fifty thousand years ago. Thus man has used language as a means of communication only during 5 percent of his history. Over 98 percent of that history passed before the agricultural revolution; human history was not recorded in writing until the last 0.6 percent; and the Phoenician alphabet was invented during the last 0.4 percent of human history. Some 0.2 percent of human history has passed since the birth of Christ, 0.03 percent since the death of Galileo, 0.02 percent since the beginning of the Industrial Revolution, and 0.01 percent since the publication of Darwin's *Origin of the Species*.

Most of human history is thus beyond any means of recall. We know virtually nothing about 98 percent of that history and very little indeed about the last 2 percent. On the other hand, science and technology have combined to produce fantastic rates of change (in population growth, energy consumption, urbanization, the accumulation of human knowledge, etc.) within the last 0.03 percent of that history. Change in many dimensions of our way of life can be described by curves such as that shown in Figure 5–1.

A social institution such as the family is poorly reflected in the archeological record. It is not part of the material culture and, therefore, leaves no artifact. Some aspects of family life can be inferred from artifacts, but the inferences are shaky. The historic record gives us a bit more insight, but, even so, most aspects of ancient family patterns are unrecorded. They simply were not interesting enough at the time.

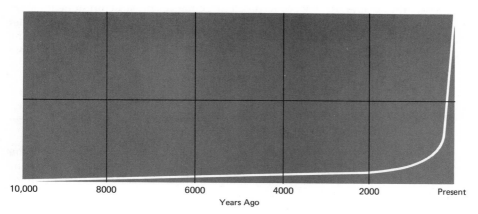

FIGURE 5–1
*Growth over the last one percent of human history. This curve can be
roughly applied to growth in several areas, for example, population,
inventions, or energy consumption.*

While the early theorists of the nineteenth century advanced grand
schemes to account for an evolution of family structures, most modern studies have limited their scope to the Industrial Revolution. Even during this
period data are not plentiful and interpretations are risky. Goode's excellent
study was of an even shorter time span (the last 0.005 percent of human history) and he concludes:

> *The difficulties of obtaining adequate data on world changes in family
> patterns over the past half-century are many and often insurmountable.
> As is so often true in social research, the time series that we can locate
> (for example the number of marriages per thousand population), are of
> only modest relevance for important social relationships. Most often, pre-
> cise data on significant relationships are missing and we have to substi-
> tute reports of travelers and explorers, foreigners who lived a long time
> in the country, or educated citizens who are amateur sociologists.*[1]

Ironically social scientists of the nineteenth century tended to have a well-
developed historic sense and were often trained to handle historic data, but
their data were grossly inadequate. Some modern sociologists, on the other
hand, who lack training in the use of historic data write as though the world
came into existence with the advent of modern science. In sociology this is in

1. William J. Goode, *World Revolution and Family Patterns* (New York: Free Press,
1963), p. 366.

elers, colonial administrators, missionaries, and others not trained to be part attributable to the widespread acceptance of structure-functionalism which concentrates on how families and other social systems work, rather than on how they began. Concomitantly, social order, for many, has become equated with social statics, and social dynamics has suffered extreme neglect.

Early Theories of Family Change

The nineteenth century saw an awakening of interest in the origin of the family as acceptance of the Biblical explanation declined and as Europeans became more acquainted with pre-industrial family patterns as a result of their explorations and colonial expansion. Lyell's *Principles of Geology* (1830) argued the *uniformitarian position* successfully for the first time: The earth is very old—much older than Bishop Usher's estimate of 4,004 B.C.—and over most of its life it has been subjected to much the same forces as act upon it in the present. Sea shells are to be found in the Alps, not because of the flood, but because they were deposited there when the Alps were being formed in sedimentary basins under the ocean eons ago. Darwin's *Origin of the Species* (1857) placed *Homo sapiens* in the evolutionary stream: Man was no longer a special act of creation. The story of Adam and Eve could no longer reasonably account for the origin of the family.

Family theorists sought to explain the development of the modern family by means of a single evolutionary scheme, although they differed as to the dynamics of the process and the stages through which the family was thought to have passed. Scholars such as John Jacob Bachofen and Lewis Henry Morgan argued for an initial stage of promiscuity.[2] Others such as Edward Westermarck and Herbert Spencer favored monogamy as the earliest stage of the family.[3] There was a strong tendency to place a stage of matriarchy before the stage of patriarchy. As late as 1927, Robert Briffault argued against monogamy as the earliest stage and contended that the proper sequence of development was group marriage, matriarchy, patriarchy, and monogamy.[4] Whatever the developmental sequence, the family was thought of as evolving through successive stages culminating in the contemporary European conjugal family—which, of course, was taken as the pinnacle of progress.

CRITIQUE

The major problem facing all of the early theorists was a lack of reliable ethnographic data. Reports about primitive people written by world trav-

2. J. J. Bachofen, *Das Mutterrecht* (Stuttgart: Krais & Hoffman, 1861). Lewis Henry Morgan, *Ancient Society* (New York: Holt, 1877).
3. Edward A. Westermarck, *The History of Human Marriage*, 5th ed. (New York: Macmillan, 1922). Herbert Spencer, *The Principles of Sociology* (New York: Appleton, 1897).
4. Robert Briffault, *The Mothers* (New York: Macmillan, 1927).

sensitive to social science techniques proved often contradictory, frequently erroneous, and all too often incomplete even in rather basic information about a particular society. It is not surprising that under such circumstances various interpretations of the same data could find a following and the ideological persuasion of the researcher could be less constrained by the data. Modern ethnographic techniques have not eliminated the problem of researcher perspective nor completely reduced the debate over interpretation. Nevertheless, it now seems quite clear that there are very few reliable data to support the assumption that family forms have passed through a particular sequence of stages. This is a much too simplistic interpretation of social evolution. The functionalists have demonstrated that many of the so-called "vestiges" of earlier stages can be shown to be functional in the current society. The evolutionary process itself is not thought of any longer as unilinear but rather as a many branched "tree."

A second major criticism arises from the more recent intensive study of kinship systems which has shown that for most folk cultures descent is primarily associated with group membership, not with recognition of genealogical ties. Therefore, certain Australian tribes who are completely unaware of biological fatherhood still emphasize patrilineal descent. Ignorance of paternity does not, in this light, seem to suggest an early stage of matriliny.

Third, the common earlier assertion that persons who are brought up together tend to develop exogamous patterns of marriage and the contention that brother-sister marriage is everywhere looked upon as incestuous are simply not supported in fact. The Angmagsalik Eskimo, for example, permit marriage between children who have been reared together. Further, the common practice of the levirate and sororate often involves members of the same extended family who are often classificatory "brothers and sisters."[5]

Finally, there is little to suggest that matrilineal societies are earlier and somehow simpler than patrilineal societies as was formerly believed:

> Among the primitive societies are the patrilineal Witoto of Amazonia, the matrilineal Kutchin of northern Canada, and the bilateral Andamanese pygmies. On the other hand, in the civilized areas of the world, are the patrilineal Chinese, the matrilineal Brahman Nayars of India, and the bilateral Syrian Christians. It is true, of course, that matrilineal cultures in general are more primitive than patrilineal ones. But it is also true that the difference is not considerable, that the similarities are very great, and that the difference may indicate nothing more than the fact that the patrilineal and bilateral Europeans and Asians have recently influenced the rest of the world extensively.[6]

A combination of family patterns is the rule rather than the exception in any given society. A great deal of debate often revolves around the criteria uti-

---

5. The levirate is the practice of requiring or permitting a man to marry the widow of his brother or another close relative; sororate requires or permits a man to marry his wife's sister after his wife's death.

6. Margaret Mead, "Family: Primitive" in R. A. Seligman (ed.), *Encyclopedia of the Social Sciences*, Vol. 6 (New York: Macmillan, 1931), pp. 66–67.

lized by a given researcher to classify a particular society as "predominantly polygamous" or "predominantly monogamous." While patterns of descent are less often mixed, many societies appear to utilize aspects of various patterns rather than adhere to a simple definition of matrilineal or patrilineal.

However, even late into this century a great deal of effort went into the study of the relationship between family structure and particular pre-industrial economies. Linton summarizes his evaluation of this effort:

> The great variety of familiar institutions found among existing "primitives" serve to show the range of possibilites but provide few clues as to what may have been developmental sequences. At most, we can say that certain forms of family are quite unsuited to particular environmental-cultural configurations. For example, no group which lives by hunting and food gathering could seclude its women in harem fashion. Nor would a group in which there was a persistent surplus of women over men be likely to practice polyandry. Beyond such simple generalizations it is impossible to go.[7]

If there is no single line of development, what can we say about family change in pre-industrial societies on the basis of the ethnographic record?

The Ethnographic Record

By examination of the ethnographic record of contemporary pre-industrial societies, it is possible to make some inference about the factors that have affected family development even though these factors have combined with others in such a fashion that many lines of development are probable.[8]

Undoubtedly the dependency of the human infant upon its mother is a significant factor affecting family form and function. Anthropologists such as Linton and Murdock favor the primacy of the conjugal or nuclear family because, they contend, it is essentially "a biological unit differing little . . . from similar units to be observed in a great variety of mammalian species." The consanguine family (or the extended family based upon blood lines), on the other hand is a "social artifact."[9] While blood relationships are as old as mating and reproduction, their utilization as a means of social organization requires great sophistication. This "explanation" is buttressed with assumptions about the conjugal family as the optimal unit for socializing young children (the social unit wherein each child can have the maximum possibility for a deep relationship with a single adult of each sex).

However such explanations overlook the fact that at best they are arguing for the importance of the mother-child relationship and the fact that fatherhood is a sociological invention, as is the recognition of blood lines. It does not seem self-evident that social organization based on blood lines is in-

---

7. Ralph Linton, "The Natural History of the Family," in Ruth Nanda Anshen (ed.), *The Family: Its Function and Destiny* (New York: Harper and Row, 1969), pp. 30–31.
   8. *Ibid.*, p. 33.
   9. *Ibid.*, p. 34.

trinsically more complicated than the formation of a partnership of a man and a woman based on economic cooperation and the division of labor. The contract is social in either case, as is particularly clear in those societies where blood relationship is assumed but not documented in structures such as clans and moieties. The natural history of mammals, furthermore, records more instances of multiple mates than of single. If we take Linton more seriously than he takes himself, it would seem that from the beginning both conjugal and consanguine families functioned. Certainly this is so in all societies known to us at present.

Indeed it is because these two types of family are found everywhere and are everywhere capable of fulfilling many of the familial functions that great care must be taken in any given society to delineate the responsibilities of each group. Sexual satisfaction and reproduction cannot be *normative* functions of the consanguine family in most societies, although as we have seen some societies do permit sexual intercourse between distant kin. Situations in which all familial functions (except those connected with reproduction) are vested in the consanguine group are characteristic of non-European pre-industrial societies. At the other pole, industrial Western societies tend to place most of these functions (initially, at least) in the conjugal family.

If the consanguine or extended family is dominant, the society is characterized by formal control over affective personal behavior, arranged marriages, status placement by ascription, and relatively slow change. The emphasis in such societies is upon repeating the patterns of the past rather than reaching into the future. Arranged marriages are stabilized by elaborate marriage finance in which the consanguine families (united in the conjugal pair) are bound together in reciprocal economic obligations. They have, thus, a vested interest in the couple's remaining together. Linton points out, however, that these economic constraints are less severe than the supernatural sanctions commonly invoked in the case of the violation of parent-child obligations.

Plural marriage is the preferred form of marriage in the majority of the world's societies, even though it is not the most common. Polyandry seems to result when economic conditions are so severe that a family unit needs more than one male in order to survive, as was the case among the Kaingang. Polygyny is not as clearly related to economic abundance, although that abundance seems to be a common factor. The Tiwi are one of many exceptions. They are able to survive in a harsh environment with a hunting and gathering economy because there are many wives to gather the vegetable food and small game. Nevertheless, some suggest that the human species may have a predisposition toward polygyny based upon the more constant sexual interest of males and their greater physical power. Moreover, it is a frequent form of mating among primates.[10] In those societies where there is a slight preponderance of females due to the more hazardous occupations of males

10. *Ibid.*, p. 40. The more constant sexual interest of the male, however, should not be taken as a given. There are cultural reversals of roles, as demonstrated in Margaret Mead's *Sex and Temperament*, and evidence of a much stronger physiological response among females in such studies as William Masters and Virginia Johnson's *Human Sexual Response*.

and the greater infant mortality of male babies, such a predisposition would be reinforced. It is socially destructive to have a large number of unmarried adults in any society. It is desirable (particularly in pre-industrial societies) that all women have the opportunity to mate and produce offspring and that these children have an adult male to teach them the proper male skills and attitudes. Polygynous marriages are, therefore, common and often exist without jealousy in many of the world's societies.

There have been numerous attempts to legalize polygyny in the United States after the two world wars. In Linton's view the problem in our society arises not so much out of a shortage of males (who are killed in the wars in greater numbers), but rather out of the unwillingness of women to accept second or third rate husbands.[11] And he believes that if polygyny does achieve acceptance in our society it will be the result of women's being unwilling to return to the *Hausfrau* role. A polygynous marriage could allow a woman to combine her career with a home and children *provided* there was another wife who was oriented to housewifery and child care. Such combinations may be difficult to find, and they may never gain acceptance, but they could provide a viable family pattern for some.

In summary, the following generalizations seem more probable than others: (1) The family based upon the husband-wife relationship (the conjugal family) is very ancient and usually involves the assumption of continuity in the mated relationship. This may occur with or without the assumption of exclusive sexual rights. (2) The conjugal family is variously related to the consanguine (extended) family. But, in general, there appears to be an increasing disengagement with increasing societal complexity. (3) In societies where the extended family dominates, marriage is typically arranged and stabilized by economic sanctions levied against its disruption. (4) Romantic love probably arose as a justification for premarital affairs in societies with arranged marriages. (5) Plural marriage is widespread. It is the *preferred* form of marriage in most of the world's societies, but it is not thereby the most common form, usually because of economic restraints. (6) Polyandry is linked rather closely to economic conditions. Under sufficient economic stress, it may develop as an alternate form of marriage in societies which have an approximately equal number of each sex. (7) Polygyny is much more common and the reason for its occurrence seems more complex. Factors contributing to its occurrence are: the more constant sexual interest of the male, the desirability in primitive societies of giving all women the opportunity to procreate, the desirability that children be raised in family or kin groups rather than in institutions, the undesirability of unmated adults as a threat to marital relations, the symbolic value of women as evidence of wealth, the desire of men to increase their leisure time, the slight but persistent surplus of females over males in most societies, and economic technological factors enabling large households to exist.

Obviously such generalizations cover but a limited range of family life and tell us nothing about the quality of family life. They are little more than suggestive of the processes by which families change, but they do alert us to

11. *Ibid.*, p. 44.

the fact that radical change in structure and function is possible given the right conditions.

Because pre-industrial societies are generally thought of as slow changing and because social scientists tend to prefer cultural or social determinism over voluntarism in their conceptual frameworks, the contributions of a single individual or a few persons are often overlooked. Margaret Mead, however, conceives of the unit of micro-evolution as the cluster of creative individuals drawn together around a common set of problems which they approach in an experimental fashion and which produce what Hall calls technical change. The concept is basic to intentional communities such as Walden II and has found expression in such divergent settings as the Oneida Community and the Israeli Kibbutz. The effectiveness of such a cluster is nowhere better demonstrated, however, than by the case of Paliau and his Lieutenants in the Admiralty Islands.

THE PALIAU MOVEMENT

In 1946 the villages of the Manus-speaking peoples of the Admiralty Islands, despite the occurrence of World War II, were living largely in what could be called a new Stone Age culture.[12] The war had exposed them to millions of American soldiers and to the tremendous amount of equipment necessary to move such a large number of men. Such an exposure created the taste for modernization and the taste for democracy.

However, after the war, the natives went back to their old way of life. Some Manus-speaking people lived in houses built out over the sea because they had no land; others lived inland on unsuitable village sites; and a few lucky ones inhabited the shoreline villages and lived comparatively well. Only the occasional "cargo cult" that assembled a number of frustrated worshippers on the beaches to await the return of the cargo ships and their many material blessings testified to the effect of the recently departed Americans.

> All this changed rather rapidly when in 1945 Paliau [see Figure 5–2], a native of the little island of Baluan, sent a letter to the 600 people of his island telling them to build a big meeting house. He was coming home and had plans. His plans were relatively simple in conception, but extremely difficult to carry out. Three major points were made: (1) The distinction between the lagoon dwellers (the Manus), the small island people (the Matankor), and the inland gardeners (the Usiai) must be eliminated. This involved a complete breakdown of economic, residential and social barriers among people who, although living close together, had been nurtured on mutual contempt. . . .
>
> (2) Change must not come about piecemeal. There must be a radical break with the past. Every item of the old culture would have to be overhauled and examined and, for the most part, rejected. Houses, clothing, manners, marriage forms, land use, trade, travel, funeral rites—everything would have to be changed, and every regression to an old

12. This material is based on the account of the Paliau Movement given in Margaret Mead, *Continuities in Cultural Evolution* (New Haven: Yale University Press, 1964).

FIGURE 5–2
*Paliau of Manus in 1954. From
Margaret Mead,* Continuities in
Cultural Evolution *(Yale
University Press, 1964).*

*form would have to be fought, since a lapse in one area would lead to
regression in other areas.*
*(3) The people of New Guinea must adopt at once long-term plan-
ning, systematic saving to accumulate capital, and a rigorous work ethic.*[13]

Out of the excitement generated by Paliau's plan, a cargo cult emerged
as the people sought immediate and simple relief from their present state. It
failed. Out of the frustration thus engendered, Paliau and his Lieutenants
were able to build a new culture within a period of about three years.

*He invited the Manus people of Mouk to move ashore onto his ancestral
lands on the island of Baluan. All the other Manus villages also moved
ashore onto small islands or combined with the gardening Usiai who
came down to the sea coast to join them.*
*A people who, under the old complex system of aid and ceremonial,
had been able to build only two or three houses in a year, now built
sixty houses in a little over two months. The new villages were designed
to express the new concepts. Every house had the same dimensions and
all had separate rooms for separate purposes. There was a central square
in which meetings were to be held. Skeleton versions of "docks" "cus-*

13. *Ibid.,* p. 209.

toms" "hostels" "hospitals" "schools" and "banks" were set up. The old practices were examined and new rules were made about the amount of expenditure that was appropriate for a wedding and a funeral. Individual economic responsibility was introduced, together with community-wide use of unused lands and community provision for widows and orphans and the sick. A common treasury was established and into this went money made during the war, to be drawn upon for the common good of the entire movement. As the break with the Mission left the population without clergy, Paliau took it upon himself to revise the Scriptures and to set up standards of clerical behavior. By 1949, he had transformed a Neolithic society into a very crude but systematic version of a mid-twentieth century society. [See Fig. 5–3.][14]

Paliau's reform was constantly challenged and constantly defended. He became personally angry when he discovered men dressed in laplaps, the traditional garb assigned to both sexes, because he understood that in order to wrestle equality from the West, males would have to be trousered. The re-

14. *Ibid.*, pp. 210–11.

FIGURE 5–3
The transformation of the people of Manus from a Stone Age culture to one with the rudiments of a modern civilization is microcosmically reflected in these photos of a Manus leader Pokanau in 1928 (left) and 1953 (right). From Margaret Mead, Continuities in Cultural Evolution *(Yale University Press, 1964).*

form abolished the old kin system under which it had been impossible for Paliau and other young men to save because any money they earned was distributed among their elders who squandered it. The new community took care of the common good by rationally conceived means and not traditional supports. In this the people of Manus, under Paliau's leadership, exhibited what Hall has chosen to call a "technical attitude toward change." Few people can subject the whole of their culture to such scrutiny for long. None can subject even a portion of it to such an examination continuously.

Thus, in less than three years, Paliau and his Lieutenants accomplished the transformation of a society based upon an extended kinship network to one based upon a conjugal family. In other societies such a transformation has taken decades, even centuries. In some it has not yet occurred, even though industrialization and urbanization have become common factors. The Manus-speaking peoples, on the other hand, are not yet industrialized and certainly not yet urbanized. They have but the "skeletons" of Western institutions in many areas and yet have been able to supplement the conjugal family functions by means of these secondary institutions in their communities.

Two Classic Theories of Family Change

Although the simplistic stages of the early theorists have largely been abandoned, there remains a strong tendency among family sociologists to think of family change as unilinear, if not unidirectional. Two classic theorists, Carle Zimmerman and William F. Ogburn, have contributed greatly to this tendency although from quite different perspectives. Zimmerman favors a *cyclical view* of family change, and Ogburn, a broad trend toward *progressive specialization*.

CARLE ZIMMERMAN

Carle Zimmerman champions a view of family change that takes in the long span of the history of Western civilization from about 1500 B.C. up to the present (the last 0.34 percent of human history). In this span he perceives broad cycles of change, a notion advanced in *Family and Civilization* written in 1947.[15] Unimpressed with anthropological data and drawing upon a rich historical sense, Zimmerman argued that it was unnecessary to rely upon data from primitive peoples outside the stream of Western history in order to account for the changes in the Western family. Indeed, such information was not only irrelevant, it was often quite misleading because family forms outside the Western tradition developed in response to quite different problems and presented solutions that were not really viable in Western families. Furthermore, they did not, in any sense, represent earlier stages of our development.

15. Carle C. Zimmerman, *Family and Civilization* (New York: Harper, 1947).

Within the experience of the West, monogamy was the normative marriage form, and the character of the family underwent successive and largely repetitive alterations as the family, the church, and the state vied for control over family members. There is, in Zimmerman's view, a close relationship between the character of the family and the character of the larger society surrounding it. Figure 5–4 illustrates Zimmerman's cyclical view.

There are three types of families in the West: the trustee, the domestic, and the atomistic. They are defined primarily by the amount of power vested in the family, the width of its field of action, and the amount of social control which it exercises. A basic polarity underlies these types. The *trustee family* represents an extreme expression of what Zimmerman called "familism" in which the rights and privileges of the individual are subordinate to the family group. At the other pole, the *atomistic family* represents the extreme expression of individualism. The *domestic family* is an expression of the creative balance of these two antagonistic tendencies.

In the trustee family the living members see themselves as trustees of the blood, property, and name of a family which has been passed on to them

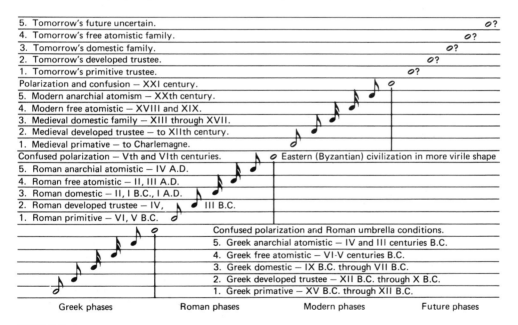

FIGURE 5–4

The cycles of cultural determinism since 1500 B.C. Zimmerman's cycles (Greek, Roman, Medieval, and Tomorrow's) end on a "whole note" of confused electicism wherein no one cultural pattern predominates. The trustee family emerges from this cultural chaos as a central institution. As the culture wanes, the centrality of the family diminishes. From Carle C. Zimmerman, The Family of Tomorrow: The Cultural Crisis and the Way Out *(Harper, 1949), p. 218.*

by ancestors who are still perceived as belonging to that family. The family itself, therefore, is immortal. The patriarch of such a trusteeship has pervasive powers—extending in the case of the Roman *protestas* to the power of life and death over his wife and children—because he is not thought of as exercising this power in his own behalf, but rather in the interests of the immortal family. This power is not absolute, therefore, but delegated for the specific purpose of carrying out his family responsibilities.

When the trustee family is dominant, the state is organized primarily on the basis of kinship structure which focuses most immediately in the *gentes* (usually a patrilineal clan which traces its descent from an original ancestor). The gentes combine to make up the state. The power of the family is thus nearly complete. In this situation, divorce does not exist as such, but the husband does retain the right to repudiate a wife who fails to support him in the integration of the family group.

Under the authority of the trustee family, a civilization moves toward greatness. By means of the primitive code of justice of the trustee family, order is created out of chaos and wealth accumulates under the edict of a rigorous work ethic. However, the unchecked authority of the family soon produces abuse of that authority. Feuding breaks out between families, and the power of the church and state is increased in order to restore order. The domestic family emerges as the state and church come to share power with the family over its members.

The domestic family's balanced authority permits a civilization to flourish. The state does not replace the family but restricts its right to punish its members and creates the concept of individual rights which must be maintained against family authority. Conceptions of divorce emerge, but actual divorce is rare. Separation becomes common.

Having set in motion the forces of individualism against the authority of the family, the power of the state waxes and the power of the family wanes. In the final stage of the disintegration of familism, the atomistic family reigns. In this stage the rights of the individual are supreme. If self-sacrificing devotion to group goals was characteristic of the trustee family, the pursuit of individual desires characterizes the atomistic family. Marriage becomes merely a civil contract and is frequently broken by divorce.

The sacredness once attached to the immortal trustee family now resides with each individual, and such individualism results in the blurring of the distinction between legitimate and illegitimate children. Whereas the trustee family might destroy such children, the state intervenes in the affairs of the atomistic family to grant such children equal rights. Other evidence of the effects of the atomistic family is to be found in rampant feminist movements, strong tendencies toward childlessness, and youth problems. As the family loses its power, it can no longer adequately carry out its task of socializing the young, and society begins to disintegrate.

It is not clear what mechanism brings about the re-emergence of the trustee family. It emerges, perhaps in part, out of a desire to restore order to a society degraded by the atomistic family. At least it has emerged in such situations in the past.

Critique: Clearly, Zimmerman is not afraid of evaluation. His atomistic family is unabashedly portrayed as pathological, despite the fact that some of the patterns he describes as pathological are, from other points of view, quite beneficial. The feminist movement is a case in point. Had Zimmerman examined the family structures of pre-literate peoples, he would have been less inclined to view any departure from the domestic family as deviant. His ethnocentrism is quite pronounced and is especially damaging because of his inability to perceive that divergent solutions to common family problems might be equally functional and desirable.

His global scale, on the other hand, makes any refutation difficult. Lacking the conceptual skills of a Max Weber, Zimmerman nevertheless ranges freely over Western history in such a fashion as to mystify all but the most erudite and historically inclined critic. It is thus easier to denounce him out of court than to evaluate his data. This seems, in fact, to be the case. There is a tendency for students of the family to be either pro- or anti-familistic as a result of his efforts.

WILLIAM F. OGBURN

William F. Ogburn was criticized by Zimmerman as belonging to the passive school of family theorists because he did not view the family as an agent of change. Ogburn confines his investigation of family change to the American family from colonial times to the present.[16] He pays great attention to the effects of the Industrial Revolution on family structure and function. As with Zimmerman, there is a tendency on Ogburn's part to view the modern American family as disorganized or, in the least evaluative perspective, as having lost many of its former functions—a point expanded by Talcott Parsons.

Ogburn's major contribution to the theory of societal change is his observation that change in the material culture tends to be cumulative and directional, because the criteria for improving tangible items—such as the internal combustion engine—are widely agreed upon (weight, cost, horsepower, durability etc.). Change in the nonmaterial culture, on the other hand, tends not to be characterized by such regularity because few will agree upon what constitutes valid criteria for making life better, happier, or more beautiful. In general, therefore, change in the nonmaterial culture lags behind change in the material culture. For example, the introduction of the automobile disrupted parental control over the recreational, dating, and mating patterns of their children. In Ogburn's view, the family itself is ill-adapted to modern technological societies. This is evident because of its loss of certain functions which has been offset only partially by an increased significance attached to the remaining more interpersonal functions.

In colonial times, the family functioned in several spheres: economic, protective, religious, recreational, educational, status conferring, and reproductive. With increasing industrialization, production was taken out of the

---

16. See William F. Ogburn, *Social Change* (New York: Viking, 1950) for a discussion of culture lag. His theory of family change is advanced in William F. Ogburn and Meyer F. Nimkoff, *Technology and the Changing Family* (Boston: Houghton Mifflin, 1955).

home, and the economic function of the family declined. Whereas, formerly, a man sought in marriage a business partner as well as a wife and all members of the family contributed to the family's productivity, the advent of the factory system transferred these functions to the company where they were carried out through largely impersonal processes. With this transfer, the woman's economic contribution declined and her status diminished. The size of the family dwelling often decreased, with children coming to be considered liabilities rather than assets.

Traditionally, the family was the primary source of protection for an individual. It provided basic medical care, economic security, and protection. These functions have been transferred to the state largely through the operation of a number of specialists such as police, firemen, welfare workers, physicians, and insurance salesmen.

Whereas the family was once the center of a personal religion, expressed in family devotions and grace at meals, and was the primary source of ethical standards, it now does not usually function in these areas. The church has assumed most of them, even though marriage increasingly has become a secular matter, and divorce has become increasingly common.

It is equally apparent that the education of children has become more formal and has passed into the hands of professionals. While in colonial times it was assumed that parents could teach their children all that was necessary to survive and could also provide academic instruction, it is patently impossible to believe that parents today could adequately instruct their children in face of the complexities of our society.

Finally, people were once respected in their community because they were the children of a family with known status and respectability. Since industrialization, the status-conferring function of the middle-class family has declined, and individuals are evaluated on their individual performance. In a modern metropolis, "the neighborhood" is frequently a rather anonymous place in which to live. Families do not seek each other out; people develop acquaintances rather than life-long friends. A family's status tends to be evaluated in terms of the husband-father's occupation, and, in an interpersonal sense, the man leaves his status when he leaves his job.

Although Ogburn is not as gloomy in his prediction of family catastrophe as Zimmerman, he does point out that several indices of "disorganization" are increasing. Divorce has increased since 1800 in America at about the rate of 3 percent per thousand. Illicit sexual activity, desertion, and juvenile delinquency are also on the increase. Despite these warning signals and the loss of function, however, the family is meeting the interpersonal needs of its members more adequately as it becomes more specialized.

Critique: Although primarily concerned with the effects of industrialization, Ogburn's time span is extended to include the colonial family. Inasmuch as Ogburn's conceptualization of loss of function is based on a model of the colonial family that has been strongly idealized, a criticism of Ogburn must attempt to present evidence against what Goode has called "the classic family of American nostalgia." While historical data on the colonial family are incomplete and any reconstruction of a type or types is at best an interpretation, it can be demonstrated that there were significant departures from the model envisioned by Ogburn, Parsons, and others. To speak of a single colonial type is, of course, an oversimplification that may only appear to be useful.[17]

Women were scarce in colonial times, especially on the frontier. Women died earlier in the struggle for survival, and they generally represented a smaller portion of the newly arriving migratory streams from the old world. So scarce were they on the frontier that companies flourished in the endeavor to entice women to move westward and become mates of pioneering men.

Engagements were short, and marriage generally occurred early. It was not uncommon for girls of thirteen or fourteen to be married. The choice of mate was strongly influenced by their parents, and, as a result, miscegenation was very rare. Unmarried women of twenty-five were commonly referred to as "ancient maids," while the unmarried women of twenty were "stale" maids. It was difficult for men to escape the married state even if they wanted to remain single. Single men were then, as today, taxed more heavily than married men. In addition they were sometimes required to perform rather ridiculous tasks as long as they were single. For example, in Eastham, Massachusetts, bachelors were required to kill six blackbirds or three crows every year while they remained single. Finally, the marriage ceremony, contrary to popular conviction, was most frequently performed by the magistrate. Indeed, in some states, the clergy were forbidden to marry a couple.

Under such conditions the status of women was generally high. Frontier women worked alongside their men and performed tasks that were equally rewarding monetarily as those that their husbands performed. They also bore children without whom the frontier homestead could scarcely hope to survive, much less expand its territory and raise its standard of living.

Many couples starting out on their married careers left for the frontier and never saw their families again. The notion of the pervasiveness of the extended family in pre-industrial days must, therefore, be qualified and not simply assumed as universally true. In the South, however, many women were pampered under a form of chivalry that could arise only because the system of slavery permitted wealth and leisure to accumulate for the aristocracy and removed the lady of the house from the drudgery of housework.

Evidence of the nearly parallel status of men and women is to be found in laws that granted essentially equal economic rights to both sons and daughters and permitted the wife to divorce her husband. Even in colonial times a few women worked outside the home in respectable careers, but for the most part, women tended to function primarily as diligent and industrious housekeepers. In religious matters men dominated, and women were punished more severely for sexual transgressions than were men.

Families of ten to twelve were quite common in colonial days. Twenty to twenty-five person families were not rare enough to cause comment. But infant mortality was extremely high. This was so not simply because of the

17. The material on the early American family is largely from Panos D. Bardis, "Family Forms and Variations Historically Considered," in Harold T. Christensen (ed.), *Handbook of Marriage and the Family* (Chicago: Rand McNally, 1964), pp. 451–59.

harsh physical environment, but also because of such quaint customs as the practice of toughening children's feet by keeping them always wet, the insistence on baptism on the first Sunday after birth regardless of the temperature of the water, the small number of physicians and resulting lack of prenatal and postnatal care, the often charlatanic method of treating children's diseases, and the generally poor sanitation. Finally, the generally widespread use of children as laborers contributed to their early death.

A major factor determining the ideology behind child training seems to have been a conviction that the child was a miniature adult who was by nature a demon. Respect for adult authority was inculcated from an early age and enforced by corporal punishment and threats of supernatural damnation. Under such a set of convictions, children could much more easily be exploited. Poor children were often sold into apprenticeship; and some companies (such as Virginia's London Company) even used kidnapped child labor from Europe.

While it is quite apparent from the statistics that divorce was much less common in colonial times than at the present, it should be obvious that it does not follow necessarily that marriage was in any sense "better." The nature of the conjugal bond was more strongly shaped by economic considerations, and alternative mate choices (especially for men) were scarce. Living in homes that were to a surprising extent self-sufficient and often geographically isolated made it necessary to contain personal disagreements. While conjugal fidelity was exhorted and fornication denounced, illegitimacy was common nevertheless. Finally, it might be assumed that since the expectations for personal "happiness" were apparently not as great for couples entering marriage in colonial times as they are today, the actual performance in the conjugal relationship could have been appreciably lower without engendering frustrations leading to divorce.

Wilbert Moore on Social Change: A Final Critique

Wilbert Moore, while not focusing directly upon the institution of the family when discussing cultural or social change, points to some further needed qualifications.[18] Attempts to understand how families change that assume a single factor to be the cause of change are clearly inadequate. Firstly, climatic trends, physiographic features, and biological characteristics change very slowly when compared to the social dynamics for which causes are sought. It is impossible to explain a variable by a "constant." Second, natural selection in the human species is always "social" selection. Under such conditions purity of casual direction is spurious. Man alters his climate, topography, and human biology. He creates a culture which in turn shapes its creator. Finally, human heredity and the nonhuman environment are always conditional and relative to the technology, social organization, and cultural values of the various human societies.

18. A concise discussion of Moore's position is presented in his *Social Change* (Englewood Cliffs, N.J.: Prentice-Hall, 1963).

In general, resorting to external causes in order to account for cultural change can produce useful typologies, but these must always be modified by internal factors. Thus in regard to natural influences, technology serves to cushion, but not eliminate, the impact of shifts and crises; and in regard to contacts between cultures, the multiplication of agencies of communication serves to reduce the isolation and thus the autonomy of societies, promoting cultural interdependence and, over the long run, homogeneity. Accounting for cultural change in terms of external "natural" or social influences after the Industrial Revolution is, therefore, an increasingly fruitless task.

When focusing upon the internal factors that make cultural change a necessary ingredient in any society, Moore looks to factors intimately related to the family. There are certain flexibilities within the system. Socialization is never perfect. Just as the generations do not genetically reproduce themselves precisely, so also there is considerable diversity in the social characteristics of generations, particularly in societies undergoing rapid change. Even if the techniques and practices of socializing agents were identical and the process capable of reproducing exact copies though successive generations, societies even at the simpler level are unable to give a precise definition of the behavior deemed appropriate to social positions. It is virtually impossible to provide absolute role specifications even in a "tightly integrated" social system. Society, therefore, allows some range of behavior as appropriate to a specific social role such as mother, father, daughter, doctor, or engineer.

There are also certain strains that are inherent in the system. There are demographic imbalances, some of which are undergone by a society only once (such as the *demographic transition* wherein a population explosion is produced in developing countries as the result of the drastic lowering of the death rate through introduction of better health care, sanitation, etc., long before the birth rate is lowered under the pressures of urbanization and industrialization), and some of which seem to fluctuate with some regularity (such as the ratio of females to males).

Second, all societies must deal with universally recognized scarcity situations. Food in many societies is a scarce item indeed, even after the "green revolution." But there are other items not ordinarily thought of in terms of scarcity such as loyalty, time, and self-esteem. The fact that all of these are quite limited and that most systems attempt to maximize their utility creates conflict that generates change.

Finally, there is a dialectical conflict between normative alternatives in all societies. By setting up polar typologies as we did in the previous chapter on kinship (unilateral versus bilateral), we tend to create the impression that the poles at least are pure. However, all achieved status systems have some elements of ascriptions within them, and all ascribed systems have some elements of achievement. These alternative ways of confronting status conflict with one another dialectically and generate change.

In determining the form and direction of change, Moore points out that such considerations first of all are clearly a function of the time period one wishes to describe, the observational units utilized, and the detail desired. Not all change that occurs in social systems is directional in any significant sense, and much may even be inconsequential to the analyst. The model or curve finally arrived at in order to describe societal change will also reflect the reliability of data available and the extent to which change is conceptualized as involving interaction in process as the analyst considers how variables at various stages in the sequence interact with one another. Thus the second Industrial Revolution comes about only after the first Industrial Revolution has generated enough food to feed the urban masses that must man the factories in order to turn out the more sophisticated agricultural equipment that will eventually reduce the rural population of developed nations to a small fraction of their total population. Finally, some changes, such as the demographic transition, occur within a society apparently only once. These changes unique to a given system nonetheless re-occur in a similar fashion in other societies undergoing development.

It must be noted that in abandoning any single-factor determinism, we do not have to accept the notion that innovation occurs with equal probability over the development of a social system. Theoretically, innovation may occur at any point in the social structure. Social structure does not itself determine a specific function, nor dictate its transformations. It does, however, impose some limit upon the range of functional alternatives and the rate of their transformation.

> *The grain of truth in technological determinism, for example, appears to be the likelihood that innovation occurs with disproportionate frequency in the means of accomplishing seemingly standard ends, with frequently unanticipated repercussions. This sequence may give rise to the sequential alternation of innovation and accommodation. . . .*[19]

In addition to the pattern imposed by such technological innovations, the alterations that are likely to occur quite rapidly as the result of the acceptance of an ideology must also be kept in mind. Goode demonstrates that the ideology of the conjugal family preceded its widespread occurrence before the advent of industrialization in countries such a Japan.

Summary

The discussion of how the family changes over time is severely limited by the fact that we do not know very much about most (98 percent) of human history. Family patterns and their mode of development can be inferred from artifacts and historical records, but these cover only the simpler aspects of family life, are based on quite limited data, and tell us little about the *quality* of family life. Recent demographic studies of family development have better data, but their generalizations apply only to a very narrow slice of human experience. Eastern and underdeveloped societies generally have poor demographic records.

Nevertheless, some generalizations are possible: (1) The conjugal family

19. *Ibid.*

is very ancient and usually involves the assumption of continuity in the mated relationship. (2) The conjugal family is variously related to the extended family, but a common pattern is increasing disengagement with increasing social complexity. (3) In societies where the extended family dominates, marriages are typically arranged. (4) Romantic love probably first arose as a justification for pre-marital affairs in societies with arranged marriages. (5) Plural marriage is widespread and is preferred in most of the world's societies. (6) Individual effort and genius can effect widespread social changes even in pre-industrial societies, as the Paliau movement demonstrated.

The classical theories of family change tend to concentrate on a single "factor" (such as Ogburn's focus on technology) to account for change in family structure and life style. Zimmerman's dynamics are not as clear, but he stresses a rather simplistic cycle of development. In his view the family evolves from trustee to domestic to atomistic as the church and state vie with the family for control over individuals. Ogburn pictured a progressive loss of function as the family's sphere of influence was increasingly encroached upon by secondary institutions such as the factory, the church, and the state. This was partially compensated for by the increasing capacity of the family to meet the emotional and interpersonal needs of its members.

The picture of family life in pre-industrial America calls Ogburn's image of family development into question. There were, for example, many situations in which the conjugal family was quite functional (e.g., on the frontier). Further, theorists such as William Moore suggest that the family does not function precisely enough to duplicate the generations. Socialization is imperfect, societal roles are imprecisely defined, the reproductive capacity of fecund couples does not respond to system needs in such a way as to produce the same number of children with the identical sex ratio from one generation to another—a fact that is compounded by all the natural and social factors that selectively kill off children of one sex or the other.

What is lacking is a clear conception of the conditions under which these variables, separately or in conjunction with one another, tend to have a determinative effect. It seems clear that natural ecological factors must be more important in societies with a primitive technology and that the contribution of genius can be discernible only when there are those who can hear and appreciate. Such, at least, was the case with Paliau.

The fact that theories of family change have been produced in a period of rapid social and technological change undoubtedly limits their utility if one is taking a long-range view of family change. It is no wonder that theories are rapidly dated and of little use to those who seek to change the character of family life. To the student of the family, however, such efforts have heuristic value in the attempt to understand the character of the family and its relationship to its culture.

In this section I examine alternative family life styles in our own society. Not all of us live in the same kind of family; our family style varies by class and, to a lesser extent, by race. There are many ethnic, regional, and religious variations also, but these tend to be subsumed under the class patterns—especially in the middle and upper classes. A major exception must be made in the case of black families. Racism excludes most Blacks from equal access to the opportunities available to most Whites. Blacks in America, therefore, not only have a unique heritage, they also have different criteria for establishing class distinctions. Families who are middle class in the black community would frequently not be considered middle class by white standards. The study of how family life style varies by class and by race in Chapter 6 refutes the common assumption that there is a single type of American family.

In Chapters 7 and 8 I carry my concern for documenting variation further. The white middle-class family, like all family types, is affected by its immediate setting. I have chosen three classic community studies, all of which were conducted in the middle fifties, in order to suggest that the way in which family members relate to one another and to outsiders is a function of setting. These differences are not reflected in the more "rigorous" studies of family interaction, because even those studies that do take class variations into account assume that all middle-class white families are essentially the same. The similarities that can be found in white middle-class families are stressed in the more traditional functional analysis that concludes Chapter 7.

In Chapter 8 I look at lower-lower-class black family patterns. A great deal of recent research has demonstrated that here too our commonly held generalizations are more misleading than helpful. There are many kinds of lower-lower-class black families, and their methods of coping with poverty are quite different. Some give evidence of incipient mobility (wherein it seems likely that the children will overcome poverty even if their parents do not) and others seem destined to perpetuate the cycle of impoverishment. I have focused on the black underclass (the lowest level of the black stratification system according to Andrew Billingsley) simply because I have personally studied these families. I found considerable strength and a striking integrity in the life style of these black families that is frequently overlooked in the discussion of their "tangle of pathology."

The reader who has intimate knowledge of any of the life styles that I sketch in these chapters will recognize many over-simplifications and omissions. That is inevitable, as I have suggested in my Introduction. A particular family's style of life is affected by a number of things, many of which are not considered in the typical study of a family's life. Its methods of coping with its problems may or may not be socially acceptable—or may be acceptable in only a small subcultural setting. In this section I therefore suggest something of the variation in the style and structure of family life in America and illustrate some of the strengths and weaknesses of alternative strategies for coping with the problems of everyday life.

FAMILIES
IN
AMERICA

6. The Family and the American Class Structure

The human family constitutes the beginning and the essential element of society. Every beginning points to some end of the same nature, and every element to the perfection of the whole of which the element is a part. Thus it becomes evident that peace in society must depend upon peace in the family, and the order and harmony of rulers and ruled must directly be actualized from the order and harmony arising out of creative guidance and commensurate response in the family.

ST. AUGUSTINE

Even though St. Augustine was talking about a family which was in some ways different from our own, we feel much the same sentiment toward the American family. We speak of the "American family" so often that we tend to assume that there is a single pattern characteristic of all Americans, if not in terms of their actual behavior, then surely in terms of their conception of the ideal family. There are certain beliefs, attitudes, and behaviors that are commonly shared that tend to support this viewpoint. These common elements include professed belief in and actual practice of monogamy; legal marriage; legal dissolution of marriage prior to remarriage; limitation of sex relations to the spouse; legitimacy of children through birth in wedlock; joint residence of husband, wife, and dependent children; financial and personal responsibility of parents for the rearing of their children; and preparation of children for their adult roles.[1]

While these elements might form the basis for a concept of the ideal family, and while most of these values are reflected in the behavior of the majority, even some of these items are more often honored in the breach than in the observance. Further, a minority of Americans living in intentional communities may disagree with the importance of these convictions, and this disagreement is reflected in their behavior as well as in their ideas of what the "good family" should be.

Social class, religion, ethnic background, region, race, and residence (rural or urban) are all variables that serve to modify significantly the character of family life in America. Since these variables do not constitute mutually exclusive categories, it is sometimes difficult to determine with any precision which factor most strongly influences the pattern of family life in a given situation. However, some conceptual clarity can be achieved by considering the major matrix to be socioeconomic class. The other factors either vary with socioeconomic class (for example, most upper-upper-class persons in America are affiliated with a protestant church characteristically Episcopalian, Congregational, or Unitarian; most working-class persons are Catholic; and most lower-lower-class persons are Baptists or belong to small sects) or their importance diminishes as one moves up the stratification ladder, that is ethnic and racial variations in family patterns are more discernible in the lower classes. To be vertically mobile in America means, in part, that one must disassociate himself from ethnic and racial influences and conform to the more broadly accepted norms of the upper classes. Ordinarily this is accomplished over several generations and with a minimum of overt coersion. Thus, upper-middle-class Blacks and Whites, protestants and Catholics, live in families that are more alike than they are different no matter whether we look at New England, the South, or the Middle West. A notable exception to this generalization appears to be the Jewish family which retains much greater involvement in its extended family than others in the upper-middle class.

The generalizations about class-based family life styles that follow are only slight improvements upon the concept of a typical American family. These too fail to do justice to the variety that obtains in our society. Many

1. Ruth Shonle Cavan, "Subcultural Variations and Mobility" in *Handbook of Marriage and the Family*, Harold T. Christensen (ed.), (Chicago: Rand McNally, 1964), p. 535.

examples can be found to contradict each generalization. As long as they are not taken as absolutes, however, these generalizations can provide a basis for conceptualizing about this variety. They do suggest how family life styles and, to a lesser extent, family structure are dependent upon the relative power and privilege a family enjoys in our society. Not only does upper-class status mean greater income and command over resources, but it represents an "accumulation of advantages" that influence socialization patterns, kin relationships, and a host of other aspects of family life.

It is possible to describe in ideal-typical fashion six types of families characteristic of *white* America.[2] Nonwhite Americans tend more to conform to these models in the upper classes and diverge quite radically in the lower class. In part, this is true because they have a separate system of stratification. In addition to class-related problems, we must deal with problems of prejudice and discrimination in a WASP society and with the emergence of an increasingly strong sense of self-identity and historicity among Blacks. For this reason I discuss white and black stratification systems separately. (In Chapters 6 and 7, I describe two family types in detail: the upper-middle-class white, and the lower-lower-class black.)

The White Stratification System

THE FAMILY AND SOCIAL CLASS

The family in America achieves its status largely through the instrumental role of the head of the house. In most families the head is a man, and his income is largely responsible for providing the family with its style of life. In about one-third of lower-class families this head is a woman. Even when the man is head of the house and principal wage earner, his income is often supplemented by additional wage earners in his own family, most frequently his wife. About one-third of all married women work. In the lower and lower-middle class, they work most often because they have to, while in the upper-middle class, women may have careers that are intrinsically rewarding. In the upper classes, a woman's work is most often voluntary—for charity. In the middle class, children supplement the family income more than they do in the lower or upper classes.

An important assumption of functional analysis is that status in the larger society, particularly as measured by capacity to earn a living and provide for the family, is a prime factor in determining a person's status within the family. This, in turn, affects the extent to which parents are able to exercise control over their children. Thus in the upper class we would expect maximum control and in the lower class, minimal control. Such a broad generalization

2. Richard P. Coleman and Bernice Ncugarten, *Social Studies in the City* (San Francisco: Jossey-Bass, 1971), have demonstrated that the residents of Kansas City, Missouri, a city of over 800,000, commonly distinguished five major classes (though analysis could make finer distinctions) in 1955. They argue, however, that the nation is tending toward a more amorphous three-class system since their study was conducted.

needs further qualification, but it can serve as a rough guide for the present

Not only is the family placed in the stratification system primarily by virtue of the occupation and income of the husband-father, but it tends to socialize its children in the pattern of life more or less distinctive of its class. Thus, lower-class children have a more difficult time in school in part because they have acquired the patterns of behavior appropriate to their class. Teachers, being largely from the middle class, tend to reward children who behave like middle-class children should and tend to punish those who do not. Therefore, the parents who are most effective in teaching their children how to cope with the world of the ghetto streets are also bringing them up in a way that will handicap them in their ability to cope with the school system.

Occupation, which on the one hand assigns status to a family and strongly affects parental authority within the family, has also been shown to have a significant affect on personal values. Recently Melvin L. Kohn has suggested that the reason middle-class parents tend to value "self-direction" (an interest in how and why things happen, good sense and sound judgment, responsibility, self-reliance, the ability to face facts and do well under pressure . . .) and working-class parents value "conformity" (obedience and staying out of trouble) in their children is that these are precisely the dominant values inculcated by their respective occupations. Careers require many decisions that must be made in the absence of specific regulations—one applies general principles to specific situations without precise "fit." Jobs, on the other hand, require diligence in following orders. Hence, both middle-class and working-class parents attempt to teach their children attitudes and behaviors that they themselves have found useful.[3]

A model of the white stratification system is found in Fig. 6–1.

THE UPPER CLASSES

In America the upper class comprises an estimated 1 to 3 percent of the population. As such, it lies well within the top 5 percent of the population which receives each year about 19 percent of the total national income. The mean income of all consumer units in 1962 was, when measured in 1965 dollars, $7,640. The average income of the top 5 percent of the nation's families was 392 percent of this amount, or close to $30,000 in 1965 dollars. In 1968, persons earning over $25,000 were in the top 3 percent of the nation's income units. Interest, dividends from investment of inherited wealth, as well as a salary from the family head are chief sources of an upper-class family's income. Because total wealth is much more difficult to estimate, an accurate reflection of this class's total command over resources is difficult to ascertain, and income alone is only a partial indicator of class.

However, Table 6–1 suggests that inequality in America is very great indeed. The top 1 percent of the nation's consumer units own 33 percent of the

---

3. Melvin L. Kohn, *Class and Conformity* (Homewood, Ill.: Dorsey, 1969).

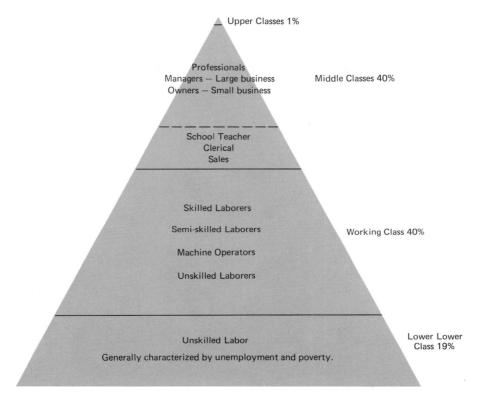

FIGURE 6–1
Social classes in the white community.

total wealth and 62 percent of the corporate stock. Furthermore, there is much greater personal autonomy in this class. In 1962 only three-eighths of the total wealth of the top 1 percent came from wages and salaries, another three-eighths from self-employment, and a final one-fourth from property income. While the dollar amounts determining both entry into the top 1 percent and the amount received from various sources varies particularly in inflationary times, the percentages remain fairly constant over time. We would infer, therefore, that the class's economic power or command over resources remains relatively constant. Specific families, however, may move into or fall out of any given class. By definition, the "established" families of the upper-upper class are not as likely to be downwardly mobile as families of other classes.

A distinction is made in the upper class between those families for whom inherited wealth is the major source of income and those who have recently

TABLE 6–1

Percent of Wealth Held or Income Received by Consumer Units When Ranked by Size of Income or Wealth

Consumer units ranked by	Lowest quintile	through 4th quintile	Highest quintile	Top 5%	Top 2%
A. Size of Wealth-Holding:					
1. Total Wealth	*	23%	77%	53%	33%
2. Corporate Stock	*	3	97	83	63
B. Size of Income					
1. Total Wealth	7%	36	57	38	25
2. Total Income	4	50	46	20	8
3. Wages and Salaries	2	53	45	15	4
4. Self-employment	1	36	63	42	26
5. Property Income	5	29	66	47	33
6. Dividends	2	15	83	65	49

Source: Edward Budd, *Poverty and Inequality*, 1962 pp. xxii.
*Less than ½ of 1 percent

arrived—the *nouveau riche*.[4] With great wealth having been a part of a family's experience over several generations, the perception of status by birthright becomes dominant. A child born into an *upper-upper-class* family does not have to worry about his social status; he is "somebody," and his socialization reinforces his self-confidence.

Characteristically, parental surrogates are responsible for the rearing of upper-upper-class children. Nurses and governesses play an important early role, followed by the teachers of successive private schools. His Ivy League education plus his extensive exposure to other cultures through travel makes the typical upper-upper-class person more sophisticated than his lower-class counterpart.

The exclusiveness of the upper-upper class is exemplified by the private clubs and the sequestered residential areas that provide visible symbols of status and separate the daily routine of this class from that of the lower classes. The proper use of money in the cultivation of culture rather than conspicuous consumption (which implies the need for status validation) characterizes the upper-upper-class person and sets him off noticeably from the *nouveau riche*.

A strong emphasis on a patriarchal extended family is discernible in

4. For a more detailed description of the characteristics of American family patterns by class variation see Ruth Shonle Cavan *The American Family*, 4th ed., (New York: Thomas Y. Crowell, 1969), Chap. 4–9. Also, for a concise description of the socioeconomic classes see "The American Class System" in *Social Stratification in the United States*, Jack L. Roach, Llewellyn Gross, and Orville Gursslin (eds.) (Englewood Cliffs, N.J.: Prentice-Hall, 1969), pp. 153–220; and Joseph A. Kahl, *The American Class Structure* (New York: Holt, Rinehart & Winston, 1962).

this class. Genealogies, records of ancestral achievements, journals and auto-biographies of ancestors, and heirlooms are important symbols of the family's traditional status. Although each nuclear family maintains its separate residence, the oldest living male member of the family ordinarily presides over its financial welfare. Loyalty to the extended family is expected, and a strong sense of solidarity usually obtains. Since the status of all depends upon the inherited wealth that is transferable in part through marital arrangements, the extended family keeps a close watch over its marriageable members. "In some large kinship groups, inter-marriage between relatives is not uncommon. The American upper-class families of the Lowells, the Lees of Virginia, and the Roosevelts all have had some kinship marriages."[5] The extended family's capacity to control mate selection is enhanced by the relative isolation of the upper-upper-class community and by the comparatively great rewards it can offer those who go along with its wishes. While in the East eight or nine generations of inherited wealth may be necessary to establish an upper-upper-class family, in the Middle West four or five generations are sufficient; in the far West, the family history may be much shorter.[6]

The family name is especially important, and therefore sons have special significance as the persons to carry on the lineage. In keeping with a strong tendency toward patriarchy:

> . . . wives are regarded as belonging to their husband's kinship group and are expected to accept the cultural elements of this group and to provide sons to carry on the name. The wife's loss of individual identity is furthered by the desire of upper-upper-class men to find wives who are not career minded and who do not necessarily have college degrees, although they require intelligence.[7]

The status of women is also low in the Episcopal Church which, among all protestant denominations, seems most identified with this class. As Parsons observed, the role of women in this class is especially associated with the refinement of culture and the preservation of a proper style of life.

In contrast to families of the upper-upper class, families of the *lower-upper class* tend to be recent arrivals. They are, therefore, more often upwardly mobile conjugal families that have become disengaged from their extended family. Families of this class are continually seeking to establish themselves through acceptance into the best social clubs, residential areas, and social circles. Although these families may have more money than the upper-upper-class, that fact alone does not gain them acceptance. They tend to be conspicuous in their consumption and insecure economically. A decline in fortune affects them more acutely, since they lack the support of a strongly entrenched extended family. However:

5. Cavan, "Subcultural Variations and Mobility," p. 546.
6. Cavan, *The American Family*, pp. 86, 87.
7. Cavan, "Subcultural Variations and Mobility," p. 546.

> . . . *the two upper classes tend to fuse, first in secondary business and professional association, and finally in primary groups and through intermarriage. The lower-upper class may be thought of as replenishing the upper-upper class, which tends to lose members through low birth rates and downward mobility.*[8]

THE MIDDLE CLASSES

Persons of the middle classes do not have the vast amount of wealth that is characteristic of the upper classes and are distinguished from the class below them by virtue of their occupation. Upper-middle-class persons often have professional and business careers ordinarily requiring college education as distinct from the white-collar, skilled, and semi-skilled jobs of the lower-middle and working classes. Most middle-class occupations require thinking as opposed to hard labor. Occupationally, members of the upper-middle class are predominantly professionals, managers of large businesses, and owners of small businesses; clerical and sales positions are characteristic of the lower-middle class. Persons in the latter class save but do not tend to accumulate a fortune. They spend most of their earnings on a comfortable style of life that includes travel and support of cultural activities.

The size of the middle class is variously estimated at 38.3 percent (Warner for Yankee City), and 30 percent (Hollingshead for New Haven, Connecticut),[9] and 40 to 50 percent (Roche *et al.* general estimate).[10] If we assume that a reasonable estimate would be 40 percent, the differentiating family income of this class was approximately $10,000 in 1968.[11] If income alone were an index of class, persons earning over this amount could be considered middle class. However, many blue-collar workers earned over this amount as did many truck drivers and persons in service-related occupations, whereas many white-collar employees (such as secretaries, bank tellers, salesmen, etc.) earned less. Therefore, income alone is never an unambiguous index of class.

The middle class is predominantly native-born white. A small ethnic community and an even smaller black contingency completes the composition. The religious affiliation of this class reflects family background and has a higher proportion of nonprotestants as well as a wider spread of protestant denominations than the upper classes.

Typically, the *upper-middle class* is the bearer of the American success syndrome. Status advance is very important to these professionals. In line with this orientation they place high value on a college education, encourage their children to read books and magazines, and are commonly civic leaders. This class strongly supports the contention that success is and ought to be

8. *Ibid.*, p. 542.
9. Kahl *op. cit.*, p. 45.
10. Roach *et al. op. cit.*, p. 166.
11. U.S. Bureau of the Census, *Current Population Reports*, Series P-60, No. 66, "Income in 1968 of Families and Persons in the United States" (Washington, D.C.: U.S. Government Printing Office, 1969), p. 17.

the result of one's personal achievement. Consequently, members are highly competitive. Upper-middle-class persons are future oriented and are willing to defer immediate gratification in order to achieve long-term goals. This is quite consistent with their conception of a career which is expected only gradually to place one in a position of prominence or relative wealth.

Families in the upper-middle class are not as isolated as those of the class immediately above them. The typical family could be called a modified extended family after Eugene Litwak.[12] Each conjugal family is typically neolocal, but a strong support network continues to function despite geographic separation. Money, gifts, letters, and telephone conversations are used to maintain these family ties, especially in times of crisis. Face-to-face reunions often occur only at weddings, funerals, and other family occasions.

Even when the wife is employed, the husband is considered to be the head of the household and is characteristically the chief provider. Upper-middle-class parents train their children to be achievement oriented. This usually means that they are encouraged in self-discipline, restraint of aggression, responsibility, initiative, and a high level of academic achievement. These are characteristics that are thought to ensure professional success.

The typical *lower-middle-class* family is second generation American, with a significant minority of families having been foreign born. Patriotism and commitment to the American dream are quite characteristic of this class as well as of the working class immediately below it. White collar, skilled, and semi-skilled jobs are common as is ending formal education with high school. Although upward mobility is valued by the younger generation, it is commonly thought of as simply obtaining a better job than one's father. During recessions or depressions these persons fear downward mobility and many become impoverished as was true in the 1930s.

Although reflecting a much wider variation of ethnic background, the families of this class are typically nuclear. The nuclear family is embedded in a much closer kinship group than is the upper-middle class. A great deal of visiting among relatives occurs, and families, while valuing a little distance, tend to live in the same community.

While the man is clearly the head of the house, the wife is typically in charge of the budget. He earns; she spends. Many wives in this class may work to supplement their husbands' incomes, but few pursue careers.

THE LOWER CLASSES

The upper-lower class is commonly referred to as the "working class." It accounts for between 30 and 40 percent of the population.[13] Occupationally, it is characterized by semi-skilled to skilled laborers and operators. It contains a high proportion of foreign born (in Yankee City 62 percent of the upper-lower class were ethnic); and some high school education seems typi-

12. Eugene Litwak, "Geographic Mobility and Extended Family Cohesion" in *Family and Change*, John N. Edwards (ed.), (New York: Knopf, 1969), p. 70.

13. Roach *et al.*, *op. cit.*, p. 180.

cal. Incomes of some families in this class may exceed the incomes of families in the lower-middle class; and so, at this level, income becomes an even more unreliable single indicator of class.

Upper-lower-class, or *working-class*, persons do not think of success in the same way as the middle classes. Having been barred (by their ethnic affiliation, lack of education, and lack of personal contact with the right persons) from obtaining success in an upwardly mobile career, persons in the upper-lower class tend to define success in terms of home ownership, an automobile, and adequate educational opportunities for their children.

Being economically quite vulnerable, working-class persons prefer job security to the risk involved with jobs that might lead to more rapid advancement. They define "work" in physical terms and value industry. Concomitantly, jobs are not ordinarily considered to be intrinsically rewarding (as are careers) and job dissatisfaction is common.[14] Jobs provide income so that pleasure may be found outside of the forty-hour week. A strong tendency to view the world in terms of concrete events and practical outcomes is reflected in child-rearing patterns that focus upon the behavior rather than the attitude of a child and the expectation that children will be gainfully employed after they leave high school.

The nuclear family of the working class is tied more securely to its extended kinship network than is the lower-middle class. The need for support in crisis situations is reinforced by a great inclination to visit and interact on a face-to-face basis. This family, more than any other, adheres to the American traditional image of the family. The father is the head of the household and the major provider by virtue of the sweat of his brow. His wife takes care of the house, rears the children, and submits to his sexual advances as a matter of obligation. While there is still a strong tendency to protect the traditional masculine and feminine images, it is less strong than in the past. Their views on child rearing, however, remain firm:

> The working class . . . emphasizes traditional values in child rearing. Respect for adults, neatness, honesty, and obedience are the central virtues which working-class adults seek to instill in their children. They want them to adhere to externally imposed standards and avoid trouble.[15]

The *lower-lower class* consists of families who are impoverished. Various estimates of the size of this class range from 15 to 20 percent of the entire population.[16] An elaborate scheme for defining poverty in economic terms has been worked out by the Social Security Administration, and a rather wide band of incomes is taken to denote poverty. The income defining poverty is a variable because factors such as rural vs. urban residence, size of family, age of children, region of the country, and increasing cost of living are taken into account in the attempt to fit the economic definition

14. See Jules Henry, *Culture Against Man* (New York: Random House, 1966).
15. Roach et al., *op. cit.*, p. 181.
16. *Ibid.*, p. 198.

of poverty as closely as possible to the facts of deprivation. A commonly used reference point in this spectrum is the income for an urban family of four. In 1966, if such a family earned under $3,335, it was considered to be in poverty. A farm family of similar composition was considered to be impoverished if it earned less than $2,345. Continuing research attempting more accurately to define poverty by income has resulted in redefinition since 1966; consequently, the number of families in poverty and their characteristics have changed. In 1968, $3,553 defined the poverty level for an urban family of four and $3,034 for a farm family.[17] An examination of Table 6–2 will indicate that what constituted poverty in 1968 was an amount of money only somewhat less than the 1941 mean income of $4,900 (in constant 1965 dollars) and considerably above the then current mean income of $2,210. What is reflected in the definition of poverty in terms of income, therefore, is an attempt to measure *relative*, not absolute, deprivation.

Persons in the lower-lower class live at or below the poverty band throughout their lives. They inherit from their parents and tend to pass on

17. U.S. Bureau of the Census, *Current Population Reports*, Series P-60, No. 68, "Poverty in the United States: 1959–1968" (Washington, D.C.: U.S. Government Printing Office, 1969), p. 11. See also the report of the Committee on Labor and Public Welfare, Subcommittee on Employment, Manpower and Poverty, *Toward Economic Security for the Poor* (Washington, D.C.: U.S. Government Printing Office, 1968), p. 8.

TABLE 6–2

Mean Family Personal Income per Consumer Unit, and Mean Income of each Quintile and Top 5 Percent of Consumer Units, Expressed as a Percentage of the Mean Income for All Consumer Units

Mean income per consumer unit	1929	1935-1936	1941	1947	1950	1954	1959	1963
Current Dollars	$2,340	$1,630	$2,210	$4,230	$4,440	$5,360	$3,600	$7,280
Constant (1965) Dollars	4,460	3,940	4,900	5,740	5,820	8,190	7,160	7,640

Mean Income of Quintile Expressed as a percent of Mean Income of All Consumer Units

	1929	1935-1936	1941	1947	1950	1954	1959	1963
Second	18%	21%	21%	25%	24%	24%	22%	23%
Third	45	46	48	55	55	56	55	55
Lowest	69	71	77	80	81	82	83	83
Fourth	97	105	113	110	111	113	113	114
Highest	272	259	244	230	231	226	228	228
All quintiles	100	100	100	100	100	100	100	100
Top 5%	600	530	480	414	428	406	400	390
Highest quintile minus top 5%	163	163	165	167	165	163	171	173

Source: Edward Budd, *Poverty and Inequality*, p. xiv

to their children an accumulation of disadvantages associated with such relative deprivation. Substandard housing, inadequate schools, overcrowded neighborhoods, and inadequate service from garbage collectors, police, housing code inspectors, and other public officials contribute to their problems. Their relatively poor performance in school reflects in part the inadequacy of their diet and the resultant poor health, the lack of privacy, and insufficient funds to buy clothing and school supplies. Few lower-lower-class persons complete high school. Occupations are characteristically unskilled, frequently seasonal jobs that provide income inadequate to overcome impoverishment. Nevertheless, the majority of the employable poor work full or part-time each year. In 1966, two-fifths of all heads of households under the age of sixty-five worked full time and one third, part of the year or part-time all of the year. Despite their efforts they remained in poverty.[18] Contrary to the common assumption of the middle class, only about one-fifth to one-fourth of the poor are "on welfare." While there is continuing debate regarding the availability of jobs for the poor, a 1968 report by the Subcommittee on Employment, Manpower, and Poverty of the Joint Committee on Labor and Public Welfare estimated that in 1966 there were 2.4 million persons for whom there were no jobs.[19] If true, such a job gap will not be closed by all the training programs the government or private industry might wish to attempt. Some new jobs must be created. [One such attempt was the modification of the New York welfare program in the summer of 1971, whereby a recipient must appear in person at the welfare office to collect his check and must be willing to accept a job (if one is available) to help "pay back" welfare.] In any case, it is in fact difficult for the average lower-lower-class person to find a job even though he desperately needs and wants one.

Faced with the realities of a rather grim life, the poor must constantly deal with feelings of hopelessness and despair. Their apparent lack of achievement motivation reflects a profound lack of trust in the social system that has excluded them from its benefits. If one is black, the realities of exclusion are manifested daily in discriminatory practices which persist despite their illegality. A deeper sense of isolation is thereby fostered.

The composition of the poor population varies depending upon how poverty is defined economically. The largest sub-groups in the present poor population are made up of persons who are white, persons who are over sixty-five, and children. The vast majority of the poor are white (68.5 percent).[20] Although urban poverty has become more conspicuous in recent years, a significant minority of the poor live in rural areas. While some 30

---

18. *Toward Economic Security for the Poor*, pp. 10, 11.
19. *Ibid.*, p. 18.
20. "Poverty in the United States: 1959–68," pp. 1, 4. In 1968 nonwhites constituted 31.5% of the poor, the aged approx. 24%, and persons under 18 approx. 42.4%. Unassimilated ethnic groups, such as Mexican-Americans, Puerto Ricans, and American Indians also make up significant segments of the poor population, as does the vast army of migrant workers that harvest our crops.

percent of our population is rural, 40 percent of the nation's poor live in rural areas.[21]

Given the deprivation and isolation to which the poor must adjust, it is a testimony to human endurance that almost two-thirds of these families have both parents present. In 1969, 37.2 percent of all families that earned under $3,000 were headed by a single parent (33.6 percent were headed by a female, and 3.6 percent were headed by a male).[22]

Lower-lower-class families are considerably larger than the average American family. Parents, in part because of an inability to provide support and protection for their children, have relatively less control over them. The husband-father in particular has a difficult role because of his falling short of the desirable conception of the father as provider. His inadequate and sporadic employment does not provide him with status in his household, and other status supports must be sought.

Typically, lower-lower-class families are not joiners. They are difficult to recruit in the services of established institutions such as the church or school. Since children tend to remain with the mother in most crisis situations, the mother-child dyad is perhaps more institutionalized than the father-child dyad, although recent studies call into question the term "matriarchy" to describe the lower-lower-class black family in particular.

Children are more likely to be born before wedlock in the lower-lower class than in other classes, and there is not as strong an inclination to marry because of an illicit conception. On the other hand, children are more readily accepted into female-headed families. The young mother may live with her parents, and the care of her child is shared by her mother and siblings.

Kin are valued, but because they cannot offer a great deal of economic support (as they themselves are frequently impoverished) the kind of exchange that characteristically takes place between the nuclear family and its kin is more in the nature of emotional and psychological support. Visiting, a place to stay when traveling or moving to a new city, and baby-sitting services are typical exchanges. For the poor who have recently moved to the city, the majority of kin may have been left behind, and face-to-face interaction with a large extended family is not as common in the city as it was in the country. Nevertheless, kin are valued above friends as persons to be depended upon in a crisis, and kin terminology is extended to nonkin symbolically dramatizing the importance of these particularly close friends.

The Black Stratification System

Since the black American has been systematically excluded from the benefits of the larger society because of his color, the factors affecting his mobility

21. The President's Advisory Commission on Rural Poverty, *The People Left Behind*, (Washington, D.C.: U.S. Government Printing Office, 1967), p. 3.
22. Derived from Table 12 of "Income in 1968 of Families and Persons in the United States," p. 34.

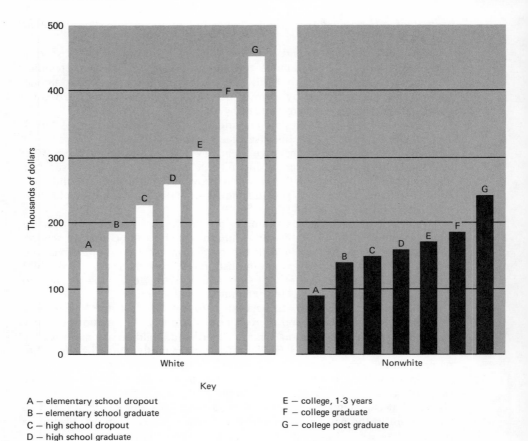

Key

A — elementary school dropout   E — college, 1-3 years
B — elementary school graduate   F — college graduate
C — high school dropout   G — college post graduate
D — high school graduate

FIGURE 6–2
*A comparison of white and nonwhite lifetime earnings, by education
completed. Adapted from* The Nation's Youth *(U.S.G.P.O., 1968), Chart 27.*

must be considered separately.[23] Some have argued that a caste system best
describes race relations in America, but this is not particularly apt since there
is some inter-marriage and integration into the "mainstream" on the one
hand and a noticeable stratification within the black community on the other.
A parallel stratification system offering black alternatives at each socioeconomic class, therefore, seems the best model to employ when describing the
condition of the black American. Figure 6–2 compares the income of com-

23. This section follows closely Andrew Billingsley, *Black Families in White America* (Englewood Cliffs, N.J.: Prentice-Hall, 1969), chap. V.

parably educated white and nonwhite males and clearly indicates why a parallel system is called for. The style of life of a black college graduate is not likely to be the same as that of a white high school dropout even though the incomes may be equal.

There seem to be several sub-systems bestowing status within the black community, each utilizing somewhat different criteria in order to assign a social position to an individual. Historically, under slavery a distinction was made between the house servant and the field hand, the former having a great deal more status in both black and white communities. (The house servants also tended to be lighter in skin color.)

Blacks, in the South in particular, who were freed before the Civil War tended to be light skinned mulattoes, and the rights vested in them as free men enabled them to accumulate property, obtain a modicum of education, and establish themselves as a kind of aristocracy. Frazier points out that skin color is less a basis of status ascription as one moves from the South to the North.[24] However, since the rebirth of black separatism around 1965, dark skin has become status enhancing, as has almost everything nonwhite. A person can be ideologically a soul brother and white although such instances are becoming increasingly rare. Skin color, therefore, is no longer as dependable an indicator of status in the black community as it once was.

Although there is an increasing acceptance of education, occupation, and income as the major indicators of a person's status (even by those who want to utilize these ingredients to fashion a distinctly separate black way of life), there is still a basic difference between the black and white communities in the manner in which they bestow status:

> Because of an over-representation of Negroes in the lower class, stratification tends to be based to a greater degree on behavioral patterns and social factors, rather than on income and occupation, which usually are considered crucial determinants in the white community. Social stratification in the black community is more likely to be determined by style of life and family background. Although a few Negroes who have amassed great wealth or achieved fame in the larger society might be considered upper class by objective standards, most blacks who are considered upper class within their own community would not be so considered if they were white. School teachers are a notable example. Within the black community they are frequently considered to be upper class; white school teachers are rarely so considered. Similarly, many individuals working as skilled workers, service workers, and even laborers are considered to be middle class because of their behavior patterns.[25]

A model for the black stratification system is provided in Figure 6–3. Billingsley argues that such a model does not indicate who associates with

---

24. Cited in Alphonso Pinkney, *Black Americans* (Englewood Cliffs, N.J. Prentice-Hall, 1969), p. 68.
25. E. Franklin Frazier, *The Negro Family in the United States* (Chicago: University of Chicago Press, 1966), p. 191.

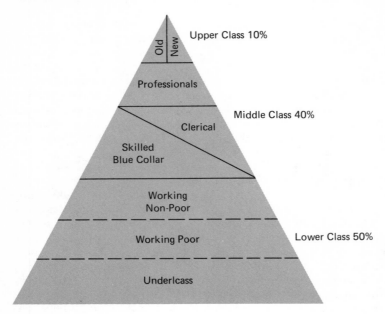

FIGURE 6–3
Social classes in the black community. From Andrew Billingsley, Black
Families in White America *(Prentice-Hall, 1969), p. 123.*

whom as is true in the white stratification system. In the black community, persons of different classes are forced by virtue of residential segregation to live in close proximity to one another. They are also much more dependent upon one another economically than would be true of persons of different classes in the white community. Nevertheless, Billingsley's model still has relevance for who looks up to (or down on) whom:

> *The importance of social class for our purposes is that the higher the social class status of a family, the greater access its members have to the resources of the wider community and the greater the level of supports they receive from the wider community, and consequently the greater will be the family's ability to meet the requirements of society and the needs of its members.*[26]

It is clear, therefore, that we cannot understand the black stratification system from the perspective of the criteria customarily applied in studying the stratification of the white community.

26. Billingsley *op. cit.*, p. 124.

THE BLACK UPPER CLASSES

Upper-class Blacks tend to associate with other upper-class Blacks, and families in this class have the greatest separation from the masses both geographically and economically. However, the parallel nature of the black system can nowhere better be portrayed than by an examination of the relative insecurity of this upper class. The old upper class is composed of families headed by men and women whose parents before them were upper or middle class: judges, physicians, dentists, high government officials, educated ministers of large congregations, college presidents, and wealthy businessmen.[27] Although there are Blacks who are millionaires, most of these upper-class black families, if ranked by the criteria of the white community, would be middle class. The vulnerability of the upper-class Black is further reflected in the fact that he earns considerably less in his lifetime than upper-middle-class Whites and frequently must rely upon the income of his wife in order to maintain his status. Significantly, the status of a black family is as much a reflection of the education and occupation of the mother as it is of the father. According to Billingsley, Senator Edward Brook of Massachusetts, Robert Weaver, Secretary of Housing and Urban Development, and Thurgood Marshall, Justice of the Supreme Court, are good examples of men in the old upper class. The success of these men reflects their opportunity in the wider society (their having had a measure of economic security denied to the vast majority of black Americans) as well as the personal effort that they exerted in their careers.[28] They are by no means "self-made" men.

The new upper class has risen to its status in one generation. Typically, these families are the families of entertainers and athletes, although recently they include such public officials as Mayor Stokes of Cleveland and Mayor Hacker of Gary, Indiana. While some of these new upper-class families come from the middle class, the majority have risen from the lower class. This is true in the case of both Mayor Stokes and Mayor Hacker who came from slum neighborhoods. The class orientation of athletics in America can be seen in the fact that upper-class black athletes in football, basketball, and tennis tend to come from middle-class families, while those in baseball and boxing tend to come from lower-class families, because the former sports have recruited players from colleges and universities.

> *Upper-class Negroes tend to associate with other upper-class Negroes. Entertaining is done in the home, except for the public events which they sponsor. They are usually Protestants, usually Congregationalists, Episcopalians, and Presbyterians. They are active in social clubs, especially fraternities and sororities, and they support civil rights activities through the National Association for the Advancement of Colored People or the Urban League.[29]*

27. Billingsley *loc. cit.*
28. Billingsley *op. cit.*, p. 125.
29. Pinkney *op. cit.*, p. 65.

Interestingly enough, another group must be classified in the new upper class—the "Shadies, those gamblers, racketeers, pimps, and other hustlers who often manage to become wealthy, to wield a considerable amount of influence, and to garner a great deal of prestige in the Negro community."[30] The inclusion of this group in the black system should give us pause to consider that the ordinary study of the white community simply omits any discussion of the class status of Mafia members and other hoodlums who manage to become wealthy and do, in fact, wield a great deal of influence by both legitimate and illegitimate means. The dismissal of this segment of the white community as simply a part of the "underworld" does not adequately reflect their position, power, and influence in our society.

Families of the black upper class are smaller than those of comparably educated whites. The number of female-headed families is comparable to the number in the white community after the family income exceeds $7,000.[31] The family structure of the black upper class is nuclear with considerably less emphasis on the extended family than is found in the white upper-upper class, but more than would be characteristic of the white middle class.

THE BLACK MIDDLE CLASSES

The life style, rather than occupation or income, sets the black middle class off from the other classes:

> . . . the middle class is marked off from the lower class by a pattern of behavior expressed in stable family and associational relationships, in great concern with "front" and "respectability" and in a drive for "getting ahead." All of this finds an objective measure in standard of living—the way people spend their money—and in public behavior.[32]

Occupations of the middle class include teaching, social work, accounting, law, and entertainment. Also included are some independent businessmen, clerical workers, service workers, and even some laborers. Middle-class Blacks are frequently Methodists and Baptists, and, unlike the lower class who profess church membership but rarely attend as adults, the middle-class Blacks are faithful church goers and are quite civic minded.

Billingsley describes the family life of these Blacks as being a precarious existence, even though in most cases their incomes are above the nation's median.[33] What is striking is that in order for Blacks to earn between $9,000 and $13,000 a year, it is necessary for both parents to work, even though in several instances one or the other parent is a college graduate. The husband-wife relationship is described as equalitarian or slightly patriarchal. There is no indication of a matriarchy in these families.

30. Billingsley *op. cit.*, p. 125.
31. Pinkney *op. cit.*, p. 71.
32. St. Clair Drake and Horace Cayton, *Black Metropolis: A Study of Negro Life in a Northern City*, rev. ed. (New York: Harper & Row, 1962), pp. 661–62.
33. Billingsley *op. cit.*, pp. 133–35.

E. Franklin Frazier is much more critical of the black middle class. As he sees it, the "Black Bourgeoisie" are a new middle class with little time for family traditions to have emerged. They tend to imitate the white society and thus have "culture without substance." The economically dependent wife is, on the whole, subordinate to her husband in the more conservative middle-class families of the South. He, on the other hand, may have a certain freedom to conduct himself in the "spirit of a gentleman," while serving as a strict censor over his wife's conduct. In the North, where women work to help maintain the family's status, there is a greater tendency toward equality. Frazier contends that there is really no generalization that one can make regarding the relationship between economic independence and conjugal status, since working wives are sometimes dominated by their husbands and dependent wives sometimes given a place of honor.[34] One of the changes that seems to be occurring within the black community as a result of the efforts of those calling for black power is a cross-class identification enlisting more and more of the middle class in a competitive struggle with the white community.

Since Frazier, there has been no extensive study of the family life of the middle- or upper-class Blacks. A major problem in comparative studies is, therefore, the overemphasis on the problems of the black lower-class family without knowledge of the proper context in which to place these observations.

THE BLACK LOWER CLASSES

Billingsley places half of the black community in the lower class. Within this class he distinguishes between the working nonpoor, the working poor, and the underclass. In 1968, Blacks constituted 33 percent of the poor population, and about 35 percent of the total black population was poor. About 60 percent of all black children live in poverty.[35] Poor black families are large, usually complete, and commonly linked through the mother to a matrilineal kinship structure. The poor Blacks have attracted much recent attention. However, a distorted picture of the lower class emerges from this concentration on the poor. Taking the characteristics of 173 families living in a black ghetto of Hartford, Connecticut, Charlotte Dunmore describes the "average" family:

> The family is Negro and Protestant. The mother was born and reared in the rural or semi-rural southern United States. She came to live in Hartford sometime after her eighteenth birthday. The family has two legally married parents and contains 4.7 members. Father is the chief breadwinner, earning $4,800 per year from his employment as a skilled craftsman,

34. Frazier *op. cit.*, p. 328.
35. Joint Report of Bureau of the Census and Bureau of Labor Statistics, BLS Report No. 332, *Current Population Reports*, Series P-23, No. 24, "Social and Economic Conditions of Negroes in the United States," (Washington, D.C.: U.S. Government Printing Office, 1967).

steward or machinist. Mother, who stays home to take care of the children, perceives them as growing, developing human beings amenable to her control, if only to a limited degree. The parents want their children to have at least some college education. They hope that their children will become skilled technicians, specialized clerical workers, or go into one of the minor professions—library science, teaching, the arts. The children are involved in at least two organized community activities (Scouts, the "Y," settlement house, etc.). . . .

Mother has achieved a rather high degree of integration into her neighborhood and is involved in a meaningful (to her) give-and-take relationship with her neighbors. At the present time, she is participating in at least two community activities. She is a registered voter and voted in the last election. She listens to the radio, watches television, and reads one of two Hartford newspapers every day.

The family is geared to obtaining a better life for its children, including more education and more materially rewarding, status-giving employment. Hartford is perceived as a racially prejudiced community, and education appears to be considered the primary method for circumventing this prejudice.[36]

Because of the tendency to lump all lower-class black families into a culture of poverty that stresses the various indices of "disorganization" (female-headed families, high rates of illegitimacy, high crime rates, high desertion, etc.), these stable lower-class types are often overlooked. In point of fact, there is a great variety of family form and structure in the lower-class black community even in the case of that portion of the community that is impoverished. These types will be dealt with more extensively in Chapter 8.

Among the working nonpoor are found black men who are truck drivers and longshoremen. These poor families are predominantly nuclear and frequently involved in their community's churches, schools, and political parties.

Below the working nonpoor is a group Billingsley designates as the working poor. "While 41 percent of all Negroes were living in poverty in 1966, only 14 percent were supported by public welfare. Thus, nationally about a third of all poor Negroes were supported by welfare. This proportion varies by communities."[37] There is no appreciable difference between Blacks who are working and yet remain in poverty and Whites who are similarly situated.

The working poor families are often headed by unskilled laborers, service workers such as elevator operators, and domestics. The unions do not find it profitable to organize these workers and, consequently, their wages remain low. Most of them are engaged in occupations that are not covered by minimum wage laws.

Finally, there is the underclass constituting 15 to 20 percent of black families. These families are characteristically headed by persons who have less than an eighth grade education, who are intermittently employed at best, and

---

36. Charlotte Dunmore, "Social-Psychological Factors Affecting the Use of an Educational Opportunity Program by Families Living in a Poverty Area" (Doctoral Dissertation, Brandeis University, 1967), chap. 3; quoted in Billingsley *op. cit.*, pp. 137–38.
37. Billingsley, *op. cit.*, p. 140.

who are often dependent upon relatives and public welfare. If they are fortunate, they live in public housing projects of the North where public welfare is generally more supportive. Vast numbers of them, however, live in the dilapidated slums of our nation's cities. Yet even in these families who may earn less than $2,000 a year, the two-parent family is characteristic.

What does it mean to be poor and black? Billingsley describes seven bases for patterning the life style of these families that suggest something of their variety: (1) Location—The conditions of life for low-income black families are most abject in the rural South, less so in the urban South, and still less so in the urban North and West. The ability of black families to meet the requirements of society, particularly for achievement, is highly associated with this geographic patterning. (2) Socioeconomic status—It makes a great difference in both family structure and achievement if the family is in the underclass, the working poor, or the working nonpoor. (3) The life style of the family varies with its structure. Among lower-class families Billingsley discerns six types: basic families with two married adults and no children, nuclear families, attenuated nuclear families with one parent missing, extended families, sub-families or augmented families with nonrelatives functioning as intimate members of the household. (4) Size is an important variable which may serve as both facilitator of achievement and an obstacle depending upon other family characteristics. (5) Patterns of decision making—the vanishing patriarchies, the resilient matriarchies, and the expanding equalitarian families. (6) Division of labor—the segmented relationship where husband and wife have their separate spheres of activity which are probably most common and the collaboration characteristic of a significant minority where there is role flexibility and mutual cooperation between husband and wife in meeting instrumental needs. (7) Attitudes toward authority and socialization of children —Some low-income black families take very good care of their children, striving to understand and shape the character of their children. An intermediate group functions less well in the controlling of their children who may be in and out of trouble. At the bottom, there is a group that is the most chronically unstable whose children are most likely to get into trouble or be neglected.[38]

> . . . it cannot be stressed too strongly that not all lower-class Negro families are poor. Not all poor families are broken. Not all single parent families are on welfare. And not all welfare families are chronic problems. A more adequate income structure would remove many of them from the arena of social concern.[39]

Social Mobility and Family Patterns

To speak as I have of patterns of family living associated with socioeconomic class in the white and black communities is to focus more on structure than

38. Billingsley *op. cit.*, pp. 143–44.
39. *Ibid.*, p. 145.

on process. Our society is to some degree an open society. One estimate suggests that about 25 percent of the nation's families are upwardly mobile in each generation and about 5 percent downwardly mobile.[40] While upward mobility may move an individual or a family in rags-to-riches fashion in one generation from the lower class to the upper class, this is a rare occurrence, more myth than reality for the average American. Ordinarily, mobility occurs between adjacent classes and may take two or more generations. The journey from the lower-lower class to the upper class is rarely made; it ordinarily takes several generations and may not include complete assimilation into the upper class even after sufficient funds have been accumulated to provide for an appropriate style of life. Downward mobility, on the other hand, is usually more rapid. Mobility in either direction generally has some adverse effects upon the family, although downward mobility is ordinarily more destructive.

As I have suggested in the previous sections, different classes have different standards for what is proper in family living and tend to regard other life styles as deviant. Mobile families thus tend to be dissociated from effective social supports.[41] While secondary relationships such as those found in business associations and civic organizations are relatively easy to enter or maintain, primary relationships tend to be broken in mobile families.[42]

The conjugal bond undergoes considerable stress in upwardly mobile families. Within the nuclear family the upwardly mobile husband may not be able to keep pace with the rising expectations generated in his wife and family by his success. Though he may be advancing, he may not appear successful in their eyes or even in his own because of his and their much greater aspirations. Families moving upward ordinarily do so by virtue of the education obtained by the husband. His wife, whose education may not be on the same level, may fall behind as he opens up a new world of ideas, attitudes, and experiences.

In the downwardly mobile family, particularly one that drops more than one class, it is common for a reversal in power and privilege to occur in the conjugal roles as the wife's income becomes more important and finally perhaps becomes the main source of support for the family. In such cases, the husband must adjust to stresses and strains within his family as well as suffer the effects of invidious comparison with others in his former class. However, a downwardly mobile husband is less likely to lose status in his family if his status is based on respect and affection or traditionally upheld ideals of patriarchy rather than on his power or his ability to provide.

Mobility may be an individual matter rather than a family affair, in which case the individual in assimilating the new style of life must also dissociate

---

40. The following section follows closely Cavan, "Subcultural Variations and Mobility," pp. 567–76.

41. Robert A. Ellis and W. Clayton Lane, "Social Mobility and Social Cohesion: A Test of Sorokin's Dissociative Hypothesis," in *Permanence and Change in Social Class: Readings in Stratification*, W. Clayton Lane (ed.), (Cambridge, Mass.: Schenkman Publishing Company, 1968), p. 298.

42. Primary relationships are those affectional, intimate relationships that are generated through face-to-face contact and occur early in a person's life, in such groups as the family.

himself from the style of life of his family of procreation. He can never "go home." His success changes his life style and the circle of friends with whom he associates. If he fails, shame is easier to bear among strangers. These generalizations seem truer of families moving from the lower class than of those moving out of the middle class where the kinship network seems to function for upwardly mobile persons as well. Perhaps this is because mobility is a much more natural expectation of families in this class (and a more realistic one at that) so that they are more experienced in dealing with the problem of success than families of the lower class.

Marriage often provides a way to achieve upward mobility for the middle and upper classes. The upper-middle-class professional man may enter the lower-upper class by marrying the boss's daughter. The middle-class woman may marry into the upper-upper class, for the patriarchal character of the family in this class permits a man to look for a woman of lesser status than himself, though one who is educated well enough to function adequately in the cultural sphere. Lower-class persons, particularly lower-class males, generally lack this route to mobility.

Speculating upon why black males more often marry white females than white males marry black females, Robert Merton suggests that in the former case it is possible for a more reciprocal exchange to take place.[43] The black male "exchanges" his relatively greater *class* position for the relatively greater *caste* position of his white wife. Not only is there ordinarily no such compensation in the case of a white male who marries a black female, but our society has not considered it necessary for such a sexual relationship to terminate in marriage. Historically, the black female has been available to white male exploitation.

The fact of upward mobility is not, in any event, a simple function of the husband's achievement in his career. Blood and Wolfe suggest four ways in which Michigan wives help their husbands get ahead: (1) collaboration in the same business, (2) wife's employment in her own career or in a supporting job, (3) emotional support and entertainment of the right people, and (4) in the case of low-status couples with little chance of mobility, the wife fulfills a housekeeper's role for the husband's comfort.[44]

The greatest disruption of family functioning occurs when mobility is rapid, particularly in a downward direction resulting in a reversal of status within the conjugal relationship, and when the mobility traverses two or more classes. Yet, in the main, despite the stresses and strains introduced by mobility, the conjugal family in America remains relatively adaptive and resilient.

Summary

The American family is strongly affected by factors associated with socioeconomic class. I have suggested that a family's size, its typical structure, its

---

43. Robert K. Merton, *Social Theory and Social Structure* (New York: Free Press, 1963), p. 173.
44. Robert O. Blood and D. M. Wolfe, *Husbands and Wives: The Dynamics of Married Living* (Glencoe, Ill.: Free Press, 1960).

mode of articulation with its larger kinship system, and its pattern of life—from the way it earns its living to the manner in which it raises and controls its children—are all functions of its status. This status is primarily determined by the occupation of the head of the household and the income that occupation provides. In the upper classes the head of the house is ordinarily a man; in the lower classes, it is more often a woman.

In brief, the following class-based patterns can be discerned: The white upper-upper-class family is inclined toward a strong patriarchal extended family very similar in function to the corporate lineage of pre-industrial societies. Children's marriages are often scrutinized by members of the extended family and an effort is made to maintain or improve upon the family fortune through the proper marriage. The lower-upper-class family, whose wealth is recently acquired, is typically concerned about social acceptability in the eyes of the old aristocracy. It is perhaps the most isolated nuclear family unit in our society. In the black system, there is a parallel distinction between the old and the new, but less of an invidious comparison. Both are considerably less secure than the white upper classes since the class is composed of professional people most of whom would be considered middle class by white standards. The black upper-class family is typically nuclear with considerably less emphasis upon the involvement with kin than is true in the white old aristocracy. Black nuclear families are smaller on the average than white nuclear families in the upper class.

The white upper-middle-class family is the most "success" oriented of all. Its pattern of child rearing reflects a strong emphasis upon achievement and competition. Litwak has called this family a modified extended family because, although the residential unit is a conjugal family, an effort is made to keep in touch with kin. In the white lower-middle class, white collar jobs are typical and economic hardship a real possibility during times of recession. While the man is clearly head of the house, the woman is in charge of the budget. It may be necessary for her to work to supplement the family income —not in order to fulfill her own striving for success, as might be the case in the upper-middle class. In the case of the black middle class both parents typically work and the conjugal relationship is likely to be equalitarian or somewhat patriarchal.

In the lower class the greatest diversity of family life styles occur. I have omitted many good descriptions of ethnic and regional variation in this class to focus on differences between and within the black and the white communities. The working-class (or upper-lower class) white family is strongly embedded in a kinship system that is realized in face-to-face relationships that contrast with the middle class's reliance upon phone calls and letters to maintain kinship relationships. The working-class family fits the common conception of what a family ought to be more than most of the other families I have discussed. A strong emphasis upon respect for adults and conformity characterize the child-rearing patterns and a marked division of labor in segregated roles is typical of the conjugal relationship. Among Blacks the working nonpoor seem to be quite similar.

Aside from the generalization that lower-class families are larger, and have a greater number of single-parent families than is true of the upper classes, it is difficult to summarize the characteristics of the many family styles found in this class. Some of the strategies for coping with poverty in the black ghetto will be discussed in Chapter 8.

7. The White Upper-Middle-Class Family of Suburbia

As an attempt to recover what was missing in the city, the suburban exodus could be amply justified, for it was concerned with primary human needs. But there was another side: the temptation to retreat from unpleasant realities, to shirk public duties, and to find the whole meaning of life in the most elemental social group, the family, or even in the still more isolated and self-centered individual.

LEWIS MUMFORD

The suburb is not the only habitat of the white middle class; this segment of the population is found in urban areas and scattered lightly throughout rural America as well. Furthermore, not all suburbs are composed of middle-class Whites. Some are working class, with a rich mixture of ethnic and minority groups. Some suburban areas referred to as "satellites" offer jobs to a significant segment of their population. A few are black. Nevertheless, the American white middle class is well established in suburbia—so much so that we commonly think of the suburb as its natural habitat. Our concern in this chapter is to focus upon the characteristic patterns of living found in white upper-middle-class families living in what has been affectionately referred to as the "dormitory" suburb—the residential retreat separated by a number of miles from the place of employment. Typically, such a suburb is the home of the professional who commutes to his job. As one writer quipped, the commuter's "heart and his treasure are twenty miles apart."[1]

Robert Winch argues that this type of suburb can be seen as the "family's response to the loss of functions."[2] Fearing the disorganization that Zimmerman felt was a necessary concomitant of the atomistic family of the industrial city, these families left the city in order to restore the family to a more central place in their lives. "The city is not a good place to raise children," suburban parents frequently remark.

Another dimension is added to this often-heard remark, however, when the subject of race is raised. The city, particularly since World War II, has become home for increasing numbers of black Americans, most of whom are from the rural South. As Blacks move in, Whites move out. The pattern is apparent all over America. Table 7–1 documents this point for nine of our largest cities. Only the Los Angeles-Long Beach area does not show a heavy net emigration of Whites from the central city.

The influx of low-income persons of whatever race means that the city must assume an increasing role in providing education, health and sanitation facilities, recreation areas, low-income housing, and public assistance. The exodus of middle-class Whites to the suburbs helps create the self-fulfilling prophecy about the city and children because with these people goes a sizable portion of the city's tax base.

Suburbs, whatever their type, tend to be one-class suburbs. On the one hand, zoning regulations restrict the type of building, while on the other hand, developers, wanting to protect the value of their new homes, restrict the price of housing available in a particular neighborhood. In some communities, "undesirables"—persons who differ in skin color, life style, or religious conviction—are "screened out" either by informal cues or by direct intervention on the part of the established residents. Residential segregation, of course, means de facto school segregation under the rubric of neighborhood schools for neighborhood children. One could thus describe the suburb of the white upper-middle class as an ethnic ghetto were it not for the fact that the inhabitants are ordinarily not thought of as a minority group and no overt constraints are placed upon them to live where they do. It is a homogeneity that is "freely" chosen.

1. Robert F. Winch, *The Modern Family*, 5th ed. (New York: Holt, Rinehart & Winston, 1966), p. 161.
2. *Ibid.*, p. 155.

TABLE 7–1   Recent Population Change in Leading Standard Metropolitan Statistical Areas (April 1960–July 1967)

Geographic area	Population, July 1, 1967 (000's)		Percent change		Net total migration (000's)		Percent nonwhite population		
	White	Nonwhite	White	Nonwhite	White	Nonwhite	1959	1960	1967
New York, N.Y.	9,726	1,750	3.4%	35.9%	−181	236	8.9%	12.0%	15.3
New York City	6,476	1,508	− 2.5	32.1	−440	165	9.8	14.7	18.4
Outside Central City	3,249	243	17.5	65.5	259	72	4.5	5.0	6.9
Los Angeles-Long Beach, Calif.	5,993	841	9.9	43.8	101	135	6.6	9.7	12.3
Los Angeles	2,237	576	8.5	38.0	54	79	10.7	16.8	20.5
Long Beach	356	23	8.0	55.0	11	3	2.6	4.3	6.0
Outside Central Cities	3,401	242	11.0	58.5	35	52	2.9	4.8	6.7
Chicago, Ill.	5,631	1,154	6.2	25.4	− 78	61	10.7	14.8	17.0
Chicago	2,522	1,028	− 7.0	22.8	−312	34	14.1	23.6	29.0
Outside Central City	3,110	126	20.1	52.6	234	27	2.9	3.1	3.9
Philadelphia, Pa.-N.J.	3,941	827	7.6	21.4	33	52	13.2	15.7	17.4
Philadelphia	1,402	640	− 4.5	19.6	−116	30	18.3	26.7	31.3
Outside Central City	2,539	188	15.7	28.2	148	22	6.6	6.3	6.9
Detroit, Mich.	3,327	787	4.1	38.9	−167	146	12.0	15.1	19.1
Detroit	969	651	−18.1	33.6	−252	101	16.4	29.2	40.2
Outside Central City	2,358	137	17.2	71.4	85	46	5.0	3.8	5.5
Boston, Mass.	3,105	126	2.9	39.0	−129	17	2.0	2.9	3.9
Boston	523	94	−16.9	36.6	−130	9	5.3	9.8	15.2
Outside Central City	2,582	33	8.1	46.5	1	8	.7	.9	1.3
San Francisco-Oakland, Calif.	2,543	445	9.6	34.8	67	57	9.4	12.5	14.9
San Francisco	540	172	−10.7	26.8	− 67	13	10.5	18.4	24.2
Oakland	255	123	− 5.9	26.6	− 21	10	14.5	26.4	32.5
Outside Central Cities	1,748	150	21.1	54.3	154	34	6.6	6.3	7.9
Washington, D.C.-Md.-Va.	2,031	666	30.4	31.5	272	75	23.1	24.5	24.7
District of Columbia	265	543	−23.2	29.7	− 85	54	35.4	54.8	67.2
Outside Central City	1,766	123	45.6	40.0	357	21	9.1	6.7	6.5
Pittsburgh, Pa.	2,206	178	− 1.6	8.9	−158	− 1	6.2	6.8	7.5
Pittsburgh	429	110	−14.6	8.3	− 83	− 2	12.3	16.8	20.4
Outside Central Ciity	1,776	68	2.1	9.9	− 74	− 1	3.5	3.4	3.7

Source: Metropolitan Life Insurance Company, *Statistical Bulletin* (Feb. 1970), 6.

141

Suburbia

The suburb may be a good place in which to bring up children, but it does not seem to be a popular place in which to grow old: upper-middle-class persons tend not to retire in the same home in which they reared their children. The variety of the dormitory suburb is thus further restricted by an overemphasis on families in the child-rearing stages of their development and a relative underemphasis on persons over sixty-five. Despite their apparent concern with children, upper-middle-class families typically have but two children.[3] Only the upper classes have smaller families. Yet because of the greater number of single persons, single-parent households, and persons past the child-bearing age in urban areas, areas surrounding the larger central cities have larger households than do the cities themselves.[4]

Table 7–2 illustrates some of the points discussed above by comparing outlying areas with central cities. The suburbs have in comparison a higher proportion of Whites, a higher proportion of young dependents (under

3. William W. Dobriner, *Class in Suburbia* (Englewood Cliffs, N.J.: Prentice-Hall, 1963), p. 134.
4. See commentary in Winch *op. cit.*, p. 159.

TABLE 7–2
Characteristics of the Population of Central Cities and Outlying Areas in Selected Standard Metropolitan Statistical Areas (1960)

Standard metropolitan statistical area	Male	White	Under 18	65 and over	14 years and over: married	Population per household
New York, N.Y.						
Central City	47.8%	85.3%	27.8%	10.5%	63.4%	2.88
Outside Central City	48.6	95.0	36.5	7.7	70.7	3.53
Los Angeles–						
Long Beach, Calif.						
Los Angeles Central City	48.3	83.2	30.5	10.2	63.1	2.77
Long Beach Central City	50.0	95.7	27.3	12.6	61.6	2.59
Outside Central Cities	49.1	95.9	36.5	7.7	70.6	3.18
Chicago, Ill.						
Central City	48.6	76.4	31.1	9.8	63.1	3.01
Outside Central City	49.7	96.9	37.5	7.1	71.3	3.50
Washington, D.C.						
Central City	46.9	45.2	28.7	9.1	57.5	2.87
Outside Central City	49.8	93.5	38.7	4.5	72.0	3.53

Source: Adapted from Metropolitan Life Insurance Company, *Statistical Bulletin*, (Feb. 1962).

eighteen years of age), a lower proportion of old dependents (over sixty-five), a higher proportion of married adults, and larger *households*.

While some support from kin and quasi-kin is common, the upper-middle-class suburban family is second only to the lower-upper class in the degree of disengagement fro ma kinship network. It is probable that the support that is given to the conjugal family comes from a relatively restricted number of kin, most commonly parents and siblings. In terms of intimate face-to-face interaction, the upper-middle-class conjugal family is relatively isolated, a fact that places great pressure upon the conjugal pair to bear each other's burdens and maintain the emotional health of the family with a minimum of kin support.

Horizontal mobility contributes to the relative isolation of the upper-middle-class conjugal family. Families, once they reach this class, are not the *most* mobile, but those who are striving to achieve professional status are *among* the most mobile in the country. The highest rates of mobility are found in the middle-income range.

The wife and children often bear most of the burden of the effects of such mobility. According to William H. Whyte, the wife, "who has only one life in contrast to the husband's two," has to adjust to new community friendships, new relationships with local stores and bank, a new house, and, often, to a new standard of living. While young children usually adjust to a move quite easily, those of junior high school age and above often view a transfer as a crisis. For them it is much more difficult to forget old friends and make new ones. Even for young children, a father's frequent transfers are sometimes a source of concern. Whyte reports the case of one executive who changed to a nontransferring company after his little boy turned to him one evening and asked, "Daddy, where do you really live?"[5]

Not all suburbs are alike, however. The life styles of upper-middle-class families differ in part as a function of setting. Here, in order of increasing affluence, are three settings wherein one is likely to find this family, as described in the mid-1950s. These three classic studies of suburbia were selected because of the fact that they all were conducted at about the same time. The differences among these communities show clearly that under similar circumstances significantly different life styles are possible. Suburbia has changed in the decade since these studies were made. The *New York Times* recently documented the increasing independence of New York's suburbs. In the 1970s the exurbanite of Rockland County is less likely to work in New York than he was in the 1950s. Nevertheless, the exclusiveness, the strong involvement of women in the politics of the school board and zoning, and the separation of job from residential setting is still characteristic.[6]

---

5. William H. Whyte, Jr., The Corporation and the Wife," *Fortune* (Nov. 1951), 109–11.
6. See the series on control of land use in the suburbs in *The New York Times*: Jack Rosenthal, "Suburbs Abandoning Dependence on Cities" (Aug. 16, 1971); Linda Greenhouse, "Rise in Jobs Poses Problem in Suburbs" (Aug. 17, 1971); and Richard Reeves, "Land is Prize in Battle for Control of Suburbs" (Aug. 18, 1971).

THREE SUBURBAN SETTINGS

Park Forest: The mobile businessman and his family find new roots in Park Forest.[7] The model man in this community "is a twenty-five or thirty-five year old white-collar organization man with a wife, a salary between $6,000 and $7,000, one child, and another on the way." The community was a mass-produced suburb opened in 1948 and designed simply to make money for the builder—lots and lots of money. Park Foresters live in anticipation of a transfer and a promotion. Many are, more properly, incipient upper-middle class. The developers built Park Forest in order to provide a captive market of about 30,000 people who would use the water and patronize the stores in the shopping center. A part of their expenditures in these areas would be returned to the developer. The dominant housing was in the form of clusters of two-bedroom garden apartments which rented for $95 a month. Around the periphery, ranch-type houses were built to sell for about $12,000. The people went to Park Forest because it was the best housing for the money.

Once there, however, they developed a vigorous style of life that made great demands on individuals and gave the developers the idea that they could better promote the community on the basis of the new style of life that was emerging:

> *You belong in Park Forest!*
> *The moment you come to our town you know:*
> *You're welcome.*
> *You're part of a big group*
> *You can live in a friendly small town*
>   *instead of a lonely big city.*
> *You can have friends who want you*
>   *and you can enjoy being with them.*
> *Come out. Find out about the spirit of*
>   *Park Forest.*[8]

The ads mirrored the reality:

> *Let's take, for example, a couple we shall call Dot and Charlie Adams. Charlie, a corporation trainee, is uprooted from the Newark office, arrives at Apartment 8, Court M-12. It's a hell of a day—the kids are crying. Dot is half sick with exhaustion and the movers won't be finished till late.*
>
> *But soon, because M-12 is a "happy" court, the neighbors will come over to introduce themselves. In an almost inordinate display of decency, some will help them unpack, and around supper time two of the girls will come over with a hot casserole and another with a percolator full of hot coffee. Within a few days the children will have found playmates,*

---

7. William H. Whyte, Jr., *The Organization Man* (Garden City, N.Y.: Doubleday, 1956), p. 300. The account that follows is based on this study.
8. *Ibid.*, p. 314.

> Dot will be kaffeeklatsching and sunbathing with the girls like an old-timer and Charlie, who finds that Ed Robey in Apt. 5 went through officer's training school with him, will be enrolled in the Court Poker Club. The Adamses are, in a word, In, and someday soon when another new couple, dazed and hungry, moves in, the Adamses will make their thanks by helping them to be likewise.[9]

Because these are families on the way up, they have not yet had time to accumulate many worldly possessions, and so they share everything from the lawn mower to babysitting time to books, silverware, and tea services.

Park Foresters are joiners. Not only, therefore, is court life intense, but participation in community organizations almost mandatory (see Fig. 7–1).

9. *Ibid.*, p. 316.

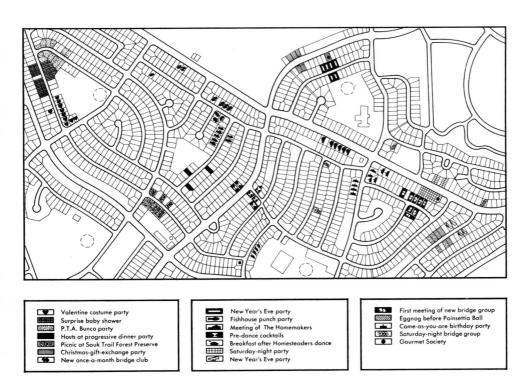

Valentine costume party		New Year's Eve party		First meeting of new bridge group	
Surprise baby shower		Fishhouse punch party		Eggnog before Poinsettia Ball	
P.T.A. Bunco party		Meeting of The Homemakers		Come-as-you-are birthday party	
Hosts at progressive dinner party		Pre-dance cocktails		Saturday-night bridge group	
Picnic at Sauk Trail Forest Preserve		Breakfast after Homesteaders dance		Gourmet Society	
Christmas-gift-exchange party		Saturday-night party			
New once-a-month bridge club		New Year's Eve party			

FIGURE 7–1
Attendance at various social gatherings in Park Forest. The intensity of court life is reflected in the extent to which close neighbors gather for such activities. Only the Gourmet Society and the Saturday-night Bridge Group reflect the dominance of a common interest over proximity. From William H. Whyte, Jr., The Organization Man *(Doubleday, 1956), pp. 338–39.*

There are sixty-five adult organizations to join. One wife remarks "Actually, neither Fred nor I are joiners like some of these silly characters around here, but it's gotten so now I practically have to make an appointment to see him Saturdays. During the week we alternate; when I have my meetings, he baby-sits for me and when he has his political meetings, I babysit for him." Even though most Park Foresters are renters, they have managed to establish a degree of political autonomy from their landlord that serves to unify them and prevents their landlord from cutting corners. Although many Park Foresters complain of the apathy of their number, most are more active than their new neighbors when they move up the ladder.

Whyte characterizes the consumer pattern of Park Forest as "inconspicuous consumption." The median equity of savings deposits in a young married group in the $5,000 to $7,500 income bracket is $700 to $800, and the median amount of loan money outstanding, $1,000.[10] Most are very poor managers of what capital they have—a rather strange paradox for businessmen. They consolidate their debts at a higher interest rate in order to lower the monthly payment and never think of using what savings they have as collateral on a loan in order to reduce the interest rate they will be charged. Most have not yet handled much money, so even the managing of a church budget of $50,-000 a year gives them valuable experience.

The construction of the courts places several duplex apartments around a common lawn. The back door is, therefore, the main door for most informal visiting. Neighbors constantly visit and never knock. The result is that it is unusual to be lonely and difficult to find privacy. One is made outgoing by virtue of the fact that if he is too shy to make the first move, someone will make it for him. A major problem emerges, however, with the childless couple. So pervasive is the concern for children that unless such couples have a great love for children, they will have a difficult time fitting in. Park Forest is made for families in the early stages of their child-rearing development, although the developer dreams of a community geared to all stages of the family's development.

As it is difficult to obtain privacy, so also is it difficult to philander.

> *The court is the greatest invention since the chastity belt. In company, young suburbanites talk a great deal about sex, but it's all rather clinical, and outside of the marriage no one seems to do much about it. There have been, to be sure, some unpleasant occurrences. In one court there was talk of wife-trading several years ago, and there have been affairs here and there since. The evidence is strong, however, that there is less philandering in the package suburbs than in more traditional communities.[11]*

On the other hand, if the efforts of a number of people to bring a couple into the group have failed and the new couple become labeled as deviants, they have problems. Their social interaction with their neighbors is

10. *Ibid.*, p. 355.
11. *Ibid.*, p. 393.

reduced, and their children are left out of the many parties. The community spirit also makes many demands upon the accepted. They are less free to express themselves in nonconforming ways. "The group is a`tyrant; so also is it a friend, and it is both at once."[12] But above all, involvement in meaningful activity is the transients' response to rootlessness.

The church also attempts to cope with rootlessness. Since the developer gave land for a church building to the people, not to a particular denomination (too many were represented), a decision was made by the residents to build a United Protestant Church. In order of importance Park Foresters felt that (1) the minister, (2) the Sunday School, (3) the location, (4) the denomination, and (5) the music were most important considerations in the building of a new church. And so in spite of denominational opposition, it was felt that one church could serve the needs of most protestants in Park Forest. "Why spend a lot of money building a lot of little churches when one church would do the job better and do it now? Why give small salaries to five so-so pastors instead of a decent salary to one good one?" The residents see the spiritual and the practical as reasonably synonymous. The church was built without denominational support and was financed by using the pledges of residents as collateral for a bank loan.

After its completion, the church focused upon the social life of its congregation rather than the refinement of doctrine. Group dynamics became fashionable. The attempt to "meet the needs of modern man" caused some members of the congregation to withdraw complaining that there was not enough attention paid to God. On the other hand, those sympathetic to the church contended that its mission was to help establish and refine the sense of community so needed by modern transient families.

Their social consciousness extended to the school as well. Park Foresters "threw themselves into the job of creating a school system with tremendous energy."[13] Teachers in the new schools were quick to observe, "Social maturity comes faster here for children like this. The adjustment to the group doesn't seem to involve so many problems for them. I have noticed that they seem to get the feeling that nobody is the boss—there is a feeling of complete cooperation. Partly this comes from early exposure to court play."[14] Parents are prone to worry about the elementary school's over permissiveness. At a PTA meeting a committee proudly agreed that learning is a "painless process." The teacher and the pupils plan together and everyone has a conscious feeling of belonging—as an individual and as a group participant."[15] The schools tend to stress the development of the whole child and skimp on academics. Parents in Park Forest agree, "The primary job of the high school should be to teach students how to be citizens and how to get along with other people."[16]

In Park Forest the response to rootlessness is involvement in community

12. *Ibid.*, p. 399.
13. *Ibid.*, p. 423.
14. *Ibid.*, p. 424.
15. *Ibid.*, p. 427.
16. *Ibid.*, p. 434.

activities that often take precedence over family activities. The school, the church, the community clubs are vigorously supported by individual family members—not by the family as a whole. Individuals, however, often behave as though they are afraid to "go it alone." They are not only other-directed, to use David Riesman's phrase, but they believe that it is right to be so. This dependence of the individual upon persons and organizations outside of the conjugal or extended family contrasts rather vividly with the common conception of the middle-class family given in Chapter 6.

Old Harbor: A somewhat different picture of suburbia emerges in the account of Old Harbor, a New England village that became inundated by suburbanites shortly after World War II.[17] In ten years (1945–1955) it doubled its population. Like Park Forest, it was studied in the 1950s.

Old Harbor is a two hour drive from New York. It is thus somewhat farther from the urban core than is Park Forest. The 8:05 commuter train provides the major means of transportation into New York. The suburban housing that rings the village starts at $22,500. The suburbanites who occupy these homes are a "high income group ($9,700) of professional men and executives. Ninety-seven percent arrived in Old Harbor married and almost ninety-four percent bought homes there."[18] They are typically protestant, have two children, and usually have at least a college education. About half commute to New York; another third work in the county adjacent to Old Harbor. The "old timers" have less income (1955 median $6,700), are middle-aged, are generally high school educated, and are in the process of sending their children to college. Suburbanites see Old Harbor quite differently than do the old-timers, or villagers:

> *I came to Old Harbor because there is still some green around here, and yet I can still get to the airport in 45 minutes. It's a nice place to live— the schools are good, and I like being near the water. It is hard to say how long we'll be here. I would like to be based further south.*
>
> *I can't think of Old Harbor as my own town or anything like that. Most of my friends live closer to the city and I work there. I don't have any feeling of living in a small community or anything like that. I guess I sleep more of my time here than anything else, but it's a good place for the kids. I've got a lot of contacts and interests outside.*
>
> *I have to go pretty much where the company sends me. I was transferred up to the office over a year ago so we bought a place out here in Old Harbor. Probably be here for three or four years then most likely I'll be sent to South America. We like Old Harbor, although the way it's building up, it will be like the city in no time. Well, it doesn't bother me much; we won't be around forever.*[19]

The Old Harbor husband-father is, therefore, a stage or so ahead of Park Forest men in his career. He has a greater command over resources and a

---

17. This account is based on the study presented in Dobriner *op. cit.*, pp. 127–42.
18. *Ibid.*, p. 134.
19. *Ibid.*, pp. 135–36.

much broader occupational horizon. The community of Old Harbor is not a place where he typically wants to find roots or encounter other people. His attitude contrasts with that of the old-time villagers who have their roots here and resent the transients' indifference.

The suburbanites have taken over the PTA and the civic organizations, while the villagers retain control of the traditional political parties and the churches. The interests of the two groups do not coincide, and conflict is constant. The villagers call for a new parish house; the suburbanites, a new school gymnasium.

Dobriner contrasts Old Harbor with Levittown, Long Island—a working-to middle-class suburb. "The Levittowns are fresh and naked, yet marked by a growing heterogeneity. The Old Harbors are split by the struggle of two communities to shape the prevailing character of the whole."[20] Yet the future is with the suburbanites, and the character of Old Harbor has changed to the hustle and bustle of the shopping centers and super highways that link it with the city.

The Exurbanites of Rockland County: Finally, A. C. Spectorsky describes the condition of a group of Madison Avenue exiles who have moved several miles further down the commuter line from New York than the average suburbanite (see Fig. 7–2) and yet remain quite attached to the city.[21] Even more than the executives of Old Harbor, these men and their families look to the city not only for their income, but for the definition of their style of life, and the center of what is happening in the world. The exurbanite earns a rock bottom minimum of $12,000 a year (1955). He is:

> . . . a displaced New Yorker. He has moved from the city to the country . . . [and] for him the change is an exile. He will never quite completely permit himself to be absorbed into the new surroundings; he never will acclimate. He may join the Parent-Teacher Association in his new home, he may attend town meetings, he will almost surely try his hand at gardening or farming; but spiritually he will always be urban, an irreconcilable whose step, after walking a hundred country lanes, is still steadiest when it returns to the familiar crowded crosswalks of Madison Avenue. Resident in the country he may be, under any of several estimable devices, e.g., "The School System is better," "It's great to get away from that carbon monoxide," "I'm a new man since I got into the rhythm of the seasons," but the customs that were his in the city remain his in the country.[22]

The exurbanite is typically an idea man—a fad setter for the masses although he may regard with derision the fashion he pushes. He is, despite his ties with the city, convinced that his move to the country has fulfilled—or at

20. *Ibid.*, p. 140.
21. This account is based on the study by A. C. Spectorsky, "The Exurbanites" in *Analysis of Contemporary Society II*, Bernard Rosenberg (ed.), (New York: Cromwell, 1967), pp. 211–59.
22. *Ibid.*, p. 219.

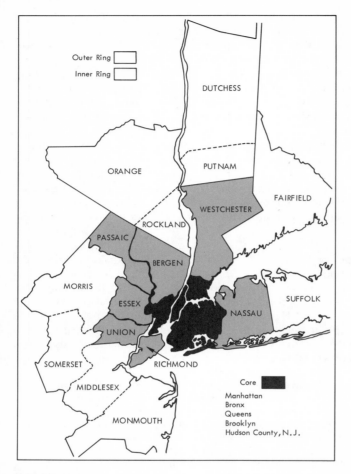

FIGURE 7–2
*The greater New York area, divided into three zones on the basis of land
development. In the mid-fifties 9 percent of the Core, 45 percent of the
Inner Ring, and 80 percent of the Outer Ring (which included
Rockland County) was available for development. Adapted from Edgar M.
Hoover and Raymond Vernon,* The Anatomy of a Metropolis *(Harvard
University Press, The Regional Plan Association, 1959).*

least pushed him toward fulfillment of—his dream, the escape from the rat-race.

The exurbanite is a rugged man. He must get up, dress, and eat break-fast at least an hour before his urban counterparts. He rides a train for at least a half hour, then copes with the traffic of Manhattan. Meanwhile, his wife, having gotten the children off to school on the bus—or driven them herself —is lonely. Take Bill and Joan:

> *When Bill is gone for the day, and the kids are in school, Joan always feels terribly alone. Sometimes this alone-feeling is accompanied by a sense of relief, sometimes she looks forward to the peaceful hours. But far more frequently Joan has to do a daily job on herself of reorientation to sudden solitude and of self-administered morale lecturing. No urban wife is ever so isolated.*[23]

Of course, Joan has much more housework to do than when she lived in the city. She must also spend a much longer time in transporting herself and her family around their country retreat—Bill to the station, the children to Scouts, herself to the supermarket—indeed almost everything that she needs requires her driving to get it. She also must become a self-styled maintenance man, because when things break down, it takes a bit of time to get them repaired, and there is no man around the house to help. She prepares for Bill's return by a rather dramatic staging of cocktails and attentiveness for the weary traveler that screens out her day of lonely monotony. Joan dreams her secret dream of doing something creative, but the children and the tasks demanded of her keep her occupied and yet alone. Spectorsky generalizes:

> *. . . the wife who moved to the exurbs at some time since 1948 is in her thirties or early forties, and looks younger. She has, usually, two children, although there are many families with three or more. She may have come here from anywhere in the country. . . . She may have married before the war; she may have married during the war; she may have married twice. In any case, the probability is that she experienced the dislocations of the war. . . . At some point before her marriage, she had a job. . . . She cheerfully, even gratefully, exchanged her career for marriage and eagerly undertook the job of both making a home and being a fit intellectual companion for her husband (or, more usually, of maintaining rather more intellectual interests than her husband). After her first-hand experiences at trying to make a home in wartime, or struggling with New York apartments, she was delighted with the idea of moving to the country. . . . For her the move came far closer to an unlimited dream: here, at last, was the opportunity to make a permanent home.*[24]

The dream has dulled amid the unsolved problems of the suburbs. The servant problem is acute and apparently unresolvable, her family has increased in size, and the separation from her husband has forced her to assume a great deal of responsibility not otherwise likely to have fallen to her. When her husband comes home, he brings office work with him, or he is tired and watches TV. He has had a good day or a bad day, but he has no

23. *Ibid.*, p. 224.
24. *Ibid.*, pp. 228–30.

tangible product against which to measure his success, and so his wife must be able to support him in the midst of his anxieties. She, better than he, knows that they are living beyond their means because she manages the household account. She must console him while finding no consolation for herself.

Typically, the sex lives of exurbanites leave much to be desired. His job confronts him with young, attractive females during his waking and productive hours. He faces his wife full of the day's anxieties and ready to sleep. Under such circumstances the exurbanite couple can easily grow apart. "Exurban physicians whose general practice brings them often in contact with exurban wives report that a most frequent complaint they make is that their husbands are sexually inadequate."[25]

As the boredom and impatience grow, there are a number of alternate coping strategies open to the exurban wife. Divorce is not as common as one might suspect. Spectorsky argues that it is lower than the national average. This is because many of these marriages are second marriages and divorce hasn't proved to be the answer in the past; and then there are the children and the home and the remembered romantic love that might be saved. Instead, exurban wives typically devote themselves to one of five areas in which they expend an inordinate amount of energy: the home, the children, drinking, outside interests, and sexual dalliance. Each area requires a design for living—a coping strategy for fighting boredom.

Children are not cut off from these problems:

> *The tensions of exurban life and marriage penetrate the child's world in uncountable ways. For some, the end-result is anxious overprotectiveness in their mothers, for others it is distracted neglect, punctuated by oral assurances that "Mummy loves you very, very much dearest—come give Mummy a big kiss." But a child needs more evidence than this that Mummy hasn't her own concerns uppermost in mind most of the time. Perhaps the most common parental attitude which adversely affects the exurban child is permissiveness. The exurban mother is frequently so permissive that her children have no structured home life to which they can adjust themselves. With no framework on which to lean, or to fight, or to accept, the children often display socially unserviceable modes of behavior, in part out of knowledge that it will, at least, elicit some definite response from mother.[26]*

A large number of exurbanites eventually dismiss their secret dream as youthful fantasy, and the limited dream is accepted "as being the best possible in this best of all possible worlds."[27] The husband has reached his niche in the hierarchy where he feels relatively secure, and the wife, now that the children have left, finds the house more of a pleasure and experiences

25. *Ibid.*, p. 234.
26. *Ibid.*, p. 258.
27. *Ibid.*, p. 259.

"muted contentment." A second group of wives attempt the impossible. They try to go back to work, finding themselves out of touch, much less attractive, and unable to adjust to the demands of the job.

Clearly the life styles of these middle-class families are affected by their specific settings as well as by their class culture. They are alike and yet different because of the special problems with which they must cope. Such descriptions serve partially to qualify any generalizations we might wish to make about middle-class families. They must be borne in mind as we explore the functional model presented below.

The Functions of the Suburban Middle-Class Family

The relationship of the suburban family to its social environment can be better understood if we examine how it handles its economic, political, socialization, educational, sexual-reproductive, and religious functions.[28] These functions are partially shaped by the problems peculiar to a family's immediate environment; given other social needs and constraints, a family will respond somewhat differently. Yet certain broad patterns should obtain.

ECONOMIC

The fact that the economic function is almost entirely the responsibility of the husband-father in the upper-middle class and is characteristically fulfilled at some distance from the home has a number of consequences for family life. (1) During the week the suburb is composed predominantly of women and children. (2) Men who work in the suburb tend to be older, have resided longer in the community, and have less education than those who commute. (3) The task of spending the family income is largely delegated to the wife-mother. (4) There are few jobs available in the community for women and children, thus accentuating their dependence upon the husband-father.

It would seem to follow that the extent to which the husband-father can participate in the life of the family is severely restricted by the time he spends on the job and in commuting. Winch argues that families move to the suburbs in order to live the good life. This would seem consistent with our case studies. And yet the time the family can spend together is often reduced by the move to the suburb, not only by the father's commuting time but also by many other factors largely involved with transporting family members to their various activities. Suburbanites are often joiners, and these activities disrupt their family life.

Further and more critically, the nature of a career as opposed to a job places the professional under quite different demands. He can opt for the

28. The following section draws heavily on Chap. 6, "Suburbia," in Winch *op. cit.*

good life at some expense to his career—usually a willingness to forego promotion or the making of a name for himself in his profession. This seems to be the route of many persons described in *The Organization Man* who reach a comfortable level of middle-management and decide to stay there. On the other hand, if a professional opts for his career and the decision to "make a contribution," then in order to be successful, he must sacrifice his family. Only those who work a "forty-hour week" with adequate income can control the amount of time they spend "on the job" as well as be relatively free from the occupational anxieties that carry over after hours.

There seems to be considerable disagreement on the financial situation of these families. Spectorsky considers them to be living far beyond their means and discusses a hypothetical exurbanite named Barber who overspent his $25,000 annual income by $7,000. He contends that men like Barber who are typical of exurbia must "operate on the necessity to earn more each year. . . . It is typically exurban to really believe that everyone else is doing better than oneself, or that those who appear not to be are intelligently budgeted, so that they live, if not well, at least in solvency."[29] So driven *men* take on extra work but wives, as a rule, do not work.

The upper-middle-class family is kept constantly on a treadmill as far as their consumer habits are concerned by their desire to acquire what Riesman and Rosenborough have called the "standard package" of consumer goods. The contents of the package are expanded as former luxuries become necessities. The content varies by region, ethnic group, life style, and class. The middle class assumes that its families will possess the minimum of an automobile or automobiles, furniture, television, radios, refrigerator-freezer, and standard brands of food and clothing. This standard package is easily transportable around the country and up the socioeconomic ladder. Furthermore, children are taught to expect this package when they reach adulthood; they want it *with* marriage and not after a few years of saving:

> *The process begins early in life when, via television and the movies, children learn what the components of the package are and witness their parents' desire to own them. The children are undergoing what sociologists call "anticipatory socialization," a process of role-playing and fantasy which leads them to anticipate the conditions of adulthood and to respond to those conditions in a predetermined way.*[30]

Although LeMasters contends that "this is the most comfortable position in the American social class system,"[31] he does concede that there are a few difficulties associated with the functioning of this family. First of all parents do not have enough wealth to ensure the status of their children as is the

29. Spectorsky *op. cit.*, p. 155.
30. Gerald R. Leslie, *The Family in the Social Context* (New York: Oxford University Press, 1967), p. 271.
31. E. E. LeMasters, *Parents in Modern America: A Sociological Analysis* (Homewood, Ill.: Dorsey, 1970), pp. 88–89.

case in the higher classes. Children have to earn their status each generation —yet in LeMasters' study this does not seem to produce any great anxiety in the children. Second, the father's career frequently takes him out of the house.

Another difficulty arises out of the fact that a business executive often enjoys a higher standard of living on the job than he does at home:

> The husband who travels on an expense account, for example, often lives much better on the road than his family can afford to live at home. He travels first class, has deluxe accommodations, eats expensive meals and so on. In the meantime his wife, who would like very much to share his good fortune, is stuck at home caring for the children, one of whom often has a cold or is otherwise difficult to manage, and eating TV dinners or the equivalent. The wife resents her husband's privileges, or at least her inability to share in them, and for his part, the husband must feign dislike for having to travel.[32]

This contrast in life styles places additional strains on upwardly mobile families.

A final comment about the economic function of the upper-middle class family concerns the growing inclination over the past decade to "do-it-yourself." Winch discounts its economic value—indeed it is more likely an economic liability even though the home craftsman frequently embarks on his tinkering career under the rationalization that it will "save money in the long run." Its positive contribution to the family may lie in the opportunities it creates "for members of families to interact in the accomplishment of some usually useful task."[33]

THE BALANCE OF POWER IN THE FAMILY

Blood and Wolfe contend that suburban families are more husband dominated than are urban families because the suburban wife sees herself as indebted to her husband for having moved her to their beautiful home.[34] This line of reasoning would be in keeping with the notion discussed above that suburban wives are more economically dependent upon their husbands, and it is consonant with the observation that wives more than husbands tend to be in favor of the move to the suburbs for the sake of the children.

On the other hand, a more common view asserts that because of the separation of the husband's job from the home and its immediate environs, the wife exercises greater domestic power. She spends the family income, she makes many of the minor decisions on the upkeep of the house (and sometimes assumes the role of repair man herself), she must decide how the children are to be taken care of, and she ordinarily keeps the social calendar

32. Leslie *op. cit.*, p. 274.
33. Winch *op. cit.*, p. 165.
34. Robert O. Blood and Donald M. Wolfe, *Husbands & Wives* (Glencoe, Ill.: Free Press, 1960), p. 36.

and thus often decides who is going to be entertained and when, and when the family is going out for its entertainment. The particularly acute plight of the exurbanite wife is described by Spectorsky:

> *The exurban wife early learns that she and she alone will cope with emergencies confronting her, the house, the car, or the children. She early grows familiar with the answer that will be given on the phone should she call New York. (The answer is: "Look honey, don't bother me now, will you? I'm busy.") The result is that when Penny falls out of a tree and fractures her skull, the exurban mother has the car out and Penny in it, has driven to the hospital sixteen miles away, and made sure that everything is under control and Penny out of danger before she will call New York and tell Penny's father what has happened. In an exurb, where houses are usually widely separated from each other, the mother is strictly on her own.*[35]

While she was probably in favor of the move to the suburbs, she had little control over when the family would move, and she may have to move again soon depending upon the demands of her husband's job. She, likewise, has little choice about which city the family will move to next.

There is another dimension of control that needs to be explored: the family's relationship to its community in the upper-middle-class suburb. Spectorsky paints a picture of minimal involvement. Dobriner, speaking about Old Harbor, contrasts the suburbanites who have taken over the PTA and civic organizations with the old-timers who control the churches and the traditional political parties. Park Foresters seem to be fully involved in their community.

The nature of community control over the family is—perhaps more than any other aspect of the political function of the family—a matter that is affected by the specific type of upper-middle-class suburb that is under consideration. What is true for the new mass-produced suburb like Park Forest does not necessarily apply to the older more established suburb, to the rather special situation of the exurbanites surrounding New York, or to the dilemmas of a reluctant suburb such as Old Harbor, where an original core village was rather rapidly inundated by suburbanites. In each case, there seem to be quite different demands made upon the family.

In Park Forest community control results from intensive interaction among families living in close proximity. Everyone is in everyone else's hair so much so that privacy is a major problem and conformity seems maximized. Whyte thus could characterize this suburb as a "projection of dormitory life into adulthood," and "a sorority house with kids."[36] In such a community parents can count upon neighbors for support, and there is a sense of security for the wife and children when the professional husband-father is called away on business.

In the isolated homes of exurbia, however, no such support can be

---

35. Spectorsky *op. cit.*, pp. 230–31.
36. Whyte, *Organization Man*, p. 280.

counted upon, and interaction between families is minimal. The daily *Kaf-feklatsch* is rare indeed. In Rockland County, Spectorsky writes, "the fettish is nonconformity, individuality, and originality."[37] In Rockland County, joining and communal enterprises are virtually unknown.

Dobriner's description of Old Harbor seems to place the rate of interaction somewhere between the extremes of Park Forest and Rockland County. Bennett Berger provides further contrast by observing that in his working-class suburb there was a minimum of interaction with neighbors because the extended family was quite functional. He quotes one informant, "I don't think it pays to have a lot of friends, maybe because we have so many relatives."[38]

We can conclude then that the factors that promote a high level of interaction such as that of Park Forest are: (1) a young community consisting of (2) young couples with children (3) with a common sense of rootlessness and of "being in the same boat" and (4) similar incomes and career objectives who (5) live in a mass-produced housing development that structurally encourages interaction. (6) The relatively low incomes of these incipient upper-middle-class families in the early stages of their development encourages instrumental help patterns and promotes greater functional interdependence. Such a pattern is not typical of upper-middle-class suburbs, much less of suburbia generally. Winch comments "In a new community there is a disposition to form friendships on the basis of residential propinquity but in established communities, friendships tend to follow similarities in education, occupation, income and the like."[39]

The ability of the upper-middle-class family to control its children is poorly documented. The isolation of the conjugal unit and its great mobility tend to work against parental effectiveness. Then, too, the inclination of upper-middle-class parents to raise their children "by the book" confronts them at one time with fads favoring permissiveness and at another, strict discipline. This subject will be dealt with in some detail in Chapters 9 and 13.

SOCIALIZATION AND EDUCATION

A number of studies have demonstrated that child-rearing practices vary significantly according to socioeconomic class. Middle-class parents more frequently discipline by withdrawing love than by using physical punishment. In general, the mother is expected to be supportive and the father the enforcer of constraints. Melvin Kohn has refined these concepts and related them more precisely to the occupational demands made upon persons in the middle class. He argues that parents in all classes socialize their children in accordance with their experience as to what constitutes successful behavior. This is

---

37. Spectorsky, *op. cit.*, p. 64.
38. Bennett Berger, *A Working Class Suburb* (Berkeley: University of California Press, 1960), p. 68.
39. Winch *op. cit.*, p. 168.

to a great extent future oriented, since it attempts to shape present behavior in terms of what is presumed will be successful when the children are adults. But the differences in child rearing result because parents' goals and experiences are different. Working-class fathers, especially, have found that conformity to the rules of the job has payed off best for them. Upper-middle-class fathers value self-direction and try to instill this quality in their children. Having some assurance that their careers will be profitable, the upper-middle class can strive to find work that is interesting, stimulating, challenging, and permits self-expression. The career must have intrinsic merit as well as monetary reward. In the performance of their tasks, professionals are characteristically expected to apply general principles to specific cases without precise guidelines. They must exercise good judgment; hence, they value their children's capacity to make good judgments, and they particularly value this capacity in their sons.

Kohn analyzes men's job preferences on the basis of social class:

> *Essentially, men of higher class position judge jobs more by intrinsic qualities, men of lower class positions, more by extrinsic characteristics. That is, the higher men's social class, the more importance they attach to how interesting the work is, the amount of freedom you have, the chance to help people, and the chance to use your abilities. The lower their class position, the more importance they attach to pay, fringe benefits, the supervisor, the co-workers, the hours of work, how tiring the work is, job security, and not being under too much pressure.*[40]

So also there appears to be a quite different orientation toward society that is reflected in occupational requirements. A belief that change can be for the good implies a certain trust in one's fellow man and the system that is derived from the experience of being personally successful—that is, of having changed things for the better in one's own case. On the other hand, the conformist's orientation is more that any change is a change for the worse. Kohn found that these generalizations were supported by his data. Upper-middle-class persons were comparatively low on authoritarian conservatism, were high on trustfulness, acknowledged a personal morality, and were receptive to change.

Finally, significant differences in self-attitude were discernible. Higher-class men were comparatively high on self-confidence, low on self-deprecation, considered themselves accountable for their actions, were comparatively less anxious, and saw themselves as generally holding independent ideas.

A tendency to value change is not generalizable to all situations in the upper-middle class. This kind of change that is referred to in Kohn's study is associated with creativity which, of course, is bounded by cultural and class definitions. Few upper-middle-class persons value change that would alter the current distribution of goods and services in favor of a more equalitarian society.

40. Melvin Kohn, *Class and Conformity* (Homewood, Ill.: Dorsey, 1970), p. 76.

Since schooling plays such an important role in the careers of upper-middle-class persons, they tend to pick their home neighborhood by the reported quality of the school. Suburbanites spend more on schooling than urbanites. (Table 7–3). Indeed, Wood argues that the greatest expenditure on the budget of the average suburb is the school appropriation. Consequently, the most important function of suburban governments is to obtain quality schooling.[41]

Table 7–3 suggests something of the inequality in education that can be expected in urban as compared with suburban schools (if per capita expenditure reflects the quality of education). In seven out of the twelve cities listed, suburban per capita income from state sources is greater than urban, and in only three instances is the urban per capita income greater. In one of these,

41. Robert C. Wood, *Suburbia: Its People and Their Politics* (Boston: Houghton Mifflin, 1958), p. 187.

TABLE 7–3
*Comparison of Revenues per Pupil from State Sources for Inner City
and Suburban Schools*

| Place | Amount per pupil: | | Percent increase: |
	1950	1964	1950–64
Baltimore City	$ 71	$171	140.8%
Suburbs	90	199	121.1
Birmingham City	90	201	123.3
Suburbs	54	150	177.7
Boston City	19	53	173.7
Suburbs	30	75	150.0
Buffalo City	135	284	110.0
Suburbs	165	270	63.6
Chattanooga City	62	136	119.4
Suburbs	141	152	7.8
Chicago City	42	154	266.6
Suburbs	32	110	243.8
Cincinnati City	51	81	78.4
Suburbs	78	91	16.7
Cleveland City	50	88	76.0
Suburbs	89	88	125.6
Detroit City	135	189	40.0
Suburbs	140	240	61.1
New Orleans City	152	239	57.2
Suburbs	117	259	121.4
St. Louis City	70	131	87.1
Suburbs	61	143	194.4
San Francisco City	122	163	83.6
Suburbs	160	261	63.1

Source: U.S. Commission on Civil Rights, Racial Isolation in the Public Schools.

however, the suburban schools are gaining rapidly on the urban schools as indicated by a much greater percentage increase in per capita income over the period 1950–1964. On the average, incomes of suburbanites exceed those of urbanites.[42]

Supporting the schools in the formal aspects of education are numerous character building organizations such as the Scouts, the "Y", church schools, and various day camps in the summer. In addition, private lessons in music, dancing, and the arts frequently supplement the formal learning imposed upon suburban children. But basically there are the schools:

> The suburbanites . . . are educational radicals; they are irrepressible spenders and cult-like in their dedication to the cause of modern education. It is an axiom among the oldtimers that the more costly a pending proposition is the more newcomers will take to it, and they are not entirely wrong. The newcomers appear willing to sacrifice all else to their children's education.[43]

Spectorsky points out that in exurbia, the schools perform another important function—relief of boredom for the wives:

> . . . There is always something for an unhappy exurban wife to do. Husbands are infrequently involved in PTA meetings, but the wives find them a fine outlet. If, occasionally, they can involve a husband or two in committee work, so much the better, but with or without husbands the wives can spend an heroic number of woman-hours in one phase or another of school life. There are charity bazaars, there are surveys to be taken of new schools, there are battles to be waged against the township's politicians, there are psychologists to be interviewed and hired, there are schools to be planned and built, and so on and on.[44]

Many upper-middle-class parents send their sons and daughters to good private schools and yet may react negatively to the education that their children receive because it is sometimes quite critical of their way of life.[45] They take it for granted that when they say they have "no plans" for their son or daughter in regard to an occupation or a college, they really mean that any occupation is "all right" so long as it is a professional or business career; and any school is "ok" so long as it is a good school. It is further assumed that their daughters will marry the right young men (from their own or a higher class), and this is usually accomplished by sending her to the right school. LeMasters contends that families that have become well established in the upper-middle class (that is, are at least second-generation upper-middle class) feel generally freer about their children's choice of occupation and school and will be more likely to permit their daughters to have a career.[46]

42. Winch, *op. cit.*, p. 159.
43. Dobriner, *op. cit.*, p. 137.
44. Spectorsky *op. cit.*, p. 250.
45. See a brief discussion in LeMasters *op. cit.*, p. 91.
46. *Loc. cit.*

Because many upper-middle-class professionals handle people rather than things, their informally acquired skills in interpersonal relations are perhaps as important as their "academic" skills. An assumption of the liberal arts *tradition* in university education, furthermore, is that the scholar—because in most cases he comes from the upper-middle or upper classes and does not have to worry about finding a job—does not *have* to be trained for a career in college. In college he is to understand himself and his society in the broadest possible perspective. He will learn the skills that are directly relevant to his career in graduate school or with the company that hires him. Thus neither the family nor the school, in the case of many an upper-middle-class male, primarily provides professional training. They hope to refine his insights and attitudes, increase his capacity to solve problems of a most general sort, and facilitate his ability to relate to people in order to provide that vaguely defined element of "leadership," or simply (and less altruistically) to provide him with the ability to manipulate others for his own personal gain.

While the matter of who controls the PTA must be a variable, in some instances it seems that the parents, who were once agents of the church, enjoined to bring up their children in the "right way," now find themselves (in some suburbs) agents of the school.

> Their parents want to know how they have fared at school: they are constantly comparing them, judging them in school aptitude, popularity, what part they have in the school play; are the boys sissies? the girls too fat? . . . After school there are music lessons, skating lessons, riding lessons, with mother as chauffeur and scheduler. In the evening, the children go to a dance at school for which the parents have groomed them, while the parents go to a PTA meeting for which the children directly or indirectly have groomed them, where they are addressed by a psychiatrist who advises them to be warm and relaxed in handling their children! They go home and eagerly and warmly ask their returning children to tell them everything that happened at the dance, making it clear by their manner that they are sophisticated and cannot easily be shocked. As Professor Seely describes matters, the school in this community (Crestwood Heights) operates a gigantic factory for the production of relationships.[47]

Thus, while the upper-middle-class family has delegated much of its educational function to the school, the parents are increasingly co-opted into the service of the school via the PTA, the cooperative preschool, and the private lesson syndrome. So also as Miller and Swanson have pointed out: "The family is again the school for the job, only now it is the school for the job's human relations, not its technical skill." It is, therefore, not sufficient simply to assert that the family has lost most of its educational function. It seems truer—in the case of the upper-middle class—to assert that it has changed the character of its involvement in the education of its children. Now

47. David Reisman, "Some Observations on Changes in Leisure Attitudes," in *Selected Essays from Individualism Reconsidered* (New York: Doubleday, 1955), pp. 136–37.

it provides skills in human relations as does the school and also assumes considerable responsibility for maintaining and upgrading the quality of education provided by the schools. This often involves much personal time as well as willingness to support higher school taxes. Having delegated the teaching of specific skills to qualified experts, upper-middle-class parents do not, and perhaps cannot, simply let go. They participate fervently in the process of education and attempt to assure that their children will receive a good education.

SEX AND REPRODUCTION

Marriage is a dominating life goal for most Americans. More than nine out of every ten eventually marry and most spend the majority of their lives in the married state. This is particularly true of the upper classes. As income increases, the number of men who have ever been married increases until, for those men who earn over $10,000 a year (1968), 96.3 percent are, or have been, married (Figure 7–3).

And yet, while in 1948 "spinster" and "bachelor" had quite negative connotations associated with sexual frustration and eccentricity, bachelorhood for the upper-income male is becoming increasingly acceptable and the "posh bachelor pads" quite popular. College educated women, meanwhile,

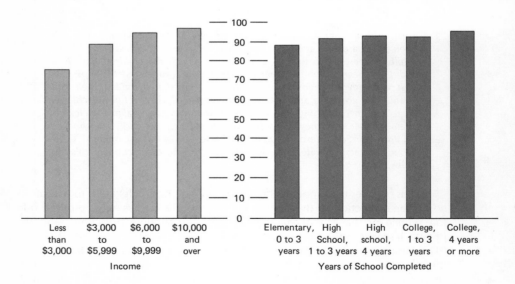

FIGURE 7–3
Percentages of married men, ages 45-54, with spouses present, by income (1967) and education (1968), Adapted from Population Characteristics *(U.S.G.P.O., 1969), p. 1.*

are beginning to establish careers as a viable alternative to marriage, and the median age at first marriage is slowly and uncertainly increasing since the low of the mid-1950s.

The meaning of marriage is changing, particularly for families of the upper-middle class. What was once widely regarded as a sacred binding together of two persons ("Those whom God hath joined together, let no man put asunder") is increasingly being considered a social or personal affair. The personal happiness of the spouses is a major concern, and young people frequently come to marriage with the expectation that it will bring them the happiness that has been so illusive during their unmarried lives. Whatever loss there is in romantic attraction after marriage should be more than compensated for by increasing satisfaction in parenthood. These expectations are simply extensions of the commonly accepted Western emphasis on love and free personal choice in the selection of a mate. Therefore, young people may enter marriage on a trial basis—despite the problems associated with this approach.

Although it is still probably accurate to assert that the norm of the upper-middle-class family holds that sex relationships should be confined to marriage, with the advent of effective contraceptives and an emerging emphasis on the positive value of bodily pleasures, sexual intercourse is becoming increasingly separated from reproductive functions and marriage. Since the lower class has not generally adhered to the norms linking sex and marriage, the sexual revolution is to a large extent a phenomenon of the upper-middle class, particularly among the younger members of this class. The characteristics of this rather complex transformation in sexual behavior will be the subject of Chapter 12.

Whatever the effect on behavior, it is clearly an ideological revolution that has made it possible for upper-middle-class wife-swappers to express their convictions freely through the mass media. These persons assert that, contrary to our cherished convictions, it is both possible and desirable for life-long monogamy *not* to involve the exclusive sexual rights to the spouse. Extra-marital sex need not be promiscuous, they assert, since it is usually limited to a relatively few persons. At any rate, the Sexual Freedom League, the Playboy Philosophy, key parties, and wife-swapping seem to be aimed more at the upper-middle class. Taken at their best, they reflect an attempt to deal with the problems facing such families in their quest for happiness.

The studies of the three different types of suburban communities do not help us much in evaluating the quality of married sexuality in the middle class. Whyte assures us that in Park Forest extra-marital affairs and wife-swapping occurred but were atypical and that the court was the greatest control mechanism since the chastity belt. Dobriner does not dwell on the matter of marital satisfaction. Spectorsky suggests that the married sexual life of the exurbanite is poor and that extra-marital affairs are common, especially for the men.

Perhaps the best study of upper-middle-class man-woman relationships to date is that of John F. Cuber and Peggy B. Harroff. On the basis of extended interviews with 437 professional men and women (whom Cuber and Harroff call "Significant Americans") between the ages of thirty-five and fifty-five, the authors conclude:

> . . . there are very few good man-woman relationships at these ages in this class. We mean by good . . . deeply satisfying man-woman relationships as appraised by the people themselves. . . . Further, of the good relationships that do exist, there is a surprisingly high incidence of them outside of marriage . . . either as enduring, relatively total associations among the unmarried, or as is more often the case, extramarital in the sense that one or both in the pair are married to someone else.[48]

Cuber and Harroff describe five types of relationships discernible among the Significant Americans: (1) The *conflict-habituated relationship* in which there is much controlled tension and conflict. Conflict is the basis of their togetherness. Rather than break up under the strain, such relationships frequently persist for a lifetime. (2) *The devitalized relationship* which is perceptably devoid of zest. Although no serious tension or conflict may exist, and some aspects of the marriage may be actively satisfying, the interplay between the conjugal pair is apathetic, lifeless, and will continue partly out of habit and partly out of the recognition that "something is there." (3) *Passive-congenial relationships* in which the existing modes of association are "comfortably adequate." "We both like classical music." "We agree completely on religion and politics." "We both love the country and our quaint exurban neighbors." "We are both lawyers." These are characteristic foci of the relationship. When these three relationships are between persons who are married to each other, they are called *utilitarian* marriages. (4) *Vital relationships* are ones in which there is a "vibrant exciting sharing of some important life experience—sex comes immediately to the mind, but the vitality need not surround the sexual focus or any aspect of it. . . . The clue that their relationship is vital and significant derives from the feelings of importance about it and that that importance is shared." (5) *Total relationships* are very rare. They are like the vital relationships in that the relationship is itself significant to the couple, but they differ in the extent to which life experiences are shared. In the total relationship a much wider sharing occurs. These last two are, in the case of the married, called *intrinsic relationships.*[49]

A significant difference between the intrinsic relationships and the utilitarian relationships is that the latter finds no use for "male-female stuff":

> A large proportion of the Significant Americans live in a diffuse marital arrangement which, they explained so often, they consider to be rational and satisfying. Their justification of it is simply that it works well for

48. John F. Cuber and Peggy B. Harroff, "The More Total View: Relationships Among Men and Women of the Upper Middle Class," in *Marriage, Family and Society* Hyman Rodman (ed.), (New York: Random House, 1965), p. 102.

49. *Ibid.*, pp. 100–102.

> *them. . . . There is a common element: "male-female stuff," joyful sex, close companionship, deep emotional involvement are not of major importance and are only occasionally present.*[50]

The effect of the sexual revolution on this sample seems to be relatively insignificant. "Many remain clearly ascetic where sex is concerned. Others are simply asexual. For still others sex is overlaid with such strong hostility that an antisexual orientation is clear."[51]

Nevertheless, for the married, infidelity is common but extra-marital involvements have meanings that differ according to the type of marital relationship a person has experienced. Infidelity occurs in all types (except the total relationship). In the conflict-habituated relationship infidelity seems to be only another outlet for hostility. Among the passive-congenial it is typically in line with the stereotype of the middle-aged man who "strayed out of sheer boredom with the uneventful, deadly prose" of his private life. The devitalized are frequently trying to recapture a lost mood. The vital, however, are sometimes adulterous too. Some are simply "emancipated—almost bohemian." To some, sexual aggrandizement is an accepted fact of life. "Frequently the infidelity is condoned by the partner and in some instances even provides an indirect (through empathy) kind of gratification. The act of infidelity in such cases is not construed as disloyalty, nor is it a threat to continuity of the relationship . . . it is simply a basic human right" which the loved one ought to be permitted to have—and which the other perhaps also wants for himself.[52] Since the latter two types of marriages, the vital and the total, were estimated to constitute but a small portion of the sample, the Cuber and Harroff data seem quite consistent with the view of exurbia described by Spectorsky.

On the other hand, the middle-class wife seems to enjoy her sexual relations with her husband to a greater extent than do wives of the lower classes, as indicated in Table 7–4. In line with the notion that personal happiness is to be sought in marriage, women in the upper classes are increasingly likely to *expect* enjoyment from sexual intercourse, while in the working and lower classes, sexual relations are more of a matter of obligation and more closely linked to the procreation of children. For the 50 percent of the middle-class wives who do not stress the enjoyment of sexual relations, it may be that in part this is because they have greater expectations of enjoyment.

RELIGION

Upper-middle-class families are predominantly protestant. After the Park Forest tradition, some suburbs have interdenominational chapels that cater to those who have gotten into the habit of "shopping around" for a church and

---

50. John F. Cuber and Peggy B. Harroff, *Sex and the Significant Americans* (Baltimore: Penguin, 1968), p. 175.
51. *Loc. cit.*
52. *Ibid.*, p. 62.

TABLE 7–4
Wife's Gratification in Sexual Relations

		Very positive	Positive	Slightly negative*	Rejection
Middle Class	(58)	50%	36%	11%	3%
Upper-Lower Class	(68)	53	16	27	4
Lower-Lower Class	(69)	20	26	34	20

Source: Lee Rainwater, *Family Design* (Chicago: Aldine, 1965), p. 64.

find one protestant denomination about as meaningful as another. Convenience frequently dictates choice of church. Whyte characterizes the religion of Park Forest as "social, pragmatic and useful"; Spectorsky sees a "subtle amorality" in the ethics of exurbanites; and Dobriner muses, "For many, education seems to have taken the place of religion."[53] In such suburbs, the language of adjustment—peace of mind, good mental health—takes precedence over the language of traditional theology. "Sin" and "Grace" are rarely heard.

The family is not the focal point of the religious life. Grace at meals, evening prayers for the children, and the reading of the Bible are not characteristics of upper-middle-class families. The church school is supposed to provide the children with religion. Many upper-middle-class parents drop their children off at church school and pick them up afterward, without attending themselves. Other families join the church as they join any of the numerous voluntary organizations in their community. They expect it to provide them with a new sense of community and the opportunity for meeting others.

One critic of the churches contends that the church has been led into captivity in suburbia. It has forsaken the city and its needs and has become a primary advocate of the suburban conception of the good life. The church attracts and holds its suburban members by drawing them into organizational activities, but, as Gibson Winter points out:

> *A puzzling feature of the organization church is the recruitment of members to do things which would be considered intolerable drudgery at home: hours of telephoning, cooking, cleaning, serving, endless correspondence. How is it possible? . . . The compulsive character of activity in religious organizations is illuminated by the notion that feelings of guilt are worked out through sacrificial action for the organization. . . . Two significant aspects emerge from this analysis of the organization church: (1) members have an opportunity to identify themselves with the religious organizations through the network of organizational activity,*

53. Dobriner *op. cit.*, p. 138.

experiencing feelings of loyalty as the congregation celebrates its own unity; (2) sacrifices of time and energy in the organization church offer members atonement for their feelings of guilt through an elaborate penitential system. . . . The search for meaning through activity and performance is typically middle-class. To be a successful middle-class person is to perform adequately. To be a middle-class Christian is to perform well on the committee. Thus, the organization church is the community of good works. . . .[54]

However, the organization church becomes quickly an introverted church placing "its own survival before its mission, its own identity above its task, its internal concerns before its apostolate, its rituals before its ministry."[55]

The organization church can quickly become superficial and its sense of community inadequate. Some observers argue that the *encounter group* is rapidly becoming the new religion of suburbia. In these small face-to-face groups frequently meeting in the homes of members, upper-middle-class persons obtain practice in *sensitivity training.* The intensive encounters with others expected in such groups, it is hoped, will open one up to the world and to others. The trust, openness, receptivity, and interdependence that become objectives of encounter groups remind one of the expectations traditionally associated with family membership. Certainly these groups are intended to become primary groups with a major function in the socialization of their members into a newer, fuller way of life.

Whether we look at the religion, education, economic activity, or the political balance of power in families and man-woman relationships of the upper-middle class, we can discern a clear quest for community and encounter. In its introverted form this quest becomes a matter of settling for security in the context of relatively homogeneous institutions. In its more outward reaching form it is an attempt to rediscover the basically human in a world that makes such human encounter difficult.

Yet the church has its critical commentaries on suburban family life. The following observations are from a pamphlet distributed by an interdenominational organization called the Family Enrichment Bureau. The complaints are directed at the "American Family," but seem particularly appropriate as commentary on the upper-middle-class family:

> *We're not even talking about the one quarter of our Christian marriages that end in divorce. They advertise their problems. Yet all of us know:*
>
> *1. There are huge numbers of "Good Christians" who are sleeping-around for "kicks."*
>
> *2. Millions of couples live in a sort of "armed truce" for much of their married life.*

54. Gibson Winter, *The Suburban Captivity of the Churches* (New York: Macmillan, 1962), pp. 97–117 passim.
55. *Ibid.*, p. 120.

3. Huge numbers of couples are afraid of their own children.
4. Still others are "too busy" to pay attention to their children.
5. Communication between husbands and wives is so bad that millions of women turn to soap operas, true romance magazines, and even casual adultery to find "love."
6. Mature, loving married sexuality and a healthy respect for sex are so rare that hard-core pornography has become a major industry.
7. Alcohol is a major source of "happiness" in many homes; it is an escape from problems.
8. Juvenile delinquency, crime, unmarried pregnancies, venereal disease — are all on the increase, and all are symptoms of family instability.
9. The image of the family is so low that we never see a TV show or movie that stresses the dignity and integrity of the home and almost never hear a sermon on the family. Instead, we hear about simple answers to human problems: answers such as money, massive rehabilitation programs, youth groups, etc.[56]

Here at least is one attempt to break out of suburban captivity, but one wonders if all of the evils described can rightly be placed at the feet of the family and, further, if some of the evils might simply cease to be discernible if the family were thought of as a variable rather than an ideal from which we are rapidly receding.

Summary

Although suburbia grew as a result of Whites leaving the city and its problems in order to establish a more central role for the family in their lives, suburban family life has its own problems. Depending upon the setting, conjugal families may be quite isolated from friends and may participate minimally in community activities, or, like Park Foresters, they may be inundated by good intentioned neighbors from the moment of their arrival.

Suburbia tends to be a homogeneous neighborhood for mother and her children and a dormitory for her husband. His job in the city commonly prevents him from being active in the neighborhood and removes him from many household responsibilities. He can often live a comparatively luxurious life on an expense account, while his wife and children manage the budget and stay at home. Marriages in suburbia tend to be utilitarian, and the relationship between the partners often lacks intrinsic satisfaction.

Suburbanites favor permissiveness in their relationships with their children, but this has some negative consequences. It is quite difficult for a child to feel secure and cared for. Parental neglect is more common than parental abuse.

The intense competitiveness and achievement orientation of parents makes them interested in the best schooling for their children. They support

56. Urban C. Steinmetz, *Family Enrichment Notes* (Fall, 1969), 4–5.

the PTA, harass the school and public authorities for better school buildings, and build a fear of failure into their children's curriculum. It would seem that rather than having suffered a loss of the educational function, the suburban family has merely changed its mode of involvement in the educational process. School activities, for these child-rearing families, often dominate their schedules.

The organization church provides a sense of belonging for transients and a means of working off guilt through church activities; it often becomes the most visible symbol of a quest for community. The church or encounter group is the center of the family's religious activities, not the home.

I will return to this middle-class family frequently in the following chapters, and I will present a more detailed analysis of its life style. This chapter is intended to give the reader a feeling for the variation in life style that is possible even within a rather narrow strata of American society, and thus to alert him to the hazards of generalizing about the American family.

8. A Black Alternative: Coping with Poverty in the Ghetto

The two primary forces that create and maintain the lower-class Negro community are economic marginality and racial oppression. . . . This means that lower-class Negro families are markedly deprived compared to others in the society in their ability to make use of the goods and services that constitute the going standard of American life. . . . Man can exist happily and healthily on much less than the American poor have available, but only if their level of living does not make them as different from and socially inferior to the great majority of their society.

LEE RAINWATER

The black lower-class family of the ghetto has been the subject of much public debate since the problem of poverty in America became a matter of general public awareness in the 1960s. Their plight has been particularly brought before the public since the 1965 publication of *The Negro Family: The Case for National Action*,[1] by Daniel Patrick Moynihan who was then Under Secretary of Labor. Despite the contention of the Kerner Commission's report that a major cause of the rioting and violence of the past decade and a half was "white racism," these disturbances are persistently attributed to black ghetto families.[2]

Terms such as "broken" and "disorganized" are used to describe the poor black family structure even though they do not apply to almost two-thirds of these families. "Deprived" and "culturally disadvantaged" are terms commonly used to describe black children, despite the fact that Blacks have a rich cultural heritage of their own. Debate continues as to whether there is a "breakdown" in the structure of the lower-class black family that can be seen as a primary cause of its impoverishment.[3] Commonly such an association is made when the phrase "culture of poverty" is used.[4] We are thus told that it is necessary to change the character of black ghetto family life before we can expect much improvement in the economic situation of these families. As a result public policy at the turn of the decade has focused on welfare reform, voluntary education in family planning, and a family approach to allotment of welfare funds rather than on the necessity to create jobs at the unskilled and semi-skilled levels, to train lower-class hard core unemployed in jobs offering some hope of mobility, and to institute reforms designed to reduce the enormous economic inequality in America.[5]

There is an ever present black rage over such indignities and a radical re-evaluation of the black experience in such slogans as "black power," "power to the people," and "all power to the straight shooters."[6] Associated

1. Office of Planning and Research, *The Negro Family: The Case For National Action*, Series P-20, No. 155 (Washington, D.C.: U.S.G.P.O., September 27, 1966). This report is also found in Lee Rainwater and William Yancey, *The Moynihan Report and the Politics of Controversy* (Cambridge, Mass.: M.I.T. Press, 1967), pp. 47–124.
2. *Report of the National Advisory Commission on Civil Disorders* (New York: Bantam Books, 1968), pp. 10 ff.
3. See particularly the discussion by Elizabeth Herzog, "Is There a Breakdown of the Negro Family?" in Rainwater and Yancey *op. cit.*, pp. 344–53.
4. An excellent evaluation of the utility of the concept "culture of poverty" can be found in Jack L. Roach and Orville R. Gursslin, "An Evaluation of the Concept Culture of Poverty," *Social Forces*, XLV, No. 3 (March 1967), 383–92. See also the more extensive critique by Charles Valentine, *Culture and Poverty: Critique and Counter Proposals* (Chicago: University of Chicago Press, 1968). The concept was first developed by Oscar Lewis. An outline of his usage appears in the preface to his *La Vida* (New York: Vintage Books, 1968). Thomas Gladwin further develops the concept in *Poverty U.S.A.* (Boston: Little, Brown, 1967). It is assumed that poverty has a culture in the Kerner Commission's Report (e.g. p. 14).
5. Daniel P. Moynihan's perspective on welfare reform and income redistribution is well set forth in his speech prepared for Governor Rockefeller's Conference on Poverty in November of 1967, "The Crisis in Welfare: The View From New York."
6. An excellent formulation of the concept of black power is found in Stokely Carmichael and Charles V. Hamilton, *Black Power: The Politics of Liberation in America* (New York: Vintage Books, 1967). See also Eldridge Cleaver, *Soul on Ice* (New York: Dell, 1968); William H. Grier and Price M. Cobbs, *Black Rage* (New York: Bantam Books, 1968); and Joyce Ladner, "What 'Black Power' Means to Negroes in Mississippi," in Norval D. Glenn and Charles M. Bonjean, *Blacks in the United States* (San Francisco: Chandler, 1969), pp. 444–57.

with these slogans is an increasing emphasis on a positive black identity, "I'm black and I'm proud." There are increasing demands that black people be given their rights and rising expectations as to what these rights ought to be. Such demands and expectations are often frustrated in America because of bigotry, ignorance, indifference, and institutionalized racism.

It is difficult in such times to bring the impoverished black family of the urban ghetto into focus in such a way that it appears not as an example of pathology or disorganization, but rather as an alternative style of life that has proven itself functional in coping with the deprivation and isolation imposed upon the majority of such families by impersonal social constraints largely beyond their control. It is difficult for Whites to see the strengths in black families and difficult for Blacks to talk about their weaknesses—in part because what is from one perspective a strength, is from the other a weakness.

With pervasive misunderstanding and entrenched stereotypic thinking characteristic of discussions between Blacks and Whites, it is beyond the power of a short chapter to "set the record straight." On the other hand, a more detailed account of family life of lower-class Blacks such as I attempted in *Coming Up Black*[7] runs the risk of seeming to place a great deal of emphasis on differences in black family life which most Whites will prematurely label "pathological" without providing adequate comparison with other family styles. Whites reading a detailed account of black family life in the ghetto tend to contrast these families with the white conception of the *ideal* family —not with vivid descriptions of what family life is actually like in white America. In the context of a book stressing functional alternatives in family life styles, however, it is hoped that a truer comparison can be made, and in my mind the attempt is worth making. The white upper-middle-class family of suburbia was examined in Chapter 7. I turn now to the lower-lower-class black family of the northern urban ghetto.

The Ghetto

Because of residential segregation, the association of poor Blacks with central city ghettos is more accurate as a generalization than is the placement of upper-middle-class Whites in suburbia. Nevertheless, not all impoverished Blacks live in ghettos. According to Table 8–1, in 1968, 54.4 percent of the poor black population were located in standard metropolitan areas, 42.4 percent were found in central cities, and 11.9 percent in the suburban fringe. In addition, 45.6 percent of all poor Blacks lived outside of these metropolitan areas. Figure 8–1 indicates that the majority of nonwhite children live in central cities.

However, the concentration of Blacks is greatest in the larger cities and has been increasing as the movement into these cities continues. In seventeen cities Blacks out numbered Whites in the public school system in the period

7. David A. Schulz, *Coming Up Black: Patterns of Ghetto Socialization* (Englewood Cliffs, N.J.: Prentice-Hall, 1969).

TABLE 8–1
Distribution of Blacks in Poverty 1968 and 1959

	1968	1959
Metro Areas	54.4%	50.4%
Central	42.5	38.4
Suburb	11.9	12.0
Outside Metro Areas	45.6	49.6
Rural (nonfarm)	37.8	
Farm	7.8	

Source: Tables H and A-1 U.S. Bureau of the Census, *Current Population Reports*, Series P-60, No. 68, "Poverty in the United States: 1959–1968," (Washington, D.C.: U.S.G.P.O., 1969).

1965–1966. To date only the District of Columbia is predominantly black, but by the end of the seventies it is quite likely that eight more major cities will have a black majority.[8]

The urbanization of Blacks has been a relatively recent phenomenon. In 1910, 75 percent of the black population were living in rural areas. By 1960, 75 percent were living in urban areas. In 1910, 90 percent of all black Americans lived in the South. By 1960, half were living in the North. Blacks have moved out of the rural South into urban areas, particularly into the North and West.[9] In the Seventies Blacks are significantly an urban, innercity people.

POVERTY AND EXCLUSION

In the city many Blacks are poor and, by virtue of residential segregation, are forced to live in ghettoes. Although it is true that the incidence of officially defined poverty in America has been decreasing for both Blacks and Whites in a generally expanding economy, the benefits of prosperity have not been equally shared by all. Blacks have narrowed the educational gap between themselves and Whites from an average of two years in 1961 to less than a half year today.[10] They have closed the income gap slightly over the period 1950–1966 so that nonwhite income in 1966 has risen to 60 percent of white (black income is 58 percent of white) from 54 percent in 1950[11] despite the fact that unemployment has remained about twice as high for nonwhites. In the first half of 1970, black unemployment rose above 9 percent, while white unemployment remained below 5 percent. Over the period 1940–1968,

8. Louis H. Masotti, Jeffrey K. Hadden, Kenneth F. Seminatore, and Jerome R. Corsi, *A Time to Burn?: An Evaluation of the Present Crisis in Race Relations* (Chicago: Rand McNally, 1969).
9. United States Department of Labor, Bureau of Labor Statistics, "Social and Economic Conditions of Negroes in the United States" Report 332 (Washington, D.C.: U.S.G.P.O., October, 1967), pp. 4–5.
10. *Ibid.*, p. 49.
11. *Ibid.*, p. 15.

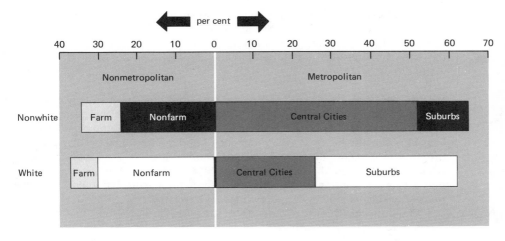

FIGURE 8–1
A comparison of white and nonwhite children's residence patterns in 1968.
Adapted from The Nation's Youth *(U.S.G.P.O., 1968), Chart 3.*

there have been substantial gains in occupational equality, although the most significant have occurred at the unskilled and semi-skilled level.[12] Although black life expectancy increased and black infant mortality decreased over the period 1960–1965, the position of Blacks relative to Whites has remained significantly unchanged in the first instance and has worsened in the second.[13]

The *quality* of education received by Blacks is generally poorer; it persists in segregated schools in the South despite legislation (in 1967, 86 percent of southern black pupils were enrolled in segregated schools) and is on the increase in the North.[14] Residential segregation increased in eight out of twelve major cities over the period 1960–1965.[15] Despite the gains in occupational equality, Thomas Pettigrew estimated in 1966 that Blacks would not attain equal status with Whites in clerical jobs until 1992, in skilled jobs until 2005, in the professions until 2017, in sales jobs until 2114, and in managerial positions until 2130, if the then current trends continued.[16]

Finally, Livingston Wingate, the director of Haryou, declared in 1966 that "If overnight Harlem houses were palaces and all its streets clean enough to eat upon, Harlem would still be afflicted by the by products of 250 years of social injustice. The spirit of the people wouldn't conform to the new physical conditions."[17]

12. Norval D. Glenn, "Changes in the Social and Economic Conditions of Black Americans during the 1960's," in Glenn and Bonjean *op. cit.,* p. 45.
13. *Ibid.,* p. 52.
14. *Ibid.,* p. 50.
15. Bureau of Labor Statistics Report No. 332 *op. cit·,* p. xi.
16. Thomas Pettigrew, *Christian Science Monitor* (May 18, 1966).
17. Livingston Wingate, *Christian Science Monitor* (May 18, 1966).

Living conditions are especially bad in black ghettoes which in many areas show a decline over the period 1960–1965 rather than an improvement. In nine of these ghettoes, the unemployment rate in 1966 was 9.3 (2.6 times the national rate) and the sub-employment (employed but with inadequate income) rate 32.7 percent.

Watts: The Watts district of Los Angeles provides illustration of typical ghetto conditions. Watts decreased in population 14 percent over the period 1960–1965, yet impoverishment dropped only 1 percent, and the number of families with female heads *rose* 3 percent. Although the unemployment rate dropped 2 percent, the median annual family income rose only $139.00, while rents rose on the average of $10.00 a month. At the same time, the percentage of housing classifiable as deteriorating rose 7 percent, and the percentage classifiable as dilapidated rose 2 percent.

The poor health of the Watts district is reflected in the fact that although it contained only 17 percent of the Los Angeles population, it contained over 40 percent of seven major illnesses and over 35 percent of two others (Table 8–2). Its death rate was 22.3 percent higher than for the city of Los Angeles as a whole. This is particularly significant since the relationship between poor health and poor school performance has been established by numerous studies. One is particularly alarming because it argues forcefully that there is a causal link between poverty and mental retardation. Rodger Hurley concludes, "Research estimates as to the percentages of cases of mental retardation caused by heredity have, over a period of many years, gradually decreased (from 77 percent in 1914 to 15 percent in 1965). . . . It is probable that future research will prove that even 15 percent is too high."[18] The im-

18. Rodger L. Hurley, *Poverty and Mental Retardation: A Causal Relationship* (Trenton, N.J.: State of New Jersey, Division of Mental Retardation, Department of Institutions and Agencies, 1968), p. 8.

TABLE 8–2
Clinical Portrait of a Ghetto Five Years Before (Watts 1960)

In 1960 Watts contained 17% of the city's population—but nearly half of its ills. For example:

48.5% amoebic infection	65 % tuberculin reactors
42 % food poisoning	44.6% dysentery
44.8% whooping cough	46 % venereal disease
39 % epilepsy	36 % meningitis
42.8% rheumatic fever	

Its death rate was 22.3% higher than the city's overall death rate.

Source: Institute of Industrial Relations, University of California, Los Angeles, Calif., cited in Rodger L. Hurley, *Poverty and Mental Retardation: A Causal Relationship* (Trenton, N.J.: State of New Jersey Department of Institutions and Aging, 1968).

pact of an unfavorable environment on black children is especially high since over half (59 percent) of all black children live in poverty.[19]

FAMILY LIFE AND POVERTY

Despite the controversy over the breakdown of the black family, some indicators ordinarily referred to in such discussions show little change over the period 1960–1966. In fact the illegitimacy rate for nonwhite women declined 1 percent (1960–1965), while the white rate rose 26 percent.[20] The percentage of unmarried children living with both parents declined, from 75 to 71, but the percentage of nonwhite families with female heads rose slightly, from 22.4 to 23.7.[21] By 1969, however, the percentage of female-headed black families reached 28.6.[22] Norval Glenn observes:

> *Although many of the discussions of Negro lower-class families are guilty of moralism and middle-class ethnocentrism, high rates of divorce, separation, and illegitimacy and a large percentage of children in fatherless homes undoubtedly do handicap the black population in its struggle for an equitable share of the "good things" of American society. Therefore, from one perspective, any decline in these phenomena is a gain for blacks and any increase a loss.[23]*

On the other hand, Hylan Lewis speaks out positively for the one-parent family as a viable family form in its own right. Among reasons he gives for such a re-assessment of the one-parent family are the following:

1. The one-parent family is with us and shows no sign of becoming less frequent.
2. There is reason to believe that children in such families are adversely affected by the negative assumptions which cluster around it.
3. Through time and space the family has absorbed a vast array of different forms and still has continued to function as the family.
4. The model American family may not be as functionally two-parent or as "patriarchal" as is sometimes assumed.
5. Analysis of research findings concerning the one-parent fam-

19. United States Department of Health, Education, and Welfare, Children's Bureau, *The Nation's Youth: A Chart Book*, Children's Bureau Publication N. 460 (Washington, D.C.: U.S.G.P.O., 1968), Chart No. 11.

20. United States Department of Health, Education, and Welfare, Public Health Service, *Trends in Illegitimacy: United States—1940–1965*, Series 21, No. 15 (Washington, D.C.: U.S.G.P.O., 1968), p. 5.

21. Glenn *op. cit.*, p. 53.

22. U.S. Bureau of the Census, *Current Population Reports*, Series P-20, No. 189, "Selected Characteristics of Persons and Families: March 1969" (Washington, D.C.: U.S.G.P.O., 1969), p. 12.

23. Glenn *op. cit.*, p. 53.

ily fails to support a sweeping indictment of its potential for producing children capable of fruitful and gratifying lives.[24]

Moynihan asserted that at the heart of the problem of black impoverishment was the disorganized family enmeshed in a "tangle of pathology" from which it was incapable of extracting itself without outside assistance. If the family were not helped, the cycle of poverty would be indefinitely perpetuated. Glenn does not place as much stress on the causal role family disorganization plays in the perpetuation of poverty, but assumes that many of the family life indicators reflect conditions that Blacks as well as Whites would want to correct. Lewis sees positive value in the female-headed family and argues for its acceptance not as a deviant family form but as a functional form in its own right. Thus the analysis of the role played by the family in the perpetuation of poverty is intimately connected with value judgments regarding what the family *should be* and assumptions as to what will happen if it is not in fact as it should be. Most studies of the lower-class black family treat it as a deviant family form (even when its structure conforms to the norm), but as Lewis asserts "the data fail to support a sweeping indictment."

CASTE VICTIMIZATION AND CULTURE

In regard to the role of the family in the perpetuation of poverty, I take a middle course. The conditions described above constitute some of the major parameters of constraint placed upon Blacks by Whites who, over the past three centuries, have been able to force Blacks to do the "dirty work of caste victimization" (that is, to turn Blacks against Blacks) because of the greater social, economic, and political power belonging to Whites. Rainwater suggests a modification of the common short-hand explanation "white cupidity creates Negro suffering" along the following lines:

> White cupidity creates
> *Structural Conditions Highly Inimical to Basic Social Adaptation (low income availability, poor education, poor services, stigmatization)*
> to which Negroes adapt by
> *Social and Personal Responses which serve to sustain the individual in his punishing world but also generate aggressiveness toward the self and others*
> which results in
> *Suffering directly inflicted by Negroes on themselves and on others.*[25]

Those Whites who can be formally related to the "white power structure" (those who have responsibility for public policy, those who deal privately but directly with the black community economically, those called upon to enforce the laws and the welfare policy, etc.) may have more obvious effect

24. Hylan Lewis, "Agenda Paper No. V: The Family: Resources for Change-Planning Session for the White House Conference to Fulfill These Rights" in Rainwater and Yancey *op. cit.,* p. 324.

25. Lee Rainwater, "Crucible of Identity" *Daedalus* (Winter, 1966), 175.

in such a process, but *all* Whites can be said to be guilty of "racism" though they need not be bigots or consciously discriminating. Through their taken-for-granted acceptance of social institutions, behaviors, beliefs, and attitudes that tend to create conditions of unequal access to the "good things" of our cultural cornucopia they tend to perpetuate the problems of black ghettoes.[26]

The black adaptation to the structural conditions imposed by white racism, however, has not been merely a passive adaptation. Blacks have made, in Ralph Ellison's word, "a life upon the horns of the white man's dilemma." This life, furthermore, is not simply the product of a response, however creative, to imposed constraints. The black man

> . . . *is no mere product of his socio-political predicament. He is a product of interaction between his racial predicament, his individual will and the broader American cultural freedom in which he finds his ambiguous existence. Thus he, too, in a limited way, is his own creation.*[27]

The positive identification with blackness increasingly prevalent in the black community and the quest for greater autonomy and power do not seem to be directly derivable from Rainwater's scheme. This is perhaps because the public expression of such autonomy and authoritativeness has not arisen from the ranks of the lower class, but has emerged from the black intelligentsia who are now spreading the gospel of power and positive identity to all Blacks. Whatever the case, it is likely that the effect of such a movement on the lower-class Blacks will be to enhance the distinctiveness and positiveness of the life they have forced upon the horns of the dilemma of racial inequality.

Since slavery, the black social institution least directly interfered with by Whites is the family. Thus the distinctiveness of black life styles derive in large measure from the character of family life.[28] As pressures for integration into the mainstream rise, it is likely that pressures to reduce the distinctiveness of this life style will increase. Such factors undoubtedly will continue to arise from outside the black community in the attempt to make assistance contingent upon conformity to white ideals, but they are also likely to arise from within the black community as increasing opportunity permits greater exploration of alternatives to the current patterns of black family life. The net result of such factors is difficult to predict, but it seems reasonable to assume that one dimension will be an increase in the number of two-parent families among low-income Blacks, because this is the major structural form at present and the ideal of most Blacks who live in one-parent families. It

---

26. Such a view does not contend that it is not the responsibility of Blacks to attempt to better their conditions; it recognizes that some indeed have overcome such social constraints and moved out of poverty at least partially through their own personal efforts. What is stressed is that we should not expect individual effort to triumph in the average case because of the much greater accumulation of handicaps that must be overcome. See especially the discussion of black mobility in Andrew Billingsley, *Black Families in White America* (Englewood Cliffs, N.J.: Prentice-Hall, 1969), pp. 97–148.

27. Quoted in Rainwater *op. cit.*, p. 172.

28. *Ibid.*, p. 178.

must be added, however, that although the structure of low-income black families may conform to that of the general norm, it does not follow that the style of life lived in such families will necessarily conform in other respects as well.

Family Patterns of the Black Underclass

As indicated in Chapter 6, half of the black community can be considered a part of the lower class, which can be further divided into the working non-poor, the working poor, and the underclass (the nonworking poor).[29] This underclass, constituting 15 to 20 percent of the black population, is most often found in the urban North, living in public housing projects, and frequently depending on welfare (only about 14 percent of the entire black community is on welfare, despite its comparatively low income levels in all socioeconomic classes). The problems of this underclass are thus generally more acute and their methods for coping with their world more different than would be true for other economic levels in the black community. In Chapter 6 I described briefly the characteristics of the average lower-class black family. I turn now to an examination of family patterns and life styles that are more characteristic of the black underclass. Most of the ethnographic material that follows (including those references taken from Lee Rainwater, Boone Hammond, and Joyce Ladner) comes from an intensive four and a half year study of a single housing project in the city of St. Louis known as the Pruitt-Igoe Project (see Fig. 8–2). The problems of this project were particularly acute, but the patterns presented in the following section seem supported by detailed studies elsewhere.[30]

LARGE FAMILIES AND HOUSEHOLDS

Figure 8–3 shows that nonwhite families are likely to be larger than white families. In 1969, the average number of children under 18 per black family was 1.80, as compared to 1.27 for Whites. Most of these black families were complete. Sixty-seven percent of all black children were living with both parents in 1969, as opposed to 91.9 percent of all white children living with both parents. However, white female-headed families were generally smaller (1.03 children) than the average white family, while black female-headed families

29. This breakdown is from Billingsley *op. cit.*, p. 123.
30. The study was undertaken by means of a grant from the National Institute of Mental Health, Grant No. MH 09189 "Social and Community Problems in the Public Housing Areas." A comprehensive report on the problems of families living in this project is to be found in Lee Rainwater, *Behind Ghetto Walls* (Chicago: Aldine Publishing Company, 1970). A detailed account of the patterns of socialization discernible in ten of these families is found in David A. Schulz, *op. cit.* Two recently released collections of studies in the black family are: Charles V. Willie (ed.), *The Family Life of Black People* (Columbus, Ohio: Charles E. Merrill, 1970), and Robert Staples, *The Black Family, Essays and Studies* (Belmont, Calif.: Wadsworth, 1971).

FIGURE 8–2
Left, *the Pruitt-Igoe projects in*
St. Louis, Missouri; below, *the*
type of housing that was torn
down in order to build the
project.

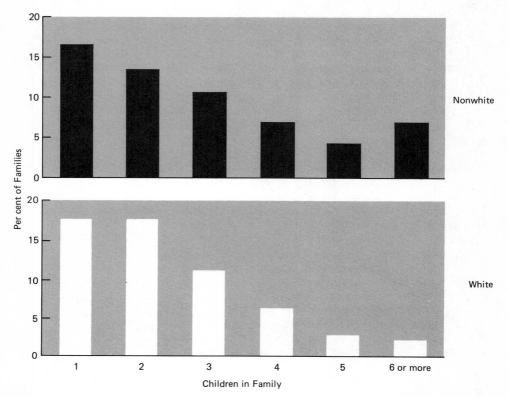

FIGURE 8–3

A comparison of the size of white and nonwhite families. Adapted from
The Nation's Youth *(U.S.G.P.O., 1968), Chart 9.*

were larger (1.95) than the average black family.[31] These large black families
occurred despite the fact that infant mortality for nonwhites is about twice as
high as for Whites.[32] On the whole, impoverished urban black families are
more likely to be female headed and larger than impoverished white families. In contrast, once the constraints of impoverishment are overcome or removed and black families become upwardly mobile, they tend to be smaller
than white families at comparable income levels and are no more likely than
white families to be headed by women.

The large female-headed family of the black ghetto is quite often found
residing in households with other relatives and nonrelatives. Thus *households*
are also typically quite large and change their composition frequently as
members come and go for varying periods of time. Children may go to live

31. *Current Population Reports*, Series P-20, No. 189, p. 12.
32. *The Nation's Youth: A Chart Book*, Chart 37.

with relatives for extended periods in order to help the mother over a particularly hard time; "outside" children[33] reaching their mid-teens leave the maternal grandparent to come and live with their mother and half-siblings; relatives from "down home" may move in for a time until they become established in the city; boyfriends may live in for a while. Therefore, the complexity of household relationships is great and ever changing.[34] This changing personnel provides support for the mother and her children while making the matter of obtaining and maintaining an intimate relationship somewhat more difficult. There is a tendency in the ghetto to extend kinship terminology to nonkin so as to emphasize the "tightness" of a relationship and broaden the base of potential economic and emotional support.[35]

These large families are not necessarily planned. Indeed several studies suggest that most lower-class mothers and fathers have more children than they desire.[36] Large families result in part because black mothers do not resort to abortion as frequently as do Whites, are not willing (or as able) to give their unwanted children up for adoption, do not experience as great a stigmatism from out-of-wedlock births, and are not as effective in contraceptive practices.[37]

SEX AND SURVIVAL

Sexual intercourse is a relatively more important form of behavior in the ghetto where there is great material and emotional deprivation than in middle-class society. Children learn about coitus early in life beginning at about the age of five. In the ghetto, young children are not thought of as asexual as is commonly the case in suburbia. One mother comments:

> *These kids grow up fast in this project. These five and six year old heifers (girls) know as much about screwing as I do. My six year old boy has already punched (had intercourse with) two or three of these fast chicks and I'm teaching my four year old boy how to be a lady killer too. I can't hide the facts of life from them because they can see them everyday on any stairway, hall or elevator in the project.*[38]

33. An "outside" child is a child born outside of wedlock.
34. The author's study of ten families suggests that it is not unusual for teenage children to have attended four or more schools in the process of getting an education. See David A. Schulz, *Negro Lower-Class Family Variations* (Unpublished doctoral dissertation, Washington University, St. Louis), pp. 437–75. The problems of mobility in ghetto families are also discussed in Eliot Liebow, *Tally's Corner* (Boston: Little, Brown, 1967), pp. 72–102 and 161–207. The problems presented by such complexity within households is discussed further in Schulz, *Coming Up Black*.
35. See particularly the detailed discussion of "Going for Cousins" in Liebow *op. cit.*, pp. 161 ff.
36. See, for example, Lee Rainwater, *Family Design: Marital Sexuality, Family Size and Contraception* (Chicago: Aldine, 1965), pp. 118 ff.; and Jessie Bernard, *Marriage and Family Among Negroes* (Englewood Cliffs, N.J.: Prentice-Hall, 1966), pp. 104 ff.
37. Lee Rainwater, *Family Design*, pp. 244 ff.; Boone E. Hammond and Joyce Ladner, "Socialization into Sexual Behavior in a Negro Slum Ghetto," in Carlfred B. Broderick and Jessie Bernard, *The Individual, Sex and Society* (Baltimore: Johns Hopkins Press, 1969), p. 50; and Kenneth Clark, *Dark Ghetto* (New York: Harper & Row, 1965), pp. 70 ff.
38. Hammond and Ladner *op. cit.*, pp. 43–44.

Sexual activities are openly discussed in the ghetto in great detail and are dominant themes in "joning" or "playing the dozens."[39] A child learns by hearing such conversation and also by observing the act of coitus. The lack of privacy, the large and heterogeneous households, and the general acceptance of sexuality as natural make observation an easy matter.[40] Finally, small children can overtly practice coitus as well, first as little more than an imitation of the adults they have seen, then with more purpose.

Hammond and Ladner suggest that sexual behavior—particularly coitus—passes quite naturally from an early stage of "sex-as-fun-and-games" to a later stage in adolescence where sex is both fun and a strategic game of survival.[41]

In the context of a milieu where "everybody does it" and the dominant masculine norm is T.C.B. (take care of business) whenever possible, the adolescent girl's choice of to "do it" or not to do it is difficult indeed. If she does it to please her boyfriend or simply as a form of recreation, a likely result in such unplanned encounters is pregnancy. This will probably terminate her schooling and confine her to low paying jobs for the rest of her life.[42] Not to do it means to give up a source of pleasure and a means (if one becomes pregnant) of acquiring status (no longer a "school girl" among peers).

The full weight of such a decision can be seen by considering other functions of sex in the ghetto:

> *In the later adolescent years . . . sex for girls takes on the important function of being a form of exchange, primarily for material goods and services (gifts, money, etc.). . . . In their day-to-day struggle for survival, males and females may have learned that delayed gratification and strong interpersonal relationships are to be viewed positively, but the insurmountable pressures of emotional and physical deprivation cause them to reject such goals. It is necessary, then, that the young child be taught to "go for himself" and to get what he can in any way necessary. Thus, girls have been known to engage in sexual intercourse in exchange for a movie date, a ride in a car, food, and other things that will take them out of the family life. The male in turn offers these things because he knows the girl is desirous of them and can offer what he wants in exchange.*[43]

Finally, sexual intercourse often occurs simply "for kicks." A thirteen year old girl remarks:

---

39. The dozens is a game where young children ridicule their female relatives—particularly their mothers—in rhyme.

40. Hammond and Ladner *op. cit.*, pp. 44–45. See also Robert J. Havighurst, "Cultural Factors in Sex Expression," in *Sexual Behavior in American Society: An Appraisal of the First Two Kinsey Reports*, Jerome Hamelhock and Sylvia Fleis Fava (eds.), (New York: Norton, 1955), pp. 191–205.

41. *Ibid.*, p. 47.

42. For a more detailed discussion of this dilemma see David A. Schulz, *Coming Up Black*, pp. 48–58.

43. Hammond and Ladner *op. cit.*, p. 49.

> *"When we are hanging around the building and don't have anything to do and boys come around, we might start playing with them and before you know it all of us are mellow (having sex)." In a similar statement another girl explains: "We sometimes do it for kicks, and you don't have to like the boy to do it with him. You do it cause you can be mellow when you don't want to play cards or watch TV."*[44]

Thus there is tremendous pressure to engage in coitus and a common result of such behavior, in lieu of effective birth control, is pregnancy. The black illegitimacy rate is several times higher than the white rate. Children born "outside" are usually raised by their maternal grandmother until they reach mid-adolescence when they may return to their mother's household. The Kinsey data suggest that the percentage of black teenage girls who have experienced coitus is three to four times higher than that of white girls in the lower class (80 percent of black grammar school educated black girls have had intercourse by the age of twenty, as opposed to 26 percent of white girls of similar age and education).[45] In general, more grammar school and high school educated black girls have experienced coitus by the age of fifteen than white boys of similar age and education.[46]

Such statistics might give the impression that sexual behavior is expressed freely and without care after the fashion of some "natural man" mythology.

> *However, close observation of peer group activities of late adolescent and early adult Negro males and females indicates that such is not the case. In the first place, attitudes toward sexual relations are highly competitive (among sex peers) and heavily exploitative (of opposite sex). Slum Negro boys typically refer to girls including their own girl friends as "that bitch" or "that whore" when they talk among themselves. Often Negro girls who do engage in sexual relations in response to the strong "lines" of the boys who "rap it to" them do not seem to find any particular gratification in sexual relations, but rather engage in sex as a test and as a symbol of their maturity and their ability to be "with it." Over time a certain proportion of these girls do engage in sexual relations out of desire as well as for extrinsic reasons. However, it seems clear that the competitive and exploitative attitudes on both sides made sexual gratification an uncertain matter.*[47]

MARRIAGE

Ghetto Blacks know what the ideal American family is like and generally consider the working-class model more desirable than many of the alternatives, given the circumstances of their existence. That is, ghetto Blacks place a high value on a two-parent family in which the faithful husband is the major

44. *Ibid.,* p. 50.
45. Lee Rainwater, "Sex in the Culture of Poverty" in Broderick and Bernard *op. cit.,* p. 136.
46. *Ibid.,* p. 137.
47. *Loc. cit.*

provider, the mother is the homemaker who is interested in her family's needs, and the children look up to and respect their parents while performing well in school. Many finer nuances can be added to this skeleton of an ideal, but the point is that ghetto Blacks realize that many of their family forms are different and—by their own evaluation—"the next best thing" to the commonly accepted normative pattern presented in Chapter 6. It is, however, unreasonable to expect them to change the character of their family life as long as they are confronted with ghetto exclusion and deprivation.

Many ghetto Blacks are not able to provide adequately for their families, even though both parents work hard at the task. Street life, with its manipulative and exploitative norms, pits the sexes against one another and makes it difficult to achieve an intimate, long-term relationship. The all pervasiveness of sex makes it difficult for teenage girls to escape pregnancy, and too many children born "outside" make marriages more difficult to achieve. Marriage, therefore, is a much more difficult contract to negotiate and maintain in the ghetto than in society at large. Nevertheless, most poor Blacks do marry and stay together for an extended period of time. It is apparent that there are fewer instrumental ties to bind ghetto adults in marriage (indeed current welfare practices tend to reduce the instrumental interdependence of husband and wife). Affectional ties are difficult to maintain in situations of chronic deprivation and emotional stress.

For many women the status of "having been married" is more significant than being married. Like first pregnancy, it indicates that the girl has become the woman. The fragility of marriage once contracted, however, means that few women will spend their child-bearing years with a single husband or boyfriend.[48] Further, the relatively greater equality between the sexes in the right of access to whatever satisfactions life offers and the relatively poorer opportunity of ghetto males to provide adequately for their families result in less pretense to patriarchy.[49]

The ideal marriage in the minds of young men who frequent the haunts of the street is the free-man–free-woman marriage where the contract reflects a minimal commitment and each is free to go his own way pretty much as he chooses. A man of twenty says:

> *The best kind of marriage is one where you've got an understanding . . . Like, you take Jil and I. She knows that I go in for other women, but we just got an understanding that we go out on one another and I don't have to lose interest in women and she doesn't have to lose her interest in men just because we are getting married.*

This ideal when put into practice, however, results in a great deal of violence. Jealousy is greater than the normative restraint implies. Men and women knife one another over infidelities.[50] In practice the woman "cuts

---

48. Rainwater, "Crucible of Identity," p. 180.

49. *Ibid.*, p. 191. See also the discussion of family forms in Billingsley *op. cit.*, pp. 142–45.

50. Schulz, *Coming Up Black*, p. 150; Rainwater, "Crucible of Identity," p. 191.

out" less than the man, and the man, if he wants domestic tranquility, handles his outside affairs with discretion. The more common types of man-woman relationships can be described in terms of a typology of male marginality.

MATRIFOCALITY AND MALE MARGINALITY

In 1967, 25 percent of all black families were headed by a female, but 42 percent of those families with incomes under $3,000 were female headed. The comparable figures for white families are 9 and 23 percent.[51] A much higher percentage of urban families are female headed than are rural families where there is a greater need for male labor.[52] Looking at the incidence of female-headed families in yet another way, Figure 8–4 shows that two-thirds of all nonwhite female-headed families earned under $3,000 in 1965.

This higher incidence (as compared to white families) of female headedness at low-income levels is one rather obvious structural component that

51. Bureau of Labor Statistics, "Social and Economic Conditions of Negroes in the United States," p. 71.
52. Rainwater, "Crucible of Identity," p. 181·

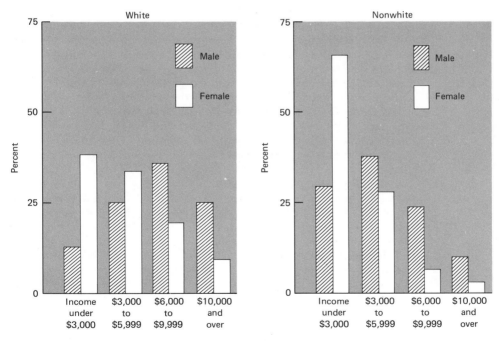

FIGURE 8–4
*A comparison of male- and female-headed families, white and nonwhite,
by income. Adapted from* The Nation's Youth *(U.S.G.P.O., 1968), Chart 15.*

has contributed to the tendency to call the black family "matrifocal." The mother-centered family is readily traceable to slavery, where the mother-child bond was more honored by slave holders than the conjugal bond. Upon the disruption of the nuclear family for whatever reason, children, then as now, tended to go with the mother.

The emphasis on matrifocality and the tendency to speak of two basic types of families (two parent and female headed) however, does not do justice to the role of the male in poor black families. In *Blackways of Kent*, Hylan Lewis mentions in passing that:

> *Gifts and some degree of support from the male are a constant in nonmarital liaisons; they are taken for granted and freely discussed. There is some informal ranking of men on a basis of the regularity and amount of gifts or support.*[53]

My own study of a small number of poor black families suggests that if one examines the strength of the adult relationship or conjugal bond; the amount, type, and extent of support provided by the man; and the extent of his care and concern for his woman's children, a seven-fold typology (outlined below) assists in understanding the extent of a man's marginality to a basic mother-child dyad.[54]

The residents of one black public housing project distinguished between "pimps"—men who "live sweet off" women (the classic case of which is the man who hustles prostitutes but the term applies to those living off women regardless of how the latter earn their income as well)—"boyfriends," and "husbands" ("old men" or "hubbies").

One can, however, distinguish seven patterns of living that reflect values, behaviors, and commitments of a more varied sort which do not seem to be mere passing phases but rather more or less persistent patterns. Four nonmarital relationships include (1) The pimp, already briefly described; (2) the supportive companion; (3) the biological father; and (4) the quasi-father. Marital relationships include (1) the indiscreet free-man; (2) the discreet free-man; and (3) the monogamous father.

The *supportive companion* is a man who is essentially looking for a clean woman with whom to have a good time. He provides her with $15.00 or so a week (1965) which she usually spends on herself in clothes or makeup. He courts his woman away from her home and children. The *supportive biological father*, on the other hand, has lost interest in the woman who bore his children, but is concerned with caring for those whom he helped to bring into the world. Without the obligation's having been imposed by the court, he cares for these children. Gifts, trips, visits, and recreational activities are typical supports other than cash that this father provides. Finally, the *quasi-father* is seeking a familial relationship with a woman and her children in the

53. Hylan Lewis, *Blackways of Kent* (Chapel Hill, N.C.: University of North Carolina Press, 1961), p. 84.

54. A more detailed discussion of this typology is found in Schulz, *Coming Up Black*, chap. 4.

text of their home. Typically the children are not his, but his care and concern extend to them as well. These relationships seem quite durable. The longest such relationship that I am aware of lasted eleven years. Five years is typical in the small sample studied.

Two of these types, the quasi-father and the discreet free-man, deserve further attention because they both represent rather effective strategies for coping with the problems imposed by ghetto living, even though it is not possible at present to ascertain just how typical they are of the black underclass as a whole.

The Quasi-Father: The distinguishing marks of this role are (1) The man supports the family regularly over extended periods of time. Commonly he goes with his woman to buy her week's groceries and pays her bill. (2) He cares for her children. He will give them allowances or spending money, attempt more or less successfully to discipline them, and will take them out (to the park or the movies, etc.) for entertainment. (3) He frequently visits the family during the week and may or may not reside with them for extended periods of time. (4) Usually the relationship is conducted in the open in full knowledge of kin on both sides, particularly the parents if they reside in the same city with the couple. In return he receives (1) some or all of his meals, (2) washing and ironing, (3) sexual satisfaction, and (4) familial companionship.

From the woman's perspective, such a relationship allows her to test a man after one or more unsuccessful marriages. A thirty-three-year-old woman who had been married twice previously expressed it this way, "If they don't care for the kids or anything then that's a bad man. . . . First he's got to love your kids before he loves you."

To understand further the importance of such a social role consider the case of Ethyl (thirty-three) and Jay (twenty-four). For Ethyl a boyfriend is indispensable:

> When I get through paying the house rent and two or three bills—insurance maybe—I don't have enough money left for food. It's not going to last a whole month. My friend he just buys groceries every week and things like that. And if I need extra money, I ask him for it and he'll give it to me. . . . He believes in survival for me and my children.

When she moved into the project with four children, Ethyl was receiving $133.00 a month ADC (Aid to Dependent Children) and paying $51.00 a month rent. This left her with $72.50 with which to feed, clothe, and in other less obvious ways support a family of five. Since she was very anemic and in poor health during much of the first year in the project, she did not work. Later her wages as a part-time domestic added about $72.00 a month to her income, but she could not count on this income every month. Her rent was raised to $66.00 a month, nevertheless, leaving $126.00 on which to live. In 1966, her total income was an estimated $3,144.00 of which about $960.00 was contributed by her boyfriend. In this year her household contained an additional two persons, her oldest daughter and her baby. Even the help of her boyfriend did not bring her family above the officially accepted poverty level (about $3,900 for an urban family of five; $5,300 for a family of seven).

Jay was once asked why he bothered to take care of Ethyl. He replied, "That's a personal question. . . . Well, first of all I help her because I love her and we're going to get married sometime, but not just now because we can't afford it."

The Discreet Free-Man: Turning now to the marital relationship, the most interesting type is the discreet free-man. This role enables a man to live effectively in two worlds. The world of the street—where the pretense of intimacy is the basis for interpersonal manipulation and where the fast buck and the cool front are the trade marks of the hustler—has an impact on ghetto families. Yet while families remain remarkably open to the influences of the street, they are not always destroyed by them—particularly if the head of the household is a discreet free-man. Such a man knows how to manage his affairs so that the world outside his legitimate family (typically involving one or more "other women") does not disrupt his domestic happiness. His "cutting out" is clearly a secondary concern which he does not use as a weapon against his wife who knows of his activities nevertheless. Typically, just as he is able to cover up or minimize activities with other women, so also he is able to carry on illegal activities (such as gambling, pimping, pushing dope) in a profitable manner without these appreciably interfering with his home life. An outside observer would undoubtedly be inclined to consider his family a very "stable" one.

An example of this type of relationship is that of the Washingtons. The Washingtons have been married for over twenty-eight years, during nineteen of which Arthur (fifty-one) was the principal wage earner. In 1965 they had eight children living in their household, and their combined income (aside from that money earned illegally) was $4,370—well below the poverty level for a family of such size.

Arthur says of his own cutting out:

> *I am this type of fellow. I talk to anybody before my wife or behind my wife. But just to go out and say I've got a bunch of women and that type of thing . . . that's all baloney. I see some women that look good to me, sure. If you push it you can get caught in the right corner and you might step out. You're human and you're a good one if you don't. If you just go out and strive directly for that, then you're going to find somebody that wants to do these things. The average woman that does it, ain't doing it because she likes to but because she wants to do something . . . different . . . it's not a big deal.*

His wife, Mary (forty-seven), presents a picture of her going along with his discreet outside activities:

> *I think I've been a nice lady. I ain't bragging on myself, but it takes a steady head I guess. I never was a wild person and liked to get out in the streets. I stayed home and took care of my children. . . .*

A major asset of such a masculine role is that it enables the father to be a much more effective agent in the socialization of his sons—given the conditions of ghetto confinement. They know the world of the street is a tough world, and the chances of moving up in the larger society are not good. Their father can show them by his own example how to survive in the world of their everyday existence without sacrificing their family life in the process. Because of his greater effectiveness (as compared to the monogamous father whose morals will not permit him to learn the ways of the city streets) in coping with the harsh realities of ghetto life, he is able to provide a more adequate role model for his sons and consequently has greater control over their behavior. Often they work alongside him in both his legal and illegal jobs.

As a typology of marginality, then, at one end the pimp seems to reflect largely an exploitative relationship between a man and a woman, and at the other the monogamous father reflects a high degree of involvement in the world of one woman and her children. In between it does not follow that "Any father is better than no father at all" because the world of the indiscreet free-man is in constant turmoil, while the quasi-father is much more supportive of his woman and her children. Inside the ghetto—given the condition of quite limited mobility—the strategy of the discreet free-man seems more effective in coping with everyday realities.

The Female-Headed Family: E. Franklin Frazier commented on the centrality of the mother-child dyad to the underclass black family:

> The dependence of the child upon the mother, who is the supreme authority in the household, often creates a solidarity of feeling and sentiment that makes daughters reluctant to leave home with their husbands and brings sons back from their wanderings. . . . The mothers on their part show equally strong attachment for their grown sons and daughters.[55]

Given the conditions of ghetto life, it is probable that, although at any given time the female-headed family is in the minority, a majority of mothers in the ghetto spend at least part of their adult life as the head of a family.

> Because men are not expected to be much help around the house, having to be head of the household is not particularly intimidating to the Negro mother if she can feel some security about income. She knows it is a hard, hopeless and often thankless task, but she also knows that it is possible. The maternal household in the slum is generally run with a minimum of organization. The children quickly learn to fend for themselves, to go to the store, to make small purchases, to bring change home, to watch after themselves when the mother has to be out of the home, to amuse themselves, to set their own schedules of sleeping, eating, and going to school. Housekeeping practices may be poor, furniture

55. E. Franklin Frazier, *The Negro Family in the United States* (Chicago: University of Chicago Press, 1939), p. 144.

takes a terrific beating from the children, and emergencies constantly arise. The Negro mother in this situation copes by not setting too high standards for herself, by letting things take their course. Life is most difficult when there are babies and preschool children around because then the mother is confined to her home. If she is a grandmother and the children are her daughter's, she is often confined since it is taken as a matter of course that the mother has a right to continue her outside activities and that the grandmother has the duty to be responsible for the child.

In this culture there is little of the sense of the awesome responsibility of caring for children that is characteristic of the working and middle class. There is not the deep psychological involvement with babies which has been observed with the working class mother. The baby's needs are cared for on a catch-as-catch-can basis. If there are other children around and they happen to like babies, the baby can be over-stimulated; if this is not the case, the baby is left alone a good deal of the time. As quickly as he can move around he learns to fend for himself.[56]

Such a household is home-base for older children. Girls expect their mother to raise their first baby. Boys (even after twenty) expect to be able to come home and live without working for extended periods of time. This does provide the grandmother with a sense of involvement and usefulness in her later years, however.

PROBLEMS OF PARENTAL CONTROL

A basic mistrust in interpersonal relationships is characteristic of ghetto life. It grows out of a long history of perceived exploitation at the hands of others—civic officials, employers, "the man," and those of one's own race of the opposite sex. (Both sexes are well instructed, but the art of manipulation seems best manifested in the pimp, the man who lives off his woman and uses her money to take other women out, thus demonstrating that he doesn't "give a damn" about his benefactress.) This mistrust is built into the socialization process very early in a child's life.

Contrary to what might be assumed from the evidence of large families and husky smiling women, it is not uncommon for ghetto women to feel themselves "overrun with children." Their tendency to feel this way seems to vary with their birth order. Those born first and consequently forced early to assume the responsibility of raising "her" (their mother's) children feel the strongest resentment. At nine they were caring for her babies, feeding them, and changing their diapers. At thirteen they were "given the children" as their major responsibility. They express a deep-seated anger and resentment against these children who deprived them of their girlhood, and a strong ambivalence over their own children, who come along later in life and restrict the freedom of their womanhood. They give evidence of experiencing

56. Rainwater "Crucible of Identity," p. 195–96.

both an intense feeling of guilt over this hatred and a strong desire to identify with their daughters, in an attempt to regain their girlhood vicariously.

This ever-present guilt causes some ghetto mothers to seek compensation by indulging their children and letting them have their way. But the
anger is not thereby dissipated. It remains always in the background and
sometimes—particularly in the case of first-born daughters who have become
mothers—breaks through their apparently easygoing and indulgent natures in
uncontrollable anger. In some cases this anger is so close to the surface that
they are afraid to discipline their children for fear they will go too far and
seriously hurt them. Thus the basic mistrust is further reinforced in the socialization process, as children sense, but cannot always define, the nature of
their mother's conflict. The male child feels this most, since he offers little
compensation by way of identification for his mother, yet demands the same
care in his early years. From about six on, boys are more likely than girls to
be socialized by their peers in gangs and with buddies.[57]

Children quickly learn from their father also that they are not an unmixed blessing. In the city, large families are liabilities, particularly when the
father is uncertain of his ability to provide for them. Caught in the pinch between desiring children to validate his masculinity, and experiencing repeated
failure in his attempt to provide, the father often deserts. Before he leaves he
may make his reason for leaving explicit: "There are just too many children
in this house." Children thus learn that they are somehow responsible for
forcing their father to leave, although they can do nothing about it.

This is not to imply that ghetto parents do not love their children, or
that they rear children incapable of love. It is intended to say that they bring
up children who must love *in spite of* this basic mistrust of interpersonal
relationships. Such conditions make the matter of parental control more dependent upon the overt concrete demonstration of parental care. Such concrete care is often quite difficult to demonstrate effectively in the context of
ghetto impoverishment. This is most clearly seen in the case of the father's
role.

In contrast to women (who even in the ghetto are more closely identified
with the home, with kin and the continuity of the family, and with the more
respectable institutions such as the church and school—all of which tend to
support an image of an almost unchallengeable respectability about motherhood), the man in many ghetto homes derives at least some of his status from
his ability to cope with the world of the street and to provide for his family

---

57. In our society, at least, boys generally seem to be socialized outside the home
to a greater extent than girls. See, for example, Robert F. Winch *Identification and Its
Familial Determinants* (Indianapolis: Bobbs-Merrill, 1962), p. 123. In the ghetto, however,
the effect of this outside socialization is heightened by the greater respectability and de-
pendability attributed to the mother's role and by the greater inclination to view the
father's role as largely nonfunctional with regard to the family and deviant with regard
to the norms of the larger society. Finally, the effects of the father's absence has perhaps
been somewhat over emphasized. At least one study—David Lynn, "A Note on Sex Differences in the Development of Masculine and Feminine Identification," *Psychological Review* (1959), 126–35—suggests that masculine identification in America depends much more
than feminine identification upon a cultural stereotype of masculinity that can be transmitted via the mass media.

by whatever means become available. The father's "bifocality" is most clearly manifested in the indiscreet free-man role. But the most significant manner in which a father becomes a nexus between his family and the street world is shown in the case of the discreet free-man who gains status in his children's eyes by his coping ability, while not offending them by bringing his "outside" interests into the home. Such fathers thus become effective agents in socializing their sons into the world of the street.

They do this in a number of ways. The first and perhaps most effective is by their successful engagement in such illegal manipulative strategies as gambling or pimping and their participation with their sons in tavern drinking, pool sharking, and other leisure activities of the street. Such fathers further provide their sons with excellent examples of how to lie effectively as they handle strangers such as bill collectors, insurance men, various government agents, and social scientists. This is not to say that nonghetto persons do not lie as a manipulative strategy, but rather that deception seems more pervasive and necessary as a survival strategy in the ghetto. Finally, such fathers are effective socializing agents insofar as their sons take pleasure in listening to their fathers' recollections of the past exploits of their youth. These tales, often told off-hand over a beer or in response to a son's questioning his father as to how to handle a particular situation, bind father and son in a common heritage of "making the best of it" and "taking care of business." Not all project fathers tell such tales, because not all have had the experience of making it on their own, living off women, pushing the numbers, or engaging in other "unrespectable" activities. But in the ghetto where the legal means of mobility are often clearly blocked, illegal means seem much more realistic in the circumstances and fathers who are skilled in such techniques have an edge over those who are not—provided they manage their affairs discreetly.

Within the family a father's status is legitimated in various ways: (1) It can be legitimated by virtue of his being able to provide adequately for his family—to offer some protection against the harshness of ghetto realities. (2) The good man, by virtue of his respectable behavior—as demonstrated by his "giving to his children" and his fidelity to his wife—earns the respect of his family and legitimizes his authority over his children to the extent that "they have nothing over him." (3) His status can be legitimated by his ability to teach other members of the family effective strategies for coping with the street. (4) Finally, it can be legitimized by his ability to be a pal and understand his children's problems—particularly his sons'.

All of these elements in a father's role can be seen as offering protection against either external threats of economic destitution and social scorn, or internal threats of alienation and separation from loved ones. The father's claim to legitimate authority within the household can be made on any or all of these. Characteristically, ghetto fathers tend to claim children *ought* to obey them for one of the above reasons, depending upon the extent of their marginality.

The following relationships are suggested:

1. The traditional *monogamous father* tends to legitimate this authority on the basis of two more or less equal aspects of his relationship to the external world, that is, (a) his ability to be an adequate provider (or the fact that his inability to provide is understood as the result of a justified disability), and (b) his claim to respectability. He is affectionate toward his wife and children, of course, but he tends to be—at least verbally—an advocate of the patriarchal type of family. He is generally not an adaptive of the street because he has been more or less able to make it by legitimate means and because his principles prohibit him from such activities.

2. The *discreet free-man*, on the other hand, tends to legitimate his authority within the household on the basis of his being a warm, loving pal to his children and an expressive companion to a more instrumentally oriented wife. He tends also to be able to muster respect for his ability to cope with the problems of street life. He expresses concern for "skeletons" in the family's closet, indicating that he would like to draw upon past respectable behavior as an example for his children, but he does not feel that he can do so.

3. The *indiscreet free-man* has least control over his children because he has little to justify his authority. If he is able to provide for his family, his status is still marred by his split in allegiance, often reflected in a marked division of his resources between his families. He generally has little justification for his authority on the basis of his expressive ability and none as a model of respectability. Whatever ability he has developed in coping with the street is not likely to be passed on to his sons because his handling of this activity generally makes them angry.

4. The situation of the *boyfriend* is simplified since only two of the four types are at all concerned with children. The *quasi-father* seems to be inclined to legitimate his authority on the basis of his instrumental effectiveness and coping ability. The *supportive biological father*, on the other hand, stresses his affective role, while at the same time offering support to the children. He, more than the quasi-father, wants the children to think of him as a "good guy"; he has a greater stake in their affection since they are biologically his. In the case of the quasi-father where the *obligation* is not as apparent, the *fact* of support can be called upon as a legitimate reason for assuming some authority over the family.

Whatever the grounds for asserting parental authority, the relative effectiveness of parental control is reduced in the ghetto. What *is* characteristic of the ghetto home is the fact that children constantly question the right of the parents to govern them, and the parents seem unable to establish their authority firmly and set limits to their children's behavior in response to such questioning. Children know that their parents (particularly their fathers) are unable to protect them adequately from the harsh realities of their world and are largely unable to offer them reliable information or dependable role models to enable them to better themselves in the world outside of the ghetto. When parents attempt to guide their children along more respectable lines of behavior, they are quite frequently reminded, "You do the same things you tell us not to do. Why can't we do them?" Parents thus watch their children's development with mixed sorrow and a peculiar pride in the fact that they are following after them, even though they know that the road leads nowhere.

Finally, parents are confronted quite straightforwardly with the fact that they need their children's love. Boys, in particular, threaten to withhold this by running away from home to live with a relative more likely to grant them what they want in terms of the small pleasures of life. Children who have been "farmed out" will hold this fact against their parents and taunt them by saying that they liked living where they were sent better than living at home.

The result is a constant threat of insurrection in the home. Parents often try to cope with this by letting a child have his way and intervening in his life only in extreme situations. Such belated intervention only further weakens the bargaining power of the parents and submits their authority to further questioning since, when confronted with a delinquent child for example, they have even fewer resources to call upon for help.

Because parental authority is constantly being subverted, a common recourse in the ghetto is to call upon some recognized authority from outside of the family. Neighbors will not do, because they are normally unwilling to intervene in another's family domestic squabbles—unless it is to defend their own child from presumed attack; past experience has told them that to attempt such an intervention would likely only increase the conflict.

The police, therefore, are quite often called upon to settle domestic troubles between parents themselves and between parents and their children.[58] Such intervention is both needed and hated because it makes it obvious that the family is unable to govern its own life. Furthermore, persons who thus intervene are very likely to acquire a closer relationship with one member of the family (ordinarily the wife) and incur the wrath of another. Outside intervention thus restores order in the household without solving or resolving any of the problems that precipitated the disorder. At the same time, such intervention heightens suspicion among family members and churns resentments likely to erupt later into further discord. Such discord tends to increase the father's marginality and his desire to desert.

58. For a further discussion of this point, see David A. Schulz, "Some Aspects of the Policeman's Role as it Impinges on the Lower-Class Negro Family," *Sociological Focus* (Spring, 1969).

TABLE 8–3   Divorce Ratio of Persons 25 to 64 years old, per 100 Married Persons, by Region

Area, race, nativity, and parentage	Ratio for men					Ratio for women				
	United States	North-east	North Central	South	West	United States	North-east	North Central	South	West
Total	3.1	2.0	3.1	2.9	5.0	4.5	3.4	4.4	4.4	6.7
Urban	3.4	2.1	3.5	3.4	5.2	5.4	3.7	5.5	5.9	7.7
Urbanized areas	3.4	2.1	3.7	3.6	5.4	5.6	3.6	5.7	6.4	8.2
central city	4.3	2.6	4.7	4.3	6.8	6.9	4.5	7.3	7.4	9.9
urban fringe	2.3	1.4	2.1	2.2	4.0	3.8	2.6	3.4	4.2	6.4
Other urban	3.1	2.4	3.0	2.9	4.3	4.9	3.9	4.8	5.0	5.7
Rural Nonfarm	2.7	1.8	2.7	2.5	4.7	2.6	2.2	2.5	2.5	3.5
Rural Farm	1.6	1.4	1.3	1.7	2.9	1.0	1.0	0.7	1.2	1.3
Native white of native Parentage	3.1	2.2	3.0	2.9	5.1	4.5	3.6	4.2	4.2	6.6
Urban	3.5	2.4	3.4	3.3	5.3	5.7	4.2	5.5	5.7	7.8
Urbanized areas	3.7	2.4	3.6	3.6	5.6	6.0	4.1	5.7	6.3	8.4
central cities	4.8	3.2	4.8	4.4	7.2	7.6	5.5	7.6	7.5	10.3
urban fringe	2.5	1.6	2.1	2.1	4.2	4.2	2.9	3.5	4.2	6.6
Other urban	3.1	2.6	2.9	2.9	4.4	4.9	4.6	4.9	4.7	5.8
Rural Nonfarm	2.7	1.9	2.6	2.5	4.6	2.6	2.3	2.6	2.5	3.5
Rural Farm	1.7	1.4	1.4	1.8	2.9	1.0	1.0	0.8	1.2	1.2
Foreign White Stock	2.5	1.7	2.6	2.5	4.6	3.7	2.8	3.6	4.6	6.2
Negro	4.1	2.9	6.4	3.2	8.1	6.8	5.5	10.1	5.3	13.5
Urban	4.6	2.9	6.3	4.0	8.0	8.0	5.6	10.3	7.1	14.0
Urbanized areas	4.8	2.9	6.3	4.2	8.1	8.3	5.6	10.1	7.3	14.4
central cities	5.0	3.0	6.4	4.4	8.9	8.5	5.7	10.5	7.7	15.2
urban fringe	3.6	2.5	4.8	3.2	5.4	6.7	5.1	8.5	5.1	11.6
Other urban	3.8	3.5	6.9	3.3	7.4	6.8	4.4	9.8	6.6	8.1
Rural Nonfarm	2.6	2.9	9.9	2.2	9.8	2.8	3.8	6.0	2.6	5.0
Rural Farm	1.4	2.4	4.7	1.3	4.8	1.2	2.1	1.3	1.2	1.6
Other Races	4.0	2.7	5.3	3.8	4.0	3.7	2.3	3.5	4.0	3.9

Source: U.S. Bureau of the Census, U.S. Census of Population: 1960, Subject Reports, Marital Status (Washington, D.C.: U.S.G.P.O.), Table 3.

BREAKING UP MARRIAGES

Marriages in the black ghetto are often broken. Table 8–3 compares the number of divorced persons per hundred married persons for Whites and Blacks, by sex, region, and residence in 1960. Table 8–4 does the same for separated persons. Black rates are much higher than White rates and reach their peak in the central cities of the Northeast in the case of separation rates for black women (22.1 percent). The divorce rates are highest for black women in the central cities of the North Central states. In both cases the data support Frazier's image of the city of destruction. The black family is clearly more likely to remain intact in rural farm areas—particularly in the South. In part this is because there the nuclear family is more firmly embedded in an extended family, and partly it is the result of relatively greater value of a man's labor.

Data from a sample survey of project families give some idea of the reasons for breaking up families. Since a person could give more than one response, the percentages do not total 100.

Sexual infidelity	*40%*
Husband wouldn't support her	*20*
Husband lost job, couldn't find another	*3*
One partner too immature	*17*
Husband drank excessively	*15*
Husband cruel, beat her	*15*
Husband gambled too much	*7*
Husband in jail	*3*
Unspecified infidelity	*22*
Husband just deserted, no reason given	*8*

Despite the fact that "having papers" on a woman entitles the husband to treat her much more roughly than he could if she were simply his girl, husbands sometimes overextend themselves, and wives can't simply "lay down and let that man walk all over them." The most commonly mentioned reasons for breaking up are infidelity and nonsupport. The former further gives the lie to the concept of marriage as a minimal commitment in the ghetto; the latter again highlights the problems of unemployment and deprivation. Marital breakup, despite its relatively greater frequency in the ghetto, is not taken lightly. A mother of five children who had been married for six years recalls her husband's change in behavior after the birth of their third child:

> Then he started drinking and staying away from home. . . . He was real cruel. He like to fight and I didn't. . . . We'd fight sometimes two or three times a week. I put up with that for almost two years. Then I left and I was too proud to go back. . . . I miss him sometimes you know. I think about him I guess . . . just in a small way.

TABLE 8—4   Separation Ratio of Persons 25 to 64 years old, per 100 Married Persons, by Region

Area, race, nativity, and parentage	Ratio for men					Ratio for women				
	United States	North-east	North Central	South	West	United States	North-east	North Central	South	West
Total	2.0	2.3	1.4	2.5	1.7	3.1	3.7	2.0	3.8	2.3
Urban	2.2	2.4	1.8	2.8	1.8	3.6	4.2	2.7	4.8	2.6
Urbanized areas	2.4	2.5	2.0	2.9	1.9	3.8	4.4	3.0	4.8	2.8
central city	3.2	3.5	2.9	3.6	2.5	5.1	6.1	4.2	6.0	3.5
urban fringe	1.2	1.4	0.7	1.4	1.3	2.0	2.3	1.2	2.3	2.0
Other urban	1.8	1.9	1.0	2.6	1.4	3.0	3.1	1.5	4.7	2.0
Rural Nonfarm	1.6	1.5	0.9	2.2	1.6	1.9	1.7	1.0	2.8	1.4
Rural Farm	1.0	1.3	0.4	1.7	0.9	0.9	0.9	0.2	1.6	0.5
Native white of native Parentage	1.4	2.0	1.0	1.3	1.5	1.8	2.8	1.2	1.7	1.9
Urban	1.5	2.2	1.1	1.4	1.6	2.2	3.4	1.5	2.1	2.2
Urbanized areas	1.6	2.2	1.3	1.5	1.7	2.3	3.4	1.6	2.2	2.2
central cities	2.1	3.3	1.8	1.7	2.1	3.0	5.1	2.2	2.5	2.7
urban fringe	1.0	1.4	0.6	0.9	1.2	1.6	2.0	1.0	1.5	1.8
Other urban	1.2	2.0	0.9	1.2	1.4	1.9	3.1	1.3	2.0	1.9
Rural Nonfarm	1.2	1.5	0.8	1.3	1.4	1.3	1.6	0.9	1.5	1.3
Rural Farm	0.7	1.3	0.3	0.9	0.8	0.4	0.8	0.2	0.7	0.4
Foreign White Stock	1.2	1.4	0.8	1.2	1.3	1.9	2.3	1.1	1.9	1.9
Negro	9.5	11.4	10.0	8.8	8.5	15.4	20.7	15.3	14.0	13.6
Urban	10.1	11.4	9.9	10.0	8.3	17.2	21.0	15.4	16.8	14.0
Urbanized areas	10.2	11.5	9.9	10.0	8.2	17.3	21.2	15.7	16.6	14.2
central cities	10.6	12.1	10.2	10.3	8.8	17.9	22.1	16.0	17.0	15.2
urban fringe	7.6	8.4	6.9	7.8	6.3	13.8	16.5	12.6	13.3	10.7
Other urban	9.8	9.1	9.0	10.0	8.9	16.6	15.7	11.4	17.4	10.1
Rural Nonfarm	8.2	12.7	13.7	7.5	11.4	10.5	13.4	12.1	10.4	7.7
Rural Farm	5.2	8.5	8.2	5.1	6.7	6.0	6.4	4.4	6.1	3.4
Other Races	2.4	5.2	3.1	3.1	1.9	2.3	4.8	3.3	3.9	1.6

Source: U.S. Bureau of the Census, U.S. Census of Population: 1960, Subject Reports, Marital Status (Washington, D.C.: U.S.G.P.O.), Table 3.

PERSONAL LIFE STYLES
FOR COPING WITH POVERTY

Lee Rainwater suggests that under the conditions of extreme deprivation and exclusion that characterizes the ghetto, the personal life styles appropriate to living outside the ghetto are not adequate.[59] The notions that one can make a life out of his career and can find maximum happiness in the "good life" by virtue of his own striving depend upon the conviction that the system is trustworthy and that the opportunity to change status is open.

In the ghetto the larger society does not seem trustworthy, and mobility seems quite unlikely. The alternatives open to ghetto dwellers are the expressive, the depressive, and the violent. In the *expressive life style* the actor—after the fashion of the hustler or confidence man—"sells himself." He makes himself attractive to others so that he can manipulate their behavior for personal gain. In the ghetto such activity is called "working game." The *depressive strategy* is commonly one of withdrawal: "I don't bother anybody and I hope nobody's gonna bother me; I'm simply going through the motions to keep body (but not soul) together." Persons following such a strategy commonly spend days watching television. The *violent* is increasingly seen in urban rioting where the pent up emotions of a thousand frustrations are released in aggressive behavior resulting in widespread destruction. Less notable (from the nonghetto world's point of view) are the high rates of violent crimes against persons committed in the ghetto everyday, most of which never reach the major newspapers and most of which are never solved. Most of these crimes are committed by the ghetto dweller against the fellow ghetto dweller and remain in the ghetto (police surveillance is much greater than police protection in most ghettos).

These styles Rainwater has termed "strategies for survival." They are not strategies for maximizing the benefits of the larger society for oneself and do not offer training in techniques that will be successful outside of the ghetto. They frequently result in suffering within the ghetto. They do, however, provide the ghetto dweller with effective techniques for living in his violent and restricted world. Most persons utilize mixed strategies that occasionally incorporate the work ethic of the larger society but, since employment is usually underemployment or sub-employment and frequently results in unemployment, such an alternative is extremely vulnerable in the eyes of a rational man making the most of a bad situation.

Summary

There is a rich variety of family forms found in the black ghetto. The dominant structural form at any one time is similar to the white working-class model. However, because of frequent unemployment, job discrimination re-

59. Rainwater, "Crucible of Identity."

sulting in under- and sub-employment and inadequate training, the role of the black father in the ghetto is difficult indeed. Therefore, it is likely that most women in the ghetto spend a portion of their adult lives as heads of households and that most children spend a part of their lives living with only one parent. The fact that a woman is head of a household does not mean that there are no men around the house. An intensive study of ten families containing 108 persons (see footnote 30) helps to describe the male's marginality to the basic mother-child dyad, but since the sample is small, it is difficult to evaluate its representativeness. The boyfriend is typically present and often assumes a quite responsible role vis-à-vis his woman and her children as a quasi-father. In the ghetto some fathers are quite marginal to their families because of their dual commitment to several families. The father who seems best able to manage the affairs of a ghetto family (given the conditions of its isolation from the opportunities of the larger society and its extreme deprivation) is the discreet free-man who makes the best of both legal and illegal means of earning a living without disrupting his domestic world.

A father's status in the family is variable. In the ghettoes some families are still patriarchal—particularly if the father is the principal wage earner—and others are equalitarians; most are matrifocal. A man's authority is a function of his marginality (with the exception of the situation of the pimp where a highly exploitative relationship obtains in conjunction with extreme marginality).

The large families of the ghetto are not the result of conscious design. Most parents would wish fewer children, and some mothers (particularly those who were first-born daughters and were saddled with the responsibility of raising children from an early age) feel overrun with children. They tend to mask their hostility through indulgence or minimum interference in their children's affairs. Given better understanding of contraceptive techniques *and* greater opportunities to engage in the occupational, recreational, and educational opportunities of the larger society, most would probably be more effective practitioners. The many needs met by sexual behavior in the ghetto make it unlikely that these mothers will become effective practitioners until some alternatives to meeting these needs are devised.

Thus both from the perspective of male marginality and from that of family planning, it does not seem likely that the character of family life will change appreciably in the ghetto until the harsh conditions of ghetto life are relieved. The various patterns of family life in the ghetto are effective—if sometimes painful—means of coping with poverty and isolation. Nevertheless, most Blacks see these ghetto alternatives as acceptable but "second best" to the more commonly accepted ideal of the two-parent family. Under more equitable situations it is probable that more families in the ghetto would have both parents for longer periods of time. This structural similarity need not imply that these families will be like the ideal American family in other ways as well. Much of the life lived in black underclass families is rich and satisfying and will be retained as a part of the black experience even under better economic conditions, because it has been tested and found better than the "ideal."

Up until this point I have considered the family and its members as primarily dependent on societal pressures. Although I have talked about adaptability and coping strategies, the bulk of the data has emphasized the constraints placed upon the family from the outside. In this section I focus on the *internal* dynamics of the family, examining in some detail its life cycle and child-rearing practice, and the process of selecting a mate.

Chapter 9 demonstrates that the family is a social institution with its own internal pressures and constraints. From its inception at marriage to its termination with the death of both spouses, the family is constantly changing as children are (ordinarily) added and then launched into careers of their own. Each stage in its development can be seen as presenting particularly critical tasks that must be satisfactorily completed or the family will suffer additional strains. The problems and the life styles of families at each stage of its development are different, thus adding further variation to the patterns of family life discernible in America.

In Chapter 10, I examine the process of mate selection—a process that has received considerable attention among American sociologists. It will soon become apparent that even though we do not typically depend upon marriages arranged by lineages for our social cohesion, we do informally restrict the range of mate choice to a rather narrow "field of eligibles." The couple who decide to go against these informal expectations regarding appropriate mate choice will find that their marriage will face many more hardships than the conventional marriage. This results in greater divorce rates, fewer children, a greater incidence of juvenile delinquency, and a host of other problems.

In the final chapter of this section I examine some aspects of our child-rearing practices. One consequence of the relatively greater isolation of the upper middle-class and lower upper-class families is a dependence upon expert advice in matters pertaining to how to raise children. In the 1930's there was considerable optimism over the possibility that this advice would eventually be so perfected that we could raise children "to order." As social scientists have investigated the problem further, however, this optimism has waned. The effect of parental behavior upon children's behavior is extremely difficult to assess. At the present time advice to parents reflects not only conflicting empirical data, but also divergent theoretical perspectives that interpret this data in contradictory ways. As a result, expert advice is fadish. I examine the broad trends this advice has taken over the past century, and attempt to clarify the issues raised by an examination of two theoretical frameworks within which the process of socialization may be viewed—Winch's concept of identification and Warriner's theory of symbolic interaction. Although the social sciences are a long way from being able to provide a manual on how to raise precisely the type of child you want, the insights obtained on parent-child interaction, nevertheless, can improve the quality of the interaction in many instances.

FAMILY DYNAMICS

9. The Family Life Cycle: Development and Crisis

For everything there is a season,
and a time for every matter under heaven:

a time to be born, and a time to die . . .

a time to embrace, and a time to refrain
    from embracing; . . .

a time to love, and a time to hate. . . .

ECCLESIASTES 3

In my concern with relating the family to its social milieu, I have heretofore largely avoided the question of the family's own internal dynamics. Like a person, the human family can be conceived of as having a life cycle. Ordinarily it is begun in a marriage, increases in size during the child-bearing years, wanes as the children are launched into families of their own, and ceases to be when both parents die. The family of a newly married couple is quite different from one with preschool children or one in which all the children have grown up and left home. These, in turn, are quite different from the family of a surviving spouse. Each has its own particular problems, bears its own peculiar burdens, and experiences different joys because it is made up of different sets of role relationships and faces quite different demands and problems. The persons who fill these roles have different needs, and the society expects different things from each type of family. We have a strong tendency to think of "the family" as a married couple with children, particularly small children. Our advertisements commonly reflect this concept of the family, because the consumer needs of such a family are great. Yet the life cycle of a family clearly is much more varied than this.

Just as a person is only arbitrarily separated from his social milieu so also the life cycle of a family is only arbitrarily separated from its society. The characteristics of the average American family's life cycle have changed noticeably over the past century and a half. Because of improvements in our medical services, diet, and general standard of living, life expectancy has steadily increased. Because men and women live longer now than they did at the turn of the century, it is not uncommon for grandparents to see their grandchildren married. Around 1900, one parent commonly died before the last child had become independent. The characteristics of the family life cycle, particularly in the periods after the children have left home, are quite different now than they were then. Part of the problem of growing old in America derives from the blessing of longer life on the one hand, and the crises presented by the necessity to redefine a marital relationship after the children have gone on the other. In turn, the problems of the aged are becoming an increasing concern to our society at large, as the number of aged increase and their independence from their children continues to be valued.

When I refer to a "typical" or "average" family in this chapter, it should be clear that these terms constitute a useful fiction. Most of the studies concerned with the life cycle of the family are not complex enough as yet to take into consideration all the effects of such factors as race, class, region, and ethnicity. Commonly it is acknowledged that it would be more accurate to talk about several typical life cycles that reflect these factors, but to date this refinement has not been introduced. The interest in the study of the family's life cycle is only a little over a decade old, and the conceptual scheme is still struggling for acceptance.

What does come into focus in this approach is that the family changes in response to its own internal demands as well as in response to the demands imposed upon it by its society. This process of change is *analogous* to the growth of an individual, but the family is not, in the last analysis, an organism. It is a social institution. To assume that its growth is essentially a process of maturation leads to an over-simplified conceptualization of developmental tasks that reminds one of the errors of the early evolutionists who assumed that societies and social institutions pass inevitably through successive stages of development. Yet the concept of developmental task, when not taken as rigidly, might cause one to ask what might be expected at a particular point in the family's development and, again, if the expected is not happening, what the consequences may be. Evelyn Duvall characterizes the genius of the approach as calling attention to the fact that each stage has its roots in the preceding stage in what is in fact a continuous process.

In this chapter I will look at the family life cycle and the developmental tasks associated with it.[1] Particular emphasis will be placed upon the problems of growing old. These problems stem in large measure from the changed characteristics of the later stages of the family life cycle. I will consider the family life cycle in its natural sequence, beginning with a brief discussion of the concepts of life cycle and developmental task.

Basic Concepts

THE FAMILY LIFE CYCLE

Although researchers agree on the outside parameters of the family life cycle —marriage and the death of the surviving spouse—deciding what aspects of the family's life cycle are to be considered critical so as to mark off a new stage is somewhat arbitrary. Table 9–1 shows that the number of stages in the life cycle can vary depending upon the conceptual scheme of a particular researcher. This is not an exhaustive treatment. A major over-arching division, however, separates the expanding from the contracting family, the first period being concerned with the problems of bearing and rearing children through adolescence, the second with the problems of launching the children on their own and the re-establishment of the relationship between the primary conjugal pair, retirement, and death.

The number of stages considered reflects the importance attached to particular developmental tasks by various researchers. For example, Sorokin et al. were really not concerned with differentiating between the various stages of child rearing. The problem of support and dependence was more important for them than any of the subsidiary problems of socialization and control likely to be stressed by the other researchers. The most elaborate scheme, described by Rodgers, takes into consideration the developmental problems of the last-born as well as the first-born child. Duvall does not do this. She argues that the family in a sense repeats the process it learned with the socialization of the first-born child as it passes through the stage with each successive child. Clearly, even Rodgers' elaboration does not match the complexity of family life, for "no two children are alike." Each must present different problems to the family, although the family has learned in a general way how

1. A brief description of this approach can be found in George P. Rowe, "The Developmental Conceptual Framework to the Study of the Family" in F. Ivan Nye and Felix M. Berardo (eds.), *Emerging Conceptual Frameworks in Family Analysis* (New York: Macmillan, 1966), pp. 198–222.

TABLE 9–1
Delineations of Stages in the Family Life Cycle

Family cycle stage	Sorokin, Zimmerman, and Gilpin (1931)	National Conference on Family Life (1948)	Duvall (1957)	Feldman* (1961)	Rodgers (1962)
I	Starting married couple	Couple without children	Couple without children	Early marriage (childless)	Childless couple
II	Couple with one or more children	Oldest child less than 30 months	Oldest child less than 30 months	Oldest child an infant	All children less than 36 months
III		Oldest child from 2½ to 5	Oldest child from 2½ to 6	Oldest child at preschool age	Preschool family with (a) oldest 3–6 and youngest under 3; (b) all children 3–6
IV		Oldest child from 5 to 12	Oldest child from 6 to 13	All children school age	School-age family with (a) infants, (b) preschoolers, (c) all children 6–13
V		Oldest child from 13 to 19	Oldest child from 13 to 20	Oldest child a teenager, all others in school	Teenage family with (a) infants, (b) preschoolers, (c) school-agers, (d) all children 13–20
VI	(III) One or more self-supporting children	When first child leaves till last is gone	When first child leaves till last is gone	One or more children at home and one or more out of the home	Young adult family with (a) infants, (b) preschoolers, (c) school-agers, (d) teenagers, (e) all children over 20
VII	(IV) Couple getting old with all children out	Later years	Empty nest to retirement	All children out of home	Launching family with (a) infants, (b) preschoolers, (c) school-agers, (d) teenagers, (e) youngest child over 20
VIII				Elderly couple	When all children have been launched until retirement
IX			Retirement to death of one or both spouses		Retirement until death of one spouse
X					Death of first spouse to death of the survivor

Source: George P. Rowe, "The Developmental Conceptual Framework to the Study of the Family," in F. Ivan Nye and Felix M. Berardo (eds.), *Emerging Conceptual Frameworks in Family Analysis* (New York: Macmillan, 1966), pp. 208–09.

*Feldman enumerates Stages IX, X, and XI to classify childless families to correspond with children in the stages of childbearing, childrearing, empty nest, and old age (Stages II to VIII).

to handle the common problems associated with the stages of development from its experience with older children.

A "typical" family cycle is based on an eight-stage cycle similar to that of Duvall (see Table 9–1). On the basis of a hypothetical three-child family it is estimated that parents will spend almost as much time together without children (about twenty-one and a half years) as they will with their children (twenty-six years). The period of time the mother is likely to spend in her family without children (twenty-nine years) is longer than the time she will spend rearing them.

And yet, as we have seen, the feminine role as normatively defined in America still assumes that motherhood will be a full-time career for the average woman. Further, the fact that "family" is normatively defined as a child-rearing institution and that preparation for marriage ordinarily does not prepare one for the tasks of redefining one's conjugal role after the children have left, means that the period of disengagement is commonly fraught with many difficulties for American parents. This period of readjustment in the later years has become a problem in part because it has tended to become longer over the years.

Figure 9–1 indicates the trends over the period 1890–1960 for significant transitional ages in the family life cycle and extrapolates to the year 1980. The age at first marriage for both husband and wife has been generally decreasing according to these calculations, although after 1960 there does seem to be a trend toward a slightly later age of first marriage which is the reason for the variation in the 1980 forecast. Women have generally been completing their child-bearing period earlier, though this too may well show a slight increase by 1980. The most dramatic change that is indicated in this figure is the transposition of the last two trends: marriage of last child and death of one spouse. In 1890, both husband and wife were likely to die about two years before the marriage of their last child. By 1940, they could expect to live about ten years after this event, and by 1980, it is postulated that they can expect to live eighteen years after the marriage of their last child—the wife having a slightly longer expectancy than her husband.

DEVELOPMENTAL TASKS

Closely associated with the concept of the family life cycle is the notion derived in large part from Erik Erikson that a family, as well as its individual members, must satisfactorily accomplish certain crucial tasks at specific stages in its development or it will not develop normally.[2] Evelyn Duvall defines a developmental task as one:

> . . . which arises at or about a certain period in the life of an individual
> [or family], successful achievement of which leads to his happiness and

2. See especially Erik H. Erikson, "The Problem of Ego Identity" in Maurice R. Stein, Arthur J. Vedich, and David Manning White (eds.), *Identity and Anxiety* (Glencoe, Ill.: Free Press, 1960), pp. 37–87.

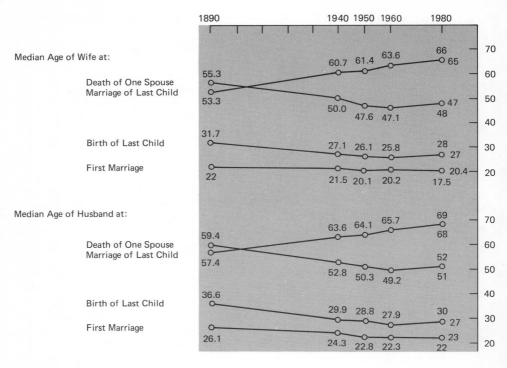

FIGURE 9–1
The ages of husband and wife at critical points in their family's life cycle,
1890–1980. Adapted from Paul C. Glick, David M. Heer, and John C.
Beresford, "Social Change and Family Structure: Trends and Proposals,"
paper delivered to the Association for the Advancement of Science,
December 29, 1959.

> *to success with later tasks, while failure leads to unhappiness in the in-*
> *dividual, disapproval by the society, and difficulty with later tasks.[3]*

As Duvall conceives of these tasks they arise from two sources: (1) physi-cal maturation and (2) cultural pressures and privileges. The individual feels constrained to accomplish certain tasks at a certain time, not only because he has biologically matured so that the task becomes possible, but also because he senses that his society—particularly his family and friends—expects that he should accomplish this task at this time. A normal child, by definition, ac-complishes each task in its appropriate time and sequence from mastering drinking out of a cup, to learning the language of his people, to assuming the responsibilities of adulthood and providing for a family of his own. A child who does not follow the expected pattern is likely to be regarded as

3. Evelyn Duvall, *Family Development*, 5th ed. (Philadelphia: Lippincott, 1969), pp. 31–32.

retarded or too precocious and may well experience a great deal of unhappiness as a result.

This concept of developmental tasks introduces a number of problems. It has a certain inherent appeal and seems to fit roughly with what we can observe in the course of our attempt to rear children and in our reflections upon our own development. It does stress the importance of cultural expectations and definitions of appropriate development which are quite obviously culture bound. But just as the approach is not interested typically in comparative material, so also it does not allow—if taken as commonly presented—for individual variation without serious repercussions. It is, in fact, not at all clear that certain tasks must be accomplished before others in order for development to occur. A particular person may alter the pattern without apparent ill effect, and a society may redefine the sequence of development. For example, becoming a satisfactory sex partner is not a task peculiar to the establishment phase of family life, but it has its roots in infancy and proceeds throughout life. It is increasingly inaccurate to assume that there is something critical about this particular aspect of human behavior during the early years of married life since pre-marriage has become more important in American society in the establishment of such relationships between future spouses. It may be that by Duvall's premises, it *should* be a developmental task at this stage, but clearly for a large number of people it is not.

The concept of developmental task seems to make more sense when it is applied to a family's development than when it refers to an individual family members' development. What is ordinarily involved in the case of a family is a change in composition resulting in a rearrangement of roles and a redefinition of the statuses of family members in order to accommodate such change. Not all stages are marked by change in composition, however, and this leads one to wonder about the hybrid nature of the conceptual framework.

Some developmental tasks do seem to be associated primarily with changes in family composition (such as those associated with Stages I, II, VII, and IX in Table 9–1) and others more closely associated with changes in the development of individual family members (for example those associated with stages III–VI). It would seem reasonable to assume that the demands made upon the developing family by each type of change (change in composition or change in an individual's development) would be different and that those deriving from a change in composition would be, in general, more stressful than those resulting from the development of individual family members. The concept of the family as a network of interacting actors or status roles allows for these distinctions and the refinement would certainly help to further distinguish the mode of the family's development from the growth of an individual.

The Developing Family

Following Duvall's scheme, the family life cycle consists of eight stages as shown in Figure 9–2. Each has its own developmental tasks which she out-

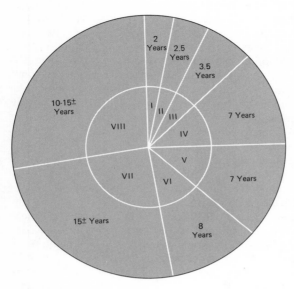

FIGURE 9–2
*The family life cycle by length of time in each of eight stages. From
Evelyn Duvall,* Family Development, *5th ed. (Lippincott, 1969), p. 121.*

lines in great detail in her text *Family Development*.[4] In this section we cannot treat the subject as exhaustively, but rather can suggest how research tends to support some of the basic notions which the developmentalists advance.

BEGINNING FAMILIES

There are many lists of the tasks assumed critical to the beginning family. Kenkel lists nine: *(1)* Developing competency in decision making. *(2)* Working out mutually satisfying and realistic systems for getting and spending the family income. *(3)* Achieving a satisfactory sexual relationship. *(4)* Developing a readiness for parenthood. *(5)* Achieving and enjoying the status of "married" in the community and among friends and relatives. *(6)* Developing ways of expressing and accommodating differences creatively. *(7)* Developing satisfactory relationships with relatives particularly husband's and wife's parents. *(8)* Learning the co-operation required in intimate pair living. *(9)*

---

4. Ibid.

Working out satisfactory household routines and schedules that facilitate smooth functioning in the world of work and pleasure.[5]

Even in such a partial list of developmental tasks, heavy weight is placed upon evaluative elements, and because what is considered satisfactory in one household might not be considered so in another, such an approach leads to an emphasis on interfamily differences. Kenkel provides for such variation by stating the tasks of the beginning family in terms of satisfaction and enjoyment, without specifying the ways in which a couple might achieve such goals. Presumably there will be greater consensus on evaluation along some dimensions than along others. As commonly used, developmental tasks reflect the norms of the researchers as much as they clarify the issues facing particular family types at any given stage in their development. The tendency at present is to assume a normative consensus. To illustrate how the framework operates, I will consider further tasks two and four.

Getting and Spending the Family Income: The matter of income is particularly pertinent to the initial stage of family development. According to the developmental task framework at this stage income procurement patterns are established and the manner in which funds are to be spent must be agreed upon with sufficient understanding so as to permit the couple to "make a go of it."

It seems that any number of reasonable adjustments may be made in regard to income procurement. What is important is that they be mutually acceptable. If the husband is to be the sole income producer from the beginning, the wife must be willing and able to adjust to what might well be a lower initial standard of living than she was accustomed to in her family of orientation. If the wife is to work, the couple must agree upon the conditions under which this is to occur. Is she to work only at first until there are children, or is this to be a lifetime career? The consequences of each choice are different for all concerned since, for example, the matter of surrogate child care must be anticipated in the latter case. The career wife further requires a greater degree of acceptance from her husband since such a pattern is atypical and counter to the common definition of a woman's role and, therefore, more likely to threaten him.

While insufficient income is frequently cited as a major reason for marital unhappiness[6], the manner in which the family income is obtained is equally important.[7] Again, many alternatives can work, but each couple must come to some understanding of how well they will work out the problem of obtaining their family income and spending it. The trend is for increasing participation of the wife in the process of income procurement. In 1900, about 5.6 percent of all married women held jobs. By 1970, over 37 percent

5. William F. Kenkel, *The Family in Perspective* (New York: Appleton-Century-Crofts, 1966), p. 409.

6. Lewis M. Terman *et al.*, *Psychological Factors in Marital Happiness* (New York: McGraw-Hill, 1938), pp. 85, 87.

7. *Ibid.*, pp. 169 ff.

were working. The employment of both marriage partners places not only a strain upon interpersonal relationships, but also creates a problem of timing. With both working there is less time to be together, and what time there is must be devoted largely to the tasks of housekeeping. This in itself creates many problems for the newly married. The development of a workable redistribution of labor so that all gets done without undue strain on one partner is an important corollary to the developmental task of income procurement and distribution.

Kenkel points out that an important aspect of spending is the realization that the income to be spent is one's own and can and should be spent according to the needs of the newly married couple.[8] There are many sources of advice from parents, friends, and professionals that, if taken too authoritatively, can cause the young couple to spend according to someone else's priorities and not their own. When advice can be listened to without the need to comply with it, a great step toward personal control of spending has been taken.

Despite the low accumulation of material wealth characteristic of newly married persons, it must be pointed out that, by many counts, such couples are quite prosperous. If the wife is working, their combined income is likely to be much more than the husband can expect to earn by himself for a number of years. Since there are but two persons to feed and clothe, their consumer demands are relatively low. If the couple does not plan ahead and save, however, the tendency to become accustomed to having money available may set a pattern that is difficult to break when children arrive and the wife ordinarily leaves her work to care for them. Should she wish to continue working for a short time after the birth of their children, a large part of the family income must be allocated toward providing care for the children. In any event, income is likely to exceed output for a large number of married couples in the beginning stage. It may not do so again for some years.

Preparation for Parenthood: Kenkel assumes that a family will have children. Nine out of ten married couples have children, and most of those who do not are not able to have them. Only a very few voluntarily refuse to have children. Nevertheless, parenthood does not "come naturally." It requires an adjustment in attitude and an assessment of readiness to assume new responsibilities. If planning a family were simply a matter of the correct use of contraceptives, then the matter would be relatively simple. E. E. LeMasters has argued that the greatest romanticism in man-woman relationships in America is not connected with the honeymoon and marriage itself, but rather with parenthood.[9] He asserts that the general folklore of our society presents a rather erroneous picture of what parenthood is all about. Rearing children is interesting and no doubt exciting, but it is not always fun. Children are not only cute, they are contrary. Since parents are not the only influence in the

8. Kenkel *op. cit.*, p. 418.

9. E. E. LeMasters, *Parents in Modern America* (Homewood, Ill.: Dorsey, 1970), chap. 2.

lives of their children, it does not always follow that children will turn out well if they have good parents. There are "bad" children as well as "bad" parents, despite the popular tendency to place the fault of children's behavioral problems at the feet of their parents. Finally, not all couples should have children. They may well be better able to live happily and productively without children. Children do not necessarily improve a marriage; they may create as many or more problems than they may resolve.

Nevertheless, romantic notions about parenthood tend to prevent the newly married couple from examining why *they* should have children. They simply assume they ought to have them. The planning of a family involves the realistic assessment of what children will mean to the family and an agreement as to when it is most desirable to have them. Parenthetically, although most couples are fertile, some assessment of the capacity to have children might be wise in the event there is any doubt. The use of contraceptives can easily prevent the recognition of fertility problems and delay the process of adoption should children be desired and the couple be unable to have them.

A strong commitment on both sides to a career, emotional or sexual problems of adjustment in marriage, a strong dislike for children, inadequate resources, genetic or phenotypic disorders, and a host of other matters can be reasons for not having children or for delaying the beginning of a family. The social consequences of a large family (over two children) should be weighed against any personal desire for a large number of children, and the possibility of adopting additional children should be considered if the couple still want more than two. Ideally these matters would be worked through and a reasonable plan for children or no children decided upon before pregnancy. However, despite the relatively high efficiency of middle- and upper-class couples in the use of contraceptives, at least two studies suggest that only about a third of all pregnancies are planned.[10] It does not follow that unplanned children are unwanted or rejected children, but it must be recognized that planning can help to reduce the problems of adjustment and maximize the potential for happiness.

FAMILIES WITH CHILDREN

I will consider the problem of socialization more fully in Chapter 11. At this point I will simply note that parents must radically change their behavior toward their children as they grow older in order to maintain a warm relationship with them. Behavior that indicates warmth to a baby is smothering for a teenager. As children grow up, they also bring to the family different tasks in response to their participation in the society outside the family as well as in response to the changing needs associated with their personal development. They finally create new demands simply by virtue of the fact that they complicate the interaction pattern of the family by creating new relationships.

When the first child is born, the family increases by one, but instead of

10. Kenkel *op. cit.*, p. 424.

there being only one conjugal relationship, there are now three relationships that must be established and maintained. "Two is company, three is a crowd" is a folk saying suggesting something of this increased complexity that applies to children as well as to the customary context of the romantic triangle. With three persons, the possibility of coalition formation emerges, and this fact, as Georg Simmel so aptly pointed out, brings about a very great change in the character of intergroup relationships. The mother-child dyad can easily become so prominent that the father is left out of any significant familial interaction. With the addition of a second child, the potential paired relationships increase to six, and the possibility for triadic coalitions emerges. As the family increases in size, the complexity of the entire network increases and the cohesion of the whole becomes increasingly difficult to maintain. Each family member affects every other and is influenced in turn by them so that the whole family affects the development of each individual member. In this simple enumeration of possible role relationships, I have not commented on the quality of the relationships and the complexities of age-sex differentials in the formation and maintenance of interaction networks. The balance of power within the family changes as new actors are added, and the changed balance presents new problems of adjustment.

Considering the developmental tasks confronting individual family members, a distinction is commonly made between those that must be met by children and those that fall to the responsibility of the parents. A great deal of conceptualizing has produced several schemes of developmental tasks that children must meet.[11] So also elaborate classifications of the developmental tasks confronting parents are extant. My concern here is to focus upon those confronting the conjugal pair. The reader is referred to the sources listed in the footnotes for a discussion of the developmental tasks confronting individual family members.

Several studies support the contention that the birth of a child, particularly the first child, is a crisis whether the child was planned or not. The crisis is precipitated by the necessity to incorporate this new being into the family circle. At the basic level it derives from the increasing complexity of the family interaction network, as has been suggested. It results in part from the necessity to reorganize the economic patterns of earning and spending the family income; in part it derives from the new demands for space, time, and attention now made upon the parents; and in part it derives from the necessity to renegotiate patterns of power and prestige and to re-establish patterns of intimacy (such as a satisfactory sexual relationship) that have been disrupted by the period of pregnancy and post-partum abstinence. For the young husband, conflicts between being a good provider and a good family man are intensified as he becomes aware of the fact that it takes work to "keep in touch with" a developing infant. For the young wife the realization

11. See Erikson *op. cit.*; Duvall *op. cit.*; Kenkel *op. cit.*; and Nelson N. Foote and Leonard S. Cotrell, Jr., *Identity and Interpersonal Competence* (Chicago: University of Chicago Press, 1955).

that child-rearing can be a full-time career becomes evident, and her own need to find a way to personal fulfillment increases. For some, traditional roles are satisfying; for many others, they are not.[12]

The presence of a child makes it necessary to re-establish a satisfactory sexual relationship under a quite different set of demands. Both parents are more likely to be tired as a result of the increased demands made upon their time and labor. Ordinarily a couple is physically able to resume sexual relations four to six weeks after the birth of their child without harm to the wife. But now the overt expression of sexual desire that previously might have been characteristic of their marriage must be controlled so that the more obviously erotic elements—as a matter of decorum—do not occur "in front of the children." Even the most liberal parents must adjust to the presence of children when they feel the need to express their erotic desire. First the infant's cries, then the toddler's demands may interrupt sexual intimacy. It is frequently considered necessary to postpone coitus until late at night so as to reduce the possibility of such invasions of privacy. Any problems in sexual adjustment that before children might have appeared minor are easily magnified afterward because of the necessity to exercise greater control over sexual activity and the frequent requirement that such intimacies occur when the husband and wife are more likely to be exhausted. It appears, too, that men and women commonly experience a reversal in relative sexual desires over the course of their marriage which creates the need for a further adjustment. Women frequently desire coitus more than men during the second half of the child-rearing period of family development.

Associated with the problems of sexual re-adjustment after the birth of children is the task of preserving the intimacy of the husband-wife relationship.[13] Conversation between the conjugal pair becomes more difficult after the arrival of children. Harold Feldman found that not only do young parents talk to each other only half as much as do newly married couples, but also when they talk, they talk about children more frequently than about themselves.[14] Several studies have noted the general disenchantment with marriage that increases over the married years.[15] The frequency of intercourse declines; the amount of shared leisure diminishes.[16] None of these common occurrences need necessarily result in a family crisis or in marital dissatisfaction if they are handled adequately. Failure to deal with them, however, increases the likelihood that the family will become disorganized or will break under the stress.

The tensions placed upon the family by the trauma of American adoles-

12. For a comprehensive study of the role of housewife, see Helena Z. Lopata, *Occupation Housewife* (New York: Oxford University Press, 1971).

13. Kenkel *op. cit.*, p. 454.

14. *Ibid.*, p. 455.

15. Robert O. Blood and Donald M. Wolfe, *Husbands and Wives* (Glencoe, Ill.: Free Press, 1960), p. 264.

16. Peter Pineo, "Disenchantment in the Later Years of Marriage," *Marriage and Family Living*, Vol. 23 (Feb. 1961), 3–11.

cence can not be overlooked nor underemphasized. The recognition that parental love is not enough and that parental authority must compete with other authorities is a difficult awakening for many parents. The limitations of parents as socializing agents has become increasingly apparent to the social scientist. Some of the problems that adolescents present to their parents will be discussed in Chapter 13.

Perhaps the major developmental task facing parents is the necessity to let their children go. We in America tend to view our children as we do our property—as something that belongs to us—when in reality we are stewards who prepare them for independence and then encourage their acceptance of it. Accepting the increasing autonomy and power of the child at the same time that one becomes aware of one's own decreasing energies is indeed difficult, but inescapable. As long as children are obviously dependent, matters of authority and control are relatively minimized. With independence comes the necessity to negotiate with children as persons with rights and privileges of their own. If child-rearing patterns have been unduly authoritarian, this re-allocation of power presents a major challenge to parents and to children.

FAMILIES IN THE MIDDLE YEARS

The family after the children have become independent has aptly been called the "empty nest." The stage Duvall designates as the middle years extends from the departure of the last child to retirement. The tendency to finish child bearing earlier coupled with increasing longevity has resulted in an average length of the stage of about fifteen years. This period of renewed independence with relative vigor after the departure of the children has been generally lengthening since the turn of the century. The formal termination of this stage at retirement, however, means that as men and women retire from the labor force earlier (as they are now doing) the period may shorten in the future even though the life span of men and women continues to lengthen. A major rationale for terminating the stage at retirement derives from the necessity to adjust to the tremendous increase in "free" time, on the one hand, and an often radically reduced income on the other.

The couple in the middle years have the opportunity to rediscover each other, regain a greater intimacy, and recapture a new sense of independence. Since middle-aged persons are generally healthier now than at the turn of the century, they can do this while still quite vigorous and with near maximum income. The possibility of a whole new rich and rewarding way of life awaits them. However, their conjugal relationship has changed over the period of child rearing. The married pair have grown apart. The wife, who may desire to return to a career, discovers that her prolonged absence has made it impossible for her to compete with those who have remained in their profession even if she should be fortunate enough to gain a professional position. Time that is free is not necessarily leisure time that is spent creatively. It can be time that weighs heavily. A wife who can no longer function as a mother, who is not inclined toward the niceties of homemaking, and who cannot enter a career faces a major problem of adjustment.

On the average, couples who begin their child-bearing period early enter the middle stage of their marriage around the age of forty-five or fifty. The need to accept the processes of aging occurs now, not in the context of confrontation with children who are pressing for independence and autonomy, but rather at a time when one is aware of the passing of a significant period of one's life—that devoted to child rearing. As a society we have not fully defined the conjugal roles of middle-aged parents without children because until recently they have been a rarity. Women end their child-bearing potential at menopause and are, in our culture, inclined to be irritable. The male experiences a decline in reproductive capacity that is more gradual, but one which apparently also has emotional components. The bodies of both men and women lose their tone, begin to wrinkle, and change their shape—physical stamina declines. In a society that worships youth, the cessation of the menses symbolizes for the woman the end of her youthfulness in a quite dramatic way.

These changes in one's body can be coped with in a number of ways: They can be accepted as inevitable. Their effect upon one's self-esteem can be reduced by careful cosmetics and dress. By retaining a full schedule as long as possible or determining to exercise for as long as possible, a person may retain his vigor. Amazingly, many of the effects of aging can be minimized for a long period of time by the proper exercise, diet, involvement in interesting and relaxing activities, and so on. Masters and Johnson, for example, tell us that men and women *can* continue an active sexual life well into their eighties, and yet many do not. For a couple to meet the task of dealing with the physiological changes of the middle years, there must be a willingness to make adjustments in the daily routine, diet, patterns of exercise, relaxation, and work. Poised against the hope to remain vigorous and the inclination to place high value on sexual pleasure even into the declining years, is the need to adjust to the realities of one's own physiology which may not, for whatever reason, permit the realization of such ideals.

For the middle-aged husband there comes a time of reckoning that is often quite difficult. He must admit that he may never be able to realize the success he had envisioned in his career. At or near the probable peak of his career, the contrast between the reality of his accomplishment and his aspirations is often unbearable. His disillusionment coincides with his wife's difficulty in coping with the void created by the now independent children, and they both need each other desperately. Yet the problem of re-establishing a bond of psychological intimacy may be too great. Certainly it is very difficult for many couples. When they should be sharing in order to rediscover one another, they discover that they do not have many common interests, that they are not accustomed to conversation, and that it is difficult to create conditions that will make these things possible.

In the midst of such struggles in rediscovery, there is the necessity to plan for retirement. The economic dimensions of this should have been taken care of many years previously, but often it has been impossible for families to put aside savings or to participate in private retirement programs that will adequately provide for the postretirement years. Certainly social security is a misnomer, since it is grossly inadequate as a major source of retirement income. It seems clear that a majority of couples in America do not adequately plan for retirement even in the very basic matter of finance.

Yet finance is but one component of a whole complex of problems centering around what can be done with the remaining years of life. While there is still an income, there is still a sense of usefulness and the possibility of overcoming some of the financial deficit now that the children have become independent. It is the matter of retaining a sense of usefulness after one ceases to be a "productive" member of society (drops out of the labor force) that must be reckoned with in the middle years. Now is the time to develop hobbies, engage in community activities that can be carried through after retirement. Clearly these are the concerns of upper-middle-class couples who anticipate reasonable income. The majority of American families can not afford such luxuries, for poverty awaits many after retirement and this threat alone is a fearful specter. In any event it is desirable, if possible, to plan to retire *to* something rather than think of oneself as retiring *from* something. The amount of income at one's disposal obviously affects the degree of freedom one has in deciding what this "something" might be.

AGING FAMILIES

That American norms support the autonomous nuclear family is made particularly clear in the case of the aged. A 1957 study found that 68.2 percent of all aged persons lived apart from their children. Twenty percent of these lived alone, 37 percent with spouse only. Women over sixty-five were more likely to be found living alone than were men (25.1 percent versus 14.4 percent). Another study conducted in 1962 found only 27.6 percent of the aged persons in its sample living in the same household with their children, although another 33 percent lived within ten minutes of their nearest child. The United States was quite similar to Denmark in this regard but differed from Great Britain where 41.9 percent of the aged lived with children and another 23.5 percent lived within ten minutes of their nearest child (Table 9–2).[17]

The 1965 survey by the U.S. census found only 9.4 percent of the men and 18.9 percent of the women over sixty-five living with relatives, although 66.8 percent of the men and 33.3 percent of the women lived together with their spouse without their children.[18]

Figure 9–3 indicates that the onset of widowhood has come later in life

17. See also Matilda White Riley and Anne Foner, *Aging and Society*, Vol. I (New York: Russell Sage Foundation, 1968, pp. 167–83, for a survey of data on the housing arrangements for aged persons.

18. Marvin R. Koller, *Social Gerontology* (New York: Random House, 1968), p. 138.

TABLE 9–2
*Proximity of Older People to their Nearest Child in Three Countries
(percentage distribution)*

	People with living children		
Proximity of the nearest child	Britain	United States	Denmark
Total	100.0%	100.0%	100.0%
Same household	41.9	27.6	20.1
10 minutes journey or less	23.5	33.1	32.0
11–30 minutes journey	15.9	15.7	23.0
31 minutes–1 hour	7.6	7.2	12.4
Over 1 hour but less than 1 day	9.1	11.2	11.2
I day or more	1.9	5.2	1.3
Number	1,911	2,012	2,009

Source: Matilda White Riley and Anne Foner, *Aging and Society*, Vol. I: *An Inventory of Research Findings* (New York: Russell Sage Foundation, 1968), p. 169.
Note: Details may not add to totals because of rounding.

as more husbands have survived through the middle years. The median age for widowhood rose from 51.4 in 1900 to 59.2 in 1964. The median age for a man to become a widower rose from 48 in 1900 to over 65 in 1964. Widows are also older in 1964 than they were in 1900 on the average (51.4 to 59.2). There are about four times as many widows as there are widowers in the

FIGURE 9–3
*Age distribution of new widows, 1900 and 1964. From Matilda White
Riley and Anne Foner,* Aging and Society, *Vol. 1 (Russell Sage
Foundation), Exhibits 7, 8.*

Median income in
thousands of dollars

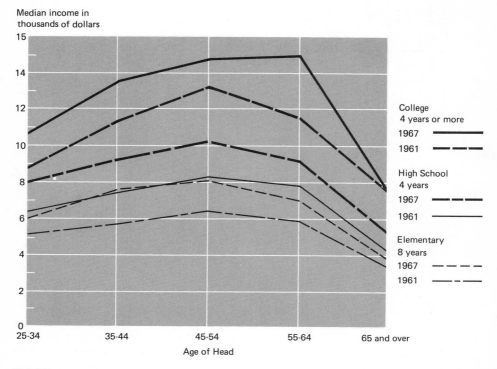

FIGURE 9–4
Median family incomes, by education and age of head. Adapted from
Current Population Reports *(U.S.G.P.O., 1969).*

United States. Consequently, older couples can look forward to a longer period of life together in their declining years, and the wife must anticipate the probability of being a widow for about eleven years on the average.

The economics of old age are dramatically presented in Figure 9–4 which compares the median income of families in 1967 and 1961 by age of head of household. Notice the most radical decline in median income occurs for families with heads over 65 in 1967. While about 13 percent of all American families are headed by aged persons, about 30 percent of all poor families have aged heads. It is commonly assumed that aged families generally spend less because their needs are fewer and their desires more subdued than those of younger families, but several studies have shown that aged families spent as much as younger families *if they have it to spend.*[19]

19. Harold L. Sheppard, "The Poverty of Aging" in Ben B. Seligman (ed.), *Poverty as a Public Issue* (New York: Free Press, 1965), pp. 98–99.

Harold Sheppard points to the problem of income procurement for aging families by comparing their income to that of younger cohorts. According to his analysis, men who were fifty-four or older in 1949 had a median annual income of $1,710. The median income of this age group decreased to $1,576 in 1959, as measured in current dollars. In constant dollars the group suffered a decrease of about 33 percent in real income. During the same period, men aged twenty-four to thirty-four in 1949 experienced a 57 percent *increase* in real income over the decade, while those thirty-four to forty-four in 1949 experienced a 34 percent increase. Thus while those who reached retirement age in 1959 were experiencing a substantial decrease, those immediately below this group in age were experiencing a substantial increase. The sense of relative deprivation is, under such circumstances, undoubtedly great.[20]

The problem of retirement is further complicated by the fact that most Americans do not have adequate retirement plans. A study conducted at the University of Michigan suggests that about 6 percent of all Americans will have no pensions whatsoever upon retirement, about 55 percent will have social security only, and about 39 percent will have social security and private pension plans of some sort. Social security was not intended to provide adequate funds upon retirement, but rather was designed to assist retiring persons in supplementing other sources. Clearly, if this sample is representative, 61 percent of all Americans will have inadequate income upon retirement. Yet the same study found that about half of the nonretired persons over thirty were doing nothing or could do nothing to add to their retirement income. Furthermore, more than a third of the middle-aged persons over forty-five had less than $5,000 in assets of any kind. It is little wonder that as retirement approaches many Americans fear old age worse than death.[21]

Because of the severe economic constraints placed upon most aging families, whether by virtue of their own lack of planning or by virtue of the society's inability to provide adequate opportunity to earn sufficient income, the problems of aging families are more apparently tied in with the problems of our economy. The developmental task approach seems to gloss over the hardships and to overemphasize the autonomy of aging families. Our society has tended to produce workers who accumulate like the waste products of our industry to be discarded and disposed of at will. Despite the data indicating that older workers are quite efficient and more reliable than many younger groups, mandatory retirement continues to come too soon in a man's life in most occupations.

Given these data, it is not difficult to understand that a major developmental task confronting aging couples is finding satisfaction as useful people. Typically the husband retires to the home and dies about five years after retirement. During the time of his retirement, he slouches around the house causing many disruptions in his wife's established routine which has

20. *Ibid.*, p. 88.
21. *Ibid.*, pp. 89–90.

changed little as a result of her husband's retirement. Conflicts that had been suppressed while children were still in the home may now take center stage and become exacerbated by the role reversals accompanying aging. The more independent breadwinner loses status upon retirement; his more dependent wife gains in status and power. Adults, also, become more dependent upon their children who may take the opportunity to seek revenge upon parents for past injustices. These hazards are real and must be overcome if the aging couple are to retire happily.

The ability to cope with the continued problems of physical aging and death is not easily acquired. Our society not only worships youth, it pretends that death does not exist. We do not die, we "pass on." There are few communities other than the church where there is even the remotest possibility of facing the reality of one's own impending death in the context of concern and shared understanding. As friends die, the intimate circle diminishes, and the aged must, by and large, come to grips with death alone. The wife, who normally survives, has the greatest burden.

The Family's Capacity to Cope with Crises

The "normal" family, by definition, meets and resolves any problems presented by the developmental tasks. Many families, however, may not meet all of these tasks on schedule with a minimum of stress. In addition to the crises which may be precipitated by failure to meet the developmental tasks, society imposes stressful situations upon the family that are unrelated to its internal development. It is useful, therefore, to analyze briefly how families cope with such crises.

Reuben Hill notes that, compared with other associations, the family is badly handicapped organizationally, is heavily weighted with dependents which it cannot freely reject, and experiences an uncertain sex composition. In addition its members receive unconditioned acceptance. If one were going to organize a group for maximum performance of a given task, the family's mode of organization would not readily present itself as a model.[22] As an organization designed specifically to cope with crises, the family thus has many shortcomings. The capacity to respond to crises is further reduced in our society by the relative isolation of the nuclear or conjugal family, particularly in the lower-upper class and the upper-middle class.

We know from our own experience that what one family would consider a crisis, another would not. One family can cope with death more easily than another. For one, teenage children are impossible; for another preschoolers are the troublemakers. Therefore, an event may be classified as crisis-

---

22. Reuben Hill, "Social Stresses on the Family" in Edward C. McDonagh and Jon E. Simpson (eds.), *Social Problems: Persistent Challenges* (New York: Holt, Rinehart & Winston, 1965), pp. 302–14. This article was reprinted from *Social Casework*, Vol. 39 (Feb.–Mar. 1958). See also Reuben Hill, *Families Under Stress* (New York: Harper, 1949).

precipitating if it exceeds a family's crisis-meeting resources, or if it is defined by the family as a crisis (regardless of its magnitude or the capacity of the family to cope with it).

For Cavan, Ranck, and Koos, to be crisis-proof a family must agree on its role structure, subordinate personal ambitions to family goals, find satisfactions within the family (because it is successfully meeting their physical and emotional needs), and share goals toward which the family moves collectively.[23] It must, in other words, have a high degree of cohesiveness plus sufficient experience in coping successfully with crises in order to be regarded as crisis proof. Others stress the importance of the relative compatibility of the married couple's personalities and the effect of their relationship on the family. Families that are adequate in these regards are less likely to experience family crises.

The second major element that contributes to the definition of an event as a family crisis is the family's definition of the event as such. Many events that are considered crises by our society (e.g. children born outside of marriage, adultery, and even the death of a member) are not so defined by other cultures. In any case, a particular family may define an event as a crisis even if its culture does not. It is this component, the family's definition of the situation, that is most important in studying *crisis-proneness*. In evaluating the crisis-proneness of a particular family, one must assess the relative inclination of the family to define events as crises when (1) the culture does not so define them, and (2) an outside observer would not so define them. If a family is prone to define an event as a crisis, this in itself is a significant indicator of crisis-proneness. Reuben Hill summarizes the argument in Figure 9–5.[24]

Crisis-proneness is thus shown to be a function of deficiency in organization plus a tendency to define hardships as crises.

A classification of stressor events is offered by Thomas Eliot and Reuben Hill:

1. Dismemberment—death of a member, war, separation, etc.
2. Accession—unwanted pregnancy, deserter returns, etc.
3. Demoralization—nonsupport, infidelity, drug addiction, etc.[25]

To which Ernest Burgess would add:

4. A sudden change in family status.
5. Conflict among family members in the conception of their roles.
6. Demoralization, plus dismemberment or accession—illegitimacy, desertion, divorce, suicide, etc.[26]

23. Hill, "Social Stresses on the Family," p. 307.
24. *Ibid.*, p. 309.
25. Thomas O. Eliot, "Handling Family Strains and Shocks" in Howard Becker and Reuben Hill (eds.), *Family, Marriage and Parenthood* (Boston: D. C. Heath, 1955), p. 617.
26. Ernest W. Burgess, "The Family and Sociological Research," *Social Forces*, Vol. 26, No. 1 (1947), 1–6.

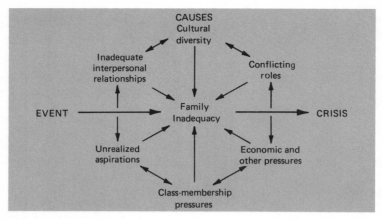

FIGURE 9–5
A schema for depicting the interplay of stressor events, contributing hardships, and family resources in family crisis. From Reuben Hill, "Social Stresses on the Family," Social Casework, *39 (February–March, 1958).*

Again it must be emphasized that culture and class variables strongly affect these factors. For example, Cuber and Harroff have shown us that extra-marital sex is not seen as infidelity among a few families who, nevertheless, give evidence of a most happy and well-rounded family life, despite the fact that the overwhelming majority of them defined such behavior as infidelity.

Marital Satisfaction and the Life Cycle

With the emphasis to this point upon problems and crises that are common occurrences in a family's development, it is well to turn briefly to an examination of several recent studies that seek to relate marital *satisfaction* to the stages in the family life cycle.[27] Table 9–3 summarizes twelve studies of marital satisfaction over the family life cycle. Rollins and Feldman interpret these studies as being quite consistent in showing a decline in marital satisfaction over the first ten years of marriage or to approximately the "school age" stage for *wives*.[28] They point out, however, that only four show a similar decline for husbands, while another four studies found no change. Their own research on 852 middle-class couples suggests that marriage has a very dif-

27. See in particular Boyd C. Rollins and Harold Feldman, "Marital Satisfaction over the Family Life Cycle," *Journal of Marriage and the Family*, Vol. 32, No. 1 (Feb. 1970), 20–28; and Wesley R. Burr, "Satisfaction with Various Aspects of Marriage over the Life Cycle: A Random Middle-Class Sample," *Journal of Marriage and the Family*, Vol. 32, No. 1 (Feb. 1970), 29–37.

28. Rollins and Feldman *op. cit.*, p. 21.

TABLE 9–3

A Summary of Twelve Studies of Marital Satisfaction over the Family Life Cycle

Study	FLC stages included*	Stage(s) lowest in satisfaction†	Number of subjects			Pattern of satisfaction change over the FLC		
			males	females	total	Decrease	Decrease then increase	No change
Bernard	I–VIII	V–VI	109	122	331	—	M, F	—
Blood	I–VIII	VIII	509	—	509	F	—	—
Bossard	I–VII	IV–VII	225	215	440	F	—	M
Burgess	I–III	II–III	526	526	1,052	M, F	—	—
Gurin	I–VIII	VII	—	—	1,867	—	M, F‡	—
Hamilton	I–IV	III–IV	100	100	200	F	—	M
Lang	I–V	IV–V	7,393	7,393	15,786	M, F‡	—	—
Luckey	II–V	IV–V	80	80	160	M, F‡	—	—
Marlowe	I & III	III	60	60	120	F	—	M
Paris	IV–VI	V–VI	62	62	124	F	—	M
Pineo	II & V	V	400	400	800	M, F	—	—
Terman	I–VII	III & V	792	792	1,584	—	M, F	—

Source: Boyd C. Rollins and Harold Feldman, "Marital Satisfaction over the Family Life Cycle," *Journal of Marriage and the Family,* Vol. 32, No. 1 (Feb. 1970), 21.

*Estimated from either age of subjects or length of time married. Definitions of the stages of the family life cycle are given in Fig. 9–2.

†In every study marital satisfaction was highest at the beginning stages of the family life cycle.

‡It is not known whether the pattern of change is for husbands or both.

ferent meaning for husbands and wives and that very different events either inside or outside the marriage affect the amount of satisfaction reported. In general, men are primarily influenced by events both before and after they have children, whereas the strongest influence on women is the presence of children. Their data suggest that child bearing and child rearing have a "rather profound and negative effect on marital satisfaction for wives, even in their basic feelings of self worth in relation to their marriage."[29] The loss of companionship consequent upon these stages is not followed by a similar dissatisfaction in the case of the husband who, consistent with previous findings, remains relatively unaffected by the stages in the family life cycle. As we might guess, Rollins and Feldman suggest that a developmental theory of marital satisfaction for wives should focus upon the contingent role of parenthood, while the occupational role seems more relevant for the husband. Thus even in the intimate arena of marital satisfaction, the occupational role seems more determinative for the husband than does the domestic role.

An area of similar assessment concerns those reporting that the present stage of their marriage was "very satisfying." Table 9–3 shows that in most

29. *Ibid.,* p. 27.

instances for both husbands and wives there is a rapid decline over the child-rearing years, and a rapid recovery as the children are launched. Since these are most likely upper-middle-class couples with the greatest potential for adequate retirement arrangements, it would be interesting to note how a sample of lower-class couples would respond. The expectation would be that the decline would continue after the children became independent.

Summary

The family, by virtue of its own development, creates new situations and new tasks to which family members must respond. As the family first expands to accommodate new members, then contracts as the children are launched into families of their own, the demands made upon family members change and the characteristics of the family as an institution—its shared values and patterns of behavior—change.

The concept of a developmental task applies most effectively to families when the task pertains to problems associated with a change in family composition. The development of the family is affected by the changes in its culture as indicated by the changing length of the developmental stages. In our highly developed technological society, the age of average entry into each of the stages changes as the technology improves our standard of living and lengthens our life expectancy. The over-all characteristics of the life cycle are quite different than would be true of primitive societies, we would surmise, although to date researchers in family development have not been particularly concerned with comparative studies.

In one of many versions of the tasks appropriate to beginning families, Kenkel suggests that they must develop competency in decision-making, managing family finances, preparation for parenthood, adjustment to married status, dealing with differences, handling inlaws, cooperating in intimate living, and working out satisfactory household routines. The arrival of children adds the tasks of handling the crisis of child-birth, recapturing conjugal intimacy, and in time learning to let children go. After children have gone, the conjugal pair must rediscover one another, accept the fact of their aging and their limited accomplishments, and plan for retirement. Aging families are quite likely to have inadequate income in the United States, many for the first time in their lives. Impoverishment complicates even further the tasks peculiar to this stage, such as coping with a feeling of uselessness and facing death.

Not all families are able to cope with these problems. Reubin Hill has pointed out the organizational handicaps that make the family particularly vulnerable in such crisis situations: poor organization, a large number of dependents it can not dispose of, uncertain sex composition, and the expectation that it give its members unconditioned acceptance. Crisis-proneness is shown to be a function of deficiency in organization plus a greater tendency for some families to define hardships as crises.

Contrary to the common assumption, study after study has shown that children decrease rather than increase marital satisfaction. Couples must recover from the experience of raising children. The typical middle-class couple reports increased satisfaction after the children have been launched, but it is postulated that problems of impoverishment common among lower-class families would lead to greater dissatisfaction.

Jack Sprat could eat no fat
His wife could eat no lean ;
And so between them both,
They licked the platter clean.

10. The Mating Game

From the romantic point of view marriages are "made in heaven." People are "destined to marry each other," "brought together by fate," "mysteriously attracted to each other," and marry even if families, friends, and their own minds demur. . . . In practice more couples are thrown together by accident than by either the magic of romance or the strategy of intelligence.

ROBERT O. BLOOD

In the United States we assume that the reason two people marry is that they are in love. In the majority of cases that is undoubtedly true. But even though the personal choices of the partners and their assessment of their love for one another do seem to affect the final choice of spouse, the choice is made—in the vast number of cases—from within a "field of eligibles" that have been "selected" by social factors beyond the awareness of the lovers. And so even though we do not place much weight upon arranged marriages, everyone does not have an equal chance of marrying everyone else in our society. The probabilities are that the spouse will be selected from among those people who live relatively close to the seeker; who are from the same socio-economic class, religion, and race; and who most likely will complement the seeker's personality.

The closed character of the "marriage market" is a powerful indicator of the extent to which social inequality is a factor to be reckoned with. Should the seeker be someone quite different from what is socially expected, he (or she) will find that he and his mate will have a harder time staying married. The problems of mixed marriages provide further data supporting the contention that the seeker is not totally free to choose whom he will marry. The emancipated persons who place personal choice above social prescription must pay a price for their deviation.

It does not take us long to realize these rather obvious generalizations once the data have been presented. We really take it for granted that such constraints exist. Often, however, such constraints are formally invoked. With regard to intermarriage between the races, as late as 1967 fourteen states still had anti-miscegenation laws providing penalties of up to $1,000 and one to ten years in prison for those who knowingly married a person of another race (particularly the Negroid). Some imposed penalties upon the person who performed the marriage ceremony as well. Many of our religious denominations openly deplore marriages outside the faith. The devout Orthodox Jew may "sit shiva"—mourn the dead—over a child thus lost to the faith. The non-Catholic who marries a Catholic may not be able to be married in the Catholic Church and may be asked to state formally that he will raise his children in the Catholic faith. Many protestant denominations feel quite strongly about mixed marriages. And, socially, there are traditional biases against marrying a person "from the wrong side of the tracks."

One may disregard any of these constraints, but not without paying a price. The fact that they are violated so infrequently testifies to their effectiveness in restricting the choice of mate. Personal choice, or falling in love, is thus a factor in the selection of a mate, but it is by no means *the* factor that determines who shall marry whom. From a comparative perspective, the most important element of mate choice in America is not so much the fact that marriage comes about largely through the operation of informal constraints rather than formal rules, but rather the fact that marriage (like status) is achieved rather than ascribed.

I have argued earlier that the factor of personal choice plays an important role in our society in large measure because we do not depend upon the kinship system to provide structure and cohesion to the same extent as do the primitive societies with unilineal kinship systems. Because national and local governments, corporations, churches, schools, and various other voluntary organizations all contribute to placing persons in the social structure (providing them with a position, giving them cues as to the behavior appropriate to that position, allowing invidious comparisons [status] to be made, and assuming much of the responsibility for organizing and controlling the interaction of groups and individuals within our society), the kinship system is less functional. The choice of partner can officially be left up to the individual because not as much is at stake (from the point of view of society) should he choose the wrong mate.

Yet society informally exerts a great deal of pressure upon individuals to marry the proper person, suggesting that it has not lost all interest in the matter of mate selection. What is at stake in our case is not so much the formal structure and organization of our society but rather the distribution of rewards and incentives, be they material goods, social status, or—correlatively—self-esteem. The choice of a partner in marriage is for some few a means of mobility, but for the majority it functions latently as a mechanism for preserving the status quo—a means of reserving the rights and privileges of a particular group for yet another generation. This is most true in the case of interracial marriage but seems applicable to the broader scene as well.

In this chapter I will examine first the factors affecting mate selection in the United States, then turn to a brief examination of the institution of premarriage as a factor in mate selection, and close with a look at the problems of "mixed" marriages.

Socioeconomic Factors: Homogamy

Although many factors affect mate choice, persons in search of a mate do not necessarily take these factors into consideration. The data presented in this discussion, by and large, simply document the extent to which mate choice is nonrandom—not the extent to which people are influenced by various factors. Most people *do* select a mate from within a field of eligibles that is defined by certain social elements, but taken together these elements may not adequately account for the choice of a particular mate.

In this section we are concerned with the principle of homogamy (like marrying like) which limits our choice of mate *even* though most of us do not consciously define our "marriage market" or have it defined for us by kin as is often done in pre-industrial societies. In the next section we turn to questions of motivation.

The principle of homogamy assumes that a person will marry someone like himself in regard to such factors as race, nationality, religion, socioeconomic class, and age. One study added education, feelings on whether the woman should work after marriage, number of children desired, and even drinking and smoking habits to this list of social characteristics indicating a high degree of homogamous choice. Data from recent studies support this principle.

Race: Although the legal barriers to intermarriage between races have been removed in most areas, there is no evidence of a rush to marry across

TABLE 10–1
Religious Homogamy

| | Religious Group | | | |
	Protestant	Catholic	Jewish	Total
Percentage of U.S. Population	66%	26%	3%	95%*
Expected homogamy due to chance	53	16	2	42
Actual homogamy	91	78	93	88
Ratio of actual/expected	1.7X	4.9X	46.5X	2.1X

Source: Representative sample of 35,000 U.S. households (Bureau of the Census). From Robert O. Blood, *Marriage*, 2nd ed. (New York: Free Press, 1962), p. 69.
*Plus 1% other religion, 3% none, 1% no answer.

racial lines.[1] David Heer estimates that, conservatively speaking, a complete amalgamation of the races will occur within the next 27,000 years, or 1,000 generations, if the current trends in race relations and intermarriage continue. A more liberal estimate concludes that it will not occur before 351 years, or 13 generations. In either case, Heer foresees no significant progress in this direction during the next hundred years.[2] When Blacks and Whites intermarry, black men tend to marry white women more than white men tend to marry black women by about three to one.[3]

Religion: Another important factor in mate selection is religion. This is particularly true when the denominations in America are reduced to the simple Catholic, protestant, Jewish tricotimy. Jews tend to marry Jews much more than Catholics marry other Catholics, who are in turn more homogamous than protestants. Table 10–1 indicates that the actual percentage of homogamous choice on the basis of religion is two and a half times what

1. August B. Hollingshead, "Cultural Factors in the Selection of Marriage Mates," *American Sociological Review*, Vol. 15 (1950), 619–27, found no interracial marriages among 2,063 marriages that occurred in New Haven, Connecticut in 1948. Randall Risdon, "A Study of Interracial Marriages Based on Data for Los Angeles County," *Sociology and Sociological Research*, Vol. 39 (1954), 92–95, determined the interracial marriage rate at less than one half of one percent for Los Angeles County prior to the repeal of an antimiscegenation law and slightly over that for a thirty-month period afterward. Paul H. Jacobson, *American Marriage and Divorce* (New York: Rinehart, 1959) estimates no more than about 2,000 black-white marriages per year—about one in every 1,200 marriages. John H. Burma, "Interethnic Marriages in Los Angeles, 1948–1959," *Social Forces*, Vol. 42 (December, 1963), 156–65, found that interracial marriages were increasing over an eleven-year period (about triple at the end) and were occurring among older persons. David Heer, "Negro-White Marriage in the United States," *Journal of Marriage and the Family*, Vol. 28 (August, 1966), 262–73, showed that the rates of interracial marriages in four states (California, Hawaii, Michigan, and Nebraska) were rising.
2. David Heer, *New Society*, August 26, 1965.
3. One hundred forty-seven out of 188 Negro-White marriages in Chicago involved black males [St. Clair Drake and Horace R. Cayton, *Black Metropolis* (New York: Harcourt Brace Jovanovich, 1945)]. Supporting evidence of a similar sort is found in John Burma *op. cit.*; Risdon, "A Study of Interracial Marriages *op. cit.*; and in Joseph Golden, "Characteristics in the Negro-White Intermarried in Philadelphia," *American Sociological Review*, Vol. 18 (1953), 177–83.

could be expected by chance. Data from the same study suggested that the rate of homogamous marriage is a function of the percentage of the population a given denomination represents. In Quebec, for instance, where Catholics constitute 88 percent of the population, only 2 percent of all marriages are interfaith. In contrast, 73 percent of the Catholics marry outside of their faith in the southeastern United States where Catholics constitute only 2 percent of the population.

In further studies of interfaith marriage, Father John L. Thomas concluded that three factors influence the rate at which Catholics marry non-Catholics: the proportion of Catholics in the community, the presence of close-knit ethnic subgroups, and the socioeconomic status of Catholics in that community.[4] For example, San Antonio, Texas, and Syracuse, New York are both about 30 percent Catholic, yet San Antonio's intermarriage rate is about half that of Syracuse because the former has an important ethnic subgroup of Spanish and Mexican Catholics. So also the higher the socioeconomic status of Catholics the greater the rate of intermarriage—in part because ethnic differences tend to diminish with socioeconomic gains. As Robert F. Winch puts it, "With socioeconomic status becoming equalized and ethnic characteristics virtually gone, religious identity has lost most of its prejudicial and discriminatory salience."[5]

Class: Research suggests that persons tend to marry spouses within their socioeconomic class. A study of New Haven, Connecticut, shown in Table 10–2, indicated that the number of cross-class pairings (587) was over twice the number expected by chance selection (277.9). A smaller study, presented in Table 10–3, produced similar pattern. Fifty-five percent of the spouses in this sample of 396 were of the same class; 40 percent were one class apart; 5 percent, more than one class apart. Of the cross-class marriages, the husband was of the higher class in 64 percent of the cases, thus supporting the hypothesis that women tend to marry up the socioeconomic ladder in our society.

Age: Age is also an important factor limiting mate choice. According to the most recent statistics, the average age difference between spouses is 2.4 years. This represents a distinct decrease in age difference since the turn of the century, when the average difference was 4.1 years (Table 10–4). Beyond this average, certain trends are discernible.

Six out of seven grooms are as old or older than their brides. The few boys who marry at age eighteen tend to pick girls a few months older than themselves, but after eighteen grooms are progressively older. At twenty-five the average boy marries a girl who is twenty-two; at thirty-seven, he would marry a girl of thirty-one, and so on until the groom's age reaches fifty, beyond which points the ages once again tend to be nearly the same.[6]

4. John L. Thomas, "The Factor of Religion in the Selection of Marriage Mates," *American Sociological Review*, Vol. 16 (1951), 487–91.

5. Robert F. Winch, *The Modern Family*, rev. ed. (New York: Holt, Rinehart & Winston, 1963), p. 336.

6. Richard Udry, *The Social Context of Marriage* (Philadelphia: Lippincott, 1966), p. 208.

TABLE 10–2
*Residential Class of Husband and Wife for 1008 Newly Married
Residents of New Haven*

Class of husband	Class of wife						Total
	I	*II*	*III*	*IV*	*V*	*VI*	
	(Chance values are in parentheses; actual values are above them.)						*Total*
I	13% (0.5)	7% (2.3)	1% (1.1)	0% (3.5)	3% (9.2)	1 (8.4)	25 (25.0)
II	8 (2.3)	56 (9.6)	8 (4.7)	12 (14.8)	13 (38.5)	8 (35.1)	105 (105.0)
III	1 (0.9)	4 (3.6)	15 (1.7)	5 (5.5)	7 (14.3)	7 (13.0)	39 (39.0)
IV	0 (3.1)	8 (12.8)	4 (6.2)	55 (19.7)	35 (51.4)	38 (46.8)	140 (140.0)
V	0 (8.5)	12 (35.5)	8 (17.4)	30 (54.8)	252 (142.8)	87 (130.0)	389 (389.0)
VI	0 (6.8)	5 (28.3)	9 (13.8)	40 (43.7)	60 (113.8)	196 (103.6)	310 (310.0)
Total	22 (22.1)	92 (92.1)	45 (44.9)	142 (142.0)	370 (370.0)	337 (336.9)	1008 (1008.0)

Source: August B. Hollingshead, "Cultural Factors in the Selection of Marriage Mates," *American Sociological Review*, Vol. 15, No. 5 (1950), 625, as modified in Robert F. Winch, *The Modern Family*, rev. ed., (New York: Holt, Rinehart & Winston, 1966), p. 337.
The number of homogamous marriages that would be expected from random mating the sum of the diagonal parenthetical values. $0.5 + 9.6 + 1.7 + 19.7 + 142.8 + 103.6 = 277.9$. The actual number is $13 + 56 + 15 + 55 + 252 + 196 = 587$.

TABLE 10–3
Relationship Between Social Classes of Mates

Social class at marriage	Number	Percent of total	Cross-class marriages	Number	Percent of total
Spouses of same class at time of marriage	215	55%	Husband one or more classes higher than the wife at marriage	116	64%
Spouses one class apart at time of marriage	160	40	Wife one or more classes higher than the husband at marriage	65	36
Spouses more than one class apart at time of marriage	21	5			
Total	396	100	Total	181	100

Source: Julius Roth and Robert F. Peck, "Social Class and Social Mobility Factors Related to Marital Adjustment," *American Sociological Review*, Vol. 16 (1951), 481.

TABLE 10–4
Median Age at First Marriage: 1890–1970

	Male	Female	Difference
1890	26.1	22	4.1
1900	25.9	21.9	4.0
1910	25.1	21.6	3.5
1920	24.6	21.2	3.4
1930	24.3	21.3	3.0
1940	24.3	21.5	2.8
1950	22.8	20.3	2.5
1960	22.8	20.3	2.5
1965	22.8	20.6	2.2
1966	22.8	20.5	2.3
1967	23.1	20.6	2.5
1968	23.1	20.8	2.3
1969	23.2	20.8	2.4
1970	23.2	20.8	2.4

Source: Statistical Abstracts of the United States, 1971 (Washington, D.C.: U.S.G.P.O., 1971), p. 60. Data prior to 1940 from *Historical Abstracts, Colonial Times to 1957* (Washington, D.C.: U.S.G.P.O., 1965), p. 45.

Socioeconomic Factors Affecting Mate Selection—A Summary: Using the cross-cultural materials presented in the first section of this book and the data on mate selection in American society presented above, we can draw some general conclusions concerning the definition of the field of eligibles. Figure 10–1 will assist us in this endeavor. A group of "insiders" is excluded in all societies on the basis of the universal incest taboo. While the relationships falling under the incest taboo differ in different societies, all societies exclude some such persons, typically the members of the nuclear family as in our case. The incest taboo proscribes sexual intercourse with these persons. The norm of exogamy pertaining to the regulation of mate selection proscribes marriages within a particular group. Commonly this group is somewhat different from the one covered by the incest taboo. For example, most states prohibit marriage between first cousins; yet this is not, strictly speaking, because of incest taboos. The normative boundary separating the insiders from the eligibles is a rigid one in most instances.

On the other hand, a group of "outsiders" is less precisely barred by the principle of homogamy—the principle asserting that like should marry like in terms of socioeconomic class. In our society these norms are not formally spelled out in terms of rules of endogamy stating that one *must* marry within a certain group, but rather they are informally understood, and mate selection in fact takes place on the basis of the homogamous principle without the necessity of formal pronouncements. The principle of homogamy defines

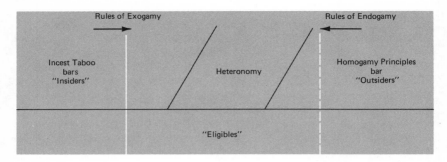

FIGURE 10–1
The relationship between homogamous and heterogamous choice.
Homogamous *principles are based on socioeconomic characteristics
such as race-ethnicity, income, and religion.* Heterogamous *choice is
made in reference to psychological characteristics with the intent
of maximizing complementariness.*

a group of persons who are typically easier to meet because they live in the same or similar residential setting and enjoy similar styles of life with similar kinds of people. Therefore, there is no problem in coming to grips with cultural or class differences, and ethnocentric biases need never be challenged. Such homogamous partners have less risk in marrying because, among other things, they are more compatible, they share the same symbolic environment, and they assume the same world to be real. Winch's phrase "ethnocentric preference" rather than "principle of homogamy" makes this clearer.

Psychological Factors: Complementarity

Within the field of eligibles, however, mate selection does not occur on a random basis nor does the principle of like marrying like define the choice of mate much further. In a study by Burgess and Wallin, only fourteen of forty-two personality traits showed a greater than chance expectation for homogamy.[7] The highest scoring of these are: degree of daydreaming, loneliness, easily hurt feelings, and touchiness. Kerckhoff and Davis contend, however, that value consensus is a further filtering factor predicting mate choice within the field of eligibles during the process of courtship.[8] If this is so, another dimension of homogamous choice must be more fully investigated.

To date the most impressive theory attempting to account for the choice of mate within the field of eligibles is Robert F. Winch's conception of com-

---

7. Burgess and Wallin, *Engagement and Marriage* (Chicago: Lippincott, 1953).
8. Alan Kerckhoff and Keith Davis, "Value Consensus and Need Complementarity in Mate Selection," *American Sociological Review*, Vol. 27 (1962), 295–303.

plementary needs.[9] This theory has received only partial confirmation.[10] In part this is because personality traits are intrinsically difficult to measure—particularly those associated with motivation—and, consequently, such a study would be quite an expensive undertaking; because some aspects of mate selection within the field of eligibles are undoubtedly explainable on the basis of other factors such as homogamy; because mate selection within the field of eligibles is not completely voluntary; and finally because, as Winch himself acknowledges, a person may experience conflict in choice of mate since any given person may not be able to gratify his entire need pattern. (For example, a person may have to choose between his need for status that could be gratified by the boss's daughter and his need for sympathy and understanding that could be gratified by another girlfriend of lower status.) Therefore, from the point of view of prediction of choice, it is necessary to establish a *hierarchy of needs*—something that the subject himself may not consciously be able to accomplish. Nevertheless, Winch's theory of complementary needs in mate selection deserves our further attention.

The theory is limited to those cultures such as our own which define the marital relationship as a rich potential source of gratification that can be realized through the voluntary (on both sides) choice of mate that is made after a culturally acceptable period of premarital testing of the personalities of a number of potential mates.[11] We see at once that many of the societies discussed in the first section do not fit these requirements.

Our own society, further, is one in which there is a great deal of emphasis upon falling in love as a motivation to marry. The character of this love is culturally defined. In our society it has an added dimension of urgency derived from patterns of socialization that are responsible for middle-class children's almost insatiable need for acceptance and security—expressed as a need to love and be loved. Such persons must affiliate with others, avoid separation, and achieve status in order to feel acceptable; hence, our personality cults, separation anxiety, and status striving. Winch concludes, "from this line of argument it appears that we have a gross psychological deficit in nurturant personalities, i.e., personalities having the need to give sympathy, consolation, protection, comfort, and so on to others.[12] Dorothy Lee points out that we tend to value people because of what they do—another way of saying that status is achieved—while societies such as the Trobrianders value people because of who they are. This is not to say that they are valued because they are members of particular families but rather because they *are*.[13]

Assuming that all behavior arises out of human needs, Winch offers the following definition of love:

9. For a complete exposition of this theory see Robert F. Winch *op. cit.*, pp. 567–607.
10. See, for example, Thomes Ktsanes and Virginia Ktsanes, "The Theory of Complementary Needs in Mate Selection" in Robert F. Winch and Louis F. Goodman (eds.), *Selected Studies in Marriage and the Family*, 3rd ed. (New York: Holt, Rinehart & Winston, 1968), pp. 517–28.
11. Winch *op. cit.*, pp. 586–87.
12. *Ibid.*, p. 579.
13. Dorothy Lee, "Being and Value in a Primitive Culture," *The Journal of Philosophy*, Vol. 46 (June 1949), 401–15.

> *Love is the positive emotion experienced by one person (the person loving or the lover) in an interpersonal relationship in which the second person (the person loved or love object) either (1) meets certain important needs of the first, or (2) manifests or appears (to the first) to manifest personal attributes (beauty, skills, status) highly prized by the first or both.*[14]

Love is difficult to define because it is based upon various patterns of needs resulting in varying degrees of gratification, and it is expressed in diverse patterns of behavior depending upon the needs that partners attempt to gratify. It does not follow that the matching of need patterns in such a way as to provide maximum gratification necessarily means that two people will experience happiness. The matching of needs can perpetuate conflict between the couple, as Cuber and Harroff suggest.[15]

Finally, love plays such an important role in our society, as contrasted to many primitive societies, because the American middle-class family is relatively nonfunctional and has few rewards to offer its members other than those derived from interpersonal companionship and the quest for intimacy. Therefore, "Americans tend to have a low threshhold of frustration in marriage and experience deep disappointment when frustrated."[16]

This theory of complementary needs in mate selection depends on the following assumptions about human behavior.

I. Propositions concerning behavior, needs, and the organization of needs:

A. All human behavior may be viewed as activity oriented to the gratification of needs.

B. Some human needs are innate; others are learned. We are particularly interested in those that are learned and expressed in interpersonal relationships.

C. Certain important needs are organized by the individual's identifications (the persons or traits with which an individual identifies or after whom he models himself).

D. The organization of needs (an individual's particular configuration of psychological needs) gives pattern to behavior and makes behavior (especially perception) selective.

E. Needs may be experienced consciously or unconsciously. Hence, a person may be completely aware, partially aware, or quite unaware of the motivation of his behavior.

II. Propositions concerning societal determinants of gratification and changing need patterns:

14. Winch *op. cit.*, p. 579.
15. See especially their discussion of the conflict habituated relationship in their *Sex and the Significant Americans* (Baltimore: Penguin, 1968), pp. 44–46.
16. Winch *op. cit.*, p. 583.

A. In all societies social interaction in congeniality groups is an important source of gratification for social needs.

B. In the American middle class, the man-woman dyad is viewed as a singularly gratifying congeniality group.

C. In a society (like that of the United States) which has numerous cultural discontinuities and a high degree of social mobility:

> *1.* Individuals are confronted with a succession of varied ego-models, with the result that they tend to develop a somewhat heterogeneous set of identifications.

> *2.* Individuals encounter shifting criteria for social approval at various ages and in various social contexts.

> *3.* As the individual passes through the age categories, new sources of gratification become accessible and some of the old ones become inaccessible, and thus the individual experiences new sources of frustration.

D. Due to the extent that the conditions in C are met, time brings about a disturbance in the adaptation of the individual and changes in his need pattern.

We can now set forth the three basic propositions of the theory of complementary needs in mate selection:

1. In mate selection each individual seeks within his or her field of eligibles for that person who gives the greatest promise of providing him or her with maximum need gratification.

2. There is a set of needs such that if one person has a high degree of need X, he will behave in a way that is gratifying to need Y in a second person.

3. These two needs, X and Y, in the two persons, A and B, are said to be complementary if:

> *a.* Type I complementariness: X and Y are the same, but the need is present to a low degree in B.

> *b.* Type II complementariness: X and Y are different needs. In this case specific predictions are made about selected pairs of needs. That is, taking account of the particular X, with respect to some Y's it is predicted that B will have a high degree and with respect to others that B will have a low degree. [An example is the case where spouse A is high in the need to be dominant (X) and spouse B is high in the need to be submissive (Y).][16]

In attempting to verify the theory, Winch discovered that two primary dimensions of complementariness seem quite common to couples in the

16. Winch *op. cit.*, pp. 584–86.

United States: *nurturance-receptivity* and *dominance-submissiveness*. These relationships reflect major dimensions of the process of socialization. They differ from those experienced during childhood, however, in that (1) conjugal relations—and those of premarriage—permit sexual gratification, but parent-child relations do not, and (2) the kinds of behavior involved in nurturing and controlling vary greatly with age.

Nevertheless, it is clear that these two dimensions of need gratification are shaped during the process of socialization and are significantly determined by the nature of the identification that occurs during this process. Complications are introduced into the notion that a person is, in effect, selecting a spouse who resembles a parent, however, with the realization that this is only *one* possible kind of identification that can be made. A child can also be influenced to behave in a fashion that reciprocates parental behavior or in a manner that is contrary to it. This gives rise to similar, reciprocal, and opposite types of identification. The matter is further complicated when we recognize that in the American middle class, children are influenced by a number of role models who may be quite different in their behavior and more influential in shaping the behavior of children than are the parents. Such complexities result in a great number of factors that must be taken into consideration in precisely predicting mate choice. The theory thus will require a great deal of additional research and insight before we can say that it is reasonably well substantiated.

Premarriage and Mate Selection

It follows from our discussion above that in the United States premarriage[17] functions to permit a person to select from within the field of eligibles that partner who most closely complements him (or her) by offering maximum gratification of basic personality needs. Even engagement has been recently redefined to mean "the final test" rather than an announcement of intention to marry. This is reflected in part in the increasing reluctance to prosecute breach of promise suits.[18] And yet this is not to say that all persons consciously utilize premarriage as such a testing device nor to imply that it functions adequately in order to ensure that the "right" persons will marry or that marriage itself has become more stable as premarriage has become more elaborate. Indeed the gross statistics indicate that the opposite is true. What can be asserted, however, is that if love (as defined above) is going to be effective in bringing people together, then some such system of premarriage must be institutionalized in order for such interpersonal "testing" to occur.

Several studies suggest that the average American couple proceed through the stages of premarriage with due deliberate speed. Burgess and

17. Premarriages, the series of institutionalized stages from dating to engagement, will be discussed further in Chapter 12.
18. Floyd Mansfield Martinson, *Family in Society* (New York: Dodd, Mead, 1970), pp. 238–39.

Wallin describe three types of courtship patterns: the telescoped, the extended, and the average. It is their impression that a sizable minority of the couples they studied progressed from first meeting to informal engagement in a few months or even a few weeks.[19] Such rapid development is attributed to (1) finding someone who fits one's ideal of a mate, (2) finding someone with characteristics similar to a person previously loved, (3) loneliness, (4) impulse, and (5) external conditions such as prosperity or war. In the first two instances premarriage is telescoped on the basis of data presumably gathered in prior relationships with similar others; therefore, the notion of testing need not be abandoned. The last three, however, indicate that some persons obviously do make a choice of mate without much testing of their personality. Such choice would further qualify the general validity of the hypotheses of complementariness. Still, the Landises report that an average of four and one half months of casual dating and eight months of steady dating occur before an understanding is reached.[20]

Further qualification of the concept of testing for complementary need patterns is derived from the observation that, although mate choice is normatively a matter of personal free choice, parents do in fact exert pressure upon their children in the selection of a mate. Most frequently middle-class parents do so by attempting to provide the proper environment for their children, but often their influence extends through advice that is sought by their children and through their own indirect expression of approval or disapproval. Thus, although a majority (58 percent) of the couples in one study reported that they made the decision to marry on their own, 35 percent reported seeking the advice of their parents, 6 percent sought advice from peers, and a few from older friends.[21] Bates reports that 97 percent of the women in his sample admit to being influenced by their mother.[22] Sussman found that parents were generally satisfied with mate choice in 145 out of 166 cases.[23] Finally, Table 10–5 indicates that homogamy is more common in those instances where one or both of the partners were still living at home when they decided to marry. Lowest rates occured when both were living away from home. All of these data do not prove that parents dictate mate choice; rather they provide some evidence of the extent of parent's influence even though, normatively, their permission to marry is not required.

Social intervention does not occur formally until the developing relationship is directed explicitly toward marriage, thus the possibility of bringing suit for breach of promise that is associated with engagement or intention to marry. Informal social intervention, however, is more pronounced. The whole process of selecting a mate is socially shaped:

19. See Judson T. and Mary G. Landis, *Building a Successful Marriage* (Englewood Cliffs, N.J.: Prentice-Hall, 1958).

20. *Ibid.*, especially Chapters 2–7.

21. Rollin Chambliss, "Married Students at a State University," *The Journal of Educational Sociology*, Vol. 34 (May, 1961), 409–16.

22. Alan Bates, "Parental Roles in Courtship," *Social Forces*, Vol. 20 (1942), 483–86.

23. Marvin B. Sussman, "Parental Participation in Mate Selection," *Social Forces*, Vol. 32 (1954), 76–81.

TABLE 10–5
Premarital Residence and Marital Homogamy

Marital homogamy	Premarital Residence at Home		
	Neither partner	One partner	Both partners
Religious homogamy	64%	80%	88%
Status homogamy	61	72	83
Minimum number of cases	22	46	36

Source: Robert O. Blood, Jr., *Marriage*, 2nd ed. (New York: Free Press, 1962), p. 70.

> . . . *a pair of lovers are sitting in the moonlight. Let us . . . imagine that this moonlight session turns out to be the decisive one, in which a proposal of marriage is made and accepted. Now, we know that contemporary society imposes considerable limitations on such a choice, greatly facilitating it among couples that fit into the same socioeconomic categories and putting heavy obstacles in the way of such as do not. But it is equally clear that even where "they" who are still alive have made no conscious attempts to limit the choice of the participants in this particular drama, "they" who are dead have long ago written the script for almost every move that is made. . . .*
>
> *Each step in their courtship is laid down in social ritual . . . and, although there is always some leeway for improvisations, too much adlibbing is likely to risk the success of the whole operation. In this way, our couple progresses predictably (with what a lawyer would call "due deliberate speed") from movie dates to church dates to meeting-the-family dates, from holding hands to tentative explorations to what they originally planned to save for afterward, from planning their evening to planning their suburban ranch house—with the scene in the moonlight put in its proper place in this ceremonial sequence. Neither of them has invented this game or any part of it. They have only decided that it is with each other, rather than with other possible partners, that they will play it.*[24]

Problems of Mixed Marriages

Some assessment of the cost of selecting a mate outside the field of eligibles can be obtained from an examination of several studies of mixed marriages. Table 10–6 indicates that families of mixed nationality have fewer children, regardless of their protestant or Catholic affiliation; 10–7 that intergenerational difficulties are more common in religiously mixed homes; and 10–8

24.   Peter L. Berger, *Invitation to Sociology: A Humanistic Perspective* (Garden City, N.Y.: Doubleday, 1963), pp. 85–86.

TABLE 10–6
*Number of Living Children in Unmixed and Mixed Nationality
Marriages, by Religion*

	Average number of living children by nationality of parents	
Religion of parents	Unmixed nationality (Both Americans)	Mixed nationalities (One American, one foreign)
Both Protestant	2.49	2.38
Both Catholic	2.76	2.42

Source: Parents of students at Brown University, Providence, Rhode Island. Adapted from Bresler in Robert O. Blood, Jr., *Marriage*, 2nd. ed. (New York: Free Press, 1962), p. 80.

TABLE 10–7
*Intergenerational Difficulties in Religiously Unmixed and
Mixed Marriages*

Intergenerational difficulties	Type of marriage	
	Religiously unmixed	Mixed
Yes	18%	90%
No	82	10
	N = 156	N = 39

Source: Robert O. Blood, Jr., *Marriage*, 2nd ed. (New York: Free Press, 1962), p. 81.

TABLE 10–8
*Arrests for Juvenile Delinquency, in Children of Religiously
Mixed and Unmixed Marriages*

Religious identity of father	Percentage of children ever arrested by religious homogamy of parents		
	Unmixed marriage	Mixed marriage	Ratio
Protestant	5.8%	11.1%	1.9X
Catholic	4.0	9.8	2.5
Jewish	5.1	41.1	8.0

Source: Families of high school seniors and of friends of their families. For simplicity, this table is limited to St. Louis but similar results were obtained in Boston, Denver, New Orleans, and Omaha. The total number of cases for the three religious groups combined was about 9,600 unmixed marriages and 1,100 mixed marriages. Adapted from Zimmerman and Cervantes in Robert O. Blood, Jr., *Marriage*, 2nd ed. (New York: Free Press, 1962), p. 79.

TABLE 10–9
*Divorces of Catholic and Protestant Women in Religiously
Unmixed and Mixed Marriages*

	Percentage divorced, by religious homogamy		
Faith of wife	*Religiously unmixed*	*Religiously mixed*	*Ratio*
Catholic	1.4%	10.6%	7.6X
Protestant	5.1	12.1	2.4

Source: All high-status couples (professional and managerial husbands) married in the state of Iowa between 1953 and 1959 who were divorced by the end of 1959. Reciprocal percentages were still married. The number of divorces represented by each of the above percentages were for unmixed marriages 225 Catholic, 2,227 Protestant, and for mixed marriages, 111 Catholic, 125 Protestant. Adapted from Burchinal and Chancellor in Robert O. Blood, Jr., *Marriage*, 2nd. ed. (New York: Free Press, 1962), p. 85.

TABLE 10–10
*Detrimental and Beneficial Ethnic Mixtures in Hawaii, by Ratio
of Divorce Rates in Unmixed and Mixed Marriages*

	Divorce rate by ethnic homogamy		
	Ethnically unmixed	*Ethnically mixed*	*Ratio*
Detrimental Mixtures			
Japanese man	14.7%	57.5%	3.9X
Caucasian woman	35.4		1.6
Chinese man	17.7	43.2	2.4
Caucasian woman	35.4		1.2
Beneficial Mixtures			
Filipino man	46.0	32.4	0.7
Puerto Rican woman	46.0		0.7
Caucasian man	35.4	24.4	0.7
Filipino woman	46.0		0.5
Caucasian man	35.4	20.1	0.6
Puerto Rican woman	46.0		0.4

Source: Divorces granted 1958–62 per 100 marriages contracted 1956–60 for the entire State of Hawaii. Adapted from Lind in Robert O. Blood, Jr., *Marriage*, 2nd. ed. (New York: Free Press, 1962), p. 91.

that arrests for juvenile crimes are more likely to occur when children are from religiously mixed homes by a factor of 1.9 for protestants to 8.0 for Jews. These tables clearly suggest that child rearing, for example, in homes where parents have not married homogamously (by religion and nationality in these cases) is likely to be more of a problem.

There is also greater stress on the conjugal bond in situations where nonhomogamous mating has occurred. Table 10–9 shows that this is more true for Catholic wives who have married non-Catholics than it is for Protestants who have married nonprotestants.

Not all heterogamy is detrimental, however. Table 10–10 indicates that under certain very select situations—in this case the peculiar tolerance of ethnic variation characteristic of the Island of Hawaii—some, but not all, interethnic marriages are beneficial. Here a Japanese man married to a Caucasian woman is 3.9 times more likely to get a divorce than if he had married a Japanese woman. The most beneficial mixing apparently is the case of a Filipino man married to a Puerto Rican woman. Had he married homogamously in Hawaii, he would have been 0.7 times more likely to obtain a divorce.

Table 10–11 summarizes the data pertaining to hypotheses about reasons for religiously mixed marriages. While none of the hypotheses can be considered as proved, several receive strong support from the current data. It is interesting that strong support is most characteristic of hypotheses pertaining to persons whose early religion was Catholic. In part this is because more research has been directed to the Catholic population in this area. The general lack of confirmation of hypotheses for the Jewish population suggests that demographic factors are much more responsible for mixed marriages among the Jews who constitute only about 3 percent of the total population and have, therefore, a more difficult time finding an attractive mate within their faith. Nevertheless, Jews tend to marry homogamously to a greater extent than do the other religious groups. The fact that Judaism is more a family-based religion than Christianity suggests that even in nonreligious Jewish homes the family exercises greater control over mate choice. When this is true, there is a greater chance that mate choice will be religiously homogamous.

Summary

Although we are formally free to choose our own mate in the United States, society does impose certain informal constraints upon marrying outside a field of eligibles—that group of persons who are similar to ourselves in socioeconomic characteristics and yet not so near to us in consanguinity that "incest" would be committed. Robert F. Winch calls the major factors shaping this field of eligibles the principles of ethnocentric preference and of incest avoidance. The choice of mate is also affected by the principle of

TABLE 10–11
Evaluation of General Hypotheses by Respondents' Early Religion

	Hypothesis	Catholic	Protestant	Jewish	Total
I	Parents of intermarried less tied to religion	*	*	————	**
II	Intermarried more likely to report dissatisfaction with early relations with parents	**	————	————	**
III	Intermarried more likely to report strifeful family interaction when young	**	————	————	*
IV	Intermarried more likely to report tenuous ties to family when young	*	*	**	**
V	Intermarried more likely to have been emancipated from parents at time of marriage	**	————	*	*
VI	Intermarried more likely to report parents had a "difficult time"	————	————	————	————

Source: Jerold Heiss, "Premarital Characteristics of the Religiously Intermarried," *American Sociological Review*, Vol. 25, No. 1 (Feb. 1960), 47.
———— Hypothesis not adequately supported.
*Some support.
**Strong support.

propinquity—the greater likelihood that persons living near enough together to interact frequently will marry—and timing—meeting the right person at the right time.

Within the field of eligibles the factors affecting mate choice are less clearly discernible. The principle of ethnocentric preference does not seem to resolve the matter, but some suggest that homogamy may apply to the search for a value concensus as a further filtering mechanism for mate choice.

Winch's theory of complementary needs is the best developed, most comprehensive theory to account for mate choice within the field of eligibles at the present time, although this theory is only partially substantiated by current research. According to Winch love is basically a matter of need gratification. Persons seek mates who complement their own psychological need pattern. This pattern is shaped by the process of socialization in American culture; therefore, love has common components when expressed by all persons reared in this culture, but it is also shaped by idiosyncratic factors pertinent to a particular individual's development in interaction with a unique constellation of significant others. The variables that must be taken into account to predict mate choice on the basis of complementary needs are many. The matter is further complicated by the fact that, as Winch contends, needs may be unconscious as well as conscious and by the recognition that one person may not be able to gratify the entire need pattern of a potential spouse.

The theory of complementary needs in mate selection also assumes that personal choice is significantly involved in the testing of persons during a period of premarriage. To the extent that personal choice is influenced by parental preference, the theory must be further qualified.

The problems likely to be encountered by persons who do not marry homogamously are reflected in the data indicating that juvenile delinquency, intergenerational difficulties, and divorce are more likely to occur among those in mixed marriages. The precariousness of such mixed marriages is further reflected in the fact that such couples tend to have fewer children than homogamously mated couples. This assumes that persons are less willing to bring children into a world in which they experience stress and strain than they would be in situations where less stress is experienced. In the more tolerant environment of Hawaii, however, some mixed marriages are actually beneficial to the extent that they are less likely to end in divorce.

11. Changing Children

Give me a dozen healthy infants, well-formed, and my own specific world to bring them up in and I'll guarantee to take any one at random and train him to become any type of specialist I might select—a doctor, lawyer, artist, merchant chief, yes, even into beggarman and thief, regardless of his talents, penchants, tendencies, abilities, vocations, and race of his ancestors. I am going beyond my facts and I admit it, but so have the advocates of the contrary and they have been doing it for many thousands of years. Please note that when this experiment is made I am to be allowed to specify the type of way they are to be brought up and the type of world they have to live in.

J. B. WATSON

The conviction that children can be raised in such a manner that their adult personalities conform in a precise way to the design of those responsible for their upbringing is perhaps nowhere better expressed than in the quotation on the preceding page.[1] Certainly if we are concerned with how to change the family, a most powerful method of doing so would be to change radically the personalities of the next generation of children so that they would "naturally" expect a different mode of family life in a different kind of society. This was the intention of the founders of the Kibbutzim of Isreal in the first decade of this century. Their collective method of raising children has indeed produced a quite different personality in the third generation but not without some unanticipated consequences. These will be discussed in Chapter 16. Similar interests have been a major concern of numerous intentional communities.[2]

Watson and others were exceedingly optimistic about the possibilities of rationally shaping human behavior. Much exciting research has given us new insights into the forces that shape human behavior and numerous applications of conditioning techniques in preschool programs, mental hospitals, and other total institutions have demonstrated that—given the proper techniques and adequate attention—the unteachable can be taught and the unreachable can be reached. Nevertheless, this early optimism is not now widely shared. A more cautious assessment of our scientific knowledge about how to produce human beings "to order" must conclude that despite the numerous books of advice on how to raise children, we really know very little about this complex process. What we do know is that (1) human behavior—unlike animal behavior—is remarkably free of instinct and strongly shaped by cultural and interpersonal factors, and (2) the range of variation in human personality types (modal personalities) is great. This range is particularly well documented in the case of sex-role development, an aspect of personality once thought to be largely determined by genetic factors.

Culture and Personality

In Chapter 12 I will discuss briefly how psychosexual differentiation can take place in spite of many biological factors, thus demonstrating than an individual does not grow only through physical maturation, but also through interaction with other human beings. In this interaction they acquire not only a psychosexual identity, but a language, a sense of self-consciousness— along with an attitude of acceptance or rejection of that self—and a way of life. This process produces markedly different personality types in different cultures. Research has shown that a people's language, for example, strongly

---

1. John B. Watson, "What the Nursery Has to Say About Instincts," *Psychologies of 1925* (Worcester, Mass.: Clark University Press, 1926), p. 10.
2. One of the strong tendencies of utopian and experimental communities from Oneida in the early 1800s to the modern "Hippie" commune is a desire to change the character of the children so that they can more fully realize the ideal world of their parents' vision. To date most have had quite mixed results.

influences the way that they perceive the world.[3] It influences the capacity to discriminate between colors, tastes, and sounds. It strongly affects how a people think about the world.[4] The distinction that the Greeks made between psyche (spirit) and soma (body), for example, has strongly conditioned Western man to think of himself as some sort of spirit imprisoned in flesh. Recent research suggests that there are even cultural differences in the perception of pain.[5]

Early research by anthropologists of the culture and personality school called attention to the extent to which culture affects personality. Different cultures "created" different modal types of human beings. Thus we read:

> *The Alorese youth is reared by a mother who feeds him sporadically, teases him a great deal, thinks his temper tantrums are amusing, does not physically punish him, but gives him no sense of control over what happens to him since there is no regular time for doing anything. He grows into a suspicious, mistrustful, anxious, and deeply insecure young man, with little self-esteem or self-confidence and—though greedy—he will do anything to avoid a fight.*[6]

On the other hand, Comanches produced a different kind of modal character:

> *The Comanche boy gets warm, noncontradictory, consistent care. His feeding is warm, loving, and unhurried. He is given no premature responsibilities and receives high praise when he emulates his parents. He is teased very little, and seldom punished. He becomes self-confident, has high self-esteem, is basically secure, friendly, and cooperative. He has few inhibitions, shows great enterprise; bold and daring, he is not anxious about injury or death.*[7]

These studies, under the influence of Freud, are most concerned with the effect of child-rearing practices upon adult personality. Most rely heavily upon the ability of the researcher to describe what he observes. The problems of eliminating researcher error and establishing indicators of behavior such as aggression that will hold from one culture to another are great. That different cultures produce different personalities seems evident even to the layman, but the process by which this takes place is only poorly under-

3. For some excellent discussions of the central concepts involved in the linguistic determination of social reality see Harry Hoijer, "The Sapir-Worf Hypothesis," in Harry Hoijer (ed.), *Language in Culture* (Chicago: University of Chicago Press, 1954), pp. 92–105; and Benjamin Worf, "Science and Linguistics," in Sol Saporta (ed.), *Psycholinguistics: A Book of Readings* (New York: Holt, Rinehart & Winston, 1961), pp. 460–68.

4. See, for example, an excellent account of the relationship between language and cultural perception of reality in Trobriand society in Dorothy Lee, "Lineal and Nonlineal Codifications of Reality," *Psychosomatic Medicine*, Vol. 12 (March–April 1950), 89–95; and *idem.*, "Being and Value in a Primitive Culture," *Journal of Philosophy*, Vol. 46, No. 401 (1949).

5. Mark Zborowski, *People in Pain* (San Francisco: Jossey-Bass, 1969).

6. Jack Conrad, *The Many Worlds of Man* (New York: Thomas Y. Crowell, 1964), pp. 152–53.

7. *Ibid.*, p. 153.

stood. The tendency among researchers has been to reduce the importance placed upon child-rearing practices and to consider socialization, the process of acquiring a way of life, to be a lifelong endeavor. I will consider socialization first, and then focus on child-rearing practices because it is these theories that are most often reflected in the advice experts give parents on how to raise their children.

The Process of Acquiring a Way of Life: Socialization

A number of terms have been offered to describe the process by which people learn the ways of a social group. Anthropologists tend to favor "culturation," "enculturation," or simple "child rearing." Sociologists favor "socialization."

A broad definition of socialization is: The whole process by which an individual develops, through transaction with other people, his specific pattern of socially relevant behavior and experience.[8] Any group, therefore, can be conceived of as a socializing agent insofar as it takes on new members and "teaches them the ropes," but it is the family's primary responsibility to socialize children into a society, although others may assist in this as well.

The study of socialization is not concerned with explaining the uniqueness of a particular individual, and it frequently restricts itself to a discussion of the impact of the group upon the individual. We must allow for the impact of the individual upon the group as well, an aspect of culture change that will be discussed in Chapter 13.

THE PRECONDITIONS

Focusing upon the capacity of an individual to acquire a culture rather than to shape one, Frederick Elkin lists three preconditions for socialization: (1) an ongoing society, (2) biological inheritance, and (3) Cooley's "human nature."[9] A human being becomes a social being by virtue of an *ongoing society* in which he is reared. An individual does not become human by maturation in isolation, but only through the process of interaction with other men. Thus a society must be stable enough for parents to be able to transmit its distinctive patterns. They never transmit them perfectly, however, and this is a source of change even in slowly changing societies. If a society is anomic or undergoing rapid social change, the process of socialization is made more difficult. But if *biological inheritance* is inadequate (if there is severe brain damage, genetic deficiency, crippling debilitations, and the like) the process of socialization may be impossible or greatly retarded. The handicapped child will not be able to realize his full human potential.

8. Edward Zigler and Irvin L. Child, "Socialization," in Gardner Linsey and Elliot Aronson (eds.), *The Handbook of Social Psychology*, 2nd ed., Vol. III (Reading, Mass.: Addison-Wesley, 1969), p. 474.

9. Frederick Elkin, *The Child and Society: The Process of Socialization* (New York: Random House, 1960), p. 7 ff.

Finally, according to Cooley, man, in distinction from the animal, possesses a *human nature* which he defines as the capacity to empathize or—more pointedly—the capacity to put oneself in another person's place. Without this capacity, Cooley argues, men could not become socialized at all.

The effects of having been reared with minimal opportunity to interact with others have been well described by Kinsley Davis. The cases of Anna and Isabelle give further support to the notion that interaction with other human beings is central to the development of the human personality.

CASES OF EXTREME ISOLATION

Two extremely deprived children who were discovered and rather extensively studied by social scientists are reported by Davis.[10] Both were about six years of age when discovered. Both were severely retarded in their learning and, some said, were incapable of learning. Both made rather dramatic progress, although one died before the full benefits of the efforts of the social scientist could be recorded.

Anna was born on March 1, 1932, and died of hemorrhagic jaundice on August 6, 1942. She was an illegitimate child, strongly disapproved of by her widowed grandfather who did not want her at home. She was thus moved about frequently during the early months of her life and finally confined to an attic room on the second floor of her mother's farm home. She received only enough care to keep her alive and was seldom moved from one position to another. Her clothing and bedding were filthy; she was given no instruction and received no friendly attention.

When she was finally removed from the room at about six years of age, she could not talk, walk, or do anything that showed intelligence. She was extremely emaciated and undernourished, having been fed viturally nothing but milk. After two years she could walk, understand simple commands, feed herself, achieve some neatness, and remember people. She appeared to have the characteristics of a normal infant of one year of age, although she was over eight.

There is the possibility, however, that Anna might have had innate mental deficiencies. Her mother was tested at an I.Q. of 50—which is the equivalent of an eight year old. Her father was probably a normal, but elderly, man. It is, therefore, fortunate (from the perspective of scientific discovery) that another child of similar history was discovered at about the same time. Isabelle was found in 1939 at the age of six and a half. She also was illegitimate. Her confinement was apparently less isolated than Anna's, since she was kept in seclusion with her deaf-mute mother, who—like herself—was a source of embarrassment to her farm family. When discovered by a welfare worker, she was unable to speak (making only croaking sounds) and was extremely rachitic because of a lack of sunshine and adequate diet. Her behavior, particularly toward men, was a mixture of fear and hostility.

10. This section is based on the material presented in Kingsley Davis, *Human Society* (New York: Macmillan, 1949), pp. 204–08.

Despite the fact that her first score on an IQ test was 19 (the equivalent of a two and a half year old) and the general impression was that she was uneducable, a systematic and intensive training program was undertaken. It was one week before she made her first vocalization, but gradually she began to respond. And then a most unusual thing happened. She went through the normal stages of learning characteristic of the years one to six in the proper sequence but far more rapidly than normal. It was as though once she had the rudiments of speech, she was gifted with extraordinary powers of learning. Two months after her first vocalization she was putting sentences together. Nine months after she was putting sentences together, she could identify words and sentences on the printed page, write well, count to ten, and tell a story after hearing it. Seven months after this, she had a vocabulary of 1,500 to 2,000 words and was asking complicated questions. She had trebled her IQ in a year and a half. By 1946, at the age of 14, she was able to pass the sixth grade in a public school.

The consideration of Isabelle's case clearly demonstrates, as Anna's does not, that isolation up the age of six, with failure to acquire any form of speech, does not preclude the subsequent acquisition of normal skills. If Isabelle were considered to be characteristic, there would seem to be an acceleration of the learning process once speech is acquired. No one learns to speak in isolation.

Additional evidence of the damage inflicted by isolation in less extreme instances is provided by Rene Spitz's study of hospitalism.[11] In this instance infants were reared by persons who, because of their heavy workload, could do little more than feed the children and occasionally turn them. They were thus in a sanitary, well-lighted dormitory, but with insufficient "mothering." Infants reared in such an environment showed markedly increased rates of mortality (commonly the result of marasma—a progressive emaciation associated with faulty assimilation and utilization of food), severely retarded development, and greater frequency of emotional disturbances than infants reared under similar circumstances in a nursing home who received loving attention from their mother or mother surrogate. It was not institutionalization as such that made the difference, but rather the type of care that the children received.

Evidence of the effects of isolation beyond the age of childhood has not been systematically gathered. What the effect of isolation until adulthood upon an otherwise normal individual might be is, therefore, not known and the contribution of maturation not fully understood. The importance of a warm mothering relationship, however, seems well established.

Although personality development is a lifelong process and socialization occurs whenever one is taken into a new group, I will focus upon the early years of childhood, for it is during these years that the family probably exerts its maximum influence. The cases of Anna and Isabelle reflect parental abuse and grossly atypical patterns of child rearing. I turn

11. René A. Spitz, *The Psychoanalytic Study of the Child* (New York: International Universities Press, 1945, 1947), Vol. I, pp. 53–74; Vol. II, pp. 113–17.

now to an examination of the historical trends in the more common practices.

Historical Trends in American Child Rearing

We Americans have not always reared our children in the same way.[12] Older people frequently admonish the young, suggesting a real or imagined change in the manner in which children are being reared today as opposed to how the oldsters were reared. We do not know enough about how children have in fact been reared in America to document these assumed intergenerational changes over the greater part of our nation's history. We can, however, make some distinctions on the basis of rather broad and somewhat arbitrary periods.

COLONIAL AMERICA

In Chapter 5, I presented some aspects of child rearing in colonial America. Children, particularly those living on the frontier, were raised almost exclusively in the context of isolated nuclear families under conditions in which the birth and death rates were quite high, all members of the family were needed for its work as a productive unit, independence and marriage at an early age were expected, and a stern Puritan Christianity strongly influenced their parents' conception of human nature. Children were considered by nature obdurate, inclined to do the work o fthe devil; they had to be broken like a horse in order to be fit for society. They were to be seen and not heard, they were to defer formally to their parents in all matters including, frequently, their marriage, and they were expected above all to be industrious.[13] Unfortunately these generalizations are based primarily upon books written by early American sages on how children should be reared and, therefore, probably reflect the ideal more than the reality. We do not know how representative any of the practices presented in Chapter 5 were. It does seem reasonable, however, to infer that, whatever child-rearing practices were representative, they were transmitted largely by imitation of traditional customs and that the general stance toward rearing children did not change rapidly, although some of the specific practices must have had regional variation and greater likelihood of change.

1850–1900

During the period of industrialization which began after the Civil War, the character of our society changed radically and the demands upon the

---

12. Excellent accounts of trends in child rearing in America can be found in Robert F. Winch, *The Modern Family*, rev. ed. (New York: Holt, Rinehart & Winston, 1969); and William F. Kenkel, *The Family in Perspective* (New York: Appleton-Century-Crofts, 1966). This section draws heavily upon Kenkel.

13. See Panos D. Bardis, "Family Forms and Variations Historically Considered," in Harold T. Christensen (ed.), *Handbook of Marriage and the Family* (Chicago: Rand McNally, 1964), pp. 403–61.

family were thus quite different. The locus of work for more and more families shifted to the city. The family changed from a unit of production to one primarily of consumption as income-producing work was more and more carried on outside of the home in the factory. Children were in great demand as laborers and it was not considered unreasonable to require them to work a twelve to fourteen hour day. Twenty-five percent of the boys between the ages of ten and fifteen were gainfully employed as late as 1890.[14] The problem of child labor did not seem to concern most people until the need for such labor declined. One can, therefore, see the establishment of the Society for the Prevention of Cruelty to Children and the later child labor legislation as reflecting not simply an awakened moral indignation, but also a change in the needs of our industrializing society. It is difficult to see how the family as an institution or the changed attitudes of parents on child rearing were especially instrumental in the enactment of Child Labor Laws, and yet, the return of children to the home and the consequent increase in their leisure time has had profound effect upon their upbringing.

The ideal adult personality of our early industrial society can be described as including such traits as: self-control, self-denial, self-sufficiency, a strong desire to get ahead, and a willingness to take risks. In part, this represented a modified carry-over from the pre-industrial pioneer period when the availability of free land was a great social leveler and the hard-working, risk-taking individual capable of getting along without too great reliance on his fellows could emerge successful. These same personality traits seemed even more appropriate for conquering the new industrial frontiers. The label of "rugged individualism" was well earned, and the password of the day was "get ahead."[15]

Although, again, no systematic data is available on child-rearing practices, the advice given to parents seems to reflect a desire to reward individualism, independence, self-denial, and competitiveness. At least such well-read manuals on the subject as L. E. Holt's *The Care and Feeding of Children* (1906) and John B. Watson's *Psychological Care of Infant and Child* (1928) reflect such a perspective. Kenkel concludes that despite the paucity of evidence, "there seems to be a basic consistency in the nature of the Industrializing Society, the ideal personality sought to live in that kind of society, and the child-rearing practices held necessary for achieving the ideal personality."[16]

1900–WORLD WAR II

With the turn of the century the era of scientific child rearing began first in the more mobile middle-class families. Shorn from friends' and kin's advice on how to rear children and deprived by the demands of industry of sufficient intimate contact with neighbors to learn by imitation, young middle-class families began to turn to the expert for advice. Kenkel sees the period since World War II as the period of the emergence of the mass society, and postu-

14. Kenkel *op. cit.*, p. 246.
15. *Loc. cit.*
16. *Ibid.*, p. 250.

lates that the child-rearing norms appropriate to the development of an ideal adult personality for a bureaucratized mass society must stress accommodation, getting along, and conformity. Reisman's other-directed member of the *Lonely Crowd* becomes the model of adjustment. The schools stress adjustment rather than achievement. Parents seek to become pals with their children and equalitarianism is extended to include the children. The data on actual practices are not yet satisfactory. Since social scientists have become interested in child development, the accuracy of the data has increased and shorter term trends are discernible. Our analysis can now become sensitive to class variables.

POST WORLD WAR II CLASS VARIATIONS

Perhaps the most significant change in child-rearing practices in the United States in the mid-decades of the twentieth century is the increasing reliance of working-class parents on expert advice. The middle-class family has a longer history of depending upon such advice as it is characteristically more detached from relatives and close friends who might be readily available for such consultation. Thus, as Bronfenbrenner observes, "the gap between the social classes in their goals and methods of child rearing appears to be narrowing."[17]

However, while there may be a slowly increasing class consensus on how children should be reared in such broad areas as discipline and sex education, the experts are not of one mind. Martha Wolfenstein's study of the advice given in the Children's Bureau's Infant Care Bulletin documents the oscillation in professional perspective over the years 1914 to 1951.[18] With the increasing dependence upon professional expertise, it is probable that the practical advice given by such highly esteemed professionals as Doctors Spock and Ginott will continue to change as new information about effective child-rearing practices becomes known.[19] This advice is likely to change much more rapidly than the advice passed on from generation to generation in the folk tradition. Thus fadism in child rearing is an increasingly likely result.

The Trend Toward Permissiveness: Bronfenbrenner has attempted to assess the effects of changing parental attitudes and behaviors on children. In 1958 he concluded that the major changes in child-rearing practices were: (1) Mothers of all social classes have become more flexible with regard to feeding and weaning over the past quarter of a century. The trend is toward demand feeding and late weaning from the bottle. (2) Class variations in feeding, weaning, and toilet training are perceivable, however. From about 1930

17. Urie Bronfenbrenner, "The Changing American Child—A Speculative Analysis," *Journal of Social Issues*, Vol. 17 (1961), 6–18, reprinted in John N. Edwards (ed.), *The Family and Change* (New York: Knopf, 1969), p. 236.

18. Martha Wolfenstein, "Trends in Infant Care," *American Journal of Orthopsychiatry*, Vol. 23 (1953), 120–30.

19. Haim G. Ginott, *Between Parent and Child: New Solutions to Old Problems* (New York: Macmillan, 1965); Benjamin Spock, *Baby and Child Care* (New York: Pocket Books, 1957).

until the end of World War II, working-class mothers were more permissive than middle-class mothers. These mothers were more likely to breast feed their babies, to feed them on demand, to wean later, and to complete toilet training at a later age than were middle-class mothers. After World War II, however, the trend was reversed. Now middle-class mothers are more permissive in each area. (3) There seems to be a correspondence between observed child-rearing practices and the advice of the experts as reflected in the Children's Bureau Bulletins, particularly in the case of middle-class mothers. (4) Methods of infant care seem to vary with cultural background, urban versus rural upbringing, and ideologies of child rearing. (5) Socialization practices are more likely to change in those segments of the population which have greater exposure to expert advice as reflected in books, pamphlets, or personal contact with physicians and counselors.[20]

With regard to child training he concludes: (6) Middle-class mothers since World War II are more permissive across the board with their young children than are working-class mothers, especially in such areas as oral behavior, toilet accidents, dependency, sex, aggressiveness, and freedom of movement outside the home. (7) Although more tolerant of their children's impulses and desires, middle-class parents have a higher expectation of their children's performing successfully in school, assuming responsibility around the home, and being able to take care of themselves. (8) Working-class mothers are consistently more likely to resort to physical punishment as a means of discipline, focusing primarily upon behavior, while middle-class parents are more likely to utilize techniques relying on reasoning or the threat of the loss of love. These latter techniques are more likely to bring about internalization of norms and values. (9) While working-class parent-child relationships are focused around maintaining order and obedience, middle-class parent-child relationships are more accepting and equalitarian. Within this context the middle-class has shifted away from emotional control toward freer expression of affection.[21]

The Companionate Family: These changes in child-rearing practices are occurring in the context of a changing complex of family roles. Burgess and Locke saw industrialization as producing a new kind of companionate family in which the bonds uniting family members were not primarily instrumental ones based on numerous social functions entrusted to the family, but were rather affectionate bonds derived from the interpersonal needs of family members in an institutional structure that was becoming increasingly equalitarian.[22] This, they assumed, was truest for the middle class. Miller and Swanson, however, who have modified this model somewhat, feel that the tendencies noted by Burgess and Locke were more related to the earlier

20. Urie Bronfenbrenner, "Socialization and Social Class through Time and Space," in Eleanor E. Maccoby, Theodore M. Newcomb, and Eugene L. Hartley (eds.), *Readings in Social Psychology*, 3rd ed. (New York: Holt, Rinehart & Winston, 1958), p. 424.

21. *Ibid.*, pp. 424–25.

22. Ernest W. Burgess and Harvey J. Locke, *The Family, from Institution to Companionship* (New York: American Book, 1945).

stages of industrialization[23] With the age of the bureaucrat, society makes different demands upon husbands, wives, and children, and complementarity —not equality—is the objective.

The distinctive characteristics of the bureaucratic order have led to what might be called a neotraditional family. The specialization on the job has entered the home, and the equal partners have been able to see that differences in talent, interest, and function, as long as they are complementary, do not threaten equality. Instead, they may enrich and promote the common life. For this reason this type of family is called the "colleague family."[24]

The equality of complementary roles is not threatened so long as society equally rewards the different roles. If it does not, then we have the re-emergence of demands for equality, for example, the feminist movement where the emphasis is once again upon the need for equality. Whatever the better conceptual model of the family may be, one thing seems common to both: the role of the father vis-à-vis the mother has been shifting. The father is becoming more affectionate and less authoritarian. The mother is becoming more important as an agent of discipline, especially for boys of the middle class. The father's extensive absence from the home contributes to the explanation of this shift.

The Effects of Permissiveness and Equalitarianism: What has been the effect of these trends on the children? Has, as Bronfenbrenner asks, the changing American parent produced a changing American child? His speculative answer to this question is "yes."

Males exposed to the "modern" pattern of child rearing might be expected to differ from their counterparts of a quarter century ago in being somewhat more conforming and anxious, less enterprising and self-sufficient, and, in general, possessing more of the virtues and liabilities commonly associated with feminine character structure.[25]

Class and sex factors affect this generalization. Fathers are more likely to treat children differently in the dimension of warmth and solicitousness on the basis of sex. They are warmer with their daughters. Sex-role differentiation tends to diminish with increasing socioeconomic status, and so it is probable that this effect is more pronounced in the lower-middle class than in upper classes. In the upper-middle class, parents tend to exercise direct discipline over their children equally. In upper-middle class families Bronfenbrenner finds a tendency to produce organization men:

> Both responsibility and leadership are fostered by the relatively greater salience of the parent of the same sex. . . . Boys tend to be more responsible when the father rather than the mother is the principal disciplinarian; girls are more dependable when the mother is the major au-

23. D. R. Miller and G. E. Swanson, The Changing American Parent (New York: John Wiley, 1959); reprinted in Edwards op. cit.
24. Miller and Swanson ibid., p. 229.
25. Bronfenbrenner, "The Changing American Child," in Edwards op. cit., p. 243.

thority figure. . . . In short, boys thrive in a patriarchal context, girls in a matriarchal. . . .

The most dependent and least dependable adolescents describe family arrangements that are neither patriarchal nor matriarchal, but equalitarian . . . The democratic family, which for so many years has been held up and aspired to as a model by professionals and enlightened laymen tends to produce young people who "do not take initiative," "look to others for directions and decisions," and "cannot be counted on to fulfill obligations."[26]

The Return to Authoritarianism: The trend toward equalitarianism and permissiveness in family relationships, however, appears to be abating. Sterner discipline and complementary parental roles seem to be in the offing. Bronfenbrenner feels that the social factor most responsible for this alteration is the advent of Sputnik and the replacement of education for adjustment by education for excellence, with the re-establishment of an emphasis upon achievement. If, as seems likely, the wife is going to assume increasing parental authority, she will have at her disposal the more powerful instrument of withdrawal of love with which to motivate her children to higher achievement. She can do this more effectively than the father whose authority is not effectively perceived until the child is older and who, of necessity, must spend more of his time away from home. She, furthermore, has a strong emotional investment in the child that should provide her with a powerful lever for evoking the desired performance. In fact several recent studies support the contention that achievement training is best fostered in matriarchal families.[27] High achievement motivation "appears to flourish in a family atmosphere of 'cold democracy' in which initial high levels of material involvement are followed by pressures for independence and accomplishment."[28]

26. *Ibid.*, p. 245. Bronfenbrenner feels that the following studies support this generalization: G. R. Bach, "Father-Fantasies and Father-Typing in Father-Separated Children," *Child Development*, Vol. 17 (1946), 63–79; A. Bandura and R. H. Walters, *Adolescent Aggression* (New York: Ronald Press, 1959); D. B. Lynn and W. L. Sawrey, "The Effects of Father-Absence on Norwegian Boys and Girls," *Journal of Abnormal and Social Psychology*, Vol. 59 (1959), 258–62; P. Mussen and L. Distler, "Masculinity, Identification and Father-Son Relationships," *Journal of Abnormal and Social Psychology*, Vol. 59 (1959), 350–56; M. Papanek, "Authority and Interpersonal Relations in the Family," (Cambridge, Massachusetts: Unpublished Doctoral Dissertation, Radcliffe College, 1957); R. R. Sears, M. H. Pintler, and P. S. Sears, "Effects of Father-Separation on Preschool Children's Doll Play Aggression," *Child Development*, Vol. 17 (1946), 219–43; O. P. Tiller, "Father-Absence and Personality Development of Children in Sailor Families," *Nordisk Psykologis Monograph Series*, Vol. 9 (1958).
27. F. L. Strodbeck, "Family Interaction, Values, and Achievement," in D. C. McClelland, A. L. Baldwin, U. Bronfenbrenner, and F. L. Strodbeck, *Talent and Society* (Princeton, N.J.: Van Nostrand, 1958), pp. 135–94; B. L. Rosen and R. D'Andrade, "The Psychological Origins of Achievement Motivation," *Sociometry*, Vol. 22 (1959), 185–217.
28. A. L. Baldwin, J. Kalhorn, and F. H. Breese, "The Appraisal of Parent Behavior," *Psychological Monographs*, Vol. 58, No. 3 (1945). See also A. L. Baldwin, "Socialization and the Parent-Child Relationship," *Child Development*, Vol. 19 (1948), 127–36; E. A. Haggard, "Socialization, Personality, and Academic Achievement in Gifted Children," *The School Review*, Vol. 65 (1957), 388–414; M. R. Winterbottom, "The Relation of Need Achievement to Learning Experiences in Independence and Mastery," in J. W. Atkinson (ed.), *Motives in Fantasy, Action and Society* (Princeton, N·J.: Van Nostrand, 1958), pp. 453–94; and Rosen and D'Andrade *op cit.*

However, such high achievers are also more aggressive, tense, domineering, and cruel. Therefore, the social costs of socialization for high achievement would seem to be great.[29]

Child Development Research

Fadism in American child-rearing practices reflects differing expert opinions on how children should be reared. This difference in opinion results from different evaluations of the desirable adult personality, on the one hand, and from different interpretations of the available data on how parental behavior affects children on the other. We are, in fact, a long way from being able to predict precisely the consequences of any given parental behavior on a child's development, although we feel more reasonably certain about some behaviors and attitudes than others. The fundamental problems confronting the expert seeking to give advice on scientific child rearing will be evident in the brief summary of the state of our knowledge on the subject as gleaned largely from experimental studies, which follows.

A basic difference in approach to the problem of rearing children scientifically is between those who are primarily concerned about changing *behavior* and those who would change *personality*. Those coming after Watson, whose primary concern is to change behavior, seem generally more optimistic about our capabilities than those who talk about changing personality. This is an oversimplification, of course, and the difference in attitude need not reflect the true state of our capacity in either case. In general, however, the optimism of the behaviorists stems largely from their successes in changing or controlling the behavior of persons in total or near total institutions and from what they take to be encouraging results from those working on animal behavior. That behavior can be modified through the careful use of reinforcements (rewards) and/or aversive stimuli (punishments) seems to be repeatedly demonstrated, though techniques vary. (In the research of Ivan Petrovich Pavlov on the conditioned reflex, the reinforcement is paired to the stimulus. In the case of B. F. Skinner's operant conditioning, it is paired with the response.) On the other hand, those concerned with changing personality are often not in agreement about what they mean by personality and are very much divided over the extent to which personality can be inferred from observable behavior. Some symbolic interactionists, for example, even question the extent to which it is useful to speak of personality as a relatively stable configuration of traits or as a "core" personality. For them personality is situationally determined and it is emergent, that is each interaction can be the occasion for the presentation of a new aspect of the self. Studies of

---

29. Bronfenbrenner does not pretend to assess the net gain of such tendencies, but such an assessment must be ventured at some point in the near future if we are to be at all ethical in the choice of socialization practices. Such an assessment, however, is hampered by all of the problems set forth in attempting to relate personality to child-rearing practices and by the diverse conceptions of what a desirable personality model should be. These issues are discussed in some detail in other chapters.

racism tend to support this perspective. A person may be discriminatory and speak against Blacks at home or at his lodge, but be tolerant and nondiscriminatory on the job.[30] In both positions change is less surprising than permanence. What is conceived of as change and how one goes about change, however, is quite different.

For example, what does a parent do to control a child's bed wetting? The way in which the same piece of equipment is utilized by both approaches can serve to illustrate some of the differences between them. One way of controlling bed wetting is to place the child on a bed pad that is wired so that when it becomes wet it will set off an alarm, thus waking the child and giving him the opportunity to complete his urination in the bathroom. The use of such a device then takes into consideration the child's personality. It assumes his willingness and ability to cooperate given the proper conditions. On the other hand, the device could as easily be used to shock the child every time he wets it. Over time successive aversive stimuli would eventually extinguish the behavior. A difference in approach might emerge between those who favor the use of reinforcements rather than aversive stimuli because of their contention that behavior is more readily modified by reinforcement than by punishment, but their preference is not really a concern with the effect of reward versus punishment on the child's *personality* nor is it a moral issue. It is based upon an assessment of relative utility. If aversive stimuli were in fact more effective, they would undoubtedly be used.

Often the problem between the two basic perspectives is joined along another issue. It seems that some of the behavior that has been changed through operant conditioning techniques reverts back to its original characteristics once the patient is removed from the rigidly controlled system of reinforcement. To put it another way, if he is not reinforced for behaving in the new way (presumably the more "normal" pattern of behavior) by those with whom he interacts outside the hospital, he will revert back to his former symptoms. Those who approach the problem of changing personality contend that in effecting such a change one in fact alters the internal control mechanisms so that long-term changes in behavior can be expected. The patient is "cured." The precise nature of what is internalized and the process by which it is internalized are problems that are a matter of great debate. Psychoanalytic theory contends, for example, that in changing behavior you often merely suppress a symptom, the cause of which hasn't been touched. What is not debatable is that once such internalization occurs, behavior is modified over relatively long periods of time. This is true even allowing for the fact that in the case of internalization of norms, values, or precepts, behavior need not always conform to the precept. Behavior must usually give evidence of a relatively greater conformity to than deviance from the norm, however, in order for us to say that the norm has been internalized.

30. For example, see Joseph D. Lohman and Dietrich C. Reitzes, "Deliberately Organized Groups and Racial Behavior," *American Sociological Review*, Vol. 19 (June 1954), 324–44.

How Does Parents' Behavior
Affect Their Child's Behavior?

An examination of experimental findings indicates that researchers arrive at divergent, often contradictory findings. Problems of methodology are compounded by differences in conceptual perspective and a general reluctance on the part of social scientists to attempt to replicate a colleague's study. Consequently, strictly comparable studies are hard to find. Yet the person seeking to improve the state of our child-rearing practices must give advice on the basis of what he perceives to be the most reliable information available. He must, therefore, judiciously choose to rely on some findings and hold others in abeyance. His dilemma will become apparent in the following summary of research in certain areas of behavior that commonly concern parents.

ORAL BEHAVIOR

Psychoanalysis suggests that the sucking behavior of infants is innate; learning theory asserts that it is an acquired drive. The data support the generalization that sucking is the product of an infant drive, but that variations in the treatment of the infant's oral behavior have important immediate effect upon this behavior. The data do not at present support any generalizations about the lasting effect of oral socialization (either before or after weaning) and later personality or behavior.[31] The most convincing support for the general association between oral socialization and later aspects of personality or behavior comes from cross-cultural studies rather than individual-difference studies. For example, Whiting[32] combined ethnographic data from thirty-seven countries with those on American patterns[33] to develop a curvilinear relationship between age of weaning and the degree of emotional disturbance. There is a positive relationship until eighteen months, and a negative relationship thereafter. That is, emotional disturbance in adult personalities seems greatest in those societies that wean children at around eighteen months and is less in those societies that wean earlier or later. There are no data to suggest that such differences in emotional disturbance would be notable in people reared within the same society but weaned at different times.

It may be that the relationship between emotional disturbance and weaning is affected by a society's norms concerning when it is appropriate to wean

---

31. Zigler and Child *op. cit.*, pp. 450–589. This section is heavily indebted to the Zigler and Child article. Most of the references cited in this section are to be found discussed by Zigler and Child, and additional information on all areas is also available in this excellent summary of the research literature.

32. John W. Whiting, "The Cross-Cultural Method," in G. Lindzey *op. cit.*, pp. 523–31.

33. R. R. Sears and G. W. Wise, "Relation of Cup Feeding in Infancy to Thumbsucking and the Oral Drive," *American Journal of Orthopsychiatry*, Vol. 20 (1950), 123–38

a child. In this case mothers might be more anxious about accomplishing the task when they *should* accomplish it, displaying a kind of maximum anxiety as the normal period approaches and showing much less anxiety (for quite different reasons) both significantly before and after the accepted normal period of time for weaning.

The two theories also would lead one to predict opposite effects from indulging the drive. If all sucking is innate, then it follows that indulgence of thumb sucking (a non-nutritive form of sucking) in infants would tend to reduce the chance of its later occurrence because the drive would presumably be satiated. On the other hand, if thumbsucking is an acquired or learned drive, then its indulgence would tend to increase the likelihood of its persistence into later childhood. Levy interprets his data to indicate that deprivation of oral sucking behavior not only results in a nonsatiated "need" to suck but also produces restlessness and interferes with optimal metabolic functioning.[34] These findings were generalized by Ribble to provide a rationale for relating a child's general well-being to oral gratification.[35] In the view of writers following Ribble, a child should not be weaned early or harshly but should be allowed maximum gratification of his oral needs. It would seem that these two positions could be tested empirically and the best conceptual framework selected, but this is not the case. Neither conceptual framework is sufficiently vulnerable to empirical testing at present, in large measure because neither's variables have not been precisely defined.

The effects of oral socialization upon later personality have not yet been established. In all areas of concern, this is the most difficult aspect of the research. It is now almost impossible to be sure that any parental behavior in child rearing has a *direct* causal relationship to later adult personality traits or behavior patterns. Even though the cross-cultural data are most suggestive, there are too many uncontrolled variables that prevent the establishment of causal sequences with a high degree of certainty. Research findings are thus quite contradictory.

DEPENDENCY

H. A. Murray defines dependence as behavior which seems to have as its goal the obtaining of nurturance from other people or which clearly indicates that reliance upon the help of others is the individual's dominant method of striving for his goals.[36] This is sometimes confused with a child's susceptibility to social reinforcement (conformity). In our society, with its high ideal of rugged individualism, we sometimes fail to recognize that, while dependence is a valued trait in infancy which must to some extent be overcome in adulthood, some degree of dependence in adulthood is absolutely necessary.[37]

34. D. M. Levy, "Experiments on the Sucking Reflex and Social Behavior of Dogs," *American Journal of Orthopsychiatry*, Vol. 4 (1934), 203–24.

35. Margaret Ribble, *The Rights of Infants* (New York: Columbia University Press, 1943).

36. H. A. Murray, *Explorations in Personality* (New York: Oxford University Press, 1938).

37. A. Bandura and R. H. Walters, *Social Learning and Personality Development* (New York: Holt, Rinehart & Winston, 1963).

Both psychoanalysis and learning theory have strongly affected the study of dependency. In the psychoanalytic frame of reference, dependence phenomena arise in association with early infancy, particularly in association with those child-rearing practices concerned with feeding. The oral personality is markedly dependent. According to the neo-Hullian version of learning theory, dependence habits develop in the presence of adults who gratify needs. These adults, through their identification with primary reinforcers (i.e. food), take on the characteristics of secondary reinforcers. Once established as secondary reinforcement, adults later become social reinforcers. For example, their presence, in itself, is rewarding.

The acceptance of an acquired dependence drive, however, does not preclude the presence of an innate drive. In advancing his concept of "attachment," Bowlby contends that actions typically thought to be acquired behavior (the tendency for the infant to stay close to its mother) can as readily be explained in terms of inborn behavior patterns which bind the mother to the child at birth. In this view, however, the range of behaviors normally included in dependence studies is reduced largely to "proximity seeking."[38]

Research seems to suggest that dependence is fostered by early rejection or frustration of a child. The deprivation studies suggest that frustration in the form of deprivation under the conditions of minimal mothering leads to greater dependence behavior. The conditions under which frustration occurs are not clearly defined as yet. We are not sure about the conditions under which frustration is likely to produce aggression and those under which frustration might produce dependence.

The relationship between parental behavior and achievement is not clear. Both permissiveness and restrictiveness on the part of parents have been related to achievement, and so we have apparently opposite parental behaviors producing the same result in children.[39] Undoubtedly further refinement of

---

38. J. Bowlby, "The Nature of the Child's Tie to his Mother," *International Journal of Psychoanalysis*, Vol. 39 (1958), 350–73; H. R. Schaefer and P. E. Emerson, "The Development of Social Attachments in Infancy," *Monographs in Social Research and Child Development*, Vol. 28 (1964), No. 1.

39. A. Conklin, "Failures of Highly Intelligent Pupils," *Teachers College Contributions to Education, No. 792* (New York: Teachers College Press, 1940); E. Jones, "The Probation Student: What he is Like and What Can Be Done About It," *Journal of Educational Research*, Vol. 39 (1955), 93–102; B. Kimball, "Case Studies in Educational Failure During Adolescence," *American Journal of Orthopsychiatry*, Vol. 23 (1953), 406–15; A. Walsh, *Self-Concepts of Bright Boys with Learning Difficulties* (New York: Teachers College Press, 1956); S. W. Becker, "Consequences of Different Kinds of Parental Discipline" in M. L. and L. W. Hoffman (eds.), *Review of Child Development Research*, Vol. 1 (New York: Russell Sage Foundation, 1964), have found permissiveness related to aggression. A. L. Baldwin, "Socialization and the Parent-Child Relationship," *Child Development*, Vol. 19 (1945), 127–36; M. J. Raelke, *The Relation of Parental Authority to Children's Behavior and Attitudes* (Minneapolis: University of Minnesota Press, 1946); P. M. Symonds, *The Psychology of Parent-Child Relationships* (New York: Appleton-Century-Crofts, 1939) have found both permissiveness and restrictiveness to be related to achievement. G. Watson, "A Comparison of the Effects of Lax Versus Strict Home Training," *Journal of Social Psychology*, Vol. 5 (1934), 102–5; David McClelland *et. al.*, The Achievement Motive (New York: Appleton-Century-Crofts, 1953); Lois Hoffman, S. Rosen, and R. Lippit, "Parental Coerciveness, Child's Autonomy, and Child's Role at School," *Sociometry*, Vol. 23 (1960), 945–1013; E. E. Maccoby, "The Taking of Adult Roles in Middle Childhood," *Journal of Abnormal and Social Psychology*, Vol. 63 (1961), 493–503 find restrictiveness related to achievement.

the conditions under which these factors produce achievement will give us more precise clues as to the optimal conditions for producing achievers—if we do indeed wish to increase the achievement motivation of our youth.

The data at present support the notion that achievement is one of many possible modes of independence. A child who is notably dependent as an infant, however, may well become achievement oriented as he grows older. Dependence and achievement are not necessarily exclusive, as many first-born children are high achievers as infants. Further, dependence may itself become a goal of achievement striving. Finally, we may view the achievement-oriented adult as dependent in a mature fashion insofar as he is striving for recognition by others rather than just by himself. The common elements in the diverse definitions of achievement orientation appear to be that:

> *Situations which evoke achievement motivation are those in which competence of performance is central. Furthermore, the general aim of achievement behavior appears to be that of obtaining positive reinforcement for demonstrated competence. Finally, achievement situations appear to be those which contain cues relevant to a "standard of excellence" which ultimately defines degree of competence or incompetence.*[40]

However, school progress may reflect motives other than achievement. Children may desire to conform to the teacher's expectations of goodness.[41] Those children with a high degree of independence may not be rated as competent by teachers and thus may experience an ambiguity between their achievement striving and school performance.

At least two generalizations can be made: (1) The development of persistent striving for achievement is strongly influenced by social approval of such striving. (2) The pattern of persistent striving is also affected by the success or failure experienced by the striver. A child's striving for achievement must not be uniformly successful—nor uniformly unsuccessful. An element of frustration, therefore, must always be present.

Cross-cultural studies relate achievement to the general approval given to achievement motivation in a particular culture.[42] The nature of the economic system is also related. Those societies with little accumulation of food (hunting and fishing societies) produce higher achievers than those where a surplus is accumulated (animal husbandry).[43] A number of studies have related achievement to socioeconomic class in our own society—in general supporting the contention that the middle class is more achievement oriented than

40. Zigler and Child *op. cit.*
41. Crandall, "Achievement," in *Child Psychology*, Pt. I (Chicago: National Society for the Study of Education, 1963), pp. 416–60.
42. McClelland, "Some Social Consequences of Achievement Motivation," in M. R. Jones (ed.), *Nebraska Symposium on Motivation* (1955); L. Berkowitz, *The Development of Motives and Values in the Child* (New York: Basic Books, 1964); Crandall, "Achievement," *op. cit.*
43. H. Barry, Margaret K. Bacon and I. L. Child, "A Cross-Cultural Survey of Some Sex Differences in Socialization," *Journal of Abnormal and Social Psychology*, Vol. 55 (1957), 327–32.

the lower class.[44] This is consistent with the view that the middle class provides greater independence training than does the lower class. Middle-class children also have been found to be more easily reinforced by "right" answers than are lower-class children.[45] But, again, the fact of confidence in the society must be considered as suggested in Chapter 8. It is usually not considered in experimental studies.

EXCRETORY BEHAVIOR

Most research in this area has ignored urinary functions and concentrated on anal behavior because of the impetus given to such investigations by Freud's conception of anal personality.[46]

The relationship between toilet training and later behavior in childhood seems somewhat better supported by research than the relationship between oral behavior and later personality characeristics or behavior. Sears *et al.* utilized "severity of toilet training" as one of several variables intended to measure frustration in socialization. While stable relationships were not found, there was some suggestion *in the case of boys only* that severity of toilet training was positively related to both aggression and general activity.[47] However, the relationships between severity of toilet training and aggression have not been consistent.[48]

The net result of studies attempting to relate the Freudian characteristics of an anal personality positively to one another suggests an important clustering of personality traits (stinginess, orderliness, obstinance, aggressiveness),[49] but evidence that this clustering of traits is related to toilet training

44. Joseph Kahl, *The American Class Structure* (New York: Rinehart, 1957); D. C. McClelland, A. Rendlishbacher and R. deCharms, "Religious and Other Sources of Parental Attitudes Toward Independence Training" in D. C. McClelland (ed.), *Studies in Motivation* (New York: Appleton-Century-Crofts, 1955), pp. 389–97; Rosen, The Achievement Syndrome . .; Rosen and D'Andrade, "The Psychological Origins of Achievement Motivation;" J. J. Veroff, J. Atkinson, Sheila Feld and G. Furin, "The Use of Thematic Apperception to Assess Motivation in a Nationwide Interview Study," *Psychological Monographs*, Vol. 74, No. 12 (1960).

45. Ann Cameron and T. Storm, "Achievement Motivation in Canadian Indian Middle- and Working-Class Children," *Psychological Reports*, Vol. 16 (1965), 459–63; G. Terrell, K. Durkin, and M. Wiesley, "Social Class and the Nature of the Incentive in Discrimination Learnings," *Journal of Abnormal and Social Psychology*, Vol. 59 (1959), 270–72.

46. B. M. Caldwell, "The Effects on Infant Care," in M. L. Hoffman and L. W. Hoffman, *Review of Child Development Research*, Vol. I (New York: Russell Sage Foundation, 1964), pp. 9–87 K. Abraham, *Selected Papers* (London: Hogarth, 1927); O. Fenischel, *The Psychoanalytic Theory of Neurosis* (New York: Norton, 1945); Sigmund Freud, "Character and Anal Eroticism," in *Collected Papers*, Vol. 2 (London: Hogarth Press, 1924), pp. 45–50.

47. Sears et al., "Some Child Rearing Antecedents of Aggression and Dependency in Young Children," *Genetic Psychology Monograph*. Vol. 47 (1953), 135–236.

48. Winterborn *op cit.*; and A. R. Holway, "Early Self-Regulation of Infants and Later Behavior in Play Interviews," *American Journal of Orthopsychiatry*, Vol. 19 (1949), 612–23, found a positive relationship. W. H. Sewell, "Infant Training and the Personality of the Child," *American Journal of Sociology*, Vol. 58 (1952), 150–59, found a negative relationship.

49. Sears, "Survey of Objective Studies of Psychoanalytic Concepts," *Bulletin of the Social Science Research Council*, No. 51, has an excellent survey of the literature of this topic. See also C. A. Barnes, "A Statistical Study of the Freudian Theory of Levels of Psycho-sexual Development," *Genetic Psychology Monographs*, Vol. 45 (1952), 105–74;

is inconclusive.[50] The best positive evidence comes again from the cross-cultural studies of Whiting and Child and here it is only suggestive.[51]

AGGRESSION

The most that can be said at this point regarding socialization and aggression is that there does appear to be a certain broad relationship between the power-assertive techniques of discipline and aggression.[52] These techniques usually include physical punishment and may include yelling, shouting, and verbal threats. This generalization is supported by Allinsmith and by Hoffman.[53] Hart warns further that the child's aggressive response tends to heighten the parental assertion of power.

In general, permissiveness in child rearing tends to increase aggressive behavior, while restrictiveness tends to prevent it in other contexts.[54] Several studies support the general permissiveness-aggression association.[55] This factor seems to interact with parental warmth and hostility producing greater aggression if the parents are hostile[56] Parental hostility and aggression also foster aggression in children. In warm parents, on the other hand, restrictiveness seems to inhibit aggression.[57]

M. L. Faber, "English and Americans: Values in the Socialization Process," *Journal of Psychology*, Vol. 36 (1953), 243–50; H. Beloff, "The Structure and Origin of the Anal Character," *Genetic Psychology Monographs*, Vol. 55 (1957), 141–72; R. Stagner, E. D. Lawson, and J. W. Moffitt, "The Krout Personal Preference Scale: A Factor-Analytic Study," *Journal of Clinical Psychology*, Vol. 11 (1955), 103–13.

50. See Zigler and Child *op. cit.*, pp. 511–16 for a fuller review and discussion.

51. John W. M. Whiting and Irving L. Child, *Child Training and Personality* (New Haven, Conn.: Yale University Press, 1953).

52. W. C. Becker, "Consequences of Different Kinds of Parental Discipline," in Hoffman and Hoffman *op. cit.*

53. B. B. Allinsmith, "Expressive Styles II: Directness with Which Anger is Expressed," in D. R. Miller and G. E. Swanson (eds.), *Inner Conflict and Defenses* (New York: Holt, Rinehart & Winston, 1960), pp. 315–36; M. L. Hoffman, "Power Assertion by the Parent and Its Impact on the Child," *Child Development*, Vol. 31 (1960), 129–43.

54. R. R. Sears, E. E. Maccoby, and E. Levin, *Patterns of Child Rearing* (Evanston, Ill.: Row, Peterson, 1957).

55. G. R. Bach, "Young Children's Play Fantasies," *Psychological Monographs*, Vol. 59 (1945), No. 2; W. W. Hartup and Y. Himeno, "Social Isolation Versus Interaction with Adults in Relation to Aggression in Preschool Children," *Journal of Abnormal and Social Psychology*, Vol. 59 (1959), 17–22; E. Hollenberg and M. Sperry, "Some Antecedents of Aggression and Effects of Frustration in Doll Play," *Personality*, Vol. 1 (1951), 32–43; H. Levin and V. Turgeon, "The Influence of Mothers' Pressures on Children's Doll-Play Aggression," *Journal of Abnormal and Social Psychology*, Vol. 55 (1957), 304–08; M. H. Pintler, "Doll-Play as a Function of Experimenter-Child Interaction and Initial Organization of Materials," *Child Development*, Vol. 16 (1945), 145–66; P. Sears, "Doll Play in Aggression in Normal Young Children: Influence of Sex, Age, Sibling Status, Father Absence," *Psychological Monographs*, Vol. 65 (1951); L. J. Yarrow, "The Effects of Antecedent Frustration on Projective Play," *Psychological Monographs*, Vol. 62 (1948).

56. Bandura and Walters, *Adolescent Aggression, op cit.*; C. Burt, *The Young Delinquent* (New York: Appleton-Century-Crofts, 1929); S. Glueck and E. T. Glueck, *Unraveling Juvenile Delinquency* (Cambridge: Harvard University Press, 1950); W. Healy and A. F. Bronner, *Delinquents and Criminals: Their Making and Unmaking* (New York: Macmillan, 1926); W. McCord, J. McCord, and I. D. Zola, *Origins of Crime* (New York: Columbia University Press, 1959).

57. E. E. Maccoby, "The Taking of Adult Roles in Middle Childhood", C. E. Meyers, "The Effect of Conflicting Authority on the Child," *Journal of Abnormal Social Psychology*, Vol. 63 (1961), 493–503; *University of Iowa Studies in Child Welfare*, Vol. 20 (1944), 31–91;

The "modeling theory" of aggression postulates that there is no need to consider either innate or acquired drives in explaining aggression. Bandura and Walters suggest that children learn aggression from watching aggressive models and will tend to continue to manifest aggressive behavior so long as it is rewarded (or at least not punished).[58] The introduction of a "disinhibitory effect" in their attempt to account for aggressive behavior via modeling has required Bandura and Walters to consider the past history of the subject. It seems likely that significant events in that past history will prove to be the child-rearing practices the child experienced. Since the authors also take into consideration models other than the parents and some characteristics of the general milieu, they conclude "the crucial psychological process in the development of aggressive anti-social patterns, in many cases, may be identification with an aggressive prototype rather than a hostile reaction to emotional deprivation."[59]

One point on which all learning theorists can agree is that *aggression continues if rewarded (positively reinforced) regardless of whether the reinforcement comes from parents, peers, or others.* This observation is particularly appropriate in a society that is tending toward greater socialization of children by peers and has been utilized by those studying gang behavior in the lower classes.

Aggressiveness has been found to vary by culture and class as different styles of life reward, punish, or ignore aggressive behavior. It seems most controlled in those societies with extended families just as all other aspects of behavior are more formally controlled. Presumably, having more people in the household makes aggression less tolerable, hence less reinforced if not punished. It is also true that in most such societies the family is the major if not sole institution giving order to the social structure and, therefore, intrafamilial aggression must be more formally controlled as there are few other secondary institutions that can provide external control.

AN ASSESSMENT OF THE DATA

It is apparent that much remains to be done if we are to perfect the science of child rearing. At present we have some understanding of small aspects of the total problem and comparatively little wisdom in regard to the application of such knowledge in the production of better children for a better world. Zigler and Child give their assessment:

> The status of knowledge about socialization is encouraging to the researcher who looks forward to the long prospect of increasing discovery and verification. But it is not very satisfactory for anyone who presses for

R. Sears, "The Relation of Early Socialization Experiences to Aggression in Middle Childhood," *Journal of Abnormal Social Psychology*, Vol. 63 (1961), 466–96.

58. Bandura and Walters, "Aggression." op. cit., and *Social Learning and Personality Development* (New York: Holt, Rinehart & Winston, 1963); Walters, "Implications of Laboratory Studies on Aggression for the Control and Regulation of Violence," *Annals American Academy of Political Science*, Vol. 364 (1966), 60–72.

59. Bandura and Walters, "Aggression," p. 370.

*immediate practical application. The practical problems which may origi-
nally motivate this research are not solved by the knowledge obtained up
to now. Anyone who has to make decisions about socialization may
reach different decisions if he is closely acquainted with this research.
He is likely, for example, to be affected in his role as parent by insights
derived from it; to hope that he will be affected for the better is, we
believe, more realistic now than it would have been a generation ago.
Yet no one is likely to be very happy about general advice based on so
tentative a body of knowledge. Whether sound manuals can ever be prepared on how parents can attain their ends in rearing children, we do
not pretend to know. But we have here a kind of knowledge which can
already—and will increasingly, we are sure, in the future—contribute to
the personal understanding which parents and others need as a basis for
wise action.*[60]

Conceptual Clarification

Even the brief summary of the research findings given above indicates the
importance of the researcher's theoretical or conceptual perspective. Perhaps
more important in affecting the research findings, however, is the fact that
families and *particularly parents are not the only socializing agents*. Nor are
parents consistent in their socializing roles. Children develop their personalities and behavior patterns in interaction with many persons, representing
quite different values and institutional perspectives. The composition of the
socializing group changes, as does the relationship with specific influential
persons. This interaction occurs in diverse settings and under different constraints. Heredity and the natural environment have an effect not readily
discernible. Not all human behavior is a function of man's capacity for symbolic reflection: Much is simply a response to stimuli. Man also behaves (at
another level of analysis) as any other physical object. If he jumps or is
pushed off a high place, he falls. Neither behavior nor personality, therefore,
is simply a function of a child's development within a family. Much less is it
a function of child-rearing practices carried out according to expert advice,
since so little of the parent-child interaction is governed by the parent *in the
role of trainee or developer*. The role of parent and the role of researcher are
not often compatible.

MODELS OF SOCIALIZATION

Some order can be provided to help us understand the complexities of
parent-child interaction by considering briefly two models of how children
are socialized in families. The first is a fusion of functional and learning
theory focusing upon the problem of how it is that parents are able (or not
able, as the case may be) to exert lasting influence upon their children. This
lasting influence Robert Winch labels "identification."[61] The identification

---

60. Zigler and Child *op cit.,* p. 555.
61. Robert F. Winch, *Identification and Its Familial Determinants* (Indianapolis:
Bobbs-Merrill, 1962).

model Winch develops attempts to relate structural-functional variables to the process of identification through the intervening concepts of "reward" and "ego ideal" or role model.

The second model, developed by C. K. Warriner, derives from the tradition of "symbolic interactionism."[62] It focuses upon the question of how roles emerge in the process of social interaction so that, on the one hand, social institutions are developed and, on the other, personality traits are discernible. These, the reader must be reminded, are but two of the many dozens of models that could be developed. They have here heuristic value insofar as they can sketch some of the parameters and suggest some of the complexities of the problem of how children become adults. Both models have one major concept in common, although they treat it somewhat differently. That concept is *social role*.

The Concept of Roles: A social role is commonly perceived by social scientists in one of two ways. Either it is thought of as a set of *expectations* of behaviors and attitudes considered appropriate to a particular social position (i.e. husband-father) or it is thought of as the *patterns of conduct* organized in response to these expectations. In either case one is studying behavior as it relates to the expectations of others in their conception of what is appropriate to a particular social position. Roles can be thought of as independent of the individuals who perform them. Likewise each individual gives his own variation to the performance of a role. No two fathers are alike, not simply as persons, but also in the manner in which they go about the business of fathering. Typically, a father in our society is expected to be the major provider for his family and the ultimate source of authority—though the patriarchal tendency is declining. How a particular father performs his role depends upon his own idiosyncratic characteristics, his family's unique interpretation of the cultural expectations regarding the role of father, and the more universally accepted definition of what is expected of an American father.

The basic difference in viewpoint between the two perspectives emerges when we ask how roles are created. In attempting to explain how persons and social systems are continuously emerging in the social process Warriner writes:

> The crux of the solution lies in the concept of role which in its primordial sense is neither personal nor societal, but is certain stabilities that emerge out of and are maintained by interaction. In their primordial form roles are situationally limited involving particular actors, a particular setting and a particular continuity of interaction, but they can be elaborated and are elaborated in two different directions to result on the one hand in personal forms and on the other in social forms.[63]

62. C. K. Warriner, *The Emergence of Society* (Homewood, Ill.: Dorsey Press, 1970).
63. *Ibid.*, p. 13.

For Warriner, therefore, role stability seems more problematic than role change. Each pair of actors generates a new version of more widely accepted roles, or they create for themselves a new role. Such perception of society relies heavily on the basic sociological insight that "situations are real in their consequences if they are defined as real by their participants" which W. I. Thomas labeled the "definition of the situation." Warriner goes a bit beyond Thomas in stressing the emergent character of roles in the process of social interaction.

On the other hand, functional theory holds that roles arise in response to system needs. That is to say, social systems are composed of institutions and roles that are maintained because they have survival value for the whole system. The functional theory of *stratification* asserts that societies must reward some roles more than others because some (for example, the President of the United States) are more important in terms of system survival than others (for example, a garbage collector).

On the level of the study of small groups, functional theory asserts that all task-oriented groups will tend to create two types of leaders: a task master and a tension reliever. Almost any person is capable of being one or the other, given the proper circumstances. It is the group's need to accomplish its task that sets requirements upon the creation of group roles. If these roles are not filled, then it is reasonable to assume that the task will not be accomplished. It is true that the precise behaviors associated with the role of task master and tension reliever might vary depending upon the individual performer, but the core requirement of the roles must be fulfilled.

The essential idea involved in the concept of role is that however derived, roles have a permanence about them. Whether conceived of as behaviors and attitudes or as expectations, they represent a socially shared definition of the situation that enables the individual actor to behave in such a manner that he neither continuously surprises other members of society nor is engaged in activities that are consistently without value to the society. From the viewpoint of the society, roles can be seen as a system of rights and obligations adhering to a particular social position. In a highly bureaucratized corporation, these rights and obligations are made formally explicit in elaborate job descriptions. In informal organizations, such as the family, roles are rarely made explicit. Appropriate behaviors for the roles of husband-father, wife-mother, and sibling-child are frequently learned by imitation and modified by the day-to-day interaction of family members.

Since socialization is largely conceived of as *the process of learning social roles and attaining competence in their performance*, there has been a strong tendency toward an "oversocialized" view of man in sociology.[64] However, neither individual behavior nor personality traits can be explained solely in terms of the acquisition of roles.

From my perspective, the concept of role is more useful in attempting to explain the recurrent patterns in social interaction than it is in attempting

---

64. See especially the criticism by D. K. Wrong, "The Oversocialized View of Man in Modern Sociology," *American Sociological Review*, Vol. 26 (1961), 183–93.

to conceptualize the process of child development. The individual is always in dynamic interaction with others in a society and frequently at variance with social expectations. Social role is, furthermore, a product of the process of socialization. The process of personality development is thus more complex than the process of socialization.

Winch's Model of Social Identification: How do parents exert lasting influence upon their children? This was the central question that Robert F. Winch sought to answer by his conceptualization of the process of *identification*. In broadening the concept identification to mean the more or less lasting influence of one individual (who may be called the ego ideal or *M*) upon another (who may be called the identifier, *I*) Winch concedes that we must distinguish between the *form* and the *content* of that influence. The latter is virtually limitless and, therefore, the investigator must be careful to specify quite precisely what aspect of the influence of parents upon children he is attempting to explain (e.g. effect of feeding upon demand, maternal warmth). The *form* of the influence can be specified along four major dimensions.[65] For our purposes the major utility in Winch's conceptualization of the process of identification is the schema by which he relates structural-functional variables that are quite impersonal to the very personal process of personality development as that is reflected in learned behaviors. Winch's model is presented schematically in Figure 11-1.

Social structure is the network of social positions and their constituent roles which specifies the number and nature of social positions with whose occupants ego must interact. In the case of the nuclear family if we consider *I* to be a child, then there must be at least two other persons with whom he must interact, his mother and father. There may be one or more siblings as well.

Social function refers to the task-oriented activity of a group or of one or more of its members which normally produces some outcome or resource. From the perspective of society, the function of the family is the replacement of members through reproduction and socialization. From the point of view of the child, the primary parental functions are nurturance and control. All members of the family derive benefits from the status-placement and emotional gratification functions of the family.

Social functions are important in this scheme because they produce resources, either material or nonmaterial. For the parent the familial function

65. The four formal distinctions are as follows: (1) Product or process: Product refers to that behavior of the identifier (*I*) which is shown or assumed to be in some relationship to the behavior of the model (*M*)—behavior here including aspirations and fantasies. Process is the sequence of events which results in the product. (2) Type of Relationship: The behavior of *I* may be interpreted as similar to, reciprocal to, or opposite from that of the *M*. (3) Level of expression: *I* may express the behavior which is seen as related to the behavior of the *M* at a conscious, covert but conscious, or unconscious level. (4) Kind: "Positional" identification refers to behavior acquired by the *I* which is interpreted as corresponding to one or more of the roles involved in some task-oriented social position through which *I* is related to *M*. "Personal" identification refers to behavior acquired by *I* which is interpreted as reflecting primarily an affective and non-task-oriented relationship with *M* (See Winch *op. cit.*, pp. 146–47).

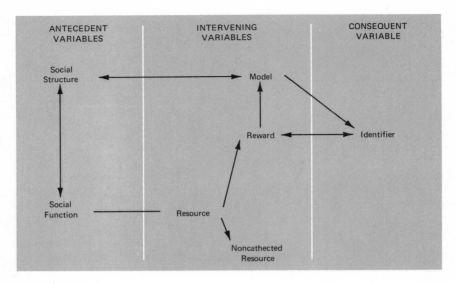

FIGURE 11–1
*Identification as an outcome of structure and function. After Robert F.
Winch*, Identification and Its Familial determinants (*Bobbs-Merrill,
1962), p. 147.*

of replacement can provide a sense of continuity with past and future generations—a kind of immortality with which to ward off the anxieties of knowing that there was a time when one was not and that there will be a time
when one will not be. In societies where the family is virtually synonymous
with social structure (in Winch's terminology, where the family is one of
maximum functionality) it fulfills more fully than it does in our society additional functions which can be labeled economic, political, and religious.
These functions also provide resources which family members, particularly
the parents, can utilize as rewards in order to influence other family members
—particularly their children.[66]

The more functional a family is—that is to say, the more the basic societal functions are fulfilled by the family rather than by secondary institutions outside the family—the more resources the family has to draw upon as
rewards with which to influence the behavior of its members and ensure
their fidelity. So also, the more functional a family is in a given society, the
more roles it is likely to acquire. Thus in a family of maximal functionality a
son may have, in addition to his filial role relationship to his father, a worker-
manager relationship, a parishioner-priest relationship, and a follower-chief
relationship. In these families identification is positional as well as personal.

66. See Winch *op. cit.*, pp. 148 ff.

With increasing loss of function, identification becomes increasingly personal and, by inference, increasingly more difficult to effect.

As we suggested in Chapter 6, socioeconomic class determines to a considerable extent the quantity and quality of the resources available to parents (*M*s) which can be utilized as rewards. Black families in the ghetto, therefore, can be expected to have less control over their children because they have fewer material and symbolic resources to utilize as rewards in the process of identification. However, since a major virtue of a *symbolic reward* is that it is not bound by the limitations of scarcity, an increase in pride in blackness should provide ghetto parents—to the extent that they can accept their blackness as beautiful—with a symbolic resource which they can utilize as a reward to increase the effectiveness of identification and their control over their children. The effectiveness of the Black Muslims in the strengthening of a small number of ghetto families would seem to support this general proposition.

Our second model is derived in the tradition of symbolic interactionism by C. K. Warriner.

Warriner's Model of Social Interaction: Warriner conceives of the social process in a somewhat different fashion. He is not concerned with relating structural-functional variables directly to the process of socialization. His focus is upon *human interaction* and the manner in which symboling in such a context shapes persons, on the one hand, and social institutions, on the other. The levels of an individual's interaction with his external environment can be seen in Figure 11–2.
Warriner writes:

> The major point of the diagram is that stimulus, percept, sign, and symbol are successive productions of the "processing" which the actor performs on the raw physical contact materials. At each stage the character of the product becomes less a function of the objective world as it immediately is and more a function of the subjective world of the actor as it immediately is.[67]

We need not go into the elaborate explanation of all of these levels of interaction. The reader is encouraged to read Warriner for a very comprehensive treatment of these complex matters. In any event, man is in some sense "behaving" on all these levels. It is at the symbolic level, however, that his uniqueness as man is most clearly expressed. It is at this level that we will examine the process of human interaction. The central question that is asked in regard to this process is "How is it that people are able to communicate with each other?"

This process of communication is more than simply transmitting messages from sender to receiver, as naïve models of socialization assume. Rather "these transactions between human beings often consist of the joint creation

67. Warriner *op. cit.*, p. 64.

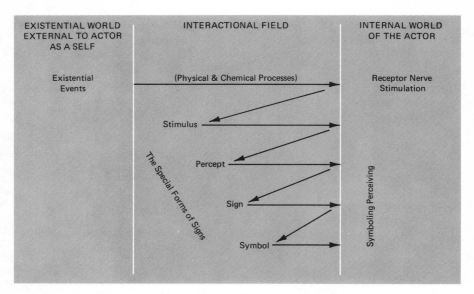

FIGURE 11–2
Phases in the process of symboling. After C. K. Warriner, The Emergence
of Society *(Dorsey Press, 1970), p. 65.*

of a meaning, rather than the simple transmission of what one or the other
or both had 'in their minds' at the start of their interaction."[68] Thus human
interaction always has the potential for the creation of symbols and symbol
systems. As symbols change, meanings change, roles change, persons change.

To the extent that the *meanings* of his experience determine what a person is, man is continuously emergent, for meanings are continually reworked
in experience and in the reflective recall of experience. Their stability and
continuity from time to time lie in their continual reaffirmation in action and
experience *rather than in any internalization as a fixture or substance or network in the individual. The individual has the continual potentiality for being
different than he was, for using new meanings in any bit of interaction. Sur-
prise should be occasioned not by change in the person, but rather by the
lack of change, by continuity.*[69]

People influence one another through communication, which can be
conceptualized as a three-part process. The first aspect Warriner designates
as the act of *reference*. When a person is faced by a sign (a gesture, a touch,
etc.) it evokes whatever past experience the actor has had with that sign. For
a child who has experienced a loving relationship and associates that relation-

68.   *Ibid*, p. 95.
69.   *Ibid.*, p. 97.

ship with a hand squeeze, a hand squeeze becomes a sign of love. The past experience is the meaning that the sign has for the person, and its recall is the act of reference.

The second aspect of communication is the act of *inference*: the actor asks himself what the sign means to the person who is giving it. Mead called this act of inference the "taking of the role of the other." Cooley designated it "human nature," as he felt that without the capacity to put oneself in another's place it would be impossible to empathize and thus impossible to become human. And yet our experience tells us that we are often surprisingly unable to perform this act of inference. This incapacitation is perhaps learned as a mechanism of defense.

Finally, the process of communication is completed in the act of *confirmation*—the establishment of the fact that one's inference is correct:

> The act of confirmation, from the perspective of either one of the actors, has two phases. I confirm my inference by observing whether the other does indeed perform the action consequences of the meaning inferred. Secondly I confirm his inference by making my meanings objective in my conduct.[70]

Without this act of confirmation the actors are essentially independent and autonomous and involved in the process of communication only at its minimal level of message transmittal.

Communication, however, is problematic. We are deceived in thinking our inferences are correct. In the final analysis, we cannot experience the other as we experience ourselves. Furthermore, interaction situations are complex events with many signs being given off. Each situation is also an episode whose meaning may be quite different to different actors—"the patient's crisis is the doctor's routine." Finally these complex sign events are continuously changing; later behavior can change the meaning of earlier events.

We are encouraged to believe that our inferences have been confirmed by the utilitarian observation that "things go right." So long as our interaction is not detrimental, produces few crises, and perhaps even "pays off" in immediately gratifying events or rewards, we assume we are right in our inference. We build up a certain confidence in people, but we can never be sure that we are not being deceived. Then, too, in social interaction we may be willing to accept less than full confirmation.

The family is a particularly significant socializing agent for the child in this frame of reference, because family members over a long period of time have had many opportunities to confirm their inefrences of the others' meanings over a wide range of situations. Thus their area of common understanding is relatively large compared to the area that any one member is likely to share with persons outside the family. This is particularly true of the young child for whom family members make up the very large part of his interaction world. The comfortable knowledge that one can be oneself at home is

70. *Ibid.*, p. 110.

really another way of saying that family members share a larger area of meaningful experience than do nonfamily actors. They are thus able to use what Mead has called significant symbols—those known to be shared in meaning —more frequently. Parents, particularly for the young child, are significant others in part as a function of this past history of having shared a symbolic universe. They, therefore, have a greater chance of influencing the child's development than do those outside the family. But of course this is truer for younger children than for older (the problems of child rearing in our time are all too apparent with older children), is more likely to occur in nonindustrial societies than in industrial ones, and is complicated by many factors pertinent to the personalities of the parents (for example, whether they are warm or hostile in their interaction). Finally, the child is also an actor and intrudes his definitions of the situation as well as accepts those of his parents and peers. He thus shapes his own personality as well as experiences its shaping. As a personality, therefore, each actor is unique.

Personality, as a system of social phenomena distinguished from society and culture, consists of a set of individual meanings. This set of meanings has its origin in the experiences of the actor with his world, which includes his own organism as well as the external world. In some cases these meanings are uniquely his own, and in other cases they have their origin in the collective meanings of the particular system of social relationships in which he participates. What distinguishes these individual meanings is their connection with and persistence in the historical continuity which is the particular individual.[71]

Summary

The possibility of changing the family by changing the behavior or personality of a new generation of children so that they will expect to live in a different kind of family and feel comfortable in it seems remote at present if we rely solely upon experimental evidence. The possibilities for significantly changing children's personalities seems particularly great if we adopt the symbolic interactionist's model of how we influence one another. However, the capacity to control the situation sufficiently so that the product—a changed personality—will conform with reasonable accuracy to a predetermined design seems beyond us. If change is approached from the perspective of behaviorism, startling modifications can be produced in institutional settings where maximum control over behavior is possible, but these dramatic changes, for the most part, seem to depend upon the continuance of such maximum control. Outside institutional settings, mental patients whose behavior has thus been modified tend to revert to their old symptoms. The long-range effect of the continuous modification of children's behavior by operant conditioning techniques has not, to my knowledge, been studied. Learning skills seem to become self-reinforcing and persist after the formal reward system has been

71. *Ibid.*, p. 154–55.

discontinued. Behaviorists are not generally concerned with the effect of such alteration of behavior upon personality.

We Americans are coming to depend more and more upon the advice of scientific experts as to how to raise children. Because of the contradictory information provided by the research findings and the divergent conceptions of what constitutes a desirable child, the advice of the experts has tended to change rather dramatically over relatively short periods of time. Actual child-rearing practices also appear to change with increasing rapidity as the needs of our society impose different demands upon parents and children. Bronfenbrenner feels that there is a consistency between the conception of an ideal personality at any given time in our history and the advice given to parents on how to produce such personalities. As this advice is dependent more and more upon experts, less upon tradition and less directly upon society's needs, the advice given to parents should become even more variable. Parental anxiety over child rearing seems likely to increase, therefore.

Our models suggest something of the complexity of the problem of rearing children by means of scientific advice with a rational conception of an ideal person as a goal. Families are not the only socializing agents; behavior and personality are affected by the environment at a number of levels, most of which fall outside of the level of symbolic interaction, on which man gives evidence of his most human characteristics (and communicates his expertise); persons are perhaps more of a historical continuity than a logical consistency or a meaningfully integrated whole; and, finally, each interaction situation presents the potential for persons to create a totally new definition of the situation and exhibit a totally new aspect of themselves.

When roles are derived from system needs, socialization is primarily the process of role acquisition, and personalities are primarily the culmination of many roles; what is problematic is change. On the other hand, when personality development is not synonymous with socialization, roles are derived, must constantly be maintained in social interaction, and each interaction situation presents the possibility for the emergence of a new role; what is problematic here is continuity.

From the perspective of social engineering where we presently seem to have the greatest control over human behavior, we seem to lack knowledge about the long-range consequences of such control. Where we are concerned with such long-range problems as personality development, we seem to lack sufficient control over the immediate situations to ensure that what we do to children now will bring about the desired adult personality later.

Nevertheless, societies have conducted some rather dramatic experiments in rearing children after a rational plan, and they have not been entirely without success. These experimental communities will be considered in the fifth section.

In this section I look at several social issues that affect our styles of family life and that suggest the need for change: the sexual revolution, Women's Lib., the generation gap, the population explosion, and the typical patterns of earning a living in America.

The sexual revolution, in part the result of an improved technology of contraception, has not only effectively separated conception from coitus, but also redefined the character of our sexual relations. The old arguments against coitus outside marriage are not so convincing when the probability of an unwanted pregnancy is greatly reduced. Sexual relations can increasingly become occasions for effective communication and intimacy between the unmarried as well as the married.

Women are raising questions about the traditional conceptions of masculinity and femininity as well as protesting the injustices in current employment practices. For men and women to have equal opportunities in employment, it is necessary that women be freed from domestic responsibilities either through a redefinition of the husband and wife roles, or by means of help from organizations outside the family such as day care centers.

Young people are calling attention to the inadequacies of the typical American family in meeting the emotional needs of its members, and seeking new forms of community in experimental communes that redefine the character of family relations.

If we are to achieve a reasonable rate of growth, many scholars point out, it will be necessary to go beyond the elimination of unwanted pregnancies through the Planned Parenthood approach. We must reduce the number of *wanted* children and this is quite another matter. For example, we must provide new forms of social recognition for women who have sought traditional fulfillment in child rearing. It might be necessary to remove some of the stigma attached to sexual behavior that cannot possibly result in the generation of children as well.

More than one observer of the American scene has noted that our means of earning a living has given our style of life a noticeable quality of drivenness. The "rat race" affects our capacity to keep in touch with other members of our family not only by making undue demands upon our time, but also by fostering respect for values that are basically anti-familial. In the past we have expected the family to change to meet the needs of industry; in the future our quest for deeper community in families may well force changes upon industries and the demands of the job.

These social issues tend to reinforce one another in their emphasis upon the need to improve the *quality* of intimate interpersonal relationships. They suggest that alternative family structures might serve our needs better than our current forms. A number of us are already living in such experimental communities; but whether or not a significant number of us do so, the issues discussed in this section will affect all our family life styles. The only real question is how much *control* we are going to be able to exert over that change. I will look at the matter of intentional change in more detail in the next section.

THE CRY
FOR
CHANGE

12. The Sexual Revolution

A sex ethos for the twentieth century has to take the resexualiza-
tion of women into account. It has to be one which reconciles the
demands made on men by their work and the demands made on
them by women. It has to be one also which reconciles the dif-
ferences between the sexes in their respective life calendars. It
has to be one, finally, which takes into account the separation
of heterosexual relations and reproduction. If the achievement of
nonprocreative sexuality has solved some issues, it has raised
many more. Nor can we anticipate what they will be. For as yet
we really do not know what the sexual renaissance implies for the
future of relations between the sexes.

JESSIE BERNARD

In the secret coming together of two human bodies, all society is
the third presence.

JEAN ROSTAND

Like the term "generation gap," "sexual revolution" is borrowed from the mass media. While the term is both sensational and diffuse, it points, nevertheless, to a transformation that is real. Nationwide surveys, for example, document the fact that attitudes toward sex constitute a major element in the conflict between generations. ". . . Nearly half of all American youth—and two out of three of the college students—say having sexual relations before marriage is not a moral issue. Nearly nine out of ten parents say it is morally wrong."[1] The "revolution" points to other changes in our style of life—the greater visibility of magazines dealing with sex, confession, and nudity, the freer interpretation of film censorship, the limited but sensational newspaper and television coverage of events occurring in the communes of the "youth culture," and the ease with which sex is frankly discussed in public.[2] "Swingers" have been able to advocate their life style on national television, psychoanalysts have been lured into the field to study the growing trend in orgiastic group sex, and Herder and Herder, a leading publisher of Roman Catholic literature, has released a pictorial encyclopedia of sexual behavior—*The Sex Book*—which deals straightforwardly with contraceptive techniques and nonprocreative sex.[3]

What is not clear, however, is who is affected by such a sexual revolution and how? Is the revolution a revolution in attitudes? In beliefs? In values? In behavior? Does it signify social or moral decay? For some who still view certain forms of sexual expression as unnatural, it undoubtedly does. For others it marks a great emancipation. I will argue that the revolution is primarily a revolution in attitudes and values, not one of behavior, at least with regard to premarital sex. We are experiencing a redefinition of the norms governing sexual behavior. As John F. Cuber remarks, "there is a profound difference between someone who breaks the rules and someone who does not accept the rules. One is a transgressor; the other is a revolutionary."[4] The revolutionaries are characteristically youth from middle-class families, but not exclusively so. The revolution goes far beyond the norms regulating coition, to rejection of the general taboo against sex and the positive affirmation of the goodness of nonprocreative sex. This has far-reaching implications for our way of life.

I will begin the discussion of the revolution with a review of what we know about sexual development and psychosexual differentiation, that is, how we develop bodily characteristics that are masculine or feminine and how we come to think of ourselves as one or the other. The fact that postnatal events

1. CBS News, *Generations Apart*, Transcript of a Television Series, Broadcast on May 20, 1969, p. 8.
2. Stanton Wheeler, "Sex Offenses: A Sociological Critique," in John H. Gagnon and William Simon (eds.), *Sexual Deviance* (New York: Harper and Row, 1967), p. 86. A most interesting commentary on the influence of pornography is found in Rustum and Della Roy, *Honest Sex* (New York: New American Library, 1968), Chap. 2. See also the controversial, *The Report of the Commission on Obscenity and Pornography* (New York: Bantam Books, 1970) which argues for the elimination of laws banning pornography in favor of sex education, citizen action, and industry self-regulation.
3. J. N. Galena, *Sex in Groups: The First Complete Uncensored Report on Group Sex in Middle-Class America* (New York: Tower Publications, 1971); Martin Goldstein, Erwin J. Haeberle, and Will McBride (eds·), *The Sex Book: A Modern Pictorial Encyclopedia* (New York: Herder and Herder, 1971).
4. John Cuber, "How New Ideas About Sex are Changing Our Lives," *Redbook Magazine* (March 1971) copyright © 1971 by The McCall Publishing Company, reprinted by permission.

have a profound effect upon how we view ourselves as sexual beings means, on the one hand, that quite radical departures from our customary way of defining sexuality are possible and, on the other, that society has a great stake in the regulation of sexual behavior through the definition of sex and gender role.

Masculinity and Femininity

THE BIOLOGICAL BASE

The process that determines a person's sexual identity—whether he thinks of himself as a male or a female—is a complex one indeed. It is neither genetically determined nor divinely ordained. It is related to, but not determined by, embryonic development, hormonal balance, and postnatal experience.

The human embryo is sexually undifferentiated through the second or third month of pregnancy. Afterwards, those with masculine genetic inheritance develop masculine morphology, while the feminine morphological components atrophy. The reverse occurs for those embryos with a feminine inheritance. Experiments with animals indicate that this process may be reversed by the application of the appropriate hormone. The treatment of certain abnormalities associated with hormonal imbalance suggest that this is true for the human species as well. Whatever might be the case with prenatal development, however, it is clear that postnatal events can override prenatal sexual development.

The neonate remains psychosexually undifferentiated until about eighteen months. During these first months of a child's life, sex reassignment can occur without complications in the case of hermaphroditic children (children who have been born with a mixture of sexual morphology) provided that (1) the parents are in agreement as to the gender of their child and raise him accordingly, (2) corrective surgery be performed to bring genital morphology in line with assigned sex, and (3) pubertal secondary sexual development be timed and regulated hormonally to conform with assigned sex.[5]

Even though these conditions are not met, many hermaphrodites are able to achieve a unitary gender role and psychosocial identity. This may occur in spite of gross contradictions in the bodily manifestations of sexuality. Thus women with a penis-sized clitoris, an exaggerated masculine physique, and a deep voice are able to develop and maintain a feminine gender role and psychosexual identity. Evidence from the study of hermaphrodites indicates that it is possible for psychosexual differentiation to occur in opposition to any or all of the following:

1. genetic sex—sex defined by chromosome characteristics
2. hormonal sex—a hormonal balance that is predominantly androgenic or estrogenic

5. John Money, "Psychosexual Differentiations," in John Money (ed.), *Sex Research: New Developments* (New York: Holt, Rinehart & Winston, 1965), p. 11.

3. gonadal sex: whether an individual has ovaries, testicles, or both
4. the form of structure of the internal reproductive organs
5. the form or structure of the external genitals[6]

Human sexual behavior, it follows, is remarkably free from hormonal control. The common illustration of this point is the greater freedom experienced by the human female. In contrast to the lower animals she is not receptive to the male's sexual advances only during oestrus. Indeed, as if in defiance of hormonal control, she is often most receptive immediately before and after her menses—a time when she is ordinarily sterile. This elementary fact would also seem to undermine the argument that sex is "naturally" for reproduction only. Human sexual behavior is so free of hormonal control that humans who have undergone operations to remove the glands producing the prime sex hormones ordinarily remain able to respond sexually and to engage in coitus. Lower animals, on the other hand, who undergo similar operations cease to manifest sexual behavior.

Masters and Johnson provide further evidence of the cultural factors affecting human sexual behavior. They discovered that, in the case of females, there was no inevitable relationship between the physiological response in orgasm and the perception of pleasure. All women responded physiologically to sexual stimulation, but not all perceived the response as the pleasurable release of tension in climax:

> The ability to achieve orgasm in response to effective sexual stimulation was the only constant factor demonstrated by all active female participants. This observation might be considered to support the concept that sexual response to orgasm is the physiologic prerogative of most women, but its achievement in our culture may be more dependent upon psychosocial acceptance of sexuality than overtly aggressive behavior.[7]

In regard to the social factors associated with the male's orgasmic experience, they report:

> For the male, these pressures have centered about the physiologic processes of penile erection and not ejaculation. Thus, cultural demand has played a strange trick on the two sexes. Fears of performance in the female have been directed toward orgasmic attainment, while in the male the fears of performance have been related toward the attainment and maintenance of penile erection, and orgasmic facility always has been presumed.[8]

Masters and Johnson thus demonstrate that sexual performance is not simply a response to hormonal urging but is culturally conditioned.

6. *Loc. cit.*
7. William H. Masters and Virginia E. Johnson, *Human Sexual Response* (Boston: Little, Brown, 1966), p. 139.
8. *Ibid.*, p. 218.

Money has demonstrated how gender can be assigned in spite of many biological constraints—in some instances. Given our present knowledge it not only is possible to correct cases of malassignment, but also—if one holds aside ethical considerations—to alter dramatically the sexual characteristics of any child (and at least some adults) using a combination of hormones, surgical operations, and appropriate learning experiences. It becomes obvious, therefore, that a major mechanism for the control of sexual behavior is the cultural definition of masculinity and femininity. The underlying assumption that there are in fact only two sexes is an essential part of our definition. The social pressures forcing individuals to define themselves as either male or female and to behave accordingly are great. Yet, despite these pressures, there clearly is no *simple* dichotomy of sexual behavior or gender role.

HOMOSEXUALITY

Homosexuals do not fit into the two-category classification, and they raise further questions regarding human sexual differentiation by calling attention to situational influences. Kinsey developed a seven-point scale of sexual behavior. On this scale "0" represents no homosexual desire or behavior, and "6" no heterosexual desire or behavior. Most human beings fall into neither of these categories, but rather can be rated from 1 to 5, depending upon their mixture of heterosexual and homosexual attraction and behavior.[9] Furthermore, many persons are able to compartmentalize their homosexual experiences so that they apparently live a "normal" heterosexual life with their wives and children and yet enjoy homosexual sex in "tea rooms" (public restrooms).[10]

Evelyn Hooker contends that it is impossible to describe homosexual behavior adequately using conceptual frameworks derived from the two-sexed heterosexual world, where males are "active" and females "passive." She concludes:

> . . . there is no apparent correspondence between a conscious sense of gender identity and a preferred or predominant role in sexual activity. Except for a small minority, the sexual pattern cannot be categorized in terms of a predominant role, and the consciousness of masculinity or femininity appears to bear no clear relation to particular sexual patterns. Comparisons of homosexual subcultures indicate that the degree to which sex role and gender roles are clearly differentiated varies greatly with the subculture. Cultural variables, as well as personality variables, appear to

9. Alfred C. Kinsey et al., *Sexual Behavior in the Human Female* (New York: Pocket Book, 1967), p. 472. Kinsey cautions "It is impossible to determine the number of persons who are 'homosexual' or 'heterosexual.' It is only possible to determine how many persons belong, at any particular time, to each of the classifications on a heterosexual-homosexual scale." He then goes on to note that the cumulative homosexual response among his male population reached 50 percent and among his female sample, 38 percent. Kinsey, of course, is not simply concerned with attraction but with its overt expression in behavioral response.

10. A detailed study of one aspect of this compartmentalization is found in Laud Humphreys, *Tearoom Trade: Impersonal Sex in Public Places* (Chicago: Aldine, 1970).

be important in defining prescribed or acceptable masculinity or femininity and/or sex roles. The relations between individual pairs appear to be additional determinants of the variations in sexual patterns and gender identity.[11]

Whether one accepts Hooker's reservations or prefers to distinguish preference in sex and gender role among homosexuals, the study of homosexual behavior causes us to talk about sexuality as a continuum, with a "neutral" ground between the two gender poles. It challenges the assumption of the "naturalness" of two sexes. When we come to understand the situation of the true invert—the homosexual with no heterosexual attraction and no hope at present of making a heterosexual adjustment—we may even come to question the assumption that there *ought* to be but two sexes. Most societies of the world acknowledge a socially acceptable "third" sex—the *berdache*, ordinarily a man who prefers to dress as a woman although he may not engage in homosexual behavior.

Gavin Arthur in his book, *Circle of Sex*, contends that many people deny their true sexual feelings because of the severe restrictions placed upon sex-role deviation by society.[12] He arbitrarily describes twelve categories of sexuality based on the interrelationships between body sex (primarily whether one has a penis or a clitoris) and sexual attraction. He believes that these categories would be almost evenly filled if all persons felt free to express their true feelings in overt behavior. Arthur contends that there are at least twelve modes of psychosexual differentiation, and these are illustrated in Figure 12–1.

PROBLEMS IN THE CULTURAL DEFINITION OF SEX ROLE

Homosexuality, transsexuality, transvestism, and the various forms of paraphilia represent types of behavior that can be thought of as deviations from the cultural definitions of sex roles, whatever their cause.[13] But, since sex role is not immutably fixed by nature, it remains for societies to define in their own peculiar way what is masculine and what is feminine and, thereby, what is deviant and what is not. It is obvious from the cross-cultural data that not only is there great variation in these definitions from one culture to another, but also that there are many problems involved in such definition. Masculinity and femininity within a particular society is assessed along many dimensions. Thus Margaret Mead writes:

11. Evelyn Hooker, "An Empirical Study of Some Relations Between Sexual Patterns and Gender Identity in Male Homosexuals," in John Money (ed.) *op. cit.*, p. 50.

12. Gavin Arthur, *The Circle of Sex* (New York: University Books, 1966).

13. "Transsexuals are persons whose gender identity and anatomy are incongruous. They are males who wish to be females or females who wish to be males. It is estimated that there are about 2,000 transsexuals who have been changed—about four men changed to a woman for every woman changed to a man. See Richard Green and John Money (eds.), *Transsexualism and Sex Reassignment* (Baltimore: Johns Hopkins Press, 1969). "Transvestites" in contrast to transsexuals do not wish to change gender; they simply wish to dress as their opposite gender. "Paraphilia" is a comprehensive label for all statistically "abnormal" sexual interests. It does not imply pathology. See Paul H. Gebhard, "Human Sexual Behavior: A Summary Statement," in Donald S. Marshall and Robert C. Suggs (eds.), *Human Sexual Behavior: The Range and Diversity of Human Sexual Experience Throughout the World as Seen in Six Representative Cultures* (New York: Basic Books, 1971), p. 215.

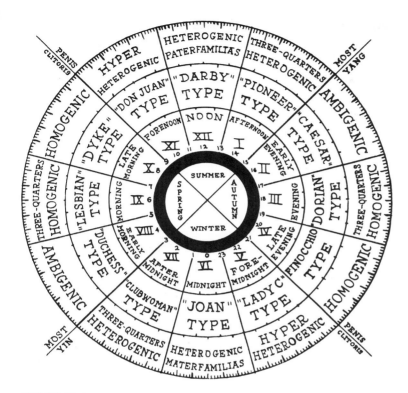

FIGURE 12–1
A typology of sexual attraction. From Gavin Arthur, The Circle of Sex
(Universal Books, 1966).

> *Our growing children are faced with another problem: How male, how
> female, am I? He hears men branded as feminine, women condemned
> as masculine, others extolled as real men and as true women. He hears
> types of responsiveness, fastidiousness, sensitivity, guts, stoicism and en-
> durance voted as belonging to one sex rather than the other. In his world
> he sees not a single model but many as he measures himself against
> them; so that he will judge himself, and feel proud and secure, worried
> and inferior and uncertain, or despairing and ready to give up the task
> altogether.*[14]

Just as human sexual development does not produce two clearly differentiated types in all cases, so also the process of socialization does not produce a simple dichotomy. Our social definition of maleness, for example,
might rate an individual high on the scale because he is a steel worker and
bravely walks the high steel, and it may rate that same individual low on an-

---

14. Margaret Mead, *Male and Female* (New York: Mentor Books, 1955), pp. 102–03.

other dimension of maleness because he is also a sensitive poetic person. Such an individual must constantly hold in tension contradictory social assertions about his sex role.

We might expect that some cultures are more consistent in the assignment of sex roles than others. The diversity actually observed in the anatomical expression of sexuality thus might be exaggerated in those societies that uncertainly assign sex role and be reduced in those that quietly build confidence by consistent sex-role assignment. Generally speaking, just as there is greater experimentation in family structure and greater expression of paraphilias, so also there is more uncertainty about sex role in advanced industrial societies where there are many dimensions of social experience along which one may be rated as feminine or masculine and where, by virtue of anonymity, greater latitude is possible in the expression of sexual behavior. The city has the potential for the development and the acceptance of a rich array of life styles.

But to say that human sexual behavior is to a very large extent learned behavior is not to say that it can be readily changed or unlearned at will. Just as the sex of the embryo cannot be changed beyond a certain point in its development, so also the definition of sex role becomes increasingly difficult to change beyond a point in a child's life. That which is not biologically determined is, nevertheless, so "fixed" socially that it is very difficult to alter the prevailing sexual mores of a people or the sex type of an individual. Thus social fixation gives the appearance at first of biological determinism. Witness the fact that in the age of the sexual revolution, homosexuality, even between consenting adults in the privacy of their own homes, is still a crime in many states, as is oral-genital contact between married persons in their own bedrooms. The affront that unisex style in dress and deportment presents to many older persons in our own society is a less dramatic but much more common example. In large measure this is so because the expression of the sexual is in fact seen to be infusing all other aspects of our way of life, and, therefore, *alteration* in the sexual suggests alteration in our life style.

If sex is not simply for procreation and is considered equally desirable as recreation, it is much more difficult to limit its expression to marriage. It is more difficult to argue that marriage is a sacrament. Marriage becomes more readily a personal contract that can be modified in terms of newly discovered preferences in the continuing pursuit of happiness. But marriage is not merely a social means of blessing coitus; it is also the mechanism for legitimizing children, the primary method of placing persons in the social structure, the legal contract involving property rights, the vehicle for the transmission of tradition, and the means for continuing the system of rights and obligations associated with kindred. Thus, if we conceive of sex in terms of Arthur's twelve types rather than in terms of two, we must also alter not only our conception of sex role but also become more inclined to permit the expression of behaviors we now deem "deviant" or "perverted." This would argue for the abolishment of a particular kind of father and mother as an ideal; marriage would not necessarily have the procreation of children as a major objective, and so on.

The sexual revolution has this potential. For most of us it has not gone far enough to cause us radically to question the structure of our institutions and our cultural definitions of sexual reality, but for some it has. Many young people express a great sense of freedom from guilt resulting from any consenting behavior, but others find such redefinition of morality repugnant: "animals mate, humans wait" their placards proclaim. It may be that it is no longer possible to talk about a dominant code of sexual behavior, but most of us are not yet ready to challenge the institution of marriage; nor are we willing—as a people—to approve "anything that turns you on, baby." As individuals many of us have begun to question the traditional sexual ethic; but as a society, we have yet to endorse the implications of the sexual revolution.

Some Dimensions of the Sexual Revolution

THE SYSTEMATIC STUDY OF AMERICAN SEXUAL BEHAVIOR

It is a lamentable fact that the understanding of the sexual revolution has not been furthered by a wealth of research on human sexuality. Against the deluge of marriage manuals, manuals for sex education, and general books of advice on sexual matters, the paucity of reliable and systematic studies of human sexuality is apparent.[15] Two decades have passed since the Kinsey studies *Sexual Behavior in the Human Female* and *in the Human Male*. The validity of the findings in these reports have been hotly contested, and the obvious limitations of the data taken from a nonrepresentative sample of less than 6,000 women and not quite 5,000 men have been pointed out. Nevertheless, they remain the best body of scientific data on the subject of American sexual behavior that has been generated. The studies by Masters and Johnson—*Human Sexual Response* and *Human Sexual Inadequacy*—have greatly improved our understanding of the physiology of sex and have suggested some very interesting hypotheses for sociologists and psychologists.[16] Nevertheless, their data are drawn from a small sample which makes it difficult to assess the sociological significance of their work.

The scientific studies of human sexuality fall into three categories: (1) anthropological, (2) clinical, and (3) survey research. These approaches each have their limitations and are quite difficult to integrate because they have been conducted in the main by scientists with very different interests. The populations studied are often diverse, and few studies claim any statistical representativeness. Nevertheless, taken as a whole, they do point to one major conclusion in regard to the sexual revolution: The revolution in premarital coital behavior occurred simultaneously with the liberation of women in the 1920s. The flappers, not the hippies, discovered the pleasures of premarital

---

15. Winston Erhman, "Marital and Nonmarital Sexual Behavior," in Harold T. Christensen (ed.), *Handbook of Marriage and the Family* (Chicago: Rand McNally, 1964), p. 597.

16. William H. Masters and Virginia E. Johnson *op. cit.* The authors' more recent book *Human Sexual Inadequacy* (Boston: Little, Brown, 1970) is much more provocative as far as its social psychology implications are concerned.

sex. The behavior of men has changed little since studies have been made; the behavior of women has changed little since the 1920s. The revolution is basically a revolution in attitudes and values. It is a rejection, not merely a violation, of Victorian norms.

> *Individual freedom of choice in many aspects of life, including sexual behavior and the choice of a spouse increased while the traditional dictates of family, community, and church declined. Women became less dependent, economically speaking, upon men and they achieved greater equality with men than had ever existed before in the history of the West. The opportunity for non-marital sexual expression contrary to the traditional mores was made possible by the anonymity of the city and the use of the automobile and by increasing scientific and folk knowledge of ways of avoiding the embarrassment and stigma of an out-of-wedlock pregnancy through the techniques of conception control and the social invention of petting. New theories about the nature of man, either implicit in the evolving human scene or explicit in intellectual formulations —political speculations on the rights of men and women, psychoanalytical and behavioristic concepts of human personality, social action theories of social interrelations, existential philosophies on the nature of being, and the resurgence of romantic love—encouraged sexual expression and sexual experimentation.·*
>
> *The advocates of free love of the 1920s epitomized and set in bold relief the characteristics of the sexual revolution at its extreme. Yet the pervasive feelings of guilt about sex so characteristic of the Christian world throughout its history continued to persist, although guilt was less potent than in some historic periods, including the one just past.*[17]

Sex and Marriage

The gap between the studies of American sexual behavior and the implications of the sexual revolution is perhaps best illustrated by the fact that many researchers still persist in categorizing forms of sexual behavior in terms of their relation to marriage, assuming the traditional norm that coitus should be confined to marriage. Thus social research is conducted on marital sex, extra-marital sex, and premarital sex, but rarely on postmarital sex or non-marital sex—much less on sex for its own sake. Cuber and Harroff's *Sex and the Significant Americans* is one of the few studies that refused to be bound by these traditional categories, studying instead "man-woman relationships" in the upper-middle class.[18]

Our society seems to be more able to separate sex from marriage than do many researchers. In some communes, a family is a group of persons who support one another for a period of time without the formal obligations of a marriage contract, but with the privilege of sexual access. Both bachelors

17. Erhman *op. cit.*, p. 592.
18. John F. Cuber and Peggy B. Harroff, *Sex and the Significant Americans* (Baltimore: Penguin Books, 1968), pp. 171–72.

and career women are becoming increasingly acceptable roles as lifetime alternatives to husbands and wives, and numerous apartment complexes "for singles only" testify to the separation of sexual behavior from marriage contracts. The commonly accepted norm of "permissiveness with affection" that Reiss contends is characteristic of a significant portion of the college population does not make it mandatory for a couple to intend—or pretend—marriage before they enjoy each other sexually. They do have to care for one another and respect each others wishes, but they do not have to become engaged in order to experience coitus. Because young people advocate the freedom of individual interpretation of what is right in a relationship, the characteristics of the current American code—or codes—are difficult to specify precisely.

MARITAL SEXUALITY

It still seems fair to say, however, that in our society the vast majority *expect* sexual intercourse to occur only within marriage. Persistent refusal to engage in coitus with one's spouse can be grounds for divorce. This has always been true. However, the sexual revolution has changed our expectations in that *both* husband and wife are expected to enjoy it. Women are expected to have a positive sex response.[19] And yet at the same time at least two studies suggest that marital sexuality for the majority of middle-class Americans is not very central to their lives or very satisfying. The first study, by Cuber and Haroff, suggests that the sexual revolution has had little impact on upper-middle-class Americans over thirty-five.

> *It is commonplace that sexual themes pervade American society. Popular literature and music express a frank preoccupation with sex, often in its rawest aspects. Madison Avenue incessantly exploits vulnerability to sexual stimuli. It is said to be almost impossible to isolate oneself or one's children from the pelvic ethos.*
>
> Yet this pervasive accent on sex seems not to have much shaped the habits and tastes of the significant Americans in line with the ubiquitous image. *Many remain clearly ascetic where sex is concerned. Others are simply asexual. For still others, sex is overlaid with such strong hostility that an antisexual orientation is clear. In sum we found substantial numbers of men and women who in their present circumstances couldn't care less about anything that they do about sex.*[20]

The second study, based on extensive clinical research and counseling by Masters and Johnson, attempts to define "sexual inadequacy" in terms of the inability to achieve satisfactory "sexual communication." The authors of *Human Sexual Inadequacy* conclude that probably half of the married couples in America are unable to communicate with one another in the sexual realm or are unsatisfied with the level of their communication.[21]

19. Mead *op. cit.*, p. 16.
20. Cuber and Harroff *op. cit.*, pp. 171–72. [emphasis added]
21. Masters and Johnson, *Human Sexual Inadequacy op. cit.*

Sexual satisfaction may or may not be related to overall marital adjustment. Cuber and Harroff conclude that the majority of the married couples in their sample of 496 significant Americans had a comfortably adequate utilitarian type of marriage in which sexuality was relatively unimportant. Komarovsky writes of the working class "because some of our less-educated women expect little psychological intimacy in marriage, and their standards of personal relationships are not demanding, they were able to dissociate the sexual response from the total relationship."[22] Masters and Johnson may expect much more out of sexuality than does the average American.

A major thrust of the sexual revolution is to raise expectations in regard to marital sexual joy. While this may indeed create additional stress and strain (particularly if sexuality is reduced to technique as it is in so many marriage manuals), the current level of living that constitutes marital adjustment and marital satisfaction for the majority of older Americans, upon examination, does not seem to be of very high quality. If this is indeed true, then a part of the rebellion of youth is a reaction against their parents' type of marriage wherein they perceive that very little is "happening." Such lack-luster marriages are not worth trying to emulate.

A complication arises when the upper-middle-class relationships are compared with working- or lower-class marriages. In this context middle-class Americans seem to fare much better in regard to sexual satisfaction in marriage. In part this is so because of a very different style of sexual behavior that is considered appropriate in the lower classes:

> *Upper level young people are much less sexually active but pet more. They tend to reserve sex for someone for whom they feel affection. Their sexual play usually has more prolonged foreplay, a greater readiness to use a variety of coital positions and a higher incidence of oral-genital contact. The males tend to treat women more as equals, and women tend to take a more active role, with the result that females at this level have a greater number of sexual postponements, masturbation is higher; college men masturbate about twice as often as those with only a grade school education. Persons at this upper level, though, have a low incidence of homosexuality. For the upper socioeducational group, sexual activity is less frequent but more variegated, more artful.*
>
> *Persons at the lower socioeducational levels have a radically different style. The frequency of male premarital sex is much higher; nearly one-half of the boys who do not go to college have intercourse by the age of fifteen. Many fewer females participate but those who do, do so with greater frequency. Persons at the lower level, especially the males, tend not to see sex as having a close relationship with affection or love. They are usually impatient with mere petting. Among this group, sexual play has greater simplicity and directness; there is less foreplay, less variety, greater speed. It tends to be male-oriented, and women at this level expect fewer orgasms and less emotional satisfaction. Masturbation is lower but homosexuality, especially among high school graduates without col-*

22. Mirra Komarovsky, *Blue Collar Marriage* (New York: Random House, 1964), p. 349.

lege educations, is higher. At the lower socioeducational level, sex is
more frequent, more restricted in formal maneuver, and more slam-bang
in approach.[23]

The working class still adheres more strongly to the double standard
than does the middle or lower-lower class. Komarovsky found that 30 percent
of her sample of working-class women were highly satisfied with their sexual
adjustment in marriage; 40 percent were moderately satisfied; and 30 percent
expressed serious dissatisfaction. The study also reported that 15 percent of
the wives in the working class felt that it was the wife's duty to "give it to her
husband whether she likes it or not."[24] In *Family Design*, Rainwater contrasts
the percentages expressing sexual satisfaction by class (Table 12–1).[25] Lower-
class women typically expressed a lack of acceptance and/or rejection of
marital coitus. These attitudes toward sexual relations with husbands reflect
the opinion of 195 women. He suggests that enjoyment of sexual relations is
a function of the degree of role segregation. (Couples who do not share activities but relate to one another on the basis of a mutually acceptable *division*
of labor live in segregated roles.) This is supported by the data presented in
Table 12–2. Those women living in a highly segregated conjugal role relationship are much more likely to be slightly negative or rejecting of sexual relations. The degree of role segregation and the amount of sexual enjoyment

23. Robert Veit Sherwin and George Keller, "Sex on the Campus," *Columbia College Today*, Vol. 15 (Fall 1967), reprinted in Meyer Barash and Alice Scourby (eds.), *Marriage and the Family: A Comparative Analysis of Contemporary Problems* (New York:
Random House, 1970), p. 338.
24. Komarovsky *op. cit.*, p. 85.
25. Lee Rainwater, *Family Design* (Chicago: Aldine, 1965).

TABLE 12–1
Patterns of Husband-Wife Sexual Enjoyment

	Middle Class (51)	Lower Class	
		Intermediate conjugal role-relationship (42)	*Highly segregated conjugal role-relationship* (44)
Both Positive			
Both very positive	45%	57%	11%
Husband only very positive	25	7	20
Both mildly positive	12	2	7
Wife only very positive	8	5	2
Wife Negative			
Husband positive	8	29	55
Husband negative	2	—	5

Source: Lee Rainwater, *Family Design* (Chicago, Ill.: Aldine, 1965), p. 71.

TABLE 12–2
Conugal-Role Segregation and Wife's Enjoyment of Sexual Relations:
The Lower Class

		Very Positive	Positive	Slightly Negative	Rejecting
White					
Intermediate segregation	(25)	64%	4%	32%	—
Highly segregated	(22)	18	14	36	32%
Negro					
Intermediate segregation	(22)	64	14	18	4
Highly segregated	(25)	8	40	32	20

Source: Lee Rainwater, Family Design (Chicago, Ill.: Aldine, 1965), p. 65.

TABLE 12–3
Husband's Assessment of Wife's Enjoyment of Sexual Relations

		Husband's assessment consistent with wife's statements	Husband says wife enjoys sex more than her statements indicate she does
Middle Class			
Upper-middle	(23)	100%	—
Lower-middle	(25)	84	16%
Lower Class			
Intermediate role-relationship	(42)	79	21
Highly segregated role-relationship	(43)	49	51

Source: Lee Rainwater, Family Design (Chicago, Ill.: Aldine, 1965), p. 71.

experienced in marital relations by wives vary by socioeconomic class. A consequence of role segregation is the husband's greater inability to assess his wife's satisfaction with sexual relations (Table 12–3).

If marital satisfaction were a simple function of reaching orgasm, then the Kinsey data would suggest that the average American woman is satisfied in her marriage. According to Kinsey the average female has reached orgasm during 70 to 77 percent of her marital coitus. The rate steadily increases with length of marriage, from 63 percent in the first year to 85 percent in the twentieth year.[26] The rate varies by socioeconomic class. Women with an

26. Kinsey op. cit. (1967), p. 375.

eighth grade education or less reach orgasm 66 percent of the time compared to 76 percent in the case of college educated females.[27]

PREMARITAL SEXUALITY

If the sexual revolution had evolved only out of a great increase in the numbers of persons who have experienced coition before marriage; then it would apply mainly to women and would have occurred in the 1920s. According to the summary of the data presented in Figure 12–2, the percentage of men and women in America who have experienced premarital coitus has increased since the 1900s, but much more dramatically so for women. Prior to the 1920s, about 25 percent had experienced coitus before marriage; by 1930 this had risen to about 50 percent. It is estimated that in 1965 about 75 percent of the adult men and about 55 percent of the adult women in the United States had experienced premarital coitus. This graph gives the impression that we know more than we in fact do, however. The major studies that give us information on premarital coitus are summarized in Table 12–4. Most of these studies have been on college students because of their greater accessibility to the researcher. The effect of class cannot be considered, therefore, but the Kinsey data suggest that those men who have only acquired a grade school education are much more likely to have experienced premarital coitus than the college graduate.[28]

Perhaps the most shocking statistic to the general public when the Kinsey Report was released was the one showing that 50 percent of the females had experienced premarital coitus. This clearly refuted the efficacy of the traditional morality with its preference for virginity even though the report went on to note that most persons were far from promiscuous.[29]

Most studies indicate that the nature of the premarital relationship is

27. *Ibid.*, p. 401.
28. Alfred C. Kinsey et al., *Sexual Behavior in the Human Female* (Philadelphia: Saunder, 1953), p. 330. The percentages for females, however, are reversed. A greater percentage of college graduates experienced premarital coitus than those with only a grade school education, p. 293.
29. *Ibid.*, pp. 291–92.

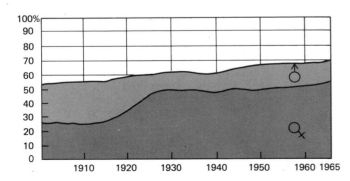

FIGURE 12–2
Premarital Sex, 1900–1965.
From Robert Veit and George
C. Keller, "Sex on Campus,"
Columbia College Today *Vol.*
15 (Fall 1967), 23–24.

TABLE 12–4 *Premarital Coital Experience in Various Populations: A Summary of the Major Research Findings*

Researcher	Date of publication	Sample size & characteristics	Findings and comments
Davis	1929	2,200 Women, 70% college graduates	7% of the married women had experienced premarital intercourse. A select sample for the time (high percentage of college women very unusual). Sample grew up around turn of century.
Hamilton	1929	100 married couples	54% of the men had experienced premarital coitus 35% of the women
Terman	1938	3,792 married couples of the middle and upper middle class of Cal.	60% of the men had premarital intercourse 37% of the women
Burgess & Wallin	1953	666 married couples	68% of the men 47% of the women
		1,000 engaged couples	45% of total had experienced premarital coitus
Kinsey	1949	c. 5,000 males	85% had experienced premarital coitus, 50% of college men by the age of 21
Kinsey	1953	c. 6,000 women	50% had experienced premarital coitus, slightly less than 20% of the college students had by the age of 20
Landis & Landis	1952	1,600 females	10% had experienced premarital coitus
Kanin & Howard	1958	117 wives of college students	43.5% had experienced premarital coitus while engaged
Ehrman	1959	? U. of Florida women	13% had experienced premarital coitus
Freedman	1965	49 senior college women	22% of the total, 16% in "serious" relationships, 6% in "uninhibited" relationships
Landis & Landis	1967	3,189 college students from 18 colleges	10% of the women who "had not had a serious love relationship" 40% of the men who "had not had a serious love relationship" 15% of those not now dating 20% of those dating: 12% of the females; 29% of the males 45% of the engaged females 48% of the engaged males
Packard	1968	?	56% of college men by age of 21 43% of college women by the age of 21

most important. This importance is reflected in the elaboration of the institutions of premarriage. The development of random dating after World War I and the invention of "going steady" that became popular after World War II marked significant steps in the institutionalization of premarriage in America. In general, the first serves as a vehicle for female experimentation with sex at the level of light petting with many partners, while the second allows the possibility of coitus without being labeled "promiscuous." Most of the research deals with the extent to which couples are willing to engage in sexual behavior within the various stages of their relationship. For example, the Bell and Blumberg study published in 1959 found that while dating, 49 percent of the girls had petted and 10 percent had experienced coitus, but while "going steady," 57 percent petted and 15 percent had experienced coitus.[30] The studies suggest that for engaged couples, the percentage who have experienced coitus increases.[31]

However a major component of the sexual revolution seems to be the increasing willingness to enjoy sexual relationships fully without their having to be institutionalized. On this aspect there is more information about attitude than behavior. For example, CBS reports "College students . . . place greater emphasis on self-expression and self-fulfillment. And a majority of the students say sexual behavior should be bound by mutual feelings, and not by formal and legal ties."[32]

John Cuber reflects on the responses to a 1968 questionnaire given to Ohio State students:

> More than the previous generation (1939) both men and women students today seem to be earnestly and self-consciously in search of the meaning of sexual expression. One young woman said, "Sex is beautiful and should be shared by two people who love each other; even if they don't get married, the love they shared at that time was beautiful." "Sex is good, natural and highly perishable," said a young man. "Why let it go to waste?"
>
> These same people, however, go on to say that they recognize numerous restraints and responsibilities. For example, they stress a deep moral obligation to use effective contraception. They condemn exploitative sex: "The gal is entitled to know whether this is for fun or whether I'm serious." And they insist on honesty: "If two people agree and are honest with each other, nothing is wrong."
>
> All this seems to me to mean that a substantial proportion of student opinion today is based on the student's own evolving precepts and judgments rather than on legal, ecclesiastical or parental codes.[33]

This code of conduct is in the best tradition of situation ethics in which a relationship does not depend upon its definition in some social fashion

---

30. Robert Bell and Leonard Blumberg, "Courtship Intimacy and Religious Background," *Marriage and Family Living*, (Nov. 1959), 358.

31. T. Judson and Mary Landis, *Building a Successful Marriage*, 5th ed. (Englewood Cliffs, N.J.: Prentice-Hall, 1968). Bell and Bloomberg *op. cit.*

32. CBS News *op. cit.*, p. 8.

33. John F. Cuber *op. cit.*, 174.

such as going steady, or being pinned or engaged. To require institutional definition is to reflect an essentially legalistic view of relationships. Even though no elaborate public ceremony might be necessary to establish the relationship, social recognition—and by implication approval—is necessary. In the former case the emphasis is upon the integrity of the couple to decide for themselves what is loving and honest in the context of their relationship. Society need not know about it. It is certainly not necessary to stipulate that the degree of sexual involvement must depend upon the stage in premarriage.

The evidence linking premarital coital experience with marital satisfaction is ambiguous. Burgess and Wallin found that orgasmic adequacy in marriage is positively related to premarital sex experience. The more sexually experienced the wife is, the more likely she is to experience a full orgasm in marital relations—provided her premarital sexual experience was with her fiancé.[34] The American Institute of Family Relations discovered an early positive relationship between premarital intercourse and orgasmic response in marriage which diminished with sexual experience in marriage, as one might expect.[35] On the basis of an examination of the data presented by Burgess and others, Paul Landis concludes that "virginity prior to marriage is most favorable to total marriage success."[36] Bell, however, interprets similar data: "On the basis of the available evidence it does not appear that premarital sexual experience has negative affects on marital coital satisfaction—in fact, the evidence suggests just the opposite. In general, premarital chastity may be favorable to overall adjustment in marriage, but premarital coitus appears favorable to sexual adjustment in marriage. However, the interpretations of these two levels of adjustment must be made with care because factors that make for good sexual adjustment may have little to do with overall marital adjustment.[37]

Expert opinion on the positive value of premarital coitus is thus quite varied. On the liberal end of the spectrum, Dr. Albert Ellis, noted sexologist, remarks:

> *Since premarital sex relations are no longer viewed as morally reprehensible or sinful by most educated and informed individuals, there need be no intrinsic guilt attached to them.*
>
> *People who are anxious and guilty about their premarital affairs are usually emotionally disturbed individuals who are also anxious and guilty about many of their nonsexual participations. On the other hand, many people today are becoming anxious and disturbed because they are not copulating before marriage.*[38]

In the middle is Paul Landis, a clinically oriented marriage counselor:

34. Burgess and Wallin, *Engagement and Marriage* (Philadelphia, Pa.: Lippincott, 1953), chap. 12; Kinsey *op. cit.* (1967).
35. Paul Popenoe, "Premarital Experience No Help in Sexual Adjustment After Marriage," *Family Life*, Vol. 21 (Aug. 1961), 1–2.
36. Paul Landis, *Making the Most of Marriage*, 4th ed. (New York: Appleton-Century-Crofts, 1970), p. 375.
37. Robert Bell, *Premarital Sex in a Changing Society* (Englewood Cliffs, N. J.: Prentice-Hall, 1966), pp. 144–45.
38. Albert Ellis, *Sex Without Guilt* (New York: Lyle Stuart, 1966), pp. 34–41.

Evidence available to date suggests that marriages of the chaste are most successful under the cultural pattern of the United States. This may merely mean that the conventional are the best marriage risks. Under a different moral order, personal and marital problems resulting from premarital sexual relations would no doubt be greatly reduced but the moral system exists and is a reality with which all must reckon. Perhaps the greatest risk in premarital sex relationships is the frequently resulting feeling of self-betrayal and the inner conflicts which this brings.

Society must operate on the principle of safety first. Here the personal impulse and group responsibility clash. The burden on society of caring for the unprotected mother and child increases yearly as mores weaken.[39]

And on the conservative end of the spectrum, David Mace, a former Methodist minister and a current authority in marriage education:

Since premarital intercourse is against the conventional code, few can seek it without subterfuge. Young people with religious associations (the majority of American youth today) suffer reactions varying from mild uneasiness to agonizing guilt. They may be consumed with remorse at having broken their code, let down their parents and earned public disapproval. This results in misery to the individual and tension in the relationship. Where one feels guilty and the other does not, the former is likely to feel exploited. These guilt feelings can easily break up a potentially promising partnership.[40]

Whatever the opinion of the experts, it is evident that attitudes toward premarital sex are changing among young people.[41]

It is probable that more than one code of conduct has adherents in American society. Ira Reiss contends that an individual's attitudes toward premarital coitus, for example, can usually be classified in one of four categories: (1) Abstinence—premarital intercourse is wrong for both the man and woman under all conditions, even when a stable relationship with engagement, love, or strong affection is present; (2) Permissiveness with affection—premarital intercourse is right for both men and women when a stable relationship with engagement, love, or strong affection is present; (3) Permissiveness without affection—premarital intercourse is right for both men and women regardless of the amount of affection or stability present, providing there is physical attraction; (4) Double Standard—premarital intercourse is acceptable for men but is wrong and unacceptable for women. A variant of the latter asserts that it is right for women under some conditions such as engagement.[42]

The dominant American codes still seem to be the double standard and

39. Paul Landis *op. cit.*, pp. 385–86.

40. David Mace, "The Case for Chastity and Virginity," in Albert Ellis and Albert Abarbanel (eds.), *The Encyclopedia of Sexual Behavior* (New York: Hawthorne, 1961), p. 348.

41. Bell *op. cit.*, p. 80.

42. Ira L. Reiss, *The Social Context of Premarital Sexual Permissiveness* (New York: Holt, Rinehart & Winston, 1967), pp. 83–84.

abstinence. Both are enforced by the religious traditions of most Americans. Permissiveness without affection is apparently a code held by a minority of Americans because it finds sex in and of itself valuable and pleasurable regardless of commitment, while most American females find the element of commitment in the relationship of major importance. Therefore, permissiveness with affection, Reiss argues, is the *emergent* norm among young Americans of the college scene. Christensen describes the problem of permissiveness or restrictiveness in regard to premarital sex as follows:

> There is a certain amount of evidence that the more permissive the culture regarding premarital sexual intimacy the higher will be the actual occurrence of such intimacy but the lower will be any negative effects deriving therefrom. And conversely, the more restrictive the culture, the lower will be the actual occurrence but the higher will be the negative effects.[43]

EXTRA-MARITAL SEXUALITY

Probably the dominant norm in the United States still holds that marriage should be a life-long commitment to one partner involving exclusive sexual rights. Adultery is the only grounds for divorce acceptable in all legal jurisdictions. We are more restrictive in our *norms* regarding adulterous relationships than we are in those applied to premarital relationships because we assume that the married are not sexually deprived and because we feel that extra-marital sexual behavior is more threatening to marriage than premarital coitus. Bell suggests that if there has been any discernible trend in our norms, it has been toward a greater equalization of "rights" to such philandering for both sexes.[44]

While Hunt points out that for the majority of Americans "adulterous love is frought with difficulties, pleasure-pain, tragedy, and sorrow,"[45] Cuber and Harroff provide us with some idea of the contextual variation in perspectives on adultery associated with their five types of marriage:

> Infidelity, for example, occurs in most of the five types, the total relationship being the exception. But it occurs for quite different reasons. In the conflict-habituated, it seems to be only another outlet for hostility. The call girl and the woman picked up in a bar are more than just available women; they are symbols of resentment of the wife. This is not always so but reported to us often enough to be worth noting. Infidelity among the passive-congenial, on the other hand, is typically in line with the stereotype of the middle-aged man who "strays out of sheer boredom with the uneventful deadly prose" of his private life. And the devitalized man or woman frequently is trying for an hour or a year to recapture the lost mood. But the vital are sometimes adulterous too;

43. Harold T. Christensen, "A Cross-Cultural Comparison of Attitudes Toward Marital Infidelity," *International Journal of Comparative Sociology* (Sept. 1962), 125.
44. Bell *op. cit.*, p. 145.
45. Morton Hunt, *Her Infinite Variety* (New York: Harper & Row, 1962), pp. 119–20.

some are simply emancipated—almost bohemian. To some of them sexual aggrandizement is an accepted fact of life. Frequently the infidelity is condoned by the partner and in some instances even provides an indirect (through empathy) kind of gratification. The act of infidelity in such cases is not construed as disloyalty or as a threat to continuity, but rather as a kind of basic human right which the loved one ought to be permitted to have—and which the other perhaps wants also for himself.[46]

Albert Ellis points out that both the Kinsey data and the Cuber and Harroff study have thrown considerable doubt upon the notion that extramarital relations are an unusual or deviant form of behavior reflecting disturbed motivations on the part of husbands and wives. He concludes on the basis of his own clinical evidence that there are healthy and disturbed reasons for having extra-marital affairs:

In my own observations of the quite unusual adulterers—unusual in the sense that both partners to the marriage agreed upon and carried out extra-marital affairs and in many instances actually engaged in wifeswapping—I have found that there are usually both good and bad, healthy and unhealthy reasons for this type of highly unconventional behavior; and if this is true in these extreme cases, it is almost certainly equally true or truer about the usual kind of secret adulterous affairs that are much more common in this country.[47]

In Ellis's view, the healthy adulterer is (1) nondemanding and noncompulsive. He prefers but does not need extra-marital affairs. (2) He usually manages to carry on his extra-marital affairs without unduly disturbing his marriage, family relations, or his general existence. He is sufficiently discreet about his adultery, on the one hand, and appropriately frank and honest about it with his close associates, on the other, so that most people he knows intimately are able to tolerate his affairs and not get too upset about them. (3) He fully accepts his own extra-marital desires and acts. (4) He does not use his adulterous relationships as a means of avoiding any serious problems. (5) He is tolerant of himself and others. (6) He is sexually adequate with all his partners and seeks extra-marital sex out of interest rather than therapy.[48]

Bell suggests that extra-marital affairs arise out of a variety of influences: (1) the search for variety in sexual partner, (2) in retaliation for a known or presumed infidelity on the part of a spouse, (3) as a result of rebellion against the monogamous mores, (4) as a result of seeking emotional (not specifically sexual) gratification outside of marriage, (5) as a consequence of friendship, (6) at the encouragement of a spouse, (7) in response to the perception of waning facility associated with aging, and (8) for simple enjoyment.

46. Cuber and Harroff *op. cit.*, p. 62.
47. Albert Ellis, "Healthy and Disturbed Reasons for Having Extra-Marital Relations," in Gerhard Neubeck (ed.), *Extra-Marital Relations* (Englewood Cliffs, N.J.: Prentice-Hall, 1970), p. 153.
48. *Ibid.*, pp. 160–61.

As in the case of premarital sexual relations, the norms governing extra-marital sex are more conservative than the practice.[49]

Sex, Sensation, and Spirit:
A Redefinition of Western Experience

The sexual revolution as a life style concerned with a transformation of erotic relationships between men and women is manifested most obviously in the "hippies" and their predecessors, the beatniks. The great attention which has been given in the folk culture and in academic, social, religious, and philosophical writings and discussions to the question of "violations" of the traditional sexual mores since the turn of the century has *frequently obscured the fact that the sexual revolution includes the development of a new social system* with respect to the erotic relations of men and women. We might advisedly speak either of a system or of systems.[50] Much of this life style seems at first glance little more than rebellion against the mores of the established society. Yet at its core is an attempt to rediscover human sexuality not as an act of "doing it" with a woman for the sake of ego enhancement or even simply for the erotic pleasure that is to be found in making love. Rather sexuality is seen as an expression of the whole of a life style and as a manner of worship after some traditions of the East (see Figure 12–3).

Alan Watts perhaps best describes this re-orientation to sexuality in his book, *Nature, Man and Woman*:

> . . . *Conventional spirituality rejects the bodily union of man and woman as the most fleshy, animal, and degrading phase of human activity—a rejection showing the extent of its faulty perception and its misinterpretation of the natural world. It rejects the most concrete and creative form of man's relation to the world outside his organism, because it is through the love of a woman that he can say not only of her but also of all that is other, "This is my body." . . . We must see that consciousness is neither an isolated soul nor the mere function of a single nervous system but of that totality of interrelated stars and galaxies which makes a nervous system possible. . . . The failure to realize the mutuality and bodily unity of man and the world underlies both the sensual and the ascetic attitudes. Trying to grasp the pleasure of the senses and to make their enjoyment the goal of life is already an attitude in which man feels divided from his experience, and sees it as something to be exploited and pursued. But the pleasure so gained is always fragmentary and frustrating, so that by way of reaction the ascetic gives up the pursuit, but not the sense of division which is the real root of the difficulty. . . .*
>
> *All this is peculiarly true of love and of the sexual communion between man and woman. This is why it has such a strongly spiritual and mystical character when spontaneous and why it is so degrading and frustrating when forced. . . . But as we have seen, the problems of sex-*

49. Bell *op. cit.*, pp. 151–53.
50. *Ibid.*, pp. 596–97.

FIGURE 12–3
*"Mithuna Couple," a 12–13th
century statue from a Hindu
Temple in Orissa, India. From
the Metropolitan Museum of Art,
Florance Waterbury Fund.*

*uality cannot be solved at their own level. The full splendor of sexual
experience does not reveal itself without a new mode of attention to the
world in general.*[51]

Watts, of course, is attempting to change the basic style of sexual behavior (and the essential character of American life) through the ancient tradition of the printed word. It is not an easy matter to determine the extent
to which such exhortation has brought about any change in the direction of
spiritual sensuality or to ascertain the extent to which the rather dramatic
changes in the behavior of "hip" young people reflect efforts such as Watts's.
The nuances and subtleties suggested by such a view are not easily recovered
in survey research, and the biases of participant observers are particularly difficult to handle in such intimate matters. This dimension of the sexual revolution, therefore, has not been adequately measured, but that it is a component
in the dramatic change affecting the lives of many Americans can hardly be
denied.

51. Alan Watts, *Nature, Man and Woman* (New York: Pantheon, 1969), pp. 185–89
passim.

Summary

Research has demonstrated that masculinity and femininity are not biologically determined. Psychosexual differentiation and gender role are not determined by entirely genetic inheritance. Thus it is possible for sex reassignment to take place without complications in hermaphroditic children before they are eighteen months old provided that the parents are agreed upon the sex of their child and take the necessary medical steps to ensure that the child's anatomy will conform to the assigned sex. Nevertheless, hermaphroditic adults are able to maintain a unitary psychosexual identity and gender role in spite of gross contradictions in physical characteristics.

Because masculinity and femininity are not fixed genetically, they can be expressed in a wide variety of ways. Cross-cultural and cross-class data and the study of homosexuality support this. Indeed, an examination of the data suggests that there is no simple *dichotomy* of sexual types. Furthermore, the cultural definition is frequently ambiguous because masculinity and femininity are evaluated along many dimensions. Thus a muscular man who enjoys poetry must hold in tension at least two different evaluations of his masculinity.

Because even the basic dimensions of human sexuality remain remarkably free from genetic or hormonal determination, and because the cultural definitions are often ambiguous, the normative control of sexual definition and behavior is a major concern of most societies. But norms are rarely completely internalized. They can be violated and even rejected. I have argued that the sexual revolution in America is best characterized as a *rejection* of the traditional norms and a positive affirmation of the goodness of sex.

The data suggest that the sexual revolution is primarily a middle-class phenomenon associated in the first instance with the emancipation of women in the 1920s. Women are now expected to have a positive sex response. They are expected to initiate sexual relations more often than was formerly the case. Norms governing sexual behavior, nevertheless, are still probably more conservative than behavior and until the two are in better balance, a great deal of guilt will adhere to sexual behavior inside as well as outside of marriage.

It is clear that while our traditional norms still proscribe coitus outside of marriage, the behavior of increasing numbers of Americans points toward increased acceptance of nonmarital coitus. For some, extra-marital coitus is a basic human right and not evidence of infidelity. Such attitudes and behavior are probably confined to a small minority of persons largely from the upper-middle class. The style of marital sexual behavior and the attitudes toward such behavior vary with class. The working class's general orientation toward marital coitus is that it is a man's right and a woman's obligation. Coitus is entered into with much less foreplay and with less anticipation of enjoyment by most working-class women. As one might expect, sexual adjustment is not as much a part of overall marital adjustment in the working class. In the lower-lower class sex is viewed as natural, and coitus is much more likely to occur outside of marriage than is true in the working class. Yet it does not seem to have the embellishments of foreplay and the concern for communication that are more common in the upper-middle class.

An emergent component in the sexual revolution is more clearly associated with the younger generation, although older "bohemian" types are also advocates. In the writings of such scholars as Watts the notion of sensual spirituality is transplanted to American soil and the positive, but not simply hedonistic, value of sex is stressed. The common polarity of spirit and body is overcome, and sex becomes a form of worship.

13. The Generation Gap

NEW YORK (AP)—A prominent New York lawyer has been ordered to resume support of his 20-year-old daughter, even though he thinks her "hippie" life "stinks." . . . "At some point," (said the family judge) "minors must have some right of their own views and needs for their independent and painful transition from minority to adulthood. . . . This court absolves the daughter from bridging the generation gap any more than she has. . . . The gap is not entirely the doing of the young, nor can it be bridged entirely by the children."

DECEMBER 1970

Children have never been exactly like their parents. They differ genetically by virtue of the fact that human reproduction requires the fusion of the father's genetic inheritance with that of the mother. Perhaps children would be more understandable to their parents if they were simply the result of a process of maturation—the "natural" unfolding of genetic or innate characteristics already present in the genes—but they are not. Instead children become adults through learning about and assimilating the culture taught to them by their parents and many "significant others," all of whom may see the same way of life somewhat differently because they will not have shared identical learning experiences.

The concern frequently expressed today (to the point that it is often taken for granted) that there is a "generation gap" in America is not based on a desire simply to point to the differences between today's youth and their parents. It is more a concern for the problems of communication between the generations, arising in part from these differences which are intensified by the crucial period of history in which we live. According to a recent CBS poll, most young people do not have problems communicating with their own parents, "What bothers parents, usually, is 'those kids,' not their kids. Three out of ten young people have trouble communicating with their own parents, but what troubles them more are the values of adult America."[1] Nevertheless, an estimated 500,000 youth are persistent runaways, and many more leave home for extended trips before they are legally of age:

> *This fall something new is happening along the generation gap. The high school kids are leaving home, but they aren't leaving town. Instead of following the pattern of the last few years and trotting off decently to the East Village or a commune, they are moving down the block or across the tracks. The kids are playing Musical Families, and many a game room in suburbia is turning into a youth hostel.*[2]

These largely middle-class youth who prefer to live away from home thus seem to indicate that problems of communication exist within families to a greater extent than the survey would suggest.

The issues frequently cited in discussions of the "gap" range from long hair, sloppy dress, and sexual permissiveness to drugs, the war in Vietnam, and the inequities of the American way of life. It is not so often the behavior of the young that sets their parents' teeth on edge as it is their attitudes and convictions. Anti-Vietnam protests, counter-cultural communes, and "mind expanding" trips are among the more dramatic expressions of a pervasive impasse. "The mess we are in" needs to be accounted for. The need for a scapegoat is great. The question of who to blame thus complicates matters, for the groups commonly blamed (Communists, hippies, corrupt politicians, profit-seeking businessmen, the Birchers) have active members from most age groups.

1. CBS News, *Generations Apart*, Transcript of a Televised Broadcast, May 20, 1969, p. 2.
2. Jane O'Reilly, "Notes on the New Paralysis," *New York Magazine*, Oct. 26, 1970, 28.

In a society in which over half the population is under twenty-five[3] and which prides itself on its youthfulness, a generation gap seems somewhat anomalous. In this chapter I will first look at the "gap" from a number of perspectives and try to assess its magnitude. Then I will offer a social-psychological explanation for why intergenerational conflict seems so great in our time. Finally, I will look briefly at the commune movement which is among the most dramatic expressions of our youth culture.

Perspectives on the Gap

Commenting on the "political rationale" for the generation gap in a symposium sponsored by the Child Study Association of America, Mark Henriquez, a high school senior, and Dr. Salvatore Ambrosino, Executive Director of the Family Service Association of Nassau County, New York, express their different viewpoints:

> *MARK: It stems basically from the fact that the older generation is upset—the generation that is in the saddle, using society's rules and concepts, social systems, customs, and so forth. Naturally once they have made it, they view with great reluctance any system change. When one spends thirty years of one's life trying to make it, and one does make it, it is very rare that one wants to change the system.*
>
> *However, the system has now been found wanting, and I think this is demonstrated most dramatically by the war in Vietnam and by the subjugation of native peoples in America. What sets me off most is the attempt on the part of the so-called capable, so-called responsible people to keep the status quo and to keep the system and to keep norms which have been outmoded by the progress of the times. In connection with this cliché, "generation gap," I think 90 percent of the concern about it is on the part of adults, because of their own shortcomings. In a society such as this, where it is such a hassle just to keep yourself together, to survive, to have food, to put the kids through school, and to pay taxes, you really are too worn out to get any kind of love or affection or any of the things that a person craves, and personal relationships are not appreciated.*
>
> *Naturally, when some kids say, "I have had enough," and when they start shouting, "Hell, no I won't go!" the parents say, "This is the generation gap." Or they blame Communist agitators, and you can't cope with this, you know.*
>
> *This is, I think, where the basic mistake lies, I see no reason in continuing a system that an overwhelming number of people think has failed.*
>
> *DR. AMBROSINO: Our increased ability to communicate and the encouragement of a more intense communication today, while very positive*

3. Children's Bureau, U.S. Department of Health, Education, and Welfare, *The Nation's Youth*, Publication #460 (Washington, D.C.: U.S. Government Printing Office, 1970), Chart 1.

and hopeful, creates in itself some problems. . . . Both adults and young people face a kind of intensification of the conflict between self-realization and the commitment to others—to family, to community, and to the world community. Of course, there has to be some kind of balance. The kind of thing I, as an adult, react to in some of the statements made by the young people here is what seems to be a self-centered orientation and preoccupation with self.

Now . . . I want these young people to be concerned about self-realization, but sometimes it seems so exaggerated and so extreme that I don't see the kind of commitment to the community that is necessary. . . .

. . . . I don't like it when somebody pins the whole rap on me as an adult—that there are no values today, and what-not—because I think this is an historical development. It is not my fault that religion has declined. It is not my fault that the family structure is changing. These are by-products of a new industrial society. It is not any one adult's fault that we're now moving more and more into giant megalopolitan centers which will demand huge bureaucratic systems, and that the individual has a completely different kind of adjustment to make today than some thirty or forty or fifty years ago.

MARK: . . . Who accuses you personally? . . . Let us understand this. When I say "the adult generation," you have to remember that I am seventeen years old, and I did not have a chance to shape the society I am emerging into. I did not have a chance to control or limit the mess that I am inheriting.

You, however, have had a chance to do this. You in person, not personally, but along with all the other people who were born in your generation, have had a chance to shape the society, and not because you especially engineered the decline of the individual or the rise of materialism, but because you, as a generation, have done nothing about it.[4]

A CBS interview contrasts the views of youth with those of their parents:

RITA FLEMING: I think the degree of difference is such that my parents will probably never really understand what I think about a lot of things, never really understand me or know me. I think it's gone almost beyond that.
MRS. FLEMING: She sort of systematically attacks everything I hold near and dear and sacred. Like, you name it—God, the flag, the king. She can't discuss religion, politics, sex, or drugs with me. You know, is there anything else? Like the weather, you know. . . .

TEX HOLMES: I think there's a large generation gap today. And I don't really think it's being exaggerated very much. Because there are an awful lot of kids who just can't talk to their parents. They can't talk about anything. Their parents just kind of shut them off and the kids, on the other hand, do the same thing. And so it's a real problem of communications.

4. The Child Study Association of America, *The Function of Rebellion—Is Youth Creating New Family Values?* Proceedings of the 44th Annual Conference, March 4, 1968 (New York: The Child Study Association of America, 1969), pp. 19, 20–23 passim.

MRS. HOLMES: They're just frustrated, I guess. I really don't know. They have every material thing they could have. And this is what their parents thought they wanted. And yet they say now they hate their parents, and their parents were wrong, so . . . I don't know what those kids want.

PAT McGRAW: It seems to me that the generation before this one, and my father in particular, were very expedient. You know, what's the best way to do it? There was no question, for example, in my father's mind, that he ought to join the army. Well, there's a very big question in my mind.
MR. McGRAW: Because they have lived under different circumstances, always at war, always problems in the cities, always problems in the rural areas of America, they are worried. They have taken the burdens and the problems of America prematurely upon their shoulders, something that my generation didn't do.[5]

Although these quotations suggest basic disagreement between youth and their own parents, the same survey revealed that many more students expressed disagreement with adult values than with their own parents. Both youth and their parents agree that there is a gap.

In a nationwide sample survey of almost two thousand parents and their children, aged seventeen through twenty-three, CBS discovered that "95 percent of all Americans believe there is a gap and a quarter of all young people —the vanguard of dissent—believe the gap is large."[6]

In its sample of over two hundred fifty student responses from fifty-three schools, the Office of Child Development found that about half of the respondents reported that the gap is viewed as a real problem among teenagers, some asserting that it is getting worse:

We don't talk about the generation gap, as such, because we all recognize it and accept it. Thus, it isn't a topic, but an assumption behind conversation. For example, the remark, "I had a pretty good talk with my Dad last night," is taken to mean that there has been a rare occurrence.
In the special case of Blacks—which I am more familiar with—this gap is even wider and the problems more difficult. The younger generation has become "aware" and is now attempting to make older Blacks and all America just as "aware." The task is harder because young aware Black students are trying to change the entire attitude of Blacks toward themselves, and America's attitude toward Blacks as a race.[7]

About a quarter responded that the gap is a problem for some and not for other teenagers, and the final quarter reported that it is no problem at all. Some of the responses from this latter group follow:

Sure maybe there is a generation gap, but I'm sure we're not the first generation that's gapped.

5. CBS News *op. cit.*, p. 2.
6. *Loc. cit.*
7. Elizabeth Herzog, *et al., Teenagers Discuss the "Generation Gap,"* Youth Report 1 (Washington, D.C.: Office of Child Development, The Children's Bureau, U.S. Department of Health, Education, and Welfare, 1970), p. 2.

From the way my grandparents talk, I'm pretty sure that my parents weren't understood either. Of course, I probably won't understand my kids either.

I am sure that each parent generation had, has, and will have objections to its younger generation.[8]

The profile of the combatants is difficult to outline clearly. What *is* clear is that the cliché "generation gap" does not do justice to the reality, because it assumes that the problem is basically one of *two* conflicting points of view —the adult perspective on the one hand and the youth perspective on the other.

In point of fact the situation is much more complex. CBS news discovered in its 1969 survey, for example, that noncollege youth held attitudes that were much more in sympathy with those of adults than were the attitudes of the college students. Within the college population the survey revealed that it was possible to differentiate among those youths who considered themselves to be revolutionary—who advocated (and presumably practiced) the use of violence to overthrow the system (approximately 3 percent of the sample), those who were for radical reform in the system (10 percent of the sample), those who were in favor of moderate reform or conformity (76 percent), and those who considered themselves to be conservative (11 percent). The CBS report estimated, however, that 48 percent of its college population sample were sympathetic with the goals, if not the tactics, of the radical left—the revolutionaries.[9] In addition, there seemed to be a difference in the perception of the problem by race. Young Blacks see themselves as having a much more difficult problem because of the necessity to reform all of white society, including those of their own generation, as well as black adults. Thus far black-white coalitions on campus seem to be tenuous at best.

Thus, the recognition of issues as being critical, the advocacy of tactics, the degree of involvement in reform, and the extent of "alienation" are not consistent among the younger generation. These factors seem to vary with age, class, and race. So also, the nonacceptance of "the older generation" by youth is not uniformly applied to the entire adult population. There are heroes of the adult generation (e.g. William Kuntsler, Dr. Benjamin Spock, Ralph Nader, Eldridge Cleaver) and numerous martyrs in the cause of reform (Malcolm X, John Kennedy, Martin Luther King) who are widely accepted by young people. Those who are most popular with youth, however, often seem most unacceptable to adults. It is clear, nevertheless, that generational lines are not *the* battle lines. Ideological alliances cross generational boundaries and compound the problem of taking sides in the continuing conflict.

Changes in the Youth Scene

A further complication in the description of the conflict occurs when one takes into account the fact that the youth scene itself is changing. Precisely

8. *Ibid.,* p. 5.
9. CBS News *op. cit.,* p. 2.

how it is changing is difficult to document, since little research has thus far been attempted. But if we allow the validity of insightful scholarship such as that of Kenneth Keniston and Kingsley Davis, we note that the profiles painted at the beginning of the 1960s differ significantly from those drawn at the close of that decade. This difference is particularly evident with regard to political participation and to the interpretation of the term "alienation" as applied to youth culture.

FROM PRIVATISM TO INVOLVEMENT

College graduates of the late-1950s were commonly referred to as "The Silent Generation" because of an almost pervasive reluctance to speak out on or engage in political issues. The more radical youth were "beat." Their elite were alienated and withdrawn. These are the students Keniston had in mind when he wrote in 1961:

> The adult world into which they are headed is seen as a cold, me-
> chanical, abstract, specialized, and emotionally meaningless place in
> which one simply goes through the motions, but without conviction that
> the motions are worthy, humane, dignified, relevant, or exciting. Thus,
> for many young people, it is essential to stay "cool"; and "coolness" in-
> volves detachment, lack of commitment, never being enthusiastic or
> going overboard about anything.[10]

Such youths were unrebellious, experiencing a widespread feeling of "power-lessness—social, political, and personal. . . . The world is seen as fluid and chaotic, individuals as victims of impersonal forces which they can seldom understand and never control."[11]

Feeling powerless, youth turned to those areas of life where they had control—their interpersonal relations and their patterns of leisure activities. This phenomenon of turning interests inward Reisman labeled *privatism*. Young people withdrew from the political sphere, shortened the time span to the more knowable *now*, and advocated a "cult of experience" exemplified in the extreme by the beatnik and his quest for "kicks."

On the other hand, reading an account of youth written in 1969 we hear a different note stressed:

> . . . the cry for power—whether it is student power or black power—
> shows a wish to be involved and a recognition that one has to act to
> be effective in society. Yet, as an absolute power means nothing. It must
> be clear: power for what? If behind these movements stands a wish for
> justice and equal opportunity for each person in this world, there is a
> valid basis for action; but power must not be sought on the basis of the
> accident of birth or position in society, or because one happens to be a
> student. We clearly must not retreat before threats; but we must accept
> the wish for justice and understand the anger, and together with young

10. Kenneth Keniston, "Social Change and Youth in America," in Erik H. Erikson (ed.), *Youth: Change and Challenge* (The American Academy of Arts and Sciences, 1961; Basic Books, 1963); reprinted in Meyer Barash and Alice Scourby (eds.), *Marriage and the Family: A Comparative Analysis* (New York: Random House, 1970), p. 363.

11. *Ibid.*, p. 365.

people we must work toward the realization of justice for all in our society.[12]

Such comments coming from an adult seem defensive. They come, however, after the significant involvement of youth in politics through the Peace Corps, Youth Corps, Vista, and the political campaign of 1968; through organized protests against the war in Vietnam, pollution of the environment, and mismanagement of our schools; and through violent reaction to oppression as in the case of young Blacks caught up in the riots of the 1960s. *Young Blacks were most active in the riots according to the Kerner Commission Report which found that:*

> *The typical rioter in the summer of 1967 was a Negro, unmarried male between the ages of 15 and 24 in many ways very different from the stereotypes. . . .*
>
> *He rejects the white bigot's stereotype of the Negro as ignorant and shiftless. He takes great pride in his race and believes that in some respects Negroes are superior to whites. He is extremely hostile to whites, but his hostility is more apt to be a product of social and economic class than of race; he is almost equally hostile toward middle-class Negroes.*
>
> *He is substantially better informed about politics than Negroes who were not involved in the riots. He is more likely to be actively engaged in civil rights efforts, but is extremely distrustful of the political system and of political leaders.*[13]

These black youths might be described as "alienated" but they cannot be described as withdrawn from political activity. On the college campus most protest and demonstration against the system comes from upper-middle-class Whites or lower-class Blacks. Both seem increasingly "aware" of the inadequacies of the system but for quite different reasons. The college unrest erupts most frequently in protest marches and speeches, less frequently in destruction and violence. While at least one observer feels that it has reached its peak, college students cannot accurately be described as "uninvolved."[14]

TRANSFORMATION OF THE RADICAL LEFT

The most conspicuous element of the youth culture has undergone a transformation from the beats of the 1950s to the hippies and yippies of the 1960s and early 1970s. Withdrawal and disengagement characterized the beats of the fifties, while radical youth now advocate "Revolution for the hell of it" and "Do it!"[15] Despite the theatricality of the rhetoric and posturing and the conviction that reality is largely subjective ("I am the revolution"), the trial

12. The Child Study Association of America *op. cit.,* pp. 12–13.
13. *Report of the National Advisory Commission on Civil Disorders* (New York: Bantam Books, 1968), pp. 128–29.
14. Robert Nesbitt, *The Washington Post,* April 19, 1970.
15. Abbie Hoffman, *Revolution for the Hell of It* (New York: Dial Press, 1968); Jerry Rubin, *Do It: A Revolutionary Manifesto* (New York: Simon & Schuster, 1970).

of the Chicago Seven has served to demonstrate some of the weaknesses of our legal system, and the defense of young activists seems to enlist the support of large numbers of youth. The precise strength of the radical left is unknown, but whatever its strength, its direction is toward involvement.

So also in the sphere of the interpersonal world, the radical left has taken on a more activist posture. It is attempting to alter radically the character of interpersonal relations—and the structure of the family itself. The commune is an experiment in living that may be but a transitory phase for many—a kind of trial marriage in some instances—but for others seems to be a long-term attempt to change the basic character of the family. This attempt will be given closer scrutiny later in this chapter.

Whether through revolution for the hell of it, through participation in political parties and established agencies working for change, or through the purely voluntary selection of vocations for social change without primary consideration of income, a large number of youth at the beginning of the seventies appear to seek involvement—to cry out for power to change things. The extent to which this image is simply a press fiction is hard to tell. Two somewhat skeptical observers assess the scene as follows:

> It is probably the case that the percentage of today's youth that can be characterized by such phrases as "rebellious" has either increased or at the very least become more conspicuous. However, it is our view that the "decline" in political involvement is still characteristic of the majority of college youth. Commitment makes headlines, apathy does not.[16]

I, for one, would be inclined to doubt the "assumed decline" of youth's involvement in politics and would instead support the view that this trend was reversed in the 1960s.

Alienation may still describe the situation of youth in America, but not because of their political disengagement. Rather, having been alienated from the more commonly held values of their parents, they are pressing for a radically different style of life. The basis of disagreement and rebelliousness is increasingly being expressed in political terms and increasingly asserts, and attempts to reinstate, the importance of the personal in an impersonal world. From this perspective youth's privatism has a strong dimension of public concern.

A Sociological Explanation

The sociological explanation offered here draws primarily upon the functional viewpoint of Kingsley Davis. This perspective attempts to link sociological phenomena to impersonal changes taking place in our rapidly changing society. The perspectives of role theory and psychoanalysis, represented here by Kenneth Keniston and Erik Erikson, also are concerned with the effects of rapid and uncontrolled change, but focus on the problem of establishing an adequate personal identity in such a society. These writers take into account

16. Keniston *op. cit.*, p. 382.

the fact that not only is there a problem of socialization—of assigning persons to an established status role in the social system—but also there is a concomitant problem of establishing an inner sense of continuity so that what one is as an adult seems consistent with what one was as an adolescent. Rapid change in our society tends, in their view, to make this transition more difficult. Thus, an individual is more likely to feel "spaced out" and poorly integrated. He experiences a sense of "identity diffusion" (to be discussed below).

Kingsley Davis in his article "The Sociology of Parent-Youth Conflict" contends that there are three universal factors that set the stage for conflict between generations in all societies. The first is the basic birth cycle differential between parents and their children. Each generation is born into a different slice of social history. "A family is not a static entity but a process in time, a process ordinarily so brief compared with historical time that it is unimportant, but which, when history is 'full' [i.e., marked by rapid social change], strongly influences the mutual adjustment of generations."[17] The birth cycle is the length of time between the birth of an individual and his procreation of another. The birth cycles of parents and their children cannot, by definition, overlap, and so each generation experiences a different segment of history. As a result, the historical time that family members share means something quite different to each generation.

A case in point is the difference in opinion over the Vietnam War. The adult population, remembering the threat posed by Nazi Germany and the subsequent development of a "containment policy," tends to see our involvement in Vietnam as a fight to contain communism. In the CBS survey already mentioned, two-thirds of the adults believed this to be true, whereas less than 13 percent of the college students so believed. For the college student, communism is not monolithic. Its popular front is often seen as part of a legitimate war of liberation. The majority of college students believe that the war is one of American Imperialism, while only a minority of adults support this view.[18]

DECELERATING RATE OF SOCIALIZATION

A generation gap, however, could not result simply from the differences in exposure to history, as Davis sees it. A second universal factor, the decelerating rate of socialization with increasing age, makes it difficult for "old dogs to learn new tricks." Because they have become committed to a point of view, adults find it increasingly difficult to give up cherished beliefs or to change old habits. Established techniques of coping with the world have proved satisfactory in the past and have, therefore, been assimilated as basic aspects of their identity. It is not that an adult cannot change quite basically, but that it costs him more in psychic energy to do so. If we further grant that human beings want to feel they have achieved a certain sense of closure—a

---

17. Kingsley Davis, "The Sociology of Parent-Youth Conflict," in Rose L. Coser (ed.), *Family: Its Structure and Function* (New York: St. Martin's, 1964), p. 457.
18. CBS News *op. cit.*

meaningful assimilation of the experiences of living—we see further the cost involved in giving up old ways. If the new way does not become assimilated adequately, a sense of estrangement may result.

RAPID SOCIAL CHANGE

Neither the birth cycle differential nor the decelerating rate of socialization would in itself necessarily cause conflict between generations. Indeed both are common to all societies, and some societies, such as that of Samoa, have very little intergenerational conflict.[19] A factor unique to industrial countries and those undergoing development is rapid social change. Each segment of the birth cycle is filled with events that significantly change the course of history and alter the life style of a people. For example, young people reaching the age of twenty-one in 1970 were born in 1949. Their parents, in all probability, were born around the mid-1920s. Before the children were born, the parents experienced the Great Depression around the age of six and the beginning of World War II when they were about fifteen. They might have had to fight in that war. The Atomic Age became a social reality in 1945—four years before our hypothetical young people were born. This second generation, on the other hand, came into a world that has remained in constant turmoil since they have been old enough to remember. Whereas their parents had to cope with the social problems resulting from the introduction of the automobile and the airplane, these young adults have had to cope with the social consequences of television, the Atomic Age, space travel, and the population explosion against the backdrop of constant United States involvement in foreign wars. An assumption in Davis's presentation is that the period of the birth cycle is particularly important because it is during this period that the most effective socialization takes place. In Erikson's scheme, the average maturing individual has established his basic identity after overcoming the threat of identity diffusion during adolescence and before he procreates. Although his identity is not "fixed" at this time, later changes are likely to be less dramatic.

Kenneth Keniston points out that rapid social change has rather different consequences in the United States because we place such a premium upon change for the sake of change—particularly change in the technological realm. "Probably more than any other society, we revere technological innovation, we seldom seek to limit its effect on other areas of society, and we have developed complex institutions to assure its persistence and acceleration."[20] Science is the major institution inducing change in our society, and Keniston asserts, "We value scientific innovation and technological change almost without reservation. Even when scientific discoveries make possible the total destruction of the world, we do not seriously question the value of such discoveries."[21] Change is institutionalized and proceeds at an ever accelerating rate in America, because we have developed complex institutions

19. See Margaret Mead, *Coming of Age in Samoa* (New York: Morrow, 1928).
20. Keniston *op. cit.*, p. 356.
21. *Ibid.*, p. 357.

to assure its persistence and have not developed any counter institutions or values that seriously restrict such change. "Lacking a feudal past, our values were from the first those most congenial to technology—a strong emphasis on getting things done, on practicality, on efficiency, on hard work, on rewards for achievement, not birth, and on treating all men according to the same universal rules."[22]

Finally, Keniston argues, we are peculiarly unwilling to control, limit, or guide the direction of institutional and social change. For the most part, "planning" is abhorrent to many Americans who see it in terms of its totalitarian or socialistic implications and who resist interference with "free enterprise," or the natural play of the market. "Given three abstract types of change—planned, imitative, and unguided—our own society most closely approximates the unguided type."[23]

In the 1970s momentum to push planning of some areas of environmental control into the political arena seems to be gathering. The ecological problems facing us as we continue to pollute the environment and overpopulate the earth cannot be evaded much longer; and more of us seem to be coming to this awareness. If this is so, then the wide-spread and well-coordinated limitation of industrial activity and technological innovation may become a part of the American way of life by the end of the seventies. It hasn't been a part of the American way of life in the past.

Lacking the willingness to plan or control social change, we are denied whatever increased accuracy in the prediction of the future might result from such efforts. As social changes that formerly would have spanned a century continue to occur within decades, the past grows more distant and the future becomes more uncertain. The present is the moment of history that is "relevant, immediate, and knowable." The exhortation of youth to live NOW is, therefore, also an exhortation to forget about the past and the future.

It is clear that not all youth are affected by the phenomenology of unrestricted technological change in the same way. As Keniston explains:

> The impact of social change is always very uneven, affecting some social strata more than others, and influencing some age groups more than others. The groups most affected are usually in elite or vanguard positions: those in roles of intellectual leadership usually initiate innovations and make the first psychological adaptations to them, integrating novelty with older values and institutions and providing in their persons models which exemplify techniques of adaptation to the new social order. Similarly, social change subjects different age groups to differing amounts of stress. Those least affected are those most outside the society, the very young and the very old; most affected are youths in the process of making a lifelong commitment to the future.[24]

22. *Ibid.,* p. 359.
23. *Ibid.,* p. 360.
24. *Ibid.,* pp. 361–62.

THE PROBLEM OF IDENTITY

The uncertainty of the future makes the achievement of an adequate identity more difficult and increasingly influenced by peers rather than parents. Such a view further points out the limitation of "socialization" as a totally adequate concept of personality development:

> If growing up were merely a matter of becoming "socialized," that is, of learning how to "fit into" society, it is hard to see how anyone could grow up at all in modern America, for the society into which young people will someday "fit" remains to be developed or even imagined.[25]

A more total view of the problem involved in growing up in America can be obtained from an understanding of what is meant by the concept of identity. If we approach the problem of the generation gap from the perspective of Erik Erikson, we can see that establishing an adult identity becomes a greater problem in America than in many Western countries. Certainly, unlike most folk cultures, Western cultures generally provide their growing young people with what Erikson calls a "psychosocial moratorium":

> . . . during which the individual, through free role experimentation, may find a niche in some section of his society, a niche which is firmly defined and yet seems to be uniquely made for him. In finding it, the young adult gains an assured sense of inner continuity and social sameness which will bridge what he was as a child and what he is about to become, and will reconcile his conception of himself and his community's recognition of him.[26]

What is normally achieved at the end of this moratorium is an *identity*, which —although continually reshaped throughout life—provides the first major integration of the adult personality.

Adolescence is viewed as a normative crisis during which the young adult is permitted to experiment with various adult roles without having to pay the consequences of full public responsibility. In primitive societies such as the Cheyenne, children do not experience such a moratorium. It is unnecessary because they are playing at their adult roles from their childhood on. The young Cheyenne hunter has a bow that is of good quality and differs only in size and strength from that of his father. He does not need to experiment with a variety of roles, because his society has already assigned him a role that will remain essentially the same for him as it was for his father. A young boy in America today, experimenting with a variety of roles, many of which his father knows nothing about, needs such a moratorium.

---

25. *Ibid.*, p. 371.
26. Erik H. Erikson, "The Problem of Ego Identity," *Journal of the American Psychoanalytic Association*, Vol. 4, No. 1 (1956), reprinted in Maurice Stein, Arthur J. Vedich, and David Manning White (eds.), *Identity and Anxiety* (Glencoe, Ill.: Free Press, 1960), p. 45.

Because of such role experimentation, inner fear and anxiety are heightened in our society. This is understandable because it is not guaranteed that a person will ever achieve an identity. He may instead suffer *identity diffusion*:

> *Identity diffusion . . . consists of a painfully heightened sense of isolation, a disengagement of the sense of inner continuity and sameness, a sense of overall ashamedness, an inability to derive a sense of accomplishment from any kind of activity; a feeling that life is happening to the individual rather than being lived by his initiative; a radically shortened time perspective; and finally a basic mistrust, which leaves it to the world, to society and indeed to psychiatry to prove that the patient does exist in a psychosocial sense; i.e., can count on an invitation to become himself.*[27]

Keniston's description of the youth at the turn of the sixties reminds one of this matter of identity diffusion. These youths seemed to be waiting for an invitation to become themselves. They were largely "other directed" in Reisman's usage. On the other hand, the assumption that adults' values are the only acceptable social values belies the capacity of the younger generation to provide adequate validation of their emerging identity.

The concept of identity as developed by Erikson and applied by Keniston does not satisfactorily handle the problem of a legitimate counter-culture, wherein a youth establishes his sense of identity on the basis of counter-values that do not provide him with a sense of sameness or continuity—for he is in rebellion—but do not qualify him for a psychiatrist's couch as an alternative. The extent to which modern youth can be described as belonging to a counter-culture of this sort is not known. Probably only a small number of young people fit into this way of life, and they have their most visible expression through the radical left. But the sympathies of youth support the values of this subculture if not its tactics.

INSTITUTIONAL PROBLEMS

Parental Roles: The increasing complexity of modern life makes the role of parents less clear. Parents are competing with other authorities in their children's eyes for adequate answers to everything from birth control and premarital sex to the proper future course of American foreign policy. Needless to say, parents are likely to be able to provide a smaller portion of the answers as the complexity of the social system increases. Youthful careers are not likely to be modeled after those of the parents because, among other things, so many alternatives are available to young people. The father may be a professional and not know anything at all about the profession his son aspires to; yet during his adolescence the son must make a significant choice in regard to professional career. Parents, particularly those in the upper-middle class, are confronted with conflicting advice from the experts on every aspect of child rearing and cannot fall back upon fully institutionalized "folk" patterns. In a relatively isolated conjugal family it is no wonder that

27. *Ibid.*, p. 57.

parents often feel themselves inadequate to the task of parenthood. This inadequacy is sometimes masked in the more general trend toward democracy and greater equality within the family structure.

Poor Integration: Increasing social complexity contributes to the heightening of parent-youth conflict in any country, but in America the complexity has even more effect because of our lack of an integrated approach to problems. The specialization of the professions and the aloofness of educational institutions have contributed to an inability to understand the problems facing our society, including the reform of the family as an institution. Many people know a great deal about small aspects of our problem, but few people know much about the relevance of the specialist's insights to specific social and political problems. There is, in short, little wisdom at hand upon which the "aware" youth can draw.

Mobility: A final variable, peculiar to industrial societies, that makes parent-youth conflict a problem is velocity of movement. American families are families on the move, as we have seen. This movement, both horizontal and vertical, means that the task of integrating and assimilating a highly complex, rapidly changing, diffuse culture, must take place in the context of rapidly changing interpersonal relationships. Fewer and fewer people have close friends upon whom they can depend for help and with whom they can talk about the things that trouble them. For example, youths talk a lot about sex, but the sharing of one's own inner feelings of sexual anxiety or inadequacy requires a trustworthy relationship, which is increasingly difficult to find. This lack of continuing, trustworthy adult relationships is at the basis of the accusation of youths that adults have lost sight of the human dimension—the sense of the joy of living and sharing with friends of the good life.

Parental Control: These factors (competing authorities, poor institutional integration, lack of trustworthy relationships) affect parental authority and mean in this dimension that parents are increasingly unable to socialize their children into their adult way of life. The problem of control is further aggravated by the fact that in industrial societies such as ours, parents and their children are frequently in direct competition for socioeconomic status and power. In the working class a son may quickly earn more than his father, even in the same type of job, and have greater job security because he is able to operate the machines more efficiently even though his father has had many more years of experience. In the professions, the expertise of the father may quickly become outdated. A son following in his father's footsteps, may, during his father's active lifetime, become a more widely recognized expert. These facts are more difficult to handle in a society in which socioeconomic status is given on the basis of achievement rather than ascription.

Finally, in Davis's view, the problem of parental control is further complicated by adults' concern for the sexual morality of the young coupled with our society's lingering taboo on sex as a "proper" topic of discussion between parent and child.

> *The extraordinary pre-occupation of modern parents with the sexual life of their adolescent offspring is easily understandable. . . . Sex is intrin-*

*sically involved in the family structure and is, therefore, of unusual sig-
nificance to family members qua family members. Offspring and parents
are not simply two persons who happen to live together; they are two
persons who happen to live together because of past sex relations between the parents. . . . In addition, since sexual behavior is connected
with the offspring's formation of a new family of his own, it is naturally
of concern to the parent. Finally, these factors taken in combination with
the delicacy of the authoritarian relation, the emotional intensity within
the small family, and the confusion of sex standards make it easy to explain the parental interest in adolescent sexuality. Yet, because sex is a
tabooed topic between parent and child, parental control must be indirect
and devious, which creates additional possibilities of conflict.*[28]

The subject of sexuality in the younger generation has been treated in more
detail in Chapter 12, "The Sexual Revolution." It is a major issue in the conflict we commonly label the "generation gap."

A breakdown in parental control is characterized by a breakdown in
communication which is often accompanied by hostility and aggression. This
phenomenon is explained by Kirkpatrick in terms of the "clash of inferiority
complexes":

*Youth feels inferior because it is untried and lacking in experience or
poise. There may be overcompensation for the inferiority of youth in an
adult world by aggression, brashness, grandiose expectations, and pseudo-
sophistication.*

*On the other hand, parents may feel inferior because of relative
lack of youthful attractiveness, declining sex powers, awareness of modest achievement, and the prospect of decreasing importance in the general scheme of things. Age without wisdom then may be glorified because age is that which parents have.*[29]

Several studies substantiate this sense of inferiority in both adolescents and
adults. Adolescents frequently express the belief that, as a group, they are
subject to condemnation, criticism, and general devaluation by adults. There
exists among adults a stereotype of adolescents as sloppy, irresponsible, unreliable, and inclined toward destructive and antisocial behavior. Adolescents
seem inclined to interpret their problems in terms of ego functions (autonomy, self-control, and judgment based on exploratory experience with adult
roles), whereas parents tend to see teen-age problems in terms of impulse
control for which they believe parental supervision and control are necessary.

SUMMARY

The factors common to all human societies of differential birth cycles and
decelerating rates of socialization with increasing age result in intrinsic uni-

---

28. Davis *op. cit.*, p. 470.
29. Clifford Kirkpatrick, *The Family as Process and Institution*, 2nd ed. (New York:
Ronald Press, 1963), p. 266. See also Albert Bandura and Richard H. Walters, *Adolescent
Aggression: A Study of the Influence of Child-Training Practices and Family Interrelations*
(New York: Ronald Press, 1959).

versal differences between parents and their children. In slowly changing societies these differences need not be the basis for parent-youth conflicts, but in rapidly changing societies personal segments of history are filled with significant events. Youths thus grow up in times that are quite different from those of their parents.

Our own situation is made even more conflict ridden by our unusual attitude toward social change for the sake of change. The partial bridge of one-way empathy (the parent being able to put himself in the youth's place because he was once a youth himself) is thus more difficult to traverse because the argument of the young, "It was not like this when you were growing up" is increasingly valid. Because things *were* different then, youths feel less necessity to conform to the advice given by their parents.

Parental authority is further undermined by competition from many other sources (experts of all sorts, other significant adults, the peer group) in a poorly integrated society where rapid mobility makes trustworthy relationships difficult to find and maintain. Not only are parents left largely on their own in our urban society, but also their children often lack enduring dependable relationships with friends. Finally, youth are often placed in competition with their parents for status, wealth, and self-esteem.

The result is a youth culture, a style of living evolving along different lines from the dominant cultural pattern. CBS discovered that:

> . . . *six out of ten young people in the United States say they want something different from life than their parents wanted. They don't necessarily want money or religion or status or conformity. They do want a far greater degree of sexual freedom and self expression. They don't easily accept adult society's reasons for fighting wars. They believe, as a majority, in the concept of civil disobedience.*[30]

Thus the stage is set for rebellion.

The Commune

With their increased disenchantment with the values and life style of their parents, a number of young people are turning to the commune in order to find in it a better way of life for themselves and (for some) their children. The number of communes in existence is difficult to determine because most fear persecution at the hands of local authorities and do not readily reveal their location and activities to the general public. The Carleton College *Collective Community Clearing House* lists 120 collective communities known to students of that school. These vary in style from the long-term religiously based communities of the Hutterites to the recently organized experimental and "hippie" communities that have not yet socialized a second generation. The term "commune" is sometimes applied to various forms of living arrangements that are not intended as permanent or long-term commitments. A *Washington Post* article indicates a growing number of communes in a local

30. CBS News *op. cit.*, p. 2.

enthusiast's assertion that "by the end of the year, there will be one hundred communes in Washington. We're finally getting it together in this city." The staff writer is less enthusiastic: "There are at least forty communes in the District of Columbia, most of them formed within the last year by refugees from the fractured hippie movement and other radicals of varying stripes. . . . Whatever their number, there is no doubt that they are on the increase as indicated by the formation of three new communes here in the past two weeks."[31]

Communes are organized around a number of different interests and objectives. In Washington, the most successful are integrated around commonly held vocational or political interests.

> . . . Communes have been organized around the activities of individual radical organizations (the SDS commune is an example); leather working . . . film making . . . helping teenage runaways . . . guerrilla theater . . . the underground press . . . rock music . . . light shows . . . a dissident religious movement . . . operation of a children's day-care center and a "liberated" preschool . . . Catholic antiwar activism . . . and an odd-jobs manpower pool and information service for the underground. . . .[32]

The life styles of these communes are also quite varied. One commentator observes that urban communes are "usually more ephemeral and more flamboyant than their rural counterparts, which in many cases have been founded by refugees from these urban communes, ousted from their quarters by city housing authorities."[33] Another comments that:

> . . . within the hippie subculture—mostly urban—not all are intelligent and promising. Some are mentally ill or not very bright; some are merely uninformed and seduced by the gross simplifications and absolute certainties that seem to result from even a rare use of LSD or a heavy use of marijuana. Mental hospitals throughout the United States report a startling drop in admissions of the two kinds of schizophrenics whose symptoms are similar to those of someone on an LSD trip; the young inappropriately laughing hebephrenics and frozenly posturing catatonics have gone to live among the hippies who tolerate them, thus discouraging their seeking psychiatric treatment.[34]

The hippie stance aims at a transvaluation of "square" values in the realm of the interpersonal, whereas the new left is more concerned with the public arena and politics. Both elements form communes of quite different character, but whatever the motivation, the fact of collective living as the expression of a revolution forces all to question seriously their interpersonal lives. The result is a wide variety of "experiments."

Some communes—a distinct minority in all probability—experiment in group marriage. Most, however, respect monogamous marriages within a much more permissive community-wide expression of affection. Some permit

31. *The Washington Post*, July 6, 1969.
32. *Loc. cit.*
33. Rita Hoffman, "The Commune—Newest Version of the American Dream," *Mademoiselle* (April 1970), 223.
34. June Bingham, "The Intelligent Square's Guide to Hippie Land," *The New York Times* (September 24, 1967); reprinted in Barash and Scourby (eds.), *op. cit.*, p. 384.

privacy, others opt for dormitory living. In some communes, drugs are important; in others, their use is minimal, and some forbid even the use of aspirin. The rural communes concentrate on the hard task of eking out a living off the land, while the urban communes haggle over the problems of getting working members to share their income with nonworking ones. The urban communes may be a place for working artists, whereas because of the difficulty of their tasks, rural communes are less likely to be so. Even in the latter, however, craftsmen often make goods to sell in order to provide the materials that cannot be produced by the commune itself. The patterns that are present in communal life are difficult to discern because there are so few studies of them and because of a general hostility toward perception of patterning in a sub-culture that prides itself on everyone's "doing his own thing." This section must depend, therefore, largely upon the observations of journalists writing for the popular press.

Comments of some communitarians seem significant and in some sense "representative" of certain types.[35] For example, Jess, twenty-seven, and Jeannie, twenty-three, state that their goal is "to create in our house a family that really means something, that is at the center of everything we do." Contending that "the idea of family has become unhappy, painful, and destructive in straight society," they moved into a house in Washington, and a married couple they knew joined them. Their house has attracted several other persons who found out about it through the local "Switchboard."[36] However, all but one of these other persons have left. The problems of the house center around money, property, and sex. In the first two areas the ideal is "from each according to his ability, to each according to his need." But this must be tempered by the realization that "you never know when someone is going to split." So the house operates on the principle of sharing equal portions of its income from all members. In the matter of sex, communalism is not practiced to the extent that it disrupts monogamous marriage. Such a commune attempts to replace the large extended family of former years with a community of nonkin who are unified by sharing, mutual aid, love, and trust.

Sometimes, however, the commune cannot harness its own resources very well, and the result is far from pleasant by middle-class standards. "We're not really into anything except our own heads," stated a nineteen-year-old female resident of one such house which has been occupied by over thirty residents in the past year (only six remain), "so it creates some problems like who does the chores." Another female member adds, "When the house started, it was structured and people had responsibility including cleaning up. . . . At the beginning it was very political. We were all into Resurrection City, and we did a lot of things together. But gradually the people changed and now we've gotten to the point where we're almost totally disorganized. . . . Everyone gets along pretty well [but] there are times when people in the house get chillingly apart." Two of the residents are "heads."[37]

Another Washington, D.C. commune consists of fifteen members includ-

35. These examples are taken from *The Washington Post*, July 6, 1969.
36. A "switchboard" is a commune dedicated to placing people in a commune seeking new members.
37. A "head" is someone who "trips"—short for "acid head."

ing children. They each contribute equal shares of the $667 a month that is required to operate the house; $185 of it goes to the rent. Members work at film-making, part-time jobs ("death jobs"),[38] and sell the "free" press to earn this money. It was formed by a hippie couple who moved to D.C. from a rural Colorado commune. John, who is twenty-eight, explains, "People use consumer goods in straight society to alleviate neuroses brought on by consumer orientation. You don't need an electric can opener, you know. I've found that there are only two property things in my whole life: my cello and a music source [a very sophisticated stereo system] in the commune living room." The house is structured "optimally" with one list of duties to be performed—"cooking and cleaning every eleven days":

> The options are no lists at all or getting into a situation where you have lists with every hour scheduled. I'm just not enough of a structure freak to put up with that. A really communal situation doesn't come from lists. What is important is integration. That's the word that flows through everything here: integration of education, of interpersonal relationships, of responsibility. Straight society is fragmented, everybody is in boxes and there is no integration, no flow. Everytime I see a co-op commune go down, it's because of overimmersion of the self on the part of the members—like in straight society. Marriage and children guard against that. Communes work if you understand what marriage and family are— not in the legal sense but in the spiritual sense. This place works because we have love and trust.[39]

The commune movement is linked with a rich tradition of experimental communities in America's past including Oneida, New Harmony, and Brook Farm. All of these past experiments failed, and I shall examine the reasons for the failure of one, Oneida, in Chapter 16. Most communes are only a few years old. Will they survive? How many youths live communally? What are the evaluations that can be reasonably made of their "experiments"? Will they have a lasting effect upon the American scene? None of these questions can be answered with certainty. The commune has not been adequately studied to date. The data are not in. Nevertheless, June Bingham cogently summarizes some of the values of the alternate life style they represent:

> At a time when Organization Man and his wife have been clutching material possessions not only for health and comfort but for prestige and a kind of security, the hippies share their food, their pad, their guitars, and such cash as they earn or are given. They would agree with Joseph Wood Krutch that true security depends upon how much one can do without, and they are proud in their own instantaneous mobility. . . .
>
> At a time when the American divorce rate is one out of four marriages (in California, one out of two), the hippies point to square hypocrisy in the sphere of sex. Many adults who have preached virginity before marriage and fidelity after it have practiced neither. . . .
>
> At a time when the "nuclear family," just two parents and their children, often must because of the father's job move away from grandpar-

---

38. A "death job" is a job that is totally lacking in intrinsic reward. It provides income only.
39. *The Washington Post*, July 6, 1969.

ents, uncles, and aunts and cousins, the hippies have established a form of the "extended family" in their pads. . . .

At a time when many squares assume that there has been no historic mutation, that nuclear warheads differ merely in quantity but not in quality from the fire raids of World War II, the hippies insist on historic discontinuity. They believe both in the infinite plasticity of human nature and also in themselves as a "new kind of human being."

Underneath the hippie refusal to sacrifice the present on the altar of the future is often a black despair which is sometimes relieved and sometimes accentuated by the drugs they take. Basically, they seem to be saying that only what they have already enjoyed cannot be taken from them. Perhaps, indeed, a hippie who faces up to the depth of his despair is more realistic than the square who blocks it out, who meticulously plans his life as if his personal future—and that of mankind—were not any longer more than a good bet. In a time of rapid change, the radical may turn out to be more solidly grounded than the stand-patter.[40]

Such counter-tendencies, however successfully they are carried out by young people, deserve the careful consideration of us all. In such efforts indeed may be the recovery of a sense of humanity though the problems faced in such ventures are not new, the "solutions" presented seem oversimplified, and the risk run by all quite high.

Summary

While the term "generation gap" is widely applied to conflicts between youth and adults in our time it is clear that the conflict does not break down simply along generational lines. It is expressed within generations as well. College educated youths, largely from middle-class families, are most likely to differ with their parents over how life should be lived. College-age youth with only a high-school education are much more likely to agree with the values of the older generation. The adult generation is also split, with many adults siding with the younger generation on issues such as Vietnam, inequality, sexual permissiveness, and even drugs.

Nevertheless, an intergenerational conflict does exist. A generation gap is much more likely to occur in industrial societies because the differences between youths and adults that are found in all cultures are intensified by rapid change, poor integration, high mobility, competing authorities, and the fact that youth are often placed in direct competition with their parents for jobs and social status. Our own society increases the intergenerational conflict further by its unwillingness to attempt the broad-scale, long-range rational planning of its development.

Perhaps the most dramatic expression of the generation gap is the commune movement wherein there is much experimentation in altering the character of the family and the definitions of sex roles. It is too soon to tell how successful these intentional communities are, or if they will have a lasting effect upon American family norms.

40.   June Bingham *op. cit.*, pp. 387–88.

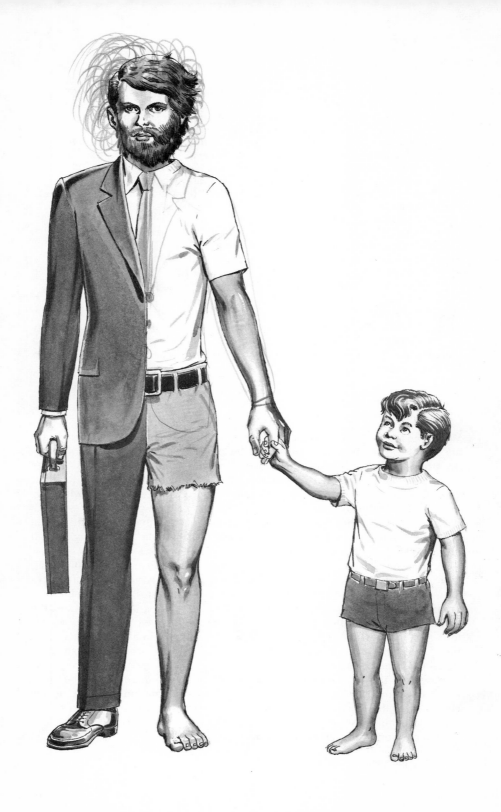

14. Careers or the Good Life

*If you have two loaves of bread, sell one
and buy a white Chrysanthemum for your soul.*

CHINESE PROVERB

One of the most powerful factors affecting family life in America is the changing demands of the job. The way a person goes about earning a living affects the way in which he lives in a family, as I have suggested in Chapter 6. I now want to look more closely at the process of industrialization and its effect on the family as well as the effect of the family on that process. This latter effect is much less well documented.

The transition from rural to urban residence for a large segment of our population came about because agriculture became mechanized, automated, and open to a whole array of scientific advances. One man on the farm could support over ten in the city. Concomitantly, laborers were not needed in large numbers on the farm, and so families left the small towns and farms and sought work in the city.

The character of the jobs that are needed in the city has also changed. From the period of time shortly before the turn of the century when large numbers of unskilled workers were needed in nonautomated industrial plants to our present condition of increasing cybernation, the general tendency has been to replace unskilled jobs with machines and demand more skills of those remaining in the labor force. This means a need for more education and training. The technical knowledge exists to make this process of replacement of men by hardware feasible up through the middle-management levels of industry, but it is unlikely that such widespread replacement will occur. Nevertheless, men are finding it increasingly difficult to think of themselves in terms of an occupational category, and their families often must face changes in income and residence—as well as self-image—as a result of the kind of work that the head of the household must perform.

The nuclear family and the alienation of the worker in the United States are directly attributable to industrialization and its concomitants. In Chapter 6 it was suggested that the strength of the nuclear family's bond to its kinship network varies by socioeconomic class. In this chapter I will examine the effects of industrialization on middle- and working-class families as they face the changing requirements of earning a living and simultaneously struggle to remain in touch with those whom they love. The demands of the job and the demands of the home are quite frequently in conflict with one another.

Urbanization and Family Life Styles

Talcott Parsons asserts that the middle-class family has become relatively cut off from its kinship network in the United States and has suffered a loss of function as secondary institutions have taken over economic, religious, political, and educational functions once reserved for the family.[1] Parsons speaks from a comparative point of view where there can be no question but that the extended family of folk societies was more functional. I now want to examine Parsons' position more closely and compare it with the views of his opponents: Is the nuclear family in America really more isolated? What does this mean concretely?

1. Talcott Parsons and Robert F. Bales, *Family, Socialization and Interaction Process* (New York: Free Press, 1955), pp. 9–10.

PARSONS' ISOLATED CONJUGAL FAMILY

In Parsons' view,

> . . . *Members of the nuclear family, consisting of parents and their still dependent children, ordinarily occupy a separate dwelling not shared with members of the family of orientation of either spouse, and . . . this household is in the typical case economically independent, subsisting in the first instance from the occupational earnings of the husband-father. . . . Relations to the family of orientation are by no means broken . . . they are attentuated.*[2]

Parsons' position asserts essentially that the extended family, with its strong emphasis on ascription, particularism, and diffuseness, conflicts with the demands of the industrial labor force which place a premium on mobility and achievement. The family, seen as the dependent variable, is modified by the stronger pressures of industrialization and urbanization from an essentially consanguine form of family to an essentially conjugal one. Notice that Parsons does not assert above that the relations with the extended family are severed—they are "attentuated" as a result of the nuclear or conjugal family's increasing mobility. The classical Parsonian position further holds that there is a close fit between the conjugal family and the industrialized society.

MODIFIED EXTENDED FAMILY?

This classical position has been challenged. The extent to which the family is isolated has been shown to be less than many followers of Parsons' position assumed. Eugene Litwak, Marvin Sussman, and Lee Burchinal among others have written about the kinds of kinship relationships that are still functional in an industrialized society such as our own (phone contact, economic support, visiting on family occasions, etc.).[3] William Goode has demonstrated that in Japan and China the extended family is quite compatible with a high degree of industrialization.[4] Further, in the Japanese case at least, the conjugal family values preceded industrialization and in some measure encouraged it, rather than followed it. Sidney Greenfield has shown that in Barbados the small nuclear family exists as the predominant family type without either extensive industrialization or urbanization.[5] The small nuclear family does not seem to be necessarily related to industrialized society.

The research on the activation of the kinship network in the American middle- and working-class family also challenges the classical position. Mar-

2. *Ibid.*, p. 10.
3. Eugene Litwak, "Geographic Mobility and Extended Family Cohesion," *American Sociological Review* (June, 1960), 385–94. Marvin Sussman and Lee Burchinal, "Kin Family Network: Unheralded Structure in Current Conceptualizations of Family Functioning," *Marriage and Family Living* (August, 1962), 231–40.
4. William Goode, *World Revolution and Family Patterns* (New York: Free Press, 1963).
5. Sidney M. Greenfield, "Industrialization and the Family in Sociological Theory," *American Journal of Sociology*, Vol. 67 (November, 1961), 312–22.

vin Sussman concludes that mutual aid is characteristic of American urban families, that it takes many forms, that it is more widespread in the middle and lower class than assumed (the amount of aid—but not the proportion of families receiving aid—varying between classes), and that the financial assistance is generally from parents to their children and not the reverse. This aid is given most commonly during the first few years of married life.

Researchers contesting the isolated nuclear family position point out that difficulties in developing satisfactory primary relationships outside of the family increase the importance of family ties. These ties are activated in get-togethers and recreational activities which outrank friend contacts in the *preference* of most urban dwellers. Distance from kin, however, limits the actual amount of such contract. The extended family of urban dwellers most often assembles for family occasions such as weddings and funerals, but these should not be discounted in their effect upon family solidarity.

Urban family members frequently provide a number of services for fellow members including shopping, baby sitting, advice giving, accommodations while moving, and general supportive behavior. Assistance to the aged is expected and commonly practiced. Again distance from kin affects the services that can readily be provided. The point is, however, that such services are desired, expected, and frequently realized in practice.

Table 14–1 shows that the direction of assistance is most often from parent to children. Only in the case of help during illness is the direction of aid most likely to be reversed. Sibling assistance is much smaller by comparison, but the reciprocity seems to be much closer to an equal exchange.

In light of this investigation, Eugene Litwak has suggested that we use the phrase "modified extended family" rather than "isolated nuclear family" to describe the characteristic American family. If the base of one's comparison

TABLE 14–1
Direction of Assistance between Kin, by Major Forms of Help

Major forms of help and service	Direction of service network				
	Between respondent's family and related kin	From respondents to parents	From respondents to siblings	From parents to respondents	From siblings to respondents
Any form of help	93.3%	56.3%	47.6%	79.6%	44.8%
Help during illness	76.0	47.0	42.0	46.4	39.0
Financial aid	83.0	14.6	10.3	46.8	6.4
Care of children	46.8	4.0	29.5	20.5	10.8
Advice (personal and business)	31.8	2.0	3.0	26.5	4.5
Valuable gifts	22.0	3.4	2.3	17.6	3.4

Source: Marvin B. Sussman, "The Isolated Nuclear Family: Fact or Fiction," *Social Problems*, Vol. 6 (Spring 1959), 338.

Note: Totals do not add up to 100 percent because many families received more than one form of help.

is limited to American society, perhaps this would be an acceptable alternative. It is doubtful if the extended family ever existed in the United States in the same functional intensity that is characteristic of it in folk societies. I know of no time in our society's history during which the extended family exercised such all-pervasive control over the behavior of family members and constituted at the same time such a major element of the total social structure of a society as is true of the extended family in these societies. (In Chapter 5, I discussed some of the data on the colonial family that would tend to support this position.) By comparison with these, the American conjugal or nuclear family is certainly isolated. I personally feel that to acknowledge the attenuated nature of its kinship network is less misleading than to suggest that it at one time was embedded in a kinship network which had such control over its member as had the extended family in folk societies. This is, however, no great matter so long as the implicit assumptions do not cloud over the reality of kin relationships in America.

It is not difficult, given the above qualifications, to accept Litwak's conclusions that the extended kin family as a structure exists in modern urban America demonstrating that extended family relations are possible in an urban industrial society. In a society such as ours, propinquity is not necessary for these relationships to be maintained. Occupational mobility seems to be unhindered by the activities of the extended family, and in some cases it has been shown to be quite supportive.[6] This family, however, can in no sense be called a classical extended family, a structure that is clearly unsuited for modern society. At best it is a "modified" extended family.

With regard to the relationship between the conjugal or nuclear family and industrialization-urbanization, therefore, it appears that the latter are sufficient but not necessary conditions for the emergence of the conjugal family. John Edwards concludes on the basis of an examination of a number of empirical studies that "It seems most reasonable to conclude at this point in the study of familial change that industrialization, urbanization, and the family are independent factors which frequently interact."[7] Their mode of interaction is only roughly perceived, but the classical view of the emergence of the conjugal family as a result of industrialization is clearly untenable.

The Major Components of Parental Roles

THE BREADWINNER

Gross and Stone found that men tend to identify themselves by occupational categories while women prefer identification by family name. In our society a job title implies status, while a name ordinarily does not. A man who is a sociologist is assumed to have certain skills, abilities, and income. While con-

6. Ann Fisher et al. "The Occurrence of the Extended Family at the Origin of the Family of Procreation: A Developmental Approach to Negro Family Structure." Paper presented to the American Anthropological Association, Denver (November, 1965).
7. John N. Edwards, ed., *The Family and Change* (New York: Knopf, 1969), p. 18.

tinued contact may prove this assumption false, there is, nevertheless, social benefit to be derived from the original assumption.

Although Morris Zelditch has provided some support for the contention that men are generally assigned instrumental roles and women expressive ones in folk as well as industrial societies, there are no data to prove that such roles are biologically determined or culturally universal.[8] In our society it is assumed that the husband is the provider for and the wife the integrator of the family unless the performance of a particular couple demonstrates otherwise. Such "atypical" performances are more likely to occur in a deviant sub-culture or among the elite and artistic members of our society.

The experience of the husband-father on his job provides the basis for some important differences in the socialization of children in working- and middle-class families, as Kohn has shown. The husband's job is generally the major indicator of his own status as well as that of his family. His job requirements are more likely to be met than are his wife's preferences, particularly when the necessity to move forces a choice between a good job and a relatively comfortable home and familiar friends. The choice (in American middle- and lower-upper class families especially) is likely to be in favor of the move to a better job.

The Instrumental-Expressive Role: Leonard Benson points out that in all probability the instrumental-expressive dichotomy is less a dichotomy than originally thought. Both men and women have instrumental as well as expressive dimensions, but they are usually manifested in appropriate sex-specific configurations. The mother is instrumental in "looking out for" her children; the father is expressive in his paternal role. The fact, however, that the father typically exercises the behaviors appropriate to both roles, being primarily instrumental on the job and expressive in his domestic relations, means that he is more likely to experience a conflict between his instrumental and his expressive demands than is his wife who behaves in both her instrumental and expressive modes toward more or less the same configuration of persons.[9]

Philip Slater further points out a basic antipathy between instrumentalism and expressiveness and asserts that the "human limitations of role differentiation" prohibit a person's cultivating *both*. Although the woman is more expressive *and* more instrumental than the father vis-à-vis the children, the father is more instrumental over all and is expected to combine subtly the elements of instrumentality and expressiveness, while his wife ordinarily is not.

In general, expressiveness is characterized by a basic tendency to please others, to be sensitive to their needs, and to respond in a way that reduces tensions between persons in their relationships. Pleasurable responses to one's efforts further motivate one to please others. In contrast, the instrumental

8. Morris Zelditch, "Role Differentiation in the Nuclear Family: A Comparative Study," in Parsons and Bales *op. cit.*, pp. 307–52.
9. Leonard Benson, *Fatherhood: A Sociological Perspective* (New York: Random House, 1968), pp. 28 ff.

concern is goal directed and encourages inattentiveness to interpersonal conflict and tension. In small groups persons who take over the role of task
leader often generate a great deal of conflict between group members in
their efforts "to get the job done." They increase the need for a complementary role of tension reducer or sociometric star who specializes in back
patting, conviviality, and helpful advice. Instrumentality is thus perceived as
an *adaptive function*, while expressiveness is considered to be basically an
integrative function. Occasionally a person is able to assume both roles in
small groups satisfactorily and becomes both the task leader and the sociometric star, but such performances are rare. The normal course is to specialize in one of two rather antithetical lines of role differentiation.

Middle-Class Coping Strategies: In upper-middle-class families, where the
success syndrome is most manifest, the conscientious husband-father is frequently presented with a painful dilemma. The demands of his job for his
time and talents and the demands of his family cannot both be satisfactorily
met. To be a success both as a father and as a provider is perceived as impossible. Lee Rainwater postulates that the middle-class American typically
utilizes two strategies for coping with his social environment: the "career"
strategy and the "good life" strategy.

Although a few can combine these strategies and although many utilize
both strategies at one time or another, most men perceive of them as alternatives. Like the Organization Man, these men opt for togetherness and immo-
bility at the expense of their careers, or they sacrifice their family life for job
advancement.

If the latter is their option, their marriage becomes what Cuber and
Harroff have described as "utilitarian." In such a relationship there is little
intrinsic reward or pleasure to be found in the companionship of spouses,
and at best home life becomes a more or less comfortable routine with little
growth in interpersonal relations. If the good life is the choice, it does not
follow that a vital relationship will obtain between husband and wife, because the American emphasis upon material comfort plays too large a role in
our common definitions of the good life, but a greater possibility for a vital
relationship exists. In either case, the husband's choice vis-à-vis his career
is the critical factor. It is the necessary but not sufficient condition for the existence of a vital relationship between himself and his wife.

If such a choice is conceived of as a purely personal one, the irony of
the American professional's career choice would not be apparent. In many
cases, however, it is *society* that requires the sacrifice of time and talent at
the expense, if necessary, of everything else in a professional's life. Without
dedicated professionals our complex system would collapse or destroy itself,
and yet with the necessity of such dedication come the unintended consequences of the corporation widow and the doctor's son whose personal happiness and development might well be reduced because of the needs of an
advanced technological society.

Although the provider role has traditionally been the man's, the recent resurgence of feminism in America has demonstrated that the career option is playing an increasingly important part in the lives of women—again primarily those of the middle class.

WOMEN'S CONTINUING QUEST FOR EQUALITY

Women have come to see job equality as quite central to their quest for social equality. However, compared with many other countries, America has always been a "paradise for women." The demand of colonial communities for the full services of all persons in order first to survive the hard winters of New England and then to push westward the ever expanding frontier meant that women and their work were critically necessary. The frontier wife's contribution to the development of the homestead was certainly on a par with that of her husband. Furthermore, when the frontier reached the West Coast, there was a critical shortage of women. The privileges granted to women in states where suffrage was open to them before the close of the century (Wyoming, 1869, and Utah, 1870) and Oregon's law of 1850 permitting women to own land can be attributed to the premium placed upon women as a result of their scarcity. In Colorado, at one time, there was only one woman for every twenty men. In California there were three men for every woman as late as 1865.[10] To their high value as labor was thus added a premium on their value as companions that was maximized by virtue of their scarcity.

And yet the fact remains that, valuable as they were, women were thought of, even in the early days of our nation, as primarily homebodies. While working women have always been a part of the American scene, they have always been in the decided minority. (In 1960 they constituted 32 percent, in 1969 36.2 percent of the working force; it is estimated they will comprise 36.9 percent by 1985.[11]) Women have been most rewarded—in terms of the approved norms governing the female role—for those activities associated with homemaking and child rearing. It was, after all, the woman who bore the large families of early America and often died before her husband in the process.

Historical Sketch: Although the rights of women were in all probability greater in early America than they were throughout most of Europe, the feminist movement really could not have caught hold had it not been for the industrial revolution. Carl Degler writes: "It was the industrial revolution that provided the impetus to women's aspirations for equality of opportunity; it was the industrial revolution that carried through the first stage in the changing position of women—the removal of legal and customary barriers to women's full participation in the activities of the world."[12]

10. Carl N. Degler, "Revolution Without Ideology: The Changing Place of Women in America," *Daedalus* Vol. 93, No. 2 (Spring, 1964). Quoted in Meyer Barash and Alice Scourby, *Marriage and the Family*, (New York: Random House, 1970), p. 310.

11. U.S. Bureau of the Census, *Statistical Abstracts* (Washington, D.C.: U.S.G.P.O., 1970), p. 214.

12. Degler *op. cit.*, p. 311.

At first the effect of the industrial revolution was to change the character and location of the husband's work. Whereas men and women often had been co-workers on the homestead prior to the nineteenth century, with the coming of the machine the work of men was increasingly away from home in the factory and the work of women assigned a more fixed relationship to the home. While prior to industrialization there was a certain overlap in the work of men and women, after the industrial revolution men and women were more likely to be performing quite different tasks. By the mid-nineteenth century, the bulk of the labor force was male.[13] Women who worked at home were not considered to be in the labor force, but were "only housewives."

However, the same industrialization that separated the home from the job and made men's work increasingly divergent from women's also created opportunities for women to work away from the home, but only in certain acceptable jobs—secretaries, typists, nurses, and the like—jobs generally requiring a low level of skill and professional training. With few exceptions, the professions remained predominantly the domain of men. Nevertheless, the opportunity to become financially independent provided by the creation of jobs away from the home gave women a major lever with which to pry for equal status.

Understandably, the first target of such striving for equality was the law. Indeed, John Stuart Mill's essay on "The Subjugation of Women," written in 1869, focused on two major dimensions of equality—the extension of suffrage to women and the elimination of their legal subordination to their husbands. In America these goals were largely realized by the end of the 1920s.

If industrialization provided the opportunity for women to be employed outside the home, then *war* increased the likelihood that they would be so employed. Both World War I and II brought large numbers of women into the labor force. Twice as many women entered the labor force during the decade of the twenties than were there in the previous decade.[14]

It was also in the twenties that women began to feel a new social freedom. For the first time it was permissible for both sexes to smoke and drink in public, and that which we have referred to as a "sexual revolution" in Chapter 12, can be called just as properly a revolution in the status of women. It has been said that during the 1920s, for the first time "middle-class men carried on their extramarital affairs with women of their own social class instead of with cooks, maids, and prostitutes."[15] The feminist of the 1920s sought equality in marriage as a voluntary contract between partners. Largely as a result of this concept of the "new marriage" the divorce rate rapidly increased (it was over 50·percent higher in 1920 than it had been in 1910). Further, two-thirds of the divorces in the 1920s were initiated by women.[16]

The overall effect of World War I, however, was not to bring a large number of women into the permanent labor force. In 1920 there were only

---

13. *Ibid.*, p. 312.
14. *Ibid.*, p. 314.
15. *Ibid.*, p. 315.
16. *Ibid.*, p. 316.

800 thousand more women working than there were in 1910.[17] New occupations were opened (e.g. elevator operator, theater usher) but some (e.g. street car conductor) rapidly returned to the male domain after the war. The depression further contributed to the problems of working women.

The effects of World War II were more dramatic. Almost 4 million additional women were brought into the labor force.[18] After 1945, the female labor force continued to increase. By 1966, 40.3 percent of the noninstitutionalized female population above the age of sixteen was in the labor force. They were employed, however, predominantly in such categories as clerical and kindred workers (32.1 percent), service workers (23.7 percent), and operatives and kindred workers (15.4 percent). That is, they worked as typists, secretaries, clerks, machine operators, sales girls, and car hops. 13.2 percent of the working women were professionally employed in 1966, and only 4.4 percent were managers.[19] In these jobs, furthermore, women are generally paid less than men comparably employed and they generally suffer a greater risk of unemployment.

Despite the employment of over 27 million women, the feminist movement has only recently begun to show signs of recovering from a long postwar slump. Alice Rossi, for example, could write in 1964:

> *In the decades since 1920 [the momentum for sex equality] has gradually slackened, until by the 1960s American society has been losing rather than gaining ground in the growth toward sex equality. . . . There is no overt antifeminism in our society in 1964, not because sex equality has been achieved but because there is practically no feminist spark left among American women.*[20]

Her explanation as to why feminism declined depends largely upon a recognition of the limitations of law as an agent of change, a reassessment of the power of our taken-for-granted style of life or culture, and a critique of the role of social scientists and the educational elite. At the same time that women have had increasing opportunity to work outside the home as a result of the generally expanding equality, the nucleation and isolation of the family and the reduction of the drudgery associated with housework have made motherhood a full-time career for the first time in human history. So also, since World War II feminists have not been able to link their efforts successfully with other reform movements as they had done in the early decades of the century. Finally, the continued acceptance even among social scientists of the assessment of feminine nature as "naturally" nurturant and expressive as opposed to the definition of the masculine role as instrumental and active has made it difficult for middle-class girls to be socialized in such a manner

---

17. *Ibid.*, p. 317.
18. *Ibid.*, p. 318.
19. United States Department of Labor, *Statistical Tables on Manpower: A Reprint from the 1967 Manpower Report* (Washington, D.C.: United States Department of Labor's Manpower Administration, 1967), p. 211.
20. Alice Rossi, "Equality Between the Sexes: An Immodest Proposal," *Daedalus* Vol. 93, No. 2 (Spring 1964). Quoted in Barash and Sourby *op. cit.*, pp. 362–63.

that they can be effective competitors in a man's world. ". . . Intellectually aggressive women or tender expressive men are seen as deviants showing signs of 'role conflict,' 'role confusion,' or neurotic disturbance. They are not seen as a promising indication of a desirable departure from traditional sex-role definitions."[21] Concomitantly women are commonly seen as persons who find complete fulfillment in their devotion to marriage and parenthood. When educated women have trouble adjusting to the routine of married life and seek a resolution from professional counselors, they are often led to believe that there is something wrong with them rather than with the opportunity structure of our society—a position deriving from our over reliance upon individualism and psychoanalysis:

> *The consequences of this acceptance of psychoanalytic ideas and conservatism in the social sciences have been twofold: first, the social sciences in the United States have contributed very little since the 1930s to any intellectual dialogue on sex equality as a goal or the ways of implementing that goal. Second, they have provided a quasi-scientific underpinning to educators, marriage counselors, mass media and advertising researchers, who together have partly created, and certainly reinforced the withdrawal of millions of young American women from the mainstream of thought and work in our society.*[22]

In the latter half of the sixties and the early seventies, however, a strong feminist movement has gained momentum, particularly among the upper-middle-class professional women who have sought to realize not only equality of opportunity in employment, but a true *social equality* which would redefine sex role and reassess the responsibility of women in the bearing of and caring for children. As such, the feminist movement involves a quite small portion of the American female population, and its appeal seems to be primarily to middle-class women who have found that the rewards of motherhood and housewifery are simply not enough. Usually these women are college graduates. Even though the present base of the movement seems to be narrow and its objectives diffuse, its critique of the role of women and its assessment of the necessary changes in family life are valid. It will undoubtedly have an effect on the character of at least the upper-middle-class family of the future.

What Does It Take To Make Women Equal? A common thread running through the women's liberation movement is the notion that women must be as free as men to pursue a career outside the home. There are women who maintain that they prefer the home to a career outside, because they feel that the role of mother and housewife is sufficiently rewarding and fulfilling. They fit the traditional American ideal of how women should arrange their lives. On the other hand, some of these women might change their minds once

---

21. *Ibid.*, p. 267.
22. *Ibid.*, p. 269. See also Betty Friedan, *The Feminine Mystique* (New York: Norton, 1963), Chapters 6 and 7; and E. E. LeMasters, *Parents in Modern America* (Homewood, Ill.: Dorsey, 1970), Chapter 7.

the alternative of an outside career were truly equally available to them, that is, if such an alternative would be prescribed in the mores, rewarded equitably in dollars and cents, and were open enough so that women would not find themselves confined to a relatively few professions. Clearly, for this to occur women must be relieved of some of the responsibility now assigned to them in their domestic role, especially the care of children.

At present women work most often to supplement their husbands' incomes or to provide the sole income for their household. They have jobs, not careers. Figure 14–1 shows that more families today have two wage earners than at any time in recent history. Over one-third of all mothers with children under eighteen are working. Mothers tend more often to work when their children are in school. Widows, divorcees, and wives with husbands absent are understandably more likely to be employed than the married woman with her husband at home. The tendency for women to work de-

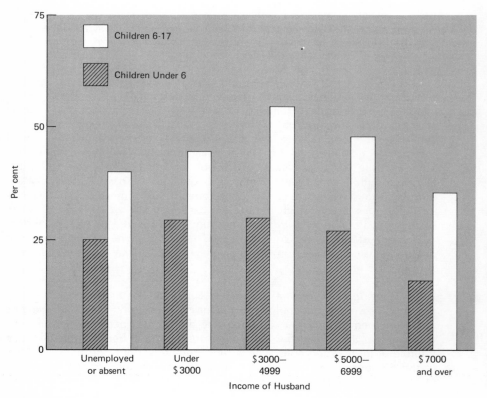

FIGURE 14–1

Percentage of mothers working, by income of husband and age of children. Adapted from The Nation's Youth *(U.S.G.P.O., 1968), Chart 18.*

creases as the husband's income increases above $3,000, regardless of the age of the dependent children. But it is precisely the wives in the higher income brackets who are more likely to have a college education and are more likely to feel unfulfilled by their domestic role. The fact that they do not enter the labor force may mean that they cannot justify it sufficiently on economic grounds and, further, that they have been socialized into accepting the notion that working mothers are bad for their children.

And yet the modern mother spends more time with her children on the average than have mothers at any other time in history. Despite the fact that socialization into adult roles is increasingly a nonfamily function shared with teachers, doctors, nurses, club leaders, and other skilled persons, the middle-class mother finds herself more attached to her children than any of her predecessors and apparently accepts motherhood as a full-time career. There is growing evidence that this is not all the good thing it is supposed to be. Mothers become neurotic, children over-dependent. It becomes apparent that the woman who must fulfill herself through the rearing of her children increasingly runs the risk of smothering them and jeopardizing her marriage at the same time.

Despite concern over working wives and mothers, there is no evidence of any negative effects on children that are directly traceable to maternal employment.[23] A major factor affecting children is how they are cared for when the mother is working. Figure 14–2 indicates that in 1965 children of working mothers were most often cared for by relatives. In 8 percent of the cases, the child cared for himself—the widely publicized "latch boy" with his key on a string around his neck being an example. In only 2 percent is some form of group care utilized. The majority of the mothers working during school hours only are those who live in families with incomes over $10,000.

Research to date supports the contention that if a child is reared by a cold non-nurturant mother or is reared in an institution lacking warmth, he will probably have personality disturbances in later life. On the other hand, if the child shares the love of his mother with a warm surrogate or surrogates in a stable environment, it is probable that he will prosper at least as well as and potentially much better than the child reared more exclusively by his mother.[24]

Alice Rossi suggests that, given the proper selection and training, a number of older women without children of their own could be productively put to work as beneficial mother surrogates to the children of mothers who want to have a career. A course in "practical mothering" could refresh them if they were once mothers themselves or acquaint them with the problems of child care in sufficient detail that they could cope with it on a part-time basis. More hopefully, however, day-care centers, perhaps sponsored by universities, could provide the major source of child care for a community. Such centers could be publicly supported and equipped to hire adequately trained personnel and could procure the best equipment at a modest cost.

23. *Rossi op. cit.,* p. 273.
24. *Ibid.,* p. 275. See also the discussion of the Kibbutzim in Chapter 16.

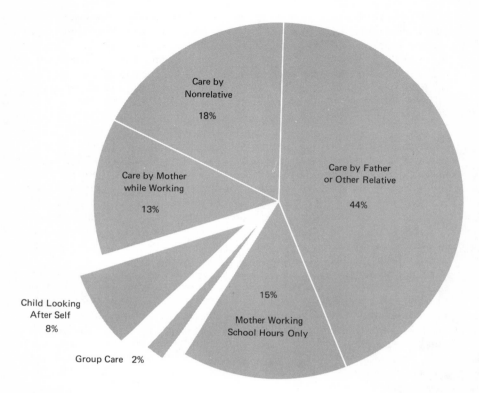

FIGURE 14–2
Allocation of child care by working mothers. Adapted from The
Nation's Youth *(U.S.G.P.O., 1969), Chart 19.*

Given proper day-care centers, Rossi believes, it would be possible for
the working mother to have two children and spend only a year away from
her career. This would make her quite competitive with male professionals,
many of whom are granted leaves of absence because they are considered
beneficial to the career in the long run.

A second pattern that must be altered, in Rossi's view, is the dramatic
separation of the home from the job that occurs when the husband must
commute from suburb to city. The inability of the husband and wife to easily
share friends known to the husband through his job, the frequent absence
of the husband from the family at times of special importance such as a
child's birthday party, and the absence of the father generally from the home
increase the differences between husband and wife at a time when there
should be greater reciprocity in the conjugal role. The father must also be returned to the family (mother deprivation vs. father absence). His presence
will help to compensate for the mother's absence should she decide upon a

career. In America it is difficult for the suburban woman who has assumed the role of spending the income to move to a productive role in the labor force. Swedish suburbs provide women greater freedom.

> *That Swedish women find work and home easier to combine than American women is closely related to the fact that Sweden avoided the sprawling suburban development in its post-war housing expansion. The emphasis in Swedish housing has been on inner-city housing improvement. With home close to diversified services for schooling, child care, household help and places of work, it has been much easier in Sweden than in the United States to draw married women into the labor force and keep them there.*[25]

A final alteration in family life style that must take place before women will have achieved equality with men is that men and women must be mutually able to perform a much wider range of tasks around the home. A wife must be able to make minor repairs, a husband must be able to feed and change the baby, etc. With the modern conjugal pair as much on their own as they are, such capacity to "pinch-hit" is an undoubted asset. The incapacitated husband who cannot manage the home when his wife is sick is a decided handicap to such nuclear family units.

Culture Against Man

We have seen how the demands of industry and the career concerns of middle-class parents have affected their domestic role performance. Now I will consider the impact of American technology upon the family in light of its capacity to set man against himself. Our industrial society has generated a culture that, in Jules Henry's words, is both for and against us. The career concerns discussed earlier are more applicable to the upper-middle-class family. What is now under consideration is much broader and much more value-laden, and it impinges upon all Americans, though no doubt in different ways.

> *Man has been so anxiously busy finding ways to feed himself and to protect himself against wild animals, and against the elements, and against other men, that in constructing society he has focused on these problems and has let even sex (not marriage) take care of itself. Within its formal legal institutions, no organized society has stipulated the procedures and guarantees for emotional gratification between husband and wife and between parents and children, but all societies stipulate the relationships of protection and support. The very efficiency of human beings in ordering relationships for the satisfaction of these external needs has resulted in the slighting of plans for the satisfaction of complex psychic needs; everywhere man has literally had to force from an otherwise efficient society the gratification of many of his inner needs. The*

25. *Ibid.*, p. 293.

*one-sided emphasis on survival, however, has provided man with an
evolutionary impulse, for in the effort to gratify himself emotionally and
to rid himself of emotional conflict with himself and his fellows, man
constantly works on his institutions and on himself and thus becomes self
changing. Meanwhile, the orientation of man toward survival, to the exclusion of other considerations has made society a grim place to live in,
and for the most part human society has been a place where, though
man has survived physically, he has died emotionally.*[26]

TECHNOLOGICAL DRIVENESS

As Henry views American society he is pained by the extent to which his own
society is turned against itself. He terms the force behind this alienation
technological driveness. This "driveness" has its roots in our achievement
strivings, competitiveness, profit seeking, mobility, quest for security, and
constant straining for a higher standard of living. Each of these dimensions of
our culture Henry defines as "drives" which are supported by an undergirding drive toward expansiveness. In contrast, our values—gentleness, kindli-
ness, generosity, frankness, simplicity, quietness, and capacity for love and
the like—are family centered. Clearly these virtues are rarely, if ever, requirements for a job or career in America, while the drives are constantly being
sought by employers. Drive is here used in the same sense as in the phrase,
"the outstanding characteristic of promotable executives is drive."[27]

Technological driveness distinguishes us from primitive cultures in that
these cultures had as their base the *fulfillment of basic needs.* We stress the
creation of needs. An expanding frontier, an expanding population that still
is seen as an asset to business in recent official statements, and extended
periods of foreign involvement helped our economy expand above the 4.5
percent annual increase in gross national product thought necessary to avoid
a recession. But there is the constant *fear* that our appetites will be assuaged
and our economy will level off. Thus the chief role of advertisement in a
technologically driven society is to create desire, to unhinge our impulse
control. "Create more desire" and "Thou shalt consume" become the first
two commandments of our way of life. The character of American society—
in its work-a-day world and its leisure hours—has always appeared to for-
eigners as off-balanced and frenzied.

At the heart of the mechanism for creating new desire is the idea of
"dynamic obsolescence." It was extolled by a president of General Motors
in a speech in Detroit in 1956:

*Continuing emphasis on change, on a better method and a better prod-
uct, in other words, on progress in technology, has been the major force
responsible for the growth and development of our country. Some call
this typical American progress "dynamic obsolescence" because it calls
for replacing the old with something new and better. From this process
of accelerating obsolescence by technological progress flow the benefits
we all share—more and better job opportunities, and advancing standard*

26. Jules Henry, *Culture Against Man* (New York: Random House, 1963), pp. 11–12.
27. *Ibid.,* p. 26.

> *of living—the entire forward march of civilization on the material side. . . .*
>
> *The promotion of the progress of science and the useful arts is of crucial importance . . . but there is a far more vital consideration. I refer to the importance of technological progress in assuring the continuance not only of American leadership in the free world, but of the democratic processes themselves.*[28]

This dynamic obsolescence in the spirit of "what is good for General Motors is good for the country" is so much a taken-for-granted aspect of our lives that we rarely deeply question its integrity. The development and production of the supersonic transport in the spirit of keeping America first among the nations of the world is a case in point. (Although the SST is officially dead at the time the book is in galley, the President has promised it will be built sooner or later.) That the social and economic costs far outweigh the calculable benefits often makes no difference in our determination to stay ahead. Our very way of life does indeed depend upon such ventures in dynamic obsolescence.

FAMILY VERSUS JOB

The family virtues are not only irrelevant in the job market, they are in truth *antithetical* to the *drives of industry*. The job, for many people in America, be they among the elite or the working class, diminishes the self. "The average American has learned to put in place of his inner self a high and rising standard of living, because technological driveness can survive as a cultural configuration only if the drive toward a higher standard of living becomes internalized."[29] Having renounced the needs of the self and one's job dream at work, Americans compensate by seeking fulfillment of their achievement drive in consumer behavior. Fixed on the job, one can try at home to keep up with the Joneses.

An indication of this lack of fulfillment on the job is the great mobility of the American labor force. More than half the American workers, for example, had two to four jobs in the years 1940 to 1949. Often feeling that they are as replaceable as the parts of the machines they operate, workers have little sense of loyalty to or identification with their occupation or their place of employment. Fringe benefits, a new boss, a few cents an hour pay increase, and the hope of greater job security can entice most younger workers away from their current jobs. Oldsters often stay on because of seniority rather than because of satisfaction. To be a success in the working class is to have job security. Opportunity for creative work and freedom of job selection is really open only to a few—the cultural maximizers who generate fashion and set new life styles via the mass media—who, even so, often find industry personally destructive and frequently leave it for the lesser paying jobs of academia.

Fear of personal obsolescence plagues the American labor force at all

28. Quoted in Henry *op. cit.*, pp. 22–23.
29. Henry *op. cit.*, p. 25.

levels of competence, especially with increasing age. Challenge has become "grim resolve" in a society that must wrestle values vital to the self from a system that seeks to destroy the personal. Thus the consumer behavior of American families is not at all free—it is driven; the patterns of relaxation not at all spontaneous—but contrived; and the quest for interpersonal encounter insatiable.

Because we are not at ease with ourselves, we carry the burden of our technological driveness into our home and into our quest for intimacy thus making that quest all the more difficult.

Henry has described his effort not as objective science but as "passionate ethnography," and so it is. Nevertheless, the tone he sets finds ample reverberation in our mass media, our literature, our leisure, and above all in our marketplace. With such a devaluation of personal values in the society at large, the task of the family to socialize, to personalize, and to provide companionship for its members is both critical and fraught with problems. The family too has been structured so that it is better able to meet its material needs for survival than to meet the emotional needs of its members.

It seems likely that things will get worse before they get better if the middle-class woman continues to diminish her responsibility for tension reduction in the home, if the working man continues to be satisfied with depersonalized rewards, if industry continues to find a market for its dynamic obsolescence, if business continues to prefer drive to virtue, and if our society in general opts for consumption rather than encounter.

Summary

The demands of the job have a great effect on family life. The family is uprooted and moved from place to place in response to the changing demands of industry or to the changing opportunities of a career. As a result, the character of the interaction between the conjugal or nuclear family and its kinship network has been modified so that by comparison to folk cultures the conjugal family in America is isolated indeed. Litwak has chosen to describe the American middle-class family as a modified extended family. It is clear, however, that the interdependence of the conjugal family and industrialization is not as close as the classical position assumes.

The husband-father is expected to be the principal breadwinner in the family, and this fact plus the separation of his place of work from his family has meant that the man, in particular, is likely to feel that he must choose between the demands of his job and the demands of his family. This can be seen as an option for the career, in Rainwater's term, or as an option for the good life. The latter is the necessary but not the sufficient condition for what Cuber and Harroff have called a vital relationship. Thus the demands of the job, by redefining the provider role so that it has increasingly become antithetical to the expressive needs of the family, have created tensions in the family.

Women, particularly those of the middle and upper classes, also are experiencing increasing strain as the status of their domestic role diminishes and they seek for social equality through job equality. As more women seek to fulfill themselves in a career so that motherhood ceases to become a full-time career for them, changes in the life style of the family must follow. Children must be taken care of by mother surrogates. The division of labor between the sexes must be increasingly less precise so that a greater interchange of activity is characteristic. The relative power of the husband will continue to diminish in all probability.

Finally, describing our culture as a technologically driven one, Jules Henry has pointed out that we have taken greater care in providing for our physical survival than for our emotional needs. The dynamism of the rat race makes the increasingly more important functions of the family (nurturance and companionship) more difficult to carry out. Cultural factors thus contribute to the tendency in our society for the demands of earning a living to frustrate the need for emotional fulfillment rather than increasing this fulfillment by providing material security.

15. Family Planning and Population Control

Doubling times in the underdeveloped countries range around twenty to thirty-five years. . . . Doubling times for the populations of the developed countries tend to be in the fifty to hundred year range. . . . There are some professional optimists around who like to greet every sign of dropping birth rates with wild pronouncements about the end of the population explosion. They are a little like a person, who after a low temperature of five below zero on December 21, interprets a low of only three below on December 22 as a cheery sign of approaching spring.

PAUL ERHLICH

The population explosion, like the threat of nuclear war, is one of the "persistent crises" of modern times. There is considerable debate over *how* populations should be controlled but little disagreement that they *should* be controlled in some way.[1] A common early effect of economic development is improved sanitation and disease control that results in a dramatic drop in the death rate while the birth rate remains high. If developing countries do not cope effectively with the problems of this demographic transition, they will not be able to provide adequate services for the dependent portion of their population, and famine, pestilence, and revolution are likely consequences.

For us in the United States the problem is somewhat different. We have already passed through the demographic transition and our rate of growth has begun to level off. We have the technology to feed our present population (if we ignore, for the moment, problems in the distribution of food that left about 10 million Americans malnourished in 1969), and we seem able to feed a much larger one in the future. The more indelicate matter of our inability to feed the *rest* of the starving world put aside, our population increase will contribute directly to our own problems of energy utilization, land use, and pollution. For us, the "population explosion" might more aptly be called an "urban explosion": many demographers argue that the more immediately critical factors pertain to population distribution and not to population per se.

Despite the "Chamber of Commerce mentality," population growth is not an unambiguous good any longer. Nor is life itself desirable under all conditions—an obvious truth that takes on new dimensions each day. Many value judgments enter into the question of what a desirable style of life is, and these color our sense of urgency in regard to what to do about population growth. These issues I will defer to the next section.

In this chapter I will look at the family in its replacement function from the perspective of family planning and its relation to population control. Clearly the family is the institution in our society that is charged with the responsibility of replacement. It does so through reproduction and socialization. It provides the major source of new members. For example, the nation's population rose 1 percent from 1969 to 1970 to a total of 204,351,000. That increase was possible because the 3,570,000 babies born in 1969 exceeded the number of deaths by 1,650,000 and because we had a net gain of 400,000 persons through immigration.[2] If the United States population continues to grow at the current rate, it will exceed 300,000,000 persons before the year 2010. Most of these 300,000,000 persons will undoubtedly be living in our already over-crowded, poorly serviced cities. Figure 15–1 shows the concentration of U.S. population in four major regions in 1960. A finer grained analysis would show that the suburban fringes of our cities are growing at a quite rapid rate while a few of our inner cities are undergoing a decline in population. The problems of controlling population migration are more complex than the problems of controlling population growth, and the former do not seem as clearly related to the family as a functioning unit of society. For

1. For a "nonalarmist" position on population see Dennis H. Wrong, "What the Census Will Show About Us in the Turbulent Sixties: Portrait of a Decade," *New York Times Magazine* (August 2, 1970), 22–30.
2. *Metropolitan Life Insurance Statistical Bulletin*, Vol. 51 (March 1970), 3.

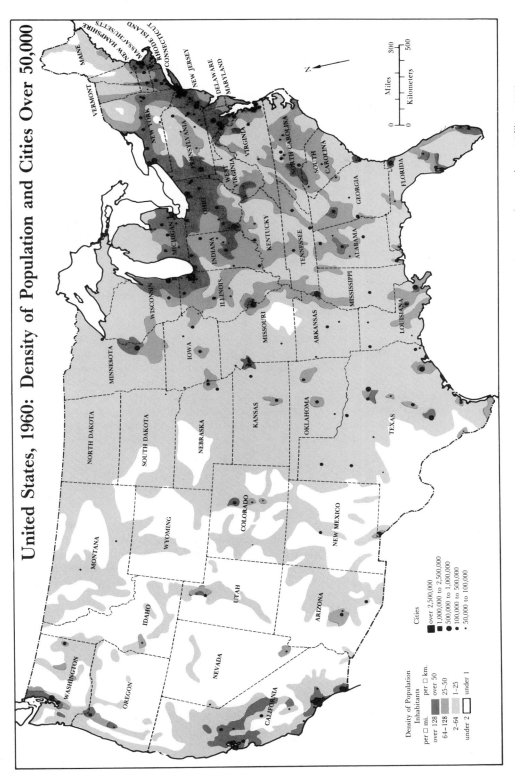

United States, 1960: Density of Population and Cities Over 50,000

FIGURE 15–1 From Lloyd Rodwin, Nations and Cities: A Comparison of Strategies For Urban Growth (Houghton-Mifflin, 1970).

Density of Population

Inhabitants	
per ☐ mi.	per ☐ km.
over 128	over 50
64–128	25–50
2–64	1–25
under 2	under 1

Cities

■ over 2,500,000
■ 1,000,000 to 2,500,000
● 500,000 to 1,000,000
● 100,000 to 500,000
• 50,000 to 100,000

Miles 300
Kilometers 500

these reasons I will focus upon what is apparently the lesser of the two problems—controlling population growth.

Family planning is gaining wide acceptance as a means of controlling our population growth. But how valid is this approach? Consider the fact that family planning will only control unwanted births when it is effective. And consider the number of couples who might want more children than would be desirable in order to maintain a zero rate of population growth.

Finally, in the last section I will examine briefly the implications of recent discoveries in the life sciences for the family. The ability to regulate the reproductive capacity of the human species so that males and females need not be *directly* involved in the reproduction of children has profound implications for family life, as books such as *The Second Genesis* suggest.[3] It is better to begin to speculate about these implications now before we have all of the necessary technology than to be startled and confused by such discoveries later on.

Growth Patterns of American Families

Even at the level of gross statistics the characteristics of American families have not remained static over our nation's history. The explanation for these changes is not totally adequate. On the other hand the data are particularly plentiful, especially over the past one hundred years. I will first examine trends in American fertility and mortality and the consequent rate of natural increase. Secondly, I will look at the changing pattern of family and household size. I will examine these data from the perspective of the family's reproductive function and how it is affected by factors "external" to the family.

REPRODUCTION AND THE FAMILY

The function of marriage, as I have argued in Chapter 4, is not so much the regulation of sex as it is the regulation of reproduction. Many societies around the world find nonmarital coitus quite acceptable, but almost all prohibit nonmarital reproduction. In some societies conception is encouraged since it is considered necessary in order to consummate the marriage. Sterility is often grounds for breaking the marriage contract. Some societies, such as Israel of the Old Testament, make allowances in such cases and permit the selection of another woman to bear children for the sterile wife. Generally speaking, children born to a married woman are considered to be her husband's—if his role as genitor is recognized by the society and he does not contest. The possibility that males can be sterile is a rather late notion to occur because of the widespread acceptance of male dominance. The social recognition that it is the male and not the female who gives birth to the child

3. Albert Rosenfeld, *The Second Genesis* (Englewood Cliffs, N.J.: Prentice-Hall, 1969).

in those societies practicing the *couvade* is further testimony to the effectiveness of male dominance.

Whatever the variation in sex role, whatever the provisions made in the case of sterility, whatever the acceptable—but not preferable—alternatives to marriage, the norms of almost all known societies prescribe that children *should be born to married persons* and, with few exceptions, should receive their basic socialization from their parents, particularly their mothers. The father's role is a sociological invention with greater variation in acceptable behavior. Normally, however, the father is an ancillary protector and provider to the basic dyad of his wife and her children.

In our society there is great pressure to enter into marriage and to have children. Children may frequently precede marriage, as in the case of ghetto Blacks, but the importance of marriage is not thereby minimized—it is simply more difficult to realize and maintain such a contract in the context of extreme deprivation and exclusion characteristic of black ghettoes. For our society the family is *the* institution charged with the responsibility of reproducing and socializing new members of our society even though it is assisted in the process of socialization and is sometimes not the major socializing agent. "Bastard" has had particularly unacceptable connotations throughout all of our history.

Figure 15–2 shows the number of children ever born to women of various age groups. In 1969 the number ever born to women between forty-five and forty-nine (those women who have ended or nearly ended their reproductive period) was 2,665 per 1,000. To replace the population at that time, it was estimated that every 1,000 women would have to produce 2,130 children. The women in this age group, therefore, exceeded the replacement rate by 535 offspring per 1,000 women. Women in the next three younger age groups have already exceeded the replacement rate. Women forty to forty-four have exceeded the replacement rate by 829 births, those thirty-five to thirty-nine by 928 births, and those thirty to thirty-four by 593 births. Undoubtedly these women will bear more children before they have completed their reproductive period, and thus we are well on our way to a population increase of 100,000,000 within the next forty years. On the other hand, women under thirty appear to have reduced their fertility rate. If such a reduction continues throughout their reproductive period, it is likely that the fertility rate will approach the replacement rate, and eventually a much lower rate of growth will be realized. This, however, cannot be positively concluded until after these women have passed their fertile period.

Figure 15–3 indicates that the crude birth rate (births per 1,000 females) is declining in the case of legitimate births (where the base is married females), and steadily increasing in the case of illegitimate births (where the base is unmarried females). It is clear that the legitimate birth rate is much more affected by the changes occurring in society—World War II, post-war affluence, improved contraception in the "pill." The illegitimate birth rate seems relatively unaffected by these events. Its steady increase suggests a much more basic redefinition of marriage and the family coupled with a steadily increasing difficulty in negotiating and maintaining marriage among

Children ever born
per 1000 women
(semi-logarithmic scale)

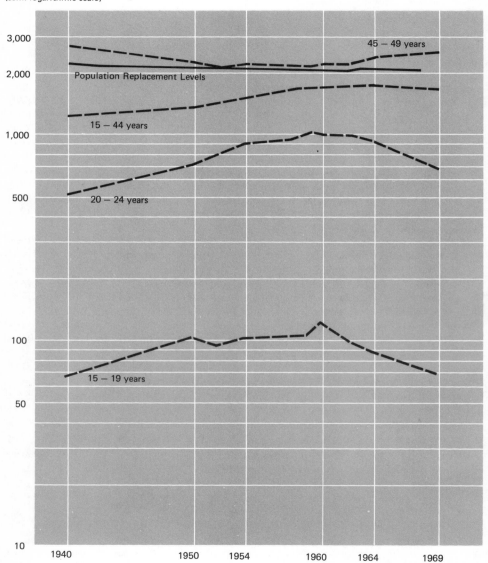

FIGURE 15–2
Children ever born per 1000 women, by age groups, 1940–1969. From
Current Population Reports *(U.S.G.P.O., 1969).*

the lower classes. In all classes, however, the *number* of legitimate births far exceeds the number of illegitimate births. The nuclear family remains the institution in which children *should* be born, and the vast majority of American children are in fact born in such a family.

TRENDS IN FERTILITY, MORTALITY, AND RATE OF NATURAL INCREASE

The birth rate is perhaps our best recorded social phenomena. We know a great deal about it descriptively, especially over the past hundred years. Despite our quite adequate accounts of what has happened, however, we do not fully understand the factors accounting for changes in the reproductive capacity of Americans.[4]

Our information on colonial America is scanty. We have assumed that at least until 1800 the birth rate was quite high in order to offset the high death rate, especially among infants and women in childbirth. Families were large (commonly over five children). The norms of Puritan New England and the demand for child labor encouraged large families. Children were economic assets, whether they were on the frontier or working in the cities.

Decreasing Fertility 1800 to 1936: From 1800 to 1936 there was a discernable downward trend in fertility. Figure 15–4 relates this downward trend in fertility to increasing urbanization. Explanations as to why the urban portion of our population has been generally unable to reproduce itself are varied. Commonly we assume that industrialization plays a significant role in changing the family from a unit of production to one of consumption. After the passage of child labor laws, children became economic liabilities in the city, and the norms assert that a family should not have more children than they can afford to rear. As the conception of the good life changes and material necessities increase (along with the amount of training generally required to achieve them), children become increasingly "expensive" for the urbanite. Concomitantly, it has been suggested that the stresses and strains of urban life, particularly among the upper classes, tend to reduce the frequency of intercourse and may have an effect upon fecundity. "A poor man's procreation is his recreation" would hold more firmly as an explanation of large families in the lower class were it not for the fact that there is reason to suspect that fecundity is reduced in these classes due to inadequate diet. Nevertheless, among the rural population and among the lower classes, many of whom are recent immigrants to the city, fertility rates are higher than among the urban upper classes.

The increasing employment of women also contributed to the decline in fertility, although, as we know from the experience of World War II, the employment of women is not necessarily correlated with declining fertility. Women in the labor force have fewer children than those not employed.

---

4. Discussion of these historical trends is found in Robert F. Winch, *The Modern Family*, rev. ed. (New York: Holt, Rinehart & Winston, 1969), pp. 190–200; Gerald R. Leslie, *The Family in Social Context* (New York: Oxford University Press, 1967), pp. 512–16.

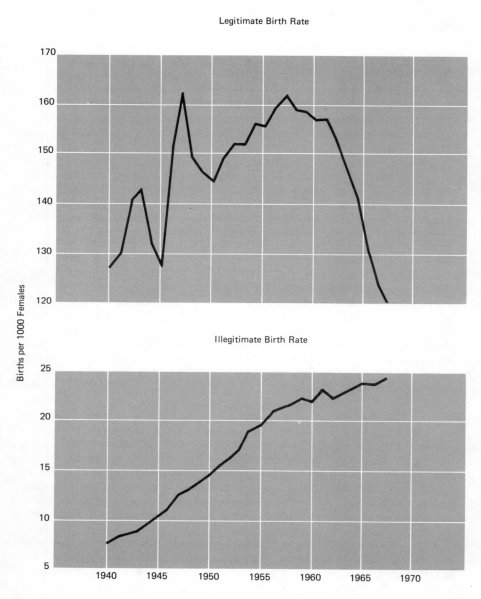

FIGURE 15–3
*A comparison of legitimate and illegitimate birth rates, 1940–1970.
From* Current Population Reports *(U.S.G.P.O., 1970).*

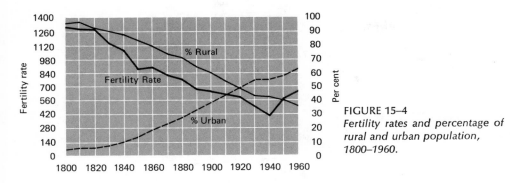

FIGURE 15–4
Fertility rates and percentage of rural and urban population, 1800–1960.

Aside from the actual time off required to give birth and to nurse the child, many arrangements can be made to free the mother for work without adversely affecting her parental role. Undoubtedly the redefinition of women's rights—which (particularly since the 1920s) has stressed the equality of opportunity for women on the job, talked down the assumed role of women as child-rearers, and sought to free as many as possible from the necessity to bear children so that ideally every child was wanted—has had an effect on urban fertility rates. Finally, freedom from the necessity to bear children is more obtainable in a society that has begun to develop effective contraceptives.

Another factor affecting fertility during this period of decline was the tendency to marry later as compared with colonial times. Women entering marriage later tend to have fewer children than those who marry younger. While the age at first marriage fell steadily over the period 1890 to 1959, it is doubtful whether the age at first marriage in the fifties was lower than in colonial days.[5] If true, the age at first marriage must have risen sharply before the end of the frontier. We have no direct evidence for this since these bits of data have not been accurately recorded for most of our history. If true, however, then that increase in age at first marriage would help account for the decline in fertility for a portion of the period 1890 to 1936.

In any event, the crude birth rate (number of births per thousand population) in 1871 was thirty-seven. By 1900 it had declined to twenty-nine, and by 1930 it was down to about nineteen—below the level of replacement. In the 1930s America was not fearing a population explosion, it was afraid that its population was not growing rapidly enough. Accordingly, welfare legislation (primarily Aid to Dependent Children) was initiated in the late 1930s in order to help overcome this feared deficit.

Increasing Fertility 1930 to 1960: Figure 15–5 illustrates the trend since 1936: a general increase until about 1957, a leveling off, and then a decline since

5. Winch *op. cit.,* p. 194.

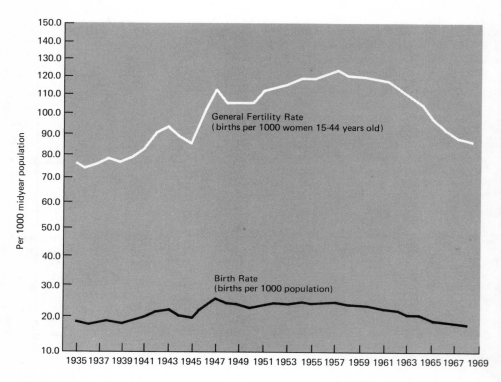

FIGURE 15–5
Annual birth and general fertility rates, 1935–1968. From Current
Population Reports *(U.S.G.P.O., 1969).*

1960. We are concerned here with the period of increasing fertility. Increasing fertility can be attributed to increasing affluence since the depression as more and more persons found jobs and married earlier. Although the number of working wives continued to increase, the increase was mainly in the forty-five to fifty-nine year old age group, those generally conceded to have completed their child bearing.

An increasing percentage of persons married, and an increasing number were fertile. Women were marrying earlier and generally having more children. World War II contributed to this in that it first had a depressing effect on fertility as men went off to war and marriages were postponed, and then it produced a "baby boom" when the men returned. Economically the nation was experiencing first a recovery from the depression, then a controlled economy of wartime, and finally a post-war boom. Over all it was a period of increasing economic security for increasing numbers of persons.

Declining Fertility Since 1960: As Figure 15–5 indicates, fertility has declined since 1960. Figure 15–2 suggests that this is primarily because of the women under thirty who have begun to reverse the trend toward larger families. In the 1960s Americans, particularly the younger ones, became aware of a great many social problems: poverty, persistent if undeclared war, inflation, and finally environmental pollution and the population explosion. America further became increasingly open to family planning as parents in the middle classes became highly conscious of the expense of providing the best for their children, and *quality* of life was an increasingly more important consideration than quantity.

Americans of the middle and upper classes are now effective users of contraceptive devices, but the evidence indicates that the average American still wants three to four children. This seems truer for those women over thirty if our inference about the lower fertility rates of those under thirty is correct. Whether there is in fact a persistent trend toward smaller families among the young remains to be seen, since these women have a number of years to go before they complete their child bearing. If there is such a trend, it seems reasonable to credit it in large part to a concern over too many children and an effective oral contraceptive. Undoubtedly among those aware of these problems, the widespread anxiety about modern living contributes to a reluctance to bring children into the world.

Focusing on the last two periods under consideration, Figure 15–6 shows that the death rate has remained amazingly constant over the period since World War II. Even that war did not affect it dramatically. Although the period of the great migrations has passed, the net immigration rate has experienced a very gradual increase since 1935, but is, nevertheless, quite low. Therefore, the net growth rate during this period is almost entirely a function of the birth rate. It rose rather sharply until 1947, remained relatively constant until 1960, and has declined since 1960. The fact that our rate of growth is declining, however, should not be construed to mean that we do not have a population problem. It may suggest that we are beginning to come to grips with the problem of expanding populations. But it must be remembered that the total number of persons in America is increasing steadily although at a now declining *rate of increase*. The nonwhite population is increasing faster than the white because its fertility rate is greater, although it too is now declining. Finally, the rate of growth in Standard Metropolitan Areas remains high.

The explanations commonly offered for the fluctuations in the fertility rate draw upon a number of factors. Human fertility is not simply the consequence of biological drives. Rather it reflects changes in the economy, state of the national security, advances in technology, religious conviction, race, and rural-urban residence.[6] At least these and other factors can be shown to

---

6. See particularly William Peterson, *Population*, 2nd ed. (New York: Macmillan, 1969), pp. 486–540; and Winch *op. cit.*, pp. 199–222.

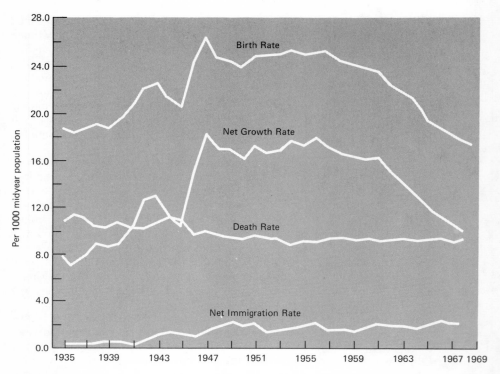

FIGURE 15–6
Annual rates of net population growth, births, deaths, and net immigration, 1935–1968. From Current Population Reports *(U.S.G.P.O., 1969).*

have a differential effect on the fertility rate. Kingsley Davis and Judith Blake have analyzed the several factors that impinge upon human conception in "Social Structure and Human Fertility."[7] It is clear from this article that the use or non-use of a contraceptive device is strongly influenced by many cultural and societal factors and that in itself such usage is not an effective means of population control. The decision to intervene in the reproductive process at the stage of conception is quite arbitrary and comes rather late in that process to be effective as a population control measure if people in a society want many more children than are necessary to replenish the population.

In a later section I ask, "Why do American's want three to four children?" Here I will consider the structural factors related to fertility.

7. Kingsley Davis and Judith Blake, "Social Structure and Human Fertility" in Rose L. Coser (ed.), *The Family: Its Structure and Function* (New York: St. Martin's, 1964), pp. 629–64.

SOCIAL STRUCTURE AND FERTILITY

In attempting to further the sociology of fertility, Davis and Blake suggest that the process of reproduction involves three necessary steps: (1) intercourse, (2) conception, and (3) gestation and parturition. At each of these three steps cultural factors affect the reproductive process. These factors are called "intermediate variables." Davis and Blake schematize them as follows:

I. Factors Affecting Exposure to Intercourse:
   Intercourse Variables.
   A. Those governing the formation and dissolution of unions in the reproductive period. A union is here defined as any heterosexual relationship in which either actual intercourse occurs or orgasm is produced for at least the male partner. Every society has a type of union (marriage) in which reproduction is expected, approved, and even enjoined. At the same time every society runs the risk of unions in which reproduction is condemned, either because they lack the legal form of marriage or because they violate one or more institutional taboos (incest, adultery, etc.).
      1. Age of entry into sexual unions.
      2. Permanent celibacy: proportion of women never entering sexual unions.
      3. Amount of reproductive period spent after or between unions.
         a. When unions are broken by divorce, separation, or desertion.
         b. When unions are broken by death of husband.
   B. Those governing exposure to intercourse within unions.
      4. Voluntary abstinence.
      5. Involuntary abstinence (from impotence, illness, unavoidable but temporary separations).
      6. Coital frequency (excluding periods of abstinence).

II. Factors Affecting Exposure to Conception:
    Conception Variables.
      7. Fecundity or infecundity, as affected by involuntary causes.
      8. Use or nonuse of contraception.
         a. By mechanical and chemical means.
         b. By other means (rhythm, withdrawal, various "perversions" etc.).

9. Fecundity or infecundity as affected by voluntary causes (sterilization, subincision, medical treatment etc.).

III. Factors Affecting Gestation and Successful Parturition: *Gestation Variables.*

10. Foetal mortality from involuntary causes.
11. Foetal mortality from voluntary causes.[8]

For some purposes it might be proper to include another variable—"Infanticide"—but ordinarily the practices associated with this variable do not affect the fertility rate. Rather, the replacement function of the family is affected by an assessment of the relative utility of the child after several months. Often, infanticide takes the form of simply restricting the food requirements so that unwanted children die of starvation over a long period of time. As such it is more properly conceptualized as a socialization variable. In any event such a category rarely applies to births in the United States.

In our discussion of the fertility trend in the United States, many of these socio-structural factors were considered. Relevant comparative material has been presented in Chapter 4. Many of these factors affect the fertility of a society as the unintended consequences of cherished institutions. Thus, in the United States, the Kinsey data suggesting that the "vast majority of premarital pregnancies terminate in induced abortion" testifies to the value we place on bearing children inside of marriage.

Nevertheless, although social-structural factors do intervene at various points in the reproductive process in order to affect the fertility rate, we have concentrated our recent effort largely in the area of contraception. Planned Parenthood has been a major factor in the dissemination of information about contraceptives and a major advocate of their use. Recently much pressure has been placed on the federal government by those who advocate the views of Planned Parenthood to make contraceptives available to the poor in particular in order to control the population growth. The fact that Planned Parenthood clinics have been generally unsuccessful in reaching the poor seems to pass unnoticed in the rush to do something about the population problem. This practical matter aside, we must now consider how effective a Planned Parenthood approach is likely to be as a means of controlling population growth.

It is obvious, first of all, that the ideology behind Planned Parenthood stresses freedom of choice—the freedom to have whatever number of children when they are wanted being reserved to parents and not the state, the church, or any other organization. Clearly such a philosophy does not help the problem of too many *wanted* births, even though the small family is a professed virtue among family planners. Many who criticize the position, however, feel that the simple advocacy of the virtue of the small family is not enough to counter the strong pronatalism that is built into our society.

8. *Ibid.*, pp. 630–31.

The Birth Control Movement and Its Opponents

William Petersen writes:

> *Neo-Malthusianism was no less an invention of the nineteenth century than, say, the vulcanization of rubber, which made possible the development of efficacious contraceptive devices.*[9]

The first book recommending contraceptive measures appeared in England in 1822. Francis Place argued that the postponement of marriage advocated by Malthus was too onerous a means of limiting population growth ever to be widely adopted. Contraceptive devices had to be utilized if families were to be limited to the desired size. In 1854, the *Elements of Social Science*, by George Drysdale, established a firm link between classical economic theory and neo-Malthusian doctrine. Its widespread publication gave a great deal of publicity to the movement.

In the United States, Robert Dale Owen wrote the first book on birth control in 1830—*Moral Physiology*. Shortly afterward Charles Knowlton's *Fruits of Philosophy* appeared. The latter, being written by a physician, gave a quite accurate account of the process of conception and its control. It was not, however, until Margaret Sanger began her crusade for birth control in 1913 that Americans became generally aware of contraceptive practices. She served thirty days in prison for "maintaining a public nuisance" after she opened her first birth control clinic.

The advocates of birth control generally have tended to support other movements (ie. pacificism, temperance, vegetarianism).[10] When the birth control movement has lacked such supporting causes, it has floundered. Traditional opposition is strong and is founded generally on convictions of the "unnaturalness" of birth control. Aside from certain strands of orthodoxy, Judaism has been generally open to birth control measures. According to some commentators, the *Talmud* permitted contraception and "the Jewish attitude never considered the function of intercourse to be for procreation only."[11] Protestants are divided over the matter. In general, Calvin and Luther both found it unacceptable. The Lambeth Conference of Anglican Bishops, however, has recently strongly endorsed the use of contraceptive devices (in 1930 and again in 1958). In 1908 they had strongly condemned their use. Protestants in the main seem supportive.[12]

The Roman Catholic position is quite another matter. The present positions of the church after *Humanae Vitae* vary. This is rather remarkable in light of the centrality with which the popes have always viewed the subject

---

9. Petersen *op. cit.*, p. 489.
10. *Ibid.*, p. 490.
11. Samuel Glasner, "Judaism and Sex," in Albert Ellis and Albert Abarnal (eds.), *The Encyclopedia of Sexual Behavior* (New York: Hawthorn, 1961).
12. See John C. Bennet, "Protestant Ethics and Population Control," *Daedalus*, Vol. 88 (1959), 454–59.

of birth control. Nevertheless, despite Pope Paul's reaffirmation of the traditional position—rhythm "for just motives" only (even in the face of the overwhelming counter-recommendations of his council of advisors)—Catholic laity and heirarchy are split into many factions.[13] Recent polls indicate that Catholics do in fact support the dissemination of birth control information "to anyone who wants it" and a significant minority favor the use of contraceptive techniques other than rhythm. Practice does not necessarily follow doctrine, but the church apparently does have an effect upon the behavior of Catholics since on most questions pertaining to contraception there is a significant difference by religion. Catholic opposition is generally stronger than that of other denominations.[14]

THE PROBLEM WITH PLANNED PARENTHOOD

The availability of contraceptives and the dissemination of information about their use are undoubtedly beneficial in helping persons to improve the quality of their family life by giving them greater control over the size of their families. As a population control measure, however, birth control has several serious disadvantages. The major are: (1) the average American wants more children than are necessary for replacement; and (2) the vast majority of Americans are already effective practitioners of birth control methods. Only the poor are not effective practitioners, but an improvement in their practice would not seriously affect the growth of our population. Our population is growing as it is because most of us want as many children as we can afford —but no more—and we commonly believe that we can afford three or four. Table 15–1 shows that at all times since 1943, more lower-class respondents have generally preferred a larger family as an ideal than the upper classes.

Leaving aside the possible undesirable side effects of a population policy aimed primarily at the poor, it can be shown that even with effective birth control practice the poor *want* larger families than the nonpoor, and this would, therefore, tend to reduce the effectiveness of birth control as a population control measure.

Table 15–2 indicates that since 1943 the large majority of white Americans have been in favor of making birth control information available to individuals who desire it. Note that the percentages are uniformly positively correlated to education—the more education, the larger the percentage favoring the dissemination of birth control information.

These tables suggest that the lower-class is least inclined of all classes toward birth control measures and that even if it were effective in its use of

13. A discussion of the various Catholic positions is presented in two volumes concerned about the defense of faculty at Catholic University in Washington, D.C. in a trial contesting the suppression of their academic freedom in response to their opposition to *Humanae Vitae*. John F. Hunt and Terrence R. Connelly, *Dissent In and For the Church: Theologians and Humanae Vitae*, (New York: Sneed and Ward, 1969); *The Responsibility of Dissent: The Church and Academic Freedom* (New York: Sneed and Ward, 1969).

14. See, for example, the summary of various national polls in Judith Blake, "Population Policy for Americans: Is the Government Being Misled?" *Science*, Vol. 164 (May 2, 1969), 522–29.

TABLE 15–1
Mean Number of Children Considered Ideal by Non-Catholic Women

Date	Age range	Level of education* College	High school	Grade school	Income or economic status† 1	2	3	4	Total respondents X	N
1943	20–34	2.8	2.6	2.6	2.9	2.7	2.7	2.5	2.7	1893
1952	21 +	3.3	3.1	3.6	3.3		3.3	3.3	3.3	723
1955‡	18–39	3.1	3.2	3.7	3.2	3.1	3.2	3.5	3.3	1905
1955§	18–39	3.3	3.4	3.9	3.4	3.3	3.4	3.7	3.4	1905
1957	21 +	3.4	3.2	3.6	3.3		3.2	3.5	3.3	448
1959	21 +	3.5	3.4	3.9	3.5		3.5	3.6	3.5	472
1960‡	18–39	3.1	3.2	3.5	3.1	3.2	3.3	3.2	3.2	1728
1960§	18–39	3.2	3.4	3.6	3.2	3.3	3.5	3.4	3.4	1728
1963	21 +	3.2	3.4	3.5	3.3	3.3	3.5	3.5	3.4	483
1966	21 +	3.1	3.3	3.7	3.2	3.2	3.4	3.7	3.3	374
1967	21 +	3.1	3.3	3.4	3.3	3.2	3.1	3.4	3.3	488
1968	21 +	3.2	3.3	3.7	3.2	3.0	3.4	3.6	3.3	539

Source: Judith Blake "Population Policy for Americans: Is the Government Being Misled?", Science, Vol. 164. (May 2, 1968), 524.
 * Highest level completed.
 † Levels 1–4 for status range in order from "high" to "low."
 ‡ Minimum ideal.
 § Maximum ideal.

contraceptives, such use would still produce much larger families than desirable to achieve a zero population growth. The poor, therefore, do not seem to be a particularly good target for public policy attempting to control the nation's population.

The primary target must be the much larger number of nonpoor Americans who are already reasonably effective practitioners, but who also want larger families than desirable to achieve zero population growth. Why do the nonpoor want "large" families (three to four children)? Judith Blake's answer is simply that our society rewards large families both explicitly in our laws and implicitly in our mores. In order to reduce the size of the desirable family we must alter this reward system:

> The existence of such pronatalist policies becomes apparent when we recall that, among human beings, population replacement would not occur at all were it not for the complex social organization and system of incentives that encourage mating, pregnancy, and the care, support, and rearing of children. These institutional mechanisms are the pronatalist "policies" evolved over millennia to give societies a fertility sufficient to offset high mortality. . . .
>
> The pronatalism of the family has many manifestations, but among the most influential and universal are two: the standardization of both the male and the female sexual roles in terms of reproductive functions, obligations, and activities, and the standardization of the occupational

TABLE 15–2
*Percentages of Men and Women in Favor of Providing Birth Control
Information to Persons Who Desire It*

| Year | Percent Men | | | Percent Women | | |
	College*	High school	Grade school	College	High school	Grade school
1943	75 (184)†	68 (284)	56 (157)	82 (216)	74 (442)	60 (207)
1945	74 (202)	62 (360)	58 (140)	83 (216)	63 (434)	56 (207)
1947	91 (84)	72 (199)	67 (66)	81 (89)	74 (228)	72 (81)
1959	88 (89)	76 (163)	66 (49)	91 (55)	79 (279)	68 (41)
1961	88 (102)	81 (188)	67 (46)	84 (81)	81 (265)	78 (50)
1962	92 (93)	83 (171)	61 (23)	84 (79)	82 (259)	66 (44)
1963	86 (105)	79 (178)	53 (40)	81 (80)	78 (251)	81 (42)
1964	92 (107)	88 (188)	83 (29)	94 (79)	85 (293)	74 (38)

Source: Judith Blake, "Population Policy for Americans: Is the Government Being Misled?",
Science, Vol. 164 (May 2, 1969), 525.
 * *Highest level completed.*
 † *Numbers in parentheses indicate total number of respondents in each category.*

> role of women—half of the population—in terms of child-bearing, child-
> rearing, and complementary activities. These two "policies" ensure that
> just about everybody will be propelled into reproductive unions, and
> that half of the population will enter such unions as a "career"—a life's
> work.[15]

The standardization of sex roles in terms of their reproductive function
is quite apparent once we realize that the human potential for varying these
roles is much greater than is normally permitted within each role. This was
the major point I attempted to establish in Chapter 12. Gavin Arthur's *Circle
of Sex*, for example, suggested a twelve-fold division of sex role instead of
our simple dichotomy. Our sex-role standardization prescribes marriage and
family patterns, and written into this prescription is the dictum that males
and females should become parents:

> This . . . takes many forms, including one-sided indoctrination in schools,
> legal barriers, and penalties for deviation, and the threats of loneliness,
> ostracism and ridicule that are implied in the unavailability of alterna-
> tives. Individuals who—by temperament, health, or constitution—do not
> fit the ideal sex-role pattern are nonetheless coerced into attempting to
> achieve it, and many of them do achieve it, at least to the extent of hav-
> ing demographic impact by becoming parents.[16]

Our casual assumption of the naturalness of our definitions of sex role
is reinforced by the fact that most of us do become parents and somehow do

15. *Ibid.*, p. 528.
16. *Ibid.*, pp. 528–29.

manage to raise our children. Yet each year some *80,000* children are beaten and maimed by their parents. Each year clinical evidence mounts supporting the thesis that some parents are inclined to select one of their children as a "scapegoat" upon whom they lay all of their own interpersonal conflict, and they literally drive the child from the family circle. The testimony of youth itself as evidenced in the generation gap suggests that our problems as parents are becoming more acute. True, all of these may well apply to a minority of parents and perhaps should not, therefore, be marshalled in support of general parental incompetence. This, of course, is not my point. They do make clear what we all know from personal experience anyway, that is, that some of us ought not to be parents. The fact that people become parents even when they themselves do not really want to become parents testifies to the coercive element in our system in favor of becoming parents. If you should decide to suggest openly that you do not want to have children when you marry, or if you are married and do not yet have children, you will know what subtle means can be utilized to bring pressure to bear upon your waywardness. Mothers who wish to become grandmothers, neighbors who lack the capacity for conversation about anything but children, friends who feel that something must be wrong with you—the general assumptions of all that a couple must have children in order to be normal—are but a part of the informal pronatalist policy. Tax structures favoring children by providing exemptions are but a part of the formal policies.

The strong tendency to define sexual perversions as sexual behavior that cannot result in pregnancy is quite formalized in our law. Some states, for example, have statutes on their books making oral sex between husband and wife illegal. The legal restrictions against homosexuals are another case in point. In a society desiring to control its population, these antinatal forms of sexual behavior have a positive value if they are between consenting adults. At a less dramatic level, the assertion that the only natural sexuality is that which can produce children must be re-examined. A number of religious denominations at present recognize the companionship function of sexuality as well as its reproductive function.

Blake's second point regarding the defining of a woman's career as child bearing and child rearing is perhaps equally important in affecting the average woman's desire to have a number of children. Research has suggested that women have children in order to resolve the dilemma between being a homebody and having an outside career. With several children, they do not have a choice in most instances. At present the working wife is penalized in a number of ways. She works for less pay in generally less desirable jobs even though she can in many instances perform at a higher skill level. She is frequently, if not chronically, sub-employed. Blake contends that the desire for a number of children is related to the average woman's desire to experience "family life" over the major portion of her life. With increasing longevity, the only way that this can be realized is by having several children. In spite of the steadily increasing number of working women, the mores still contend that a "woman's place is in the home." Until this is no longer true and until women can find acceptable and rewarding alternatives to motherhood, most women in our society will want several children.

In order to change this, Blake argues, it is necessary to remove the coercion of present pronatalist policies:

> This will involve the lifting of penalties for antinatalist behavior rather than the "creation" of new ways of life. This behavior already exists among us as a part of our covert and deviant culture, on the one hand, and our elite and artistic culture on the other. Such antinatalist tendencies have also found expression in feminism which has been stifled in the United States by means of systematic legal, educational, and social pressures concerned with women's "obligations" to create and care for children. A fertility-control policy that does not take into account the need to alter the present structure of reproduction in these and other ways merely trivializes the problem of population control and misleads those who have the power to guide our country toward completing the vital revolution.[17]

These are quite disturbing words, no doubt, to most of us. Even after coming to understand something of the variability in sexual behavior that has served other people in other cultures well, we are reluctant to examine our own mores in this matter. Much of this re-examination, as we have seen, is being conducted "experimentally" by our youth. It is and has been a part of both our elite and our deviant sub-cultures for a long time, as Blake points out. To recognize that not only is the family a variable with many functional alternatives, but also that sex role can be redefined is unnerving for many. It is perhaps too much to ask the average American to accept these as possibilities. To hope that he can accept them in others without attempting to repress them is in itself a great expectation. Nevertheless, if Blake and those who accept her general position are correct, such must be the case if we are to control our fertility.

LIFE SCIENCE, SCIENCE FICTION, AND FERTILITY CONTROL

In *Brave New World* Huxley described the ultimate in fertility control—test-tube babies. Children born outside a mother's womb "in vitro" are not yet possible so far as I know. But the possibility that we can so "create" life seems much closer than it did when Huxley wrote. Social scientists have difficulty taking into consideration the discoveries in other sciences, but it is clear that the revolutionary discoveries in the life sciences have had in the past (and will continue to have even more in the future) a profound effect upon the family.

Writing in 1962, Meyer Nimkoff observed:

> . . . our review of developments in the biochemistry of man during approximately the last decade (1950–1960) shows great progress in birth control, promising although much slower achievement in sex control, and

17. *Loc. cit.*

intermediate degree in control of sex characteristics via hormonal therapy and of the biological problems of aging. In all these fields there is no major problem of opposition from the mores; rather American society is favorable to most biological research. The uneven progress in the several areas is partly the result of uneven demand. The simplest scientific problem is that of birth control; somewhat more difficult from a theoretical standpoint is the problem of the control of the sex of the child; and much more complex are the problems of the control of aging and sexual characteristics. As to social demand, that for control over the process of aging is probably greatest, that for improved contraceptives is considerable; that for increased control over the sex characteristics is less; and that for control over the sex of the child is least. The greatest control, then, has been achieved in contraception where the scientific problems are the simplest and the demand is great. For the long pull, however, the greater promise lies in fundamental research. It is intriguing to speculate upon what another review a decade hence may show as to the nature of the living cell and the location of the genes which control the constitution of man.[18]

Since Nimkoff wrote these words, the oral contraceptive has been perfected and its side affects duly noted, the genetic code has been broken, men have synthesized DNA, and a single gene has been located. Sterile couples have been assisted and many have brought forth multiple births. With the utilization of frozen sperm, sterilization in the male need not be permanent. The Masters and Johnson studies greatly improved our understanding of human sexual behavior and convincingly demonstrate that women have a far greater capacity to enjoy coitus than do men. The multiorgasmic female is not a rare phenomenon, but a common one. A great deal has been discovered in the laboratory that is by no means ready for general use. Even the oral contraceptive needs further refinement. But amazing strides that have been taken in the sixties and the seventies show no sign of a let-up.

In animal experiments eggs have been fertilized in vitro and the embryo developed through several elementary divisions. Problems connected with the mechanical suspension of the embryo seem to be the major impediment to further development at the moment.

The possible gains from such discoveries seem great. With the location of the gene, genetic surgery seems no longer a remote possibility. The predetermination of the sex of a child also seems closer to realization. With the ability to develop a foetus in vitro the accessibility of the foetus to micro surgery preventing many types of birth defects becomes a possibility. The problems of pregnancy will have been overcome—at least those associated with the bearing of the foetus and its birth.

Along with these possible gains are some possible costs. The surgeon's knife can slip, the foetus grown in vitro could conceivably have a much different reaction to stimuli as a result of its much greater exposure to them

18. Meyer F. Nimkoff, "Biological Discoveries and the Future of the Family," *Social Forces*, Vol. 41 (December 1962), 127.

than if it had developed in the womb. The psychology of motherhood would undoubtedly be changed. We know that it is not necessary to carry a child around in one's womb in order to be able to love it, but might not the mothering relationship be affected in more subtle ways?

The reproductive function of the family would be, of course, quite dramatically altered with the advent of test-tube babies. Love may not then—as now—be a direct force in the reproductive process, and the nature of its instrumentality will not be as immediate. Sexuality will have been quite radically separated from reproduction. The horror of *Brave New World* that we associated with children reared by the state in state-operated nurseries is one extreme modification of the relationship between family and reproductivity. Much less extreme would be a couple, or couples, deciding that they—collectively—would want to have a baby and going down to the local clinic to select its characteristics, which would conceivably be an appropriate mixture of the characteristics of all four. There would no longer be any apparent relationship between the nuclear family structure and the reproductive function. In short, the number of possible family forms associated with procreation would increase.

In regard to sex role and the discovery of women's characteristically greater capacity to enjoy sex as far as her physiological potential is concerned —might not this result in a radical reversal of sex role? Picture the shy male of the future being pursued by the impassioned female. One commentator speculates:

> Whatever the outcome, the increasing laxity in regard to the discovery of the pleasures of sexuality will bring about radical alterations. The concept of adultery would disappear, words like "premarital" and "extramarital" would become meaningless, and no one would think of attaching a label like "promiscuous" to sex activities. After all why not be as free to experiment with a variety of sexual partners as with a variety of foods and restaurants? Love, marriage, and the family have been around for a long time and have served us well. But it is clear that they may not survive the new era unless we really want them to.[19]

Some of the radicalness of this statement is removed when we realize that the author is reacting to the impact of these discoveries on our rather unique definitions of love, marriage, and the family. What will happen is, as comparative data suggests, that they will not disappear. They will be redefined, and this is quite another problem.

The increasing capacity to control the reproductive process is both frightening in its implications and deeply encouraging. The possibilities for change, in any event, are greatly increased as a result of these discoveries. With such capacity the problem of controlling the size of our world's population will seem relatively insignificant compared to the more difficult matters with which we must cope.

19. Albert Rosenfeld, as reported in Louis Harris, "Science, Sex and Tomorrow's Morality," *Life Magazine*, 1969.

Summary

America's rate of population has declined, and there seems to be a trend toward small families among young mothers under thirty. Our growth has occurred unevenly and has meant that our cities have borne much of the burden in the past and will continue to do so in the future. To term our population problem an urban explosion might give the better emphasis. Nevertheless, increasing numbers of people are directly involved in related problems where the distribution of the population is important but is not the major concern. Environmental pollution, exhaustion of our natural resources, the energy crises, our chronic inability to put people to work and keep them at work over long periods of time are all critically related to the problem of our increasing population. A zero rate of growth seems a most desirable goal —one which we may be realizing even before we have fully become aware of the problem as a nation. It will take us another generation at least before we can be sure.

An examination of the family's reproductive function in our society indicated the extent to which fertility is encouraged by a number of pronatalist "policies" still extant. The definition of sex role as primarily a reproductive role and the assignment of the major responsibility in child bearing and rearing to women as their major career make it difficult for American middle-class women to want small families. Until the coercion of these policies is lessened, Judith Blake argues, we are not likely to witness a long-term trend toward small families.

Finally, a brief glimpse at some possible implications of recent and "near future" developments in the life sciences suggests that major factors responsible for future changes in our way of family living may well be largely unanticipated consequences of our increased capacity to control the character of the reproductive process. The science fiction test-tube baby seems much closer as a technical possibility in the seventies than it did in the sixties. Unquestionably the social-psychological consequences of such an event will be great.

Because our capacity to alter our family forms in some degree outstrips our understanding, it is necessary to examine in this final section three attempts to intentionally change the character of the family: the Oneida Community, the Russian Experiment, and the Kibbutzim of Israel. From each we can learn about conditions under which it is possible to change the character of the family and some of the consequences of such change.

I then discuss the prospects and proposals set forth by social scientists for family change in our own society. A projection of present trends assumes that the family will be essentially the same structure tomorrow as it is today. But with the best data available, the forecaster does not know for certain if present trends are short term or long term. Therefore, the family of the future is only dimly perceivable by present techniques.

There are those, however, who propose that the family be changed quite radically in order to create a better life and base their proposals not on present projections, but upon their conception of what is desirable. They presume that we can and should choose radical alternatives and are less concerned about the processes by which such proposals are realized.

In the Afterword I will describe what I believe to be one mode of desirable family change. As a personal perspective, it cannot claim to reflect the interests or the needs of anyone other than myself. It has arisen out of my experience, and reflects my biases and misconceptions as well as my understanding of how families function and what is most desirable in family life. It is included because it is the stance from which I see the family as I am able presently to articulate it. As such, it has undoubtedly influenced the development of this book.

CHANGING
THE
FAMILY

16. Pathways in Utopia

The era of advanced Capitalism has broken down the structure of society. . . . The socialistic task [of rebuilding] can only be accomplished to the degree that the new Village Commune, combining the various forms of production and uniting production and consumption, exerts a structural influence on the amorphous urban society. The influence will only make itself felt to the full if, and to the extent that, further technological developments facilitate and actually require the decentralization of industry; but even now a pervasive force is latent in the modern communal village, and it may spread to the towns. . . .

So long as Russia has not undergone an essential inner change—and today we have no means of knowing when and how that will come to pass—we must designate one of the two poles of Socialism between which our choice lies, by the formidable name of "Moscow." The other, I would make bold to call "Jerusalem."

MARTIN BUBER

When the family is examined with a concern for understanding its relationship with its society, it is usually thought of as largely reactive to its society and as acting upon its members. As such the many constraints placed upon family members become manifest, and family change as a result of their efforts seems almost impossible. When we further realize that not much is known scientifically about how the family functions (much less how it changes) the possibility of planned change seems even more remote.

And yet there have been numerous attempts at changing the family according to some new vision of what the good life is. I will discuss here three of the more successful of these, analyze the conditions under which change occurred, and assess the extent of the change insofar as this is possible. The Oneida Community is the most successful American experiment in "Utopian" Socialism to date. It began in the 1840s; its radical family form lasted about thirty years, and at its peak it served 288 persons. The Russian experiment began after the revolution of 1917, was radically altered in 1936, and, with continual modification, has persisted to the present day. It seems, however, in this case that what began as an attack on the conjugal family as the stronghold of bourgeois capitalism has turned into a strong defense of a family system not unlike our own. However radical the early experiment must have seemed to the West, the present urban Russian family is now hardly distinguishable from the typical family of our own hemisphere. The Kibbutzim of Israel are still able to maintain a quite radical departure from both the traditional Jewish family of the European ghetto and the nuclear or conjugal family more characteristic of the West. The first Kibbutz was founded in 1910. The movement has attracted Jews from all over the world and at present about 93,000 persons live in 225 separate communities. Many of these communities are rearing the third generation of "kibbutzniks."

Each of these three examples offers the opportunity for us to examine how it was possible for a group of people to chart out a pathway in utopia. Although Oneida no longer exists as the perfect socialist community it once was, and even though both the Russian and the Israeli experiments are giving greater weight to the conjugal family at present, all three created quite radical departures in family form and functioning. They argue against those who would say that the conjugal family is the best family form—or even that it is the basic family form in the sense of being structurally necessary.

Oneida

This community grew out of the flames of revivalism in the "burnt over" section of mid-state New York.[1] Its founder, John Humphrey Noyes (Figure 16–1), a young Dartmouth graduate intent upon the practice of law, heard the word of the Lord at a revival held in his mother's house and gave up the law for the ministry. After instruction at Andover Theological Seminary and the Yale School of Divinity, he was licensed to preach. He had received only a

1. This section is heavily indebted to Maren Lockwood Carden's study, *Oneida: Utopian Community to Modern Corporation* (Baltimore: Johns Hopkins Press, 1970). That work includes a complete bibliography on the Oneida community.

FIGURE 16–1
*John Humphrey Noyes, founder
of the Oneida Community. From*
The Religious Experience of
John Humphrey Noyes, *George
Wallingford Noyes (ed.).*

few dollars for his services as a minister when he announced in 1846 that he was perfect—sinless. This bold profession of perfection alienated him from the mainstream of Christian orthodoxy, cost him his license, and forced him to re-examine his own principles. He never gave up his basic conviction regarding his own salvation from sin, although he experienced many "crises of the spirit."

In 1846 he established the Putney Community in his sister's home, published perfectionist literature, and initiated the first stage of *complex marriage*—a form of group marriage that was to be the basis of Oneida's social structure. In 1848 his little band of followers were driven out of Putney, Vermont by irate neighbors, and took up residence on the banks of Oneida Creek in mid-state New York. The community continued to grow until it disbanded. Table 16–1 gives some idea of how Oneida grew.

Perfectionism as a theology of the revival enjoyed a widespread audience. John Humphrey Noyes's version of perfectionism always generated great controversy especially when it addressed itself to family life. Because his unconventional views were widely discussed, Oneida was able to recruit selectively from a much larger population of his admirers. Clearly the personality and the professed beliefs of this one man were quite central to the origin and life of the community.

TABLE 16–1
*Membership of the Oneida and Wallingford Communities
by Selected Years 1849–1880**

	1849	1853	1856	1866	1871	1875	
Oneida	87	130	180	209	225	253	
Wallingford†	—	17	—	45	45	45	
Total in 1880							288

Source: Maren Lockwood Carden, *Oneida: Utopian Community to Modern Corporation* (Baltimore, Md.: Johns Hopkins Press, 1970), p. 41.
**The proportion of men to women changed little. In any age group there were
almost always a few more women than men.*
† Wallingford was a branch of the community in Wallingford, Connecticut.

COMPLEX MARRIAGE

Strictly speaking, Noyes preached a nullification of marriage, not a plurality,
yet he established a form of group marriage. He quoted biblical texts (Matt.
22:30) that proclaimed that in the Kingdom marriage would be abolished,
and pointed out that Jesus said that his followers should become as one
(John 17:21–23):

> *Monogamy makes a man or woman unfit to practice the two central
> principles of Christianity, loving God and loving one's neighbor. "Exclu-
> sive attachment" to a spouse turns the attention from God and one's
> fellow man. It is preferable for a man to love everyone equally and to
> give the greatest love to God. If there are sexual relations in the kingdom
> of heaven, then the ideal state is one in which all men are viewed as
> married to all women. If the kingdom is to be established on earth, it
> must include such a system of "complex marriage."*[2]

Monogamous marriage was thus replaced by a form of group marriage, and
even romantic involvement with one person was discouraged. Any man or
woman could request sexual relations with any other woman or man. The
freedom to accept or decline the invitation was assured because such re-
quests were to be submitted through a central committee and not directly to
the person desired as a partner.

Contraception: Ordinarily the "principle of ascendancy" made it more common for younger persons to have coitus with older, presumably more perfect, members of the community. An important function served by this practice was that it enabled young men inexperienced with the practice of male
continence to develop control in their sexual behavior with minimum risk of
conceiving a child.

2. *Ibid.*, p. 16.

Male continence is a form of contraception in which the male engages in coitus without any mechanical or chemical contraceptive but prevents conception by controlling ejaculation.

A member of the community wrote in 1911 about this practice:

> *In intercourse the male inserted his penis into the vagina and retained it there for even an hour without emission, though orgasm took place in the woman. There was usually no emission in the case of the man, even after withdrawal, and he felt no need of emission. The social feeling of the community was a force on the side of this practice, the careless, unskillful men being avoided by women, while the general romantic sentiment of affection for all the women in the community was also a force.*[3]

Since the community resolved not to rear children during the first twenty years of its existence, male continence was of the utmost importance. A few children, nevertheless, were born accidentally.

Stirpiculture Children: When the community further decided to implement its perfectionist beliefs in the development of a new breed of children, a committee was appointed to decide who among the adult population would have the right to reproduce. "Stirpiculture" was the name the community gave to its eugenics program. Eventually, fifty-three women and thirty-eight men were selected as potential parents. All others were to remain voluntarily childless, although, because of the effectiveness of male continence, they were free to engage in coitus.

Those who participated in the stirpiculture program generally selected their own mates, although about one-fourth of all unions were suggested by the central committee. The women ranged in age from twenty to forty-two years with a median of thirty; the men from twenty-five to sixty-eight with a median of forty-one. Fifty-eight children were born at Oneida during the decade 1869 to 1879. Thirteen (22.4 percent) were accidental, although all were classified as stirpiculture children.[4]

The extent of personal commitment to Noyes was reflected in the resolution signed by the women who participated in this program:

1. That we do not belong to ourselves in any respect, but that we do belong first to God, and second to Mr. Noyes as God's true representative.

2. That we have no rights or personal feelings in regard to childbearing which shall in the least degree oppose or embarrass him in his choice of scientific combinations.

3. That we will put aside all envy, childishness and self-seeking, and rejoice with those who are chosen candidates; that we

---

3. Havelock Ellis, *Sex in Relation to Society, Vol. VI: Studies in the Psychology of Sex* (Philadelphia: F. A. Davis, 1911), p. 553.
4. Carden *op. cit.*, p. 63.

will, if necessary, become martyrs to science, and cheerfully resign all desire to become mothers, if for any reason Mr. Noyes deem us unfit material for propagation. Above all, we offer ourselves as "living sacrifices" to God and true Communism.[5]

Oneida was thus quite remarkable in being able to initiate and maintain a fairly successful program in planned parenthood before contraceptives were perfected and in general use. Male continence undoubtedly had an effect upon sexual relations as well, but the precise effect is difficult to ascertain. It does seem reasonable to infer that men and women were enabled to enjoy sexual relations since complex marriage and male continence were not, in themselves, given as reasons for the community's giving up its marital communism. Both men and women, further, gave evidence of their personal satisfaction with sexual activities.[6]

After the first fifteen months of their lives, children were raised communally in their own "children's house." They were thought of as children of the community—not of the particular pair that conceived them. Outside the community such children were known by critics of the community as "Christ's children" or simply as bastards. The whole community participated in some of the activities of the children's house, but the major responsibility for developing stirpiculture children was given to community appointed nurses and instructors. Children participated in the work and play of the larger community, especially in the various "bees." Most of the accounts given by members of the community indicate that it was a happy community—at least during its first two decades.

Patterns of Everyday Life: After the Mansion House was built, each member had a private room, the children had their own wing, and a number of rooms were common rooms: dining room, library, theatre, and general living rooms and parlors (Figure 16–2). Private property was not permitted, although privacy was possible.

A central feature of the daily routine was the evening assembly (Figure 16–3). During this period of the day members gathered together in the common room to listen to Mr. Noyes and the elders expound the principles of perfectionist socialism and to engage in mutual criticism. During his training at Yale, John H. Noyes joined a group of student ministers who practiced this mutual criticism as a way of improving their conduct, and Noyes found such criticism extremely beneficial. In Oneida, however, he himself was never criticized by others, although he occasionally criticized himself. All others were

5. *Ibid.*, p. 62.
6. It is questionable whether such satisfaction should be termed "a toned down" expression of the erotic compatible with the deeply religious nature of the community. See Gerald Leslie, *The Family in Social Context* (New York: Oxford, 1967), p. 129. Since under such conditions of prolonged coitus without ejaculation women frequently become multiorgasmic, the erotic tone for women could quite reasonably have intensified. This too is quite compatible with religion as the religions of the East more amply demonstrate than in Christianity as commonly practiced in the West.

FIGURE 16–2
The Oneida Community building in 1878. From Handbook of the
Oneida Community.

subjected to the most minute examination. So forthrightly was the criticism
expressed during these evening sessions that it became a means of determining who of the new postulates had the mettle to remain a permanent member of the community.

The community was to a surprising extent self-sufficient, owning an adequate farm and deriving considerable income from a few small industries,
particularly a steel trap company that made traps for hunters. They were
much in demand, and the sale of the products of this company alone
was largely responsible for the eventual solvency of the community. Can-
ning, sewing, silversmithing, and other crafts contributed to the community's income, as did the private capital of new members which became
common property upon their joining the community. Indeed, Oneida spent
ten years and $40,000 in formerly private capital before the community itself
began to show a profit. Wealth was not, however, a major criteria for admis-
sion to the community. Some joined with few worldly possessions. Nevertheless, after an initial struggle with poverty, the community had to remind
itself continually that it must not let its accumulating wealth interfere with
its service to God and its socialist principles. So successful was this venture

FIGURE 16–3
An "outsider's" view of a community meeting. Note the contrast between the formal behavior in the foreground and the activities on stage. From Robert Allerton Parker, A Yankee Saint *(G. P. Putnam's Sons).*

in utopia that after the dissolution of the community, the Oneida Company Ltd., was formed in large measure to preserve the capital accumulated. If the community's property were sold, the members stood to lose a large portion of the $600,000 book value of their holdings. Whatever the basis of the disagreement between the contending parties, it was not great enough to cause them to exact this price of themselves.

The culture of the community—its cuisine and theatre, its conversation and literary style—was widely talked about in the area of Oneida Creek and among perfectionists throughout the country. Good public relations were maintained at all times by inviting neighbors to participate in the life of the community, especially on its festive occasions. Hardly a meal was served without visitors. Oneida further extended its good neighbor policy by being generous in its business transactions with local people and in providing jobs for a few hundred persons when its industries and farm were running at their fullest.

THE END OF THE COMMUNITY, THE BEGINNING OF THE CORPORATION

In 1880 the community gave up its distinctive style of life, its complex form of marriage, and its stirpicultural children. The members formed monogamous marriages, retained their accumulated capital, and launched Oneida Company Ltd., a venture in silversmithing that still continues today (Figure 16–4). The style of this corporation life was much influenced by idealism, and its board of directors and managerial staff frequently took cuts in salary in order to help the company's economy. This practice, along with the habit of generally low wages for executives, has disappeared as the company has had to compete with the larger market for top executives.

The explanations for the community's disintegration are varied. Internally, the aging Noyes was apparently unable to turn the leadership over to his son, or, put another way, the son was unable to exert the same influence over the community as his father had. While John Humphrey Noyes was a charismatic preacher devoted to the community, his son was more interested in biology than in experimental communities. While the power of the community was formally vested in the council of elders, the elder Noyes usually tipped the balance of power in matters that concerned him. He was unable, however, to provide for his succession.

FIGURE 16-4
Oneida Ltd.'s plant, which includes the original Willow Place Factory built by the Community. From Pierrepont B. Noyes, A Goodly Heritage (Rinehart & Co.).

During the entire life of the community, and especially during its latter years, the elder Noyes absented himself from the community, residing at times in New York, at other times in the Connecticut branch of the community, and sometimes with friends. Once he fled into Canada fearing that he would be indicted for statutory rape, since it was rumored that many of the young women under the age of consent participated in the complex marriage.

Certainly the community outraged official morality, but to what extent worsening community relations or outside state intervention directly contributed to the disbanding is unknown. There was no formal complaint brought against the community that resulted from its social structure or the style of its life. The few occasions that it was brought into court concerned business matters, and the complaints were always resolved with a minimum of conflict and to the satisfaction of its adversaries. Complex marriage had been maintained and fifty-eight stirpiculture children reared without direct intervention from outside.

As Noyes began to age, his leadership became quite erratic. He seemed to be his own worst enemy. He was unable to contend with the factions developing within. Division within the community resulted from differences in opinion on matters of privilege and priority afforded Noyes and some of the elder members of the community. For example, it was Noyes's custom to initiate the young virgins into the sexual life of the community—a practice recalling the *jus primae noctis*. Some of these were apparently under the age of consent. Further, it was notable that Noyes himself sired ten stirpiculture children, more than any other male in the community.

Some observers point to a conflict between generations as younger members objected to the principle of ascendency, and some even fancied they preferred monogamous marriage over complex marriage. And yet the major political divisions within the community did not break down along age lines, though the conflict between generations doubtless contributed to the debates.

During Noyes's absence and when his leadership in the evening meetings of the community became increasingly difficult to exercise because of his weakening voice and declining vigor, other elders questioned his right in such matters.

He also became increasingly less self-consciously charismatic. Interestingly enough, stirpiculture was not justified on theological grounds but on social grounds—a desire to build a better species of men. This was the first major revision of life within the community that Noyes did not bother to support theologically. In his later years, as he became more of a social scientist, he apparently became less effective as a leader of men. In 1877 Noyes resigned as the leader of Oneida. In 1879 he left for Canada and shortly thereafter the community dissolved.

HOW WAS SUCH A COMMUNITY POSSIBLE?

Although social scientists can point to the fact that Oneida was a failure since it was unable to socialize the second generation of Oneidans, the fact that such a radical experiment in family living was initiated and maintained in the America of the early 1800s should cause us to pause and examine some of our assumptions about family change. What does it mean when we say that Noyes was a charismatic leader? Do we account for the success of the entire venture on the basis of this charisma? Clearly it was an element that was basic to the founding of the community, and yet perfectionism as an ideology independent of personalities was in the wind. Revivals stirred men's souls, and certain districts and certain types of people were more stirred than others.

It seems clear that Oneida had few, if any, lower-lower-class persons in its membership. It was dominated by upper-middle-class literate persons. It drew upon the prior organization of perfectionist circles. For example, although there was not much money initially, there was the offer of a farm on which to build and a reserve of good will among perfectionists to support the experimenters and to provide a pool from which they could recruit new members. This ability to be selective was an important factor in the perpetuation of the community, because only those persons who could subject themselves to public community examination of their character and behavior could become members.

Selective Recruitment: The recruitment policy was also an important factor in the initiation of the venture. Noyes's reputation preceded him and enabled him to assemble those most likely to be in sympathy with his initial views. Furthermore, the working out of the perfectionist philosophy in the Putney community, a community composed of close friends and family, was a boone to Oneida. While many stopped reading the *Witness* (a widely circulated perfectionist journal) with Noyes's announcement of his views on marriage, those who continued to read and to profess allegiance to such convictions experienced something of the burden of labeling while still outside of the community. Residence within the community (should they be accepted as members) therefore, was likely to be perceived as a haven in a storm. In similar fashion those who sought membership were in some degree already proven insofar as they had remained faithful to perfectionist principles while outside of Oneida. All along, then, Noyes's involvement in perfectionist circles and his dissemination of perfectionist theology contributed to the greater likelihood of the Oneida community's recruiting members who would be able to form a more cohesive group.

Internal Dynamics: The cohesiveness of this community was maintained by several factors. The farm on Oneida Creek was relatively isolated, and members were expected to make a complete commitment to the community, the rejection of its principles revealing their own guillibility. Further, if we accept Carden's analysis, that the community attracted those persons who were particularly bothered about their own burden of guilt and sin (and therefore sought in perfectionism the release from such a burden), the community's built-in mechanisms for guilt release (mutual criticism, the perfectionist principles, male continence, and the daily routine itself) were a positive force for retaining loyalty. Carden also suggests that religious communities, more than other types of communities, have the capacity to put principles above self-interest and, thus, the principles themselves became a major mechanism for maintaining the community.

Doctrinal Flexibility: The structure of the community, as well as the interests of individuals, was modified when it was thought that such was necessary in order to put perfectionism into practice. The principles were thus broad enough and Noyes was skilled enough in leadership during the earlier days of the community that numerous adjustments in the specific application of principles could be made. Oneida's life was to be continually modified in order to express better the changing revelation of perfectionism. This required constant surveillance, constant evaluation, and constant revision. This commitment to remaining aware of the community's development and one's own progress toward a more perfect being were further factors contributing to social solidarity, for one could not accomplish either dimension of this task without the help of the community:

> The community prospered, too, because the main principles upon which it was based—communalism and self-perfection—loosely defined as they were, could be adapted to allow for changes in organizational needs. If the application of ideals had been specified more precisely or if Noyes had been less prepared to accept change, the community's economy would have failed and the experiment would have been disbanded many years before it was. It is, in any case, a vague and misleading oversimplification to assign to a leader full responsibility for the success or failure of a Utopia. . . . Although Noyes cannot be separated totally from his message or his methods, they, not he, were basic to Oneida's success. The key was not the presence of a leader but the practice of Perfectionism.[7]

In the case of Oneida, any explanation offered must be less than adequate because much of the data—the diaries and the personal accounts of the community—were burned to protect the reputations of those involved after the establishment of the corporation. All that remains is in the recollection of children of members and the published accounts of the community's life. We have no way to contrast these with observation or with records not preserved for public dissemination. Consequently, the case of Oneida can function mainly to raise questions that must finally remain unanswered.

The Russian Experiment

The character of the attempt to change the family is radically different in the Soviet experiment. From a venture involving fewer than 300 persons to one involving a vast multitude is a great step. It is difficult to place any precise boundary around the population involved in the Russian experiment. Perhaps 200 million persons were affected in some degree. An urban minority (about 30 percent of the total population) was most affected. The family structure of

7. Carden *op. cit.*, pp. 110–11.

the rural peasantry (80 million persons) was largely unaffected by official Soviet policy.

HISTORY

Many peoples have been joined together in the Union of Soviet Socialist Republics. The Slavic peoples made up about four-fifths of pre-revolutionary Russia and worshipped in the Eastern Orthodox tradition. The non-Slavic peoples were largely Muslims. A number of family forms were thus to be found. The dominant form, however, was a bilateral conjugal family that tended toward an extended family, particularly in the upper classes.[8] It was sternly patriarchal. Eastern Orthodoxy supported the contention that women were morally weaker tha mnen. Evil had an affinity for women, as was exemplified in the deception of the first woman, Eve. From the thirteenth century onward male dominance increased. The Bolshak (head of the household) could drive the disobedient son from his house with nothing but the clothes on his back and his crucifix. Russian folk adages supported the patriarch: "Beat your son in his youth and he will comfort you in your old age;" "If a son will not obey his father he will obey the whip." Wives also fell under the same authority, as a husband was father to his wife. Advice to the loving patriarch included the following:

> . . . and no matter how guilty the wife is, the husband should not hit her eyes or ears, nor beat her with his fist or feet under the heart; nor strike her with his staff or with anything made of iron or wood. . . . But to beat carefully, with a whip, is sensible, painful, fear inspiring and healthy. . . . In case of a grave offense, pull off her shirt and whip politely holding her by the hands and saying, 'Don't be angry, the people should not know or hear about it; there should be no complaints.'[9]

Of course these pertain to norms and not necessarily to practice. Nevertheless, the folk adages support a strong patriarchy as does a large portion of pre-revolutionary Russian literature.

The landed gentry, the urban upper classes, and the Eastern Orthodox faith represented three concentrations of power and wealth against which the revolutionary movement was directed. The ideology of the revolution fused Marxism with a strong feminist movement. Engels' treatise on *The Origin of the Family, Private Property and the State* condemned the conjugal family as a stronghold of bourgeois capitalism and a major means of subjugating women:

> The modern monogamous family is founded on the open or disguised domestic slavery of women. . . . A wife differs from a prostitute only

---

8. Gerald Leslie *op. cit.,* p. 133. This section particularly draws upon information quoted in Leslie; William F. Kenkel, *The Family in Perspective* (New York: Appleton-Century-Crofts, 1966), pp. 104–37; and Kent Geiger, "The Soviet Family," in Meyer Nimkoff (ed.), *Comparative Family Systems* (Boston: Houghton Mifflin, 1965), pp. 301–28.
9. Elaine Elnett, *Historic Origin and Social Development of Family Life in Russia* (New York: Columbia University Press, 1926), pp. 32–35.

in that she does not offer her body for money by the hour like a commodity, but sells it into slavery once and for all.[10]

Such words seemed particularly true in Czarist Russia. Marxist Socialism was supported by a strong feminist movement that sought radical redefinition of the woman's role. Marriage and family life were to be stripped of the element of possessiveness. Such concepts as "my husband," "our children," and "our home" were to be abolished. Sex was to become as natural as a drink of water and devoid of emotional involvement. Any good comrade should be willing to offer his body to any other of opposite sex. This was a factional but dominant view of the early revolutionists.

The 1920s: After the revolution an official family policy was established. The attempt to realize the ideal family then became manifest in a number of laws directed at the institutions of marriage, private property, and parent-child relationships. In addition programs designed to bring about greater equality for women by encouraging greater participation in all segments of Soviet life were begun. The official revolutionary view of the family was that it should be an expression of the personal freedom of even the average man. The state was to record what the individuals intended; it was not to dictate marriage choice, nor demand monogamy, nor make divorce prohibitive. The mutual consent of the partners was the prime prerequisite for marriage. The wife need not assume her husband's last name, and he could not dictate where the family should live.

The Code of 1926 did not even require that marriages be registered. It only recommended that they be so. A marriage was legal if there was:

> . . . the fact of cohabitation, combined with a common household, evidence of marital relations before third parties or in personal correspondence and other documents, mutual financial support, the raising of children in common if supported by circumstantial evidence, and the like.[11]

By such decrees the legal status of marriage was removed from the control of either the church or the state.

Each spouse was entitled to support from the other. Children were not assumed to be the prime responsibility of the wife after divorce. The official divorce law in the early years of the revolution provided that only one partner need appear before the registrar, provide evidence of marriage, and record the divorce. Thus by minimizing the official requirements pertaining to both marriage and divorce, the base of the traditional family was undermined, and women were granted a new freedom under the law.

Laws affecting sexual behavior were dropped or modified. For example, abortion was legalized in 1920. The intent of this decree was (1) to permit

10. Friedrich Engels, *The Origin of the Family, Private Property and the State* (Chicago: Charles H. Kerr, 1902), p. 86.
11. Alex Inkeles and Kent Geiger (eds.), *Soviet Society: A Book of Readings* (Boston: Houghton Mifflin, 1961), p. 531.

such operations to be performed freely and without any charge in Soviet hospitals, where conditions are assured of minimizing the harm of the operation, (2) absolutely to forbid anyone but a doctor to carry out the operation, (3) to ensure that any nurse or midwife found guilty of making such an operation would be deprived of the right to practice and be tried in the People's Court, and (4) to call to account in a People's Court any doctor carrying out an abortion in his private practice with mercenary aims. Clearly the code was concerned primarily with ensuring that such operations would occur under the most favorable circumstances. It was not intended to encourage abortion. This was also in keeping with feminist ideology of making women truly equal and child bearing a matter of free choice. However, there were abuses. In Moscow in 1924 there were twenty-seven abortions performed for every hundred live births. In 1930 there were 175,000 abortions in Moscow alone— 55,000 of them in a single abortion clinic. The most common reasons given for seeking an abortion were social—a fact hailed by the feminists as a great victory.

Laws concerning adultery, bigamy, and incest were dropped from the list of punishable offenses.[12] Contraceptive devices were made readily available and all official stigma removed from illegitimacy. Sexual behavior was to be a matter of free consent with no reactionary bourgeois morality. Interestingly enough, an attack on prostitution followed from similar lines of reasoning. The buying and selling of flesh was a form of bourgeois capitalism. The number of prostitutes in Moscow was reported to have dropped from 3,000 to 400 within a few years after the revolution, according to official documents.

The party view of child rearing was that the state should give women the opportunity to be equal participants with men in the new society by providing adequate community care for their children. Such centers could also more easily indoctrinate the youth into revolutionary ideology and bring their behavior under greater control of the state. "Creches" were child-care centers located in or near factories to provide children with the new collectivized mode of education. Mothers left their children in the creches while they worked. A nursing mother could return for that purpose only, but need not concern herself with her baby until evening. A Park of Culture provided care for her children on the mother's days off. Youth groups such as the Komsomol, Octoberists, and Pioneers took care of the older children. In such organizations children were given physical examinations, medical care, food, clothes, collectivized play, and education. In them, toys belonged to groups, not to the individuals. Such toys or blocks were often too big for one child to lift by himself thus requiring him to seek help.

At first women took the less skilled jobs because they were untrained, but soon women occupied skilled positions as well. By 1930 over two-thirds of the able bodied women were working outside the home. In 1960, 45 percent of all the jobs in Russia were held by women. Thirty percent of all construction workers, 70 percent of all teachers, and 70 percent of all doctors

---

12. Nicolas S. Timasheff, "The Attempt to Abolish the Family in Russia," in Norman W. Bell and Ezra F. Vogel (eds.), *A Modern Introduction to the Family* (New York: Free Press, 1960), p. 56.

were women. Women were able to fill skilled jobs because they were nearly equal in education to men. For example, in 1960, 49 percent of all college graduates and 53 percent of secondary school graduates were women.

A number of programs were initiated that were only partially successful. Among these were communal kitchens and a broad based social insurance program. The working husband and wife found the communal dining rooms useful, but over time these have tended to drop out of use and the private kitchen has become taken for granted as part of the average urban dweller's life. The social insurance program still leaves a large number of people without adequate coverage.

The Reform of 1936: Soviet policy has changed significantly over the years. The official decrees discussed in the above sections pertain to the period before 1917 to the beginning of World War II. By 1936, the 1920 abortion law was modified. Abortions were forbidden except for medical reasons. Divorce was made more difficult in that it was to cost 50 rubles for the first divorce, 150 for the second, and 300 for the third. Freedom of choice was thereby limited. Child bearing was encouraged in 1936 by a stipend system granting the mother 2,000 rubles for each child over six and under ten. For the eleventh child she was to receive 5,000 rubles. The abortoria had effected a decline in the Russian population, and large families were now encouraged.

Post World War II: World War II had a devastating effect upon Soviet society. Those of us untouched by war can hardly realize what it must have been like for a nation to lose 20 million citizens—more than half of them civilian. In the Ukraine, half of the means of production was destroyed. Eighty-two thousand schools serving 15 million children were destroyed. Half of Russia's ships, port facilities, machinery, farm equipment, and railroads were destroyed.

The failure of the various family policies became more critical as a result of the destruction of war. The rise in divorce rate, decline in the birth rate, and the increase in juvenile delinquency were each in part a result of this failure in policy. These problems the family could handle better after the state's failure. Accordingly, the 1944 Code reinstated the regularization of marriage. Only registered marriages would confer rights to individuals. The state now enriched the ceremony, and marriage parlors became popular. Divorce became even more expensive (500 to 2,000 rubles) and was now a lengthy procedure requiring the couple to seek professional help to save the marriage. Further, People's Courts could refuse divorces. Women were now given assistance for their third child (400 rubles). Finally, under the 1944 reform, unwed mothers were not entitled to support from the father, but only from the state. Thus a greater degree of stigma was attached to illegitimacy.

THE MODERN SOVIET FAMILY

What is family life like in the Soviet Union today? Kent Geiger and others provide us with a sense of the problems confronting the "typical" Russian family, but do not provide us with much insight into the joys and successes of such family life. Clearly rather basic hardships are more common in Russia than in our own society today. Water is often not piped into one's private quarters but requires a trip to the basement, court yard, or community well (in the smaller towns). Communal dining halls still in existence require the patrons to line up before meals. Family concerns reflect a class base. The upper-class person seems most concerned to find more time at home with his family, the middle-class man more concerned with better housing, and the lower class much more beseiged by basic problems and therefore not as describable in terms of a modal problem.

The masculine and feminine roles of Soviet citizens have been altered radically. The war and military service have more adversely affected the male population. In the 1959 census, for example, there were almost twice as many women as men. Despite the emphasis on feminine equality, men seem reluctant to assume "feminine" jobs around the home—dishes, child care, etc. Women do not work simply because they want to even though they are "liberated." Aside from those comparatively few career women, women work because of economic need and a sense of duty and out of the conviction that housework is unimportant—essentially the same reasons women give for working in the United States.

Geiger suggests three basic family types: (1) the female-headed family with the mother working is a common country type; (2) a conjugal family of minimal functioning (cooking, child care, etc., being provided by the state); (3) a conjugal family in which many of the family's functions are performed by another person—particularly the *babuska* (grandmother).[13] He distinguishes several patterns of authority in these types: extended families ruled by the old men and those where, in general, the male dominates are typical of the peasant population. The family stressing equality of the sexes is an urban revolutionary pattern and the strong woman type a by-product of revolution and war. The overall tendency is still from male dominance toward equality within the family. As one might expect, the impact of ideology is much more difficult to discern when a large population is concerned since there are so many groups within the population who respond differently. A multiplicity of family forms and authority structures results. The greatest changes have occurred among the urbanites. Yet the dominant family form of the Soviet city seems hardly distinguishable from the Western urban types.

HOW EXTENSIVELY HAVE SOVIET FAMILIES CHANGED?

Data on the change in family and structure, even if accurate, do not tell us much about the character of family life. Official publications are more inclined toward rationalizations of ideological positions than clarifying changes in family life. Outsiders are generally prohibited from studying such inside matters. Consequently, we are prevented from a fine-grained analysis of the change in Soviet family life.

13. Geiger *op. cit.*

Nevertheless, there is much conjecture. Geiger contends that the change has been minimal. "The important thing is that the old ways are tenacious, not easily changed and that when change is nonetheless demanded by the new situations offered by life, it has to be accounted for, justified, rationalized."[14] He contends further that the ideological revolution has not brought about a significantly new family. "There is no evidence that the changes in property law brought by the revolution have made the 'socialist family' any more stable, solidary or otherwise better than the family in a society where it is legal for individuals and families to own productive property."[15] As he sees it, family behavior seems to be governed by individual personality factors which do not permit patterns to be predicted and, further, where change in the family has occurred it seems to be more in the character of the larger society than in the character of the family itself. On the other hand, proportionately twice as many Soviet women work as do American women, and about five times as many Soviet children are cared for in groups (creches) as is true in America. These facts in themselves would suggest that whatever change toward an equalitarian family has occurred, it has progressed further in the Soviet Union than in the United States. Whether this is radical change or change due mainly to ideological factors associated with socialism are other questions much more difficult to answer.

What seems clear is that there has been a continuous struggle over the past thirty years between official ideology and the practice of family life with the continuing uncertainty as to where to draw the line between the rights of the individual and legitimate interests of the regime. "The debate is public in the 'no man's land' between regime disapproval and no legal constraints."[16] It goes on clandestinely in the areas of clear prohibition. The typical modern urban Soviet family may differ little in composition and style from the typical urban family of the West, but—even so—this family is quite different from the extended patriarchal family of Czarist days. The new family being forged under socialist reform is as yet a minority pattern, but its equalitarianism seems much more realized in fact than is true for similar patterns in our own society. For some families in the Soviet Union, the change from prerevolutionary days has been great indeed. For large numbers of peasants and rural folks, the old ways persist largely unchanged.

The Kibbutzim

Our best source of information on planned family change comes from the study of the Kibbutzim of Israel.[17] These experiments in utopia began with the founding of Degania in 1910. Today, many Kibbutzim are in their third

14. *Ibid.*, p. 325.
15. *Ibid.*, p. 324.
16. *Ibid.*, p. 327.
17. This section draws heavily upon Dan Leon, *The Kibbutz: A New Way of Life* (Oxford, England: Pergamon Press, 1970); Leslie *op. cit.*; Yonina Talmon, "The Family in a Revolutionary Movement—The Case of the Kibbutz in Israel," in Nimkoff *op. cit.*; and Dorothy Blitzen, *The World of the Family* (New York: Random House, 1963).

lation of 93,210 persons (Table 16–2). They constitute about 4 percent of the generation. They comprise 225 settlements which had (in 1967) a total popu-population of the state of Israel. Politically these settlements are organized into three main streams and several minor movements (Table 16–3) each with its own particular ideological flavor and characteristic style of life. I am concerned in this section with the Kibbutz Artzi Hashomer Hatzair, the largest of these federations comprising 73 settlements and producing about 11 percent of Israel's total agricultural output. In many regards it represents ideologically a middle position between extreme leftist socialism and rightest Zionist patriotism. The locations of these Kibbutzim are given on the map (Figure 16–5).

HISTORY

The founding fathers of the Kibbutz came principally from western European ghettoes. The typical family of the Jewish ghetto was a large extended patriarchal family which had corporate characteristics in that members frequently owned property in common and expected economic as well as emotional support from one another. This patriarchal family was thus highly functional and strongly supported by the Jewish faith. Under such a system the patriarch was obliged to provide food and shelter for a large number of relatives, and younger members of the family were expected to give of the fruits of their labors to support the older members. As members of a persecuted minority group, Jews were not permitted to own land in a large number of European countries and thus were dependent in the main upon small businesses and mercantilism.

The first Kibbutzniks were typically single adolescent youths, most of

TABLE 16–2
The Kibbutz Movement and Jewish Population of Israel

Date	Jewish population	Kibbutz population	Percentage
1 Oct. 1930	175,000	4,506	2.57%
1 Oct. 1940	492,400	25,900	5.24
1 Oct. 1945	592,000	37,400	6.32
1 Oct. 1950	1,152,000	64,029	5.56
1 Oct. 1955	1,580,000	80,348	5.09
1 Oct. 1960	1,902,000	80,155	4.21
1 Oct. 1965	2,284,300	87,162	3.82
1 Oct. 1967*	2,372,000	93,210	3.93

Source: Dan Leon, *The Kibbutz: A New Way of Life* (Oxford: Pergamon Press, 1970), p. 201.

*A New York Times *article of Jan 11, 1970, "Kibbutz Worried," contends that the 1970 population of the Kibbutzim ". . . represents only 3.7% with less than 100,000 members." Such figures could, of course, reflect a continued growth in absolute numbers.

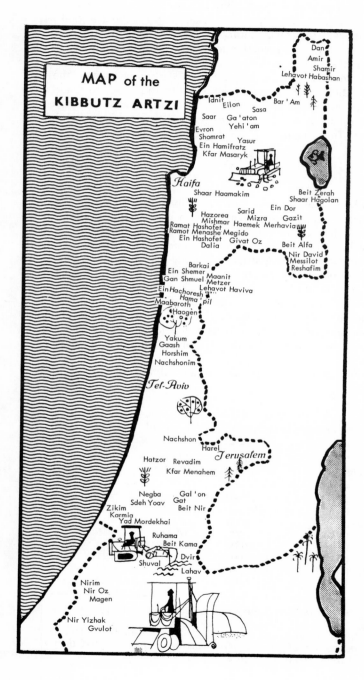

MAP of the
KIBBUTZ ARTZI

Dan
Amir
Shamir
Lehavot Habashan

Idnit
Eilon
Saar   Ga'aton   Sasa   Bar'Am
Evron   Yehi'am
Shomrat
Ein Hamifratz   Yasur
Kfar Masaryk

Haifa
Shaar Haamakim
Beit Zerah
Shaar Hagolan

Ein Dor
Hazorea   Sarid
Mishmar   Mizra   Gazit
Ramat Hashofet   Haemek   Merhavia
Ramot Menashe   Megido
Ein Hashofet   Givat Oz
Dalia   Beit Alfa
Nir David
Messilot
Reshafim

Barkai
Ein Shemer   Maanit
Gan Shmuel   Metzer
Lehavot Haviva
Ein Hachoresh
Hama'pil
Maabaroth
Haogen

Yakum
Gaash
Horshim
Nachshonim

Tel-Aviv

Nachshon
Harel   *Jerusalem*
Hatzor   Revadim
Kfar Menahem

Negba   Gal'on
Sdeh Yoav   Gat
Zikim   Beit Nir
Karmia
Yad Mordekhai
Ruhama
Beit Kama
Dvir
Shuval
Lahav

Nirim
Nir Oz
Magen

Nir Yizhak
Gvulot

FIGURE 16–5
From Dan Leon, Kibbutz:
A New Way of Life
(Pergamon, 1970).

TABLE 16–3
The Kibbutz Population, September 30, 1967

Federation	Number of Kibbutzim	Population	Percentage
Whole kibbutz movement	225	93,210	100%
Kibbutz Artzi Hashomer Hatzair	73	32,061	34.5
Ichud Hakvutzot V'hakibbutzim	75	28,936	30.4
Hakibbutz Hameuchad	57	25,609	27.7
Hakibbutz Hadati	10	3,987	4.2
Haoved Hatzioni	5	1,300	1.7
Poalei Agudat Yisrael	2	448	0.7
Others	3	869	1.0

Source: Dan Leon, *The Kibbutz: A New Way of Life* (Oxford: Pergamon Press, 1970), p. 200.

whom were male and embued with a Marxist-Socialist-Zionist ideology. They were intent upon reforming the Jewish people by developing once again a strong and prosperous Jewish peasantry.

> When the strong hand of the Jewish peasant once more guides the plough, the Jewish problem will be solved. [Herzl]

Palestine, the historic home of the Jewish people, became a symbol of a new unification of the Diasporic Jew and a locus of hope for these youths. By settling in Palestine and reclaiming the land from the desert, they hoped to rebuild the Jewish people and overcome the unnatural economic base that mercantilism provided. The Zionist Jews who came to Palestine seeking liberation at the close of the nineteenth century had to give up their venture because they quickly became either employers of cheap Arab labor or vassals of Jewish philanthropists abroad. They failed to establish sufficient economic autonomy to enable them to carry on the implementation of their vision. Their failure was known to the youthful pioneers of the twentieth century.

Dan Leon summarized the influences which motivated the foundation of the first Kibbutz groups as including the following:

The supreme test of settlement, colonization and physical security could best be tackled by the joint effort of a group united by common aims, and fortifying the will and staying power of the individual through complete mutual aid and responsibility.

This would facilitate the transition to agricultural labor of young people unaccustomed to its rigours, especially in the harsh and primitive conditions of the new land.

It would make possible the absorption and integration into the new life of new settlers from future waves of immigration.

This group would be founded on the individual consciousness of every settler, and the whole framework would be entirely voluntary, lacking any form of external coercion.

It would be based exclusively on self-labor by Jewish workers, and they would undertake every type of work, however hard, including the guarding of their own security.

The group would be democratically self-governed, and completely equalitarian. Equal rights woud be granted to all, and there would be full equality for all in everything. This would include equality between men and women, between original settlers and newcomers, and between all members regardless of the work performed.

The Kibbutz would play a pioneering role not only in settlement, but also in shaping the image of the new socialistic society in the Jewish homeland.[18]

These should be considered to be rough guiding principles, not precise plans for a community. As rough guides they were in part reactions against the hierarchy of the ghetto family and its high degree of familism as well as an attempt to establish a society that could withstand the pressures of discrimination and prejudice. These principles stress the importance of pioneering and working with the hands as a redemptive element and place great emphasis upon cooperation in a face-to-face democracy where the concept of household was really transferred to the community at large rather than a resident group or conjugal family. A strong emphasis upon equalitarianism is also apparent, not only between generations but also between the sexes. Blitzen argues that the family form that characterized the early settlements (in which marriage was abandoned, mating was deemed a personal affair, and housekeeping and child rearing were largely communal, thus freeing the parents for work and for defense of the community) was an attempt to realize an adolescent dream as much as any political ideal.[19] The desire to escape from child-rearing responsibilities and the easy access to sexual gratification are characteristic of adolescent society. On the other hand, the composition of the early communities, the harshness of their struggle for survival, and the Marxist-feminist ideology of equalitarianism were also factors that contributed to the abandonment of the nuclear family. Early settlements were, in any event, quite primitive. The Kibbutz today, however, may be quite modern and comfortable (Figure 16–6).

18. Leon *op. cit.,* pp. 8–9.
19. Blitzen *op. cit.*

FIGURE 16–6
*Above, the beginnings of Kibbutz Artzi, which was established in 1922
with Kibbutz Biet Alta; below, Kibbutz Artzi in the 1960s. From Dan
Leon,* The Kibbutz: A New Way of Life *(Pergamon, 1970).*

THE KIBBUTZ FAMILY PATTERN

It is fair to say that the Kibbutz has transferred to a surprising extent family
loyalty from extended family to include the whole of a community of perhaps
250 to 1,000 people. Within this community a three generational family may
exist as a group of persons bound together by blood and marriage (which

has been re-introduced since the founding of the state of Israel in 1948), but it does not exist as an independent economic or socializing unit. The members of its several conjugal families do not reside together, nor do they spend a major portion of their day together. Married couples, however, do share a room. Their children are reared communally in age groups which become the major socializing influence in their lives according to Bruno Bettleheim. A conjugal family of such low functionality at first unmarked by a formal marriage ceremony led early writers such as Milford Spiro to comment that the nuclear family was not universal.[20] It simply did not exist in the Kibbutz. A better perspective acknowledges the existence of the structure and points to the many ways in which parents and their own children are recognized as a functioning unit, but admits that this unit has been greatly submerged in the structure of the community as a whole which receives center-stage importance.

Education: At the heart of the Kibbutz society are the principles of collective education:

> *The fundamental aim of the educational system in the Kibbutz Artzi, which is known as collective education, is to ensure the continuity of Kibbutz values. Though over the years it has developed into a school of education in its own right, it is not detached educational theory, but endeavors to translate into educational terms the basic values of Kibbutz society—labour, equality, collectivism, democracy and voluntarism. Its educational precepts are inseparable from the theory and practice of Kibbutz life, from the ideology of the Kibbutz as a value in itself and as an instrument for the national and social liberation of the Jewish people.[21]*

Kibbutz children are reared by these principles from birth onward. Table 16–4 indicates their progression from one stage to another. Each stage has separate housing facilities designed to meet the needs of this particular age group, and each stage is overseen by community appointed nurses or metaplets. For the first six weeks after a child's birth, his mother is relieved of her other work responsibilities to the community so that she may feed, change, and care for her baby, but the baby remains in the infant's house. She puts her child to bed and goes to her own quarters. Further, her treatment of her baby during the day is supervised by metaplets (which proves to be a boon especially to young inexperienced mothers).

At about fifteen months a metaplet who has been with the children in the infant's house assumes responsibility for the care of six children in the toddler's house. There the children learn proper eating habits, cleanliness, and discipline. At four or five in the afternoon the children return home for the "children's hour" with their parents. Each parental room has a children's corner where the child's personal toys are kept (a recent concession to pri-

---

20. Milford E. Spiro, "Is the Family Universal?—The Israeli Case" in Bell and Vogel *op. cit.,* pp. 55–63.
21. Leon *op. cit.,* p. 37.

TABLE 16–4
Stages for Kibbutz Children

	Age	No. in group	Educ. workers	Study hours	Work hours
Infants' house	Birth to 1¼	—	Infants' nurse Metaplet	—	—
Toddlers' house	1¼–4	6	Metaplet	—	—
Kindergarten and transition-kindergarten (Grade 1)	4–7	18	Kindergarten teacher, 2 Metaplet	Flexible	Flexible
Children's community (Primary School Grades 2–6)	7–12	18	Teacher, Metaplet	4–6 hours per day	Up to 1 hour
High school	12–18	25	Teacher, Metaplet	34 hrs. per week	12–13: 1 hr. 14–15: 2 hrs. 16–18: 3 hrs.

Source: Dan Leon, *The Kibbutz: A New Way of Life* (Oxford: Pergamon Press, 1970), p. 99.

vate property). After visiting and relaxing with his parents the child returns to the toddler's house and the metaplet puts him to bed with a snack and a story or song. In the last year two groups which have been living together side by side are joined by a third group of six to make the basic unit for a kindergarten class.

The kindergarten group of eighteen children share a common building that contains their eating, sleeping, and learning quarters. Here, as elsewhere in the system, they are not segregated by sex, but share bedroom, table, toilet, and shower with members of the opposite sex. Activities of the kindergarten years include gymnastics, musical education, clay-modeling, crafts, acting, nature trips, story telling, and training in the arts of conversation and discussion. Emphasis is upon a child's developing his senses and physical skills. During the last year (ages six to seven), he is introduced to reading, writing, and arithmetic and expected to master the basic skills by the age of eight.

The children's community (composed of children from seven to twelve), runs its own farm where the children look after ducks, rabbits, pigeons, sheep, and other domestic animals. Group loyalty and solidarity are developed, and the election of functioning committees within the children's community is encouraged with the supervision of the metaplet. Training in collective living, Kibbutz style, is formally begun.

High school education frequently takes place in a school that is jointly owned and operated by several Kibbutzim, although the larger communities may have their own. This school, in any event, is set apart from the rest of the community with its own grounds and recreational facilities. About 4,000 students studied in 27 Kibbutz Artzi high schools in 1967.

> *All Kibbutz children without exception receive a full high school education. Since free and compulsory education in Israel covers only elementary school, this is a great financial burden on a workers' community like the Kibbutz involving an expensive building, a large staff and smaller classes than those in town. . . . Insofar as this is humanly possible, the Kibbutz gives the lie to the cynical idea that all people are born equal but that some are more equal than others. For it is not only a highly child-oriented society, but its education is unreservedly non-selective. In accordance with this principle of non-selectivity, no grades are given, no formal examinations held and no pupils held back a class. Though its academic standards are high, Kibbutz education is not concerned to cram the pupil with the maximum amount of pure knowledge. Real education—in the sense of the development of intellect, of personality, of character and of social values—and instruction, the inculcation of pure knowledge, are inseparable in the Kibbutz school.*[22]

In spite of the utopian character of such a venture, the Kibbutz students compare favorably with non-Kibbutz Israelis in national examinations and surpass the average Israeli in meeting the requirements of the various branches of the armed forces.

Ordinarily after graduation from high school both boys and girls serve two years in the army and recently have assumed a third year of service to the movement helping young settlements to become established. The service these young people provide to the state and to the movement is widely acclaimed. During service to the state they are exposed to the larger world of cities, and some decide not to return. The percentage of youth not returning to the Kibbutz has never exceeded 25 percent, and the average Kibbutz would not expect to lose more than 15 percent of its youth. Accordingly most Kibbutz were composed of at least 50 percent Kibbutz-born (Sabras) in 1970. The movement is continuing to grow, although at a slower rate than the rate of growth of the population of the state of Israel as a whole (Table 16–2).

Marriage: Courtship is strongly influenced by collective education, the rebellion against bourgeois morality, and the lingering heritage of a conservative religious tradition. At first there was no marriage at all. Sexual relations were to be based upon personal need and consent. "My husband," "my wife," and "my children," in keeping with Marxist ideology, were capitalistic labels. A couple who wished to establish a lasting relationship stated their intention to become "a couple" by applying for a common room. After 1948, marriage ceremonies were frequently performed only after the birth of a child because the state required such to legitimize the birth. Any "uncoupled" adult was a

22. *Ibid.*, p. 22.

potential sexual partner for any other person of similar status, but of opposite sex. However, because of the sibling-like nature of the peer group within which one was educated, many preferred to marry outside their own Kibbutz. Promiscuity was never much of a problem, however, and most young adults voluntarily sought monogamous relationships eventually. At first divorce rates were relatively high. Now they are lower than in the state of Israel as a whole.

The Kibbutz desire to make sex a natural matter has not meant that in fact it has gone unregulated. Indeed while coitus is not condemned after high school and before marriage, conception is frowned upon under such conditions. Whether a new sexual morality has indeed developed is hotly contested. Those within the movement are convinced that such has developed. Some outside observers are skeptical. Bruno Bettelheim is one such example:

> *The new Jew, in the new society, would not be bound by these age-old sexual anxieties; all such taboos would be done away with. It was a liberating experience the founders meant to provide for their children: From infancy on everything would be open about sex and the body. Nothing would be hidden as shameful.*
>
> *Actually such arrangements lead to sexual stimulation. This forces one either to act upon it—as occurs typically among children who share life together very "openly" under slum conditions—or leads to early and far-reaching sex repression, and these to the development of a deeply puritanical attitude toward sex. But Kibbutz children have little option. Because they are not only asked to be "natural and open" about their bodies, it is expected that this will make them "pure" about it. That is they should not only not have sex, but should not even desire it.[23]*

Because Bettelheim comes to the Kibbutz with Freudian notions about repression, it is not unusual that he would make such an observation. If indeed it is true that this openness and naturalness about sex is intended to create a new form of puritanism because, presumably, there is now no longer the need to act upon one's erotic impulses, then it would seem that not much has been liberated. On the other hand, most studies on the Kibbutz give the impression that a great deal of acting on these impulses does in fact occur—at least to the extent that couples typically experiment rather widely before settling down to monogamy. If the latter is the case, then it is hard to see the weight of Bettelheim's point. At best he is arguing against the *manner* in which sex is regulated or—for those who may be blinded by their ideology into thinking that sex that is natural is unregulated—he is emphasizing the point that it is regulated indeed.

Given the fact that both husband and wife were nearly equal contributors to the Kibbutz economy there was little basis for male dominance in the household (Table 16–5). Men helped their women with the little housework that was necessary to keep their room in order, and women participated in

23. Bruno Bettelheim, *Children of the Dream* (New York: Macmillan, 1969), p. 237.

TABLE 16–5
Comparison of Men's and Women's Responsibilities in Kibbutz Artzi

	Women	Men
No task	55.4%	40%
Membership in a committee	24.6	18
Chairman of a committee or branch-organizer	16.3	34
Central task (Secretary, Treasurer, outside movement work)	3.7	8

Source: Dan Leon, *The Kibbutz: A New Way of Life* (Oxford: Pergamon Press, 1970), p. 130.

all aspects of the community's work. Women have, however, tended to become concentrated in a few areas of work and are relatively scarce in others (Table 16–6). They have also tended to stress feminine dress and decorum after work as the settlements have become established. Thus equality in the Kibbutz has not meant an identity of masculine and feminine roles and has not yet been realized to the extent that Kibbutz women desire:

> The women want to be equal, but not the same, not only in the choice of clothes or furniture. . . . They want to preserve their femininity, and the Kibbutz needs their emotional warmth, their discretion in taste, their ability to make a room into a home, their feeling for beauty and refinement. . . . Women in the Kibbutz have . . . achieved a degree of equality which cannot be compared to that in other societies, and a unique degree of independence. Equality is guaranteed—but its potential is yet to be exploited to the full.[24]

As the hardships of the desert are overcome, the standard of living improved, and the need for an increasing rate of growth recognized, more weight has been given to the conjugal family unit which might seem to the founders (whose principles placed more weight upon the collective) to be a crucial concession. Rooms have become homes where once they were bare and uninviting. In some Kibbutzim children sleep with their parents (not in the Kibbutz Artzi movement, however). More time and money are thus vested in the conjugal unit, but the collective spirit remains strong. The Kibbutz have not become cooperatives. That type of community is for the Moshave movement which remains in constant dialogue with the Kibbutzim.

ECONOMIC BASE

The equality in the Kibbutz is realized by various techniques of distribution. In some settlements each member is granted a fixed number of exchange units per year and may buy anything he wishes with that "money." The cen-

24. Leon *op. cit.*, p. 134.

TABLE 16–6
Women's Roles in Kibbutz Artzi

Education	36.1%
Clothing (clothes-store, sewing, laundry)	18.5
Kitchen and dining-hall	13.2
Agriculture	8.9
Administration (includes accountancy)	4.3
Health	4
Industry	3.9
Full-time public activity	1
Outside work	0.6
Miscellaneous (crafts, illness, feeding mothers, etc.)	9.3

Source: Dan Leon, *The Kibbutz: A New Way of Life* (Oxford: Pergamon Press, p. 132.

TABLE 16–7
Distribution of the Labor Force of Kibbutz Artzi

	Labor force	Agriculture	Industry	Outside work
1962	8350	69.7%	15.2%	15.1%
1964	8850	67.2	16.4	16.4
1966	9190	64.5	17.4	18.1

Source: Dan Leon, *The Kibbutz: A New Way of Life* (Oxford: Pergamon Press, 1970), p. 38.

tral committee must decide the value of each item produced in the Kibbutz or brought in from the outside. Even gifts from relatives must be evaluated and this value deducted from the fixed income of the member. Food in community dining halls presents no problem since each may eat what he wishes according to his needs. Such an equality of distribution is easier in communities based upon agriculture, because there is not as broad a variation in skills required in such communities as is the case in industrial societies. Indeed early in the movement members rotated jobs so that no one remained in one for long.

However, as the settlements have prospered and the state has required more of the service of members, each settlement must set aside a portion of its labor force for outside work in the movement and in the state (ordinarily about 18 percent). As industries are brought in, managers must acquire increased skills, and the ability to rotate them declines. Table 16–7 shows that although the labor force of the Kibbutz is still predominantly agricultural, an increasing percentage is being devoted to industrial work. Indeed in 1966, 82 percent of the Kibbutz Artzi population lived in settlements with industries.

Because of the increased output, these plants are able to prosper in spite of their inability to hire and fire at will or to expand their size beyond the size deemed critical to maintaining community cohesion. Nevertheless, many plants must hire outside workers, and these workers are not imbued with the spirit of the movement. They must also be paid competitive wages, a fact that upsets the Kibbutz economy and its ideal of equality of income. Kibbutzim are working to eliminate such contradictions and reduce the number of outsiders, but during the transition to industry such adjustments seem inevitable. Leon argues that Kibbutz industry will remain competitive with Israeli industry, and that industry will provide an increasing portion of the movement's income. If the Kibbutz can meet the challenge of industrialization without the loss of its spirit of equalitarianism, it will indeed have taken a great leap forward.

Summary

Although such case studies must remain unique instances of change in some degree, they have a number of commonalities, particularly with regard to structure. Each type of community advocated communal child rearing for the express purpose of liberating the woman from this primary responsibility and in order to facilitate the inculcation of community and collectivist norms. Each was an attack upon the conjugal family as an expression of bourgeois capitalism and morality. The Soviet attack seems, at least initially, most anti-conjugal family because a normative alternative to monogamous marriage was not specified. Each asserted a socialist vision of equality, although Oneida's was tempered by perfectionist theology, the Kibbutz by Zionism, and the Russian by a humanist secularism. In this dimension as well, the Russian experiment seems to be more against certain social factors—such as capitalism and Eastern Orthodoxy—than it was *for* some viable alternative. The large-scale nature of the revolutionary movement did not permit as ready a formulation of an alternative ideal that was acceptable to the majority as was the case with Oneida and the Kibbutz. Both of these latter, furthermore, had the added advantage of being able to recruit their members from a much larger body of persons dedicated to principles (perfectionism and Zionism) in some measure supportive of the new communities. The party in the Soviet Union has not enjoyed a similar position nor has it been able to isolate its experiment spatially from the general public in order to maximize the effects of its selective recruitment of members.

The size of the reform effort thus seems critical. In all three instances a social ideology sought expression in concrete social organization. In terms of effecting the maximum amount of alteration in family structure over the longest period of time, the Russian attempt seems least successful. In large part this is so because not everyone shared the same vision, and those who held to a more perfect vision could not be—or were not in fact—separated from the masses so that through selective recruitment they could bring their principles to more effective expression. The problem of socializing the second generation was thus maximized because a distinctive culture was not established within a bounded community. Competing authorities compound the problem of maximizing change in a single direction.

Size is critical internally as well. Internal cohesion through direct democracy is not possible when the population is measured in the millions. Laws do not function as adequately as mutually agreed upon principles in enforcing conformity. Although Oneida was in fact an oligarchy at best, it reaffirmed its consent to be so governed each evening in the community meetings. In the Kibbutz the whole settlement participated in the decision-making process.

The effect of external threats in bringing about internal cohesive action must also be seen as related to the size of the experimental endeavor. Both Oneida and the Kibbutz settlements were relatively small in comparison to the hostile forces beyond their community boundaries. They knew for a fact that they must surely "all hang together or they would all hang separately." Again, in the case of the Russian experiment the threat of capitalism was much more diffuse and the response much more diverse.

It seems fair to say that the vision of family reform expressed in Soviet policy has tended to be much more dogmatic. The state formulates the policy, the citizen is expected to acquiesce to the authoritarian statement of truth. Even Noyes was able to remain flexible enough on the issue of principle to allow various attempts at its expression. Both Oneida and the Kibbutz can be seen as "experimental" in this sense and the Russian less clearly so.

The great advantage of the Kibbutz over the Oneida community is that the former is based upon the principle of direct democracy, encouraging the establishment of the broadest possible base of leadership, while Oneida was overly dependent upon its elders and infatuated with the charisma of Noyes. To date the Kibbutz has been able to cope with the problem of succession and is now socializing the third generation. The Kibbutz thus seems to have built in much greater capacity to adapt to new situations than even its recent critics maintain. Its principles remain virtually unchanged, but the policy emanating from them has permitted continual modification of the economic base and the educational system. Furthermore, the external threat to the Kibbutz has been maximized with the increase in Arab hostility. Oneidans never had to fight for their lives.

On the other hand, Kibbutzim have lost some of their status in the larger society with the establishment of the state, and they can rely less upon immigration to fill their numbers. Whether continued modification of family roles will re-instate the type of conjugal family typical of Western industrial societies remains to be seen. While some critics see this as a possibility, the fact remains that the family as found in the Kibbutz today is quite different. With all of its problems, the Kibbutz seems to have become a permanent part of Israeli society. But even if it should be swallowed up in the state or modified into a form of cooperative, it has demonstrated quite successfully that men are able to change the character of their family life to fit their vision of the good life. This venture in utopia seems durable indeed.

17. Trends and Proposals

The family of the future must not be defined in terms of more structure but in terms of less explicit structure. It must at once be flexible enough for increasingly individuated people, yet a stable basic unit for human life. The family as a commitment implies freedom in the definition of the marital relationship in order to meet the demands of the particular way of life of the two people involved.

CHARLES W. HOBART

What will the family be like in the future—say the year 2000? This question invites two types of response. The first is an attempt to project from present trends broad propositions about this future family assuming relatively little innovation is possible. The second assumes that some intentional intervention is possible and that a present trend need not continue as one might predict. Ordinarily this latter approach analyzes the ills of current family forms and proposes solutions that will make the family more functional and more in line with the conception of what the ideal family should be.

Neither approach at present is well grounded in reliable information. Our capacity to predict is, therefore, quite limited. Predictions based on statistical trends have often proved to be inaccurate in the past. Even those attempting to assess the net gain or loss in such broad features of family life as familism have ordinarily not specified the time period over which they were attempting to predict. Therefore, it is impossible to tell whether they are accurate, not only because of the lack of operational clarity in their variables, but also because of the lack of a target date. And yet it is natural that we continue to attempt to predict. Such attempts can help refine variables and can force us to reconceptualize the family as a unit of analysis. Presumably the more we understand, the more accurate will be our predictions. However, there is an element of self-fulfilling prophecy that plagues all predictions. In some degree the family in fact will be like the experts say it will be only because they say it will be so. The family is also affected by experts' conceptions of what it *ought* to be. This effect has been partially confirmed by Martha Wolfenstein and others in their studies of child-rearing practices, and there is no reason to believe that expert advice does not have an effect upon other aspects of family life as well.

I will begin this chapter with an examination of attempts to project current family trends into the future. These projections tend to assume that the form of the family will be essentially the nuclear or conjugal family and its derivatives, although some redefinition of role and function might be possible. The second section will discuss several proposals for family change. These tend to be more radical in their prescriptions and appeal to our capacity to intentionally alter the structure and dynamics of our family life. They do not predict what the family *will* be, but rather offer suggestions as to what it *should* be. Implementation of such programs, in general, presupposes freedom of choice and the courage to affirm one's convictions in action. Nevertheless, these prescriptions for change are also based upon scientific information about how the family operates.

Projections

It is not possible to project present trends into the future without considerable analysis.[1] Even the attempt to predict what is happening to such relatively precise statistical variables as "age at first marriage" cannot be simply a projection of the curve plotting age at first marriage against time into the

1. Most of the articles referred to in this section are assembled in John N. Edwards, ed., *The Family and Change* (New York: Knopf, 1969).

future. Other factors such as the number of potential spouses available at any given time also influence the age at which persons marry. These factors, in turn, are dependent upon many other factors such as the sex ratio, fertility rate, war, the state of the economy, and probably several unknowns as well. It is not, then, a matter of applying curve to graph paper.

METHODOLOGY

Reuben Hill discerns four methods for projecting the contemporary family into the future: extrapolation from present trends, inferences from three-generational studies, inferences from an assessment of the impact of technology upon the family, and assessment of the effects of family specialists and their advocacy upon the family. Turning to the first method, which he labels the most hazardous, Hill notes:

> Projection of current trends in marriage and the family into the future involves predictions in the following areas: trends with respect to proportion married (higher), age at first marriages (younger), family size (larger), divorce and separation (higher), remarriage (higher), births out of wedlock (higher), premarital intercourse (higher), power structure (more equalitarian), division of tasks and responsibilities (more flexibility), communication, affectional patterns, delegation of family functions, child-rearing beliefs (developmental), and policies and practices (permissive).[2]

Because Hill wrote from the perspective of family trends in 1963 to 1964, his assessment (included within parentheses) would not be identical with one made today. Two trends have statistically reversed themselves (age at first marriage has been slowly increasing for both males and females since 1966[3]; average family size has been decreasing slowly since 1966).[4] Since these reversals are quite recent, it is difficult to assess with confidence whether they are short-term or long-term changes. In addition, as has been noted in Chapter 11, some observers now see a trend toward a more authoritarian treatment of children. Finally, it is clear that such projections do not allow for class variation and seem to pertain most clearly to middle-class families. For these reasons alone, the simple attempt to project current trends into the future is not likely to be reliable. It has failed consistently in the past, and is likely to do so in the future unless "assumptions about the social and economic order were made crystal-clear and predictions were charted accordingly."[5]

The second approach—inferences from three-generational studies—was first utilized by Hill and his colleagues. On the basis of a study of 300 families over a three-generation span (100 per generation) conducted in the metro-

---

2. Reuben Hill, "The American Family of the Future," *Journal of Marriage and the Family,* Vol. 26 (February 1964), 20–28.
3. U.S. Bureau of the Census, *Statistical Abstract of the United States: 1970,* 91st ed. (Washington, D.C.: U.S.G.P.O. 1970), p 10.
4. *Ibid.,* p. 35.
5. Hill *op. cit.,* reprinted in Edwards *op. cit.,* p. 355.

politan Minneapolis-St. Paul area involving five questionnaires administered over the period of one year, a number of intergenerational changes were noted: (1) The educational superiority of wives over husbands steadily declined to near equality (12.4 to 12.6). (2) The age at first marriage declined over the three generations showing a concomitant decrease in the gap between the age of spouses at marriage. (3) The number of children born and their spacing was curvilinear—the youngest generation had a larger average family size than their parents (approximating their grandparents) but ended their child-rearing period earlier as a result of closer spacing. (4) A pattern of accelerated advancement on the job was noted. (5) The youngest generation is accordingly least fatalistic, moderately optimistic, and future oriented. (6) The trend is toward developmental child rearing, equalitarian division of labor, improvement in family value consensus, greater planning in economic matters, but deterioration of role integration. Hill summarizes:

> *Surely these data are adequate to demonstrate the possibilities of utilizing generational changes as the basis for capturing the American family of the future. From this analysis a picture emerges of increasing effectiveness, professional competence, and economic well-being, of greater flexibility in family organization with greater communication and greater conflict between spouses. There is little evidence in this generation of the phenomenon of reaction formation which is supposed to explain the turn to the right politically. This is a generation which has enjoyed the material amenities and has already chosen to elaborate the nonmaterial values of home and children. Their educational aspirations for their children are the highest of the generations.*[6]

While the three-generational model is undoubtedly useful, it too has certain limitations. Clearly the effect of developmental stage is not easily controlled. Families in earlier stages with younger parents and children compared to families in retirement will undoubtedly show differences, but that these differences can be shown to be predictive of future family forms is not clear. The support for Hill's position thus far is the fact that his intergenerational study yields results not too different from trend studies—and we have seen that these have their weaknesses. Nevertheless, used in conjunction with other approaches, this work seems promising.

The third method—assessment of the impact of technology on the family—has been discussed in Chapter 15 and is largely the result of the efforts of Ogburn and Nimkoff.

Finally, Hill summarizes the expert's position. The mate selection machinery should be re-organized to ensure that couples of similar background will meet and be tested for compatibility over a prolonged period of courtship and engagement; the intimacy of premarital sex should depend upon the conscience of the couple and the strength of their relationship; the experts should be consulted in an increasing number of cases in order to help cou-

---

6. *Ibid.*, p. 359; see also pp. 355–59 *passim.*

ples make the "right choice"; the objectives of marriage should be "the continued matching and stimulating of companionship, mutual understanding, common interest and joint activities, as well as building a system of planning and problem solving"; there is evidence of additional need for education in regard to parenthood; the chief objectives for the family can be listed in accordance with its stage of development (see Chapter 9) as family size control, physical maintenance, socialization, and gratification of emotional and motivational needs of all members. In order to accomplish these tasks the family needs a higher degree of group organization.

All methods of prediction indicate that the average family will enjoy increasing flexibility in family organization, an improvement in planning and decision making competence, and an accelerated upgrading in its standard of living. These predictions, it should be noted, are in contradiction to the commonly held view that the family is a disintegrating institution.

There are further indications that the future family will continue to be strong in many regards. Robert Parke and Paul C. Glick project the basic demographic trends to 1985. They predict that: (1) Persons now (1966) in their late twenties and their early thirties are more likely to marry at some time in their history than any other group on record. (2) The teenage marriage will continue to decline for a while then level off. (3) The relative oversupply of young women will tend to produce a further rise (over the next ten years) in the age of first marriage for women. (4) The continued decline in the difference of age at first marriage of husband and wife will reduce the frequency of widowhood and increase the likelihood of joint survival to retirement. (5) To the extent that there are reductions in poverty and improvements in the socioeconomic status of the population, divorce and separation rates should decrease. (6) The small average size of the American family as a residential unit is not likely to change much. (7) In the next twenty years five out of six aged individuals not in institutions will keep house on their own, and more than half of the adult individuals of other ages will do so.[7]

On the other hand, looking at the matter from the point of view of what is valued, Ivan Nye draws conclusions that differ from those of Parke and Glick: (1) Increasing number of families will experience a complete role reversal with the wife becoming the major provider. (2) Contrary to the above prediction of Parke and Glick the divorce rate is likely to *increase* as women become more occupationally oriented and financially independent. (3) Nursery and day-care centers will provide care for an increasing number of children as the number of full-time homemakers decreases. (4) The sexual lives of women are likely more nearly to approximate those of men as women travel more and become less dependent economically. (5) The birth rate will continue to decline as women are rewarded for other activities. (6) The age at first marriage for girls is likely to increase—not because of the marriage squeeze resulting from girls coming of marriageable age sooner than boys as

7. Robert Parke, Jr., and Paul C. Glick, "Prospective Changes in Marriage and the Family," *Journal of Marriage and Family*, Vol. 29 (May 1967), 249–56.

Parke and Glick would have it, but because education will be seen by women as more beneficial to them as it earns them higher status in the job market.[8] These predictions Nye labels as "probable latent consequences" of the fact that increasingly more of the normative family behavior is held to be instrumentally valuable rather than intrinsically valuable. Things that are valued primarily for their utility, he reasons, are more susceptible to change.

On the broader consideration of the relative importance of the family as an institution, the professional opinion is equally divided. Charles W. Hobart contends that because of essentially nonfamilial values (such as our emphasis on achieved status and materialistic rewards), because of the continued loss of familial functions to other institutions, and because of our increasing mobility the modern family is rapidly weakening. *If the family is to survive as a humanistic institution, it must assume a less explicit structure and tolerate a higher degree of individualism which stresses the intrinsic worth of members.* Increased leisure time will provide the opportunity for increased involvement in family affairs and potentially increase the meaningfulness of this involvement.[9]

John Edwards takes exception to Hobart's position, arguing that rather than a revolution in values, there will be an increased interdependence between the family and the economic sphere. This will bring into closer alignment familial rewards which are largely affective with those provided through other institutions which are to a great extent instrumental.[10] On the other hand, Robert and Rhona Rapoport assume that the sphere of work and family will continue to be differentiated even further. They point out, however, that this need not mean that the family sphere will continue to diminish in importance. In fact they suggest that critical role transitions in both the familial and the career sphere tend to occur simultaneously in an advanced industrial society, thus increasing the importance of personality variables in *both* spheres.

For example, the professional career requires a training period corresponding to engagement in the family sphere, a choice of career lines corresponding to the honeymoon, and a period of early establishment corresponding to early marriage. "Fitting participation patterns in work and family together, like coping with the tasks posed within each sphere, is partly a matter of an individual style that emerges as the individuals meet each successive situation, rather than the outcome of conformity to or deviance from a pre-existing normative pattern."[11] Thus, in their view, both work and family tend to benefit to the extent that these critical role transitions occur

---

8. F. Ivan Nye, "Values, Family, and a Changing Society," *Journal of Marriage and Family,* Vol 29 (May 1967), 241–48.

9. Charles W. Hobart, "Commitment, Value Conflict and the Future of the American Family," in Edwards *op. cit.,* pp. 325–38.

10. John N. Edwards, "The Future of the Family Revisited," *Journal of Marriage and the Family,* Vol. 29 (August 1967), p. 505–11.

11. Robert and Rhona Rapoport, "Work and Family in Contemporary Society," *American Sociological Review,* Vol. 30 (June 1965), 381–94.

simultaneously and to the extent that career (and marriage) opportunities are sufficiently available to permit selection on the basis of personal style. This most nearly obtains in the case of upper-middle-class and upper-class males at present.

Continuing the line of argument that change even in structure is not necessarily bad, Clark Vincent points out that the family's greatest asset is its ability to adapt:

> *The author's thesis remains that an industrialized society characterized by rapid social change necessitates a highly adaptive family system. This adaptiveness of the family will be interpreted by some as evidence of weakness and by others as evidence of strength. Those who view it as weakness may point to the family's loss of power and authority, while those who interpret its adaptability as strength may see the dependence of the larger social system on the flexibility of the family and see the family's adaptive function as crucial to its socialization and mediation functions. The family's internal adaptiveness may well prove to be a key variable in socializing the child for the flexibility needed in future adult roles within a rapidly changing society.[12]*

IS THE FAMILY OBSOLETE?

Finally, Barrington Moore, Jr., asserts that there is evidence to suggest that the family as an institution may be obsolete. Rather than simply a reduction in function and an increasing specialization in the remaining functions of socialization or nurturance, the family in toto may be a "survival" and may soon disappear because it will become apparent that *all* of its functions can now be better performed by other institutions. Evidence that the family does not perform the task of socialization well is abundant. As I have pointed out in Chapters 9 and 13, this in part accounts for the fact that it is difficult to determine with any precision the effect of parental behavior on children. The generation gap gives further evidence of this failure at a later stage. As for the family's providing emotional support for its members, Moore suggests that it quite probably inflicts as much pain as it provides pleasure, threatens as much as it supports. When the family functioned as an economic unit, with the father clearly in authority, the emotional atmosphere was one of cooperation. With industrialization this changed. Increasingly bureaucratic institutions have taken over functions formerly performed by the family, including some of the routine aspects of raising children. Moore argues that in some instances an institutional environment can be "warm and supportive," whereas obligations and conflict often make family relationships painful. While he does not feel this transfer of responsibility will solve "all personal problems," Moore

---

12. Clark E. Vincent, "Familia Spongi: The Adaptive Function," *Journal of Marriage and Family*, Vol. 28 (February 1966), 29–36.

suggests that in the future some may praise contemporary institutions for having given "greater scope to the creative aspects of the human personality than did the family, which had begun to damage rather than develop the personality." Moore sees the trend toward bureaucratic arrangements (such as the division of labor) within the family as well as outside it, and suggests that the family will suffer the fate of other traditional institutions.[13]

The Need for Alternatives

Throughout this book I have assumed that a discussion of the various types of families found in the United States and the commonly recognized family problems would suggest the need for change. But I have not been explicit about this matter. Now it is necessary to be so.

Whether one takes the position that the nuclear family is in crisis and in need of resuscitation or that it is undergoing evolutionary or revolutionary change that should be welcomed, the net effect is that many if not most people have unmet needs in the current arrangement. Looked at from the perspective of the society as a whole, some of these needs stand out more or less independently of one's personal evaluation, and others depend quite heavily upon one's notion of the ideal society.

Unbalanced Sex Ratio: In the first instance it is quite apparent that the unbalanced sex ratio—the fact women come of age for marriage in our society sooner than men and the fact that they tend to outlive men by about seven years—means that there are large numbers of involuntarily single women in our society at present. One source estimates that they number 5 to 10 million.[14] The mores at present consign such women to involuntary chastity, although these women may behave otherwise with varying degrees of guilt. Even though our projections lead us to believe that their number will be reduced in the next twenty-five years (perhaps even to the extent of a reversal in marriage opportunity), it is not likely that the marriage market will operate with 100 percent efficiency under even the most ideal conditions. A sizable number of persons will undoubtedly remain involuntarily single during part or all of their lives. They have a great need to be incorporated into an intimate circle of people as they more or less once were under an extended kinship system. Is it not only possible but highly desirable to alter the mores and institutions so that they may live fuller, richer lives?

Defective Nurturance: There is mounting evidence that the family does not meet the emotional needs of its members adequately. This is particularly true of marriage. Cuber and Harroff document the dryness of the upper-middle-class marriage of convenience. The rising divorce rate, while indicat-

---

13. Barrington Moore, Jr., *Political Power and Social Theory* (Cambridge, Mass.: Harvard University Press, 1958), pp. 160–78.

14. Rustum and Della Roy, *Honest Sex: A Revolutionary Sex Ethic By and For Concerned Christians* (New York: The New American Library, 1968), p. 119.

ing that marriage has become more voluntary, also indicates that more and more marriages are not satisfying to both partners for some reason or other. It does not follow that all is well because those who have been disappointed try again as indicated by the increasingly high rate of remarriage. Must we continue to assume that the reason that the divorce rate continues to rise is that the conjugal family is not like it used to be and should simply be patched up in order to work better?

Inadequate Population Control: In the age of the American sexual revolution it is still possible for marriage counselors to encounter marriages in which the partners are ignorant of rather simple techniques that would increase the likelihood of their having children. On the other hand, while the birth rate is falling, the population continues to grow, and according to one school of thought will soon exceed desirable limits even in America. At the same time that the legitimate birth rate continues to fall, the illegitimate birth rate rises dramatically. Clearly we as a people are not yet proficient in pregnancy control.

We are, judging from the material discussed in Chapter 12, even less proficient in utilizing sex as a form of communication and recreation. Sexual intimacy is apparently quite difficult to achieve in our society inside or outside of marriage and, if Masters and Johnson's studies are representative, the majority of us suffer from sexual inadequacy. Aside from coitus, there is an obvious inability to express affection, particularly between adults of the opposite sex who are not married to each other. From one perspective this is a vast misuse of the human potential for joy and happiness.

Ineffective Socialization Agent: As a socializing agent, the conjugal family is declining in importance and seems increasingly ineffective in its capacity to produce well developed, adequately socialized, creative children. The generation gap is only the most obvious expression of this. This failure is not limited to the family as others have begun to assume significance as socializing agents and must share the responsibility. Yet the mode of their involvement (often professional and aloof as school teachers, counselors, doctors, clergy, etc.) leaves much to be desired. Can we assume any longer that parents are able, if willing, to compensate for the general lack of warmth and understanding when an increasingly small portion of their time is spent with their children and their authority is under constant attack?

Insufficient Social Justice: From my perspective we stand in need of greater equity and justice along a number of dimensions. The first involves the redefinition of sex roles so that women can achieve *in fact* a greater measure of fulfillment. The second has to do with expanding the role of children to open up to them a greater voice in the affairs of their society at all ages. Third, within the economic sphere the great inequity in wealth must be overcome. All of these will have an impact upon the character of American families. The last perhaps more than the rest, because we do not at present seem to be moving in this direction at all, whereas in the case of women and children we are at least en route. The implications of greater equity in wealth suggest a new type of American with a new set of values and a new mode of seeking social prestige and status. Parenthetically, the crises in our environment also call for a new American with a new set of priorities in many ways consonant with those supporting income redistribution. At the heart of both is the need to foster greater public responsibility and concern and less rugged individualism.

Finally, there are those whom we label sexual deviants who—from all that we presently know—are so involuntarily and will likely remain so for a long time to come if not permanently. Need they also remain untouchable? Might not homosexuals (true inverts), for example, be legally permitted to marry each other and required to observe the same ethic as heterosexuals with regard to fidelity and mutual care and concern? In the broader view, is it really desirable to exclude those who are different from us because they do not fit the proper categories of gender or because they choose to live in a family structure that is non-normative or participate in sexual behavior that is atypical or considered unacceptable?

Proposals

Proposals for bettering family life are a constant feature of our society. It is impossible to do justice to the variety of such proposals that have been offered. Most have not been tested in practice. They are often in opposition to projected trends in family living and sometimes even considered unworkable (for the average American) by the proposer. Nevertheless, they deserve our attention because they arise from those who have studied the family and its problems and who are convinced that it is improvable even if not completely along the lines they suggest. We can treat them here under the rubric "I wonder what would happen if . . ."[15]

TRIAL MARRIAGE

Bertrand Russell, in his *Marriage and Morals* first published in 1929, approaches the subject of reform from the perspective of developing a rational ethic, "An enlightened approach to sex and love." He was writing during the first decade of the emancipation of women and the concomitant greater freedom they espoused in sex, marriage, and divorce. A rational ethic would be based upon an assessment of human need rather than reliance upon traditional ethical practices which, in Russell's view, rather poorly reflect that need—particularly in the light of man's changing control over his environment.

From Russell's perspective, civilized men and women can find happiness in marriage only if a number of conditions are met:

> *There must be a feeling of complete equality on both sides; there must be no interference with mutual freedom; there must be the most com-*

15. Most of the articles in the following section are assembled in Herbert A. Otto (ed.), *The Family in Search of a Future: Alternate Models for Moderns* (New York: Appleton-Century-Crofts, 1970).

plete physical and mental intimacy; and there must be a certain similarity in regard to standards of values. (It is fatal, for example, if one values only money while the other values only good work.) Given all these conditions, I believe marriage to be the best and most important relationship that can exist between two human beings. If it has not often been realized hitherto, that is chiefly because husband and wife have regarded themselves as each other's policeman. If marriage is to achieve its possibilities, husbands and wives must learn to understand that whatever the law may say, in their private lives they must be free.[16]

Given these conditions, marriage can become the best regulator of love as it is intended to be. In spite of the attacks leveled against the book because of its frank treatment of trial marriage and free love, Russell did not believe that love should be unregulated:

. . . but love is an anarchic force which, if it is left free, will not remain within any bounds set by law or custom. So long as children are not involved, this may not greatly matter. But as soon as children appear we are in a different region, where love is no longer autonomous but serves the biological purposes of the race. There has to be a social ethic connected with children, which may, where there is conflict, override the claims of passionate love. A wise ethic will, however, minimize this conflict to the uttermost, not only because love is good in itself, but also because it is good for children when their parents love each other. To secure as little interference with love as is compatible with the interests of children should be one of the main purposes of a wise sexual ethic.[17]

It follows from this position that a rational ethic would not place as much weight upon a marriage with no children as it would on one with children. The former should be easily dissolvable; the latter should require greater effort on behalf of its preservation. Russell advocated Judge Ben B. Lindsey's conception of a "companionate marriage." In this view young persons should be encouraged to marry early. There should be no intention of having children, and so long as there are no children divorce should be possible simply by mutual consent. In the event of divorce, the wife should not be entitled to alimony. This, in effect, is a form of trial marriage enabling young people to carry their relationship a great deal further than would be possible under premarriage (even with the current sexual permissiveness) because the public contract would be a minimal one. Russell observes:

At present a marriage is null if sexual intercourse is impossible, but children, rather than sexual intercourse, are the true purpose of marriage, which should therefore not be regarded as consummated until such time as there is a prospect of children.[18]

16. Bertrand Russell, *Marriage and Morals: An Enlightened Approach to Sex and Love* (New York: Bantam Books, 1969; originally published in 1929 by Horace Liveright, Inc.), p. 37.

17. *Ibid.*, p. 87.

18. *Ibid.*, p. 118.

The companionate marriage would thus publicly recognize the importance of the non-natal components of human sexuality, yet reserve a special place for the bearing of children in a fully consummated marriage.

Margaret Mead elaborates upon these ideas in her recent article in *Redbook* entitled "Marriage in Two Steps":

> *I should like to see us put more emphasis upon the importance of human relationships and less upon sex as a physical need. . . . I should like to see children assured of a lifelong relationship to both parents. . . . I would like to see a style of parenthood develop that would survive the breaking of the links of marriage through divorce. . . . At present, divorce severs the link between the adult partners and each, in some fashion, attempts—or sometimes gives up the attempt—to keep a separate contact with the children, as if they were now a wholly individual relationship. This need not be. . . .*
>
> *These goals—individual choice, a growing desire for a lifelong relationship with a chosen partner, and the desire for children with whom and through whom lifelong relationships are maintained—provide a kind of framework for thinking about new forms of marriage.*[19]

Mead proposes two forms of marriage to meet these objectives: "individual marriage" and "parental marriage." Individual marriage would be a licensed union between two individuals who would be committed to each other as long as they wished to remain together but with the understanding that there would be no children. The central obligation of the partners in this contract would be ethical, not economic. This could be a lifetime contract if the couple so choose.

> *Individual marriage, as I see it, would be a serious commitment, entered into in public, validated and protected by law and, for some by religion, in which each partner would have a deep and continuing concern for the happiness and well-being of the other. For those who found happiness it could open the way to a more complexly designed future.*[20]

Individual marriage would be the necessary preliminary to every parental marriage, which, in contrast to individual marriage, would be difficult to contract. It would be contracted after each partner knew the other quite well and both decided that they wanted to become a family. During the individual marriage, couples could acquire the skills and the income necessary for ensuring the economic well being of the family without having to fall back upon parents. Children could be fully planned, not only medically, but socially, psychologically, and ethically as well, and if, after a thorough investigation the couple would decide that they *ought not* to have children, they need not separate nor feel that they somehow have a second-class marriage. Parental marriage would be quite difficult to dissolve, and if divorce should occur, the divorce would not legally affect the parent-child relationship.

19.   Margaret Mead, "Marriage in Two Steps," *Redbook Magazine,* (July 1966) copyright © 1966 by The McCall Publishing Company, reprinted by permission; in Otto *op. cit.,* pp. 79–80.

20.   *Ibid.,* pp. 81–82.

> *The family, as against the marriage, would have to be assured a kind of continuity in which neither parent was turned into an angry ghost and no one could become an emotional blackmailer or be a victim of emotional blackmail. . . .*
>
>   *By strengthening parenthood as a lasting relationship we would keep intact the link between grandparents, parents, and children. Whether they were living together or were long since divorced, they would remain united in their active concern for their family of descendants. The acceptance of two kinds of marriage would give equal support, however, to the couple who, having foregone a life with children, cherish their individual marriage as the expression of their love and loyalty.[21]*

Thus the tradition of trial marriage, companionate marriage, or marriage in two steps has enjoyed considerable attention over the last half century. Russell, Lindsey, and Mead aim at clarification of our vision of what marriage and the family should be, but beyond suggesting changes in the law, do not tell us how such alterations in values and behaviors can come about. Posited is that the image of men and women is sufficiently rational so that once their vision has been clarified, they will act to bring greater congruence between that vision and reality. At another level, however, is the supposition that in some degree social pressures are pushing us in the general direction of the vision and that clarification of goals will help in their earlier realization.

THE HUMAN POTENTIAL PERSPECTIVE

Other writers concern themselves with ways and means of making marriage a more fulfilling, rewarding experience. A number of these writers—but not all—identify themselves with the human potential movement. Common to this perspective of man is the assumption that:

> *. . . in principle [man] has the possibility of re-creating himself at every moment of his waking life. It is difficult but possible to reinvent one's identity, because man is human, the embodiment of freedom; his body and his situation are raw material out of which a way to be can be created, just as a sculptor creates forms out of clay or steel.[22]*

And, with regard to the marriage relationship:

> *It is possible to play games with a relationship, to experiment with new forms, until a viable way is evolved. What seems to thwart this kind of interpersonal creativity is failure in imagination on the part of either partner, dread of external criticism and sanctions, and dread of change in oneself.[23]*

Jourard contends that economic barriers to such experimentation are rapidly disappearing and that in the most affluent society on earth we have the po-

---

   21. *Ibid.*, p. 83.
   22. Sidney M. Jourard, "Reinventing Marriage: The Perspective of a Psychologist," in Otto *op. cit.*, p. 44.
   23. *Ibid.*, p. 45.

tential to ground a "fantastically pluralistic society." Within marriage he envisions the possibility of "serial polygamy to the same person" arising out of the fact that couples feel reasonably secure enough to experiment with their relationship usually after a period of separation during which time each remains faithful to the other:

> *There is a period of estrangement, a period of experimentation, and a remarriage in a new way. In this view anything can and should happen so long as it contributes to the experience of freedom, confirmation, and growth on the part of the participants.*[24]

The same emphasis upon development of the human potential in the marriage relationship is found in Virginia Satir and Herbert Otto who concern themselves primarily with the conventional structure. As Satir argues, marriage should be a five-year, renewable contract—not a life-long obligation. Otto would have "the involvement of both partners in the adventure of actualizing each other's potential" as the basis for the marriage contract. Satir concerns herself with the matter of child rearing and would endorse also a period of trial marriage. In both cases the intent is to expand the human potential in all directions and especially in the capacity to experience joy. However, what is proposed is not a specific objective (since the outer limits of the human potential remain unknown); it is rather that alternatives must be found to the present experience in which most human relations—especially those of the family—are constraining rather than liberating. As Satir puts it:

> *The current Western marriage contract has been derived from a chattel economic base, which stresses possessing. This frequently gets translated into duty and becomes emotional and sometimes literal blackmail. The quality of joy is lost in the game of scoreboard. 'Who loses, who wins, and who is on top?' The result is . . . grimness.*[25]

Satir makes numerous suggestions as to how marriage and parenthood could be changed in order to maximize the possibility of fulfillment and joy for all family members. Included among these is the suggestion that we *not* assume that everyone should rear children and that parenthood be valued as the most challenging and interesting job for each adult who can engage in it. To encourage these objectives several steps should be taken: (1) Each neighborhood should have a Family Growth Center within walking distance; (2) Birth should be a family concern, and all three (mother, infant, and father) should "room in" for at least the first two weeks; (3) Child-rearing practices should be altered so that each child is treated as a person and not as a dependent; (4) Children should be free to experience the emergence of the sexual self openly; (5) The goal of being human should be to become real,

---

24. *Ibid.*, p. 49.
25. Virginia Satir, "Marriage as a Human-Actualizing Contract," in Otto *op. cit.*, p. 63.

loving, intimate, authentic, and alive as well as competent, productive, and responsible.[26]

> *If we were taught from childhood on that our most important goal as human beings is to be real and in continuing touch with ourselves, this in turn would ensure a real connection with others. Were we taught that creativity, authenticity, health, aliveness, lovingness, and productivity were desirable goals, we would have a much greater sense of when this was achieved and would also find it much easier to do so.[27]*

Finally, I will consider several authors who examine the possibilities of specific structural alternatives to our current approaches to marriage and the family.

FOCUS ON STRUCTURE

Albert Ellis considers the possibility of group marriage a real one but only for a small number of people. Certainly it will never become the dominant mode of marriage in America if for no other reason than that it is too difficult. His assessment is based upon his intimate knowledge of about a dozen such marriages. These have lasted from a few months to a few years and then have broken up for largely nonsexual reasons.

The disadvantages that make group marriage an unlikely candidate for persistent popularity with large numbers of people are the following: (1) It is difficult to find a group of four or more adults who can live together harmoniously. The types who are ordinarily attracted to group marriage are utopian-minded persons who often cannot accept the limitations and greater self-discipline that group marriage requires. (2) Given divergent tastes, interests, work habits, etc., even healthy, practical types find that such communal living requires stepping on toes and creates a great deal of conflict. (3) The selection process is quite difficult. The sexual compatibility of four or more persons is more difficult to establish than the sexual compatibility of two persons, and we have not done well in this limited area. (4) Problems of sex, love, and jealousy arise once such a community is established and are exceedingly difficult to handle. (5) At present fewer females than males are interested in group marriage. An unbalanced sex ratio increases the problems.

On the other hand, if these can be managed there are some advantages: (1) Group marriage affords a high degree of sexual variety. (2) It widens and enhances love relationships for many people. (3) Family life can be increased and enriched by group marriage. (4) There are considerable economic advantages that can be worked out if the group marriage is a compatible one. These range from sharing baby sitting to achieving a higher standard of living for all than monogamous couples could afford separately. Thus such groups can more easily own expensive equipment and are more likely to maintain a good measure of economic security. This is based on the assumption that

---

26. *Ibid.,* pp. 58–61 *passim.*
27. *Ibid.,* p. 65.

adult members who are able to work do work, which is often not the case in fact. (5) Group marriage tends to add an experimental dimension to life that can be exhilarating. (6) A deeper sense of the humanity of man can be realized.[28]

> *Group marriage, then, is a logical alternative to monogamic and to other forms of marriage for a select few. In practice, marriage tends to be monogynous (that is, a man and a woman living fairly permanently, though not necessarily forever, only with each other and their children) all over the world, even when other forms of mating are legally allowed. The chances are that this kind of practice will largely continue, but that a sizeable minority of individuals will devise interesting variations on this major theme or else live in thoroughly non-monogamic unions, including group marriage.[29]*

Polygamy, particularly in its polygynous form, has received consistent support from a number of sources over the years. The Mormons were, of course, the most famous practitioners in our society during this century. There have been numerous attempts to legalize polygamy in the United States and all have failed. Ralf Linton, recognizing the difficulty of establishing polygynous unions in a society where mate selection tends to be highly possessive, speculates on the role that such a union might play in our society. He concludes that the need for such a form is likely to increase.

> *The real problem is less that of providing for the sexual and psychological needs of women who cannot find husbands than that of providing for women who will not be satisfied with second- or third-rate husbands. It seems inevitable that the number of the latter group of women will be increased by the development of independence and self-confidence in those whom the war brought into responsible and well-paid positions ordinarily pre-empted by men.[30]*

Such households could provide children of working wives with better care than they would receive in other institutions (as is the case in societies where polygyny is permitted and wives allowed to work). Such an arrangement could also help ease the problems associated with sex-role definition permitting those women with domestic leanings to be good housewives and those who want careers to have them without demeaning either.

Linton goes on, however, in a rather pessimistic vein regarding the likelihood of polygyny being recognized.

> *There is no pressing need for it in terms of group perpetuation even in the present world situation, and its formal recognition would do violence to many of our most strongly entrenched mores. . . . Changes in such a basic aspect of social organization as family structure cannot be*

---

28. Albert Ellis, "Group Marriage: A Possible Alternative?" in Otto *op. cit.*, pp. 92–96 *passim*.

29. *Ibid.*, p. 97.

30. Ralf Linton, "The Natural History of the Family," in Ruth Nanda Anshen, ed., *The Family: Its Function and Destiny*, rev. ed. (New York: Harper and Row, 1959), p. 44.

> *imposed suddenly by legislative fiat. They can only come about through a series of small but cumulative modifications on habits and attitudes. The family of the future will be a direct outgrowth of present familial conditions and trends, and in order to predict its possible forms it is necessary to have an understanding of the current situation.*[31]

Anthropology overcame speculation and Linton, in the end, relegates little weight to human intentionality.

To others, however, polygyny remains a possible solution to the needs of our society. Victor Kassel points out the desirable aspects of such a marriage form for those over sixty. As long as the number of aged women continues to be greater than the number of aged men and as long as the aged in general tend to have increasingly better health, it is natural for them to wish to live in family units rather than in institutions which tend to be impersonal and stultifying. The advantages of polygyny after sixty as Kassel sees them are: (1) It would allow more women to remain married throughout their lives. (2) They could also have the opportunity to re-establish a meaningful family group wherein they participate as intimates, not as babysitters as is common where they now live with their children. (3) It is likely that diet would improve, as eating with others is always more conducive to better food preparation than eating alone. (4) There is more possibility of economic security in polygynous households. (5) Care when ill would be assured when it need not extend to hospitalization. (6) Homemaking would undoubtedly improve. (7) A polygynous relationship would permit many more aged persons to express rather than repress their sexual desires. (8) Undoubtedly personal grooming would improve for those able to live in such households. (9) Depression and loneliness could be much better coped with in such households. (10) There might be greater benefits available to such groups through group health plans.[32]

On the other hand, there are those who argue that polygyny is far from a viable solution to the problems of the aged. George Rosenberg assesses the conditions under which polygyny occurs and concludes that among the many deficits to such a marriage arrangement for the aged would be a further reduction in the importance of the male role which has already suffered from the effects of retirement. Wives typically assume the preponderance of the work responsibility around the house in polygynous settings, and thus the need for a husband as a part-time worker around the house would cease to exist. Further, the aged retain strong value commitments to monogamy which would be extremely difficult to alter. Rosenberg contends that, contrary to Kassel's argument, widowhood does not mean *greater* economic dependence since many widows are often better off economically after the death of their spouse:

> *Therefore, it seems fair to state that although polygamous marriage in principle may provide an alternative to the status of monogamous spouse, it is neither regarded as significant nor rewarded by the predominantly*

31. *Ibid.,* p. 45.
32. Victor Kassel, "Polygyny After Sixty," in Otto *op. cit.,* pp. 137–42.

conjugal values which are retained from earlier socialization to an experience in monogamy. The ideological stress on egalitarianism in the conjugal relationship, the emphasis on women's rights to choose a husband, and the romantic love pattern which assumes that because a husband loves his wife, she has a certain degree of influence over him, would all appear to militate against polygynous marriage for the aged. Thus, the marital status highly valued in Western societies today does not seem to fit with the role of polygynist as a realistic substitute for that of a monogamous spouse.[33]

A final point against polygyny in the West, Rosenberg argues, is that it would disrupt kinship relationships and divert the energies of old people from the important expressive role that they tend to play in integrating the extended family network.

Finally, several proposed structural alterations need to be mentioned that do not focus upon the conjugal bond. Continuing the tradition of the encounter group, Frederick H. Stoller contends that an intimate network of families would indeed be a new structure.

Briefly defined, an intimate network of families could be described as a circle of three or four families who meet together regularly and frequently, share in reciprocal fashion any of their intimate secrets, offer one another a variety of services, and do not hesitate to influence one another in terms of values and attitudes. Behind this definition is a picture of a brawling, noisy, often chaotic convocation which develops its own set of customs for the purpose of coming together in terms of rich experiences rather than merely being "correct" and, in the process, achieves movement in terms of its own views of its arrangements and ways of operating. Such an intimate family network would be neither stagnant nor polite but would involve an extension of the boundaries of the intimate family.[34]

This circle of families would meet regularly and frequently, share as openly as possible the secrets, joys, and sorrows of their worlds, exchange services and strive toward the development of a new set of shared values about human relationships. In such an arrangement there would always be a dynamic tension between separateness and connectedness or privacy and participation. The working out of the balance between these two would be a major task for such an intimate circle.

Rustum and Della Roy explicitly carry the sharing much further than Stoller contending that it might well be the loving thing to do in certain circumstances to extend the "erotic community" to those outside the family. In the case of the involuntarily single this could compensate (without necessarily involving polygamy or extra-marital coitus, though the authors allow for the possibility of the latter to occur as the ethical and loving thing to do

33. George S. Rosenberg, "Implications of New Models of the Family for the Aging Population," in Otto *op. cit.,* p. 178.
34. Frederick H. Stoller, "The Intimate Network of Families as a New Structure," in Otto *op. cit.,* p. 152.

in certain situations) for other marriage structures. Returning to the needs of single women the Roys comment:

> *What does it require, then, for deep sustaining relationships to be established between single women and married men in our society? First we can remove some of the emotional objections to thinking if we eliminate, initially, considerations of intimate sexual relations in such cases. Should married couples remain consciously open to the establishment of relationships with single women? In a particular case, having established a relationship with both husband and wife, should a single girl develop further the relationship with the husband? . . . Surely Christian freedom not only permits but in the absence of other solutions cries out for these deep longrange relationships among married men and single women. In such a solution there are many real difficulties to be overcome, and many others which turn out to be bogeymen. Among the latter is the specter of an orgy of extramarital sex, happy homes being broken up, the crumbling of the institution of marriage and the shaking of the foundations of society. . . . If every single female above thirty and under sixty-five were attached to a married man, only one married couple in about ten would be affected. . . . This idea would hardly change society's sexual behavior measurably. The proposal, then, for deep and continuing relationships between married men and single women is not a proposal which will greatly alter extramarital sexual behavior though even such a price must surely not deter us. The proposal does envisage a radical change in the co-marital relationship structure of society.*[35]

The Roys are concerned with the quality of the relationship and the ethical demands for a couple to meet more deeply the needs of their fellow men than they have done in the past. In this context, the structure of the relationship is secondary and the rigidity of the mores something to be overcome rather than accepted or viewed as insurmountable.

Taking as the point of departure the knowledge that the father for various reasons is absent most of the time in most American homes and assuming that the trend is likely to worsen, not abate, Carl Levett proposes that attention be given to the development of a professional male parental presence in future families. As Levett envisions such a person he would be well educated, highly paid, and intimately connected with several families who would each have to work out their own mode of operation with the professional. This male parental presence seems to be an extension of the Big Brother Program but with an upgrading of skills and responsibilities. Levett envisions many benefits to be derived from such an intimate professional in the home. He would begin to work with children when they are in the first grade, establish a workable and of necessity intimate relationship with the mother—a more superficial one with the father. The third parent's presence could mediate effectively between siblings and, given the establishment of an expanded program, provide many recreational benefits to groups of children (along the lines of the Boy Scouts, the "Y," etc., but again with deeper in-

35. Rustum and Della Roy *op. cit.*, p. 120.

sights and responsibilities); he could become a meaningful presence in the school so that the teachers would be well informed of a male's perspective on the work and children would have someone beside their parents in whom to confide. There are obviously many problems of interpersonal relationships that must be worked through especially in the case of the father who may resent such an intrusion into his family. However, as wtih the Trobriand father, such intrusions may be seen as beneficial in the long run when the son and father can re-establish a relationship in maturity.

THE FAMILY IN WALDEN II

B. F. Skinner has redesigned a whole community in his *Walden II*, and within it the family. What many reviewers of this work miss is that Skinner is not an old fashioned utopian—that is, he is not offering the ultimate answer to the human problems posed by present institutions. Rather he is giving a picture of what, to him, is a desirable series of modifications of *present* practices with the basic conviction that they must be continually modified on the basis of experience. The experimental community he proposes would constantly revise its culture in order to achieve its objectives more effectively:

> *We have no reasons to suppose that any cultural practice is always right or wrong according to some principle or value regardless of the circumstances or that anyone can at any time make an absolute evaluation of its survival value. So long as this is recognized we are less likely to seize upon the hard and fast answer as an escape from indecision, and we are more likely to continue to modify culture design in order to test the consequences.*[36]

Skinner wrote this in his *Science and Human Behavior*, and it is in this spirit that *Walden II* is offered.

The picture of the family presented in *Walden II* has been influenced by scientific research as well as humanistic values. Accordingly, Frazier, the leading figure in this fiction, begins with a critique of current practices:

> *The significant history of our times, Frazier began, is the story of the growing weakness of the family. The decline of the home as a medium for perpetuating a culture, the struggle for equality for women, including their right to select a profession other than housewife or nursemaid, the extraordinary consequences of birth control and the practical separation of sex and parenthood, the social recognition of divorce, the critical issue of blood relationship or race—all these are parts of the same field. And you can hardly call it quiescent.*
>
> *A community must solve the problem of the family by revising certain established practices. That's absolutely inevitable. The family is an ancient form of community, and the customs and habits which have been set up to perpetuate it are out of place in a society which isn't based on blood ties. Walden II replaces the family, not only as an economic unit,*

36. B. F. Skinner, *Science and Human Behavior* (New York: Free Press, 1953), p. 436.

but to some extent as a social and psychological unit as well. What sur-
vives is an experimental question.[37]

Some of the features of this experimental question can be sketched,
however. One provision for privacy in the context of a cooperative community of several hundred persons living together in common houses is private
rooms for husbands and wives:

> *We asked all husbands and wives who were willing to do so to accept*
> *separate or common rooms on the basis of a drawing of lots. . . . The*
> *result was clear-cut. Living in a separate room not only made the indi-*
> *vidual happier and better adjusted, it tended to strengthen the love and*
> *affection of husband and wife.*[38]

As with many of the alterations in family life style proposed in *Walden II*,
this is not in itself very striking. But the principle by which it was arrived at is.
These are things that can be put to the test. If the test yields significant results, the rational community will change its structure and living arrangements
in the direction indicated by the experiment.

So it is with every principle of organization. *Walden II* encourages free
affection between sexes, having been successful in establishing the norm "seduction not expected." The proof of the validity of the encouragement of
greater intimacy between the sexes is a happier, healthier life, because what
in the world outside *Walden II* might have become a clandestine affair is
allowed—encouraged—to become a lasting friendship.

The experimenters of *Walden II* did not feel it necessary to alter the
marriage contract significantly. Monogamous marriages contracted after short
engagements (made possible because the young couple did not have to worry
about financial matters and because each knew the other in a commune like
Walden II) were entered into in earnest, retained their fidelity for the most
part for life even though divorce was a socialized (but not preferred) alternative available to all.

In *Walden II* the most significant alterations in family life pertain to the
parent-child relationships. These were attentuated by design. Following the
example of the Kibbutz, children were reared communally by nurses of both
sexes. They were thought of as belonging to everyone in the community,
were not singled out by their biological parents for special benefits, and remained on a first-name basis with all adults. These measures untied the overly
dependent relationship with mother, made the childless members of the community feel less conspicuous and more involved in family, and prevented
damage to the children resulting from divorce. Furthermore, Frazier observed:

> *. . . many parents are glad to be relieved of the awful responsibility of*
> *being a child's only source of affection and help. Here it's impossible to*
> *be an inadequate or unskillful parent, and the vigorous, happy growth of*

37. B. F. Skinner, *Walden II* (New York: Macmillan, 1948), p. 114.
38. *Ibid.*, p. 115.

> our children is enough to remove any last suspicion that we have been
> deprived of anything.[39]

Skinner answers the question of identification problems that might be raised as a result of communal child rearing through his spokesman, Frazier:

> We know very little about what happens in identification. . . . No one
> has ever made a careful scientific analysis. The evidence isn't truly ex-
> perimental. We have seen the process at work only in our standard fam-
> ily structure. The Freudian pattern may be due to the peculiarities of that
> structure or even the eccentricities of the members of the family. All we
> really know is that children tend to imitate adults, in gestures and man-
> nerisms, and in personal attitudes and relations. They do that here, too,
> but since the family structure is changed, the effect is very different.
>
> Our children are cared for by many different people. It isn't institu-
> tional care, but genuine affection. . . . Remember that the adults who
> care for our children are of both sexes. We have broken down prejudices
> regarding the occupations of the sexes, and we have worked particularly
> hard to keep a balance in the nursery and school system. . . . By bal-
> ancing the sexes we eliminate all the Freudian problems which arise from
> the asymetrical relation to the female parent.[40]

As the child matures in *Walden II*, he singles out particular people as models, but they need not be the biological parents. He has a much wider range of adults whom he knows intimately and thus can more reasonably find a model closer to his own needs for fulfillment than would be true if he were reared in a nuclear family.

Finally, women are fully emancipated in *Walden II*. Frazier's critique is biting:

> What does the middle-class marriage amount to? Well, it's agreed that
> the husband will provide shelter, clothing, food and perhaps some
> amusement while the wife will work as a cook and cleaning woman and
> bear and raise children. The woman has no choice, except between ac-
> cepting and neglecting her lot. She has a legal claim for support, he has
> a claim for a certain type of labor. . . . She is made to believe that she
> is necessary . . . but the intelligent woman sees through it at once, no
> matter how hard she wants to believe. She knows very well that some-
> one else could make the beds and get the meals and wash the clothes,
> and her family wouldn't know the difference. The role of mother she
> wants to play herself, but that has no more connection with her daily
> work than the role of father with his work in the office or factory or
> field. . . . The community has changed the place of women more radi-
> cally than that of men. Some women feel momentarily insecure for that
> reason. But their new position is more dignified, more enjoyable, and
> more healthful, and the whole question of security eventually vanishes.[41]

39. *Ibid.*, p. 118.
40. *Ibid.*, pp. 119–20.
41. *Ibid.*, pp. 121–22.

The book is written as though the experiments had already been accomplished and the evidence evaluated, but of course that is a fictional element elected to enhance the style of the presentation. Nevertheless, the speculations as to what the results of the experiments might be are edifying—and, in 1948 when the book first appeared, they were quite shocking to the general public. That they do not seem so today is partial testimony to the effect of many much more radical experiments that have been conducted—often with minimal skill—by numerous groups in the late fifties and sixties. Some have even tried to put Skinner's idea of the experimental community to the test, but to date the results of these attempts are not in.

Afterword

The bulk of this book has been devoted to a discussion of the constraints placed upon intentional change by socioeconomic factors largely beyond the control of individuals. Indeed, individual choice has rarely entered into my considerations explicitly. Yet, despite the lack of knowledge and in spite of these constraints, men and women have been able to intentionally change the character and structure of their family life. I have suggested a few cases in point—the utopian or experimental communities discussed in Chapter 16, and the more private decisions to participate in swinging, limit the size of one's family, or to extend one's erotic community discussed elsewhere in the text. While the weight of individual preference seems insignificant in a discussion of a family policy for the nation, it has great weight when individuals sit down to consider how they might change the style of their own families. This is an area over which many of us have some control and one in which, for the moment at least, we seem to have some freedom of movement. The alternatives discussed in Chapter 17 each have their own peculiar costs as well as their anticipated benefits. What is at stake personally in each case is difficult to discuss in the abstract. Therefore, I want now to briefly discuss my own preferences in this matter as I now understand them.

In turning to my own conception of an ideal family and how it might be achieved, I am aware that for me the "family" is a small group wherein my human capacity to love is freest because I can be myself to a greater extent than it is possible for me in other settings. I suspect that the quest for alternatives to the conjugal family in our time has merged with a quest for community arising out of a widespread sense of alienation and isolation. The encounter group movement, for example, has become a multi-million dollar business promising "instant intimacy" to over six million people according to *The New York Times*. As I see it, the time people spend in such groups is ordinarily too short, and their stake in the venture too small to effect lasting change. Nevertheless, by realigning families so that they can in fact encounter each other over extended periods of time and in a variety of contexts, I feel that significant improvements will be made even if structural alterations are minimum. But how can such an intimate community be realized?

A number of considerations which enter at an early stage into the shaping of my ideal community place quite severe restraints upon what is reasonable for me to expect of such an adventure. At present these seem most important and therefore rather than change *them* I feel inclined to accept their constraints—though at a later date I may feel otherwise. The first is *size*. I do not want to hassel through the problems of integrating a large number of families. Three or four conjugal families seem ideal, because I want to get to know a few people well rather than a large number less well. It may be that in fact the best way of achieving this would be to join a larger group and seek out a clique within it, but I don't know of such a group and doubt that, in the last analysis, forming such a coalition would be beneficial to the larger group.

The second consideration is that the community must be an *open one*. I want to get to know others deeply, but not at the expense of losing contact with the larger society in which I live. Individuals should be free to work in the larger society, free to involve themselves in its problems, free to come and go on vacation, and to visit friends outside the community. This value is in some degree in conflict with the implied "privatism" of a small group of intimates. The dynamics of working out a balance between participation in the immediate community and involvement in the society surrounding it will inevitably be a major concern to the members. On the other hand, opting for a small size group makes this matter of openness a necessity, for it is unlikely that such a small group could become reasonably self-sufficient in any area. It could not effectively educate its children for today's world: They would have to go to school outside. It certainly could not become economically self-sufficient—even if it owned a farm, it would not likely possess the skills necessary to sustain itself. And besides, I like my work, and would hope that those who joined with me in this venture liked theirs. I also enjoy the relatively high standard of living my job offers. I would be willing to lower that standard a bit for the sake of community but it would be difficult for me to live at the primitive level necessary if economic independence were going to be an ideal to be maximized. At a later stage of the community's life it might indeed be possible for me to give up a great deal in order to progress further along the line of mutual support and fulfillment. I must say in all honesty, however, that Oneida's relative wealth appears to me to have been more of an asset than a liability.

Thirdly, I want *privacy* without excessive privatism. The Kibbutz places inordinate pressure upon people to participate in the corporate life of the community. Even the emphasis upon neighborliness that obtained in Park Forest seems to me to be excessive in some areas because the desire to be alone was considered somewhat deviant (though provided for in the rule of the closed window shade) and the emphasis was upon conformity. I want spatial privacy and I do not seek emersion in a corporate self. In the last analysis I do not believe that my integrity as a person depends upon that degree of commitment to a group. On the other hand, I want more interaction, more sharing of hopes and despairs, more doing things together than I have now (both within my conjugal family and within a larger group such as an intentional community).

Fourthly, I would want to stress *equality* within the community. The commitments made by each conjugal family to the corporate life should be as equal as it is possible to make them. This assumes that all who join should be upper-middle-class so that each conjugal family enters with about the same economic risk and can contribute roughly similar amounts of support to the common venture. I think this is important initially because an unequal commitment (reflected in part in an unequal economic risk) increases the likelihood of withdrawal, as well as tempering the character of participation by inviting invidious comparison. I am uncertain about the extent to which this equality should be expressed in communalism over and above a general desire to share more of myself and my property than I currently do. At the outset I don't think that the sharing of spouses at the level of coition is desirable although I have no conviction that it ought not to follow as the group grows more intimate.

There are obviously many sides to this issue, but I opt for monogamy with exclusive sexual rights at least initially (and perhaps permanently) because I want to encourage a linkage between coition, love, responsibility, and commitment to the corporate venture. I can certainly see how it is possible—and perhaps desirable—to disengage these, either through the mode of the swinger, who sees sexual behavior primarily as a form of recreation and enjoys the erotic for its own sake, or from the position that it is natural and, therefore, ought not to be regulated by such restrictions. My personal persuasion, however, is that I would rather opt for equality at the level of economic support and merge on this basis, rather than coming together out of a conviction that sex is enjoyable and that everyone should have equal access to every other adult sexually. I'm personally just not ready for sexual communalism.

Given these constraints that I find important elements in the *initiation* of an intentional community, it might be well to ask why come together at all. Most of my reservations (or values depending upon how you look at what I have said) run counter to inclinations of utopian socialists and suggest quite a different form of community than those we have discussed in Chapter 16. They seem closer to Skinner's *Walden II* which I discussed in Chapter 17. None of what I have suggested thus far violates any of our basic mores—though it may call for a modification of their expression. I do not seem to want anything very radical.

I am seeking a deeper mode of involvement with other people that cuts across sex boundaries as an expression of "free affection" not "free love" as commonly understood. I want to involve my children in the experience of a broader community and believe that they will profit from deeper exposure to other adults who can serve as alternative role models and can provide insight and assistance in the process of growing up. I would like to participate in a community that would help me face myself and my world more honestly, openly, and vigorously—one that would deepen my sensitivity to others. Paradoxically, all that I want to receive, I want to be able to give.

The reader will at once recognize that, in essence, what I desire is often attributed to the extended family of rural America although I am not convinced that it ever in fact functioned like this for most people. I am sure it once did for some. On rare occasions organizations such as the churches move in this direction in particular parishes, but most do not. My aspirations are certainly not new. My conception of what is required initially in order to express them is not radical. The most "far out" component of my ideal thus far is a willingness to remain open, in principle if not in practice, to a wide variety of structures within which these aspirations might be realized. Even this is already true of our practices but not of our mores or laws. I really need to know much more about the experimental communities now underway in America before I can say if I could live and be happy in them. From what I have seen, I imagine that I would have a very hard time living in most because I do not have either the strong revulsion against the society in which I live, or the strong drive toward communalism that seems to be at the base of most of these attempts.

But what do I see as required of me to realize even my limited dream?

The first most pressing demand is for time. I want to do this in the context of being open and, therefore, the attempt to develop an intentional community must be at the expense of other things I am presently doing. "If you are committed to something you will find the time to do it." Of course, but it isn't that easy. My wife and I have not talked about all of the implications of such an attempt and are not together on how much *we* are ready to risk. This takes time. We do not know of others who are interested (although we can think of a few friends who might be). To discover one another takes time. Although I am intellectually committed to the notion that my time could not be spent in a better fashion, the routine of work, home, and family, the patterns of recreation and the demands of friendships that we have already developed are difficult to change. At one level it is easier to make a complete break and leave job, home, and current habits behind for something altogether different than it is to incrementally alter present patterns to allow something quite new and different to gradually emerge. At another level one can argue that radical structural change is always premature because the people who suddenly go to live in radically different structures haven't really changed. They have simply brought their "hang ups"—and their effective and comfortable patterns—with them. In the new situation "hang-ups" may perhaps become more conspicuous (and, therefore, more readily altered) or their rigidity may prove to be the undoing of the new venture. The decision as to how much to get your feet wet—and when—is at least a function of the extent to which one is dissatisfied with one's present state, attracted by an ideological dream to establish a more perfect state, free (economically, emotionally, sociologically) to act, and able to sustain the courage of one's convictions. I'm a wader at present.

In my vision of incremental commitment (cautious wading) a group would go through the sequence of close neighboring (and/or a past friendship without present close residence), a series of "encounter" type sessions in order to hash out the basic conception of who they were and what they were about, and then possibly rent a common facility (such as a summer camp lodge in the winter time) in order to work out the problems of living together for a period of a month or more. After such an experience, I would expect that all concerned would be able to decide whether they wanted to push further or not. This experience should also help the group to decide on the most desirable physical expression of this community. Should there be a large single house with private apartments and common rooms? A cluster of private residences with or without a common house? How much isolation from the larger society is necessary? Can such a residence be located in a suburb, exurb, or should it be entirely apart but within easy commuting distance from places of work? My own preference at present would be a cluster of private residences in close proximity (but without common house) in an exurban or rural setting. A particular group must decide these matters for itself even though its choice may be affected by information about how other groups have operated.

After an extended period of living together the common conception of a desirable familial structure within the larger community would become clearer also. I do not feel that a change in the marriage contract or the structure of the conjugal family, or in the residential unit of a conjugal family is necessary. One option, as far as I am concerned, is that they remain the same but become revitalized through the enriching contact with others who care and are committed to one another. On the other hand, the progression toward deeper intimacy within the group might well lead to a sharing of spouses at all levels and a community mode of child rearing. The structure of the family would thus be coextensive with the community after the fashion of the early Kibbutzim. This, too, seems a reasonable and ethical possibility as far as I am concerned.

Ideally, whatever conception of the family became the guiding one for the community, the commitment to greater intimacy in terms of structural alterations in the current family should be made voluntarily and with as full an awareness of the likely consequences as it would be possible to discern. The consequences for a particular group would, of course, be highly dependent upon its past history. As I see it, an important aspect of that history would be the extent to which the community placed its commitment *to one another* above its commitment to a particular expression of community or family, for this would determine its freedom to experiment with what seemed the most reasonable (and the most loving) thing to do at any given time.

It seems especially clear that if such a community were to persist over a long period of time its needs would change. What is desirable for married couples in their thirties with children would be quite different than what would be so for older couples free of the responsibility of child care, or for widows and widowers. Therefore, it must be possible at all times for persons to leave the community without feeling that they have betrayed others in so doing. This, in itself, is quite difficult to achieve in practice and the extent to which the intentional community could effectively establish such a climate permitting guiltless disengagement would be as much a mark of its "maturity" in my mind as its capacity to recruit new members.

If the ideal of a small community persisted over time it is clear that the life of such a community would be most likely limited to a single generation perhaps even to a single stage of family development. Children raised in such an environment may or may not wish to remain and bring their spouses. It is quite likely that they would *not* want to do so, having been imbued with a spirit of independence as well as one of greater corporate sensitivity. I cannot really conceive of an ideal family form or community structure for myself when I am fifty-five (perhaps this is closely related to the fact that I would rather not think about such matters at this time). I would hope, however, that whatever intentional community I might join would be sufficiently flexible so as to permit me to stay when I grew older if I so desired. But this would be quite difficult to accomplish in a small group that intended to stay open to the larger society.

Looking at the matter from the perspective of the larger society for a moment, I would like to see a situation in which men and women were much freer to experiment with new forms of relationships. A great number of experiments are now being carried out in the United States but most of them bear the additional burden of social ostracism and stigmatism. Our laws legislate against freedom to express ourselves sexually much more than they need to because we have bought the packaged deal that the only fully legitimate relationship in which to engage in coition is marriage, that the purpose of coition is procreation, and that the only legitimate form of the family is the conjugal family or one of its truncated forms. In effect we have legalized Aquinas' constrictions on sexual behavior to a surprising extent—sex for the right purpose, with the right person, and in the right way. This is an oppressive form of legalism and represents in part the failure of the theological venture within the Christian tradition to remain sensitive to the changing needs of today's world and the changing technology that has given us much greater control over these matters than men had in the days of Aquinas.

It seems to me quite unlikely that the majority of Americans will radically alter either their mores or their behavior enough to appropriate a greater freedom than they have at present. I would hope, however, that they not attempt to coerce others—using the force of violence or the law—into living as they do.

I would like to see a society in which people can live their lives, if only a small portion of them, within a community intent upon openness and dialogue in the pursuit of happiness; a society in which people are free to live in whatever form of family seems most expressive of their love and concern for one another. This would probably mean that two different modes of community would be open to all Americans free enough to move between them: one subculture devoted to the work of an industrial society; alongside it another intent upon the resuscitation of the human community and the recclamation of warm loving "familial" values in human interaction. Its focus would be the family and the home. Given the greatest social freedom, some of us may choose to live all of our lives within one or the other subculture and some of us may choose to alternate once or many times between them.

I believe that it would be possible for the nation to get its work *and* its loving done to the best interest of all concerned—each person doing what he wanted to do most. It just might be that some such scheme is necessary if we are to meet the problems posed by our present way of life and to continue as a people.

D. A. S.

Credits

We would like to thank the following publishers and authors for permission to re-print material.

Aldine: L. Rainwater, *Family Design*, © 1965 Social Research Inc. The American Museum of Natural History. *American Sociological Review*: J. Hess, "Premarital Characteristics" (1960); A. B. Hollingshed, "Cultural Factors" (1950); J. Ross & R. F. Peck, "Social Class and Social Mobility" (1951). The Bobbs-Merrill Co.: R. F. Winch, *Identification and Family Determinants* © 1962. C.B.S. News: "Generations Apart" © 1970 Columbia Broadcasting System, Inc. Child Study Association of America. *Daedalus*: L. Rainwater, "Crucible of Identity" (1966); A. Rossi, "Equality between Sexes" (1964). The Dorsey Press: C. K. Warriner, *The Emergence of Society* (1970). Doubleday & Company Inc.: P. L. Berger, *Invitation to Sociology* © 1963. Harper & Row Publishers: C. C. Zimmerman, *The Family of Tomorrow* © 1949. Harvard University Press: E. M. Hoover & R. Vernon, *The Anatomy of a Metropolis* © 1959 the Regional Plan Association. Hawthorn Books: J. F. Cuber & P. B. Harroff, *Sex and the Significant American* © 1968. Holt, Rinehart and Winston, Inc.: E. A. Hoebel, *The Cheyennes* © 1960; I. Hogbin, *A Guadalcanal Society* © 1964; W. Madsen, *The Mexican-Americans of South Texas* © 1964; B. F. Skinner, *Walden II* © 1948. The Johns Hopkins University Press: C. B. Broderick & J. Bernard, *The Individual, Sex and Society* © 1969; M. L. Carden, *Oneida* © 1970. Houghton Mifflin Company: L. Rodwin, *Nations and Cities: A Comparison of Strategies for Urban Growth* © 1970. *Journal of Marriage and the Family*: B. C. Rollins & H. Feldman, "Marital Satisfaction" (1970). Dan Leon. J. B. Lippincott Company: E. Duvall, *Family Development*. Liveright Publishing Corp.: B. Russell, *Marriage and Morals* © 1929; © 1957 by Bertrand Russell. The Macmillan Company: B. Bettleheim, *Children of the Dream* © 1969; R. O. Blood, *Marriage* © 1962 The Free Press; G. P. Murdock, *Social Structure* © 1949. Metropolitan Life. The Metropolitan Museum of Art. The New American Library, The Times-Mirror Co.: R. & D. Roy, *Honest Sex*. *New York Magazine*: J. O'Reilly, "Notes on the New Paralysis" (1970). The New York Times Company: J. Bingham, "The Intelligent Square's Guide to Hippieland" © 1967. Keith Otterbein. Oxford University Press: H. L. Shapiro, *Man, Culture and Society* © 1960. Pergamon Press Ltd.: Dan Leon, *The Kibbutz*. Prentice-Hall, Inc.: A. Billingsley, *Black Families in White America* © 1968; W. J. Goode, *The Family* © 1964. Random House, Inc.: J. Henry, *Jungle People* © 1964 by Jules Henry; A. W. Watts, *Nature, Man, and Woman* © 1969 by Pantheon Books. *Redbook*, The McCall Corp.: J. F. Cuber, "New Ideas about Sex" (1971); M. Mead, "Marriage in Two Steps (1966). The Russell Sage Foundation: M. W. Riley & A. Foner, *Aging and Society* (1968). *Science*: J. Blake, "Population Policy" (1969). Simon & Schuster Inc.: W. H. Whyte, Jr. *The Organization Man* © 1956 by William H. Whyte, Jr. *Social Casework*, Family Service Association of America: R. Hill, "Social Stresses" (1958). St. Martin's Press: Coser, Blake & Davis, *The Family*. University Books: R. F. Barton, *Autobiography of Three Pagans in the Philippines* (1963); G. Arthur, *The Circle of Sex*. Yale University Press: M. Mead, *Continuities in Cultural Evolution* (1964); J. Whiting & I. Child, *Child Training and Personality* (1953).

EPIGRAPHS

Chapter 2: Claude Lévi-Strauss. "The Family," in Harry L. Shapiro (ed.), *Man, Culture and Society*. New York: Oxford University Press, 1960, p. 266.

Chapter 3: Bernard Willard Aginsky. "An Indian's Soliloquy." *American Journal of Sociology*, 46 (1940): 43–44.

Chapter 4: Margaret Mead. *Coming of Age in Samoa*. New York: William Morrow & Company, 1928, p. 105.

Chapter 5: William J. Goode. *World Revolution and Family Patterns*. New York: The Free Press, 1963, p. 380.

Chapter 6: St. Augustine. *The City of God.* Bk. XIX, Ch. 16.

Chapter 7: Lewis Mumford. *The City in History.* New York: Harcourt, Brace, and World, 1961, p. 494.

Chapter 8: Lee Rainwater. *Behind Ghetto Walls.* Chicago: Aldine, 1970, p. 370.

Chapter 10: Robert O. Blood. *Marriage* (2nd. ed.) New York: The Free Press, 1969, p. 36.

Chapter 11: John B. Watson. "What the Nursery Has to Say About Instincts." *Psychologies of 1925.* Worcester, Mass.: Clark University Press, 1926, p. 10.

Chapter 12: Jessie Bernard. "The Fourth Revolution," *The Journal of Social Issues*, 22 (1966): 86–87.

Chapter 15: Paul R. Erhlich. *The Population Bomb.* New York: Ballentine Books, 1968, pp. 22–26.

Chapter 16: Martin Buber. *Paths in Utopia.* Boston: Beacon, 1949, pp. 148–49.

Chapter 17: C. W. Hobart. "Commitment, Value Conflict, and the Future of the American Family." *Marriage and Family Living*, 25 (1963): 410.

PHOTOS

page

  16: Ken Heyman

  40: Denver Public Library, Western History Collection

  62: Wayne Miller, © 1970 Magnum Photos

  88: The Bettman Archive

  112: Rivera, Mexican National Tourist Council

  138: Ken Heyman

  170: Ken Heyman

  230: The Bettman Archive

  250: Ken Heyman

  284: Ken Heyman

  310: World Wide Photos

  352: World Wide Photos

  378: Ken Heyman

  410: Margaret Mead, Ken Heyman; Bertrand Russell, The Bettman Archive; B. F. Skinner, Ken Heyman

Selected Bibliography

1. INTRODUCTION

Bruyn, Severyn. *The Human Perspective in Sociology.* Englewood Cliffs, N.J.: Prentice-Hall, 1966.

Goode, William J. *The Family.* Englewood Cliffs, N.J.: Prentice-Hall, 1964.

Polanyi, Michael. *Personal Knowledge.* London: Routledge and Kegan Paul, 1958.

———— *Science, Faith and Society.* Oxford: Oxford University Press, 1954.

Strauss, Anslem (ed.). *The Social Psychology of George Herbert Mead.* Chicago: University of Chicago Press, 1962.

2. DO ALL OF US LIVE IN FAMILIES?

Henry, Jules. *Jungle People.* New York: Vintage Books, 1964.

Levy, M. J., and L. A. Fallers. "The Family: Some Comparative Considerations," *American Anthropologists,* 61 (1959): 647–51.

Murdock, George Peter. *Social Structure.* New York: Free Press, 1965.

Nye, F. Ivan, and Felix Berardo. *Emerging Conceptual Frameworks in Family Analysis.* New York: Macmillan, 1966.

Reiss, Ira. "The Universality of the Family: A Conceptual Analysis," *Journal of Marriage and the Family,* 27 (1965): 445–55.

Lévi-Strauss, Claude. "The Family" in Harry L. Shapiro (ed.), *Man, Culture and Society.* New York: Oxford Press, 1960.

Zelditch, Morris. "Family, Marriage and Kinship" in R. E. L. Farris (ed.), *Handbook of Modern Sociology.* Chicago: Rand McNally, 1964.

3. THE WEB OF KINSHIP

Eggan, Fred. "Kinship" in *International Encyclopedia of the Social Sciences,* Vol. 8 (1970).

Goody, Jack. "Kinship: Descent Groups" in *International Encyclopedia of the Social Sciences,* Vol. 8 (1970).

Madsen, William. *The Mexican Americans of South Texas.* New York: Holt, Rinehart & Winston, 1964.

Mead, Margaret. *Sex and Temperament.* New York: Mentor Books, 1950.

Newman, Philip. *Knowing the Gururumba.* New York: Holt, Rinehart & Winston, 1965.

Parsons, Talcott. "The American Family: Its Relation to Personality and the Social Structure" in Talcott Parsons and R. F. Bales (eds.), *Family: Socialization and Interaction Process.* New York: Free Press, 1955.

———— "The Kinship System of the Contemporary United States," *American Anthropologists,* 45 (1943): 22–38.

Stephens, William N. *The Family in Cross-Cultural Perspective.* New York: Holt, Rinehart and Winston, 1969.

4. MARRIAGE AND FAMILY STRUCTURE

Bott, Elizabeth. *Family and Social Network: Roles, Norms and Extended Relationships in Ordinary Urban Families.* London: Tavistock, 1957.

Dubois, Cora. *The People of Alor,* Vols. I, II. New York: Harper & Brothers, 1944.

Ford, Clellan S., and Frank A. Beach. *Patterns of Sexual Behavior.* New York: Harper & Brothers, 1951.

Goody, Jack. "A Comparative Approach to Incest and Adultery" in Paul Bohannan and John Middleton (eds.), *Marriage, Family and Residence.* New York: The Natural History Press, 1968.

Hart, C. W. M., and Arnold R. Pilling. *The Tiwi of North Australia.* New York: Holt, Rinehart and Winston, 1960.

Lewis, Oscar. *Tepotzlan: Village in Mexico.* New York: Holt, Rinehart and Winston, 1960.

Malinowski, Bronislaw. *The Sexual Life of Savages.* New York: Harcourt, Brace and World, 1929.

Mead, Margaret. *Coming of Age in Samoa.* New York: William Morrow, 1928.

5. TIME AND CIRCUMSTANCE: THEORIES OF FAMILY CHANGE

Bardis, Panos. "Family Forms and Variations Historically Considered" in Harold T. Christensen (ed.), *Handbook of Marriage and the Family.* Chicago: Rand McNally, 1964.

Childe, V. Gordon. *Man Makes Himself.* New York: Mentor Books, 1951.

Gillespie, Charles. *Genesis and Geology.* New York: Harper and Bros., 1951.

Goode, William J. *World Revolution and Family Patterns.* New York: Free Press, 1963.

Linton, Ralph. "The Natural History of the Family" in Ruth Nanda Anshen (ed.), *The Family: Its Function and Destiny.* New York: Harper and Row, 1969.

Mead, Margaret. *Continuities in Cultural Evolution.* New Haven: Yale University Press, 1964.

Ogburn, William F. and Meyer F. Nimkoff. *Technology and the Changing Family.* Boston: Houghton Mifflin, 1955.

Zimmerman, Carle. *Family and Civilization.* New York: Harper and Row, 1947.

6. THE FAMILY AND THE AMERICAN CLASS STRUCTURE

Billingsley, Andrew. *Black Families in White America.* Englewood Cliffs, N.J.: Prentice-Hall, 1969.

Cavan, Ruth Shonle. *The American Family* (4th ed.). New York: Thomas Y. Crowell, 1969.

————. "Subcultural Variations and Mobility" in Harold T. Christensen (ed.), *Handbook of Marriage and the Family.* Chicago: Rand McNally, 1964.

Coleman, Richard P., and Bernice Neugarten. *Social Status in the City.* San Francisco: Jossey-Bass, 1971.

Kohn, Melvin. *Class and Conformity.* Homewood, Ill.: Dorsey, 1969.

7. THE WHITE UPPER-MIDDLE-CLASS FAMILY OF SUBURBIA

Cuber, John F., and Peggy B. Harroff. *Sex and the Significant Americans.* Baltimore: Penquin, 1968.

Dobriner, William W. *Class in Suburbia.* Englewood Cliffs, N.J.: Prentice-Hall, 1963.

LeMasters, E. E. *Parents in Modern America: A Sociological Analysis.* Homewood, Ill.: Dorsey, 1970.

Rainwater, Lee. *Family Design.* Chicago: Aldine, 1965.

Spectorsky, A. C. "The Exurbanites" in Bernard Rosenberg (ed.), *Analysis of Contemporary Society II.* New York: Crowell, 1967.

Whtye, William H. Jr. *The Organization Man.* Garden City, N.J.: Doubleday, 1956.

Winter, Gibson. *The Suburban Captivity of the Churches.* New York: Macmillan, 1962.

8. A BLACK ALTERNATIVE: COPING WITH POVERTY IN THE GHETTO

Clark, Kenneth. *Dark Ghetto.* New York: Harper & Row, 1965.

Ladner, Joyce Ann. *Tomorrow's Tomorrow.* Garden City, N.Y.: Doubleday, 1971.

Liebow, Eliot. *Tally's Corner.* Boston: Little, Brown, 1967.

Rainwater, Lee. *Behind Ghetto Walls*. Chicago: Aldine, 1971.

————, and William Yancey. *The Moynihan Report and the Politics of Controversy*. Cambridge: M.I.T. Press, 1967.

Scanzoni, John H. *The Black Family in Modern Society*. Boston: Allyn and Bacon, 1971.

Schulz, David. *Coming up Black: Patterns of Ghetto Socialization*. Englewood Cliffs, N.J.: Prentice-Hall, 1969.

Staples, Robert (ed.). *The Black Family: Essays and Studies*. Belmont, Calif.: Wadsworth, 1971.

Valentine, Charles. *Culture and Poverty: Critique and Counter Proposals*. Chicago: University of Chicago Press, 1968.

Willie, Charles V. (ed.). *The Family Life of Black People*. Columbus, Ohio: Charles E. Merrill, 1970.

9.   THE FAMILY LIFE CYCLE

Burr, Wesley R. "Satisfaction with Various Aspects of Marriage over the Life Cycle: A Random Middle-Class Sample," *Journal of Marriage and the Family*, 32 (1970): 129–37.

Duvall, Evelyn. *Family Development* (5th ed.). Philadelphia: Lippincott, 1969.

Hill, Reubin. *Families Under Stress*. New: York Harper, 1949.

————, and Roy Rodgers. "The Developmental Approach" in Harold T. Christensen (ed.), *Handbook of Marriage and the Family*. Chicago: Rand McNally, 1964.

LeMasters, E. E. *Parents in Modern America*. Homewood, Ill.: Dorsey, 1970.

Nye, F. Ivan, and Felix Berardo. *Emerging Conceptual Frameworks in Family Analysis*. New York: Macmillan, 1966.

Rollins, Boyd C., and Harold Feldman. "Marital Satisfaction over the Family Life Cycle," *Journal of Marriage and the Family*, 32 (1970): 20–28.

10.   THE MATING GAME

Berger, Peter. *Invitation to Sociology: A Humanistic Perspective*. Garden City, N.Y.: Doubleday, 1963, pp. 93–121.

Kerckhoff, Alan, and Keith Davis. "Value Consensus and Need Complementarity in Mate Selection," *American Sociological Review*, 27 (1962): 295–303.

Murstein, Bernard I. "A Theory of Marital Choice and Its Application to Marriage Adjustment" in Bernard I. Murstein (ed.), *Theories of Attraction and Love*. New York: Springer, 1972.

Rodman, Hyman. "Mate Selection: Incest Taboos, Homogamy and Mixed Marriages" in Hyman Rodman (ed.), *Marriage, Family and Society: A Reader*. New York: Random House, 1965.

Sussman, Marvin B. "Parental Participation in Mate Selection" *Social Forces*, 32 (1954): 76–81.

Winch, Robert F. *The Modern Family* (3rd. ed.). New York: Holt, Rinehart & Winston, 1971. pp. 261–95.

———— "Motivation and Role: A Comment on Balance, Reinforcement, Exchange, Psychosomatic, and S.V.R. Theories of Attraction" in Murstein *op. cit.*

11.   CHANGING CHILDREN

Bronfenbrenner, Urie. "The Changing American Child—A Speculative Analysis," *Journal of Social Issues*, 17 (1961): 6–18.

———— "Socialization and Social Class Through Time and Space" in Eleanor Maccoby,

Theodore M. Newcomb, and Eugene L. Hartley (eds.), *Readings in Social Psychology* (3rd. ed.). New York: Holt, Rinehart & Winston, 1958.

Lee, Dorothy. "Being and Value in a Primitive Culture," *Journal of Philosophy*, 46 (1949).

———— "Lineal and Nonlineal Codifications of Reality," *Psychosomatic Medicine*, 12 (1950): 89–95.

Warriner, C. K. *The Emergence of Society*. Homewood, Ill.: Dorsey, 1970.

Winch, Robert F. *Identification and Its Familial Determinants*. Indianapolis: Bobbs-Merrill, 1962.

Wolfenstein, Martha. "Trends in Infant Care," *American Journal of Orthopsychiatry*, 23 (1953): 120–30.

Worf, Benjamin. "Science and Linguistics" in Sol Saporta (ed.), *Psycholinguistics: A Book of Readings*. New York: Holt, Rinehart and Winston, 1961.

Wrong, D. K. "The Oversocialized View of Man in Modern Sociology," *American Sociological Review*, 26 (1961): 183–93.

Zigler, Edward, and Irvin Child. "Socialization" in Gardner Linsey and Elliot Aronson (eds.), *The Handbook of Social Psychology* (2nd. ed.), Vol. 17 (1961).

12. THE SEXUAL REVOLUTION

Arthur, Gavin. *The Circle of Sex*. New York: University Books, 1966.

Bell, Robert R., and Jay B. Charles. "Premarital Sexual Experience among Coeds, 1958 and 1968," *Journal of Marriage and the Family*, 32 (1970): 81–88.

Christensen, Harold T. "A Cross-Cultural Comparison of Attitudes Toward Marital Infidelity," *International Journal of Comparative Sociology* (September, 1962).

Goldstein, Martin, Edwin J. Haeberle, and Will McBride (eds.). *The Sex Book: A Modern Pictorial Encyclopedia*. New York: Herder & Herder, 1971.

Humphreys, Laud. *Tearoom Trade: Impersonal Sex in Public Places*. Chicago: Aldine, 1970.

Masters, William H., and Virginia E. Johnson. *Human Sexual Inadequacy*. Boston: Little, Brown, 1970.

———— *Human Sexual Response*. Boston: Little, Brown, 1966.

Money, John. "Psychosexual Differentiation" in John Money (ed.), *Sex Research: New Developments*. New York: Holt, Rinehart and Winston, 1970.

Reiss, Ira. *The Social Context of Premarital Sexual Permissiveness*. New York: Holt, Rinehart and Winston, 1967.

Roy, Rustum and Della. *Honest Sex*. New York: New American Library, 1968.

Sherwin, Robert Veit, and George Keller. "Sex on Campus" in Meyer Barash and Alice Scourby (eds.), *Marriage and the Family: A Comparative Analysis of Contemporary Problems*. New York: Random House, 1970.

Watts, Alan. *Nature, Man and Woman*. New York: Pantheon, 1969.

Walshok, Mary Lindenstein. "The Emergence of Middle-Class Deviant Subcultures: The Case of Swingers," *Social Problems*, 18 (1971): 488–95.

13. THE GENERATION GAP

Bingham, June. "The Intelligent Square's Guide to Hippieland" in Meyer Barash and Alice Scourby (eds.) *Marriage and the Family*. New York: Random House, 1970.

Child Study Association of America. *The Function of Rebellion—Is Youth Creating New Family Values?* New York: Child Study Association of America, 1968.

CBS News. *Generations Apart*. Mimeographed Transcript of a Televised Broadcast, May 20, 1968.

Davis, Kingsley. "The Sociology of Parent-Youth Conflict" in Rose L. Coser (ed.), *The Family: Its Structure and Function*. New York: St. Martins, 1964.

Erikson, Erik H. "The Problem of Ego Identity" in Maurice Stein, Arthur T. Vedich, and David Manning White (eds.), *Identity and Anxiety*. Glencoe, Ill.: Free Press, 1960.

Herzog, Elizabeth *et al*. *Teenagers Discuss the 'Generation Gap.'* Washington, D.C.: U.S. Dept. of Health, Education and Welfare, 1970.

Keniston, Kenneth. "Social Change and Youth in America" in Meyer Barash and Alice Scourby (eds.), *Marriage and the Family*. New York: Random House, 1970.

14.   CAREERS OR THE GOOD LIFE

Benson, Leonard. *Fatherhood: A Sociological Perspective*. New York: Random House, 1968.

Degler, Carl N. "Revolution Without Ideology: The Changing Place of Women in America," *Daedalus*, 93 (1964).

Friedan, Betty. *The Feminine Mystique*. New York: Norton, 1963.

Goode, William. *World Revolution and Family Patterns*. New York: Free Press, 1963.

Gordon, Michael, and Penelope J. Shaw Kweiler. "Different Equals Less: Female Sexuality in Recent Marriage Manuals," *Journal of Marriage and the Family*, 33 (1971): 459–66.

Greenfield, Sidney. "Industrialization and the Family in Sociological Theory," *American Journal of Sociology*, 67 (1961): 312–22.

Henry, Jules. *Culture Against Man*. New York: Random House, 1963.

Litwak, Eugene. "Geographic Mobility and Extended Family Cohesion," *American Sociological Review* (June, 1960): 385–94.

Rainwater, Lee. "Crucible of Identity: The Negro Lower Class Family," *Daedalus* (Winter, 1965): 172–216.

Rossi, Alice. "Equality Between the Sexes: An Immodest Proposal," *Daedalus*, 93 (Spring, 1964).

Sussman, Marvin, and Lee Burchinal. "Kin and Family Network: Unheralded Structure in Current Conceptualization of Family Functioning," *Marriage and Family Living* (August, 1962): 231–40.

15.   FAMILY PLANNING AND POPULATION CONTROL

Blake, Judith. "Population Policy for Americans: Is the Government Being Misled?" *Science*, 164 (1968): 522–29.

Davis, Kingsley, and Judith Blake. "Social Structure and Human Fertility" in *Economic Development and Cultural Change*. Chicago: University of Chicago Press, 1956.

Farley, Reynolds. *Growth of the Black Population: A Study of Demographic Trends*. Chicago: Markham, 1970.

Nimkoff, Meyer F. "Biological Discoveries and the Future of the Family," *Social Forces*, 41 (1962).

Petersen, William. *Population* (2nd. ed.). New York: Macmillan, 1969.

Rosenfeld, Albert. *The Second Genesis*. Englewood Cliffs, N.J.: Prentice-Hall, 1969.

16.   PATHWAYS IN UTOPIA

Bettleheim, Bruno. *Children of the Dream*. New York: Macmillan, 1969.

Carden, Maren Lockwood. *Oneida: Utopian Community to Modern Corporation*. Baltimore: The Johns Hopkins University Press, 1970.

Engles, Frederick. *The Origin of the Family, Private Property, and the State.* Chicago: Charles H. Kerr, 1902.

Kephart, William M. "Experimental Family Organization: An Historical Cultural Report on the Oneida Community," *Marriage and Family Living*, 75 (1963).

Inkeles, Alex, and Kent Geiger (eds.). *Soviet Society: A Book of Readings.* Boston: Houghton Mifflin, 1961.

Leon, Dan. *The Kibbutz: A New Way of Life.* Oxford: Pergamon Press, 1970.

Noyes, Pierrepont. *My Father's House: An Oneida Boyhood.* New York: Holt, Rinehart & Winston, 1937.

Spiro, Melford. *Children of the Kibbutz.* Cambridge: Harvard University Press, 1958.

———— *Kibbutz: Venture in Utopia.* Cambridge: Harvard University Press, 1956.

Timasheff, Nicolas S. "The Attempt to Abolish the Family in Russia" in Normal Bell and Ezra Vogel (eds.), *A Modern Introduction to the Family.* New York: Free Press, 1960.

17. TRENDS AND PROPOSALS

Edwards, John (ed.). *The Family and Change.* New York: Knopf, 1969.

Hill, Reubin. "The American Family of the Future," *Journal of Marriage and the Family* 26 (1964): 20–28.

Linton, Ralf. "The Natural History of the Family" in Ruth Nanda Anshen (ed.), *The Family: Its Function and Destiny* (rev. ed.). New York: Harper & Row, 1959.

Moore, Barrington Jr. *Political Power and Social Theory.* Cambridge: Harvard University Press, 1958.

Otto, Herbert A. (ed.). *The Family in Search of A Future: Alternative Models for Moderns.* New York: Appleton-Century-Crofts, 1970.

Parke, Robert Jr., and Paul C. Glick. "Prospective Change in Marriage and the Family," *Journal of Marriage and the Family*, 29 (1967): 249–56.

Rapoport, Robert and Rhonda. "Work and Family in Contemporary Society," *American Sociological Review*, 30 (1965): 381–94.

Russell, Bertrand. *Marriage and Morals: An Enlightened Approach to Sexual Laws.* New York: Bantam Books, 1969.

Skinner, B. F. *Walden II.* New York: Macmillan, 1948.

Vincent, Clark E. "Family Spongia: The Adaptive Function," *Journal of Marriage and the Family*, 28 (1966): 29–36.

Index

Macro-functional approach, defined, 5
Madsen, William, 51
Malcolm X, 316
Male continence, as form of contraception, 383, 384
Male dominance
  in kibbutzim, 405
  in modern Russian families, 395
Malinowski, Bronislaw, 28, 37, 77, 86
Maltreatment of children, 371
Manus society
  avoidance behavior in, 49–50
  effects of Paliau movement on, 97–100
Marginality of male roles in ghetto families, 187–92
Marital relations
  in middle-class families, 155–57
  in primitive societies, 51
Marital sexual satisfaction (orgasmic responses)
  family life cycle and, 226–28
  patterns of, 297
  premarital intercourse and, 302
Marital sexuality, 294–99
  in middle-class families, 163–65
    effects of sexual revolution on, 294–96
  social class and, 296–98
Marquesan society
  deference behavior in, 52, 53
  extramarital intercourse in, 69
  family structure in, 28–33
  marriage in, 84
Marriage and Morals (Russell), 420
"Marriage in Two Steps" (Mead), 422
Marriages, 63–87
  age at first, 413, 415
  of Angmagsalik Eskimos, 93
  changing meaning of, 163
  child bearing and, 76–78
  of Chiricahau Apaches, 85
  of Chuckchee Eskimos, 33, 84
  in communes, 328–29
  complex, 382–86
  conjugal family and, 31, 33
  defined, 64
  family structure and, 78–86
  as goal, 162
  human potential perspective on, 423–24
  of Kaingang, 21–23, 84, 95
  in kibbutzim, 404–6
  in modern kinship system, 59
  of Nayar, 26, 85
  plural, 95, 96
  projections on, 415
    individual marriages, 422
  reproduction regulated through, 356–60
  sexuality and, 64–76
    sexual revolution and, 294–306
  teenage, 415
  trial, 420–23
  view of, by ghetto blacks, 185–87
  See also Divorces; Husbands; Wives
Marshall, Thurgood, 129
Masculinity
  biological base of, 287–89
  sex roles and, 290–93
Masters, William H., 219, 288, 293, 295, 296, 373, 419
Mate selection, 231–49
  need to change machinery of, 414

premarriage and, 242–44
psychological factors in, 238–42
regulation of, 74–76
socioeconomic factors in, 233–38
Matrifocality in black lower-class families, 187–92
Matrilineal descent, defined, 44
Matrilineal societies
  Haida as, 47–48
  in evolutionary stages of family, 92, 93
Matrilinear *taravad*
  described, 26
  economic cooperation by, 27
  function of, 26
Matrilocal residence, defined, 54
Mead, George H., 6
Mead, Margaret, 63, 64, 97, 279, 280, 290–91, 422, 423
Men, role of, in black lower-class families, 187–92; *see also* Fathers; Husbands; Masculinity; Polyandry
Merton, Robert, 135
Meteplets, 9
Mexican-Americans, extramarital sexuality among, 69–70
Micro-functional approach, 5
Middle-class families
  black, 130–31
  child rearing in, 259–60
  white, *see* White middle-class families
Mill, John Stuart, 341
Mixed marriages, problems of, 244–48
Mobility
  generation gap and, 325
  horizontal, 143
  social, 133–36
Modeling theory of aggression, 271
Modern Soviet families, 394–96
Modified extended families, 335–37
Mohave society, mate selection in, 75
Money, John, 289
Monogamous fathers, described, 195
Monogamous households, Marquesan, 29
Monogamy in ideal community, 436
Moore, Barrington, Jr., 411, 417
Moore, Wilbert, 106–8
Moral Physiology (Owen), 367
Morgan, Lewis Henry, 92
Mortality
  infant
    black, 175
    in colonial times, 105–6
  trends in, 360–63
Moslem societies, marriages in, 85
Mother-child relationships, importance of, 9
Mothers
  deferent behavior toward, 53
  working, 345–46
Moynihan, Daniel Patrick, 4, 11, 172, 178
Mumford, Lewis, 8, 139
Mundugumor society, joking behavior of, 49
Murdock, Geoge Peter, 5, 81, 94
  family structure and, 23–31, 35, 37
  kinship system and, 46, 47, 50, 55
  marriage and, 84
  sexual behavior and, 65–69, 71
Murngin society, premarital sexuality in, 68–69
Murray, H. A., 266
Mutual aid in urban families, 336